TRADE, COMPETITION AND DOMESTIC REGULATORY POLICY

Trade, Competition and Domestic Regulatory Policy presents a unique combination of analysis of both international trade and investment policies, and competition and regulatory policies. Increasingly, policymakers, businesses and the law and economics professions need to better understand how changes and policy developments in international trade and competition developed and how their interaction impacts on global business.

In addition to providing a comprehensive analysis of the attempts of international trade theory and practice to deal with tariffs, non-tariff barriers, market distortions and failures to protect various kinds of property rights, this book contains a detailed treatment of how property rights protection, including intangible property rights, are a critical element of ensuring open trade and competitive markets. It examines how these rights have developed over time, and how they have been integrated into trade and competition policy.

This book will be of significant interest to students of international business, professors of economics, law and business, and policymakers at the intersection of trade, investment, competition and property rights.

Shanker A. Singham is one of the world's leading international trade and competition lawyers/economists. He is the CEO of Competere and a former cleared advisor to the United States Trade Representative. Mr Singham is a former advisor to the Secretary of State for International Trade of the UK.

Alden F. Abbott is a Senior Research Fellow at the Mercatus Center, focusing on antitrust issues. Before joining Mercatus, Mr. Abbott served as the Federal Trade Commission's General Counsel from 2018 to early 2021, where he represented the Commission in court and provided legal advice to its representatives.

TRADE, COMPETITION AND DOMESTIC REGULATORY POLICY

Trade Liberalisation, Competitive Markets and Property Rights Protection

Shanker A. Singham and Alden F. Abbott

Routledge
Taylor & Francis Group
LONDON AND NEW YORK

Designed cover image: diane39

First published 2023
by Routledge
4 Park Square, Milton Park, Abingdon, Oxon OX14 4RN

and by Routledge
605 Third Avenue, New York, NY 10158

Routledge is an imprint of the Taylor & Francis Group, an informa business

British Library Cataloguing-in-Publication Data
A catalogue record for this book is available from the British Library

ISBN: 978-0-367-33987-6 (hbk)
ISBN: 978-0-367-33988-3 (pbk)
ISBN: 978-0-429-32333-1 (ebk)

DOI: 10.4324/9780429323331

Typeset in Bembo
by codeMantra

Access the Support Material: www.routledge.com/9780367339883

CONTENTS

FIGURES

TABLES

1

PURPOSES OF TRADE LIBERALISATION AND COMPETITIVE MARKETS

The purpose of trade liberalisation, as set out originally in the work of Adam Smith and David Ricardo, is to ensure that global consumers can benefit from the working out of the basic law of comparative advantage. In this way, resources can be properly allocated and not wasted. The resulting efficiencies lead to benefits for consumers around the world. Under the law of comparative advantage, nations can benefit from trading with each other by leveraging the fact that trade is a non-zero-sum game. Ricardo's theory is based on the fact that where two countries trade, and one country is better at producing product A than product B, then trade may be beneficial to both countries even where the other country is less good at producing both A and B than the first country. This occurs because the first country has a comparative advantage in producing product A, even though it has an absolute advantage (compared with the second country) in producing both A and B. The first country will therefore tend to produce more of product A, and trade with the second country to satisfy its needs in product B. This occurs even though the first country is empirically better at producing product B.[1] In simple terms, the law of comparative advantage produces a non-zero-sum game, where trade leads to benefits for both the better producer as well as the less good producer as long as one country has a comparative advantage in one product.[2] The law of absolute advantage sets up a zero-sum game, where trade leads to one country gaining and the other losing. This is a very important distinction as we expound on our theory of the interaction between trade and competition policy in the course of this book. Time and again, in actual case studies we discuss on the application of domestic regulation, governments apply a zero-sum/absolute advantage view of liberalisation. This leads to a producer welfare orientation (as opposed to one that advances consumer welfare in the narrow economic sense) and has important and negative consequences for trade flows and for consumers.

DOI: 10.4324/9780429323331-1

Based on Ricardo's doctrine, a move was made to lower tariffs and trade barriers. While attempts to remove barriers and obstacles in international trade pre-date Smith and Ricardo, the removal of the Corn Law in Great Britain in the 19th century was one of the first modern-day manifestations of the application of this theory. Interestingly, the catalyst for the repeal of the Corn Laws was the classification by repeal proponents of the tariff as a tax. The famous rallying cry of "do not tax the people's bread" resounded with the political thinking of the day and drew out a constituency of consumers to countervail the powerful vested interest elites of the day.

Adam Smith's *Wealth of Nations*, published in 1776, expressed the notion that the invisible hand of the market or market forces would do a better job of ensuring total social welfare in the economic sense than government's attempts to influence change. The repeal of the Corn Laws (the system of corn tariffs that protected England's corn farmers) in the mid-19th century represented the practical culmination of Smith's ideas. How it happened, though, speaks as much to politics as it does to economics. As early as 1780, Pitt the Younger had focused on free trade as a way to avoid the wholesale smuggling that was then occurring. However, these early developments[3] did not lead simply and steadily to the repeal of the Corn Laws. The Napoleonic wars prevented change, as a combination of a wartime economy, and the fact that Napoleon had cut off trade between England and the European continent together meant that English farmers had a virtual captive market for the domestic supply of grains. This led to higher prices between 1793 and 1815. The subsequent fall in corn prices led English farmers to demand an institutionalisation of the corn monopoly they had formerly enjoyed in the country. The government of Lord Liverpool then introduced the Corn Laws in 1815. Some of the arguments used find resonance in very similar arguments used today to promote agricultural protection. Lord Binning noted:

> Numbers of persons had been turned out of employment, and the pressure of the poor rates [had] become intolerable…Most enormous losses had been suffered in the last year; and if some speedy remedy was not administered by the wisdom and firmness of the legislature, the agricultural interest of the country might soon be completely ruined.[4]

The Corn Law provided that no foreign grain could be imported until domestic grain prices reached a certain level. The effect of this was to subject food prices to high and fluctuating levels. The landowners benefited enormously, and since they were the only group represented in Parliament, the law looked bullet proof. As food prices went up, consumer demand for manufactured goods shrank. There were some MPs who understood what the impact of the Corn Laws would truly be. For example, one MP said:

> If we artificially raise the price of provisions, we shall raise the price of labour, and in the same proportion we shall assist our rivals against ourselves.[5]

There was strong opposition to the Corn Laws but it was organised around the central principle of the impact on consumer welfare of laws that artificially increased the price of provisions. The enactment of the Corn Laws in 1815 was accompanied by trade-related riots. While matching some of the riots that have occurred more recently around the subject of trade and globalisation in anger, they came from an entirely different source. This source was best expressed by the Declaration of January 1819 that came out of a meeting of the radicals.

> The conduct of the late Parliament in passing the Corn Bill, which was obtained under false pretensions…was oppressive in its design and cruel in its operation; being neither more nor less than a vile conspiracy between the great Landholders and the Ministers, to extort from the industrious labourer and mechanic, through the very bread they eat, an immense portion of taxes for the support of the borough system, and to enrich themselves and their pensioned minions, by the sweat of the poor man's brow.[6]

As a result of the Corn Laws, food prices were kept so high that the domestic manufacturing market was negatively affected. As sales of these manufactures decreased, so unemployment increased setting up a depression cycle.

The Corn Laws were ameliorated in 1828, lowering the threshold price at which duty-free imports could occur and introducing a sliding scale between a lower price where imports were gradually introduced.

The industrial revolution provided the other mechanism to stimulate the opposition to the Corn Laws. The cotton industry which was centred in Manchester relied on imports and exports. It was no surprise then that much of the opposition to the Corn Laws came from two Manchester newspapers, the Manchester Times and the Guardian. The latter was expressly created to spread ideas of free trade and reform. The cotton industry as a purchaser of imports for its mills was perhaps the most powerful consumer group of its day. Political reform (through the 1832 Political Reform Act) gave these industrialists greater power in Parliament and allowed the consumer side of the debate to have a platform which it had hitherto lacked.

Two of the most important actors in the process that ultimately led to the repeal of the Corn Laws in 1846 were Richard Cobden and John Bright. Both were instrumental in setting up the Anti-Corn Law League ("ACLL"). The special gift, in particular, of Cobden was reducing the obscure concepts set forth by Smith into something that untrained people could easily grasp. Both Cobden and Bright organised on a massive scale.

One of the great successes of the ACLL was that it gave its campaign the semblance of a religious crusade.[7] In one of his many speeches, Cobden got to the heart of the trade and competitive market interface:

> How can protection, think you, add to the wealth of a country? You may by legislation, in one evening, destroy the fruits and accumulations of a

> century of labour; but I defy you to show me how, by the legislation of this House, you can add one farthing to the wealth of this country. You guide that intelligence; you cannot do better than leave it to its own instincts. If you attempt by legislation to give any direction to trade or industry, it is a thousand to one that you are doing wrong...[8]

Cobden's rhetoric was not directed towards lowering the price of corn for the sake of the benefits that a lower price would bring. Instead, he argued that the price should be the natural one that was dictated by the world's market:

> We do not seek free trade in corn primarily for the purpose of purchasing it at a cheaper money rate; we require it at the natural price of the world's market, whether it becomes dearer with a free trade...or whether it is cheaper, it matters not to us, provided the people of this country have it as its natural price, and every source of supply is freely opened, as nature and nature's God intended it to be...we state that we do not believe that free trade in corn will injure the farmer; we are convinced that it will benefit the tenant-farmer as much as any trader or manufacturer in the community. Neither do we believe it will injure the farm labourer; we think it will enlarge the market for his labour, and give him an opportunity of finding employment, not only from the [land, but also from the opportunities in towns].[9]

Cobden was noting the practical reality of what Adam Smith and David Ricardo had originally contemplated theoretically – that if comparative advantage is unleashed through free trade, prices will move towards a consumer welfare-enhancing equilibrium in the absence of some other anti-competitive practice.

Adam Smith: Before the Trade and Competition Divide

Smith's seminal book is as much a treatise on competition as it is on trade.[10] To Smith, both areas came from the same intellectual well-spring, the notion of consumer welfare. One of his most famous quotes is the oft-repeated section counselling that businesses rarely come together except in a conspiracy to harm the consumer.[11] Similarly, his passages on trade foreshadow the work on comparative advantage theory of David Ricardo and focus on the benefits to consumers of import competition.

Indeed, he notes that:

> Consumption is the sole end and purpose of all production; and the interest of the producer ought to be attended to, only so far as it may be necessary for promoting that of the consumer. The maxim is so perfectly self-evident, that it would be absurd to attempt to prove it. But in the mercantile system, the interest of the consumer is almost constantly sacrificed to that of the

> producer, and it seems to consider production, and not consumption, as the ultimate end and object of all industry and commerce.

The key themes that emerge from Adam Smith include the recognition that stopping imports retards the country that is doing the obstructing because it prevents them having access to essential inputs. Smith noted that old families of inherited wealth were rare in commercial countries. It is interesting that Adam Smith does not make the rigid distinction between trade and competition that practitioners (particularly in the US) have subsequently imposed. Smith discusses economic development, trade and the dangers of monopoly in the same breath. Indeed, he notes that the "benefits of trade [with the colonies] may sometimes be overwhelmed by the negative effects of the monopoly of such trade."[12] He regards merchants with suspicion, warning his readers to be careful of distributors, traders and shopkeepers whose interests are very often at variance with the interests of the population as a whole. He notes with breathtaking clarity that monopoly of one kind or another is the sole engine of the mercantilist system,[13] which operates by the encouragement of exportation and the discouragement of importation.[14] He further notes that the interests of consumers are always sacrificed to the interests of producers.[15] He explains the costs of agricultural protectionism as it impacts other industries and highlights the fact that China's decline in manufacturing industry in the 18th century is connected completely to the deliberate favouring of agriculture. Specifically in discussing the trade with the American colonies, Smith notes that while the overall trade is good for Britain, monopoly of such trade can have distortive effects. He states[16]:

> We must carefully distinguish between the effects of the colony trade and those of the monopoly of that trade. The former are always and necessarily beneficial; the latter always and necessarily hurtful.

Smith evaluated how the monopoly distorted the colony trade and led to consumer welfare harm. In the case of Britain's colony trade, he concludes that the overall positive effects of the trade outweigh the negative impacts of the monopoly, but in the case of Spanish and Portuguese trade, he concludes that their trade benefits are outweighed by their monopoly effects.

It is worth examining more closely what Smith says about monopoly and mercantilism, given that he states that monopoly of one sort or another is the *sole* engine of the mercantilist system. Not one of the engines but the sole engine. Why does Smith make this somewhat dramatic statement? The context of Smith's statement is that the regulations under which the mercantile system flourishes distort the natural distribution of stock. This disarrangement, Smith argues, is achieved because of the monopoly. In other words, Smith argues that it is the monopoly that drives the disarrangement of stock which is the key to the mercantilist system. He goes on to note that this mercantilist system leads to inflated profit margins for shopkeepers and distributors and damages consumers.

In analysing the matter in this way, Smith notes the central importance of competition policy in determining whether trade is beneficial or not. He concludes quite differently between the examples of British trade with the colonies, as opposed to Spanish and Portuguese trade with their colonies. Smith concludes that in Spain and Portugal, "the bad effects of the monopoly, aggravated by other causes, have, perhaps, nearly overbalanced the natural good effects of the colony trade. These causes seem to be, other monopolies of different kinds."[17]

Smith's point is that merely having colony trade did not automatically mean that manufacturing industry in a country would be benefited (or could be maintained). After making this initial point, Smith cites various examples of issues that would prevent colony trade from leading to benefits:

- i Degradation of gold/silver below its value in other countries;
- ii Exclusion from foreign markets by export taxes;
- iii Narrowing of the home market by improper transportation taxation internally and
- iv Irregular/partial administration of justice and its abuse to protect debtors from the legitimate claims of creditors.

While divisions have developed between competition/antitrust on the one hand and trade on the other, since Adam Smith's time, it is clear that it has not always been thus, and that at least as the basic principles of trade and competition policy were being expounded, they were seen as part of a single general principle. It is important to note this because the disciplines have developed separately over the intervening period. However, it is important to note that the differences are very much man-made and are not reflective of the economic underpinnings of the global marketplace.

We will analyse these disciplines in this book, sometimes separately and sometimes together by reviewing a number of case studies in different sectors in the hope of building towards a more general theory of the interaction between trade and competition policy – a theory with which Adam Smith might have concurred. We will also integrate these disciplines with property rights protection in all its forms which is a crucial pillar of economic development as property is what firms compete with. By doing this, we can develop a more holistic theory of anti-competitive market distortions where distortions which impact property rights, as well as domestic and international competition, can be formulated as a normative framework.

What Is the Purpose of Trade Liberalisation?

As explained above, the purpose of trade liberalisation is to unlock the gains that would come from the efficient operation of the principle of comparative advantage. The purpose of trade liberalisation is not to ensure that the producers of one's own market have better access to external markets. The purpose of liberalisation is not to create more jobs in one particular market. These two last objectives are merely side-effects of significant trade liberalisation. These barriers act as the sand in the gears of the very comparative advantage on which so much of trade theory is based. Once trade is liberalised, the resultant better economy certainly should spin off more jobs all other things being equal. And certainly as these barriers diminish, exporters to that market are better off. But it is key to note that it is in order to increase global welfare that trade liberalisation is pursued, by limiting the inefficiencies and distortions in the market, and optimising consumer welfare. This is the fundamental lens through which all those involved in the trade policy world should view the issues.

Once this lens is used, then those involved in trade liberalisation efforts have a response to those groups that would seek to advantage themselves at the expense of the consumer. These benefits can be expressed clearly and can be communicated to individuals and thus can buttress the arguments of consumer groups who should be the prime beneficiaries of trade liberalisation. Viewed through this lens, much of trade policy and trade negotiations look a lot like mercantilism, protectionism and producer welfare secured at the expense of consumers. It is necessary to redress this imbalance, and once again bring consumer arguments firmly into the centre of the debate and not on the sidelines where they have so far been relegated. The very language that trade negotiators use, describing tariff reductions as concessions and utilising the so-called request/offer process reinforces the rhetoric of mercantilism, and strengthens the hand of producer lobbies in negotiations. This is not to say that producer welfare is unimportant in considering total social welfare. However, our contention is that consumer welfare concerns have played little role in framing trade negotiations thus far. It is also a common misconception that consumers are the individuals that sit at the end of the production and the supply chain. However, most producers are also consumers of something. Indeed, it is hard to name any producer that is not also a consumer (even of raw materials). However, not every consumer is a producer. In arguing for a market equilibrium that enhances total social welfare, it is therefore very important to redress the balance and place more emphasis on consumer welfare.

While the notion that border barriers should be the exclusive province of traditional trade theory may have had some validity when those border measures were very restrictive (for example, when tariffs were very high), domestic regulatory effects, in particular the level of competition inside the border, become the major impediment to trade when border barriers decrease. Just as the classical mechanics of Newton is an approximation which describes the macro world, so traditional trade theory is an approximation which describes a world where tariffs are high. However, as tariffs come down, internal market effects dominate and traditional trade theory breaks down, just as classical mechanics breaks down in the micro and quantum worlds. This does not mean that either Newtonian mechanics or traditional trade theory is wrong – it merely recognises that they are both approximations which break down when the world to be analysed is different. A theory that combines traditional trade theory with competition – a general theory of trade and competition can accurately describe the new world where regulatory protection has to some extent supplanted (or at least supplemented) the world of tariffs and quotas. This theory should therefore be regarded as supplementing existing trade and antitrust principles.

As liberalisation moved from purely border tariff or quota issues, newer inside the border issues began to emerge as fundamental obstacles. It is in this discussion that the new trade theory is emerging. This emergence started in earnest with the negotiations on rules and also services which began during the Uruguay Round. It became clear that services negotiations were in reality negotiations about domestic regulation, in particular the regulatory structures that were the background for provision of services in particular markets. The simultaneous privatisations that occurred in what had been hitherto described as essential services to be provided only by governments such as energy, telecommunications and transportation acted both as a stimulant to the desire for greater levels of liberalisation that could be achieved in the Uruguay Round and also set in motion the types of issues that such liberalisation would be forced to address. Unlike goods, which could be easily observed as they moved from one market to another, services could not be so easily observed. The barriers which service providers faced were more insidious than mere tariffs. They faced regulatory barriers that threatened to vitiate any market access that would be given through a privatisation or in any other capacity. Now in order to deal with these regulatory barriers, it became necessary for rules of the World Trade Organization to focus on issues of domestic policy, which had become a very thorny area indeed. Countries resisted the notion that the rules of the international trade system should be applied to their domestic policies. For the most part they felt that as long as they did not discriminate against foreign service providers in an obvious way, they did not believe that further reform or corrective action was necessary. However, trade liberalisation in the area of services in the context of the General Agreement on Trade in Service (GATS) negotiations ran head on into problems with domestic regulatory systems.

The most challenging aspect of trade liberalisation in services is the issue of domestic regulation. Under the GATS, countries make commitments in the area of national treatment and non-discrimination. The barriers to services access in markets tend to be of a domestic regulatory nature and relate to the level of competition in that particular market. Within ten years of the conclusion of the GATS agreement, services trade had increased and accounted for approximately 20% of the share of total global trade. We are thus being forced to confront these issues much more quickly. Services trade has continued to grow and has also included the so-called "servitised" goods trade where trade in goods necessarily implicates services provided, such as after care services in the case of computers and cars. E-commerce has grown exponentially, particularly rapidly accelerated during the pandemic.

Given that in many services related cases, the provision of the service was reserved to the government by way of a statutory monopoly, these issues are inevitably tied to the privatisation of these providers. We now have a wealth of experience in this area after over 20 years of privatisations around the world. We also have a wealth of case studies indicating to us how not to proceed, where much touted privatisation processes have resulted in failure, or more accurately failure for the consumers who were supposed to have been empowered as a result of the privatisation. In general, as the reader will see from the case studies and specific regulatory examples, this has been because the privatisation process has not been about developing a competitive market but has been more about enriching national treasuries. One point that is worthy of stressing and re-stressing is that privatisation does not automatically guarantee competitive markets. In fact, often, privatisation without a pro-competitive regulatory system leads to the enrichment of the licence-holders or economic gatekeepers with no benefit accruing to consumers.

Trade Liberalisation in Highly Regulated Markets

A March 2004 World Bank study analysed the impact of regulation on the ability of countries to increase growth through trade liberalisation.[18] This study compares the impact of increased trade liberalisation on countries where domestic regulation is open and where it can be characterised as closed, or where countries are more heavily regulated. There is a school of thought that increased trade forces countries to improve bad institutions. This school of thought believes that lowering border barriers inevitably leads to competitive markets and the institutions that support them. However, the study suggests that regulatory changes must accompany or precede trade liberalisation. While the focus of the study is excessive regulation (e.g. red tape) on the domestic private sector, it does show that trade (or border) liberalisation on its own will not lead to the benefits that would come with competitive markets as well. The study is also interesting because of its review of the interaction between trade and institutions. The impact of import competition on making the domestic private sector more competitive with all of these benefits occurs in countries where the network of domestic regulation is pro-competitive or open, but does not occur where domestic regulation is markedly anti-competitive (for example, in the former Soviet Union). The precise regulations reviewed for the purpose of this work include labour and business entry regulations. The regressions run in the study suggest that trade does not yield long-run growth in economies that are highly regulated. This analysis is echoed in our own attempts to measure the effects of distortion which we set out in Chapter 4. However, the authors note that it is possible that heavily regulated economies become more dependent on trade in the long run because of their inflexible domestic environments. The authors do capture the central point when they note:

> If the regulatory environment severely distorts domestic prices, then expanded trade can lead to lower income.[19]

The missing consideration is the impact, not just on growth, but also consumer welfare enhancement in the countries considered. Certainly, if the regulatory system distorts the market, then any benefits of border liberalisation will not necessarily accrue to consumers. In addition, the study is evidence that these benefits may not even lead to higher growth, if the institutions and regulatory frameworks are missing or uncompetitive.

Notion of Public Interest Regulation

A recurring excuse which regulators, who are looking for excuses to engage in anti-competitive regulation that favours incumbent companies, use is the public interest regulation defence. Public interest regulation is regulation that is designed to secure some regulatory objective that the market might not yield. Examples include media regulation to promote local culture or universal service regulation in the case of telecoms, postal or other services that are intended to ensure that all citizens have access to certain basic services. Prudential regulation, such as health and safety regulation or sanitary and phytosanitary regulations to protect animal or human health, would similarly be covered. Any attempt to reform such regulation in favour of consumers is met with the public interest regulation or prudential defence. But this defence needs to be unpicked and re-examined in the light of cases, the results of privatisation and attempts to bring a pro-competitive regulatory structure to markets.

While regulatory objectives may be non-economic, it is often forgotten that the public interest is also favoured by pro-competitive regulation that enhances consumer welfare. We would submit that this public interest frequently outweighs other producer-driven interests which too often dominate regulation. Consumer welfare-enhancing regulation may also ensure that the other public interest regulatory objectives can be more quickly met. This is not to say that you would not apply prudential regulation if an anti-competitive effect is shown. Frequently, the prudential concern is so overwhelming that you would do it anyway. However, it is important, even in these cases, that the anti-competitive cost of the regulation is made explicit, so policymakers can make informed decisions.

Countries have struggled to find the right balance between the pro-competitive and innovation aspects of regulation and satisfying important public interest in, for example, health and safety. There is clearly a link between a country's domestic regulatory settings and its external trade policy. If countries err on the side of unnecessary anti-competitive restrictions in their domestic policy, they are likely to imperil their external trade policy as well. This is because exporting companies from trading partners will complain about the regulatory restrictions as a behind the border barrier to trade.

In the areas of sanitary and phytosanitary measures affecting agricultural products, the WTO SPS agreement makes it clear that domestic regulations should be based on sound science and impose the least trade-restrictive requirements necessary to achieve a particular regulatory goal. Similarly, the WTO's Technical

Barriers to Trade Agreement provides that countries should not discriminate between WTO members in their technical regulation.

The International Competition Network in its work on competition advocacy has suggested that governments should do competition assessments of regulatory proposals to minimise their negative effects on competition. This recommendation echoes the recommendations of the OECD in both its regulatory toolkit and its competition assessment documents.[20]

Impact of Lack of Competitive Markets on Trade

There is a very real impact on trade caused by a lack of competitive markets. If there are anti-competitive practices, rules or restrictions in one market, these may have spill-over effects in another market, causing a higher level of exports from the first market than would ordinarily be the case if this market was competitive. Similarly, producers in the second market may find it harder to access the first as a result of the regulatory or otherwise anti-competitive barriers in it. In the former case, producers complain about the high level of imports, and seek tariff, safeguard or other methods of protection which do not differentiate between imports caused by greater efficiency and those caused by lack of a competitive market. In the latter case, competitors, unable to access another market, demand greater market access through trade negotiations – if their demands fail, their only sanction is to punish the export market by closing up aspects of their own market to other (and innocent) exporters from it. Clearly, both of these processes do little to protect the interests of consumers and merely express the producer interest. A better way of dealing with the issue is to attack the problem at its source, which is the anti-competitive practice, rule or other issue (collectively known as an "Anti-Competitive Market Distortion" or "ACMD") that gives rise to the problem in the first place. We illustrate in the course of the rest of the text examples of how this would apply to existing case studies (Figure 1.1).

Vy is the volume of exports from market *Y* that would normally be exported to *X* without anti-competitive barriers. The presence of ACMDs or other barriers will lead to an additional export volume ΔVy, if these ACMDs lower the cost of production. ΔVy is proportional to the level of ACPs in Market *Y* (Figure 1.2).

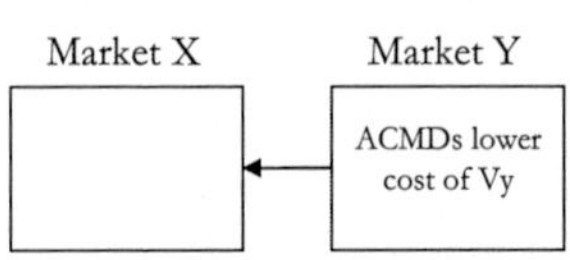

$$Vy \rightarrow x = Vy + \Delta Vy$$

Where Vy is the volume of exports from market Y that would normally be exported to X without anti-competitive barriers. The presence of ACMDs or other barriers will lead to an additional export volume ΔVy, if these ACMDs lower the cost of production. ΔVy is proportional to the level of ACPs in Market Y.

FIGURE 1.1 Impact of Distortions on Trade Flows (1)

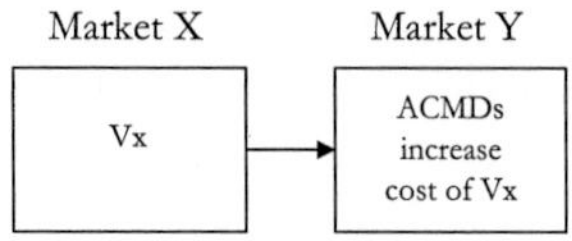

$$Vx \rightarrow y = Vx - \Delta Vx$$

FIGURE 1.2 Impact of Distortions on Trade Flows (2)

Vx is the export volume from Market *X* that would normally be exported to Market *Y* absent ACMDs in *Y*. These ACMDs increase the cost of *Vx* and lead to a reduction in export volume by ΔVx, where ΔVx is proportional to the level of ACMDs in Market *Y*.

Impact of Lack of Protection of Property Rights on Trade

The three pillars on which economic development rests are (1) trade liberalisation, (2) competitive markets inside the border and (3) the protection of property rights. Naturally, if property rights are not protected, then the value that accrues to those rights cannot properly be extracted. This has a direct impact on investment. This means that the lack of protection of property rights also has a direct impact on consumer welfare enhancement. Essentially, the protection of property rights also confers a consumer welfare benefit in an economic sense just as a competitive market does. The failure to protect such rights leads to an overall loss of consumer welfare in the long run. Here, two fundamental philosophies are in tension. Some countries adhere to the view of property rights as a fundamental and natural property right that stands outside of the relationship between a government and its citizens. The notion that property rights are either "natural" or are derived from the work done to generate revenue from the property – but certainly do not flow from governments – is a vital one for a functioning market economy. These property rights should be protected from government takings which includes not only direct confiscation or nationalisation of property but also so-called regulatory taking, where an investor is taxed at a prohibitive rate or made subject to regulation (for example, excessive environmental regulation) which can take away or substantially reduce the benefits of the investment in the first place.

The Importance of Property Restitution

There has been a sea change in the approach to the issue of private property restitution since the Second World War, at least from the perspective of the US, the UK and major developed countries. In the early part of the 20th century, the sovereignty of the state was generally supreme. The idea that victims of state confiscatory policies actually had rights simply did not exist. The great change occurred with the Second World War and the unprecedented atrocities that occurred at that time. This gave rise to the notion that some reparation ought to be made for these atrocities. This led to the actual application of the philosophical principles behind property restitution – that where people had their property taken from them without compensation, there should be some mechanism to restore that property to them, when the regime that had conducted the confiscation was gone. However, even in the case of Holocaust property restitution, many decades had to pass before there was meaningful property restitution. After the end of the cold war, restitution of confiscated property has been on the agenda as a result of transition from communism (see Central and Eastern European cases) as well as more recent cases involving cases of civil war and confiscations which occurred during various conflicts (Bosnia, Kosovo, Rwanda, Guatemala).

It is worth briefly explaining the nature of property rights and how they have developed over time. Property rights have long been recognised as a basic human right protected by a variety of treaties. For example, the European Convention for the Protection of Human Rights and Fundamental Freedoms states:

> Every natural or legal person is entitled to the peaceful enjoyment of his possessions. No-one shall be deprived of his possessions except in the public interest and subject to the conditions provided for by law and by the general principles of international law...[21]

On 10 December 1948, the General Assembly of the United Nations adopted and proclaimed the Universal Declaration of Human Rights. Article 17 states that, "Everyone has the right to own property alone as well as in association with others.... No one shall be arbitrarily deprived of his property."[22]

In November 1990, the Conference on Security and Co-operation in Europe (CSCE) adopted the Charter of Paris, which designates the right to own property and to exercise individual enterprise as one of the most fundamental of human rights.[23]

These treaties are merely expressions of a much more fundamental notion. The right to private property is a well-recognised theme of international law. From the time of Grotius and Pufendorf[24] and even before this to the Roman legal scholars, the notion that private property should be protected from state interference has been enshrined in international law. The common underlying theme is that property rights are fundamentally independent of state sovereignty, and hence changes in state sovereignty or government do not affect them. Private property rights exist outside the realm of the powers of the state (even the state's police powers). Therefore, even lack of governments has no impact on private property rights. In cases of military occupation, "immoveable private enemy property may under no circumstances or conditions be appropriated."[25]

International law has therefore recognised a "natural" right to property that is beyond any state conferred or sanctioned right. This stems from the notion that property rights exist independently of States, one of whose many purposes is to protect those property rights. John Locke clarified this view by saying that it was a man's labour that gave rise to the property right. This vision was exemplified in the Spitsbergen Archipelago problem. Here, barren islands were mined by US companies before any country claimed ownership of the islands. When Norway claimed ownership, the US asserted that this did nothing to affect the pre-existing property rights of its mining companies. In that treatment and subsequently, there is a real distinction among legal systems, with the Anglo-American legal system strongly in favour of the concept that property rights exist separate and apart from the State ("natural rights"), contrasted with those systems which adopt a positivistic approach (where property rights are conferred by the country's legal regime, and are therefore more in the nature of state grants, like a patent, for example). This kind of approach is to be found in primarily civil law jurisdictions.

These property rights also critically include both tangible and intangible property rights. The protection of intellectual property rights is therefore consumer welfare enhancing and is part of the three-legged stool of trade liberalisation, competition and protection of property rights which are the basics of economic development. Far from tension existing, as many assert, between intellectual property policy and competition policy, in fact the two policies have the same overall goals – the stimulation of productivity which is derived from specialisation and the stimulation of innovation which is a byproduct of strengthened inter-firm competition.

We will explore this subject in greater detail in Chapter 11 on the triple interface between trade, competition and intellectual property.

Impact of Market Failure on Trade Liberalisation

We have seen the impact of market failure on trade liberalisation attempts which have not yielded benefits as a result of domestic market failure. We have seen this particularly in cases where privatisation has converted public monopoly with regulation into private monopoly without regulation and where the privatisation process has not led to the unleashing of the forces of competition. The primary purpose of a privatisation is to unleash these forces, so consumers have better choice and lower prices and so business is more efficient. The fire-sale value to a government of an inadequately thought-out privatisation is vastly outweighed by the cost of an essentially unregulated private monopoly extracting monopoly rents out of the economy. We illustrate this with a number of examples from network industries where these problems tend to be acute.

These issues tend to be particularly serious in the context of privatisation. There have been a number of privatisations in the last 20 years which have faced problems which are on the cutting edge of the interface between trade and competition. Many privatisations give opportunities for market access to both domestic and foreign new entrants. However, these benefits can be forestalled in cases where these privatisations do not go forward in a pro-competitive manner.

Mercantilism in Trade Negotiations

We will examine the history of trade negotiations and the development of the WTO in more detail in Chapter 2. However, we must note, by way of introduction, that recent trade negotiations in the WTO and in the regional/bilateral arena have demonstrated that the concept of mercantilism very much influences trade negotiations if not trade theory as set out above. While it is clear that trade theory rests on the principle of comparative advantage, trade negotiators often employ pure mercantilist, zero-sum game arguments in their negotiations. Initially, the Cordell Hull inspired mechanism for negotiating tariffs, embodied in the Reciprocal Tariffs Act of 1934, harnessed this mercantilist impulse for a noble purpose – by setting up a tariff-setting negotiation between the country which was the principal consumer of a product and the principal supplier on a tariff, and then applying that "deal" through the most favoured nation principle to all trading partners. This was a very clever way of ensuring that tariffs would be systematically ratcheted down. However, while it might work for tariffs (and even this is debatable), it clearly has no place in the negotiation of rules that embody much of the more recent work of the WTO. Indeed, the problem that what was once a useful mechanism which harnessed the mercantilist impulse for a positive purpose has now become something that merely enhances the mercantilist impulse. The notion that a country will prevent the negotiation of certain rules that would help its consumers, in exchange for some gains in an unrelated area that would ultimately help certain of its producers, is clearly not a sensible approach. Yet precisely this is happening in trade negotiations around the world. Indeed, the rise of the G-20 (a coalition of developing countries headed by Brazil and India focused on securing agricultural concessions from developed countries) was founded on such a trade-off. The G-20 have resisted negotiations in services and non-agricultural market access, until gains in agricultural market access are secured for developing countries. The collapse of both the Free Trade Areas of the Americas and the length of time it took for the EU-Mercosur trade negotiations to conclude highlighted these issues as well.[26] The trade-off was that in exchange for agricultural concessions from developed countries, the developing countries would consider the possibility of opening up their services and industrial sectors and admit the possibility of greater rules-based agreements.

We contend that it is imperative that trade negotiations be infused once more by the normative principles of consumer welfare enhancement – which we argue would be a return to their original roots. The initial repeal of the corn tariff, as we have seen, was an attempt to craft a trade solution which would allow comparative advantage to work properly. It led to a unilateral tariff "concession" in modern (and mercantilist) parlance. Yet what was being conceded was the right to have a tariff which would harm English consumers, while allowing local producers of corn to engage in rent-seeking behaviour, by limiting competition. In this case, the consumer welfare interest trumped the local producer interest, which, although difficult, was achieved. It required, as we set out early in this book, an extensive campaign. Encouragingly, the Corn Tariff was repealed, despite Adam Smith's recognition that local producers are good at persuading people in their countries that what is in their interests is in the interests of the country as a whole. Consumer interests did, for a period, trump mercantilist interests in this case. Hence, we believe that this is a precedent for the principle that we advocate. There is another reason why trade negotiations will be more likely to be informed by competition policy in the future. We are reaching a point in trade negotiations where more and more of the actual negotiation is a negotiation on domestic regulation. These are essentially competition-type negotiations where consumer welfare interests require pro-competitive regulation. Mercantilist negotiators often say that this is an intrusion into national sovereignty or that their policy space is being limited. But the reality is that the sovereignty to harm one's own consumers has been limited since the introduction of the GATT, 1947. An example of this is GATT Article III's limitation on a nation's internal laws governing taxes, sale and distribution which prevents them from applying different rules as between different producers in other countries. In addition, other GATT rules such as the disciplines on state trading enterprises in Article XVII and the nullification and impairments rules in Article XXIII do restrict some policy space or impose limits on sovereignty. The question that consumers around the world should ask when faced with these bogus arguments is whether governments have the right to abuse the fundamental principles of international trade for the sole purpose of visiting harm on consumers in order to enrich a relatively small proportion of local producers. As trade barriers in the traditional sense (such as tariffs and certain non-tariff barriers) are eroded, so internal market effects become more and more important in potentially distorting international trade, even as they distort domestic markets. There is nothing in a trade agreement which precludes any type of government action; they merely require the offending government to pay for them. We will show in the following chapters the many areas where competition rules are already in the WTO, and how they have already limited effective national sovereignty as a logical extension of the most basic of GATT principles. If one accepts the fundamental doctrine of Smith and Ricardo as set out above, one has already accepted the idea that one's policy space being practically circumscribed by the notion of the competition principle as a normative governing economic principle. Mere accession to the WTO is an implicit acceptance of this notion, even though countries often seek to reject this. Negotiations with all WTO members will get increasingly difficult in the future as negotiations deepen in these areas but deeper negotiations with those members that have accepted this principle may well be possible. Indeed, we have seen this in the regional agreement process following the collapse of the WTO Doha Development Agenda, and the rise of initiatives like the Comprehensive and Progressive Trans Pacific Partnership. The recent UK accession negotiations here show that these initiatives are not mere regional agreements but represent a coalition of willing nations, or as UK Foreign Secretary Liz Truss has called them, a "network of liberty."

Indeed, we will also show that competition policy principles already infuse the WTO, particularly in the areas of Articles III, XVII and XXIII. They are even more persuasive in the context of the GATS agreements, such as the Basic Telecommunications Agreement, and in particular the Reference Paper on Competition Safeguards. In addition, other services sectoral papers, such as the Financial Services Annex, also contemplate domestic regulatory or competition policy. The current built-in (to the Uruguay Round) agenda of services involves negotiations on government procurement, and domestic regulation as well as market access. We argue that a domestic regulatory negotiation is basically a competition policy negotiation, which includes a discussion of how to deal with market failure.

Notes

1 David Ricardo, *On the Principles of Political Economy and Taxation* (Dover Publications 1817).
2 *Id.*
3 Vergennes Treaty, GB-Fr, 1786.
4 Parliamentary Debates, 1st Series, Vol. 29 (1815) Col. 984.
5 *Id.*, Col 811–817.
6 Declaration from Meeting in Manchester (1819), *reprinted in* Donald Read, *Peterloo: The Massacre and its Background*, Manchester University Press (1958).
7 Dr Pye Smith, "Report of the Conference of Ministers of all Denominations on the Corn Laws" (1841) ("the doctrine and practice of free trade [was] in harmony with the essential principle and the benevolent design of the gospel") https://books.google.com/books?id=wL2gvhdTVmcC&printsec=frontcover#v=onepage&q&f=false.
8 Richard Cobden, M.P., Free Trade, Speech XXI, Com Laws, House of Commons, 28 Feb 1846, *in* Speeches on Questions of Public Policy (1870).
9 Richard Cobden, M.P., Free Trade, Speech XXI, Com Laws, House of Commons, 28 Feb 1846, *in* Speeches on Questions of Public Policy (1870).
10 *See* Adam Smith, *An Inquiry into the Nature and Causes of the Wealth of Nations* (Roy H. Campbell, Andrew S. Skinner, and William B. Todd eds., Liberty Fund 1981) (1776).
11 *Id.*, I.x.c.27 ("People of the same trade seldom meet together, even for merriment and diversion, but the conversation ends in a conspiracy against the public, or in some contrivance to raise prices.")
12 A*n* I*nquiry Into the* Nature *and* C*auses of the Wealth of* Nations, *supra* note 10, IV.vii.c.
13 *Id.*, IV.viii.
14 *Id.*, IV.viii.4.
15 *Id.*, IV.viii.
16 *Id.*, IV.vii.c.
17 *Id.*, IV.vii.c.
18 Bineswaree Bolaky and Caroline Freund, *Trade, Regulations, and Growth*, World Bank (March 2004).
19 *Id.*, at 23.
20 Materials on the OECD Competition Assessment are available at https://www.oecd.org/competition/assessment-toolkit.htm; Materials on the OECD Regulatory Toolkit are available at https://www.oecd.org/gov/regulatory-policy/oecd-regulatory-enforcement-and-inspections-toolkit-9789264303959-en.htm; Material on the ICN's competition advocacy work is available at https://www.internationalcompetitionnetwork.org/working-groups/advocacy/.
21 European Convention for the Protection of Human Rights, Article 1, https://www.echr.coe.int/documents/convention_eng.pdf.

22 G.A. Res. 217 A (III), U.N. GAOR, 3rd Sess., U.N. Doc. A/810 at 71 (1948).

23 "Charter of Paris for a New Europe," Organization for Security and Co-operation in Europe (21 Nov 1990), https://www.osce.org/files/f/documents/0/6/39516.pdf.

24 Hugo Grotius, *The Rights of War and Peace* (Archibald C. Campbell trans., M. Walter Dunne 1901) (1625); Samuel Pufendorf, *Of the Law of Nature and Nations* (William Percivale, Jean Barbeyrac, and Basil Kennett trans., L. Lichfield 1710) (1672).

25 Lassa Oppenheim, *International Law; A Treatise 403* (Hersch Lauterpacht ed., 7th ed., Longmans, Green, and Go 1948).

26 For more information about the EU-Mercosur negotiations, see EU-Mercosur Trade Agreement, EU-Arg.-Braz.-Para.-Uru. (28 Jun 1999), https://ec.europa.eu/trade/policy/in-focus/eu-mercosur-association-agreement/.

2

INTRODUCTION TO INSTITUTIONS UNDERPINNING GLOBAL TRADE AND REGULATIONS

On 1 July 1944, while the war in Europe was approaching its conclusion, a conference with the participation of 45 countries was held at Bretton Woods, New Hampshire. The conference was entitled the "United Nations Monetary and Financial Conference," and it was here that the great pillars that were to underpin the global trade order well into this century were built. At this conference, the key players, the US and Great Britain, initiated the process that led to the International Monetary Fund (IMF) and the International Bank for Reconstruction and Development (IBRD), and recognised the need for an organisation to support the rules which governed world trade, which was to be called the International Trade Organization (ITO).

However, even the initial path of free trade did not run smoothly. The Bretton Woods conference was mainly devoted to monetary and banking issues but the critical drive for the ITO fell at the door of the US Congress. The General Agreement on Tariffs and Trade (GATT) was introduced as a contract among trading partners and as a preliminary step before the ITO legislation was to be passed by Congress. It took another 47 years before the WTO agreements took effect and the World Trade Organization was created.

The International Monetary Fund (IMF)

Structure and Scope

The IMF was officially established on 27 December 1945, when 29 of the participating countries at the conference of Bretton Woods signed its Articles of Agreement. Its financial operations were inaugurated on 1 March 1947. The IMF, which today consists of 184 member countries, is an international organisation designed to be a lender to developing countries.

DOI: 10.4324/9780429323331-2

The principal focuses of the IMF are set out in Article I of the IMF's charter: The purposes of the IMF are as follows:

- i To promote international monetary cooperation through a permanent institution which provides the machinery for consultation and collaboration on international monetary problems.
- ii To facilitate the expansion and balanced growth of international trade and to contribute thereby to the promotion and maintenance of high levels of employment and real income and to the development of the productive resources of all members as primary objectives of economic policy.
- iii To promote exchange stability, to maintain orderly exchange arrangements among members and to avoid competitive exchange depreciation.
- iv To assist in the establishment of a multilateral system of payments in respect of current transactions between members and in the elimination of foreign exchange restrictions which hamper the growth of world trade.
- v To give confidence to members by making the general resources of the Fund temporarily available to them under adequate safeguards, thus providing them with opportunity to correct maladjustments in their balance-of-payments without resorting to measures destructive of national or international prosperity.
- vi In accordance with the above, to shorten the duration and lessen the degree of disequilibrium in the international balances of payments of members.

The Fund shall be guided in all its policies and decisions by the purposes set forth in this Article.[1]

However, the primary focus of the IMF has been to ensure orderly transactions in financial markets. Its policies have evolved since its creation. Rather than mission creep as some suggest, we consider that this is an organic evolution based on a changing global economic environment. For example, early reliance on the gold standard was abandoned and replaced by fixed exchange rates. The elimination of the gold standard had the effect of removing one of the primary purposes of the IMF, as it was no longer required to maintain currency value in relation to gold. The IMF began to adopt the role more of an economic development institution by extending subsidised loans to less developed countries in the early 1970s.

The IMF has the following operating functionalities: a surveillance function over member countries' exchange rates, financial assistance and technical assistance.

Surveillance

Among the IMF's responsibilities is "surveillance." Surveillance refers to the process of the IMF's dialogue with its member countries on the impact of national and international actions on economic and financial policies. This process includes both a monitoring and a consultation process.

IMF surveillance activities are as interesting for what they do not cover as for what they do. Article IV[2] and a Decision in 1977[3] provide the set of issues which are subject to IMF surveillance. The 1977 Decision provided that the IMF must look at the general economic situation and policy decisions of the borrower country. The covered issues include primarily the exchange rate, and monetary and fiscal policies. Structural issues such as international trade were added to the IMF's surveillance in the 1980s – also included were labour market issues and power sector reform. In the 1990s, with the increased number of financial crises, surveillance began to include a watching brief over the financial sectors of countries through the Financial Sector Assessment Program (launched with the World Bank in 1999). Finally, institutional issues such as corporate governance have been added to the Fund's remit, largely in response to massive failures in both developed and developing country members alike.

We therefore see a growing body of issues, starting at purely measures related to the interaction between members and then looking at structural policies of those members themselves who are increasingly subject to IMF surveillance. However, the IMF only reviews these to the extent that they have a direct macro-economic impact and does not focus attention on the micro-economic policies of borrower countries. Nonetheless, reviewing the underlying trend of the IMF to focus increasingly more and more attention on behind-the-border issues (such as financial stability of the banking sector, which is ultimately an issue of domestic regulation), it would be fair to say that micro-economic policies of borrowers could and should come increasingly under the IMF microscope, just as the micro-economic policies of borrowers in the private sector are checked by lenders in determining whether they are good credit risks.

Financial Assistance

The Fund has a number of different, tailored facilities that it uses depending on the type of borrower. In this respect, the Fund operates just as any bank that tailors its loans to borrowers based on their particular and peculiar characteristics. IMF lending has increased with the rise in the number of transition countries (Central and Eastern Europe and the former Soviet Union) and countries emerging from import substitution economics.

Technical Assistance

The IMF already provides technical assistance in its core areas of competence. As one would expect, the technical assistance provided follows the surveillance functionalities that define IMF core competence. However, it is in the legal technical assistance that one begins to discern a greater focus on domestic regulatory issues. For example, technical assistance will be given to assist countries in writing bankruptcy laws so as to build fiscal stability. Legal technical assistance also extends to customs and tax laws. Bank regulation is also expressly covered by IMF technical assistance programmes. The Fiscal Affairs Department, for example, does consider tax and customs policy in some detail, although the perspective often errs on the side of revenue generation for governments rather than ensuring that freer trade is enhanced.[4]

The World Bank

Structure and Scope

The IBRD was established at Bretton Woods to supply loans for reconstruction after the Second World War. As it turned out, IBRD did not play the foreseen instrumental role in the reconstruction of Europe but the institution quickly evolved into the world's biggest development organisation and became known as the World Bank. The Articles of Agreement[5] for this organisation were signed by 29 countries by the end of December 1945. Its first loan of $250 million was to France in 1947 for post-war reconstruction. Today, the World Bank consists of 184 member countries, with the Democratic Republic of East Timor having become the 184th member on 24 June 2002.

The World Bank slowly began branching out. In 1955, with the establishment of the Economic Development Institute (EDI), the Bank began training developing-country government officials to improve the economic well-being of their citizens. The Bank also established the following: (i) International Financial Corporation (IFC) (1956); (ii) International Development Association (IDA) (1960); (iii) International Centre for **Settlement of Investment Disputes (ICSID) (1966) and (iv) Multilateral Investment Guarantee Agreement (MIGA) (1988).**

The IFC's mission is to promote sustainable private sector investment in developing countries. The IFC is the largest multilateral source of loan and equity financing for private sector projects and development in the developing world. The three parts of the IFC's work focus on financing developing-world private sector projects, facilitating developing-world private companies to access international financial markets and providing technical assistance to developing world businesses and governments.

World Bank members provide contributions based on the size of their economies, and the larger and wealthier the economy, the more the country is likely to give. A country's voting power is based on the amount of its contributions. Since the US is the biggest donor, it therefore has the most voting power. The Bank's funds are also derived from investments that the Bank makes in financial markets. The Bank sells bonds and other debt securities to pension funds, insurance companies, corporations, other banks and individual investors. Its original source of income, however, remains the contributions by member countries. Countries receiving loans are charged an interest rate, adjusted every six months.

Functions

The World Bank initially financed infrastructure projects such as dams, bridges, railways, roads, ports, power plants and communication facilities. Electricity supply, often connected to large dam projects, represented half of total lending. During the 1970s, World Bank lending increased dramatically. Even if the Bank during this period stressed investments in the social sector, the increase in lending came mainly in the traditional sectors like infrastructure.

The original mandate of the Bank was to provide loans on a project-specific basis. This mandate evolved with the international debt crisis of the early 1980s. By the end of the decade, roughly 25% of the Bank's lending went to the restructuring of developing-country economies through structural adjustment programmes. In countries with structural adjustment programmes, these loans have amounted to 50% or more of total lending. The conditioning of loans upon structural adjustment implies devaluations, reductions in public sector spending and cuts in subsidies. In many cases, this includes subsidies on basic food supplies. The programmes have often involved export orientation based on raw materials and natural resources. Environmental concerns also began to play a role in Bank lending policies in the 1980s. In the 1990s, the Bank began to focus on issues related to civil society as a means of creating sustainable development.

The World Bank has significant influence on the formulation of policies and development strategies of recipient countries due to its ability to provide loans. The Bank's influence is enhanced by its role as a coordinator of development aid in a large number of countries.

Over time, some of the differences between the World Bank and the IMF have faded, as the Bank now stresses short-term macro-economic policy (originally the IMF's field), while the IMF has started to talk about development on a long-term scale.

The International Trade Organization

After the World Bank and the IMF were created, the United Nations (UN) Economic and Social Council held a conference on trade and employment issues in February of 1946. This would eventually lead to the draft of a convention establishing the ITO. A Preparatory Committee, after two meetings in London (1946) and Geneva (1947), produced a first draft. At the UN Conference on Trade and Employment, held in Havana (Cuba) from November 1947 to March 1948, the text of the Charter for the ITO (Havana Charter) was adopted, and the Interim Commission for the ITO (ICITO), consisting of 52 countries, was created. The ICITO established an Executive Committee that held several meetings, but by 1950 it had become clear that the Havana Charter was not going to be accepted by the US Congress, even though the US had supported it in the first place and was a signatory country. All efforts to establish the ITO were then abandoned.

The Havana Charter[6] included chapters on employment, economic development and reconstruction, commercial policies, restrictive business practices, commodity agreements and dispute settlement. It is evident that the original ITO had a broad agenda that covered many areas beyond tariff liberalisation in industrial goods. The original ITO vision was for a comprehensive Charter and an organisation that would deal with a number of trade-related areas in a holistic fashion.

Article 1 of the Charter set out the purpose and objectives of the ITO. Of its six principal objectives, one directly concerned the way in which trade should be conducted and organised: "To promote on a reciprocal and mutually advantageous basis the reduction of tariffs and other barriers to trade and the elimination of discriminatory treatment in international commerce." Another exclusively concerned economic development: "To foster and assist industrial and general economic development, particularly of those countries which are still in the early stages of industrial development, and to encourage the international flow of capital for productive investment." Two dealt with the founding principles of the world trade order:

> To further the enjoyment, by all countries on equal terms, of access to markets, products and productive faculties which are needed for economic prosperity and development; and to enable countries, by increasing the opportunities for their trade and economic development, to abstain from measures which would disrupt world commerce, reduce productive employment or retard economic progress.

The link between trade liberalisation and competitive markets was already well established by the ITO Charter, as well as the link between these two policies and economic development. Stepping forward, the decision to call the trade negotiations that were launched in Doha in 2001, the Doha Development Agenda was essentially tautology. As expressed clearly in the ITO Charter, trade liberalisation between countries should lead to economic development particularly for those countries in the early stage of their development.

Another objective of Article 1 sought "To facilitate through the promotion of mutual understanding, consultation and cooperation the solution of problems relating to international trade in the fields of employment, economic development, commercial policy, business practices and commodity policy."

The theoretical understanding behind the Havana Charter was that countries would have to make national adjustments to international forces when international trade was expanding rather than contracting. Further, countries had to make an equal commitment to eliminate all forms of arbitrary and discriminatory barriers that the state and market actors routinely erected for public or private profit. In the imperfect world of the late 1940s (much like our own), countries everywhere employed export subsidies, quantitative restrictions and commodity agreements for commercial ends.

However, the ITO was never established largely because of opposition within the US Congress, which considered the establishment of the ITO to reach too deeply into domestic policy. Many of the arguments that were made then in the US are being made today in developing countries, as to why the WTO (the successor to the GATT, see *infra*) should not reach behind borders and impact domestic policies in various fields.

These arguments are usually framed in terms of preserving policy space for national legislators to promulgate their own regulations. First, national legislators are free to do what they want – they merely have to pay for it if it violates trade rules and harms trading partners. However, it is important to point out that the policy space to damage one's own consumer is not a policy space worth protecting. Given that legislators tend to be pressured into favouring domestic producer interests at the expense of local consumers, policy space is frequently used to diminish consumer welfare, and in many cases can damage a country's overall economic development if producer welfare concerns are allowed to systematically trump consumer welfare concerns.

It is important to note that there was a general understanding at the launch of the Bretton Woods institutions, as well as at the signing of the ITO Charter, that one could not simply liberalise tariffs on industrial goods and hope that this would lead to meaningful liberalisation, competitive markets and economic development or that countries would actually benefit from the process of liberalisation without deeper reforms. Unfortunately, the import substitution economics that were then followed by some countries did much to shore up the power of vested-interest elites that benefited from protection, thus making it even harder now (as opposed to in 1946) to make trade gains, and to return the globe to the state in which it was originally intended to be – free trade without barriers, to ensure the economically efficient allocation of resources.

The General Agreement on Tariffs and Trade (GATT)

History of GATT Negotiations Culminating in the World Trade Organization (WTO)

While the work on the ITO was proceeding, members of the Preparatory Committee engaged in tariff negotiations, and on 30 October 1947, 23 countries signed a Final Act authenticating the text of the GATT in Geneva, Switzerland.[7] This was based on the Commercial Policy provisions of the Havana Charter, and the text was amended in 1948 to reflect the final version of the Charter. Rather than adopt GATT by means of its provisions on acceptance, the participants in the negotiations concluded a Protocol of Provisional Application by which they agreed to apply GATT from January 1948. The countries that joined after this date may be regarded as having joined the arrangements constituted by the combination of the Protocol and the General Agreement.

The signatory countries committed to participate in regular negotiations on tariff reductions. These regular multilateral trade negotiations later became known as the Rounds of GATT, in which countries exchanged comments to reduce tariffs and agreed to extensions of the GATT rules.

The following table summarises the GATT/WTO Rounds held so far:

Geneva	*1947*	*Adoption of GATT*
Annecy	1949	Tariff Cuts
Torquay	1950–1951	Tariff Cuts
Geneva	1956	Tariff Cuts
Dillon	1960–1962	Tariff Cuts
Kennedy	1963–1967	Tariff Cuts, GATT negotiation rules
Tokyo	1973–1979	Tariff cuts, Non-Tariff Barriers (NTBs): government procurement, customs valuation, subsidies and countervailing measures, anti-dumping, import licencing, conditional MGN approach, the beginning of the opening of the GATT to broader issues.
Uruguay	1986–1994	Broader: limit agricultural subsidies, include services, include intellectual property, establishment of WTO, comprehensive legal (non-political) dispute settlement understanding.
Doha	2001–Incomplete	NTBs, Services, Non-Agricultural Market Access, Transparency in government procurement

In the Annecy (France) Round (1949), the Torquay (Great Britain) Round (1950–1951) and the Geneva 4th Round (1956), the focus was maintained on tariff reductions. In Annecy, 5,000 tariff concessions were made and 10 more countries signed the agreement. In Torquay, 8,700 tariff reductions were added and the number of participating countries rose to 38. In the 4th Round in Geneva in 1956, the trade covered by the tariff reductions was of USD 2.5 billion.

As can be seen, these earlier rounds were launched in fairly rapid succession. There is little to indicate that they were driven by anything other than the interests and concerns of trade ministers pursuing their own particular mandates to roll back the highly destructive protectionism of the interwar era. The tariff reductions negotiated in these rounds were accompanied by the dismantling of quantitative limits on imports and exports and various payment impediments that hampered international commerce. Broader issues "behind the border" were not even discussed. By the time the agreements arising from these four rounds were completed, the average weighted tariff in the major industrialised countries had fallen to about 15%.[8]

The Dillon Round

The Dillon Round (1960–1962)[9] was the last Round to focus solely on tariff cuts. The Dillon Round was largely initiated to deal with the US and other concerns about the trade implication of the launch of the European Economic Community (EEC) and the European Free Trade Association (EFTA).

Specifically, the negotiations were intended to resolve claims arising under GATT Article XXIV with respect to the just-created EEC, as well as to examine the Article XXIV consistency of the EEC and the EFTA, which had been established by the West European countries (Norway, Switzerland, Iceland and Liechtenstein) that had chosen not to join the EEC. Both exercises ended inconclusively, setting the precedent for future such investigations of consistency of regional free trade arrangement with Article XXIV, which specifies the conditions under which such arrangements comport with multilateral rules (for a more precise analysis of Article XXIV, see *infra*).

The Kennedy Round

While the Kennedy Round (1963–1967) resulted in important tariff cuts, it is an interesting question as to why it took until 1963 to launch a serious tariff-cutting exercise (the Round employed a "formula approach": industrial tariffs were reduced by 35% over a period of five years). In reality, only two of the five preceding rounds had resulted in major tariff cuts: one of these had occurred prior to the formation of the GATT, in the first negotiation in Geneva in 1947, and the second in Torquay. The negotiations in Annecy and the second round of negotiations in Geneva both produced disappointing results, as did the Dillon Round. Meanwhile, a clear-cut trade policy agenda had long been advocated from the Haberler Report of 1958, which had made recommendations that the panel of experts[10] had been asked to examine. Specifically, the Report recommended:

1 shifting to a systemic approach to tariff cuts to replace the product-by-product approach;
2 addressing trade in agricultural goods; and
3 giving developing countries greater flexibility to use trade restrictions to promote infant industrial development, particularly key industries that would spur further industrialisation, to address balance-of-payments issues (which they would be more likely to face), and more generally to "turn the international terms of trade… in [their] favour."

The Haberler Report coincided with a period of time (in the late 1950s) when some economists led by Raul Prebisch, a Latin American central banker, started to suggest that import substitution might be a way to protect and develop the economic systems of newly industrialising countries. Prebisch drew on the work of Friedrich List and even Alexander Hamilton before that. The infant industry argument was born out of this thinking. The problem, as we shall see repeatedly in the course of the next few chapters, is that these infants rarely become adult. But while they are infants, they can suck the life out of the economy by gorging themselves on monopoly rents and eroding consumer welfare.

It is worth noticing that two of the Haberler recommendations, trade in agriculture and developing-country issues, were still featured prominently in the failed DDA, and are as controversial as they were many decades ago. The Haberler Report is riddled with the notion that one has to choose between liberalisation and development. In the language of this book, the Haberler Report fell squarely onto the producer welfare side of the economic ledger. We can see in the way these issues are playing out now that this same zero-sum economic thinking is remarkably resilient.

The new negotiations were agreed to at the meeting of ministers of the GATT Contracting Parties in Geneva in May 1963 but were formally launched a year later. The negotiations were initiated in 1964 and concluded in 1967. The length of the negotiations reflected the fact that, for the first time, trade negotiations embraced issues beyond the tariff itself.

Throughout the Kennedy Round, balance-of-payments issues dominated the economic policy concerns. Sixty-six nations participated and the draft of an "Anti-Dumping Code" emerged from this round, in addition to the tariff reductions. An agreement was also reached on dealing with the trade of developing nations and on new GATT negotiation rules (the "formula approach").

The Anti-Dumping Code was designed to deal with a world where firms were seeking to replace the protection; they had lost through successive tariff reductions. They sought an alternative border measure to the tariff. This alternative measure affected trade at the border and was the application of anti-dumping laws. As these laws were interpreted in ways that were more based on price than cost (a producer welfare vision), the number of imports that were blocked by anti-dumping actions was almost equal to the number of complaints brought. This effectively means that every time local producers were affected by imports, these imports were blocked. Hence, the impact of this on the flow of trade was so significant that something had to be done about the producer welfare orientation and application of these laws. We discuss this in much greater detail in Chapter 4 on trade remedies.

The Tokyo Round

While the Tokyo Round (1973–1979) resulted in broad tariff reductions, it is more noted for several supplementary agreements, as well as strengthening GATT's dispute resolution mechanisms.

Ninety-nine countries participated in the Tokyo Round and the overall reduction of tariffs (covering more than USD 300 billion of trade) was of an average level of 35% and 5%–8% among developed nations.[11] Non-Tariff Barriers

(NTBs) were the focus, the Anti-Dumping Code was revised and codes for the following areas were established: Government Procurement, Customs Valuations, Subsidies & Countervailing Measures and Technical Barriers to Trade (TBT). Preferential treatment was accorded to the developing countries.

Not surprisingly, given this agenda and how it developed, there was disagreement until 1977. Much of the plurilateral countries were free riding off the commitments of others. The 1970s were a particularly turbulent period. Dramatic events such as the Yom Kippur War, the first oil crisis, Watergate and the impeachment of President Nixon, and the collapse of the Bretton Woods system, as well as the emergence of Japan as a major economic actor on the international scene conspired to set the stage for a change in direction for the GATT.

The Tokyo Round also adopted the so-called Enabling Clause that legalised partial trade preferences among developing countries, as well as one-way partial preferences by developed to developing countries. The latter provision legitimated the Generalised System of Preferences (GSP) that had come to exist since at least 1971. The Enabling Clause was never formally incorporated into GATT but its provisions have been clearly influential in the creation of many partial Preferential Trade Agreements (PTAs) and in legitimating the GSP (see more *infra*).

The Uruguay Round

The Uruguay Round was undoubtedly the most far-reaching of all multilateral trade negotiations and agreements to date. With its full implementation, the expectation is for as much as 75% of world trade to be under the discipline of GATT.

The Round was initiated in 1985 and formally launched in September 1986 at Punta del Este. The Uruguay Round consisted of 120 countries. The US proposed that services, intellectual property and foreign investment restrictions be included on the agenda. In addition, the EC was persuaded to accept the inclusion of agriculture. Five contentious areas were identifiable as subjects of the round negotiation: agriculture, textile and "new areas," such as services, intellectual property and investment. The US insisted on the fact that negotiations on new areas were to be conducted separately from those on goods: therefore, consensus was reached that no attempts would be made to link an offer of concessions in the goods area to demands for concessions in new areas.

Agriculture, the traditional bugbear of trade negotiations, was the most controversial area. By 1990, it looked like disagreement on the scope of the agricultural negotiations would doom the round. Indeed, it was only the threat by then President George H.W. Bush of a multi-billion-dollar farm bill that brought the European Union back to the negotiating table.[12] Much of the current difficulties surrounding agriculture today in the Doha Development Agenda carry the same trade baggage. After the Farm Bill and the related discussion, by November 1992, the US and EC had agreed on terms for reducing EC export subsidies.

This paved the way for further negotiations on agriculture and other issues, and ultimately the conclusion of the Uruguay Round in December 1993.

WTO Structure: Overview

"The Final Act Embodying the Results of the Uruguay Round of Multilateral Trade Negotiations," signed by ministers in Marrakesh on 15 April 1994, was the most comprehensive series of trade agreements hitherto agreed. We attached at Annex 1 a list of all Uruguay Round Agreements.

The major contribution of the Uruguay Round is the WTO and its dispute settlement mechanism which forms part of the single undertaken and comprehensive agreement. The prior GATT dispute resolution mechanism was an inherently political process where the party that lost the Panel Decision had the right to veto the Panel Decision itself. This embroiled Panel Decisions in a political morass with very little forward progress. The role of dispute resolution in ensuring compliance to GATTs disciplines was stymied. Under the new WTO dispute settlement mechanism, the rulings of the Panel become legally binding and enforceable, subject to an enforceable system of trade sanctions. In addition, the Appellate Body (an appeals court to whom parties who lost in Panel Decisions could take their claims) was set up, initiating the development of a distinct body of WTO law. The constitutional architecture of the global trading system, foreshadowed by the ITO decades previously, was beginning to take shape. The WTO structure is headed by a Ministerial Conference meeting at least once every two years. The General Council oversees the operation of the agreement and ministerial decisions on a regular basis. The General Council acts as a Dispute Settlement Body and a Trade Policy Review Mechanism reviews the WTO compliance of member countries. A series of councils supporting each of the main agreements was set up. These include the Goods Council, a Services Council and a TRIPS Council.

The WTO framework[13] ensures a "single undertaking approach" to the results of the Uruguay Round – thus, membership in the WTO entails accepting all the results of the Round without exception.

As the WTO Secretariat has explained, it is important to note the Single Undertaking nature of the WTO agreements. Therefore, with the exception of some of the plurilateral agreements all the WTO agreements stand together as a single binding contractual arrangement among members. The agreements can be divided into the following constituent parts:

- The Agreement establishing the WTO itself.
- Agreements for each of the three broad areas of trade that the WTO covers (goods, services[14] and intellectual property).
- Dispute settlement understanding.
- The Trade Policy Review Mechanism, where country's trade policies are reviewed by a TPRM to ensure compliance with a country's obligations.

Broad Agreements

The GATT for goods, the General Agreement on Trade in Services (GATS) for services and the Agreement on Trade-Related Aspects of Intellectual Property Rights (TRIPS) for intellectual property, though presently TRIPS has no additional parts.

Annexes deal with specific sectors.

Sector-Specific Commitments

These are made by individual countries, allowing specific foreign products or service-providers access to their markets. For GATT, these take the form of binding commitments on tariffs for goods in general, and combinations of tariffs and quotas for some agricultural goods. For GATS, the commitments state how much access foreign service providers are allowed for specific sectors, and they include lists of types of services where individual countries say that they are not applying either MFN or national treatment principles.

Plurilateral Agreements

Plurilateral agreements initially developed as a result of the Tokyo Round in response to the idea that some countries were free riding off the commitments of others. They are a significant departure from ordinary WTO law where the concept of the Single Undertaking is so important. The concept underpinning the plurilateral agreement is that only WTO members that want to can join, thus creating a "coalition of the willing" who would be prepared to countenance much deeper levels of integration. The plurilateral process can thus act as a spur to the liberalisation process by encouraging countries to emulate the practices that lead to other successful economies. However, these agreements can also lead to a two-speed WTO leading to trade diversion. After the Uruguay Round, however, there remained four agreements, originally negotiated in the Tokyo Round, which had a narrower group of signatories: Government Procurement, Civil Aircraft, Dairy Products and Bovine Meat (the last two were terminated in 1997, handled now under the Agriculture and Sanitary and Phytosanitary Agreements).

The Doha Development Round

Since the formation of the WTO in 1995, five Ministerial Conferences have been held. It is worth reviewing the results of these different ministerial conferences.

Singapore (1996)

Three new working groups were initiated: on trade and investment, on competition policy and on transparency in government procurement. The Ministers also instructed the WTO Goods Council to look at possible ways of simplifying trade procedures, "trade facilitation." Because the Singapore conference kicked off work in these four subjects, they were known as the "Singapore issues." We will look carefully at these issues.

Investment

Seven major themes within investments were discussed: the scope and definition of "investments"; transparency; non-discrimination; modalities for pre-establishment commitments based on a GATS-type, positive list approach; development provisions; exceptions and balance-of-payments; safeguards; and consultation and the settlement of disputes between Members. The issue of scope is based on either a narrow (enterprise- or transaction-based) definition or a broader (assets-based) definition. It is worth considering the fate of the investment group, in parallel to the discussions that took place within the OECD on a Multi-lateral Agreement on Investment. The OECD discussions began in 1995 but thanks largely to a high degree of pressure from Non-Government Organisations (NGOs) was aborted in 1998. Many developing countries were also extremely sceptical of this agenda and their scepticism played out in the context of WTO negotiations. The resistance to the notion that there should be discipline on what governments can do to international investments stems in large measure from what countries perceive is their policy space. This notion is a replaying of the Calvo doctrine which prevailed in Latin America in the early 20th century. We discuss this in greater detail in Chapter 8.

Competition Policy

At the WTO level, discussions have focused on peer review and cartels.[15] Peer review is a method by which countries can assess the quality and effectiveness of their policies, legislation, policy environments and key institutions. It provides a forum where policies can be explained and discussed, where information can be sought and concerns expressed, on a non-confrontational and non-adversarial basis. One of the main assets of peer review is as a transparency mechanism. Greater transparency is particularly valuable in relation to trade and competition issues. Peer review creates some transparency, which may mitigate the influence of rent-seeking, local-producer vested interests.

The detection and prosecution of hard-core cartels was the other focus of the competition agenda. Cartels – whether in the form of price fixing, output restrictions, bid rigging or market division – raise prices and restrict supply, enriching producers at consumers' expense, and act as a drag on the entire economy. Cartels by their very nature have an anti-competitive effect, and involvement in such behaviour is sanctionable criminal action. Greater globalisation has made international cartels more prevalent. However, this group's work has been delayed to beyond the conclusion of the DDA. The competition agenda failed largely because it fell between two stools. The initially comprehensive agenda that would have dealt with public sector restraints (more appropriate for the work of the WTO in any event) was pared back to a very limited agenda that it was difficult to get the business community to focus on. Critics of the competition agenda have opposed it on the basis that competition is a Trojan horse for market access. The interface between competition and trade was much broader than the WTO Group considered it to be and we set out in this book the parameters of that relationship. It merits noting, nonetheless, that international cooperation on anti-cartel enforcement has been encouraged in recent decades by institutions other than the WTO: specifically, by the International Competition Network (a voluntary virtual network of national competition agencies, established in 2001, that promotes international competition law convergence) and the OECD.

Transparency in Government Procurement

Like the issues of competition and investment, this group has been delayed to a later negotiating time. Transparency in government procurement means the publication/distribution of each country's laws, policies, rules and practices for bid purposes. In order for government procurement processes to be transparent, the following is needed: (i) adequate and timely notice; (ii) neutral standards; (iii) objective criteria; (iv) public bid opening; (v) awards based on the pre-established criteria and (vi) dispute settlement and bid protest, including arbitration. The value of government procurement transparency is not only that foreign companies will be better able to take part in these processes but that domestic companies will also be able to gain better access as the old non-transparent procurement processes are replaced by more transparent ones.

The negotiation was intended to enshrine some of the core principles of transparency in government procurement processes in the Single Undertaking which would automatically apply to all WTO Members. The existing plurilateral[16] on government procurement only applies to those 20 or so countries that have signed up to the plurilateral itself. However, most countries ought to be in principle in favour of transparency and therefore should sign onto the agreement. Problems occurred when the agreement was perceived to be a bargaining chip or could be discussed in the context of a trade-off as opposed to for the sake of its own principles. Once again, as with other Singapore issues, developing countries expressed concern that transparency in government procurement was really a Trojan horse for market access in government procurement.

Trade Facilitation

The overall objective of trade facilitation measures is to improve trade efficiency, in particular the speeding up of customs processes, through the application of WTO core principles to official trade procedures: transparency (availability of information, predictability, establishment of local enquiry point, due process); non-discrimination between consignments and traders, based on the application of objective criteria and controls; and the principle of "proportionality."

The other ministerial meetings took place as follows:

- i Geneva, Switzerland (1998).
- ii Seattle, United States (1999).
- iii Doha, Qatar (2001). After the well-publicised failure in Seattle, an agreement was finally reached on the mandate for the next round of WTO multilateral trade negotiations, the "Doha Development Agenda," because of the emphasis placed on the concerns of developing countries and transition economies. The mandate is set out in the Doha Declaration and was set to be completed by the beginning of 2005. However, as we note in the section below, talks are currently stalled.
- iv Cancún, Mexico, 2003. The Doha Agenda set a number of tasks to be completed before or at the Fifth Ministerial Conference in Cancún, Mexico, 10–14 September 2003. On the eve of the conference, on 30 August 2003, an agreement was reached on the TRIPS and public health issue (but not incorporated into TRIPS). This was a concession by the developed world to address the perception by the developing world that the Uruguay Round required more concessions from the developing world than from the developed world. Members remained deeply divided over a number of issues, especially the "Singapore Issues" and Agriculture. The developing world pushed for a reduction in domestic subsidies by the developed world in agriculture and resisted most of the Singapore issues, particularly investments (the US -EU Common Proposal was refused by G-20, a group of countries led by Brazil, India and South Africa). The conference ended without a consensus and the subsequent deadline of January 2005 was not met.

  The Trade Facilitation work did proceed without objection from WTO members after the General Council Summer Package in 2004. Annex D of that General Council decision did note that the purpose of the trade facilitation work was to build on GATT Article V, GATT Article VIII and GATT Article X, and that the work was focused on further expediting the movement, release and clearance of goods. The work was also designed to increase cooperation between customs agencies and to increase technical assistance.

A first consolidated text was submitted in 2009 and this text was adopted at the Bali Ministerial Conference in 2013. The agreement entered into force in 2017.

WTO Snapshot, Current Situation

Little progress had been made in the Cancun ministerial in 2003 and DDA deadlines were starting to be missed on a regular basis by the time trade negotiators met in Hong Kong in 2005. Throughout the course of 2006, a series of deadlines were missed and the DDA negotiations were essentially on life support by the end of 2006.

The DDA has since died a gradual death. This means that as of writing there has been a 28-year period of hiatus since the last big multilateral round of trade negotiations. This is unprecedented in GATT/WTO history. It means that for over a third of the lifetime of the GATT, there has been no concluded round. There have been some positive actions at a multilateral level. The Trade Facilitation Agreement covering all of the WTO's membership is not an insignificant event. However, there has been no agreement covering the most challenging and pernicious of modern trade practices which are behind-the-border barriers or market distortions. Instead, we have seen more plurilateral negotiations covering the more difficult areas, such as anti-competitive market distortions.

Plurilateral negotiations have now been launched in areas as disparate as e-commerce and services, but progress has been slow in services. The key problem area in services is domestic regulation, where an agreement has been reached. In many ways, a services negotiation is a domestic regulatory negotiation. Of the recent agreements, the agreement on domestic regulation (the Agreement on Services Domestic Regulation) is a significant one. But the level of ambition is less than when the negotiation was originally conceived. The scope of the domestic regulation provisions is limited to government rules, procedures, standards and requirements which firms must satisfy in order to market their services. It does not apply to any exempted sectors in a country's GATS schedule. There are hortatory provisions encouraging members to mutually recognise professional services qualifications. The agreement enshrines a number of key regulatory principles such as the principle that governments must give adequate notice of regulatory changes and allow reasonable comment periods.

In addition, regulators and those involved in issuing licences must be independent of the industries they regulate and there are hortatory provisions encouraging members to develop or contribute to the development of technical standards in a transparent manner.

The key provisions of the Agreement on Services Domestic Regulation are those regarding the manner in which regulations are promulgated and the rules that apply to that process. The Agreement (at Para 22) provides that measures must be based on objective and transparent criteria, must be impartial and procedures must not in themselves unjustifiably prevent the fulfilment of requirements (i.e. the process of promulgating regulations itself should not be a trade barrier).

However, the Agreement on Services Domestic Regulation does little to impact the major problem in services trade which is the corpus of regulation which has a negative effect on trade or market competition.

There are specific provisions on financial services which support the prudential carve-out of the GATS Financial Services text. This misses an opportunity to bring more clarity to the financial service prudential carve-out. There is a danger to trade and competition if the prudential carve-out is used without a nuanced approach. A better regulatory approach would be to understand the impact on trade and competition of a particular regulatory approach and then ask the question whether such an approach is justified based on the prudential concerns that the regulatory system is designed to deal with. We discuss this in more detail in the chapters of the book that deal with regulation.

The key areas of difficulty have been and continue to be as follows:

Agriculture

There has been very little movement on agricultural trade in the WTO thus far. The key issues as discussed before are as follows:

- i Market Access
- ii Export Subsidies
- iii Domestic Programmes

Little progress has been advanced on these issues.

Services

Services negotiations, part of the built-in agenda of the Uruguay Round, have lagged agricultural progress. The G-20 block, which has emerged as a powerful grouping, led by Brazil and India[17] has cast the negotiations as hinging on progress in the agricultural negotiations.

The plurilateral negotiations on services (TISA) are the result of an effort to move the services agenda forward which begin in mid-2008. Full negotiations were launched in April 2013 but are making slow progress. By then, it was clear that the DDA was dead, and that the range of offers that countries were making under the GATS was extremely limited and early anticipation that countries would be adding to covered sectors was not being realised. There has been comparatively little progress on the TISA but it was intended to cover four main parts:

1. Text which includes and builds on GATS obligations.
2. Commitments on market access and national treatment with a list of exceptions for non-conforming measures.
3. Sectoral regulatory annexes.
4. Institutional measures.

Innovations beyond GATS include the US suggestion of including rules on state-owned enterprises. These measures track quite closely modern thinking on SOE chapters which can be found in the Comprehensive and Progressive Trans Pacific Partnership (CPTPP, for example). Another innovation is the use of a hybrid list, covering negative and positive list approaches. Market access measures are to be negotiated under a positive list approach (these must be put on the table for negotiation by parties), but a negative list approach is used for the national treatment provisions. There is therefore more ambition in the national treatment area where countries must not discriminate between trading partners. The use of a positive list for market access ensures the GATS agreement's lack of ambition in covering these issues. The core areas which could be prone to a negotiation of sectoral annexes (based on likely US asks) are as follows:

1 Audiovisual. This is a key sector for both the UK and the US from an export perspective but has historically been a defensive sector for France and the EU. Canada is also likely to oppose the inclusion of this sector.
2 Express Delivery. This has always been a major US ask in trade negotiations. It is also likely to be a significant ask of the UK and the EU. The US/UK/EU position will be to push on market access but also to cover issues related to anti-competitive cross subsidisation by Post Offices, and the handling of public service commitments like the Universal Service Obligation.
3 E-commerce/Digital Trade. The major developed nations such as the US, the UK, the EU and Japan are growing increasingly concerned about data localisation and restrictions on cross-border data flows. The US, the UK and Japan will also be likely to prioritise data flow, whereas the EU's approach is much more protective of privacy concerns and much more likely to impose restrictions for prudential reasons.
4 Financial Services. The UK and the US are aligned on the approach to data in financial services and not aligned with the EU approach (see above). Regulatory cooperation on financial services will also be important to ensure pro-competitive regulation applies in this area. Agreements to take similar positions in external fora such as Basel and IOSCO would also be important.
5 Maritime services. This annex will pit most developed countries against the US, although the US has shown signs of relaxing its very restrictive rules on cabotage in some cases.
6 Professional services. Mutual recognition of professional services has been expressly covered in the separately negotiated Services Domestic Regulation plurilateral.
7 Telecommunications. The Basic Telecoms Agreement and its Reference Paper on Competition Safeguards is one of the most advanced GATS-era agreements. Nevertheless, this annex would seek to build on that agreement.

Non-Agricultural Market Access ("NAMA")

Progress on NAMA has been similarly held hostage to the progress, if any, on agriculture. The G-20 countries have largely refused to give meaningful NAMA commitments absent more progress in agriculture.

As many predicted, and for some of the reasons set out in this book, the DDA has failed to materially meet any of its deadlines. It missed its April 2006 modalities deadline, and when the July 2006 deadline was missed, the talks were officially suspended by then WTO Director-General Pascal Lamy.

The GATT Contract

As was discussed above, the GATT agreement represents the compromise solution to the critical failure of the ITO at the hands of the US Congress. This consisted of what was intended to be a temporary agreement, pending the successful ratification of the ITO. Few at the time thought that the ITO's ratification would take another five decades. The GATT is therefore a contract between a group of countries. It is founded on two fundamental principles, the principle of Most Favoured Nation and the principle of national treatment.

Both these principles taken together can be seen as an incomplete rendering of the core principle that we have articulated elsewhere in this book – the consumer welfare principle. Clearly, rules and regulations that violate the MFN or national treatment principle will lead to market distortion, although not all market distortions will result from MFN or national treatment violations. And not all market distortions are anti-competitive. Let us unpack these different principles.

Most Favoured Nation (MFN) Principle

The principle of Most Favoured Nation (Article I GATT) means that any benefit which is given to one country must be given to all trading partners. Any tariff benefit which is given to one trading partner must be automatically extended to all partners. The process for embarking on the negotiation draws on the principle by providing that the country with the greatest interest in ensuring that a tariff be reduced (the principal consumer) negotiates with the country that is the principal supplier of a certain kind of product. This system was originally envisaged in the US Reciprocal Trade Act of 1934, and the great advantage is that it harnesses the mercantilist impulse to give concessions only when benefits can be gained, and the MFN principle to systematically ratchet tariffs down.[18] The benefits that result from that negotiation are bound (the so-called tariff bindings). A binding means that while the country is free to lower its tariff (and it often does so), it may not raise its tariff over the bound rate.

In practice, many countries do in fact lower their tariffs below the bound rate (the so-called "applied rate"). GATT negotiations commence with a country's bindings.

Conditional and Unconditional MFN

Prior to the 1922 Trade Act, the US had relied on conditional MFN. Under conditional MFN, if a country grants a preferential tariff to another country, then it must extend that benefit to its other trading partners only if they pay for it with tariff cuts that are reciprocal in nature. Conditional MFN was later used by the US in the Tokyo Round, after the 1974 Trade Act provided that the US negotiators must use conditional MFN principles in trade negotiations. A concern was expressed that many GATT members were benefiting from the trade barrier reductions of larger members, while not making tariff cuts themselves. This led to the introduction of a number of plurilateral agreements in the Tokyo Round, only applying to those GATT Members that actually signed them. However, the prevailing trade orthodoxy has been and remains unconditional MFN. It should be remembered that the 1922 Trade Act which returned the US to this orthodoxy also ensured a higher net tariff level (albeit on an MFN basis) and could therefore be regarded as a protectionist measure.

Exceptions to MFN

There are exceptions to the MFN principle. A strict application of the MFN principle would mean that no WTO member could embark on separate negotiations to form either more regionally limited free trade areas or customs unions. Article I itself accommodates the trade preferences that existed prior to 10 April 1947.

Article XXIV GATT

The European Union, NAFTA and the US-Israel agreement were all negotiated after the GATT was launched. These agreements are tolerated by the WTO as an exception to the MFN principle under GATT Article XXIV. In the last ten years, there has been an explosion of free trade agreements. There are now over 500 FTAs, all of which are technically subject to Article XXIV. Although Article XXIV was frequently referred to and used to challenge the early trade agreements such as the EC and EFTA, and even the US-Canada agreement, more recently the Committee on Regional Trade Agreements has been quiet. Many FTAs can no longer be described as purely regional as some of these agreements span regions, e.g., the Chile-China agreement, the Japan-Morocco agreement or the new round of US-bilateral agreements all over the world. Most recently, the UK is in the accession process for the CPTPP.

Conclusion

We can see from classical trade theory and how it has developed over time that initially, when the ITO was being discussed, it was not intended that trade and competition issues should be so rigidly separated. We note that this dates back to Adam Smith's classical framing of the issues. This stems from the notion that the disciplines of trade and competition were indivisible as early as when human beings first met each other's needs in voluntary exchange. Ensuring that voluntary exchange is not impeded justifies a broader theory or normative framework of anti-competitive market distortions in which both issues related to international competition (traditional trade theory and its focus on MFN and national treatment) and domestic competition (including domestic regulatory settings) rest. It is this normative framework that this book explores.

The GATT itself was a compromise arrangement, borne out of the need to have some part of the 1947 arrangements stick when the entire arrangement was going to fall on the sword of the US Congress. However, what started as a compromise rapidly became the standard way that trade negotiations were pursued in the following decades.

Little attention was paid to the precise way that domestic regulatory barriers affected trade flows, and competition in domestic markets. Partly that was because trade negotiations were largely conducted by the quad countries – the US, Europe, Canada and Japan with little input from other GATT members, and in these countries (with the exception of Japan), competitive markets were much more the norm, and therefore the impact of a lack of competitive on trade flows was less pronounced, especially with high tariffs and other border barriers. Indeed, none of these regions had yet experimented significantly with import substation economics or with command economies. The remnants of these economic theories have meant that there is much regulation and law that is market-distorting in countries emerging from these failed experiments. Now, the real impact of China in the global marketplace is bringing these issues sharply into focus.

Notes

1 Articles of Agreement of the International Monetary Fund, *Article I – Purposes* (22 Jul 1944), https://www.imf.org/external/pubs/ft/aa/pdf/aa.pdf.
2 *Id., Article IV - Obligations Regarding Exchange Arrangements.*
3 *Surveillance over Exchange Rate Policies, Decision No. 5392-(77/63),* International Monetary Fund (29 April 1977), as amended by *Decision Nos. 8564-(87/59),* IMF (1 April 1987); *8856-(88/64),* IMF (22 April 1988*; and 10950-(95/37),* IMF (10 April 1995).
4 For an example, see *Report of the Appellate Body* in *Argentina - Measures Affecting Imports of Footwear, Textiles, Apparel and Other Items*, AB-1998-1, WT/DS56/AB/R (98–1190), World Trade Organization (27 Mar 1998). This decision begins to address the difficult problem of the relationship between WTO legal obligations and other international legal obligations. Although the other legal obligations raised by Argentina in this case – ostensible commitments to the IMF – have a rather unique nature, the Appellate Body's approach is instructive. The Appellate Body rejected Argentina's claimed defence because the IMF obligations (i) were not shown to be legally binding, (ii) did not raise an irreconcilable conflict with WTO law and, most importantly for future cases, (iii) were not received into the WTO legal system.
5 *See Articles of Agreement,* International Bank for Reconstruction and Development (as amended effective June 27, 2012). ff.
6 United Nations Conference on Trade and Employment, Havana, Cuba, 21 Nov 1947 – 24 Mar 1948, *Final Act and Related Documents: Interim Commission for the International Trade Organization*, U.N. Doc. E/Conf. 2/78 (Apr 1948).
7 *Final Act,* The General Agreement on Tariffs and Trade General Agreement on Tariffs and Trade, Oct. 30, 1947, 61 Stat. A-11, 55 U.N.T.S. 194.
8 As reported in Bernard M. Hoekman and Michel M. Kostecki, T*he Political Economy of the* World *Trading System*: F*rom* GATT *to* WTO 18 (1996).
9 The round was named for C. Douglas Dillon who, as the US Undersecretary of State in the Eisenhower Administration, suggested its launch.

10 The panel, which was chaired by the distinguished economist Gottfried Haberler of Harvard, was set up by the GATT in 1957, shortly after conclusion of the 4th Round in Geneva.
11 A Guide to the Uruguay Round Agreement (ed. WTO Secretariat, 1999).
12 *See* for example, Robert L. Paarlberg, *The Uruguay Round and Agriculture: International Path to Domestic Policy Reform*, Working Paper, Weatherhead Center for International Affairs at Harvard University, Paper No. 96-01 (30 Jan 1996).
13 *See* A Guide to the Uruguay Round Agreement, *supra* note 11.
14 The agreements for the two largest areas – goods and services – share a common three-part outline (even though the detail is sometimes very different).
15 Though these are important issues, the more pervasive and pernicious issues are structural and ones on which countries ought to focus their competition efforts – specifically those of public sector restraints and the restraints that governments impose in favour of domestic producers. These are high-visibility issues, and their resolution would have a much greater effect on consumer welfare.
16 The current WTO agreement consists of the Single Undertaking as well as those agreements that are committed to by countries outside of the Single Undertaking via a country-by-country process (the plurilateral agreements).
17 The G-20 consists of the following countries: Argentina, Bolivia, Brazil, Chile, China, Cuba, Ecuador, Egypt, Guatemala, India, Indonesia, Mexico, Nigeria, Pakistan, Paraguay, Peru, Philippines, South Africa, Tanzania, Thailand, Uruguay, Venezuela and Zimbabwe. *See Groups in the WTO,* World Trade Organization (updated 18 Dec 2017).
18 For a good treatment, *see* Kenneth Dan, "Cordell Hull, The Reciprocal Trade Agreement Act, and the WTO," Brookings (10 Oct 2004), https://www.brookings.edu/wp-content/uploads/2016/06/20041010dam.pdf.

3

THE ROLE OF CONSUMER WELFARE IN COMPETITION IMPLEMENTATION AND ENFORCEMENT[1]

A parallel development has been taking place alongside the progressive trade liberalisations of the 1990s and early 21st century that we have referred to in Chapters 1 and 2. This development was also brought about by the general acceptance of the market economy as the economic system most likely to deliver growth and development. That led to the spread of competition laws in many countries in the world. In the late 1980s, competition law was really only applied by the US, Canada and the European Community among major trading nations. By 2021, over 130 countries had some form of competition law and a competition agency that was actually functional. It is no coincidence that a more open trade environment has been accompanied by a growth in competition laws. Embracing a market economy means not only opening up one's market to foreign competition, but also ensuring that the market is competitive and is not adversely affected by the kinds of restraints or anti-competitive practices that could make it difficult for exporters to properly access these markets. However, merely having a competition law is no guarantee of a competitive market. Whether the market is competitive or not will depend in large measure on how that competition law is implemented. It also depends on the extent to which laws or government regulations create anti-competitive market distortions (ACMDs) that cannot be reached by competition law.

The widespread development of competition laws around the world has meant that there has been a focus on how implementation of competition law actually works from country to country. We focus on both the European Union (EU) and US cases as examples of well-developed bodies of competition law and describe the clear trend in which the US and EU laws have become much more economics-based. In addition, it is clear that both the EU and US laws have become more focused on consumer welfare enhancement as the guiding light of

DOI: 10.4324/9780429323331-3

competition enforcement. This focus is particularly needed in new technology markets in which rapid change and other factors must be accounted for in the competition analysis.

Background: Principles behind Competition/Antitrust Enforcement

In this section, we study the underlying principles that underpin competition policy and draw some conclusions about how competition law is implemented. In this analysis, it is important to note that a country's chosen policy which often incorporates the views of others outside of the competition agency can drive the actual application of competition law. In studying the interpretation of antitrust or competition law on a comparative basis, it is vital to understand the reasons that the law first came into being. The fundamental reason for the US antitrust law was the power of the private trusts and the perception that by wielding considerable market power, these private trusts were able to maintain prices above levels that a free market would ordinarily dictate. In this respect, the reasons for the US antitrust enforcement were very different from the reasons for European competition law enforcement.

European competition law, by contrast, arose out of the interference that European governments had made in the economy in the lead-up to the Second World War. Hence, European competition law enforcement included provisions regarding state aids that are anti-competitive and distort markets from the outset. The concern in Europe with respect to private behaviour was that what the European Member States had agreed to in terms of the reduction of border barriers between them should not be undone by private cartelising behaviour by European firms. This is one of the reasons that European competition law is more restrictive in its analysis of vertical behaviour than the US law, as vertical restrictions are generally used to divide up markets geographically.

In order to understand the basis of competition law, it is instructive to look at the US and European systems by comparing and contrasting their underlying goals.

Since the US system is largely predicated on minimising welfare losses to consumers (see post), it is deemed to be most important to prevent anti-competitive practices such as price fixing and cartelisation. Sections 1 and 2 of the Sherman Act state, in pertinent part:

> Section 1. Every contract, combination in the form of trust or otherwise, or conspiracy, in restraint of trade or commerce among the several [s]tates, or with foreign nations, is declared to be illegal…
>
> Section 2. Every person who shall monopolise, or attempt to monopolise, or combine or conspire with any other person or persons, to monopolise any part of the trade or commerce among the several States, or with foreign nations, shall be deemed guilty of a felony…[2]

The Clayton Act[3] gives private rights of action to individuals who are adversely affected by behaviour which is prohibited by the antitrust legislation.[4]

The EU competition law is governed by Articles 101 and 102 of the Treaty Establishing the European Economic Community.[5] Article 101(l) states that:

The following shall be prohibited as incompatible with the common market: all agreements between undertakings, decisions by associations of undertakings and concerted practices which may affect trade between Member States and which have as their object or effect the prevention, restriction or distortion of competition within the common market, and in particular those which:

a directly or indirectly fix purchase or selling prices or any other trading conditions;
b limit or control production, markets, technical development or investment;
c share markets or sources of supply;
d apply dissimilar conditions to equivalent transactions with other trading parties, thereby placing them at a competitive disadvantage;
e make the conclusion of contracts subject to acceptance by the other parties of supplementary obligations which, by their nature or according to commercial usage, have no connection with the subject of such contracts.[6]

Article 101(2) states that such agreements shall be automatically void. Article 10(3) allows exceptions in certain cases, either by specific application to the European Commission or by a system of negative clearance designed to facilitate business transactions.

Article 102 provides that:

> Any abuse by one or more undertakings of a dominant position within the common market or in a substantial part of it shall be prohibited as incompatible with the common market insofar as it may affect trade between Member States.

Such abuse may, in particular, consist of:

a directly or indirectly imposing unfair purchase or selling prices or other unfair trading conditions;
b limiting production, markets or technical development to the prejudice of consumers;
c applying dissimilar conditions to equivalent transactions with other trading parties, thereby placing them at a competitive disadvantage;
d making the conclusion of contracts subject to acceptance by the other parties of supplementary obligations which, by their nature or according to commercial usage, have no connection with the subject of such contracts.[7]

These two articles have a direct effect under Article 105 of the European Treaty, and therefore may be relied on by any private individual in his national court. However, this ability has not been fully exploited and national courts have shown a marked reluctance to involve themselves in actions based on Article 105, which has primarily been relied on as a defensive weapon, at least in the UK courts.

There are a number of substantive and procedural differences that are regularly exposed in the analysis of the differing decisions on the increasing number of transatlantic mergers. This will be analysed in detail later but some preliminary points are worth noting now. Analysis of the case law and the manner in which Sections 1 and 2 of the Sherman Act and Articles 101 and 102 have been interpreted illustrates that there are differences in the US and EU approaches. Article 101 has been applied more formalistically than Section 1, placing a greater emphasis than its Sherman Act analogue on exemptions and formal classifications in assessing behaviour. The differences between Article 102 and its rough American analogue, Section 2, centre on the question of what constitutes monopoly power (in the US language) or dominance (in the EU terms). European law merely precludes the abuse of that position once attained. While the European law is suspicious of those with dominant positions, the US antitrust law has a higher threshold requirement before monopoly power can be found. We will explore these differences in detail later in the chapter.

The evolution of US antitrust law has arisen out of a deep-rooted distrust of political and economic power.[8] For many decades, the US antitrust laws were often used to shield small businesses, without regard to the negative effect on business efficiency and innovation. Gradually, however, in response to the realisation that this approach had damaged the economy, economic efficiency, directed towards consumer welfare, became the most important thing to consider in the administration of US antitrust laws. This new thinking reflected the scholarship of the "Chicago School" of law and economics, which was influential on the Reagan Administration (1981–1989). Since price fixing and bid-rigging cartels were inefficient and harmed consumers, enforcement against these entities took centre stage during the Reagan years. Mergers were rarely challenged.

In Europe, as we have noted, competition law developed for very different reasons. Jean Monnet's vision of a unified Europe was founded on two basic theses. The first was that greater unity was a moral imperative after the ravages of two wars. The second was an economic imperative. The businesses of the crippled European economies needed to be able to better compete with their rivals in the US and elsewhere. In order to be competitive on efficiencies of scale and so forth, the Europeans needed to be able to encourage transnational mergers. However, once the region was unified, it became necessary to ensure that businesses themselves did not cartelise the region. The desire to stimulate entrepreneurial activity as well as redistribution policies made it easy for the EU competition law to be seen as a way to lead the playing field.

Hence, European law contains the Article 102 provisions on abuse of dominant position. Dominance is much easier to prove than monopoly under Section 2 of the Sherman Act. As such, dominant firms are precluded from a range of practices, such as predatory pricing and so forth. Examples of Article 82 actions abound, whereas Section 2 of the Sherman Act actions are comparatively rare. Similarly, merger law, specifically in the form of a merger regulation, in the European Commission developed much later, since one of the goals of the European Commission in the first place was to encourage such merger activity. A merger regulation has only been in place since 1991. Under the European merger law, the Europeans are concerned not only with price increases but also with the merger's potential exclusionary effects on smaller competitors, and proof of output reduction is not the only guide.

European competition law is much broader than its US counterpart. Free movement is an integral part of EU competition law. European competition policy extends to the area of government action in the form of state aids. European Competition Commissioner Karel van Miert initiated in the mid-1990s a policy of aggressively enforcing the Article 107 prohibition on competition-distorting state subsidies (state aids), which has been carried on by his successors.

EU-US Cooperation

It is worth noting that the European Commission and the US agreed in 1991 (the 1991 EU/US Competition Cooperation Agreement) to cooperate in the application of their competition laws, though the initial agreement was first voided on a technicality and then reapplied. A report produced by the European Commission on the application of this agreement was published on 8 October 1996.[9] The report reveals that the agreement itself provides that cases which concern the important interests of the other party be notified to them. Exchange of information on general matters is mandated. Both parties' competition authorities must cooperate and be coordinated. Each party must take into account the interests of the other when it takes measures to enforce its competition rules. Either party may take appropriate measures in respect of anti-competitive behaviour that takes place on its territory, but whose effect is felt in the territory of the other party. The 1991 Agreement also provides for regular bilateral meetings to share information on current enforcement activities and priorities; on economic sectors of common interest, to discuss policy changes, and to discuss other matters of mutual interest relating to the application of competition laws.

The initial 1991 EU/US Competition Cooperation Agreement was supplemented by a 1998 EU/US Positive Comity Agreement. Under the rules of positive comity, one party may request the other party to remedy anti-competitive behaviour which originates in its jurisdiction but affects the requesting party as well. The agreement clarifies both the mechanics of the positive comity cooperation instrument, and the circumstances in which it can be availed of. Positive comity provisions are not frequently used as companies (i.e., complainants) prefer to address directly the competition authority they consider to be best suited to deal with the situation.

In 2002, a set of best practices on cooperation in reviewing mergers was agreed. These best practices were updated and revised in 2011. These best practices are not legally binding but simply intend to set forth an advisory framework for interagency cooperation. They put in place a structured basis for cooperation in reviews of individual merger cases.

Most of the notifications that have taken effect to this point have been in the mergers area. The European Commission, once it notifies the US, must notify the Member States whose interests are affected. Timing is obviously key. The Microsoft case is an example of how coordinated action can be taken at the same time. An attempt has been made for case handlers on each side of the Atlantic to assess each other's view of the competitive effects of the transaction or behaviour in their market.

Parties to merge and conduct investigations routinely waive confidentiality protections to facilitate cooperation.[10] Waivers are particularly valuable to the agencies and can benefit parties by reducing information production burdens and avoiding incompatible remedies. In 2013, the FTC and the Department of Justice (DOJ)'s Antitrust Division issued a joint model waiver of confidentiality for use in merger and civil non-merger matters involving concurrent review by the US and non-US competition authorities. The model waiver is designed to streamline the waiver process to reduce the burden on individuals and companies as well as to reduce the agencies' time and resources involved in negotiating waivers.

Although the ability of the European Commission and the US to exchange confidential information has become less of a stumbling block, problems still exist in harmonising merger reviews, especially if the two authorities adopt different definitions of the market. Moreover, Kimberly-Clark/Scott Paper[11] shows that even if the product market is identical, a different geographic market can lead to different results and requirements for divestiture. The US and European Commission cooperated in the Glaxo/Wellcome joint venture,[12] where there were a number of quite distinct product markets. This case demonstrated the different approaches that the FTC and the European Commission take. The European Commission required that the merged company licence one of the two anti-migraine treatments and so retain a competitor, while the FTC required full divestiture of Wellcome's R & D for this particular anti-migraine treatment. Regarding geographical market analysis, the European Commission and the US authorities tend to focus on effects in their own markets exclusively. There are, however, some examples where the European Commission already recognises a global market: in Lockheed Martin/Loral,[13] the European Commission accepted that the satellite market was a global one. Nevertheless, the US authorities took the view that the US was the relevant market because of, among other things, differences in price, quality and/or technology between the US and non-US manufacturers.

In certain cases, if the parties consent, the US and European Commission authorities may discuss information. There is a process by which the European Commission may respond to requests for information.[14] In addition, there are areas where the authorities have cooperated to help each other to locate information, which is of public record, but may not necessarily be information to which the authority unassisted would have been directed. For example, in the Lockheed Martin/Loral merger, the FTC drew the European Commission's attention to information filed with the SEC, which was public, but which the European Commission would not necessarily have looked for without such notification. Cooperation is also important when clarifying a point of foreign law which is relevant to the agreement or to the efficacy of a remedy. Waivers can also be useful in allowing the different agencies to discuss remedies in specific cases, and to exchange documents disclosing anti-competitive behaviour.

The positive comity provisions have now been invoked,[15] though it is too early to tell how effective the positive comity doctrine will be in its application. Also, there have been many examples of the authorities delaying their own action, pending the action of the others, and keeping in close contact with that action. The European Commission has gone on record as saying that it would welcome European businesses' response to whether and how best it should seek to use the positive comity provisions to push the US authorities to investigate examples of where anti-competitive behaviour in the US threatens the ability of Europeans to compete. Although the European Commission report focuses on cooperation in the merger area, greater possibilities for cooperation may present themselves in non-merger cases, such as international price cartels. In these areas, the restrictions on the exchange of confidential information have been felt at their keenest. This is particularly so in the difficult investigation phase.

It will be a significant element of antitrust policy to determine whether certain behaviour should be classified as per se illegal, whether a rule of reason should be universally applied, or whether antitrust policy should be informed by concepts of dominance (more prevalent in the European system). Concepts of dominance are thought to encourage small competitors to compete against their larger rivals, as opposed to a pure allocative efficiency analysis which promotes efficiencies and focuses on behaviour which lowers price for consumers. It should be pointed out that small companies are also consumers of new materials and other inputs. Ensuring that these input costs are minimised can ensure a more competitive environment for small businesses.

Differences between the EU and US Laws

The EU and US competition law prohibitions employ somewhat different frameworks. Generally, in the evaluation of vertical restraints, the US law applies a rule of reason analysis as described above. However, under the EU law, one would have to ascertain whether the restrictions contravene Article 101(1), and if they do, to seek a block exemption or an individual exemption from the European

Commission.[16] This procedure has proved successful in promoting a certain and predictable business climate. The European Commission does issue comfort letters, and this procedure has been followed in Venezuela, for example. However, the comfort letter procedure (which is non-binding) has been criticised as not providing much comfort.

Private enforcement is still comparatively rare in Europe, though it is starting to grow. Its expansion through litigation before in EU Member State courts is explicitly encouraged by the EU as a key element of "competition modernisation." In the US, most enforcement is done at the private party level, largely because, unlike in Europe, juries decide damages, and in the area of antitrust, treble damages apply.

Joint ventures are classified differently. If a venture is classified as a consolidation in Europe (rather than a collaboration), then it is analysed under the Merger Control Rules, and if it falls below the reporting thresholds, it will certainly not be challenged. In the US, joint ventures are regarded as creatures in between full mergers and agreements among separate entities, to which a rule of reason analysis will be generally applied.

Differences between the US and European laws have been illustrated in their approach to vertical arrangements. This difference was highlighted in the Boeing/McDonnell-Douglas merger review, which led to completely different results when analysed by the European authorities and the US authorities, who were analysing the same market (the worldwide market for large commercial aircraft). Most of these differences are found in the different approaches to vertical restraints.

In the US, vertical restraints are analysed in two categories, those that can lead to collusion, and those that can lead to exclusion. However, the US antitrust recognises that vertical restraints may lead to real efficiencies, by better aligning the incentives of producers and distributors (by, for example, incentivising dealers to promote a particular manufacturer's product or by eliminating "free-riding" by zero frills dealers on information provided by "full service" dealers). Vertical restraints in the EU are analysed differently, bearing in mind the overriding goal of ensuring closer economic integration within the EU. The US authorities will generally be more lax than European authorities about allowing territorial restrictions to stand, on the basis of their efficiency-enhancing aspects.

Similarly, in vertical merger cases, efficiency claims (as a defence in a merger case) carry much more weight in the US, than currently in the EU. We will now consider specific exemptions of the difference in approach by the EU and US officials in certain key vertical relationships.

Exclusive Dealing Agreements

Exclusive dealing arrangements are another area of difference between the EU and US systems. A key difference is at what level of market foreclosure will the antitrust authority find an exclusive dealing agreement problematic. The

European law is generally more suspicious of exclusive dealing contracts, and a lower level of foreclosure would be needed before the European authorities would typically find these invalid. This is clearly illustrated in the different approaches to the exclusive supply agreements between Boeing and various airlines which was analysed in the Boeing/McDonnell-Douglas merger.

The Europeans found that Boeing had a dominant position in the market and abused that dominance by entering into exclusive supply contracts with a number of airlines. The dominance of the seller is the main factor. Dominant position in a US analysis would be only one of many factors in an overall rule of reason analysis. The analysis is found in *Tampa Electric v. Nashville Coal.*[17] First, the court defined the product and geographic markets and then sought to determine whether the contract foreclosed competition in a substantial share of that market. A contract would only be declared invalid if opportunities for other traders to enter into or remain in that market were significantly limited. But any anti-competitive effects such as the strength of the parties, the percentage of commerce involved, and the present and future effects of foreclosure on effective competition in the market are weighed against any efficiency arising from the exclusive arrangement. It may well be that there is a safe harbour for exclusive dealing contracts which foreclose even up to 20%–30% of the market.[18] By contrast, under the European law, it is only really the *Delimitis v. Henniger Bräu* cases[19] that adopted a foreclosure analysis where the Court held that exclusive purchasing agreements do not restrict competition unless they make a significant contribution to the foreclosure of competitors from the market. Nevertheless, pre-existing case law suggested that a European court would simply condemn exclusive dealing arrangements, if the seller had a dominant position.[20] Cases after *Delimitis* suggest that even when the exclusive contract amounted to 10% of the market, a violation could still be found.[21]

In the *Boeing* case, the European Community and the US analysed Boeing's exclusive supply contracts differently. How exclusive contracts are analysed in Latin America will be very important in assisting countries in the region with one of their stated objectives, that of increasing foreign trade and investments. In industry sectors where entry barriers are high, exclusive contracts are an important tool to be able to compete. It may be that applying a European-style approach would have a chilling effect on such trade and investment flows.

Vertical Mergers[22]

The treatment of vertical mergers will also be very important in any developing economy where foreign investment is encouraged. There is likely to be significant integration between manufacturers seeking to integrate their distribution networks, or between two manufacturers where there is likely to be technology transfer.

The US has analysed vertical integration by looking closely at the impact of any resulting foreclosure on competition. The *2020 Vertical Merger* Guidelines[23] describe three theories of possible competitive harm from a vertical merger.

One falls under the rubric of foreclosure and raising rivals' costs. Specifically, a merger may increase the vertically integrated firm's incentive or ability to raise its rivals' costs by increasing the price or lowering the quality of a related upstream or downstream product required by rivals. The merged firm could also refuse to supply rivals with the related products altogether ("foreclosure"). Second, a merger may give the combined firm access to and control of sensitive business information about its upstream or downstream rivals that was unavailable to it before the merger. For example, a downstream rival to the merged firm may have been a premerger customer of the upstream firm. Post-merger, the downstream component of the merged firm could now have access to its rival's sensitive business information, enabling it to disadvantage its rival. Third, in some cases, a vertical merger may diminish competition by enabling or encouraging post-merger coordinated interaction among firms in the relevant market that harms customers. The *2020 Guidelines*, however, also recognise that vertical mergers may allow the combination of complementary economic functions and assets and may eliminate contracting frictions, thereby benefiting competition and consumers. Under the *Vertical Merger Guidelines*, American enforcers will not challenge vertical mergers unless anti-competitive effects described above are likely, and outweigh pro-competitive efficiencies.

A word of caution is, however, required. American agency enforcement guidance pertaining to vertical and horizontal mergers is in a state of flux. In January 2022, the US antitrust enforcers (the Justice Department and the Federal Trade Commission) requested public guidance on "how the agencies can modernise enforcement of the antitrust laws regarding mergers",[24] as a prelude to producing new guidelines. It is generally understood that new Biden Administration leadership intends to have the antitrust enforcement agencies adopt a far more aggressive posture towards mergers, perhaps more in tune with the EU's approach. Such an approach might place less of an emphasis on consumer welfare and more on preserving the independence of smaller firms. It is far from clear, however, that the US Supreme Court (which for four decades has emphasised consumer welfare and economics analysis in its antitrust opinions) and lower federal courts would support such a change in direction and uphold more aggressive merger challenges by the agencies.

As we have noted, in Europe, market integration is the overriding goal. This strongly impacts the analysis of vertical arrangements.[25] In Europe, merger control is governed by the 1989 regulation 4064/89 – the Merger Regulation. Here, the EU is particularly concerned by firms that integrate manufacturing and distribution and can exert power over their suppliers. This is the case because the exercise of this kind of power can distort the market.

Concentration

The EU and the US also have differed in their approaches to market concentration. The approach to collusion differs as between the US and the EU in merger analysis. Historically, the US used the Herfindahl-Hirschman Index (HHI) as an indication of coordinated effects, whereas the EU considered only dominance. A unilateral effects analysis has been more recently employed in the US, and American cases have come to focus far more on unilateral effects than on coordinated effects. The European starting point is to look at the market share controlled by leading suppliers. The European Commission is unlikely to authorise a merger which results in or reinforces a position purely on the basis of efficiencies, whereas the US agency position has been a bit different. As indicated above, however, the US agencies are expected to adopt a more interventionist EU-like approach, though the position of US reviewing courts towards such a change remains in doubt.

In the US, merger analysis has moved towards a more dynamic analysis of markets. Mergers that benefit from efficiencies have been broadly recognised, particularly in the vertical area. In the case of distribution efficiencies, the presence of another brand properly distributed in the market might well lead to a more efficient market, with the potential for an increase in interbrand competition and lower prices to consumers. A static merger model, based only on existing market shares, results in a snapshot of competition in a particular industry.[26] Importantly, international competitiveness and the drive towards technological superiority are being expressly recognised in merger analysis, and innovation benefits arising from such analysis for technology transfer are so important to economies in transition that such concepts should be encouraged and utilised by those countries' antitrust agencies. Increases in efficiency likewise should be considered. Regrettably, this may change in the US, as Biden Administration merger policy is contemplating adopting a more sceptical attitude towards merger efficiencies and mergers in general.

Currently, analysis focuses at least, in part, on the possibility that the merged firm would alter its behaviour unilaterally following the acquisition by elevating price and suppressing output. Specifically applying to vertical integration, the FTC and DOJ recognise raising rivals' costs and foreclosure as potential competitive harms of vertical mergers, either input foreclosure (denying access of essential inputs to downstream rivals) or downstream foreclosure (denying downstream outlets for production, thus raising upstream rivals' costs).

Impact of Vertical Differences on Trade

These differences do have effects on trade. Many vertical arrangements are cross-border in nature. Hence, if the EU has a more restrictive approach, this will tend to limit what foreign suppliers can do in European markets, and so have a negative impact on trade. Similarly, if other countries have a more competitor-welfare-enhancing view when it comes to vertical arrangements, then these will have a more distortive impact on trade. This will limit the effectiveness that might have arisen as a result of vertical integration across borders. Changes in the US merger enforcement policies, however, may muddy this picture.

With this brief overview of the key areas of difference between the most well-known and well-tested competition systems, it is worth analysing the history of US and EU policies and look precisely at how these differences arose.

History of US Antitrust Enforcement

US antitrust enforcement has gone through a number of different phases since the original enactment and implementation of the Sherman Act in 1890. These have included an initial phase during which very little enforcement occurred at all; an early phase in which the underlying principles of consumer welfare were set but broader approaches also occasionally appeared; the rise of competitor-protection tendencies during the 20th century, which often harmed competition and consumer welfare; and finally a gradual return to the consumer welfare principles and a growing reliance on economic analysis in furtherance of these principles.

As noted above, the US antitrust law was designed from the outset to discipline private sector and only private sector behaviour. Antitrust enforcement was limited in the first couple of decades of the Sherman Act's existence (1890–1910), with the antitrust agency (DOJ) having to face down entrenched elite power, something it found very difficult to do. A close reading of the Sherman Act itself, however, illustrates how it has been formulated as an economic law from its inception. The concepts contained in the Sherman Act are economic concepts and nowhere does it refer to disciplining companies simply because of their size. This is an important point because the economic goals of consumer welfare enhancement often are at variance with a policy that would discipline large companies simply because of size. A survey of the early cases of antitrust enforcement in the US illustrates this.

Early US Cases Reflecting a Consumer Welfare Approach

It is often argued that the US antitrust consisted of a number of different types of approaches at different times. The conventional wisdom suggests that the FTC and DOJ moved to an increasingly competitor-welfare-oriented vision of antitrust in the first 70 or so years of enforced, and then retrenched back to a period of less intervention in business affairs, based on the discovery articulated by the Chicago School of Economics of the importance of efficiencies in antitrust enforcement. Upon closer and more rigorous analysis, this conventional view misses the fact that the early cases had a strong consumer welfare orientation as did the original law.[27]

Analysis of the earlier cases is instructive and pays careful analysis. This analysis demonstrates the central importance of consumer welfare analysis in even the earliest days of competition analysis in the US.

The *Trans-Missouri* case (1897)[28] was a price-fixing case involving a horizontal pricing agreement among members of a railroad association. Before the Supreme Court, there was a debate between Justice Peckham and the other justices, led by Justice White, in which Justice White wanted to regulate the market by setting a "reasonable price" standard for the services involved. Justice Peckham, meanwhile, believed that there was no way to determine what a "reasonable price" would be because that was for the market itself to determine. He therefore argued for a per se prohibition on horizontal agreements to fix prices because they always restrained competition, no matter what the intention of the parties to them. Meanwhile, Justice White's proposed reasonableness approach helped pave the way for a rule of reason approach for other aspects of antitrust enforcement. In some ways, this early dichotomy was to inform antitrust analysis for years to come. Justice Peckham had adopted a legalistic approach; one in which if a particular kind of behaviour fitted a box, then it would be illegal, whereas Justice White's approach was much more of an economic analysis. There are countries, such as Brazil, that have adopted normative principles based on what Justice White had proposed. In Brazil, a relativity rule (or rule of reason) applies to all conduct whether it is horizontal or vertical.

In *Addyston Pipe and Steel* (1898),[29] the government brought a case against cast-iron pipe manufacturers who had agreed to fix prices and divide up territories. Judge Taft of the Second Circuit Court of Appeals again proposed a per se prohibition against what he described as "naked" restraints on trade. He rejected Justice White's reasonable price standard on judicial (not economic) grounds. Judge Taft differentiated between "naked" restraints – whose sole purpose was to restrain competition – and "ancillary" restraints – whose competition-restraining effects were ancillary to their main purposes. He argued that vertical restraints could be legal if they were merely proportioned to and ancillary to the legitimate main purpose of the contract. The "rule of reason" methodology he suggested for distinguishing between naked and ancillary restraints enabled the court to consider efficiency-enhancing concepts that led to enhanced consumer welfare.

Another railroad rate agreement was struck down in the *Joint Traffic* Supreme Court decision (1898).[30] Here, Justice Peckham responded to the argument that his per se rule against restraints on trade would prevent any commercial agreements at all. Instead, he pointed out that there were many economic partnerships that would not implicate the antitrust laws, including partnership contracts, company formations, leases or purchases by farmers of new warehouses or factories, as well as other examples drawn from the business world. Antitrust commentators (including Judge Robert Bork[31]) have seen this as a nod towards the notion that efficiency concerns played a role in competition enforcement even at this early stage in competition enforcement.

In the well-known *Standard Oil* case (1911),[32] Justice White focused on the reduction of output caused by the monopolist and thus laid the foundations for consumer welfare to be the only policy goal ascribed to the Sherman Act. This altered the view of the Sherman Act and its interpretation from a set of rules or precedent to an economic vision. As we look at the European examples, we will see that frequently a rules-based vision of competition law enforcement can get in the way of such an economic approach with resulting harm to the economy. The other notable characteristic that was inherent in Justice White's decisions in *Standard Oil* and *American Tobacco*[33] was the fact that the Sherman Act was to be interpreted dynamically, and this dynamic interpretation could evolve and alter as economic understanding progressed.

Departures from Consumer Welfare Goal

Following these earliest antitrust enforcement cases, the court continued to struggle with how to contain what was essentially an economic law in a judicial framework. The tension was in understanding the economic purposes behind the law and ensuring that it did not become unduly rule-oriented or "distorted by a largely inappropriate mass of precedent."[34] This tension can be seen in several other early cases that appeared to adopt a broader approach to antitrust enforcement that went beyond the consumer welfare goal. It was in these early cases that the seeds of producer-welfare/competitor-welfare analysis were sown that were later to inform antitrust analysis with catastrophic results for the US economy.

In one early case foreshadowing a shift to the producer-welfare vision of antitrust that was to so severely damage antitrust enforcement in the years to come, the Supreme Court in the *Dr. Miles* case (1911)[35] found resale price maintenance illegal and equated vertical restraints with a horizontal price cartel. In doing this, the court made a fundamental error of economics. The case was a classic example of pressure brought to bear by a competitor aggrieved by the actions of one of its rivals that actually benefited consumers. By finding the resale price maintenance agreement illegal on a per se basis, the Court was merely responding to that competitor pressure without an adequate enquiry into the actual impact of this behaviour on the market and on consumers.

The next significant development came in the *Chicago Board of Trade* case (1918).[36] Here, the Brandeis Supreme Court analysed the "call" market in the Chicago Board of Trade. This market was created by a "call" rule, which limited the volume of trading in a particular product or commodity during certain parts of the business day. The Supreme Court considered allegations that the "call" rules violated the Sherman Act as an unreasonable restraint on competition. Justice Brandeis examined the intent as well as the effects of the rule – although considering intent is not a consumer welfare approach. The Court found the arrangements to be legal, based upon what appeared to be a resurrected rule of reason approach, which suggested that market conditions were actually improved by the restriction. The Court's opinion, however, reflects the beginnings of the notion that antitrust law should be used to level the playing field among competitors, or to build up weaker players who might not otherwise be able to compete. We also see in this opinion the beginnings of the promotion of national champions, mercantilism and even protectionism. We therefore see the producer-welfare side of the economic ledger, which approach has visited such devastation on the economies of countries and the world. Countries that are embarking on antitrust enforcement should read this decision with great care, as in it the seeds of economic destruction were sown.

By the time of the *Alcoa* decision (1945),[37] it had become clear just how far-removed US antitrust law had come from the original consumer welfare enhancement goals that underpinned the Sherman Act itself. In that decision, Judge Learned Hand of the Second Circuit Court of Appeals stated that preserving a social landscape of a multitude of smaller players was one of the goals of antitrust policy *at whatever cost*. The poor competitor that Judge Hand was seeking to protect has since taken many guises, but in none of them is he as helpless as he claims. This point also underlines the difficulties inherent in imposing structural remedies for antitrust violations, given that it is impossible for judges to determine the optimal structure for a market. Judge Hand sought a role for judges in interposing their view of what constituted benefits and harm to competition, and thereby moved a long way from the consumer welfare standard reflected in the earliest cases.

By the time of the *Brown Shoe* case (1962),[38] fragmentation of a market by the courts was seen as an end in itself and favouring the small producer against larger rivals was considered to be one of the guiding lights of the antitrust laws. The Supreme Court in this case noted that Congress, in enacting the antitrust laws, intended to "protect small, viable, locally-owned businesses," even where this "resulted in higher costs."[39] In other words, the notion of consumer welfare or efficiency as the primordial purpose behind the antitrust laws had been turned on its head. Since the original leaning of the court in the *Standard Oil* case of 1911, the next 50 years had seen a complete reversal in what the courts considered to be the fundamental purpose of the antitrust laws. The courts had shifted almost entirely to a producer-welfare vision of economic law. The problem with this producer-welfare approach, however, is that it limits efficiency, and therefore denies to consumers benefits such as lower prices and increased innovation.

History of European Union Competition Enforcement

As noted above, the origins of competition law in the EU are very different from those of US antitrust law. The competition law provisions enacted as part of the Treaty of Rome had as their primary objective not promoting competition as such, but rather furthering economic integration and eliminating national discrimination in the European economic system. Thus, while the US antitrust law was intended to be focused upon the limited economic goal of consumer welfare with respect to private behaviour, the EU competition law by contrast expressly was intended from the beginning to deal not only with private behaviour but also with the public sector restraints that also distorted the market equilibrium from a consumer-welfare-enhancing perspective. Another goal of European competition law was specifically targeted at preventing either private parties or governments from dividing the single European market. The European project, as it was envisaged shortly after the Second World War, would depend in large measure on the integrity of the single market.

These different origins help to explain some of the differences in scope between the US and EU laws. For example, the US law has become comparatively tolerant of vertical restraints on competition, such as exclusive distributorships or certain pricing arrangements between suppliers and dealers. Many EU cases, meanwhile, have been stricter on these issues because of concerns regarding the protection of national champions and the need to integrate the suppliers and distributors of the various member states.

Another important difference in the origins of European competition law is that it began as a much more rules-based system than did the US antitrust law. This led competition authorities to take a much more formalistic or legalistic approach to enforcement matters, as opposed to a more flexible approach based upon economic principles as seen in the US. The rules-based approach also contributed to European competition authorities taking enforcement actions against activities that often had overall positive effects on consumer welfare and economic efficiency. These types of differences must be kept in mind when comparing competition law provisions and policies of different jurisdictions.

Since 1995, the EU competition law has undergone a series of reforms similar in many ways to the changes that occurred in the US antitrust law a decade earlier. These reforms include, most notably, the Notice on Vertical Restraints, the Modernisation Initiative, the new leniency policy, the Technology Block Exemption Report and the Merger Process Reform. A significant step in these reforms came in 2001 when Mario Monti became the first Competition Commissioner to declare that consumer welfare is not only "a" goal of competition policy but "the" goal.[40] The reforms also have featured a significant integration of economic analysis into EU competition policy and regulations.

As a result of these reforms, the EU competition law and the US antitrust law have undergone a gradual (though incomplete) convergence with respect to their focus on consumer welfare as the appropriate policy goal, and their reliance on economic analysis in assessing what policies further that goal. Unfortunately, however, there are some troubling recent signs that the EU and the US antitrust enforcement policies may now be moving away from the consumer welfare standard.

Possible Retreat from Consumer Welfare towards Interventionist Antitrust?

In the last few years, the rise in economic importance of high-technology digital "platforms," such as Google, Amazon, Apple and Facebook, has led to aggressive EU competition cases against those entities, based on abuses of dominant position. (The antitrust prosecution and regulatory oversight of these problems are discussed further in Chapter 14.) The theories of competitive harm have focused primarily on producer welfare – they have centred on platform conduct that may disadvantage certain competitors, while neglecting to show any actual or plausible harm to consumer welfare. Cases of this sort not only move away from a consumer welfare approach but they sanction potentially innovative conduct, thereby discouraging the sort of competition that drives dynamic economic welfare improvements. These EU prosecutorial initiatives have been dubbed a form of "precautionary principle" antitrust,[41] in that they condemn novel little-understood business arrangements, merely because they might in the future enhance a dominant platform's market power.

Although the US enforcers have not yet explicitly adopted a precautionary antitrust approach with respect to digital platforms, there are significant indications that American antitrust enforcement may also be wavering in its commitment to consumer welfare.[42] Beginning around 2016, a number of interventionist-minded critics began to assert that current antitrust enforcement has become ineffective and needs to be redefined. To bolster their case, they cited an alleged rise in American market concentration and diminution in American competitive vigour (claims which have been contested but with little effect thus far on the public policy debate). Some analysts stressed abandoning antitrust's overarching consumer welfare goal and its replacement with a multifactor weighing of diverse interests, including those of fairness, democracy, small business, labour and the environment, among others. Research reports and congressional hearings in 2020 and 2021 prompted congressional introduction of legislative proposals to limit or prohibit acquisitions by large firms and impose far tougher monopolisation standards. Lawsuits filed in late 2020 by the Justice Department and the Federal Trade Commission (joined by various states) against Google and Facebook, respectively, stressed harm to competitors, and were in tension with a truly consumer welfare-centric approach to antitrust.[43] Both federal complaints also raised the possibility of a corporate "breakup" to cure the claimed antitrust violations, a drastic remedy that has seldom been employed in American monopolisation cases.

These developments, combined with the rewrite of merger guidelines previously noted, suggest the real possibility of a return to a more restrictive approach to antitrust, perhaps featuring "big is bad" populism in the US and a greater reliance on a rules-based oversight of dominant firms in the EU. Another possibility is the partial deemphasis of antitrust in favour of regulation in the case of dominant platforms.[44] Indeed, in December 2020, the European Commission issued the Digital Market Act (DMA),[45] a form of direct regulation of digital platforms. The DMA, which becomes effective in 2023, requires that digital "gatekeepers" (entities that provide digital "core platform services" characterised by huge scale economies, strong network effects and lock-in, among other factors) comply with a list of requirements, including, for example, allowing third-party interoperability with the gatekeeper services and enabling businesses access to data they generate in the platform. Substantial fines and (as a last resort) behavioural and structural remedies are to be imposed for violation of DMA obligations.

During 2020, 2021 and 2022, other key jurisdictions, including France, Germany, the UK, Japan and Australia, among others, also pursued digital platform-related regulatory initiatives, leading a former Canadian Competition Commissioner to warn of an "emerging patchwork of digital regulation [that] further amplifies existing incoherence and uneven application of competition regimes on the technology sector and digital markets across the globe."[46] The existence of new regulation does not formally displace antitrust but it adds a new layer of obligations that may impose new and potentially inconsistent burdens on large digital companies, depending upon where they operate. While the US has avoided the imposition of new competition-like regulatory requirements on top of antitrust obligations in recent decades, some influential American commentators are now calling for regulation as an adjunct to antitrust in dealing with "big tech" companies.[47] Also, in March 2021, the FTC served notice that it might consider promulgating rules to prohibit unfair methods of competition[48] and in December 2021, the FTC released a "Statement of Regulatory Priorities" that disclosed plans for competition-related rulemakings.[49] Furthermore, during 2022, legislative proposals to impose new antitrust limitations on large companies (including tight restrictions on mergers and various other requirements) remained under consideration in the US House and Senate.

Despite these recent developments, it is still far too soon to proclaim the end of consumer welfare-based antitrust, at least as a general matter. Antitrust enforcement in the US and the EU has come to rely heavily on economic analysis, which lends support to welfare-based measures. Furthermore, particularly in the US (but to some extent in the EU as well, as demonstrated by the February 2022 EU General Court's *Intel* decision[50]), courts remain in place as a major check on the quick abandonment of decades of doctrinal development focusing increasingly on economic efficiency and consumer welfare promotion. To be sure, the increased focus on public regulation in many jurisdictions (including potentially the US) and the contemplation of possible statutory revisions to American antitrust law may counteract judicial limitations on changes in antitrust policy direction. Up to now, of course, big digital platforms have been the primary targets of those calling for a major competition law overhaul. Firms outside of "big tech" may be a bit less affected. In short, at this time, it is impossible to say whether market-oriented consumer welfare-based antitrust will "weather the storm" and remain more or less intact or be swept away in favour of expansive governmental micromanagement of the terms of competition.

The best weapon to combat the recent fascination with aggressive government antitrust interventionism (and thereby to successfully promote the global acceptance of economics-based consumer welfare analysis) may be a pragmatic focus on the policies that underlie innovation and economic dynamism. In recent decades, the US advanced the most robust consumer welfare approach to antitrust in the world, and the least regulatory approach to the treatment of innovation. During this period, the US brought forth the internet, leading digital technologies and standards, almost all of the world's great digital platforms, most of the world's successful new pharmaceuticals, and the world's greatest biopharma innovations (consider the mRNA technologies that underlie successful COVID-19 vaccines and will likely generate many other medical breakthroughs).[51] There is every reason to believe that this enviable record of welfare-enhancing discoveries owed much to the general American environment of relatively "permissionless innovation,"[52] which featured a far more market-friendly approach to regulation and to antitrust (embodied in the consumer welfare standard) than elsewhere. Hopefully, the marshalling of evidence pointing to this reality could do much to dampen the enthusiasm for sudden and dramatic pro-regulatory changes in antitrust policy.

Public Sector Restraints: State Aids

Under the European law, restraints on public sector activities were envisaged from the outset. The European state aid law, which is rather convoluted and rife with exceptions, is set out in Articles 107–109 of the European Union Treaty.[53]

Article 107(1) provides that state aid is incompatible with the common market to the extent that it affects trade between member states. State aid is "any aid by a Member State or through State resources in any form whatsoever which distorts or threatens to distort competition by favouring certain undertakings or the production of certain goods." Article 107(2), however, provides three broad exceptions that exempt aid having "a social character" that is granted to consumers; aid to make good the damage caused by natural disasters or exceptional occurrences; and aid granted to Germany to compensate for damages arising out of German unification. Article 107(3) also lists five other possible ("may be considered to be compatible") exceptions that allow state aid: (1) for areas facing economic underdevelopment and social challenges; (2) to deal with an important project of common European interest or with a serious national economic disturbance; (3) to facilitate the development of certain economic activities or areas; (4) to promote cultural and heritage conservation; and (5) as specified by decision of the Council on a proposal from the Commission.

Article 108 authorises European Commission review of proposed state aid projects, and to order states to abolish or not grant aid incompatible with Article 107(1). EU Member States may challenge Commission decisions in court, or request the European Council of EU Member States (by unanimous vote) to decide that otherwise incompatible state aid is nevertheless justified due to "exceptional circumstances."

Article 109 authorises the European Council, on a proposal from the Commission and after consulting the European Parliament, to make any appropriate regulations for the application of Articles 107 and 108.

In sum, there are broad exemptions under Article 107 that cover, for example, regional aid to parts of Germany, and social aid to individuals (as opposed to firms). In these cases, the aid is deemed to be compatible if it does not exceed the amount that is absolutely necessary to achieve a legitimate social end. In the case of the Article 107(3) exemptions, which cover things like aid to promote the execution of a project that is important to European interests, or aid to promote certain economic activities, the Commission has discretion as to what type of aid is compatible with the single market. State aid is assessed based on its impact on the market, not the form which it takes.

As is common for other aspects of European competition law, there has been some historic tension between a formalistic interpretation that would look more at how the aid is disbursed and an economic view that would look only at actual impact of the state aid.

In *PreussenElektra*,[54] for example, the advocate-general had compared state aid where the funding of the state aid had come from competitors. He had stated that in many ways such funding was even more anti-competitive than a state aid funded solely by taxpayers. However, in the end in that case, the state aid was not found to be incompatible with the common market. This was because under Article 87(1) (now 107(1)), it was required that the state aid must confer an advantage to an undertaking or the production of certain goods must be granted by the state through state resources, and must be liable to distort competition and affect trade. This was a very formalistic approach which could lead to the unfortunate result where a very high universal service fund, for example, in the telecoms area could be saved from being an actionable state aid if it was paid for through a tax levied against the incumbent telephone company's competitors. In other words, the very thing that distorts the market the most (a levy directed against an incumbent's competitors) would be what saves the particular state aid from being actionable – clearly ludicrous result. The statement by Advocate-General Jacobs recognised that the state aid law was really an economic concept shackled by legalism.

How ludicrous this is from an economic standpoint is determined by the Commission Decision on UK electricity producers where the government imposed a tax on consumers that was paid directly to the electricity companies in order to avoid the government handling it. This alone was deemed enough to mean that the monies were not coming from state resources and the action was deemed to not be a state aid.[55] This is true of competition and trade concepts generally. The early legalistic approach taken in Europe had limited the ability to make the law work economically but this has changed as we have noted above. However, vestiges of the old legalistic form-ridden approach remain. State aids must be notified to the Commission and approved which starts to smack of ex ante regulation.

The EU in evaluating whether there is an actionable state aid relies on the market economy investor principle.[56] Another expression of the market economy investor principle was made in the opinion of Advocate-General Jacobs in *Spain v. Commission*.[57] Here, it was noted that the test was that the state provided funds that a private investor would not have made in the normal course of events applying commercial considerations and disregarding other considerations of social, political or philanthropic nature. We will see that this test echoes the language of GATT Article XVII on the limitations on state trading enterprises, which we discuss at length in Chapter 6. What precisely "commercial considerations" actually meant was litigated in the *Canada Wheat Board* case.[58] In the end, the panel and appellate body in that case moved away from an economic test that would have been based on competition principles. However, in this context, the EU state aids law is part of European competition law, and therefore it stands to reason that normative competition reasons must be applied. The explicit nod to market economy principles buttresses the notion that "commercial considerations" in this context means the behaviour of a private firm, i.e., a profit maximiser.

Services in the General Economic Interest: The EU Approach

A particularly difficult issue is what to do when the state aid is to satisfy public service obligations. We will discuss some of the EU case law specifically in this context in the chapter on telecoms and postal services. For the moment, we will merely address the basic application of the EU law in this area. The seminal case is the *Altmark* case.[59] In the case, which we discuss again in some of the sectoral chapters, the European Court of Justice laid down four conditions:

a The public service undertakings must be clearly defined and laid down in a law or regulation or in some other legal arrangement.
b The amount of the obligation must be determined in advance in an objective and transparent manner.
c The USO amount must not be greater than what is necessary to cover the costs of carrying out the specific service.
d If there is no public procurement process to select the undertaking to provide the service, the amount of the USO must be cost-based.

In other words, the USO must merely offset costs, and anything more than this could lead to a finding of incompatible state aid. The twin concepts of necessity and proportionality are very much to the fore. The precise measure of costs as we note in other sections is a particularly controversial and sensitive area.

The *Altmark* conditions are interesting because they can be compared with the US state action exemption doctrine as first set forth in *Parker v. Brown* and elaborated in *Midcal.*[60] In these cases, the state action exemption was found to only apply when there was a clearly articulated state policy to displace competition, and the action was in furtherance of that state policy.

Non-Obvious State Aids

It is clearly easier to point to examples of where cash is directly handed from the government to a particular undertaking, but frequently the aid takes the form of something much more difficult to detect. This can be in favourable loan terms, relief from the payment of certain taxes and the like. It is well established under the European law that fiscal measures are to be judged by their effect not simply by their form, and the mere fact that they are fiscal measures will not protect them from being found to be state aids that are incompatible with the common market. In particular, we have to be very careful with tax benefits as these can take many forms. For example, since 2013, the European Commission has been challenging various alleged state subsidies in the form of favourable tax rulings granted major multinational companies (such as Apple),[61] with mixed results before the courts.[62] The application of bankruptcy laws and the non-enforcement of debts by the public sector can also be seen to be state aids. Some commentators have suggested that there should be a much more "effects-based" approach which would catch a lot of non-obvious state aids.[63]

Recent State Aid Policy Developments: Clarifying Commission Policy

The 2009 global financial crisis spawned many "bailout" proposals by European states targeted to assist financial institutions and other struggling enterprises. On the whole, the European Commission's state aid review system responded remarkably well, and fears that political pressures would lead to the suspension of state aid rules were not realised. As then-EU Competition Commissioner Joaquín Almunia explained in 2010:

> Early action by the European Commission helped ensure a common approach by Member States to financial sector bail-outs. Member States may have adopted different measures – those which they felt were best-suited to their respective situation – whether guarantee schemes, recapitalisation measures, or impaired asset relief measures, or a mixture of these. But the European Commission required that all of these measures complied with certain fundamental principles – non-discriminatory access to national schemes, subsidies limited to what was necessary, mechanisms to prevent abuse of State support, restructuring measures for certain financial institutions that received large amounts of aid. This helped keep to a minimum any distortions of competition between banks within and across national borders, and helped preserve the integrity of the EU internal market. It prevented costly and damaging subsidy races between Member States, with each trying to outdo the other in an attempt to prevent business moving away.[64]

In short, Commission guidance ensured that state aid arising out of the financial crisis continued to meet EU Treaty criteria and thereby limited the subsidies' distortive effects.

The Commission has continued to provide guidance to EU Member States on the permissible boundaries of state aid, in light of new general EU policy directives and initiatives. For example, in April 2021, the Commission adopted revised EU Guidelines on Regional State Aid,[65] setting forth the rules under which Member States can grant state aid to companies to support economic development in disadvantaged areas of the EU. The revised Guidelines entered into force on 1 January 2022. According to Commission Executive Vice President Margrethe Vestager, in addition to supporting regional development initiatives, the revised Guidelines will bolster major EU strategic priorities, including the European Green Deal and the European Industrial and Digital Strategies:

> support the least favoured European regions in catching up and to reduce disparities in terms of economic well-being, income and unemployment. These cohesion objectives are at the heart of our Union. We have also increased possibilities for Member States to support regions facing transition or structural challenges such as depopulation, so that the Guidelines fully contribute to the green and digital transitions while ensuring a level playing field between Member States.[66]

In sum, state aid guidance, while cabined by the requirements of Articles 107–109, is dynamic and evolves over time. It is refined in tandem with other aspects of overall EU economic policy and is revised in light of changing EU strategic initiatives. We now turn to focus more specifically on the issue of market distortions, the central economic problem that state aid restrictions seek to minimise.

What Is a Distortion

The European case law has looked at the issue of what constitutes a market distortion. There are a number of different kinds of distortion that apply – one is distortion between firms that are operating in the market. This would be where aid is given to one of the firms. Distortion can also arise where the aid gives rise to inefficiency. The former distortion is based on competitor welfare; the latter stems from consumer welfare (or damage to such welfare). Sometimes, the aid can lead to increased market power, allowing one firm to set price to monopoly levels. In some cases, aid given leads to a distortion of the economic calculus that firms use to guide investment decisions. This distortion can lead to consumer welfare damaging impacts.

Distortion effects can in particular be significant when looking at public subsidies given to satisfy a universal service obligation. This is because these kinds of subsidies are not the best way of dealing with what is perceived to be a market failure (but as we have noted is usually simply caused by market restrictions imposed by the same government that now wants to subsidise the service). Commentators have noted that even a rigid application of the *Altmark* conditions may not be enough to enough to prevent the recipients of aid from having an unfair advantage over their competitors.[67] The problem with this kind of subsidy, as is the problem with any kind of subsidy, is that it does not create downward pressure on costs (in fact the subsidy releases that pressure, thereby promoting all kinds of inefficient practices to creep into the behaviour of the entity being subsidised). One way of ensuring that this downward pressure on costs is achieved is to encourage competitive bidding of the public service obligation itself. We deal with this in greater detail in the specific sections that deal with trade and competition issues in postal and telecommunications.[68]

Anti-Competitive Market Distortions ("ACMDs")

ACMDs are market distortions that lessen competition. The lessening of competition is determined by reference to the impact of the distortion on consumer welfare in the economic sense. (In other words, by reference to its impact on productive and allocative efficiency, as discussed subsequently in this chapter.) ACMDs involve government actions (embodied in laws, regulations or policies) that empower certain private interests to obtain or retain artificial competitive advantages over their rivals, be they foreign or domestic.[69] ACMDs fall outside the scope of competition and trade laws, and thus cannot be reined in through enforcement actions. In the US, this has been largely because of the state action exemption in antitrust law (as noted herein), and, more broadly, a general deference to governmental regulatory actions that do not violate constitutional norms. ACMDs have not been well addressed by the trade authorities because they frequently do not implicate national treatment violations. Many ACMDs, although they do harm foreign firms, also harm domestic firms and hence will not necessarily give rise to trade violations. However, ACMDs still very much harm export interests (by undermining the ability of foreign exporters to compete with domestic beneficiaries of ACMDs) as well as domestic economies. We will analyse (in Chapter 4) some possible remedies which might be used to deal with ACMDs. Central to addressing this problem is understanding and agreeing what metric is appropriate to use to measure distortion. This metric must describe the actual impact of the ACMD on the market. The answer to this question is to be found in competition, rather than trade law, which is why we discuss competition law first.

Recent Inadequate Efforts to Address the ACMD Problem (with a Focus on China)

International trade agreements thus far have not dealt with ACMDs. A good example of predatory ACMD behaviour is China. China has clearly telegraphed its intention to become a leader in a whole range of advanced technology sectors.[70] And, it seems to be using ACMDs in order to gain global dominance in those industries.[71] International trade agreements thus far have not dealt effectively with these distortions. Whatever trade tools are used to deal with the problem should follow at least the spirit of international trade liberalisation principles (in order to ensure that the US, the UK and other G7 countries can maintain the moral high ground with their trading partners), and they must be effective in disciplining Chinese behaviour.

Although there have been several ad hoc efforts in recent years to address the ACMD issue (including Chinese ACMDs), but they have not been very effective.

The first response has been to expand the scope of industrial subsidies. However, these impact only trade in goods and not services, which are significantly affected by ACMDs. A subsidy approach also does not attack the problem at its source which is the impact of the distortion on competition.

The second approach is to make ad hoc trade deals with China, as the Trump Administration sought to do. As is now known, the China deal negotiated by the Trump Administration did not succeed in disciplining distortions in any meaningful manner. Because the Trump tariffs and the Phase 1 deal based on a "forced" market share are clearly contrary to at least the spirit of international trade liberalisation, the US administration also lost the moral high ground for the mechanism proposed.

The third response is for some key countries to collaborate to deal with ACMDs. The WTO trilateral group (the EU, Japan and the US), for example, has focused on reducing market distortions in third countries. The EU has come up with a new approach to investigating and countering competition-distorting subsidies by non-EU governments, which will be implemented shortly (see discussion above of the European Commission regulation on foreign subsidies).

Finally, a multilateral approach is being attempted. Atlantic Charter and G7 announcements in the UK have both prioritised fair trade and a reduction of market distortions, but these bare-bones proposals require further development.

Regrettably, none of these initiatives have frontally attacked the core problem, which is the impact of government distortions on competition in the market. Nor have they suggested remedies that could actually have a positive impact and stand a chance of changing the behaviour of the distorting countries.

Fortunately, the UK Trade and Agriculture Commission (TAC) recently proposed a solution that is designed to resolve the ACMD problem more fully. We now turn to that proposal.

Responding to ACMDs Comprehensively: UK Trade and Agriculture Commission (TAC) Proposal

In 2021, the UK TAC issued a report which, among other proposals, recommended a novel trade mechanism to deal with ACMDs that harm international trade and undermine efforts to promote economically beneficial trade liberalisation. This mechanism, which is discussed below, provides a possible solution to address new challenges that confront nations in trade negotiations. This novel approach seeks to overcome the inadequacies of recent ad hoc efforts by various nations to address the ACMD problem.

Background

The TAC Report recognises that ACMDs have replaced tariffs as the preferred method of protection in many areas. The global trading system has not been able to deal with this reality appropriately. The Report also reflects the understanding that a number of issues outside of the traditionally trade remit have been brought into the trade agenda. These include issues like labour and the environment, and now, climate change. This has renewed calls for border tax adjustments or dual tariffs on an ex ante basis. This is in sharp tension with the World Trade Organization's (WTO's) long-standing principle of technological neutrality and focus on outcomes as opposed to discriminating on the basis of the way products are produced. The problem is that it is too easy to hide protectionist impulses into concerns about the manner of production, and once a different tariff applies, it will be very difficult to remove. The result will be to significantly damage the liberalisation process itself, leading to severe harm to the global economy at a critical time as nations seek to recover from COVID-19.

TAC Tariffication Mechanism to Deal with New Problems

The TAC has proposed the following mechanism to deal with the issues outlined above.

It proposes a tariffication of distortion mechanism which could be used in trade policy to deal with situations where countries agree to lower their tariffs but protect their markets and give their producers an artificial edge by distorting their markets through ACMDs. The result of the mechanism is a tariff based on the scale of the distortion which operates like a trade remedy. The mechanism can also be used offensively where a country is preventing market access for the exporting country through the ACMD, or defensively, where an ACMD in a foreign market leads to excess exports from that market.

Details of the Mechanism and Its Application

Offensively, one could envisage provisions on ACMDs in trade agreements that discipline their use and allow dispute resolution when they are applied in violation of the agreement.

Defensive Mechanism

An aggrieved country would have to show:

An ACMD (i.e., deviation from an agreed standard inserted into an FTA or other trade agreement).

a An impact on competition.
b Excess exports as a result of the distortion.

c Damage to the aggrieved nation's producers.
d In addition to the cases above, an ACMD could result from the deliberate derogation from a country's own law in order to promote trade or competitive advantage.
e The questions to be resolved would be as follows:
f Is there an international standard which covers the issue?
g Is country X deviating from that standard for trade or competitive advantage?
h Is there an effect on trade and competition? To match other GATT provisions, this could be an equality of competitive opportunity test.
i Are there excess exports from Country X into country Y as a result?
j Are country Y's producers adversely affected and can you prove both damage and causation?

If yes to all, then the tariffication mechanism can be applied.

Reflections on the Mechanism and Its Advantages

The tariff would be calibrated to the scale of the ACMD and would apply only to the product category in which the distortion is occurring. The advantage of this over a more conventional trade remedy is that it is based on cost as opposed to price, and is designed to remove the effects of the distorting activity. It would not be applied on a retaliatory basis in other unrelated sectors. The TAC proposal is to use this mechanism to deal with distortions in order to maintain a commitment to zero tariffs and zero quotas in agriculture, a notoriously difficult piece of trade liberalisation but crucially important for international trade.

The mechanism seeks to ensure that where countries derogate from commitments made in FTAs, or ultimately internationally to the WTO, and do so for trade and competition advantage, there is a real means to discipline them through the application of a tariff. But the TAC proposal also looks at the offensive agenda and how disciplines on ACMDs can be used to limit trade barriers in other markets as part of the UK's FTA agenda. This mechanism would also effectively deal with defensive issues without the dangers of an ex ante dual tariff and the protectionist concerns that could result.

Potential to Use ACMD Mechanism Offensively to Deal with Government Distortions that Block the Aggrieved Country's Exports

Where an ACMD is being used to protect a particular domestic industry, using the ACMD mechanism to apply a tariff for the exports of that industry would help, but this may not apply where the purpose is protective and the industry does not export much. In this case, it would be important to ensure that FTAs include disciplines on these ACMDs which if breached could lead to dispute settlement and the potential for retaliatory tariffs for sectors of the culpable trading partner that do export. This is certainly a normal WTO-sanctioned practice and could be used here to encourage compliance. It is clear from the experience in dealing with countries that engage in ACMDs for trade or competition advantage that unless there are robust disciplines, mere hortatory language would accomplish little or nothing.

The mechanism is applicable generally to a broad array of trade negotiations and has far broader implications than the UK trade policy. It could be a much more nuanced solution to current US-China trade disputes, one which would not be as damaging for global trade as national security-based tariffs but would recognise the fact that the impact of Chinese market distortions on global trade is severe. This type of mechanism could also feed into the work of the trilateral group on market distortions in the WTO and be a complement to existing measures allowed under the Agreement on Subsidies and Countervailing Measures (ASCM).

A calibrated tariffication-based mechanism to address ACMDs, embodied in the TAC Report mechanism, could be used flexibly for offensive and defensive purposes. Such a mechanism obviously could be refined and made the subject of future negotiations; it is not at this time a "silver bullet" for solving the ACMD problem. Nevertheless, it represents the type of problem solving and innovative thinking that the international trading system needs as it faces a range of challenges that threaten liberalisation itself and the hard won gains of the post-war GATT/WTO system.

The TAC Mechanism and the UK-EU Trade and Cooperation Agreement

As part of the Brexit process following the UK's withdrawal from the EU, the UK and the EU entered into negotiations for a UK-EU Trade and Cooperation Agreement (TCA).[72] A key aspect of these negotiations was the establishment of a level-playing field for open and fair competition. The main level-playing field provisions are set out in Title XI of Part Two of the TCA. The EU and the UK recognise that to prevent distortion of "trade or investment" between the parties, conditions are required to ensure a level-playing field for open and fair competition. The TCA says that while the UK and the EU are committed to maintaining and improving their respective high standards, they reaffirm their right to regulate and recognise that the purpose of the commitments is not to harmonise those standards. The TCA has complex and bespoke provisions for dispute settlement between the parties. This involves consultations, recourse to an independent arbitration tribunal, and temporary cross-retaliation. The Court of Justice of the EU (CJEU) has no role in the dispute settlement provisions. The provisions on competition policy and taxation are excluded from the dispute resolution.

The most innovative aspect of the Agreement's dispute settlement is a rebalancing mechanism for the level-playing field. If significant divergence in subsidy policy, labour and social policy, or climate and environment policy arises between the UK and the EU, and this has material impacts on trade or investment, both parties have the right to take countermeasures, subject to arbitration. In simple terms, if one side raises its standards and the other does not, the former can take reciprocal action. These rebalancing measures could include temporary suspension of parts of the Agreement or tariffs but are not defined beyond that.[73]

Significant policy divergences noted above that have material impacts on trade or investment and qualify for rebalancing under the TCA may also be characterised as ACMDs, if they impose competitive harm in one jurisdiction. In cases where the UK was the competitively harmed jurisdiction, it could elect to employ the TAC's mechanism in order to counteract the EU ACMDs at issue, given the flexibility in the TCA's rebalancing mechanism.

In short, the TCA establishes an ideal regulatory environment for the practical application of the TAC's anti-ACMD methodology to specific matters. As such, the TAC's approach can be tested under real-world conditions and refined as necessary. Properly handled, this testing may facilitate the broader adoption of the TAC's mechanism in international agreements, and further the cause of subjecting ACMDs to international enforcement discipline. The development of a body of case law holdings could go a long way towards demonstrating the soundness of the TAC's mechanism. It must be emphasised, however, that appropriate application and invocation of the TAC's approach will require a reliance on modern competition law economics, centred on concern for the promotion of economic efficiency and consumer welfare. Sound economic analysis is key to the ultimate goal of correctly spotting and counteracting ACMDs. With that caveat in mind, we turn now to spotlighting sound economics-based modern principles of competition law that should be applied equally to both private anti-competitive restraints and government-imposed ACMDs.

Subsidy and State Aid

Clearly, the WTO has rules in its ASCM agreement that are designed to deal with cases where governments subsidise a particular industry. State aid is focused on cases where governments give money to particular undertakings as we have seen. Generally, because state aid applies to a broader series of government-type activities, it is broader than the ASCM-prohibited subsidies.[74] The EU has had some success in including state aids measures in some of its external agreements (such as the European association agreements with incoming members of the EU). However, increasingly more and more of these kinds of provisions are stripped out by the EU's trading partner prior to the conclusion of negotiations. Sometimes, it is the EU itself that would prefer not to give countries it is negotiating with the ability to use the agreement to attack EU exporters. This occurred, for example, during the EU-Chile trade negotiations. It is unlikely therefore that some multilateral state aids disciplines in the context of EU negotiations with other countries, except insofar as the EU itself is enlarging. We must not forget that the EU itself is perhaps the largest and deepest example of the integration of trade and competition policies. Despite the criticism of it by other countries, it remains the deepest model of integration and certainly points the way to a set of disciplines that could limit government interference in the economic space that will have a negative impact on the market and a damaging impact on consumer welfare as a result.

A May 2021 OECD Recommendation on Competitive Neutrality[75] furthers the cause of pursuing limitations on competition-distorting state aids and, more generally, on avoiding ACMDs. As the OECD explains:

> It is a fundamental principle of competition law and policy that firms should compete on the merits and should not benefit from undue advantages for example due to their ownership or nationality.
>
> Government actions can sometimes prevent, restrict or distort competition within a market....
>
> The Recommendation establishes a set of principles ensuring that governments' actions are competitively neutral and that all enterprises face a level playing field, irrespective of factors such as the enterprises' ownership, location or legal form. It recommends adopting and maintaining neutral market rules so that adhering governments ensure that the legal framework is neutral and that competition is not unduly prevented, restricted or distorted. It also recommends avoiding selective advantages and measures that may unduly enhance an enterprise's market performance and distort competition.[76]

Modern Principles of Competition Law

The purpose of competition is not simply rivalry or the process of competition itself – it is rather to ensure that the free market be actually able to deliver to consumers its accompanying efficiency gains. When we talk about efforts to achieve consumer-welfare-enhancing equilibria, we are really talking about the stimulation of efficiencies that lead to lower costs of production and therefore higher output and lower quality-adjusted prices.[77] Where private (or for that matter public) behaviour distorts this market, consumer welfare enhancement, which is built on liberating these efficiencies, is eroded. When we use the language of competition, we really mean rivalrous conduct that is directed towards maximising consumer welfare. In other words, a competitive market is characterised not by relative levels of market share, but rather by how close the market is to achieving this optimum. (Market share does not really tell us how a given market works and thus sheds no light on the central consumer welfare question.) Whenever we talk about competition, we should be talking about business rivalry directed at benefiting consumers.

It is important to note what consumer welfare enhancement is *not* about. It is *not* about consumer protection, with which it is often confused. Consumer protection – for example, those laws that protect health and safety and truth in advertising – is designed to protect present consumers. However, consumer welfare enhancement means the enhancement of future consumers. While there are cases where the interests of present and future consumers are similar, there will also be cases where their interests are opposite and in tension. Future consumers are interested in efficiency not only because this reduces costs and therefore prices, but also because it stimulates innovation that can also deliver new and better products.

With consumer welfare as a guiding principle, trade-offs must still be made – namely, the efficiencies associated with certain types of monopoly may need to be sacrificed in order to secure price benefits for consumers. However, this is a very different situation from a trade-off that compares economic efficiency on the one hand with social concerns supporting a fragmented market on the other. This is at the heart of what it means to have consumer welfare as a normative principle for the market economy.

The Nature of Efficiency

Efficiency is a consumer-welfare-enhancing concept because the benefits of increased efficiency are passed to consumers in the form of lower prices. Competition policy discussions must consider two different forms of efficiency – allocative efficiency and productive efficiency.

Allocative efficiency relates to the allocation of the available productive forces. Simply put, allocative efficiency occurs when firms produce those goods and services most valued by society. This means that scarce resources are utilised in a manner that maximises this type of consumer welfare. It is found by matching marginal cost to marginal benefit. If marginal cost is less than marginal benefit for a particular good, production should be increased. If it is the other way round, then production should be reduced. This equilibrium is Pareto-optimal, since to deviate from it would detract from one person's situation by more than it would improve any another person's situation.

Productive efficiency by contrast relates to the means of production for each line of industry. Productive efficiency involves using the least amount of resources to produce a given good or service. When productive efficiency is maximised, output is produced at the lowest possible unit cost.

By contrast to recent developments we have outlined, we believe that the goal of competitive markets, as developed through the competition law, is to promote a consumer-welfare-enhancing market equilibrium. The measure of whether such an equilibrium has been achieved is through the maximisation of productive and allocative efficiencies. Consumer welfare is damaged, and consumer and consumer/producer surpluses are converted into deadweight losses when the efficiencies are impaired either through private anti-competitive behaviour or through public sector restraints which we describe as ACMDs. While antitrust law has traditionally focused on private behaviour, some of the most significant adverse welfare effects occur in the public sector, as a result of public sector restraints of trade.

The Organisation for Economic Cooperation and Development (OECD) has produced a "Competition Assessment Toolkit" that "helps governments [if they so choose] to eliminate barriers to competition by providing a method for identifying unnecessary restraints on market activities and developing alternative, less restrictive measures that still achieve government policy objectives."[78] More specifically, the Toolkit calls for governments to examine actual or proposed legal provisions that limit the number or range of suppliers; limit the ability of suppliers to compete; reduce the incentive of suppliers to compete; and limit the choices and information available to consumers. It then sets forth means for evaluating the actual effects of such restrictions and provides helpful case studies. In short, the Toolkit provides a ready-made mechanism for governments to identify and study actual and potential ACMDs, with an eye to their elimination, if they are so inclined. Use of the Toolkit is, of course, entirely voluntary. Thus, while the Toolkit offers a good diagnostic methodology, it is not a formal legal mechanism for combating ACMDs.

In order to understand how these ACMDs should be treated, it is first necessary to understand what metrics have been utilised by competition policy as it has been implemented by the countries that have the most experience with it, especially the US and the EU. Both competition systems have differed markedly in their treatment of competition issues. In the next section, we will review how the US antitrust law and European competition law have evolved in this treatment of competition issues. We will highlight in particular those areas where the US antitrust law or European competition law have fallen into error with negative consequences for the economies of both regions.

Curbing Market Power in Its Incipiency: A Policy with Costs

The dangers of incipient market power have been somewhat overstated throughout the history of US antitrust enforcement. The theory of incipiency suggests that the dangers of market power can be forestalled before market power is reached. The problem with this theory, however, is that incipiency may relate to building efficiencies and economies of scale, as well as merely to market power. Efficiency and economies of scale of course are actually positive for economic development and can lead to enhanced consumer welfare. To forestall them based upon an incipiency theory therefore is to forestall consumer welfare, and to damage the economy.

During the 1960s, there was a shift towards a more interventionist competition policy whose goal was to ensure a particular market result – more fragmented markets – resulting from some of the cases that we have discussed as well as the public perception that there was some merit to a de-concentrated market. These fragmented markets, so the theory went, were in-and-of-themselves laudable aims, *even if there was a cost to attain them, measured by a loss of efficiency.* President Johnson's Neal Task Force even went so far as to consider introducing legislation to break up particular industries and to impose structural remedies to ensure their fragmentation.[79] The notion that there was some direct mathematical link between the concentration of a market and its levels of competition had gained substantial ground.

A 1971 FTC Annual Report specifically referred to the fact that the FTC's enforcement goals continued to be the "elimination of monopolistic practices and restraints of trade in their incipiency."[80] The heavy focus of the FTC on incipiency reached its high point in the *Von's Grocery* case (1966).[81] The *Von's Grocery* case was a merger case in which the Supreme Court held unlawful the merger of two grocery market chains in Los Angeles that held only a combined 7.5% market share in Los Angeles, and the top *eight* firms accounted for only 40.9% of the market. In finding the merger unlawful, the Court did not engage in any analysis of its potential competitive effects, other than to note a trend towards increased concentration in the market.

Certain commentators, meanwhile, rightly were sceptical of the claimed linkage between market concentration and competitive effects, even at the time that the incipience theory was reaching its apex. Harold Demsetz, for example, writing in 1968, stated as follows:

> We have no theory that allows us to deduce from the observable degree of concentration in a particular market whether or not the price and output are competitive.[82]

In fact, there is no good economic reason to find an antitrust problem with a concentrated market simply because it is concentrated. Rather, there are great dangers associated with discouraging the pursuit of monopoly power since that is what all businesses seek to do. The pursuit of a monopoly (by legal means) is, in business language, merely the desire to increase one's market share. Not only is there nothing wrong with this desire, it is actually an important and vital part of doing business. Indeed, it is the essence of competition itself. Firms compete against each other in the all-important game of improving market share, and it is the red heat of this competition that leads to consumer welfare enhancements as demonstrated by improved quality and lower prices. By attacking low levels of market share based on the supposition that they may lead to much higher levels of market share in the future, competition agencies act as regulators stifling innovative activity and thwarting the very competitive impulse that they seek to promote.

Other Countries and Regions

As more and more countries embrace a free-market economy and start to adopt and enforce laws that regulate those markets, it is becoming increasingly relevant to ask how those laws are to be implemented and enforced. For example, all of the countries in Central and Eastern Europe adopted the provisions of European competition law encapsulated in Articles 1055 and 1066 of the Treaty Establishing the European Community.[83] Largely, this was done in order to assist them in their bids to join the EU itself. In Latin America, some countries have adopted European-style concepts in their antitrust laws (for example, Venezuela), and others (like Brazil or Mexico) have adopted laws that more closely resemble the Sherman Act of the US.[84] It is not at all clear, however, that the wholesale adoption by emerging economies of the provisions of one or another of these two systems would be in the interests of the countries, short-term or long-term[85] Certainly, a careful analysis must be conducted in assessing which antitrust policy must be used to inform the enforcement decisions of the individual country's antitrust authorities.

By 2021, it could safely be said that the administrative principles of the EU's civil antitrust system have proven more influential than common law-oriented American antitrust in the adoption and implementation of new antitrust statutes.[86] It could not be said, however, that all countries were moving lockstep towards opening up their economies and freeing their markets. Indeed, for example, Venezuela, once a major energy producer, had developed a socialist market model that retained antitrust on the statute books but in practice paid little heed to free-market antitrust principles.

Since 2001, efforts to promote the "soft convergence" among antitrust laws have proceeded under the aegis of the International Competition Network (ICN), a virtual network of antitrust agencies from most countries around the world.[87] While ICN recommendations are non-binding, the ICN leadership (heavily influenced by the US and European enforcers) has sought to promote non-binding procedural and substantive "best practices" and "recommended practices" in competition law. In particular (at least up to 2021), the advancement of consumer welfare was central to various ICN documents. Although there has been some convergence, many jurisdictions' antitrust laws seek to advance a number of goals in addition to strengthening consumer welfare and competition. Thus, significant differences among competition law goals remain. In light of antitrust agencies' pursuit of varying goals (including labour protection, industrial policy and so forth) and imperfections in administration of the laws, it is difficult to say whether the proliferation of antitrust statutes has truly benefited consumers and national economies. If antitrust enforcement worldwide is to achieve its pro-consumer pro-innovation pro-growth potential, a great deal more work needs to be done.

Impact of UK Leaving the EU on the UK Competition Policy

On June 2016, the British people voted to leave the EU, and on 31 January 2020, the UK left the EU. By 1 January 2021, the transition period had ended and the UK is now fully outside the EU and its institutions. Section 60A of the

UK Competition Act removes the requirement to interpret the UK competition law in accordance with corresponding principles of EU competition law after the transition period. There are some early signs of the direction of travel of UK competition law and policy.

We will very briefly analyse these early signs, using the economic basis for competition policy based on the maximisation of both productive and allocative efficiencies as outlined above as a benchmark. There are disturbing indications that the UK seeks to prioritise the protection of competitors much as the US did in the 1950s and 1960s. This is particularly true when applying competition policy to the tech sector.

The new post-Brexit perspective of UK competition policy may be gleaned from two significant policy initiatives and one recent specific regulatory determination by the Competition & Markets Authority (CMA), the UK's competition agency.

In March 2021, the CMA issued new *Merger Assessment Guidelines*,[88] which stressed the need for "concrete changes to the CMA's [previous 2010] Merger Assessment Guidelines to address the risk of under-enforcement," particularly in relation to digital markets. Citing two reports by outside consultants calling for more aggressive merger enforcement than in the past, the new 2021 *Guidelines* explained that "[t]he findings as set out in the [consultants'] reports referred to above have been carefully considered (and largely adopted) in the updates to these Guidelines." Of particular note, the 2021 *Guidelines* noted the failure by enforcers (including the CMA) to block acquisitions by large digital firms and stressed that "in dealing with digital markets that have high levels of uncertainty and move quickly, competition authorities need to recalibrate how they assess some mergers because underenforcement can be very costly." Although it is too early as of yet to assess the changes in CMA merger enforcement policy wrought by the revised *Guidelines*, this explicit language certainly suggests that a more interventionist bias may be expected in future investigations.

In July 2021, the UK Government announced a consultation regarding the formation of a "Digital Market Unit" (DMU) within the CMA, charged with "addressing both the sources of market power and the economic harms that result from the exercise of market power" in rapidly evolving digital markets.[89] As proposed by the consultation, firms with market power in at least one digital activity will be classified as having "strategic market status" (SMS), and be subject to an enforceable code of conduct setting out how they are expected to behave (thereby "shaping firms' behaviour to prevent bad outcomes before they occur"). The DMU will be empowered to intervene and "address the root causes of substantial and entrenched market power in digital markets." The DMU "will require robust powers to deter and tackle noncompliance." What's more, CMA-administered rules are being considered to toughen merger enforcement in digital market (the rules are aimed "to ensure merger activity is more proactively monitored and that harmful mergers are blocked where they further enhance or entrench the powerful positions of firms with SMS"). Although these proposals have not been finalised and their details have not all been filled in, it may safely be assumed that they represent the near-term future of UK competition policy regarding digital markets.

All told, the DMU SMS-related consultation proposals go beyond mere precautionary antitrust to establish a de facto regulatory regime applicable to highly successful digital firms. Although they claim to be designed to promote competition, in effect they represent arbitrary government intervention into the business activities of highly successful digital firms that have showered countless benefits on consumers. They bespeak an elitist conceit that enlightened government regulatory manipulation of highly dynamic markets will improve competition and welfare. History, however, belies the assumptions that underlie this conceit, which represents yet but one more example of what Nobel Laureate Friedrich Hayek termed "the pretence of knowledge" by government officials.[90]

We turn now to a recent CMA decision imposing oversight over Amazon, a digital platform that has greatly invigorated competition in retail sales to consumers.

The Amazon digital sales platform has been noted for the many benefits (including low prices) it has conferred upon consumers.[91] As such, imposing new competition-based regulations on Amazon, absent a clear showing of competitive harm, would risk consumer welfare harm and be counterproductive.[92] Nevertheless, in February 2022, the CMA decided to designate Amazon (and its UK subsidiaries) as a UK retailer subject to the Groceries Market Investigation Order, which requires the UK's large grocery retailers to follow the Groceries Supply Code of Practice. In announcing its decision, the CMA explained:

> This Code, which applies to retailers with an annual turnover of more than £1 billion from grocery sales, ensures that they treat their suppliers fairly. For example, it restricts firms from making changes to supply contracts at short notice. It also requires retailers to give an appropriate period of notice if they no longer want to use a supplier and provide reasons for ending the contract.
>
> Households across the UK are increasingly using Amazon to buy food and other essential items. Today's decision to designate Amazon helps to ensure a level playing field for companies active in the groceries sector as people's buying habits evolve.
>
> These rules mean that the thousands of companies supplying Amazon with groceries are now protected from potential unfair business practices.[93]

In short, CMA has decided to regulate Amazon's business dealings with other firms to ensure the "fair treatment" of those companies, a classic statement of favouring competitors over competition and the consumer interest. In taking this action, the CMA made no suggestion that Amazon had in any way harmed consumer welfare through its actions.

Taken together, the 2021 *Merger Assessment Guidelines*, the establishment of the Digital Markets Unit and the 2022 imposition of regulation on Amazon are of great policy significance. They plainly manifest an unfortunate post-Brexit CMA fixation on the interest of competitors (particularly in the area of digital platforms), which is at odds with a pro-competitive focus on consumer welfare maximisation and allocative efficiency. If CMA authorities truly wish to promote vibrant competition and consumer welfare enhancement (which they have frequently cited as a key goal) in the UK post-Brexit, they should take a close look at their post-Brexit policy initiatives and consider a major course correction. In particular, they would do well to eschew regulation of successful competitors and intervene only to prevent harmful business activity and mergers that undermine competition and harm consumers.

Case Study: Latin America

The economic liberalisation in Latin America has meant that there is increasing evidence of more reliance on antitrust enforcement in Latin America. The liberalisation of Latin American economies may lead to a firmer view of such anti-competitive practices as price fixing and division of markets. There will be a number of areas where highly concentrated markets remain, and it is important for these to be properly addressed. The growth in international joint ventures will lead to a greater emphasis on mergers review. In addition, it is important that antitrust enforcement not stifle the flow of foreign investment into the countries of the region. Consideration of what actually constitutes the market will become relevant. It will become increasingly important to consider the global or at least sub-regional welfare effects in performing market analysis. The countries of Central and South America are considering which competition system to favour, the European or the US system, both in its implementation and in its philosophical basis.

Until the beginning of this decade, competition policy in Latin America had taken a back seat. Competition laws were enacted prior to this, to be sure, but in environments where government intervention in markets was the norm these laws were not properly implemented. However recently, Latin American countries have started to enact more modern competition laws. Many of the Latin American countries have enacted legislation addressing the competition issue and setting up institutions that can implement competitive policy. Argentina enacted such a law in 1980, Brazil in 1994, Colombia amended its law in 1992, Chile in 1979, Costa Rica in 1994, Mexico in 1992, Panama in 1996, Peru in 1991 and Venezuela in 1991. A number of other countries are currently discussing legislation. Regionally, only NAFTA includes competition provisions although there is some discussion of this within MERCOSUR and CARICOM. The view of the Organisation of American States (OAS) is that laws in the region target the promotion of freedom in industry and commerce, equitable participation of small- and medium-sized enterprises, and the decentralisation of economic power. Emphasis should be placed on preventing monopolistic behaviour, and abuse of dominant position, much more like the European system. Indeed, a number of Latin American laws are very closely modelled on the European law. Many countries have carved out certain sectors from the application of competitive law. Mexico, by way of example, does not apply its competition laws to the petroleum, natural gas sectors or to export cooperatives. Chilean competition law excludes mining and petroleum. In Costa Rica, insurance activities, alcohol distillation, fuels, activities carried out by the concessionary regime and telephone, telecommunications, electric energy and water services are excluded from competition. In Colombia, household public services, and the financial and insurance sectors are excluded. However, of course, the US also has such exemptions, both by statute and by the application of the state action doctrine.

There are a number of commonalities among all Latin American laws. For example, certain matters are prohibited, and these include:

a Price fixing;
b Restriction of market access for new competitors by making the sunk costs of potential competitors more onerous;
c Bid-rigging or coordination in presentation of bids at public procurement auctions;
d Restraint of output agreements by quota imposition;
e Market and consumer division agreements; and
f Predatory practices adopted by a dominant company to force out or prevent entry of competitors by selling at prices below production cost.

Certain vertical agreements are also generally illegal:

a Price discrimination agreements;
b Resale price maintenance;
c Territorial restraint agreements by which a supplier confines a distributor to market a product in a certain territory;
d Exclusive agreements under which a distributor obtains the right to sell and market a product under the condition of not trading the other product;
e Tying arrangements and
f Refusal to do business based on a supplier's stronger negotiation position.

The US-style per se/rule of reason classification has not generally been used in the design of laws by countries in the region except in the cases of Mexico, Panama and Costa Rica. In Brazil, all potentially anti-competitive behaviour is analysed by a rule of reason. In Argentina and Brazil, in order for behaviour to be anti-competitive, there must be a demonstrable threat to a nation's economic interests. In Venezuela, horizontal agreements are per se unlawful, and a rule of reason analysis is applied to vertical agreements. This looks like the US law but the Venezuelan law is based also on European dominance concepts. In their enforcement, all countries rely on the US jurisprudence.

In Latin American competition law, with the exception of Mexico or Costa Rica, it is an abuse of a dominant position, not the attempt to monopolise, which is to be penalised. This is something of a double-edged sword. The reason is that although the European law seeks to find out what is actually being done by the monopolist and the US law penalises attempts to become a monopolist, it is in practice a lot easier to demonstrate that someone has a dominant position, than that they are in fact a monopolist under the US antitrust laws. Generally, in Latin America, the abuse of a dominant position is predicated on the following factors:

a Degree of concentration of the market, existence of barriers to entry and dynamics of competition in the relevant market.
b Abuse of that position through the performance of additional anti-competitive acts.

In order to ease analysis, Colombia, Chile and Venezuela actually specify the type of conduct that constitutes abuse of dominant position. This includes things like price discrimination, restriction of output and distribution, refusal to deal for the purchase or performance of services, discriminatory practices to impose unequal conditions for performance of services and tying agreements.

Economic concentrations are universally disapproved of, because this establishes the platform for abuse of a dominant position. However, doing the necessary analysis to establish how an increased level of concentration can affect competition is no easy task. This analysis requires a tremendous amount of economic and legal analysis associated with considerable manpower. Broadly, the guidelines used by these countries include:

a Relevant market defined by product and geographic content.
b Pre- and post-operation concentration levels, measured by sales volume, and the value of assets, and the value of the transaction.
c Level of competition among participants in terms of number of competitors, production capacity and product demand.
d Barriers to entry of competitors.
e History of competition and rivalry between participants in the sector or activity.

In Brazil, Colombia and Venezuela, this evaluation allows us to take into consideration the increases in efficiency which the new operation might produce. The analysis includes the possibility that the merger took place purely to strengthen certain companies, and not necessarily to boost efficiency. Brazil, Chile, Jamaica and Venezuela follow a model whereby certain exceptions are authorised for practices that help enhance economic efficiency with respect both to market participants and to consumers. This mirrors the European approach. These exceptions have been specifically applied to:

a Export agreements.
b Agreements on research and development.
c Exclusive distribution and purchase agreements.
d Agreements which help to improve output, quality and marketing of goods or services.
e Exclusive agreements, as in the case of exemptions and territorial representations.

Mexican, Brazilian and Venezuelan laws also have de minimis exceptions.

Many of the countries' competition laws are connected with the deregulation of the economy. Determination of the limits of state intervention is very important in developing country markets, particularly those whose industries have been shielded from competition for so long and have levels of inefficiency built up over a period of years, if not decades. Hence, in many countries, the laws allow the competition agencies to issue orders or regulations to amend or rescind existing legislation when such legislation generates barriers to the entry of participants. The wave of privatisation must be closely monitored to ensure that the potential for the build-up of private economic concentrations is controlled. Agencies in Mexico, Brazil and Venezuela have the power to evaluate the effect that a privatisation might have on competition.

One question which will occur in Latin America as elsewhere will be the extent to which competition law is being implemented in such a way as to limit the ability of new entrants to break into markets. An approach to dominance, based on the European model, can lead to decisions that take on the hue of competitor-welfare analysis, keeping firms out of markets and this tendency has to be carefully guarded against.

Many other countries have gone through similar processes and are asking very similar questions.

Examples from Asia

Many of the competition laws of the Asian countries draw on Japanese and German precedents (which, in turn, were substantially drawn from the US precedents).[94] South Korea's law, which is the most developed after the Japanese in the region, was itself modelled on German law.

In many of the Asian countries, competition law was a reaction to a period of heavy emphasis on import substitution or building up national champions. This policy had to great inefficiencies on and consequent harm to the economy. In the case of South Korea, there was a recognition that the highly cartelised and Chaebol-dominated economy had laid the groundwork for the financial crisis that followed in the mid-1990s. Economic concentration therefore became the bugbear that had to be guarded against by a new competition law. Recognising that structural defects in the economy had caused the malaise leading to the financial crisis, the Korean Fair-Trade Commission (KFTC) has placed considerable emphasis on competition advocacy, the process whereby competition agencies advocate pro-competitive principles to other branches of government.

Similar factors, in particular the collapse of Indonesia's economy after the Asian Financial Crisis, led to an enhanced role for competition in the Indonesian economy. Once again, regulatory and policy barriers to competition pervaded the Indonesian economy.[95] The large presence of state-owned companies was also problematic. Indonesia's competition law (enacted 5 March 1999) was therefore designed to protect the competitive process.

One factor common to various Asian competition laws is an emphasis on "unfairness" and inequalities in bargaining power. A concern about protection of smaller competitors, among other factors, rather than mere consumer welfare promotion, is a key feature. Enforcement of Asian competition laws has become far more aggressive in recent years, featuring increased fines and other sanctions. Increased attention has been paid to cartels, mergers and large digital platforms.[96]

China's Competition Law

The most significant Asian (and perhaps global) antitrust development in the 21st century has been China's enactment (in 2008) and robust enforcement of a competition law (the Antimonopoly Law or AML), currently administered by one powerful government agency, the State Administration for Market Regulation (SAMR). The AML is a civil law statute that borrows heavily from the German legal tradition. It covers all aspects of competition, including intellectual property, business registration, mergers and acquisitions, pricing policy, food security and consumer protection.

While the AML has all the trappings of a modern competition law regime, the authoritarian nature of China (which raises questions about the vitality of the rule of law) and the lack of a true consumer protection orientation are problematic. A 2021 Asia Society study of Chinese competition law concluded that, though China has made "developing an environment for fair competition" a priority, "long-standing instincts favoring the interests of state-owned enterprises (SOEs) over consumers – and domestic firms over foreign ones – are still embedded in the Chinese system, with little regard for consumer welfare or fair competition."[97] Given the enormous importance of China for the world economy, and the international trading system, the future evolution of Chinese competition law will be of great policy significance.

New Technology and Competition Enforcement

Competition enforcement has been greatly impacted by new technology. Markets affected by new technology move at much higher speeds than they have historically. This pace means that potential entrants are much more likely to break into these new markets, and barriers to entry may be considerably less than they were before.

One of the most significant areas where technology has fundamentally altered analysis is the area of monopolisation or dominance. The new type of market is additionally examined in Chapter 14, but in this context, it principally means that firms with high levels of market share are restrained in their behaviour by external factors such as the likelihood that the technology which they currently dominate may become obsolete or overtaken by new technologies.

The economic case for attacking incipiency has never been strong but it is particularly weak now as applied to markets in which changing technology has led to accelerated change in the way firms do business. As market definition becomes a more flexible concept, this has meant that in the high-tech markets, incipiency is less of a concern. In more traditional environments, incipiency could mean an imminent threat of monopoly. However in a new technology environment, incipiency is much less of a concern because the causal connection between having incipient power and ultimately having an illegally acquired monopoly is broken. Indeed, the entire market could change in the period between incipiency and what would have been monopoly. This means that incipient market power, and in some cases market power itself, is of much less concern in high-technology markets.

Impact of Technology on Markets

New technology does have impacts on the competitiveness of markets, particularly in technology-based information industries, because of a number of factors. These include the following:

1. There are powerful *network effects* in information industries. These effects create a positive feedback loop, which instils both demand-side economies of scale, as well as supply side economies of scale. These effects reinforce each other and mean that there is a premium on competitors reaching the broadest market possible. It also means that slight differences in quality can be the difference between success and failure, and that whole industries can disappear and emerge very quickly depending upon their perceived quality.
2. *Positive feedback* is the result of these economies of scale and scope. Positive feedback is based on Metcalfe's rule that the value of the network increases with the square of the number of users. Positive feedback operates to ensure rapid growth in industries (typically high-tech, internet industries), where the technology is working, and consumers want it. However, if there are perceived problems with the technology or there is some barrier in the way of its success, positive feedback will work through a vicious cycle and could render an entire technology obsolete in a very short timeframe. This is a very different situation to the old economy, where negative feedback operated to

restrain any dramatic changes in market share. In the old economy, the market tended to an equilibrium position, and any attempt to increase market share met with the gravitational force of this equilibrium. This did not mean that changes were impossible, merely that they were difficult. The opposite is true for the high-tech economy. Here, by contrast, there is a tendency for any, even minor perceived differences to be amplified so that they can quickly lead to a positive feedback loop leading to some competitors being removed from the market altogether.

3 We should note that *not all network industries are characterised by rapid rates of innovation*. The financial services industry is generally subject to network effects, but their innovation rates are not as high as in the software industry, for example. Lock-in is therefore likely to be a bigger problem in network industries such as financial services as opposed to in industries where there is a far higher degree of innovation. Therefore, you are more likely to see lock-in and path dependence the less innovative the network industry actually is. Lock-in effects will be less dramatic for very high-tech industries.

4 Schumpeterian *creative destruction* has to be viewed through a *dynamic lens*. Too often, regulators view a snapshot of the market to determine and explain market behaviour. This is a flawed analysis. Hence, using market share as a proxy for market power is an extremely flawed way of trying to understand how the market actually works. This is particularly true of markets that are highly dynamic and subject to constant change. Although one could argue that all markets are changing, the only difference between a so-called innovative market and a less innovative market is the rate of change. In either case, market share is a weak proxy for market power, but it breaks down altogether at high levels of innovation.

There are two schools of thought for assessing competition enforcement issues in high-technology industries. The first is the network externalities school which suggests that because there are network externalities associated with high-tech products (i.e., strong demand-side economies of scale), monopolisation is likely in this sector and carries with it the great harms of consumer lock-in and path dependence. These harms are caused by strong demand-side economies of scale leading to consumers opting for the particular technology so as to join an increasingly valuable installed base. If this happens to a significant extent, then whole technological choices of societies will be determined by the ability of firms to monopolise this installed base. This would be a particular concern to developing and transition countries where technological choices could determine the economic fate of the country.

The second school of thought notes that the high-tech industry as a whole demonstrates certain public goods characteristics. This is because consumption of products does not take away from the availability of those products to other consumers. This would apply to communications services, internet products and software, by way of example. This means that the industry is characterised by a declining marginal cost curve (which actually declines to zero), which is very different from the U-shaped marginal cost curve that characterises most traditional industries. This means that the industry is likely to be characterised by product markets that appear and disappear (almost overnight). The industry will also be characterised by powerful positive feedback loops that make success highly successful and failure complete. Any differences between companies' products can quickly lead to very pronounced market share effects, leading to "monopoly" or failure. Hence, the competition that is consumer-welfare-enhancing is the competition for these short-term monopolies (akin to the race to find a patentable invention). This leads to multiple platforms capable of competing against one another under a notion of monopolistic competition. Each platform is protected by intellectual property, thus leading to substantial interbrand competition among platforms.

The competition that is sought in order to guide technological development is actually the ferocious competition to attain what will likely be only a temporary monopoly. In other words, high-tech businesses will always spend enormous resources in pursuit of either the killer application or an incremental change that makes a product a "winner". This is what limits path dependence and lock-in effects. Once companies achieve this, they admittedly will have a temporary monopoly. But as long as they do not use illegal means to maintain a monopoly (such as entering into cartels with others), it is a legitimate reward for the fact that in order to build an installed base, they may have had to virtually give away the application itself. If the temporary monopoly were treated as a regulated industry the moment it was achieved, there would be no incentive to pursue it, just as the search for an AIDS vaccine would be limited if companies knew they would have to give it away once they discovered it.

Analysing Market Power in Technology Markets

The meanings of market power and market access are changing dramatically. Market share alone is no longer a good proxy for market power. In the industries characterised by negative feedback – the equilibrium of a number of companies with market share changing slowly – market share was a better proxy for market power. Because market shares did not change rapidly in such industries, market share was a closer indicator of the power that a firm could exercise over price. However, in the high-technology world, where positive feedback plays such a strong role, market shares can change rapidly over short periods of time. Indeed, whole industries can be eliminated or created in very short periods of time. Positive feedback also tends to make the strong stronger and the weak weaker, with little in between.

In addition, the rate of change of market share with time, dM/dt, and the second differential of that rate of change (i.e., the rate of change of the rate of change of market power with time), D^2M/Dt^2, are indicators of rising market share and potential market power. However, regardless of market share, if these are small in the case of the first differential or negative in the case of the second, then there is no issue as to market power. Where the market share of a company in a positive feedback environment is declining, there is little that the company can do to control prices. Indeed, in such an environment, the company's future itself is in question. This needs to be considered in determining the correct approach for antitrust to such industries.

Compatibility is also a major issue affecting market power in the new high-tech world. Compatibility standards can be used by firms as a weapon in the competitive battle and, once again, positive feedback applies in this context. There is therefore a premium on building an installed base; an installed base provides a firm with a group of customers already inclined to purchase the firm's products or services. Similarly in high-tech industries, there is much more alliance formation and joint cooperation on common standards. These factors also increase the positive feedback effects in high-tech industries. Rivals must vie for their technologies to be chosen as the standard, as this can ultimately mean the difference, not just between gaining and losing market share, but between life and death for entire companies.

Competition Law Remedies in High-Tech Industries

Another important issue in competition enforcement relating to high-tech industries is identifying the appropriate remedy that preserves competitive markets in the event that anti-competitive activity is found. The question is whether this appropriate remedy changes when you are dealing with a high-tech world.

The High Costs of Structural Remedies

Judge Richard Posner has noted that "Structural remedies such as divestiture are, as we know, slow, costly, frequently ineffectual, and sometimes ineffective…."[98] Judge Posner argues that the normal remedy in antitrust cases should be a monetary fine, which should be set at a level sufficient to discipline the violator (i.e., it should be some multiple of the actual cost to society of the offence to deter firms from attempting to simply commit offences and conceal them).

Competition enforcers and courts should pursue the remedy that is the most economically efficient and produces the greatest consumer welfare benefit. Commentators have considered various ways of evaluating the optimal remedy. Shelanski and Sidak have suggested the following approach:

> Step one is to evaluate whether the static (short-term, holding technology constant) efficiency consequences of a proposed remedy will yield a net gain. Do the gains in allocative efficiency (that is, reductions in price and increases in output) exceed the losses in productive efficiency (that is, ability to reduce production costs), if any, associated with a particular remedy? If so, then step two is to compare the static efficiency gains from the first step with any effects that the remedy is likely to have on dynamic

> (long-term, with technological change) efficiency. Examples of dynamic efficiency include innovation that reduces production costs or develops new products and services for consumers. If the net gain is positive, then step three is to evaluate the remedy in terms of its enforcement costs, broadly defined. The optimal remedy is the one that produces the greatest overall efficiency gains net of enforcement and administrative costs.[99]

The issue of how the new economy works is relevant to the understanding of how remedies should work. There is no doubt that increased network effects lead to expanding markets and so forth, but there is some disagreement as to whether this leads to Schumpeterian rivalry where companies emerge and are destroyed in a sort of economic natural selection (one that Jeff Bezos of Amazon.com hinted at when he referred to the new economy as a primeval soup from which companies would emerge through an evolutionary process). An alternative vision is that precisely these same effects can lead to a "lock-in" effect for consumers – in which consumers initially choose a particular provider's technology or standard and subsequently are "locked-in" to that provider's products or services – and therefore can increase the dangers of monopolisation.

It is certainly true that in the new economy, with vast demand-side economies of scale, and public goods characteristics, the marginal cost tends to decline to zero, which means that we will see highly competitive behaviour where firms must engage in very low price offers for products (often at levels that might be deemed predatory) or even giveaways of technology to secure market share. Moreover, the new multisided digital platforms compete for consumer attention and provide many services to consumers at a nominal zero price – though consumers typically "pay" implicitly by being exposed to advertising (consider, for example, Google's facilitation of consumer searches for desired information, Google-owned YouTube's provision of entertaining videos, Facebook's offering of valuable social networking experiences). We must look at this conduct from the perspective of the consumer and consider whether it is economically efficient. In the Schumpeterian universe, it clearly is, because consumers will have access to more and better technology on an on-going basis. Certainly, Shapiro and Varian argue that winners will be short-lived as new industries emerge, but that for the period of victory, winning does tend to mean total dominance.[100] Indeed, this dominance is required in order to accommodate the costs of striving to achieve it. Hence, we can expect ferocious competition initially for limited periods of dominance. If this is indeed the background against which firms are competing, then utilising competition remedies that are based on competitor-welfare norms will be counterproductive, as it will erode rather than enhance the competitive process.

Case Study: The AT&T Divestiture

The landmark divestiture remedy in a network industry is the Modified Final Judgment ("MFJ") in the case of *United States v. AT&T* (1981).[101] In this case, the major motivation was the fact that AT&T was using its regulated telecommunications monopoly to engage in anti-competitive practices in competitive markets to the detriment of both its competitors and its consumers alike. The reasoning behind the divestiture was that the separation of the regulated and unregulated components of AT&T would eliminate such practices. Even in this scenario, the government elected not to pursue complete dissolution as a potential remedy, implicitly accepting the concept that there were some benefits associated with vertical integration.

There are difficulties in enforcing structural remedies in any industry. Contrary to the view that these remedies are easier than behavioural remedies because they do not require subsequent monitoring, it can also be difficult for an enforcer to ensure that core requirements of structural remedies are being enforced. These difficulties can include:

1 Ensuring no information exchange between the separate components.
2 Ensuring proper accounting separation between structurally separated components.

Another problem with structural remedies is that there is an inevitable arbitrariness in how a divestiture remedy can be applied. In the AT&T case, the government proposed a remedy which was intended to be a middle ground. Not all of the Bell operating companies were separated but the government arbitrarily decided to group them into seven regional operating companies (in addition to a separate competitive long-distance provider and two research and development entities). The rationale for this decision was an evaluation of at what point market shares would begin to raise competitive questions. This type of rationale reflects a competitor-welfare orientation and an undue focus on the structural shape of the market as opposed to its dynamic nature. Many commentators have argued that the divestiture goal of reducing AT&T's market share was successful. From a competitor-welfare standpoint, it was.

However, while there has been little treatment of the impact of the divestiture on consumers, it is clear that this impact has been negative and substantial.

As in other cases, we see in the AT&T divestiture a tension between the lower court and the Court of Appeals in terms of its approach to competition policy. The MFJ decision said that if a regulated monopolist uses its position to disadvantage competitors in competitive markets, it could be barred entirely from competitive markets. The Court of Appeal overruled the MFJ decision, stating that the monopolist could only be barred on a case-by-case basis, depending on its actual behaviour. The MFJ seemed, at least according to the Court of Appeal, unduly focused on the impact of competitor welfare and the impact of the regulated monopolist's behaviour with respect to competitors. The remedy itself, far from being a one-off fix, required a considerable amount of monitoring.

It is important to bear in mind that the antitrust system is a deterrence-based system, and not a regulatory one. (Antitrust may, however, be in the process of developing regulatory attributes in dealing with high-tech platforms, as discussed previously in this chapter.) While divestiture remedies in Sherman Act Section 2 violations (for monopolisation or attempted monopolisation) are comparatively rare, such remedies are much more common in merger cases. It is useful to look at potential divestiture remedies in these cases, in order to understand the use of divestiture as a remedy.

A New Approach to Remedies for Technology Markets

The choice of remedy is an integral part of the competition policy process. The application of remedies that emanate from the competitor-welfare side of the ledger can be equally distortive to trade as merely finding harm on this basis. We will spend some time discussing remedies under competition law in order to assess the impact of the remedy on the market and its possible role as a barrier.

In general, competition remedies fall into three broad categories:

i Behavioural remedies – these include injunctions to stop the antitrust law violating behaviour (i.e., to stop agreeing prices, or dividing up markets).
ii Structural remedies – these include splitting up a firm found guilty of antitrust violations.
iii Fines – the government may impose fines and penalties on those guilty of antitrust violations (including jail sentences for offenders).

Depending on how these remedies are imposed, there may be an impact on markets, and or entrants in those markets. Particularly in the services sector, but also in other areas, if antitrust remedies are overly broad, then legitimate business activity in the cross-border segment might be unnecessarily impaired. In particular, an over-reliance or structural remedies may distort foreign investment choices and restrict the ability of foreign traders and investors to be successful in these markets.

In high-technology markets, remedy choice is also affected by the dynamics that drive those new markets.

The Philosophical Underpinnings of Remedy Choice

Under a consumer welfare approach to competition policy, any structural remedy proposed must give rise to productive efficiencies. If productive efficiency cannot be demonstrated, the structural remedy should not be considered. The government must then weigh the allocative efficiency gains against productive efficiency losses if productive efficiencies cannot be demonstrated. Hence, the government must weigh dynamic losses against static efficiencies resulting from any ordered break-up. Any consideration of the overall welfare gains from competition remedies also must consider the costs of monitoring the particular remedies.

There is also a question of expertise. As a general rule, courts and competition agencies should avoid fashioning remedies for which they are unlikely to have the expertise and resources to execute. Agencies and courts instead must be able to explain and reasonably supervise remedies. In particular, courts and agencies should avoid the temptation to start to act like regulators.[102] Here, the difference between a competition agency and sectoral regulator is important. The goal of the competition agency is to ensure that nothing stands in the way of the market's efficient operation. The goal of the sectoral regulator, by contrast, is to ensure that the regulatory environment enables certain pre-determined regulatory goals to be achieved. These differences are significant. A competition agency is not functioning to its highest and best use when it tries to act like a regulator. Clearly, the danger of this is exacerbated if the industry in question is unregulated to begin with. It should be noted that in the case of the AT&T MFJ, the court was dealing with an industry that was already regulated.

Behavioural injunctions generally should be preferred to structural remedies because they can be more narrowly tailored to the particular anti-competitive harm at issue. However, the downside of a behavioural injunction is that it might actually be costly to enforce. But structural remedies also impose their own costs. In the case of the AT&T divestiture, for example, structural remedies were avoided precisely because they would have made the network almost impossible to operate.[103]

Clearly, the design of the remedy will depend on the specific facts of the high-tech industry involved, in particular whether network externalities are at play or whether the industry possesses public goods characteristics. In some cases, both economic effects will be present and the precise choice of remedy therefore can tip between them. The remedy chosen also could result in rent-seeking behaviour by tipping this balance. If the net effect of the remedy is to create a regulatory structure that yields supra-competitive returns to certain competitor companies, then the net effect is damaging to overall consumer welfare. Here, the remedy is very dependent on whether the industry was regulated to start with. If the industry was regulated to start with, then a structural remedy that looks regulatory in nature is less pernicious than where the industry was not regulated to start with. Shelanski and Sidak have summarised this by saying that in order to determine whether a remedy was efficient, courts or agencies must assess the following factors:

> Expected price reductions will offset any production cost increases or losses in consumer sale-side network externalities; that the net gain from such price reductions will not entail offsetting costs in the form of inefficiently reduced innovation incentives; and that the remaining net gains can then not be achieved at a lower cost through an alternative remedial plan.[104]

Sufficiency of Damages as a Remedy

Structural remedies tend to be favoured where monetary damages are found to be an insufficient remedy. This of course begs the question of what is an insufficient remedy. Broadly, damages calculations are designed to discipline the wrongdoing while not penalising efficient activity. However, there will be examples where damages awarded must be higher than the actual damage caused because otherwise the wrongful practice would be encouraged and not deterred (this is because the detection rate is less than perfect). This is the major reason for the treble damages penalty in the US antitrust cases.

Damages remedies can address many different issues. If a violation results in an increased cost of inputs, these costs can be factored into monetary damages. Lost profits as a result of anti-competitive behaviour similarly can be factored in by money damages. Injunctive relief, however, is a special case – useful when irreparable harm is threatened. Where businesses are in imminent danger of being driven from the market, as opposed to merely injured, then an injunctive-type remedy is particularly applicable. Injunctive relief is also particularly appropriate in those cases where there has been a history of dealing with the defendant and monetary damages have in the past been used but have not led to an improvement in conduct.

Behavioural vs. Structural Remedies

It is commonly thought that behavioural and structural remedies are different in kind rather than degree. Behavioural remedies, so the argument runs, are more difficult to enforce as they require some kind of on-going court or agency supervision. Structural remedies meanwhile are easier to enforce because they are a one-off remedy that changes the incentives for engaging in anti-competitive practices. The reality, however, is that there are elements of behavioural remedies encompassed in a structural remedy, and even structural remedies can be difficult to enforce and can require substantial supervision. This is because structural remedies frequently also require some changes in behaviour.

One example of a long-running case that eventually required a structural remedy is the *United Shoe Machinery* case,[105] where there was initial litigation in 1912, and a final divestiture in 1969, after a history of what was an exceptionally durable monopoly held. Structural remedies such as divestiture may be appropriate in such cases where the monopoly in question is particularly durable. Even the divestiture in the *AT&T* case became a long-running and much-disputed administrative obligation for the courts. The MFJ in that case actually became a secondary level of regulation, as waivers that were required in order for the Regional Bell Operating Companies ("RBOCs") to enter new markets became subject to long backlogs.[106]

In the case of the *Paramount Pictures* consent decrees, the lower court would have imposed a behavioural remedy enabling exhibitors to obtain movies from the defendant film studios through competitive bidding. The Supreme Court rejected this remedy on the basis that it would do nothing to decrease the studios' market power. When the case was remanded, the lower court ordered divestiture in reaction to the Supreme Court's notion that a behavioural remedy involved the court "in the daily operation of this nationwide business."[107]

Compulsory Licencing

One alternative to divestiture in many cases is compulsory licencing of intellectual property ("IP"), where patent or copyright owners are required to licence certain IP rights to other parties and have no right to refusal. Such licencing could be ordered either with or without a fee paid by the licensee. This remedy has some interest in high-tech cases because the IP owned by the defendant often is the perceived source of the anti-competitive effects. However, compulsory licencing has met with almost uniform criticism in the economic literature.[108] The problems associated with it are (a) its advantages are generally outweighed by its administrative difficulties because it is difficult for a court to properly evaluate what a licence or royalty fee should be, and (b) the difficulty of on-going supervision by the courts. Hence, it has been noted that compulsory licencing is a rarity in the patent system[109] and that while it may be used as a remedy, "it must be used sparingly."[110] Compulsory licencing's most significant disadvantage, however, is that it degrades the values of the affected intellectual property and therefore disincentivises investments in innovation-inducing IP – to the detriment of technological advancement and economic growth.

Importance of Intellectual Property Protected Platforms

We deal with the interface between intellectual property, competition and trade more specifically in Chapter 10 but it is worth making some introductory remarks on the subject now.

For countries with relatively new competition agencies, this is a very important area. Many people see the goals of competition policy and intellectual property policy as being in tension with each other. Many countries' competition agencies regard the patent as a monopoly, and the goal of competition policy is to ensure that the monopolist or patent-holder's behaviour can be reined in. However, this analysis mischaracterises the nature of the intellectual property right. The intellectual property right is in fact more like a property right (such as the right to exclude someone from one's house or preventing someone from stealing your television set). However, it is also an economic right, and the patent system is designed to strike a balance between granting a complete and absolute monopoly to an inventor for a particular innovation and giving the right for too short a period of time, such that no one would spend the money and effort on coming up with an invention.

Even assuming all of this, the patent cannot be viewed as conferring a monopoly as that term is understood by antitrust law unless it confers market power in a particular defined product market. It is comparatively rare for a patent by itself to confer this sort of market power. One can think of examples where a new drug is discovered and for a short time is the only way to treat a particular disease. However, usually new treatments are discovered and are themselves patented and so vigorous competition ensues between the various brands. Rarely does the 20-year patent period confer market or monopoly power, as those terms are understood by antitrust law, for its entire duration. Indeed, this point has been noted by the DOJ and FTC in their 2017 *Antitrust Guidelines for the Licensing of Intellectual Property*,[111] in which the agencies jointly note that intellectual property does not necessarily create market power in the antitrust context. The *Guidelines* state that while the IP right may confer the power to exclude with respect to specific process or product, there will often be sufficient actual or potential close substitutes for such products, processes or works to prevent the exercise of market power. Furthermore, the *Guidelines* stress that (1) even if an intellectual property right does confer market power, that market power does not by itself offend the antitrust laws; (2) nor does such market power impose on the intellectual property owner an obligation to licence the use of that property to others (a rejection of compulsory licencing, except when it may be used to remedy the illegal acquisition of market power or other anti-competitive behaviour).

Competition agencies are often asked to "regulate" how the owner of intellectual property must treat rivals. Many competition agencies have suggested in decisions or statements that the intellectual property right confers some form of essential facility that the rights holder must give others access to, or else face competition proceedings. Once again, this view is deeply tied to the belief that the intellectual property right is a monopoly. The question of whether a refusal to licence is a competition issue will depend on whether the person exercising that right has market power in a properly defined market. Even if they do, a key question will be whether there are alternatives available to the party to whom the licence was not granted.

Under the original US essential facilities case, *MCI v. AT & T*,[112] four elements had to be met in order to show an essential facility. These elements were as follows:

1 Control of the essential facility by a monopolist.
2 A competitor's inability to practically or reasonably duplicate the essential facility.
3 The denial of the use of the facility to a competitor.
4 The facility of providing the facility.

The Second Circuit, in the *Twin Labs* case,[113] specifically approved the leading antitrust treatise's view of what might constitute an essential facility: "facilities that are natural monopoly, facilities whose duplication is forbidden by law, and perhaps those that are publicly subsidised and thus could not be built privately."[114] We must note, however, that the US Supreme Court jurisprudence has recently severely restricted (and some would argue de facto rejected) the application of this essential facilities doctrine.[115]

The Metrics to Measure ACMDs

We have seen through the evolution of various antitrust doctrines in many countries a gradual acceptance that consumer welfare should be the guiding light of competition implementation and enforcement. The same principles should guide the measurement of consumer welfare effects of ACMDs found by governments. We discuss the metrics of ACMDs in detail in the next chapter.

The question because how can these be measured? First, it is necessary to provide a taxonomy of ACMDs. The OECD Toolkit, discussed previously, supplies such a taxonomy, and in so doing describes a wide variety of specific ACMDs.

Having established a suitable taxonomy, it is necessary to make some observations regarding how the ACMD can be evaluated based on its welfare effect. We propose conducting this analysis in the following manner.

1. Identification of ACMD.
2. Evaluation of Market prior to the distribution.
3. Product and market analysis; definition of relevant product and geographic markets.
4. Imposition of the ACMD on the market.
5. What is the likely result of the ACMD?
6. Evaluation of the market, post-distortion.
7. Use of various indices to determine the impact of the ACMD such as the HHI and the Lerner Index to assess the impact of competition on the product and geographic markets.
8. Other ways of assessing anti-competitive harms.

We analyse proposed models for measuring ACMDs in the following chapters.

Conclusion

We have seen that there is a common thread that runs through the application of competition law, and that thread is consumer welfare enhancement in an economic sense. While it is sometimes said that the US has adopted two schools of thought with respect to the enforcement of antitrust law, a closer look at the cases demonstrates that these schools of thought were not sequential but simultaneous. The guiding purposes of competition law and policy have always been about consumer welfare enhancement and allowing economic efficiencies to play an undistorted role in optimising the competitive process, so that costs are reduced, and prices lowered. This fundamental understanding informs all approaches to competition policy. It guides how competition agencies view themselves – either as a facilitator of an undistorted market or as a regulator whose role is to shape the market. It guides the approach the agency takes with respect to remedies, as well as shaping the approach that is taken with respect to the type of behaviour which is subject to scrutiny. Very recent initiatives in the US and the EU, and other jurisdictions to move away from a strict consumer welfare analysis in dealing with big digital platforms (including the introduction of direct regulation) are not necessarily at odds with a desire to improve consumer welfare. Rather, they may reflect a concern (well-founded or not) that the new digital giants pose a novel and unique threat to markets and consumers over the long-term, that must be counteracted by government intervention in the short-term. It is premature to say the least to conclude that this recent targeted modification to antitrust enforcements norms represents an abandonment of general consumer welfare-based antitrust principles, particularly given the continuing role economists play in the administration of competition law. Furthermore, the role of reviewing courts in restraining major shifts away from a consumer welfare approach is another constraint that antitrust enforcers must keep in mind. Nevertheless, it must be acknowledged that recent opposition from various quarters to an emerging consumer welfare-centric antitrust consensus has generated some costly uncertainty as to the future direction of antitrust policy worldwide.

Precisely how countries implement and enforce competition laws will determine whether the overall goal of trade liberalisation as we have discussed in the first two chapters is accomplished by a consumer-welfare-enhancing approach to competition policy inside the market. As we will see in succeeding chapters, these concepts underpin many areas of trade policy and can help shift trade policy from a mercantilist, producer-welfare-dominated vision to the consumer-welfare-oriented vision which was the original vision of the framers of the modern free trade movement. The precise manner in which countries actually implement competition laws internally will determine the quality of the competitive market inside the border. This will, in turn, determine the ability of participants in that market to engage in international trade. A consumer-welfare-enhancing approach will serve both domestic and foreign new entrants.

We have also made recommendations as to how first to deal with ACMDs. We have noted the existence of the OECD Toolkit and have suggested our own checklist that might be consulted when we analyse them. We have also developed a metric for a "distortions index" that includes a metric that can be used to estimate the actual size of particular ACMDs.[116] (That metric has been applied to estimate the welfare losses attributable to ACMDs in India.[117] In the next chapter, we will look at what tools and remedies could be used to move markets around the world to more pro-competitive outcomes, understanding that there are real politically powerful forces that have a vested interest in the anti-competitive status quo. Crucial to fighting these resistive forces will be coming up with a robust metric to measure ACMDs, and a normative framework to understand distortions in which trade policy, competition policy and regulatory policy sit.

Notes

1 For a good comparative overview of EU and US antitrust law and its application to other regions, see generally Barry Hawk, *Antitrust and Competition Laws* (Juris Publishing, 2020). The discussion in this chapter also draws upon James Keyte, Frédéric Jenny and Eleanor Fox, *Buckle Up: The Global Future of Antitrust Enforcement and Regulation*, 35 Antitrust No. 2, 32–40 (2021).
2 Sherman Antitrust Act, 15 US C. § 1–7 (1890).
3 Clayton Act, 15 US C. §§ 12, 13, 14–18, 20, 21, 2–27 (1914).
4 *See id.* § 18(1)(1).
5 *See* Treaty establishing the European Economic Community (EEC), 25 March 1957, Doc. 11957E/TXT, art. 101–102.
6 *Id.*, art.101(1).
7 Treaty establishing the European Economic Community, *supra* note 5, art. 82.
8 *See* Eleanor Fox, *Antitrust, Trade and the Twenty-First Century–Rounding the Circle*, 48 REC. NYC BAR.ASSN 535, 539 (1993).
9 European Commission, XXVIth Report on Competition Policy, § III.lo (1996) (*hereinafter* "Commission Report").
10 See Randolph Tritell and Elizabeth Kraus, *The Federal Trade Commission's International Antitrust Program*, Federal Trade Commission (2021), at 5.
11 Commission Report, *supra* note 9.
12 Commission Decision of 28 Feb 1995, Case IV/M.555, Glaxo/Wellcome Plc, 1995 O.J. (C 65), at 3.
13 Commission Decision of 27 Mar 1996, Case IV/M.697, Lockheed Martin/Loral Corp., 1996 O.J. (C 314), at 9.
14 *See* Council Regulation 17/62, 1962 O. J. (013 P. 0204–0211), art. 11.
15 *See* Commission Report, *supra* note 9.
16 *See* Commission Regulation 1983/83, 1983 O.J. (L 173), at 1; Commission Regulation 1984183, 1983 O.J. (L 173), at 5; Commission Regulation 417/85, 1985 O.J. (L 53), at 1; Commission Regulation 418/85, 1985 O.J. (L 53), at 5; Commission Regulation 4087/88, 1988 O.J. (L 359), at 46.
17 Tampa Elec. v. Nashville Coal, 365 US 320, 327–335 (1961).
18 *See* Jefferson Parish Hosp. Dist. No. 2 v. Hyde, 466 US 2, 17 (1984*ff.*
19 *See* Case C-234189, Stergios Delimitis v. Henninger Bräu AG, 1991 E.C.R. 935, I-944-4.
20 *See*, e.g., Case 85/76, Hoffmann-La Roche v. Commission, 1979 E.C.R. 461.*ff.*
21 *See* Commission Decision 93/406/EEC, 1993 O.J. (L 183/19), at 19, 22.
22 *See* Robert Pitofsky, Chairman, US Federal Trade European Commission, *Vertical Restraints and Vertical Aspects of Mergers-A US Perspective*, Address at the Fordham Corporate Law Institute 24th Annual Conference on International Antitrust Law and Policy (16–17 Oct 1997).
23 *See Vertical Merger Guidelines*, US Department of Justice & The Federal Trade Commission (2020).
24 *See* "Request for Information on Merger Enforcement," U.S. Department of Justice & Federal Trade Commission (19 Jan 2022), https://www.justice.gov/opa/press-release/file/1463566/download.
25 *See* Juan Briones Alonso, Head of the Merger Task Force, European Commission, *Vertical Aspects of Mergers, Joint Ventures, and Strategic Alliances,* Address at the Fordham Corporate Law Institute 24th Annual Conference on International Antitrust Law and Policy (16–17 Oct 1997).
26 Thomas N. Dahdouh and James F. Mongoven, *The Shape of Things to Come: Innovation Market Analysis in Merger Cases*, 64 ANTITRUST L.J. 405, 406 (1996).
27 For a closely argued analysis of the early cases in greater detail, *see* Robert Bork, *The Antitrust Paradox: A Policy at War with Itself* (Free Press, 1978).
28 United States v. Trans-Missouri Freight Ass'n, 166 US 290 (1897).

29 Addyston Pipe and Steel Co. v. United States, 85 F. 271 (6th Cir. 1898).
30 United States v. Joint Traffic Ass'n, 171 US 505 (1898).
31 *See, e.g.*, *The Antitrust Paradox*, *supra* note 27.
32 Standard Oil of New Jersey v. United States, 221 US 1 (1911).
33 United States v. American Tobacco, 221 US 106 (1911).
34 *See The Antitrust Paradox*, *supra* note 27, at 34.
35 Dr. Miles Medical v. John D. Park and Sons Co., 270 US 373 (1911).
36 Board of Trade of the City of Chicago v. United States, 246 US 231 (1918).
37 United States v. Aluminium Company of America, 148 F.2d 416 (2d Cir. 1945) ("Alcoa").
38 Brown Shoe Co. v. United States, 370 US 294 (1962).
39 *Id.*, at 344.
40 Mario Monti, *The Future for Competition Policy in the European Union*, Address at Merchant Taylor's Hall, London (9 Jul 2001).
41 *See* Aurelien Portuese, *European Competition Enforcement and the Digital Economy: The Birthplace of Precautionary Antitrust*, in *The Global Antitrust Institute Report on the Digital Economy* (Joshua D. Wright and Douglas H. Ginsburg eds., 2020), at 597–651.
42 *See generally* Alden Abbott, *US Antitrust Laws: A Primer*, Mercatus Center at George Mason University (2021), https://www.mercatus.org/publications/antitrust-policy/us-antitrust-laws-primer.
43 *See* Thomas Lambert, "Why the Federal Government's Antitrust Case Against Google Should – and Likely Will – Fail," Truth on the Market (18 Dec 2020), https://truthonthemarket.com/2020/12/18/why-the-federal-governments-antitrust-case-against-google-should-and-likely-will-fail; Dirk Auer, "Facebook and the Pros and Cons of Ex Post Merger Reviews," Truth on the Market (11 Dec 2020), https://truthonthemarket.com/2020/12/11/facebook-and-the-pros-and-cons-of-ex-post-merger-reviews/.
44 *See generally* Gabriella Muscolo and Alessandro Massolo, "Will the Biden Presidency Forge a Digital Transatlantic Alliance on Antitrust" in *The new US antitrust administration* (Concurrences 2021), https://www.concurrences.com/IMG/pdf/03.concurrences_1-2021_on-topic_biden_antitrust-2.pdf?65669/bbc9e79042d0e1899a5ed1e956d8e80f21021d002629ba2d6278d76d5baafb05.
45 *Proposal for a Regulation of the European Parliament and of the Council on contestable and fair markets in the digital sector (Digital Markets Act)* (COM (2020) 842), European Commission (2020); *See* also, "Deal on Digital Markets Act: EU rules to ensure fair competition and more choice for users," Press Release, European Commission (24 Mar 2022), https://www.europarl.europa.eu/news/en/press-room/20220315IPR25504/deal-on-digital-markets-act-ensuring-fair-competition-and-more-choice-for-users (As discussed in the press release, the DMA will be enforceable six months after publication in the European Journal, which will occur 20 days following the finalization of DMA language and approval by both the European Parliament and Council.
46 John Pecman and Antonio Di Domenico, *In Comity We Trust: Utilizing International Comity to Strengthen International Cooperation and Enforcement Convergence in Multijurisdictional Matters,* 3 Antitrust Chronicle 2021, Issue 1, at 23.
47 *See* Tom Wheeler, Phil Verveer, and Gene Kimmelman, "The Need for Regulation of Big Tech Beyond Antitrust," Brookings Institution (23 Sept 2020), https://www.brookings.edu/blog/techtank/2020/09/23/the-need-for-regulation-of-big-tech-beyond-antitrust/. On 21 January 2021, Kimmelman was named a Senior Counselor in the Biden Justice Department. Shiva Stella, *Senior Advisor Gene Kimmelman Resigns from Public Knowledge to Join Justice Department*, Public Knowledge (21 Jan 2021), https://www.publicknowledge.org/press-release/senior-advisor-gene-kimmelman-resigns-from-public-knowledge-to-join-justice-department/.
48 "FTC Acting Chairwoman Slaughter Announces New Rulemaking Group," Press Release, Federal Trade Commission (25 Mar 2021), https://

www.ftc.gov/news-events/press-releases/2021/03/ftc-acting-chairwoman-slaughter-announces-new-rulemaking-group.

49 *See* "Statement of Regulatory Priorities," Federal Trade Commission (2021), https://www.reginfo.gov/public/jsp/eAgenda/StaticContent/202110/Statement_3084_FTC.pdf.

50 Judgment of the General Court, Case T-286/09 RENV Intel Corporation v Commission, 2022 ECLI:EU:T:2022:19. General Court of the European Union, Press Release No. 1622, The General Court annuls in part the Commission decision imposing a fine of € 1.06 billion on Intel (26 Jan 2022), https://curia.europa.eu/jcms/upload/docs/application/pdf/2022-01/cp220016en.pdf. As a leading global law firm analysis explains:

[t]he [General Court] judgment demonstrates that infringement decisions must be supported by economic analysis, and not rely on form-based condemnation of rebate schemes, and that companies can rely on economic analysis to assess the antitrust compliance of their rebate schemes, which the EC must carefully review in case of investigation.

Skadden, Arps, Slate, Meagher and Flom LLP, *EU General Court Overturns Intel Antitrust Fine* (7 Feb 2022), https://www.skadden.com/insights/publications/2022/02/eu-general-court-overturns-intel-antitrust-fine

51 *See* Derek Thompson, "How mRNA Technology Could Change the World," The Atlantic (29 March 2021), https://www.theatlantic.com/ideas/archive/2021/03/how-mrna-technology-could-change-world/618431/.

52 *See* Adam Thierer, *Permissionless Innovation: The Continuing Case for Comprehensive Technological Freedom* (2nd ed., Mercatus Center 2016).

53 For a more detailed overview of this topic, *see* Eleanor M. Fox and Damien Gerard, *EU Competition Law* (Elgar 2017), at 311–333; Conor Quigley, *European State Aid Law and Policy* (3rd ed., Hart Publishing 2015).

54 Case C-379/98, PreussenElektra AG v Schhleswag AG, 2000 ECR I-2159.

55 Commission Decision Case N.661/99, 2002 O.J. (113/3).

56 *See*, for example, France v. Commission (Stardust Marine) [2002] ECR I-4397; Comune di Milano/European Commission [2020] CJEU ECLI:EU:C:2020:1012.

57 Cases C-278/92 and C-280/92, Spain v. Commission, 1994 ECR I-4146.

58 For a detailed treatment, *see* Chapter 7.

59 Case C-280/00, Altmark Trans GmbH and Regierungspräsidium Magdeburg v. Nahverkehrsgesellschaft Altmark GmbH, and Oberbundesanwalt beim Bundesverwaltungsgericht, 2003 ECR I-7747.

60 Parker v. Brown, 317 US 341 (1943), California Liquor Distributors Association v. Midcal, 445 US 97 (1980).

61 See *EU Competition Law, supra* note 53, at 329–333. (This led the Commission to bring tax-related state aid proceedings against Ireland for aid to Apple; the Netherlands for aid to Starbucks; Luxembourg for aid to Fiat. McDonald's, and Amazon; and Belgium for operating an excess profit exemption scheme.) See Fox and Gerard, pp. 329–333. This led the Commission to bring tax-related state aid proceedings against Ireland for aid to Apple; the Netherlands for aid to Starbucks; Luxembourg for aid to Fiat. McDonald's, and Amazon; and Belgium for operating an excess profit exemption scheme.

62 In September 2020, the Commission appealed to the European Court of Justice the General Court's July 2020 ruling that annulled the Commission's 2016 decision that Ireland had granted illegal tax breaks to Apple. *See* "Statement by Executive Vice-President Margrethe Vestager on the Commission's decision to appeal the General Court's judgment on the Apple tax State aid case in Ireland," Press Release, European Commission (25 Sept 2020), https://ec.europa.eu/commission/presscorner/detail/en/statement_20_1746. In May 2021, the General Court confirmed the Commission's June 2018 decision that Luxembourg granted illegal State

aid to Engie through selective tax breaks but it annulled the Commission's October 2017 decision that Luxembourg granted illegal State aid to Amazon. *See* "Statement by Executive Vice-President Margrethe Vestager following today's Court judgments on the Amazon and Engie tax State aid cases in Luxembourg," Press Release, European Commission (12 May 2021), https://ec.europa.eu/commission/presscorner/detail/en/statement_21_2468.

63 *See* Hans W. Friederiszick, Lars-Hendrik Roller, and Vincent Verouden, *EC State Aid Control: An Economic Perspective*, in The EC State Aid Regime: Distortive Effects of State Aid on Competition and Trade (Michael Sanchez Rydelski, ed., Cameron May 2006), at 145–182.

64 EU Competition Law, *supra* note 53, at 322–323 (citing remarks by Joaquín Almunia, Vice President and Commissioner for Competition, 9th Global Forum on Competition, Paris, 18 February 2010).

65 "State Aid: Commission Adopts Revised Regional Aid Guidelines," Press Release, European Commission (19 Apr 2021), https://ec.europa.eu/commission/presscorner/detail/en/ip_21_1825.

66 *Id.*

67 *EC State Aid Control, supra* note 59, at 587.

68 *See* the postal discussion in Chapter 15 where we consider auctions of the universal service obligations.

69 *See* Alden F. Abbott and Shanker A. Singham, *Enhancing Welfare by Attacking Anti-competitive Market Distortions* (15 Dec 2011). 4 Consurrences (2011); Shanker A. Singham, *Freeing the Global Market: How to Boost the Economy by Curbing Regulatory Distortions*, Council on Foreign Relations (2012).

70 China Innovation Project, *A Guide to Understanding China's Next Wave of Innovation*, Newsletter, Harvard University (2021).

71 James McBride and Andrew Chatzky, *Is 'Made in China 2025' a Threat to Global Trade?*, Background Note, Council on Foreign Relations (2019).

72 See *The UK Trade and Cooperation Agreement: Level Playing Field,* House of Commons Library (2021).

73 Article 411 (1) to (3) sets out the rebalancing mechanism. Further provisions allow for a review of the 'Trade' heading of the TCA. This is in case of a persistent dispute, including on the application of the relevant level playing field commitments. This mechanism opens up the possibility of the entire trade part of the agreement being suspended.

74 The prevailing view is that it is broader but there are exceptions; see, for example, M. Slotboom, *Subsidies in WTO Law and in EC Law, Broad and Narrow Definitions*, 36 J. WORLD TRADE 517 (2002).

75 "Recommendation of the Council on Competitive Neutrality," Organization for Economic Co-operation and Development (30 May 2021), https://legalinstruments.oecd.org/en/instruments/OECD-LEGAL-0462. The OECD underscored the importance it accords to promoting competitive equality by including it as a featured topic at the 2022 OECD Competition Open Day; *see* "OECD Competition Open Day (2022)," Organization for Economic Co-operation and Development (n.d.), https://www.oecd.org/competition/oecd-competition-open-day.htm.

76 OECD, "Competitive Neutrality in Competition Policy (2022)," (accessed 10 Feb 2022), https://www.oecd.org/competition/competitive-neutrality.htm.

77 The leading American antitrust treatise writer has characterised the consumer welfare standard as focused on behaviour that tends towards maximising output (taking into account quantity, quality and innovation) in a way that is consistent with sustainable competition. *See* Herbert Hovenkamp, *Federal Antitrust Policy: The Law of Competition and Its Practice* (6th ed., West Academic, 2020), at 102.

78 OECD, Competition Assessment Toolkit (revised 2019 version), https://www.oecd.org/competition/assessment-toolkit.htm.

79 *See* Phil C. Neal, et al., *Report of the White House Task Force on Antitrust Policy*, 2 Antitrust L. & Econ. Rev. 11 (1968).
80 *Annual Report*, Federal Trade Commission (1971), at 21.
81 United States v. Von's Grocery Co., 384 US 270 (1966).
82 Harold Demsetz, *Why Regulate Utilities*, 11. J. LAW AND ECON. 55, 59–60 (1968).
83 Treaty Establishing the European Community, arts. 85–86, 7 Feb 1992, 1992 1 C.M.L.R. 573, at 626 (*hereinafter* "EC Treaty"), *incorporating changes made by* Treaty on European Union, 7 Feb 1992, 1992 O. J. (C 224), 1992 1 C.M.L.R. 719, 31 I.L.M. 247 (*hereinafter* "TEU"). The TEU amended the Treaty Establishing the European Economic Community, 25 Mar 1957, 298 U.N.T.S. 11, 1973 Br. Brit. T.S. No. 1 (Cmd. 5179II) (*hereinafter* "EEC Treaty"), *as amended by* Single European Act, 1987 O. J. (L 169), 1987 2 C.M.L.R. 741 (*hereinafter* "SEA").
84 Sherman Antitrust Act, 15 U &C. §§ 1–3 (1994).
85 *See* Spencer Weber Waller, *Neo-Realism and the International Harmonization of Law. Lessons from Antitrust*, 42 U. Kan. L. Rev. 557 (1994), at 564–565, 582.
86 See Alden F. Abbott, *The Globalization of Antitrust,* Mercatus Center at George Mason University (2021).
87 For an overview of convergence efforts and differences among competition laws, *see id.*
88 *Merger Assessment Guidelines*, Competition & Markets Authority (2021).
89 *See A New Pro-Competition Regime for Digital Markets*, Presented to Parliament by the Secretary of State for Digital, Culture, Media & Sport and the Secretary of State for Business, Energy and Industrial Strategy by Command of Her Majesty (July 2022).
90 See Friedrich von Hayek, Lecture to the memory of Alfred Nobel, December 11, 1974, *The Pretence of Knowledge*, https://www.nobelprize.org/prizes/economic-sciences/1974/hayek/lecture/.
91 *See* Chris Marchese, "How Amazon Wins: By Benefitting Sellers & Consumers," NetChoice (22 Dec 2020), https://netchoice.org/how-amazon-wins-by-benefitting-sellers-consumers/#:~:text=Amazon%2C%20in%20fact%2C%20is%20even,products%20and%20their%20closest%20competitors.
92 *See* Lazar Radic and Geoffrey Manne, "Amazon Italy's Efficiency Offense," *Truth on the Market* (11 Jan 2022), https://truthonthemarket.com/?s=amazon&orderby=relevance&order=DESC.
93 "CMA Designates Amazon as a Grocery Retailer to Protect Suppliers," Press Release, Competition and Markets Authority (9 Feb 2022), https://www.gov.uk/government/news/cma-designates-amazon-as-a-grocery-retailer-to-protect-suppliers.
94 *See* Cassey Lee, *Model Competition Laws: The World Bank-OECD and UNCTAD Approaches Compared*, in Competition Policy in Asia: Models and Issues (Cassey Lee and Cheong M. Fong, eds., 2006).
95 *See id.*, at 141.
96 *See generally, e.g.*, "Antitrust in Asia," F*reshfield* B*ruckhaus* D*eringer* (Feb 2018).
97 *Competition Policy Reform*, The China Dashboard, Asia Society (Winter 2021).
98 Richard Posner, *Antitrust Law: An Economic Perspective* (University of Chicago Press, 1976), at 268.
99 Howard Shelanski and J. Gregory Sidak, *Antitrust Divestitures in Network Industries*, 68 U. CHI. L. REV. 1, 11–12 (2001) ("Shelanski & Sidak").
100 *See* Carl Shapiro and Hal R. Varian, *Information Rules: A Strategic Guide to the Network Economy* (Harvard Business Review Press, 1998).
101 *US v. AT&T,* 552 F. Supp. 131 (D.D.C. 1982), *aff'd* 460 US 1001 (1983).
102 Phillip Areeda, *Essential Facilities: An Epithet in Need of Limiting Principles*, 58 ANTITRUST L.J. 841 (1990).
103 Per comments of network engineer, Joseph Weber, in Peter Temin and Joseph Weber, *The Modification of Final Judgment: Its Logic and Errors*, 8 U. FLA. J. L & PUB. POL. 201 (1997).

104 Shelanski and Sidak, at 135.
105 United States v. United Shoe Machinery Co., 247 US 32 (1918).
106 Paul H. Rubin and Hasem Dezhbakhsh, *Costs of Delay and Rent-Seeking Under the Modification of Final Judgment*, 16 MANAGERIAL & DECISION ECON. 385 (1995). According to Rubin and Dezhbakhsh, by 1994, this backlog had reached 54.7 months.
107 United States v. Paramount Pictures, Inc., 334 US 131 (1948).
108 *See* Shanker A. Singham, *TRIPS and the Interface Between Competition and Patent Protection in the Pharmaceutical Industry*, 26 BROOKLYN J. INT'L L.J. 363, 390–395 (2001).
109 Dawson Chemical Co. v. Rohm & Haas Co., 448 US 176, 215 (1980).
110 Phillip Areeda and Herbert Hovencamp, Antitrust Law, Vol. III, §705 (Rev. 1996).
111 *Antitrust Guidelines for the Licensing of Intellectual Property*, US Department of Justice (2017).
112 MCI Communications Corp. v. AT&T Co., 708 F.2d 1081 (7th Cir. 1983).
113 *Twin Labs v. Weider Health and Fitness, 900 F. 2d. 566 (2nd Cir. 1990).*
114 *See* Antitrust Law, *supra* note 100, §736.2 (Supp. 1988).
115 See, e.g., Law Offices of Curtis V. Trinko v. Verizon, 540 US 398 (2004).
116 *See* Shanker A. Singham and A. Molly Kiniry, Introduction to Anti-Competitive Market Distortions and the Disortions Index, Legatum Institute (2016).
117 *See* Alden Abbott, "Legatum Institute Publishes an Eye-Opening Case Study on the Benefits of Eliminating Anticompetitive Market Distortions (ACMDs) in India," Truth on The Market (7 June 2016), https://truthonthemarket.com/2016/06/07/legatum-institute-publishes-an-eye-opening-case-study-on-the-benefits-of-eliminating-anticompetitive-market-distortions-acmds-in-india/.

4

A BRIEF INTRODUCTION TO THE THEORY OF ANTI-COMPETITIVE MARKET DISTORTIONS

As we have noted previously, anti-competitive market distortions, or ACMDs, refer to government-imposed restrictions on competition. If a country seeks to have a market economy, then it must accept that the heart of the market is competition.[1] It must therefore accept the widely held view that competition on the merits should be the organising principle of the economy. Any deviations from that competition on the merits through laws, regulations or actions can be described as an ACMD. These distortions may occur as distortions of international competition (trade distortions) or they may be distortions of domestic competition, or they may be distortions of property rights protection (that with which firms compete). Distortions across any of these pillars could have a negative effect on economic growth.

Singham has written extensively about market distortions for over 20 years.[2] Singham also dealt with the issue extensively in his 2007 book, A General Theory of Trade and Competition: Trade Liberalisation and Competitive Markets (CMP) (2007). Formally, Abbott and Singham[3] have defined ACMDs as those that "involve government actions that empower certain private interests to obtain or retain artificial competitive advantages over their rivals be they foreign or domestic."

Singham also discussed market distortions in a working paper for the Council on Foreign Relations, Freeing the Global Market by Curbing Regulatory Distortions (October 2012, Council on Foreign Relations). This paper included an inventory of distortions and explained why they have a pernicious impact on international trade.

Having identified that ACMDs present a pernicious problem in international trade, the lack of a quantum of the impact of these distortions made it very difficult to evaluate the scale of the problem. Without a sense of the impact of the ACMD, it has proved difficult for policymakers to develop tools and mechanisms

DOI: 10.4324/9780429323331-4

to discipline these practices. It was therefore necessary to research different ways of evaluating the harm posed by ACMDs. Singham and Rangan embarked on this exercise with a series of papers from 2014.[4] Singham and Rangan also published two papers introducing the economic analysis of ACMDs in 2016 for the Legatum Institute.[5] That work is the precursor to further papers on the subject, which include modifications and adaptations to the model used.

It is only by fully understanding the metrics of ACMDs that we can really evaluate their impact. ACMDs can damage international trade flows as well as distort markets in ways that reduce competition and destroy wealth out of the economy. Hence, ACMDs are just as relevant to the international trade agenda as they are to the domestic regulatory agenda. Policymakers would greatly benefit from understanding the cost of ACMDs and how they relate to domestic regulatory promulgation. The OECD in its regulatory toolkit and competition assessment has advised policymakers to promulgate regulation in ways that are the least anti-competitive possible consistent with a publicly stated, legitimate regulatory goal. Many countries include this sort of competition assessment in the ways they promulgate regulations, including taken into account the views of competition agencies. However, absent a robust metric to measure distortion, it is difficult for governments to properly evaluate the harm caused by certain types of regulation, and it is also impossible for publics to fully understand the impact of regulation so that they can properly weigh the costs and benefits of regulation and determine if the harm is justified by the importance of the regulatory objectives.

ACMDs can be particularly harmful (as distinct from private anti-competitive behaviour) as they are imposed by the government. Therefore, they enjoy state-backed power and the force of law.

Economists have long recognised the prevalence and pernicious consequences of ACMDs. The complexity and breadth of this issue, however, have made it an especially difficult one for policymakers to tackle. Our work to date attempts to break down the impact of ACMDs on productivity.

If we are able to develop metrics to measure ACMDs, there are a number of policy consequences that are of great value. These include allowing governments to tarifficate market distortions in the markets of trading partners which allows a nuanced approach to issues like the US-China trade dispute (as opposed to the imposition of a tariff regardless of evidence of ACMDs in China). Such a policy would have the advantage of actually incentivising the party which has the ACMDs to lower them (and thereby benefit from the lower tariff), as well as enabling countries to signal to their trading partners that they are open to imports which are efficiently produced because of the consumer welfare gains for their economies.

Policymakers can also improve the quality of their own regulatory promulgation processes. Under the OECD Regulatory Toolkit and Competition Assessment, governments should regulate in ways that are the least damaging to competition consistent with a publicly stated, legitimate regulatory goal. If policymakers had a sense of the effect of ACMDs in their own markets on their own economic output, this would be tremendously valuable in coming to better regulatory decisions. It would also be invaluable in ensuring that legislators can properly evaluate the regulatory goal and the cost of the ACMD and make informed decisions.

Such a metric would also inform the public debate and ensure that this is actually being carried out in a manner that balances the regulatory objectives that need to be properly and clearly stated, and the cost of the ACMDs to the economy. Too often in public debate, a knee jerk response to a perceived market failure occurs without any attempt to present, much less understand the economic evidence.

A metric will also tell us something about the scale of the economic impact of ACMDs. It has been assumed that reduction of border trade barriers is where the largest economic gains are to be found, and reduction of distortions is important but not of the same order of magnitude. A metric will enable us to evaluate this impact. A sense of the scale of this impact was developed in a preliminary fashion by Cebr in 2019.[6] According to the Cebr report, imposing a distortion inside the border as opposed to at the border in an agency-based model led to a 37% reduction in output versus an 11% reduction of output for an equivalent border measure. This suggests that the impact of ACMDs might be much higher than previously supposed.

Impact of ACMDs on External and Internal Trade: A Schematic Representation

ACMDs can be reduced by a country's domestic policy choice or as a result of a trade negotiation. The schematic below illustrates this point.

Pro-Competitive Regulation

$R_{r,i}$ = Real System of Regulation for sector i

$R_{0,i}$ = Optimal systems of regulation and for sector i

C_o = Maximisation of production and allocation efficiency

After C_o on the $R_{r,i}$ curve, competition becomes cannibalistic and C_α is no longer maximised.

In the $R_{0,i}$ system, there are no ACMDs or competition distortions. This means that we will automatically remain at the C_o level (Figure 4.1).

The schematic graph above illustrates that there is an equilibrium point where a particular regulatory system maximises consumer welfare (i.e. is pro-competitive) but that ever-increasing levels of competition (including cannibalistic competition) can lead to a reduction of overall output. In other words at every low levels of competition or at cannibalistic levels of competition, economic output is damaged. This hypothesis is tested in the various models we have referred to below.

C_o

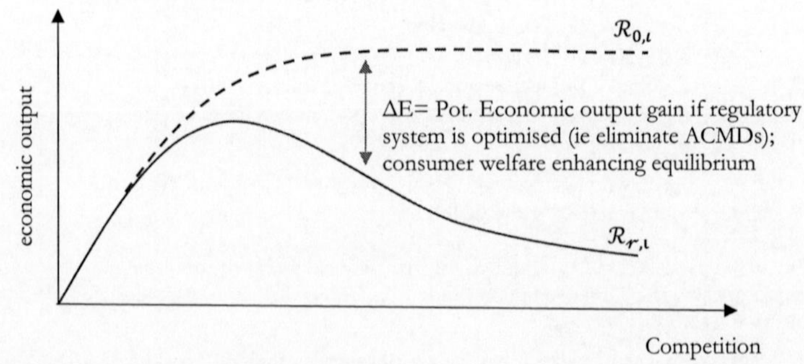

FIGURE 4.1 Pro-competitive Regulation

Our assumption is that ΔE far outweighs the frictional trade cost of different regulatory systems. This assumption can only be tested when a robust metric to measure ACMDs is developed.

The Singham-Rangan-Bradley (SRB) model tells us what the GDP cost of ACMDs is in country,[7] or

where R_α^A is the regulatory setting for product α in country A, ϒ R_α^B is the regulatory setting for product α in country B (and so on). Country A can unilaterally reduce its ACMD for R_α^A. It can also negotiate a reduction of B's ACMD for R_α^B (Figure 4.2).

$$\text{Hence, } \sum_{i=A}^{Z} \text{ACMD}_i = \sum_{i=A}^{Z} \text{ACMD}(R_\alpha^C)$$

If A reduces ACMD $\left(R_\alpha^A\right)$ to [ACMD $\left(R_\alpha^A\right) - x$] and negotiates a reduction in B to [ACMD $\left(R_\alpha^B\right)$ − y], $\sum_{i=A}^{Z}$ACMD(R_α^C) is reduced but ACMD $\left(R_\alpha^C\right)$ continues to damage the global system.

To the extent that an ACMD in country B negatively impacts a producer in country A, country A should be able to tarifficate that distortion. Distortions in country B also negatively impact the economy of the total global system and in some cases the economy in country B itself (although some producers in B are benefited). In order to determine what is the appropriate level of such a tariff, it is necessary to be able to quantify the impact of an ACMD. This is the only way that the tariffication can be narrowly tailored to the actual scale of the distortion so that it is the lowest amount necessary to correct the distortion.

We now describe the SRB economic model which is designed to quantify the scale of the distortion and its impact on GDP (as a measure of productivity).

The SRB model is designed to identify the impact on productivity and thus on global output for a given set of ACMDs. We can identify the impact of ACMDs at the country level based on the metrics we are able to use. Later in this chapter, we will develop a specific inventory of ACMDs.

$\mathcal{R}_{r,\iota}$ = Real System of Regulation for sector ι
= Optimal systems of regulation and for sector ι
C_0 = Maximisation of production and allocation efficiency
After C_0 on the $\mathcal{R}_{r,\iota}$ curve, competition becomes cannibalistic and C_α is no longer maximised.

In the $\mathcal{R}_{0,\iota}$ system, there are no ACMDs or competition distortions. This means we will automatically remain at the C_0 level.

Our assumption is that ΔE far outweighs the frictional trade cost of different regulatory systems. This assumption can only be tested when a robust metric to measure ACMDs is developed.

The Singham-Rangan-Bradley (SRB) model tells us what the GDP cost of ACMDs are in country[i], or

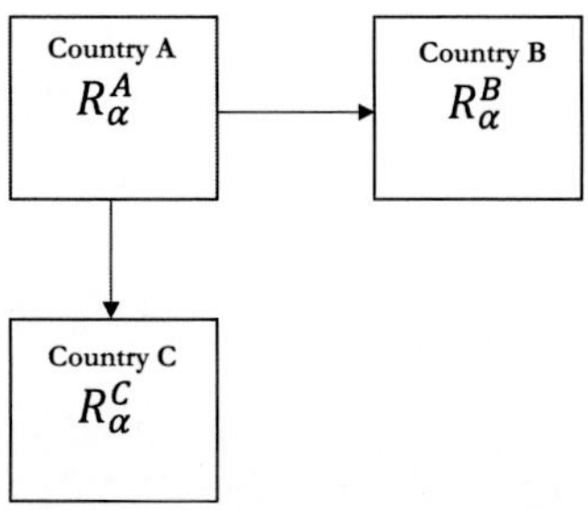

Where R_α^A is the regulatory setting for product α in Country A, γR_α^B is the regulatory setting for product α in Country B (and so on). Country A can unilaterally reduce its ACMD forR_α^A. It can also negotiate a reduction of B's ACMD for R_α^B.

Hence $\sum_{i=A}^{Z} ACMD_i = \sum_{i=A}^{Z} ACMD(R_\alpha^C)$

If A reduces ACMD (R_α^A) to [ACMD (R_α^A)-x] and negotiates a reduction in B to [ACMD(R_α^B) – y], and $\sum_{i=A}^{Z} ACMD(R_\alpha^C)$ is reduced but ACMD (R_α^C) continues to damage the global system.

[i] See discussion in Shanker A. Singham and U. Srinivasa Ragan, *Anti-Competitive Market Distortions: A Typology,* 38 ECON. AFFAIRS 339 (2018).

FIGURE 4.2 Trade Flows under SRB Model

Towards a Quantum for Measurement of Distortions: Model for Anti-Competitive Market Distortions

The model which we have developed is based on the notion that the three pillars of economic development are property rights protection, domestic competition and international competition.[8] Broadly, anti-competitive government policy affects the way the market functions through these three pillars. Essentially, the way this happens is explained below.

Property Rights

The foundation of a productive economy is property rights protection. If property rights are left unprotected, the incentive to invest, compete and innovate is lost. If the returns from effort cannot be captured, can be taken away or cannot be regained if wrongly taken away, what incentive is there to exert effort? Furubotn and Pejovich[9] describe the nature of property rights in this way:

> ... property rights do not refer to relations between men and things but, rather, to the sanctioned behavioural relations among men that arise from the existence of things and pertain to their use... The prevailing system of property rights in the community, then, can be described as the set of economic and social relations defining the position of each individual with respect to the utilisation of scarce resources.
>
> *(p. 1139, italics are the authors')*

The authors add in a footnote that "Roman Law, Common Law, Marx and Engels, and current legal and economic studies basically agree on this definition of property rights." In other words, the very nature of an economic transaction is defined by the right to property and this definition is not disputed. Property rights allow four things to occur: (1) investment to create the property (as in the case of intellectual property or IP and machinery); (2) investment to make the property more productive (as in the case of land, machinery and IP); (3) exploitation to get the maximum productivity out of it (as in the case of land, machinery, IP, etc.); (4) transfer of property to another who might be able to do a better job of the first three instead of the current owner of the property (as in the case of land, machinery and IP). All these lead to increased productivity, higher incomes and thus wealth and prosperity. So, a lack of property rights protection effectively undermines the ability of economic agents to operate effectively. It also undermines the process of competition because property rights are what firms compete with. In developing countries in particular, establishing and enforcing property rights play a significant role in creating the preconditions for growth.[10] Therefore, all other factors influencing economic outcomes depend on the level and quality of property rights protection. We account for the fact that the effect of domestic competition and international competition on other factors depends on the level of property rights in our model and will discuss how we capture this in the next section.

The property rights Protection indicator is constructed as follows. Intellectual property rights are themselves a type of property rights and are a crucial aspect of economic development.[11] Including this measure as a part of a property rights protection indicator was obvious and necessary. The other six subcategories are different ways in which a policy can ensure that the effort of agents cannot be wrongfully expropriated, that when a person's rights are violated, the process for righting that wrong is not prohibitively expensive[12] and that the legal system itself has integrity. The subcategories of the property rights protection indicator follow the Heritage Foundation Index of Economic Freedom's criteria for grading countries in terms of property rights protection.[13]

Domestic Competition

Domestic competition plays a significant role in the efficiency of both domestic and foreign firms. Competition among firms encourages innovation and upgrading of production processes, as well as positive externalities in local markets.[14] Each of these features of competition has a positive impact on welfare, which justifies its inclusion as part of this index.

Typically, the term "competition policy" refers to activities – and the enforcement of these activities – concerning restraint on competition created by private parties. Our domestic competition indicator is, instead, meant to capture the extent to which government policy itself restricts competitive behaviour.[15] Timothy Muris (2005)[16] highlights the importance of understanding and correcting restrictive government actions – not just private restrictions. He compares these two sources of competitive restrictions to the forks in a stream and states that "Protecting competition by focusing solely on private restraints is like trying to stop the water flow… by blocking only one channel." Muris goes on to say that creating a system which prevents anti-competitive behaviour by firms but allows a government to dictate the same anti-competitive outcome that would have resulted from private action has not eliminated the problem, "It has simply dictated the form that the problem will take." Domestic competition here refers to the domestic policies affecting the way in which firms make decisions and interact with one another. Any policy which limits profit-maximising firms' ability to make their own decisions will reduce the score for domestic competition for a country.[17] If a policy reduces the ability of some subset of firms to make their own decisions while not restricting others in the same way, then the domestic policy score will be reduced. However, this does not mean that a country with no regulations controlling the decisions of firms will receive the highest score. The goal of this index and the scores it generates are to allow comparisons between countries regarding the degree to which policy is welfare-maximising. If welfare is to be maximised, then some government regulation may be appropriate in many contexts. For example, if a market can be characterised as a natural monopoly, appropriately tailored government regulation may be crucial for welfare maximisation.[18] If there are true market failures that are not being handled adequately through purely private action (severe adverse health effects from pollution, a shortage of funds for post-secondary education, harmfully discriminatory practices, etc.), then government regulation may be necessary.[19] These antitrust or industrial organisation types of regulations are part of the domestic competition score. No judgment is made as far as the exact specification of the regulation. Instead, the effectiveness of antitrust policy and the cost of adhering to different policies are the measures used.

The domestic competition score is higher when firms are able to make their own decisions because we are trying to evaluate how well domestic policies promote competitive behaviour. It is constructed as follows. Competitive behaviour refers to the behaviour firms exhibit in a particular market which will maximise welfare within the market. Therefore, the domestic competition score is higher when policies respond to market failures and antitrust violations efficiently but otherwise do not interfere with or dictate firm behaviour. This is because the behaviour of profit-maximising firms – faced with demand from the market, the decisions of competitors, no market failures and no antitrust violations – will produce and charge a price which generates the welfare-maximising equilibrium. That is, once any market failures are corrected for, firms will behave in a way which maximises welfare. Of course, in practice, it is often very difficult or impossible to fully correct a market failure. However, some countries will do a better job than others in choosing and implementing policies that actively respond to market failures. The closer a country is to actually eliminating a market failure, the closer it will be to moving a market towards its welfare-maximising equilibrium.[20]

The domestic competition indicator is defined by because infrastructure[21] and the policies concerning how firms make decisions. Infrastructure and the efficiency with which it is built have serious implications for the competitiveness of a country. Reliable, well-maintained infrastructure is a crucial component of efficient markets. Here, infrastructure reflects each type of infrastructure in an economy. Labour regulations are defined by how free firms are to hire and fire employees, as well as how firms are then allowed to utilise those workers. Restrictions on the hiring and firing process or deployment of labour decisions will reduce the score for domestic competition. The less flexible policy makes the labour force, the higher the cost of production will be because firms will have to work around or suffer the restriction of each policy. Regulatory promulgation process refers to how laws are created. If the government is allowed to make decisions based on favouritism and the process is not transparent, ACMDs can be created at will. There will be no need to disguise them as market failures, or if they are disguised, they will be very difficult to recognise. Industrial organisation policies refer to the regulations which firms must adhere to in order to exist in a market and how antitrust behaviour is dealt with if it arises. All of these areas impact a firm's ability to make their own profit-maximising decisions.

International Competition

International competition refers to the degree to which a country allows foreign firms to access its domestic market and the degree to which it allows domestic firms to access foreign markets. Any restriction on the free flow of trade which is not the correction to a market failure will reduce the score for international competition. Greater access to a wider variety of goods benefits consumers and greater access to less expensive or higher quality inputs benefits firms. Also, exposing firms to potentially more efficient foreign firms promotes innovation. All of these forces combine to generate gains in welfare.[22]

The policies which reduce the score here are those that make it more costly or burdensome to transact internationally. The indicator is constructed as follows. Tariffs and procedural burden directly affect the flow of goods. Financial restrictions affect the flow of capital. The freedom of foreigners to visit is a measure reflecting the general openness of the economy to free movement of people. A policy which restricts visitation by foreigners would make it more difficult for foreign firms to have a presence in an economy. If any of these categories is restrictive, it will be more difficult for trade to occur. The Washington Consensus[23] also noted the importance of eliminating distortionary trade policies applied differently in different areas.[24] Import liberalisation is seen as particularly important because it eliminates the export disadvantage created by restricted access to less expensive imported intermediate goods. This type of ACMD is exactly what we are trying to capture with our international competition index.

Combined Effects

An important point to be made is that if one of these three areas is improved while the other two are left in poor condition, the impact on productivity will be reduced or reversed. For example, if domestic competition is improved by making it faster and less costly for domestic firms to start a business but property rights are left unprotected and international competition is prevented, the impact on productivity will likely be zero because firms will still be uncertain about entering the market (because their property can be expropriated, for example) and will not need to compete as fiercely as they would in the face of foreign competition.

Each of the three categories has an impact on how an improvement in the other categories will be realised in terms of productivity. As stated previously, without property rights protection agents cannot act in their own economic interests. This means that without property rights protection improvements in the other two categories will have no effect on the determinants of productivity. Domestic competition determines the structure of a domestic market which determines the equilibrium of each domestic market. If firms are not allowed to decide how they will behave, then imported foreign goods will enter an inefficient market and face inefficient constraints on their position in that market. It is possible that distorted domestic competition may help or hurt foreign firms. Similarly, international competition policies can prevent foreign firms from entering the domestic market or may prevent domestic firms from reaching foreign markets. In either case, the total effect in the long run will be a reduction of welfare.[25] Also, improving each of these three areas simultaneously will have a combined effect. If a country can correct the ACMDs in every area, it can move towards its optimal welfare level. Leaving ACMDs uncorrected in any area will negatively affect the benefits from correcting other ACMDs.

We have further developed the economic model of ACMDs, and this material is attached in the e-resource part of the book available at www.routledge.com/9780367339883

Notes

1 *See*, for example, *Oversight of the Enforcement of the Antitrust Laws: Hearing before the Subcomm. on Antitrust, Competition Policy, and Consumer Rights, S. Comm. on the Judiciary*, 114th Cong. (statement of Assistant Attorney General Bill Baer) ("As the Supreme Court [in Standard Oil vs FTC, 340 US 231 (1951)] has said, 'the heart of our national economy long has been faith in the value of competition'"); *see* also *Report and Recommendations,* Antitrust Modernization Commission (April 2007), http://govinfo.library.unt.edu/amc/report_recommendation/toc.htm, ("free-market competition is, and has long been, the fundamental economic policy of the United States").

2 *See,* for example, Shanker A. Singham, *Market Access and Market Contestability: Is the Difference purely semantics?* 25 Brook. J. Int'l L. 337 (1999); Shanker A. Singham, *Advancing the Competition and Trade Policy Agenda: Public Sector Restraints on Trade in the Free Trade Area of the Americas,* Int'l Antitrust Bulletin (2001); Shanker A. Singham and D. Daniel Sokol, *Public Sector Restraints: Behind the Border Trade Barriers,* 39 Tex. Int'l L. J. 625 (2004).

3 Alden F. Abbott and Shanker A. Singham, *Enhancing Welfare by Attacking Anticompetitive Market Distortions*, Revue 4 Concurrences (2011).

4 *See* Shanker A. Singham, Robert Bradley, and U. Srinvasa Rangan, *The Effect of Anticompetitive Market Distortions (ACMDs) on Global Markets*, Concurrances (2014).

5 *See* Shanker A. Singham, U. Srinivasa Rangan, Robert Bradley, and A. Molly Kiniry, *Anti-Competitive Market Distortions and their Impact; A Case Study of India*, Legatum Institute (2016); *see,* also, Shanker A. Singham and A. Molly Kiniry, *An Introduction to Anti-Competitive Market Distortions*, Legatum Institute (2016).

6 See *An Agent Based model of Trade; Market Distortions and Output*, Cebr (2019), https://img1.wsimg.com/blobby/go/bf4d316c-4c0b-4e87–8edb-350f819ee031/downloads/Cebr%20Market%20Distortions%20Trade%20Report.pdf?ver=1603533215968.

7 See discussion in Shanker A. Singham and U. Srinivasa Ragan, *Anti-Competitive Market Distortions: A Typology*, 38 Econ. Affairs 339 (2018).

8 As proposed and argued in Shanker A. Singham, *A General Theory of Trade and Competition: Trade Liberalisation and Competitive Markets* (Cameron May, 2007).

9 Eirik G. Furubotn and Svetozar Pejovich, *Property Rights and Economic Theory: A Survey of the Recent Literature*, 10 J. of Econ. Lit. 1137 (1972).

10 A lack of property rights protection creates what De Soto calls "dead capital" – the poor cannot leverage the assets they do accumulate, which prevents entrepreneurialism. *See* Hernando De Soto, *The Mystery of Capital: Why Capitalism Triumphs in the West and Fails Everywhere Else* (Basic Books, 2000).

11 For a detailed treatment of the importance of intellectual property rights, see later chapters of this book.

12 Either financially or through time commitments.

13 That is, Heritage Foundation describes why a country receives each level of score and this, in turn, provides a framework for the aspects of policy which we considered in building our indicator. "2022 Index of Economic Freedom: Property Rights," Heritage Foundation (2022), http://www.heritage.org/index/property-rights.

14 Michael E. Porter, *The Competitive Advantage of Nations* (The Free Press, 1990) *as cited in* Mariko Sakakibara and Michael E. Mariko, *Competing at Home to Win Abroad: Evidence from Japanese Industry*, 83 The Rev. of Econ. and Stat. 310 (2001) (positive externalities include, "…supplier availability, easier access to technology and market information, and specialised human resource development").

15 As part of our domestic competition indicator, we include an indicator of the success of policy in limiting the ability of private entities to restrict competition through the "Effectiveness of Anti-Monopoly Policy" variable in the "Industrial Organisation Regulation" subcategory.

16 Timothy J. Muris, *Principles for a Successful Competition Agency*, 72 U. of Chi. L. Rev. 165 (2005).

17 Similarly, the Washington Consensus includes privatisation as one of the ten key areas of development because of the belief that "private industry is managed more efficiently than state enterprises, because of the more direct incentives faced by a manager who either has a direct personal stake in the profits of an enterprise or else is accountable to those who do. At the very least, the threat of bankruptcy places a floor under the inefficiency of private enterprises, whereas many state enterprises seem to have unlimited access to subsidies." This theory is the backbone of our domestic competition indicator. However, regulation of private markets is not discussed in the Washington Consensus. We correct this oversight by emphasising the importance of policies which allow firms to make their own decisions. Originally conceived in John Williamson, *What Washington Means by Policy Reform*, in Latin American Adjustment: How Much Has Happened? (John Williamson ed., 1990) at 5.

18 When changing market characteristics, such as new technologies, eliminate natural monopoly conditions, however, maintaining government regulation may become counterproductive and welfare-inimical, and such regulation should be lifted.

19 Before the government acts, care should be taken to ensure that the private sector cannot adequately rectify the market failure at issue, and that the costs associated with government intervention are not likely to outweigh the benefits that flow from eliminating (or reducing) the market failure.

20 The welfare-maximising number and size of firms will depend on the market (type of good, substitutes, demand, etc.).

21 The ideal infrastructure measures would be those that reflect the policy for awarding contracts for infrastructure projects (specifically, for building, managing or maintaining infrastructure). However, the primary data available is concerned with outcomes, with only a couple of exceptions in financial infrastructure.

22 For a description of the theory, *see* Claustre Bajona, Mark J. Gibson, Timothy J. Kehoe, and Kim J. Ruhl, *Trade Liberalisation, Growth, and Productivity* (Federal Reserve Bank of Minneapolis, 2008), *as prepared for* "New Directions in International Trade Theory," Conference, University of Nottingham (8–9 Jun 2007). These authors also highlight the fact that trade openness does not always lead to increased GDP and that the theory does not predict an increase in GDP from openness. The theory does predict greater welfare from openness, though. We will use GDP per capita as our proxy for welfare because we do not have a direct measure of welfare. There are many sources which do find a positive relationship between openness and GDP. A few examples include Jeffery A. Frankel and Davin H. Romer, *Does Trade Cause Growth?* 89 Am. Econ. Rev. 379 (1999) *as cited in* Bajona et al. (2010); Robert E. Hall and Charles I. Jones, *Why Do Some Countries Produce So Much More Output per Worker than Others?* 114 Q. J. of Econ. 83 (1999) *as cited in* Bajona et al. (2010); and Francisco Alcalá and Antonio Ciccone, *Trade and Productivity*, 119 Q. J. of Econ. (2004) *as cited in* Bajona et al. (2010).

23 *What Washington Means by Policy Reform*, *supra* note 17.

24 Though, again, no emphasis was given to the competitive environment within a country except for the stress on privatisation.

25 *See The Effect of Anticompetitive Market Distortions (ACMDs) on Global Markets*, *supra* note 4.

5

TRADE POLICIES AND TRADE REMEDIES THROUGH THE LENS OF COMPETITION AND CONSUMER WELFARE

Rarely do we look at trade policy in general and trade remedies in particular through the lens of consumer welfare. Although, as has been noted in previous chapters, consumer welfare underpins the comparative advantage theory that itself underpins trade liberalisation, the language of trade negotiators has become one of mercantilism. Trade policy debates are characterised solely by producer versus producer interests with little interest focused on the consumer side of the debate. Frequently, a country's offensive trade policy interests are viewed through the lens of how aggressively its own producers can break open foreign markets. The impact of trade policy on domestic economies is also not viewed through a consumer or competition lens. Instead, the impact of trade policy on domestic economies is limited to the impact on domestic producers. If domestic producers are adversely affected, then it is assumed that the country is being adversely affected. In reality, this bears out something that Adam Smith wrote about in the Wealth of Nations:

> … the interest of our manufacturers has been most peculiarly attended to; and the interest, no so much of the consumers, as that of some other sets of producers, has been sacrificed to it …[1]

In reality, consumer welfare is certainly not always guaranteed by maximising producer welfare.

So, what does trade policy through a consumer lens really mean? It means a renewed focus on markets and verifying that markets actually function in consumer-welfare-enhancing ways. It means ensuring that results of trade policy lead to competitive markets and consumer welfare optimisation. So, what are examples of trade policy instruments that could have either a positive or negative

DOI: 10.4324/9780429323331-5

impact on competitive markets and consumer welfare? In the course of the rest of the book, we discuss these issues in great detail in the context of the different rules which underpin the GATT, GATS and other rules of the world trading system. Here, I will focus on national laws that have an impact on trade flows and their impact from a competition standpoint.

Anti-Dumping and Countervailing Duty Measures

Many countries now maintain anti-dumping (AD) and countervailing duty (CVD) measures. These are measures that countries use in order to prevent imports from countries which are lower than the price at which they sell in the home country. The CVD laws are used to penalise those who subsidise their products with export subsidies. The original AD and CVD laws of the US represent some of the earliest AD and CVD laws, and so it is worth examining these laws and how they have developed.

The US AD law of 1917 focused on purely price effects. By comparing price and not purely costs, the AD law of the US has paved the way for a purely producer-orientated approach to trade problems. Indeed, the practice of dumping is not unlike price discrimination, which triggered the Robinson-Patman Act. In the case of dumping, foreign producers elect to charge different prices in different countries. There are a number of reasons for engaging in this activity, some based on prevailing market conditions, for example, when pharmaceutical manufacturers price at different levels in different countries. However, this price discrimination is very often exactly what consumers want. The complaints brought by local producers seeking to prevent the access of foreign-produced cheap products are redolent of the complaints brought by mom-and-pop grocery stores complaining about the advance of larger supermarket chains in the 1930s. These complaints led to the introduction of the Robinson-Patman Act which barred price discrimination. There are clues in the treatment of the Robinson-Patman Act and how it has been interpreted over the years by the US courts that shows a change from the initial approach which was very much a producer-orientated approach to the more modern consumer-based approach which holds important lessons for the way in which the AD and CVD laws could become more consumer-welfare-oriented.

Initial Legislative Build-Up to the Robinson-Patman Act

The Robinson-Patman Act is a good example of what happens when consumer interests are subsumed by purely producer (or competitor) welfare interests. The initial response which gave rise to the Robinson-Patman Act was a concern among small grocery store owners about the potential threat from much larger supermarket chains that could out compete them. Because the larger chains had access to more products and could sell them in greater numbers, they were able to engage in marketing techniques that small grocers simply could not engage in. For example, these big chains were able to offer products at different prices to different categories of consumers. However, from a purely consumer-welfare-enhancing standpoint, the big supermarket chains were good for consumers. They led to more competition and gave consumers access to lower prices and more choice.

Although the history of the Robinson-Patman Act begins in 1914, when section 2 of the Clayton Antitrust Act expressly prohibited price discrimination, the actual legislative passage of the Act itself began in 1936, when section 2 of the Clayton Act was amended by the Robinson-Patman Act. The 1936 Congress was concerned about a number of possible harms that large firms could engage in. These included (a) domination of markets through a predatory activity, (b) extraction of price concessions from sellers that smaller firms could not extract. Indeed, the major legislative purpose behind the Robinson-Patman Act was to provide "some measure of protection to small, independent retailers and their independent suppliers from what was thought to be unfair competition from vertically integrated, multi-location chain stores."[2]

This legislative purpose can be seen to be a competitor-welfare-based purpose. The intent was to protect the smaller stores. A consumer-welfare-oriented purpose might have been to prevent the erosion of competition that might result from buyer power, with consequent monopolistic effects. However, notwithstanding how the statute came to be applied, it is important to see that this was not the original purpose of the Robinson-Patman Act itself. The same Supreme Court case stated that the Act was based on a fundamental principle:

> to assure, to the extent reasonably practicable, that businessmen at the same functional level would stand on equal competitive footing so far as price is concerned.

The major bar, enshrined in section 2(a), is therefore that all sellers must sell to everyone at the same price. Section 2(f) requires all buyers with requisite knowledge to buy from a particular seller at the same price as everyone else.

These provisions, viewed in isolation, could have profoundly damaging economic effects. They could prevent a host of pro-competitive and pro-consumer behaviour. They would prevent sellers of products from offering bulk discounts to large-scale buyers, thus leading to a decline in overall economic efficiency. They could prevent airlines, hotels or other service providers from distinguishing and thus tailoring their products to individual passenger or client profiles. Indeed, they would prevent any sort of profiling of this nature which could have profound economic efficiency positives. That these eventual effects were not realised is really because of another fundamental principle that also underpins all of antitrust, the principle that all of the antitrust laws should be interpreted according to the broader policies of the antitrust laws.[3]

In a speech on the Robinson-Patman Act by Donald S. Clarke, then Secretary of the Federal Trade Commission, in 1995, the secretary of the Commission noted that:

> The best way to effectuate this objective is to interpret the Act so as to emphasise the prohibition of discriminatory practices that injure or threaten to injure competition.[4]

By incorporating this principle in how the Act should be interpreted, the FTC paved the way for a consumer-welfare-enhancing interpretation of a statute whose "fundamental purpose" was competitor and not consumer welfare. The Supreme Court, in *Brooke Group Limited v Brown and Williamson Tobacco Corporation*, confirmed that the Robinson-Patman Act only barred price discrimination only if there was a potential threat to competition, stating that "Congress did not intend to outlaw price differences that result from or further the forces of competition."[5]

But it is important to note that the Act contained defences which could be broadened to prevent competitor welfare concerns dictating how the Act would be interpreted. These included the meeting competition and cost justification defences. This could lead to an application which was more consistent with the maximisation of consumer welfare and economic efficiency.

The courts have gradually eroded the scope of the Robinson-Patman Act. The Act does not apply to long-term leases, to mere offers to sell, acting as an intermediary between sellers and customers, to licencing computer software. The Act does not apply to intangible products.

The sale of almost anything now is exempted from the Act, unless the "dominant nature" of the transaction is the sale of goods.[6] The First Circuit Court of Appeals has stated that for the purposes of the Robinson-Patman Act, a company and its wholly owned subsidiary could not be characterised as a single seller for the purposes of the Act.[7]

The seminal *Brook Group* decision introduced two additional elements:

1 The lower price had to be below an appropriate measure of the rival's costs.
2 The person who engages in below-cost pricing has to have a reasonable prospect, or a dangerous probability of recouping its investment in below-cost prices.

In this case, the Supreme Court applied the kind of test that was applied interpreting section 2 of the Sherman Act. In the monopolisation context, the potential monopolist has to have market power (or dangerous possibility of acquiring it) and has then to engage in some anti-competitive activity such as below-cost pricing. This is necessary in order to show some adverse effect on the market. Hence, understanding the lower prices are in the interests of consumers, it is important to note that the risk to the market occurs only when the prices are so low that all competitors will be knocked out, and then there is a reasonable possibility that the monopolist can raise prices to the monopoly level. What is interesting to see is that even starting with the raw material of a statute whose purpose was the protection of competitors, and not consumer welfare, succeeding courts have been able to alter the application of the law so that its fundamental purposes have been realigned to support consumer welfare. This has occurred because courts have read the Act in alignment with the general purposes of the antitrust laws. It is the fundamental principles of antitrust – the competition principle, if you will – that has saved the Robinson-Patman Act from becoming a tool, which could be used by competitors to ensure more rather than less anti-competitive practices. There is a lesson in here for the AD laws. Application of the principle was originally established in the *FTC v. Morton Salt Co.* case, where the emphasis was placed on finding an inference of requisite competitive injury, i.e., damage to the market itself, as opposed to damage to competitors.

So the competition principle has led to a more rigorous test in order to establish price discrimination but it has also led to an expansion of the defences available under the Robinson-Patman Act. These defences include meeting competition. A seller can establish this defence in cases where he can:

> show the existence of facts which would lead a reasonable and prudent person to believe that the granting of a lower price would, in fact, meet the equally low price of a competitor.[8]

The Supreme Court has said that the territorial price differences that are responses to competitive conditions satisfy the defence.[9] Given that sellers can now charge lower prices to attract new customers as well as to retain new ones, and that it can respond on a territorial basis means that this defence has in reality become a very broad one indeed. A seller can also defend against allegations that it has violated section 2(a) by arguing that the lower price at issue was functionally available to the allegedly disfavoured purchaser.[10] In the *Texaco v. Hasbrouck*[11] decision, the Supreme Court noted that if a price differential "merely accords due recognition and reimbursement for actual marketing functions," then it was not illegal. In the case, Texaco was found to have engaged in price discrimination largely because there was no evidence that the functional discount to any savings enjoyed by Texaco. Because of this the discounts to selected distributors were found to have adversely affected competition. However, the Supreme Court made clear that a rigorous mathematical proof of the link between the discount and the costs saved was not necessary, again helping those who seek to establish the defence. It should be noted that in demonstrating below-cost pricing, a complex analysis is generally required. This shifting of the burden of proof also limits the ability of the Act to be used in a way that enhances competitor welfare at the expense of consumer welfare.

In its most recent Robinson-Patman Act decision, *Volvo v. Reeder*, the Supreme Court underscored the contemporary judicial view that the Act should be construed in a way that promotes the consumer welfare goal of the antitrust laws and that focuses on competition, not the protection of individual competitors. It stated:

> Interbrand competition, our opinions affirm, is the primary concern of antitrust law. The Robinson-Patman Act signals no large departure from that main concern. Even if the Act's text could be construed [in a different manner,]...we would resist interpretation geared more to the protection of existing *competitors* than to the stimulation of *competition*. In the case before us, there is no evidence that any favored purchaser possesses market power, the allegedly favored purchasers are dealers with little resemblance to large independent department stores or chain operations, and the supplier's selective price discounting fosters competition among suppliers of different brands. By declining to extend Robinson-Patman's governance to such cases, we continue to construe the Act consistently with broader policies of the antitrust laws.[12]

FTC Enforcement Actions and Considerations

The Robinson-Patman Act has had a rich, if somewhat chequered history. Late 20th-century FTC actions have been useful in establishing how the Federal Trade Commission is now dealing with its powers to enforce the Act. This is also instructive in seeing how the overarching competition principle has been used to guide how the Commission proceeds on this issue. The first proceeding is the 1988 administrative complaints against book publishers for charging lower prices to large book retail chains than prices charged to smaller independent booksellers. On larger orders, the chains paid lower prices per book. In this case, the publishers maintained that their behaviour was cost justified as the book publisher representatives had only to visit headquarters of the chain, rather than multiple stores. The matters were withdrawn from adjudication, since the FTC could not find any evidence of consumer harm or that the competitive process itself had been impaired in any way.

In 1998, independent booksellers again tried to sue the larger competitors, this time Barnes and Noble and Borders (interestingly, neither of these companies existed at the time of the 1988 lawsuit, although many of the independents did. In the case, US District Judge William Orrick noted that the discounts which large bookstores enjoyed could not be shown to have harmed consumers. It is interesting to note that the motivating purpose of the lawsuit came exactly out of the competitor or producer welfare school of thought. Indeed, Avin Mark Domnitz, representing the American Booksellers Association, said:

> Borders and Barnes and Noble are using their clout and influence with publishers to get discounts and preferential treatment. This poses a threat [to Independent Bookshares] survival and the diversity of American bookselling. They are being asked to compete with one hand tied behind their backs.[13]

As we will see in the chapter on the New Media Economy, these producer welfare considerations were also suggested under the guise of cultural considerations. Although the case was ultimately settled, the concern that it brought was the notion peddled by the independent booksellers that the large chains were harming competition simply because they were able to attract customers from the smaller chains.

On 31 March 2005, the independent Antitrust Modernisation Commission was set up by Congress to investigate whether the US antitrust laws needed to be modernised. In its 2007 Report to Congress, the Commission recommended on policy grounds that the Robinson-Patman Act be repealed:

> The Commission recommends that Congress finally repeal the Robinson-Patman Act (RPA). This law, enacted in 1936, appears antithetical to core antitrust principles. Its repeal or substantial overhaul has been recommended in three prior reports, in 1955, 1969, and 1977. That is because the RPA protects competitors over competition and punishes the very price discounting and innovation in distribution methods that the antitrust laws otherwise encourage. At the same time, it is not clear that the RPA actually effectively protects the small business constituents that it was meant to benefit. Continued existence of the RPA also makes it difficult for the United States to advocate against the adoption and use of similar laws against US companies operating in other jurisdictions. Small business is adequately protected from truly anticompetitive behaviour by application of the Sherman Act.[14]

Although Congress failed to act and the Robinson-Patman Act remains on the statute books, it effectively has been eviscerated in the courts and repudiated by antitrust scholars. This then represents perhaps the low water mark for competitor welfare under the antitrust laws. Once again, the only reason that this Robinson-Patman Act journey could have reached this stage was because the driving force behind antitrust law enforcement was the notion that only behaviour that had an adverse impact on the market, or on competition as measured by consumer welfare, was problematic. Behaviour that merely harmed competitors without harming the actual process of competition was not problematic and indeed could be pro-competitive. We see therefore that notwithstanding what the legislature said at the beginning of the life of the Robinson-Patman Act, normative competition principles thwarted what was an essentially anti-competitive legislative goal.

By contrast, the AD laws, without this defining or organising competition principle, have become tools to stop foreign competition and protect domestic industry. This has occurred because price comparisons and not cost considerations have prevailed. When a foreign company engages in "dumping," the AD laws discipline that activity when the dumping is below the competitors' cost of production, but also when the foreign company's price is merely below the price it charges in its home market. In addition, safeguard legislation applies in cases of temporary import surge – something that can happen for reasons wholly unrelated to below-cost pricing. Instead, if a normative competition principle applied in the anti- dumping world, then we would be able to move more in this direction – just as the US courts moved in the interpretation of the Robinson-Patman Act.

However, there is a way that the Anti-Dumping and Countervailing Duty Laws can be applied in a pro-competitive way, along the model of how the Robinson-Patman Act has been interpreted and challenged.

Shifting Anti-Dumping Law to a More Competition-Based Framework

In any analysis of revisions to AD law, it is important to note that the political reality that gave rise to the AD laws still exists. Indeed, it is perhaps even stronger today than it was when the US AD laws were introduced in 1916. The arguments advanced by (usually) developed countries' trade ministries as to why vigorous enforcement of AD laws are required are as follows:

1. Dumping distorts the principle of comparative advantage on which free trade rests.
2. Dumping is only made possible by market isolation of the exporting country.
3. AD action ensures the maintenance of "fair" competition.
4. Producer welfare includes consumer welfare because consumers also work in the producer industries.
5. AD laws help free trade regimes. Without the protection of AD, people would protest against the entire free trade process.[15]

The first argument is pretty fundamental. We have asserted in these pages that for the law of comparative advantage to work effectively in a world of relatively low border barriers, there must be functioning and competitive markets inside borders. The problem with the first argument is that it does not differentiate between a lower export price that arises from efficiency and the one that arises through a predatory motive (or worse some artificial cost lowering such as a state aid). If the dumping arises through a predatory motive and there is a predatory effect, then it is the importing countries' consumers that will bear that cost. If it arises because of a state aid, then consumers in both the exporting and importing countries will bear the cost. If the price arises merely through efficiency, then there will be no cost to be borne by consumers in either country (the loss being instead visited on inefficient producers in the importing market).

The second argument has more validity if it can be proved. However, the better way of dealing with this problem is to actually isolate it and discipline the anti-competitive practice where it occurs. Otherwise, the AD law could have equal application to a case of anti-competitive practices inside the exporting country giving rise to cheaper export prices, as to a case where the exporting producer is merely more efficient, and makes pricing decisions in different markets for its own internal economic reasons. In the former case, there is an actual competition problem. In the latter, it may be possible to envisage a safeguard-type action, where the safeguard is linked to the demonstration of anti-competitive practices inside the border of the exporting country. We deal with this subject at greater length at the end of the chapter.

There are real problems with the argument suggesting that AD actions ensure the maintenance of fair competition. The word "fair" is a loaded term. If "fairness" refers only to where the "dumping" is below cost such that there may be super-competitive pricing in the future, then the notion of unfairness is made out. If the low price is brought about because there are state aids or other artificial methods that reduce cost for the exporting firm, then unfairness may be made out. However, in both of these cases, there are better ways than the AD laws to discipline this kind of behaviour.

The notion that consumers work in producer industries is also a poor justification for the way AD laws are implemented now. It is important to properly evaluate the costs and benefits of legislative and regulatory actions. If consumer welfare is being evaluated, it should be properly evaluated and producer welfare is a poor proxy for it. This does not mean that producer welfare or total social welfare should be ignored, merely that in evaluating the impact of anti-dumping, consumer welfare should be separately evaluated. If legislators acting on behalf of the people they represent believe that producer welfare trumps consumer welfare, then there should be some process whereby the two are separately evaluated without simply relying on inaccurate proxies.

As conventional trade barriers come down and foreign imports increase, it is natural for domestic producers and their workers to complain about how this rise in imports affects their economic well-being, or their protected position in a domestic economy. The AD laws were intended to secure some protection for these producers and their workers from "unfair" foreign imports. In this regard, the situation is not unlike the Robinson-Patman Act which attempted to protect small retailers from their larger competitors. As in both cases, the superficial arguments look justified. To the extent that unfair trade practices distort markets and increase inefficiencies, such behaviour should be punished. To the extent that discriminatory prices damage the process of competition, it too should be restrained. Unfortunately, the precise mechanism that underpins how the AD laws and investigations work comes from a trade protection motivation rather than a motivation to make markets function properly.

Prusa and Blonigen, in The Cost of Anti-Dumping: The Devil is in the Details,[16] note the disconnect between competition policy and AD protection. They note with irony that:

> There has been more than a century of legal analysis of what constitutes anti-competitive behaviour through the application of antitrust laws. Yet

> the definition of "unfair" trade practices and application of antidumping remedies has been allowed to develop a life of its own and bears no resemblance to established standards of anti-competitive behaviour.

Since it is low prices that the AD laws are designed to rectify, a competition approach would be to identify as harmful only those low prices which carry with them an anti-competitive risk. Such low prices would be prices that are below some measure of cost. Areeda and Turner have noted that for these purposes, average variable cost serves as a proxy for marginal cost.[17] Hence applying a competition standard, the AD laws would only discipline pricing that is below average variable cost of a rival, so that it is clear that the price charged is a tactic to remove competition and then charge at super-competitive prices. However, this is not how AD laws actually work.

The current focus of most countries' AD legislation is to look at whether an "unfair price" is being charged and whether this "unfair price" is causing material injury to the country's domestic firms that compete in the market. While the anti-dumping laws were the exclusive preserve of the US, Canada, Australia and the European Union (EU) until relatively recently, now the number of countries that rely on the AD laws to block foreign imports is skyrocketing. Between the 1980s and 1990s only, the number of countries relying on AD laws had tripled.[18] Most countries define dumping as occurring when firms sell products at less than a fair value. Fair is determined by reference to the price the exporting firm charges in its own market for the same product and the constructed cost of the product itself. The cost-based element comes from WTO negotiations that sought to limit the fact that the anti-dumping laws were being used as tools of trade protection. We are still a long way, however, from a competition-based system. The key is to look at how the antitrust authorities analyse predatory pricing cases and compare this with how AD authorities analyse constructed cost in an AD proceeding.

Antitrust Analysis of Predatory Pricing

Economically, a concern only arises when a firm is pricing below its marginal cost. There can be but one reason for charging below marginal cost and this is to knock out competitors so that the firm is left as the only source of supply. In this case, the firm will be able to raise prices to monopoly (or at least super-competitive) levels. However, when countries' AD officials measure constructed costs, they generally use a cost figure which is far above the marginal cost standard. Indeed, they include fixed costs and their own estimate of a profit element. This approach is really a cost-based approach in name only. When coupled to the requirement to find material injury to a domestic producer, we are really looking at a law that has the most anti-competitive elements of the Robinson-Patman Act – a mere price discrimination law. In the case of the anti-dumping laws, we have found that the language of "unfairness" is very different, indeed almost the opposite of the language of "anti-competitive" and has little to do with consumer welfare and everything to do with producer welfare and protecting competitors in a narrow sense. There is also evidence that anti-competitive practices are actually facilitated by use of the AD laws, including parties using the AD laws to discipline those who would cheat on a price cartel.

Constructed Cost in Anti-Dumping Analysis

Naturally, there has been much attention focused on how price is calculated in anti-dumping cases. Early US practice on this point was changed as a result of the WTO's rules on AD which are set forth in the WTO Anti-Dumping Agreement.[19] The WTO AD code provides that an AD duty can only be found if there are dumped imports, material injury to domestic industry and a causal link between the two. Article 2 provides that dumping must be calculated on the basis of a fair comparison between normal value (price of the imported product in the ordinary course of trade in the country of origin or export) and the export price. Both these prices have to be calculated in a WTO-consistent manner and the fair comparison must be WTO-consistent also.

The basic WTO-consistent rule requires a comparison of the export price and the comparable home country price. If there are no domestic sales of the like product, in the ordinary course of trade, the export price is compared with the price charged in an appropriate third country, or the cost of production in the country of origin, plus a reasonable amount of administrative, selling and general costs and profits. These elements are to be calculated by reference to the actual amounts incurred and realised for this general category of products, the weighted average for *other* exporters/producers in the country of origin.

The comparison itself must also be fair, taking into account different levels of taxation, exchange rates, terms of trade and other factors affecting price comparability.

The WTO Agreement now sets floor or base requirements that countries must use in their AD laws. It is thus sometimes referred to as the WTO Anti-Dumping implementation agreement. Where laws or practices deviate from the norms set out above, there may be WTO violations occurring. The question is do these norms move AD law and practice in more consumer-welfare-enhancing directions. The answer is that by including a cost element, they certainly move in the right direction, but as we shall see in our discussion of the way in which costs are calculated in the newly privatised industries of energy and telecoms, a cost-plus type of model does not lead to downward pressure on price. While the WTO AD agreement removes the worst (most producer-welfare-enhancing) practices, it also enshrines into practice a cost-plus methodology which is prone to abuse (as is the case for any arbitrary calculation of a profit element).

Impact of Anti-Dumping Laws on Trade

The mere presence of these laws changes the economic behaviour of firms. Instead of focusing on profit maximisation goals, firms engage in lobbying for protection activities or steps that are more likely to lead to favourable AD investigations (this usually consists of signalling that foreign competition is having a materially adverse impact, even if that is not actually the case). In addition, firms invest in economically wasteful activities such as lobbying to convince trade ministries to activate AD proceedings against them.

It is possible to retain trade remedy laws but apply them in a more competition policy-orientated fashion, and indeed some countries are moving in this direction. However as in any application of the principles of competition policy, one has to countervail powerful producer lobbies with arguments that favour the consumer standpoint.

Some countries have considered this quite seriously. Chile and Canada agreed to suspend the use of AD laws in their free trade agreement. New Zealand also considered this in its discussion paper: Trade Remedies in New Zealand; Chapter 3. New Zealand governmental authorities have considered a more competition policy-oriented AD law.[20] In the EU, a case involving magnesium oxide from China[21] states that:

> In assessing the Community Interest...prevent distortions of competition arising from unfair commercial practices and thus to re- establish open and fair competition on the Community market...In addition, in general, while there might be a short-term price advantage to end users if no duty is imposed, to refrain from establishing fair competition on the Community market would, in the longer term, lead to less competition and higher prices.

This highlights the approach in the EU that asks what legitimate purpose is served by implementing the AD laws (to ensure that anti-competitive practices do not lead to predatory pricing in export markets). One is reminded of Richard Cobden's injunction to find a market price for bread, not just a lower price. That must be the ultimate purpose of all economic laws, not just the AD laws. It is this purpose to which the word "fairness" must apply in the context of a normative competition approach to the anti- dumping laws. So what would this normative approach entail?

Normative Approach to Anti-Dumping

Useful examples of what this might be can be seen in the relationship between Australia and New Zealand or within the borders of the EU. In the case of the Australia–New Zealand trade relationship, full free trade in goods and the harmonisation of competition laws represent the way of dealing with the issue. The EU's internal market does not apply AD of any sort to internal EU trade. Canada and Chile do not apply AD laws to each other. In the case of the EU or Aus/NZ, these are extreme examples when integration is far more advanced than it is in the case of other countries. It will be many decades and many more rounds of trade negotiations before most countries achieve this kind of level of integration. In the meantime, how can AD laws be better informed by competition concepts?

There are two key areas. The first is using competition terms and competition principles to dumping, and the second is to actually imbue dumping investigations with a competition-like analysis.

Competition as an Organising Principle for Anti-Dumping: Some Suggestions

As a normative principle, AD actions should only be maintained if a demonstrable adverse impact on the process of competition or a distortion of the market can be demonstrated. Hence, the test of whether a "dumping" claim can be made is if the pricing leads to a lessening of competition. Hence, the test of whether such a thing is likely will turn on whether the exporting firm's low price is below some measure of cost. This cost measure would include analysis of any governmental or other measures that lead to an artificial reduction in the cost base of the exporting firm, such as governmental aids, subsidies or other distorting practices. The resultant cost standard will be an average variable cost plus standard. The plus reflects the evaluation of government benefits of one kind or another given to the exporting firm. These benefits can take a number of non-traditional forms. In addition to the obvious state aids and subsidies, they could include preferential treatment in terms of licencing and other privileges necessary to conduct business, toleration of cartel activity, even government toleration of intellectual property violations to give the exporting firm an unfair cost edge.

Most AD laws have a material injury to local producers' element. Under normative competition principles, this material injury would be a competition injury. In other words, if pricing can be established as predatory (albeit with a modified costs standard), then the material injury is already made out. Competing producers are caught up in the general harm to consumers in the importing country. This parallels the test that would be applied in the case of demonstrating standing in an antitrust case. In antitrust cases, it is necessary to demonstrate that the plaintiff is the type of person the antitrust laws were intended to protect, i.e., the kind of person who is caught up in the consumer harm caused by the allegedly anti-competitive practice.[22]

We note that there is a difference between the analysis and the kind of analysis that would be applied if one was looking at the issue purely as a predatory pricing/monopolisation case. In the latter case, one would have to show that the person guilty of the below-cost pricing had market power. Otherwise, he would not be able to maintain the below-cost pricing for more than an intermittent or short period. However, this element is not required in proving a Robinson-Patman claim as it is currently interpreted. It is from this interpretation of the Robinson-Patman Act that lessons for pro-competitive AD laws can be learned. The other difference is that under this analysis, it is appropriate to ask why the dumping is occurring and factor in non-efficiency-orientated reasons. For example, if the dumping occurs because of governmental aids, then the impact of these can be weighed into the costs considerations because the impact of the state aid can be seen to artificially lower the cost base of the exporting firm – something that the rival cannot replicate. The material injury test could be broadened so that any competition harm visited on consumers and downstream producers could be factored in also (based on a relevant product market analysis).

Dumping Pricing

The current method for looking at dumping pricing is to compare the dumped price with home country arm's length transactions or prices charged to other countries. In the alternative, constructed prices based on costs are used, but these factor in fixed costs and an element for profit as noted above. The difference between this and an antitrust test is that antitrust targets below average variable cost pricing. Clearly, the addition of other elements must be carefully handled as this is where producer/competitor welfare thinking might lead to increases that artificially increase cost and make the test more like a constructed price test.

There also needs to be a mechanism to deal with non-price predation, such as misuse of governmental processes or legal processes to secure an increase in rival costs or a decrease in one's own costs. There could be a claim for a safeguard based on non-price predatory behaviour in the home country market that leads to changes in overall costs that distort the export market.

Cartel Behaviour

While there is anecdotal evidence to suggest that AD actions are sought to discipline those who break cartels, it is also possible that cartels may allow members to dump in certain markets in order to keep prices higher in certain other markets.[23] In a Federal Trade Commission working paper, Christopher Taylor challenges the notion that withdrawn AD investigations are often the result of collusion in the affected industry (3 August 2001). In the paper, Taylor notes the earlier work of Calvani (1986) and Prusa (1992) in this area.[24] However, Taylor does accept the evidence that cartels have used AD laws to perpetuate cartel activity. He noted the 1984 Ferro-Silicon cartel which set a collusive price and then withdrew capacity from the US market. The US firms then used this reduction as a ground for AD cases against foreign rivals. Once the AD duty had rendered these companies non-competitive, the US firms could manage the cartel and raise prices. Commentators have further suggested that a withdrawn anti-dumping petition is a signal that the foreign and domestic industries have reached a price agreement. If there are agreements that lessen competition behind a dumped price, then in addition to relying on the usual antitrust mechanisms to defeat the international cartel, there could be a temporary safeguard linked to this kind of anti- competitive behaviour. This would therefore link the level of competition in the home market with export effects in the export market.

Magnitude of Anti-Dumping Duty

The magnitude of the AD duty and how it is arrived at is itself an important issue as very high AD duties can act to change business behaviour, even without being actually applied. A competition approach would lead to fines and potentially injunctive relief as opposed to imposition of duties because the competition remedy would be designed to change the behaviour that had given rise to the problem not to assist affected competitors.

Duration of Anti-Dumping Orders

Another concern is the permanence of AD orders. Some have lasted for over 25 years, before the WTO Anti-Dumping Agreement imposed a five-year sunset provision. Still five years is a very long time and could lock in an inefficient activity, by giving certain companies protection from competitive forces.

In addition, below average total cost pricing is a legitimate business tool that is relied on by many different businesses and is engaged in by domestic companies with no legal constraint. Since the AD laws effectively prevent this, then domestic companies are at a considerable advantage with respect to their foreign rivals – something which further impacts the likelihood that free trade will deliver consumer benefits to local consumers. There is evidence that when the AD laws were first introduced, dumping was defined in a way that "approximated predatory pricing."[25] Since that time, the interpretation of AD laws has, according to the CBO testimony:

> evolved along a path of ever-increasing protection for US firms from imports and decreasing concern for consumers and the economy as a whole.

Between 1980 and 1992, the Department of Commerce found dumping in 93% of the 339 cases that came before it for final determination. The ITC, in this same period, found injury in only 66% of cases before it. What this means is that for at least one third of cases where dumping duties were imposed, there was no economic harm to competing firms.

The CBO testimony focuses on how the US economy benefits from pricing that is above average variable cost but below average total cost – precisely the margin where AD duties would be applied, but where antitrust law would find no harm. The CBO testimony notes that:

clearly, the US economy benefits when it purchases a product for less than the cost to produce it. The alternatives are to produce the product domestically – and thereby incur the entire cost of production – or else to purchase it elsewhere for a price equal to or greater than the cost of production. Either way, the cost to the economy is greater than the cost of purchasing the dumped product.

Similarly, the US economy also benefits when it obtains a product at a lower price than other countries can obtain it. When such products are purchased by firms that produce other goods, the lower price gives the US firms a competitive advantage over foreign firms. For example, if the AD laws result in a substantial increase in the price of semi-conductor chips or flat panel displays in the US, computer manufacturers have an incentive to take their production operations overseas in order to get their chips and displays at lower prices. Similarly, actions that increase the price of steel increase the problems that US automobile manufacturers have competing with manufacturers in Japan.

In the case of products purchased by final consumers, US consumers obviously benefit by being able to purchase products at lower prices than consumers in other countries must pay.

Domestic companies that export are also hurt by AD laws. They are hurt by retaliatory AD laws. They are most significantly hurt by the inability of foreign countries to buy the exports of the producing country because their exports are blocked by AD laws. This is actually the playing out of any number of economic arguments which illustrate the danger of protection. It would be useful to look at the number of cases where domestic firms competing with foreign importers rely on predatory pricing claims as opposed to AD actions. The number is very low/zero simply because it is so much easier to bring an AD action.

The reality is that where antitrust has evolved (see the changing application of the Robinson-Patman Act), the AD law has grown worse from a consumer welfare perspective. The fact that the AD laws did not start from a producer/competitor welfare orientation mirrors how the US antitrust laws have developed – a path that we chart in Chapter 3. This suggests that unless consumer welfare interests are the main objective of economic regulations, political reality will bend those regulations to competitor or producer-welfare-enhancing ends.

The reality is that where antitrust has evolved (see the changing application of the Robinson-Patman Act), the AD law has grown worse from a consumer welfare perspective. The fact that the AD laws did not start from a producer/competitor welfare orientation is in marked contrast to how the US antitrust laws have developed – a path that we charted in Chapter 3. This suggests that unless consumer welfare interests are the main objective of economic regulations, political reality will bend those regulations to competitor- or producer-welfare-enhancing ends.

We will, in the course of the next few chapters, look precisely at how trade rules can be applied in a manner that enhances consumer welfare, based on competition principles. This will help us understand how competition should be at the root of the rules that underpin the trade system.

Notes

1 *See* Adam Smith, *An Inquiry into the Nature and Causes of the Wealth of Nations* (Roy H. Campbell, Andrew S. Skinner, and William B. Todd eds., Liberty Fund 1981) (1776), IV. viii.
2 *See* Boise Cascade Corp. v. F.T.C, 107 FTC 76 (1986), rev'd & remanded 837 F. 2d 1127 (D.C. Cir. 1988).
3 Brooke Group Limited v. Brown and Williamson, 509 US 209 (1993).

4 Donald S. Clark, Secretary to the Commission, Federal Trade Commission, *The Robinson-Patman Act: General Principles, Commission Proceedings and Selected Issues,* Speech before the "Ambit Group Retail Channel Conference for the Computer Industry," San Jose, California (7 June 1995).
5 *Supra* note 217.
6 *Metro* 984 F.2d 739 Metro Communications v. Ameritech Mobile Com., 984 F.2d 739 (6th Cir. 1993), (where plaintiffs simply acted as intermediaries between Ameritech (services seller) and its customers); Microsoft v BEC Computer Co., Inc., 818 F. Supp. 1313 (C.D.Cal. 1992).
7 Caribe BMW v. Bayerische Motoren Werke Aktiengesellschaft, 19 F. 3d 745 (1st Cir. 1994).
8 US. v. US Gypsum, 438 US 422 (1978).
9 Falls City v. Vanco Beverage, Inc., 460 US 448 (1983).
10 *See* FTC v Morton Salt., 334 US 37 (1948); Shreve Equipment, Inc. v. Clay Equipment Corp., 650 F. 2d 101 (6th Cir,) cert. denied, 454 U.S 897 (1981).
11 Texaco, Inc. v. Hasbrouck, 490 US 1105 (1990).
12 Volvo Trucks North Am., Inc. v. Reeder-Simco GMC, Inc., 546 US 164, 181 (2006).
13 Janelle Brown, "Barns & Noble and Borders Sued by Booksellers," Wired Magazine (13 Mar 1998), https://www.wired.com/1998/03/barnes-noble-and-borders-sued-by-booksellers/.
14 Civil and Criminal Remedies, in, Report and Recommendations, Antitrust Modernization Commission (April 2007), http://govinfo.library.unt.edu/amc/report_recommendation/toc.htm.
15 *See* "Trade Remedies," Ministry of Business, Innovation & Employment (n.d.), https://www.mbie.govt.nz/business-and-employment/business/trade-and-tariffs/trade-remedies/.
16 Bruce A. Blonigen and Thomas J. Prusa, *The Cost of Antidumping: The Devil is in the Details*, 6 Pol'y Reform, no. 4 233 (2003).
17 Phillip Areeda and Donald F. Turner, *Predatory Pricing and Related Practices Under Section 2 of the Sherman Act*, 88 Harv. L. Rev. 697 (1975).
18 Thomas J. Prusa, *On the Spread and Impact of Antidumping*, 34 Canadian J. of Econ. 591 (2001).
19 Agreement on Implementation of Article VI of the General Agreement on Trade and Tariffs, 1994.
20 New Zealand Ministery of Commerce, Trade Remedies in New Zealand: A Discussion Paper (1998)
21 Council Regulation 1473/93, 1993 O.J. (L 145) 4 (EC).
22 *See*, for example, *Altantic Richfield Co. v. USA Petroleum Co.*, 495 US 328 (1990).
23 *See* Bruce A. Blonigen and Thomas J. Prusa, *The Cost of Antidumping: The Devil is in the Details,* 6 Pol'y Reform, no. 4 233 (2003), at f.n. 14.
24 *See* Terry Calvani and Randolph W. Tritell, *Invocation of United States Import Relief Laws as an Antitrust Violation*, 31 Antitrust Bull. 527 (1986); Thomas J. Prusa, *Why Are So Many Anti-Dumping Petitions Withdrawn?*, 33 J.of Econ. 1029 (1992).
25 CBO Testimony, Statement of Jan Paul Acton on Proposed Anti-Dumping Regulations and Other Anti-Dumping Issues before the Subcommittee on Trade Committee on Ways and Means, US House of Representatives, 23 April 1996.

6

THE GENERAL AGREEMENT ON TARIFFS AND TRADE

A Temporary Fix but a Constitutional Foundation

As was discussed above, the GATT agreement represented the compromise solution to the critical failure of the ITO at the hands of the US Congress. GATT consisted of what was intended to be a temporary agreement, pending the successful ratification of the ITO. Few at the time thought that the ITO's successor's ratification would take another five decades. The GATT is therefore a contract between a group of countries. It is founded on two fundamental principles, the principle of Most Favoured Nation and the principle of National Treatment. We briefly introduced the two central themes of the GATT in the first chapter. We will now discuss these themes in greater detail, as well as the rule excepting regional trade agreements from general MFN requirements. These two themes are extremely important in WTO law as they represent the constitutional architecture of the global trading system.

We discussed the MFN and National Treatment principles in Chapter 2. These are the fundamental building blocks of the WTO. As noted previously, there are exceptions to the MFN principle. A strict application of the MFN principle would mean that no WTO member could embark on separate negotiations to form either more regionally limited free trade areas ("RTAs"), or customs unions (CUs). Article I itself accommodates the trade preferences that existed prior to 10 April 1947. However, RTAs are subject to GATT provisions, specifically Article XXIV. In the last 30 years, there has been an explosion of Free Trade Agreements, coinciding with a slowdown in the pace of global trade negotiations. There are now over 500 free trade areas (FTAs), all of which are technically subject to Article XXIV. So what does GATT Article XXIV actually allow.

Article XXIV GATT

The European Union (EU), North American Free Trade Agreement (NAFTA) and the US-Israel agreement were all negotiated after the GATT was launched.

DOI: 10.4324/9780429323331-6

These agreements are tolerated by the WTO as an exception to the MFN principle under GATT Article XXIV. In the last 30 years, there has been an explosion of Free Trade Agreements.

As an exception to the MFN principle, Article XXIV permits the formation of FTAs and CUs, whereby two or more WTO members eliminate trade barriers among themselves in a preferential way, with respect to other WTO members. Under an FTA, such as the NAFTA or US-Canada-Mexico ("USCMA" as it is now known), each member retains its own external tariffs, while under a CU, such as the EU, the members adopt a common external tariff on each product. These arrangements naturally introduce WTO-allowed discrimination between FTA or CU members and outside countries.

The key elements of Article XXIV are that the FTA must cover (a) substantially all trade and must be (b) trade-creating and not trade-diverting. There is no agreed definition or interpretation on the trade coverage that would constitute "substantially all trade," either quantitatively or qualitatively. The WTO Appellate Body has affirmed in the case *Turkey – Restrictions on Imports of Textile and Clothing Product* that "'substantially all the trade' is not the same as *all* the trade, and also that 'substantially all the trade' is something considerably more than merely *some* of the trade."[1] The unofficial rate for coverage of trade in goods that would meet the "substantially all trade" criteria in the case of FTAs is between 80% and 95%[2] of the trade between the members of an FTA. Although this ratio provides a conceptual anchor to the meaning of the "substantially all trade" criteria, the manner in which it should be applied remains a point of diverging views among the Members of the Committee on Regional Trade Agreements (CRTA), as it did among the contracting parties of the GATT.

However, few WTO members would bring an Article XXIV case against another WTO member, given the fact that most major trading nations are also members of FTAs at this time.

There has been a proliferation of FTAs in the period since the last major concluded multilateral round (1994). In the first 46 years of the GATT, between 1948 and 1994, 124 such agreements were signed (many of which have since expired), an average of 2.7 per year. Between 1995 and 2004 alone, the WTO has been notified of more than 130 such agreements, an average of more than 15 per year.[3] By 2002, 43% of international trade occurred under Free Trade Agreements, and that share would reach 55% by 2002.[4] At present, there are almost 500 FTAs in the world. Notwithstanding GATT Article I, FTAs are a legal fact of life in international trade.

The rules that underpin whether an FTA is GATT-legal or not are important, as WTO members may wish to challenge certain types of agreements that confer strategic advantage to certain other WTO members without requiring them to make key concessions in other areas. An example of this would be the EU FTAs with developing countries that expressly exclude disciplines on agriculture (such as the EU-Mexico FTA). It is certainly arguable that these RTAs lead not to free, but rather to manage trade.

The "Enabling Clause"

The second exception to Article I GATT-MFN is the one introduced by the 28 November 1979 GATT Decision on "Differential and More Favourable Treatment, Reciprocity and Fuller Participation of Developing Countries," better known as the Enabling Clause. Paragraph 2(a) of the Enabling Clause calls for the establishment of "nonreciprocal and non-discriminatory preferences" under GSP schemes, while paragraphs 3(a) and 3(c) require that preferences be designed to "facilitate and promote the trade of developing countries" and "respond positively to the development, financial and trade needs of developing countries."

The Enabling Clause also allows two or more developing countries to exchange partial trade preferences with one another. In these cases, internal tariffs need not be eliminated entirely, nor is it required that substantially all products be covered. The Enabling Clause also permits one-way preferences by developed to developing countries. These preferences, as exemplified by GSP, may be partial and can be granted on selected products. The EU and the US grant developing countries specific preferences based on actions related to, inter *alia*, combating illegal drugs, protecting the environment or upholding certain labour standards. We have started to see new RTAs between developing countries which would be subject to less rigid scrutiny than Article XXIV because of the Enabling Clause. These include Brazil's negotiations with India, China and South Africa.

In a landmark ruling on the EU's GSP scheme on 7 April 2004,[5] the WTO Appellate Body pronounced that developed countries are not prohibited by WTO rules from granting different tariffs to products originating in different developing countries under the GSP, provided that such differential treatment meets certain conditions under the Enabling Clause. Before the panel, India challenged the WTO consistency of tariff preferences accorded under the drug arrangements with the MFN. India claimed that the drug arrangements were "discriminatory," as the benefits the EU granted were available only to certain specified developing countries. India argued that countries excluded from the scheme experienced adverse impacts on certain exports to the EU.

In particular, India pointed out that Pakistan's entry into the scheme has affected USD 250 million of Indian textile exports, which faced higher tariffs than their Pakistani equivalents on the EU market. This was very much a foreign policy decision that had wide-ranging trade impacts.

The Appellate Body decision is the outcome of an appeal lodged by the EU against an earlier decision of a WTO Panel in this case. That Panel[6] had interpreted the word "non-discriminatory" in the case of the Enabling Clause to mean that identical tariff preferences under GSP schemes be provided to all developing countries without differentiation. The Appellate Body, however, disagreed with this interpretation and concluded that the word "non-discriminatory" does not prohibit developed countries from granting different tariffs to products originating from different GSP beneficiaries, provided that such differential tariff treatment meets the conditions of the Enabling Clause.

Nevertheless, the Appellate Body cautioned that in granting such differential tariff treatment, preference-granting countries are required by virtue of the term "non-discriminatory" to ensure that identical treatment is available to all "similarly-situated" GSP beneficiaries that have the "development, financial and trade needs" that the treatment in question is intended to respond to.[7] In particular, the Appellate Body highlighted the point that the EU Council Regulation on GSP,[8] under which the drug arrangements are administered, provides no mechanism or objective criteria that would allow for other developing countries that are similarly affected by the drug problem to be added to the list of existing beneficiaries. Hence, the GSP preferences were not justified under the Enabling Clause. Moreover, the regulation in question offers no criteria according to which a beneficiary would be removed from the drug arrangements on the basis that it is no longer "similarly affected by the drug problem."

Also noteworthy was that the Appellate Body stated in dicta that the EC's "special incentive arrangements for the protection of labour rights" and the "special incentive arrangements for the protection of the environment" (not at issue in this case) included detailed provisions regarding procedure and substantive criteria for beneficiary status. This was in contrast to the drug arrangements, which lacked such criteria. We believe that this suggests that such detailed criteria are WTO-compatible.

Waivers to Article I GATT

Finally, in the past, the GATT contracting parties have granted waivers from the application of Article I. The United States-Canada Automotive Products Agreement of 1965, which established an FTA between the two countries in the automotive sector, operated under such a waiver. During 1971–1981, GSP also operated under a similar waiver.

National Treatment and the Application of Article III to Distortionary Taxes and Regulations

The second pillar of the WTO system is the principle of National Treatment. National Treatment means that WTO members may not discriminate against other WTO members in certain domestic laws (that chiefly affect the sale, distribution and taxation of produce), thus putting local producers on a better footing than foreign producers. The National Treatment concept is enshrined in the GATT in Article III. Article III provides that:

> 1 The contracting parties recognise that internal taxes and other internal charges, and laws, regulations and requirements affecting the internal sale, offering for sale, purchase, transportation, distribution or use of products, and internal quantitative regulations requiring the mixture, processing or use of products in specified amounts or proportions, should not be applied

to imported or domestic products so as to afford protection to domestic production.

It is important to note that the National Treatment principle immediately reaches behind the border issues by applying to domestic regulations that affect domestic taxation and domestic distribution rules. Thus, we can see that even the GATT (even in its provisional nature) saw fit to deal directly with domestic rulemaking, and thus fettered national sovereignty, where that sovereignty was essentially being used to reduce the overall level of competition simply by applying different rules to foreign competition. Article III has two key provisions which we will discuss in detail: Article III.2, which prohibits discriminating taxation, and Article III.4, which prohibits discrimination in the sale and distribution of goods.

Scope

What is a measure under Article III? Panels generally take a broad view of what constitutes a measure. In GATT decisions, even written undertakings given by investors, conditional on approval of the proposed investment, made pursuant to a law and considered legally binding amounted to a measure (see undertakings given by investors under Canada's Foreign Investment Review Act ("FIRA") – *Canada – FIRA* case).[9] In the *EEC – Parts and Components* case,[10] even voluntary obligations assumed in order to obtain an advantage from the government were deemed to be measures.

In the *Japan – Measures Affecting Photographic Film* case,[11] the interpretation of the word "measure" was particularly important because the measures that the US was challenging related to schemes that arose out of a network of government decisions and private sector practices. The Panel noted that the terms "law, regulation and requirements" should include a "broad range of government action, and action by private parties that may be assimilated to government action."

The *United States Section 337* case[12] considered the issue of what constituted an actionable measure. The case concluded at paragraph 5.10:

The Panel noted that the text of Article III.4 makes no distinction between substantive and procedural laws, regulations or requirements and it was not aware of anything in the drafting history that suggested that such a distinction should be made.

In the *Italian Discrimination Against Imported Agricultural Machinery* case,[13] the Panel said that:

> the selection of the word 'affecting' would imply... that the drafters of the Article intended to cover in paragraph 4 not only the laws and regulations which directly governed the conditions of sale or purchase but also any laws or regulations which might adversely modify the conditions of competition between the domestic and imported products on the internal market.

In the *United States Section 337* case, it was clear that enforcement procedures could not be separated from the substantive procedures they were designed to serve. WTO members cannot avoid the substantive National Treatment provisions by applying enforcement techniques that apply differential treatment against foreign members. Article III.4 also applies even where procedures are applied to persons rather than products, since the factor determining whether persons might be susceptible to Section 337 depended on the source of the challenged products.

In the *European Communities – Bananas III* case, the Appellate Body held that the administration of licence distribution procedures and the eligibility criteria for the distribution of licences were within the scope of Article III.4. It is important to note that in the case, it was not the import licencing requirements themselves that were being considered, but rather the EC procedures and requirements for the distribution of import licences for imported bananas among eligible operators within the European Communities. The Appellate Body found that the rules went beyond the scope of mere import licencing requirements and intended to cross-subsidise distributors of EC and ACP (African Caribbean and Pacific States) bananas, and to ensure that EU banana-ripeners obtained a share of the quota rents. As such, the rules fell within the scope of Article III.4.

Article III.2: Application of National Treatment Rule to Domestic Taxation

The National Treatment principles apply slightly different rules to taxation than to other domestic regulation which implicate Article III.4. Article III.2 deals with domestic taxation, and provides that:

> 2 The products of the territory of any contracting party imported into the territory of any contracting party shall not be subject, directly or indirectly, to internal taxes or other internal charges of any kind in excess of those applied, directly or indirectly, to like domestic products. Moreover, no contracting party shall otherwise apply internal taxes or other internal charges to imported or domestic products in a manner contrary to the principles set forth in paragraph 1.

Article III.2 has been extensively reviewed by GATT, WTO Panel and WTO Appellate Body decisions. There is therefore a relatively clear case law on Article III.2, which enables us to gain a better understanding of how WTO Panels will review discriminatory tax laws.

As noted by the Appellate Body in *Japan – Taxes on Alcoholic Beverages*,[14] Article III.1 contains general obligations, but Article III.2 contains specific obligations regarding internal taxes and internal charges (at para 18). The general provision informs the rest of Article III. Article III.1 provides the context to Article III.2. Therefore, Article III.2, first sentence means that any tax measure that applies domestic taxation on imported products in excess of like products is inconsistent with Article III. In other words, there is no requirement where we are dealing with like products that "so as to afford protection" to domestic products plays any part in the analysis. Less favourable taxation constitutes a "per se violation" of Article III, regardless of the impact on the competitive relationship between imports and domestic products.

Like Products

The first question is whether the products are "like products." The test for what defines a like product is set out in a number of the Article III.2 cases. The *Japan – Taxes on Alcoholic Beverages* notes that "like products" should be construed narrowly, because of the per se nature of the violation if applied to this product category. The Appellate Body notes that how narrowly "like products" should be determined depends on the tax measure being considered. This is interesting because it suggests that the placement of products in this narrow product market does not depend on the characteristics of the products alone, but also on the particular measure concerned. In other words, the trade impact of the measure can be factored into an analysis of whether the products themselves are like products. This recognises that some consumer-preference lock-ins or price differences can be brought about by the tax measure itself, and that the effect of these cannot be discounted in the analysis of what constitutes a like product for the purpose of Article III.1, first sentence.

The earliest good analysis came in the Working Party Report on Border Tax Adjustments (BISD 18S/97) at para 18, which contemplated that the following factors should be part of the case-by-case analysis:

a Product's end uses.
b Consumer tastes and habits.
c Product's properties, nature and quality.

The Appellate Body notes that the decision is a discretionary decision of the Panel but that there is no one fixed approach. It also notes that "like products" may be differently read according to different provisions of the WTO agreements themselves. In other words, the definition of "like products" depends on product characteristics, the type of tax measure itself and also on the very fact that we are dealing here with Article III.2 as opposed to another article of the WTO. The Appellate Body adds to the Working Party decision that the tariff classification of products can be helpful in determining whether two products are like. This reference, it must be noted, is to the harmonised system, a uniform classification of tariff nomenclature, and is not intended to refer to the specific tariff bindings classifications which countries use in Article II negotiations which differ from country to country.[15]

There are also some panel reports that examine the definition of "like products" that are worth reviewing closely.

In the *Korea – Taxes on Alcoholic Beverages*, for example, the Panel examined what would be directly competitive or substitutable products first (this being a broader category, *see infra*).[16] The Appellate Body looked to the ordinary meaning of the term "directly competitive or substitutable" for the case. In doing so, they also examined the first sentence of Article III.2 and stated that "'Like' products are a subset of directly competitive or substitutable products."[17]

Like Product Analysis: The Japan Panel Ruling on Alcoholic Beverages

The *Japan: Taxes on Alcoholic Beverages* case concerned the Japanese liquor law (Shuzeiho), Law No. 6 of 1953. This law laid down a system of internal taxes applicable to all liquors. The EU, the US and Canada complained that the Shuzeiho law applied less favourable tax treatment to imports (such as whiskey, gin and other similar products) than to the Japanese spirit, Shochu. The Complainants brought the matter to a Panel, having failed to convince the Japanese government to rectify the situation in consultations. The "like product" analysis centred on which of these many spirituous liquors were like. In the case, the EU claimed that both categories of Shochu were like products with vodka, gin, white rum and genever. The US claimed that all spirits, including white and brown spirits (which included whiskey), were like products, but that in the alternative all white spirits were like products.

The EU in its argument said that like products should not be confined to identical products but could cover non-identical products that had the same or near identical end uses. Minor differences in taste did not defeat this test. Canada did not claim that the spirits were like, preferring to rely on arguments brought under Article III.2, second sentence (see post). The US suggested that the like product analysis was bound up in the analysis of the impact of the regulatory system. Japan relied on the 1992 *Malt Beverages* decision where the Panel said:

> The purpose of Article III is thus not to prevent contracting parties from using their fiscal and regulatory powers for purposes other than to afford protection to domestic production. Specifically, the purpose of Article III is not to prevent contracting parties from differentiating between different product categories for policy purposes unrelated to the protection of domestic production.
>
> *[para 5.25]*[18]

The Panel then found that high alcoholic beer was not a like product to low alcoholic beer.

The Japan Panel noted very importantly that the precise definition of like product was different as between Article III.2 and other WTO provisions and, as a result, jurisprudence covering Article III.2 was not helpful in assessing the scope of "like products" in Article III.4 or, indeed, in other WTO provisions.

One of the reasons for this, as we will explain at length in the section on Article III.4, is that Article III.4 only refers to like products (and so competitive products do not factor into an Article III.4 analysis). Applying the same definition of "like products" to both Articles III.2 and III.4 would mean that these sub-articles had substantially different coverage.

The Panel decision in *Canada – Wheat Board* (circulated 6 April 2004), however, has applied Article III.2 findings to an Article III.4 case.[19] Canada argued that for the purposes of the *Canada Grain Act*, all grades and varieties of grain are not like. While it was not claiming that no US grain is like Canadian grain simply due to origin, Canada maintained that different quality standards existed between the two types of grain and that thus, the different treatment did not amount to less favourable treatment under Article III.4. The Panel disagreed:

> We recall relevant WTO jurisprudence, which supports the view that where a difference in treatment between domestic and imported products is based exclusively on the products' origin, the complaining party need not necessarily identify specific domestic and imported products and establish their likeness in terms of the traditional criteria – that is, the physical properties, end-uses and consumers' tastes and habits. Instead, it is sufficient for the purposes of satisfying the 'like product' requirement, to demonstrate that there can or will be domestic and imported products that are like.
>
> *Para 6.164*

Footnote 246 of the Panel Report explains that the "relevant WTO jurisprudence" invoked by the Panel is the Panel decision in *Argentina – Hides and Leather*. While that case identified an Article III.2 "like product" definition, the vital content of the footnote is that this decision is carried over to an Article III.4 case:

> In *Argentina - Hides and Leather*, in dealing with a claim under Article III.2 of the GATT 1994, the panel found that where a Member draws an origin-based distinction in respect of internal taxes, a comparison of specific products is not required and, consequently, it is not necessary to examine the various likeness criteria… While this finding pertained to Article III.2, we consider that the same reasoning is applicable in this case *mutatis mutandis*.

The Panel concluded on the issue that:

> In the present case, there may be legitimate reasons for Canada to treat domestic grain and like imported grain differently, for example, because the latter has not been subjected to the Canadian quality assurance system, which imposes certain restrictions and conditions on Canadian grain, including with respect to production. However, as the Appellate Body found in *Korea - Various Measures on Beef*, different treatments as between

> imported products and like domestic products must not result in the imported products being treated less favourably.

It should be noted that Canada filed a notice of Appeal on 1 June 2004, and the Appellate Body while finding no violation of the separate Art. XVII ruling (see post) did uphold the Panel's finding that the Canada Grain Act did violate Article III.4.

Returning to the *Japan – Taxes* case, the Panel there found that the interpretation of like products must go beyond a narrow "identical products" finding. The Panel noted the underlying purposes of Article III in a prescient section of its report (at 6.21):

> …one of the main objectives of Article III.2 is to ensure that WTO Members do not frustrate the effect of tariff concessions granted under Article II through internal taxes and other internal charges, it follows that a parallelism should be drawn in this case between the definition of products for purposes of Article II tariff concessions and the term "like products" as it appears in Article III.2. This is so in the Panel's view, because with respect to two products subject to the same tariff binding and therefore to the same border tax, there is no justification, outside of those mentioned in GATT rules, to tax them in a differentiated way through internal taxation.

Tariff classification is therefore an important element in the classification of products. The statement by the Panel, however, is more wide-ranging than this because it recognises the interface between domestic measures and border measures and applies a parallel test to them. Regarding like products, the Panel confirmed that the tariff classification was an important criterion for making the decision. The Panel, in considering that there should be a narrow definition, also noted that there was no *de minimis* exception for like products (see also *United States – Taxes on Petroleum and Certain Imported Substances*, para 5.1.9).[20] Commonality of end use is a necessary, though not sufficient, criterion to establish like products (see 6.22, *Japan – Taxes on Alcoholic Beverages*). Importantly, in actually applying the test to two products, vodka and Shochu, the Panel used the processes which gave rise to the products (the distillation and filtration systems) as evidence that they were like products. The Appellate Body noted that like product classifications and what this meant was more useful when applied to precise tariff classifications as opposed to higher level tariff classifications.

Like Product Analysis: The Korea Panel Ruling on Alcoholic Beverages

In the *Korea – Taxes on Alcoholic Beverages* case at para 118, the Appellate Body noted that "like products" were a subset of directly competitive or substitutable products. In the Korea case, the EC and the US claimed that Korea, under its general Liquor Tax Law and Education Tax Law, imposed a lower tax on the traditional Korean distilled spirit soju than that applied to other distilled spirits, such as whisky, brandy, vodka, rum and gin. Taxes on other spirits were as much as three times as high as those on soju. According to the EC and the US, in 1996, soju accounted for as much as 94% of the Korean liquor market. Imports of soju to Korea are insignificant. The EC and the US claimed that Korea applied its internal tax laws on vodka in excess of taxes applied to soju and was therefore in breach of its obligations under Article III.2, first sentence of GATT 1994.

In the Korea case, what was important was the equality of competitive opportunity between imports on the one hand and directly competitive or substitutable products on the other. It does not matter how much trade is affected, nor does it matter whether there are any imports of the directly competitive or substitutable products. These products can include both products that compete now and those that may potentially compete with the products in question.

Like Product Analysis: The Chile Panel Ruling on Alcoholic Beverages

In *Chile – Taxes on Alcoholic Beverages*, the measure at issue was the "Impuesto Adicional a las bebidas Alcoholicas" ("ILA") contained in Law No. 19534 of 1997.[21] The ILA was an excise tax levied on the sale and importation of alcoholic beverages, and it was an ad valorem tax. The case concerned ongoing attempts by Chile to bring its tax system into WTO compliance. The Old Chilean system differentiated between three types of distilled spirits – pisco, whiskey and other spirits – and applied differential rates of taxation among these different classes. The New System, which was the subject of the case, was more complex, as the ILA abolished the distinction between these three classes of spirits, but applied taxes based on the degree of alcohol content. All spirits with an alcohol content of 35 degrees or less suffer a 27% tax rate. From there, the base rate escalates in increments of 4 percentage points for each additional degree of alcohol up to a maximum rate of 47%. Of interest here is that none of the Complainants suggested that the different spirits affected were like products. The European Community made the assumption that whisky, other spirits and pisco were not like products, and instead sought to bring them under the head of directly competitive or substitutable products. It should be noted that pisco is a wine distillate and so is more different from other spirits than, say, shochu and vodka.

Like Product Analysis Where There Are No Imports Because of a WTO-violating Import Ban

In some cases, there is no comparable "like" imported product because imports themselves are banned. In this case, it is important to look at a hypothetical import and to test whether it is a like product. The appellate body in the *Canada periodicals case* provided a clue as to how this could be done at para 20:

> and as there were no imports of split-run editions of periodicals because of the import prohibition [found to be violative of GATT Article XI], hypothetical imports of split-run periodicals have to be considered.

Note that domestic competition agencies have looked at the issue of defining product markets in this area for antitrust analysis. The two most important definitions are those of the EU and the US.

In the EU:

> A relevant product market comprises all those products and/or services which are regarded as interchangeable or substitutable by the consumer, by reason of the products' characteristics, their prices and their intended use (demand-side substitutability). Supply-side substitutability may also be taken into account when defining markets in those situations in which its effects are equivalent to those of demand substitution in terms of effectiveness and immediacy. This means that suppliers are able to switch production to the relevant products and market them in the short term without incurring significant additional costs or risks in response to small and permanent changes in relative prices.[22]

The US has a similar product market definition. Under the Department of Justice/Federal Trade Commission Horizontal Merger Guidelines, a product market is a market in which the firms could effectively control prices if they were to coordinate their actions. A product market encompasses all products that can be substitutes and have a high cross-price elasticity.

The DOJ/FTC evaluates the next-best substitute as a product that consumers switch to in response to a price increase. To consider a product as a substitute, the DOJ/FTC examines (1) evidence that buyers have shifted or have considered shifting purchases in response to a price increase, (2) evidence that sellers base business decisions on the prospect of buyer substitution, (3) the influence of downstream competition and (4) the timing and costs of switching products.[23] Where you can have price discrimination, the DOJ/FTC uses a different model:

> If a hypothetical monopolist could profitably target a subset of customers for price increases, the Agencies may identify relevant markets defined around those targeted customers, to whom a hypothetical monopolist would profitably and separately impose at least a SSNIP. Markets to serve targeted customers are also known as price discrimination markets. In practice, the Agencies identify price discrimination markets only where they believe there is a realistic prospect of an adverse competitive effect on a group of targeted customers.... The Agencies also often consider markets for targeted customers when prices are individually negotiated, and suppliers have information about

customers that would allow a hypothetical monopolist to identify customers that are likely to pay a higher price for the relevant product. If prices are negotiated individually with customers, the hypothetical monopolist test may suggest relevant markets that are as narrow as individual customers (see also Section 6.2 on bargaining and auctions).

Nonetheless, the Agencies often define markets for groups of targeted customers, i.e. by type of customer, rather than by individual customer. By doing so, the Agencies are able to rely on aggregated market shares that can be more helpful in predicting the competitive effects of the merger.[24]

For both the US and EU product definition models, the product analysis is different than that under the WTO jurisprudence. The competition policy models of product market definition do not take into account that the tax itself shapes preferences and helps to determine what is included as a relevant product. Hence, a traditional antitrust test will not capture some of the discriminatory taxation abuses involved in a WTO case concerning directly substitutable or like products, including those that distort the market. Let us take, for example, the FTC consent order involving the Diageo acquisition of Seagrams. As part of the consent order, Diageo agreed to divest its Malibu rum business in order to acquire Seagrams. The FTC determined a number of product markets: (a) premium rum, (b) popular gin, (c) deluxe Scotch, (d) single malt Scotch and (e) Cognac.[25] Among the concerns of the FTC was that had Diageo not agreed to divest its Malibu rum business worldwide, it would have controlled 95% of all US premium rum sales. This product market is different from the one in Korea, where the relevant price difference was at a level 20 times the two products and therefore two rums might well be in different product markets.

The difference is that like products in the trade sense must account for the built-in tariff preferences and the impact of the distorting tax measures. However, as these barriers are progressively reduced, one would expect the like product analysis to gradually approximate an antitrust/competition policy product market definition. This expresses the fact that as countries reduce barriers, pure consumer welfare analysis (such as discussed in detail in Chapter 3) should govern, and the trade list should more closely approximate traditional antitrust-type tests. If products are in the same product market in an antitrust/competition sense, then clearly any differential treatment could be market-distorting at that point. We will see in the next chapter on GATT Article XVII and State Trading Enterprises similar principles at work. Here, the test of what constitutes predatory approximates a pure antitrust test the more regulation becomes transparent, and the less the STE can sustain below-cost pricing.

Excessive Taxation

If the products are found to be like products, all that remains to be proved in order to show that there is a violation of Article III.2, first sentence is for there to be less favourable taxation for the imported like products. Here, as the *Japan – Taxes on Alcoholic Beverages Appellate Body* notes, any excess is too much. There is no *de minimis* rule. The *Japan panel* quoted the *United States – Measures Affecting Alcoholic and Malt Beverages* (confirmed by the Appellate Body at p. 25):

> The prohibition of discriminatory taxes in Article III.2 first sentence, is not conditional on a "trade effects test" nor is it qualified by a *de minimis* standard.

If Products are Not Like Products: Article III.2, Second Sentence

If the like product test is not met, then it is necessary to show that the products in question are directly competitive or substitutable. This arises from the precise wording of Article III.2, second sentence. The *Japan Appellate Body decision* sets out how Article III.1 informs the second sentence of Article III.2 (at p. 25):

> Article III.1 informs Article III.2 second sentence, through specific reference. Article III.2 second sentence contains a general prohibition against "internal taxes or other internal charges" applied to "imported or domestic products in a manner contrary to the principles set forth in paragraph 1." "Article III.1 states that internal taxes and other internal charges "should not be applied to imported or domestic products so as to afford protection to domestic production". Again, *Ad* Article III.2 states as follows:
>
> A tax conforming to the requirement of the first sentence of paragraph 2 would be considered to be inconsistent with the provisions of the second sentence only in cases where competition was involved between, on the one hand, the taxed product and, on the other hand, a directly competitive or substitutable product which was not similarly taxed.

The *Ad* Article III clarifies the meaning of Article III.2, second sentence.[26] In other words, if we do not have like products, we need to show the following:

1 Are the imports and the domestic products directly competitive or substitutable?
2 Are the two products not similarly taxed?
3 The dissimilar taxation must be applied so as to afford protection to domestic production.
4 Are the two products not similarly taxed?
5 The dissimilar taxation must be applied so as to afford protection to domestic production.

Each of the above three points must be established separately in order for an Article III.2, second sentence violation to be made out. We shall take each, in turn.

Directly Competitive or Substitutable

At first check, this looks reminiscent of an antitrust-type standard. After all, is this not the same basis for ascertaining whether products are in the same antitrust product market? While there are some similarities, there are some important differences that highlight the interaction between competition and trade policy. Under competition rules, a product market is defined to include products that are also substitutable. The test that is used is the significant, non-transitory price increase test. When faced with two products, we ask whether a small, significant but non-transitory price increase in one product would cause consumers to switch to the other. Typically, the effect of an increase of 10% iis considered, although the precise percentage can vary based on the conditions of the market. If consumers would switch to the other product, then this is evidence that both products are in the same product market (see *US v. Dupont*,[27] and the 1992 US Merger Guidelines as amended[28]). However, this market assumes that products have equality of competitive opportunity, whereas in the case where imports compete with local products, imports face vastly increased barriers to entry (the payment of a tariff, having to clear customs procedures and so forth, not to mention the very tax policies complained of). For this reason, such a test inadequately takes account of consumer preferences that may be locked-in precisely because of the government tax or other policies, and inadequately takes account of potential competition which would arise if governmental preferences were removed.

The *Japan – Alcoholic Beverages* Panel examined a number of different tests that included product characteristics, common end-use and tariff classification, but also at-market-place issues. The Appellate Body noted that it would not be inappropriate to examine cross-price elasticity of demand, although this was not necessarily the final determinant of the test. The Appellate Body supported the Panel's discussion of the test, and it is therefore worth looking at the Panel Report in greater detail. The Panel noted that, independently of similarities with respect to physical characteristics or tariff nomenclature classifications, greater emphasis should be placed on elasticity of substitution. The Panel relied heavily on economic studies which looked at cross-price elasticity of demand. The Panel notes carefully that cross-price elasticity will tend to give us information on whether products are in the same competitive market, "all other things being equal" (See 6.31). The Panel goes on to say at 6.31:

> However, all other things are not equal. When working with a set of (potentially) substitutable products, it is necessary to recognise that underlying trends in the data may affect the apparent relationship between the variables examined (serial and auto-correlation). In addition, the variables may in actuality be closely related. For example, outside factors (i.e. those not measured directly) may affect the markets that are examined jointly (multicollinearity). Moreover changes in income may affect demand in all the markets studied, and this effect may vary systematically across the markets...

The particular flaw that the Panel found in the Japanese government's data was that the simple analysis, which relied on a very static model, did not fully control for autocorrelation and multicollinearity. More simply put, a number of extraneous factors, such as the fact that different price sensitivities arose specifically because of the government preferred tax rate, were simply not taken into account in the studies. Quoting the *Japan – Customs Duties, Taxes and Labeling Practices on Imported Wines and Alcoholic Beverages*, the Panel at para 6.28 noted that:

> A tax system that discriminates against imports has the consequence of creating or even freezing preferences for domestic goods.[29]

The *Korea Panel* reviewed the negotiating history of Article III.2, second sentence and *Ad* Article III and noted the following:

> The Geneva Session of the Preparatory Committee provided an explanation of the language of the second sentence by noting that apples and oranges could be directly competitive or substitutable. Other examples provided were domestic linseed oil and imported tung oil and domestic synthetic rubber and imported natural rubber. There was discussion of whether such products as tramways and buses or coal and fuel oil could be considered as categories of directly competitive or substitutable products. There was some disagreement with respect to these products.
>
> *[Korea Panel, Para 10.38]*

The Korea Appellate Body also stands for the proposition that grouping can be done in the directly competitive or substitutable analysis. In addition to the other methods of finding that products are directly competitive and substitutable is to look at the channels of distribution and the point of sale. As the Panel noted in the Korea case:

> Considerable evidence of overlap in channels of distribution and points of sale….is supportive of a finding that the identified imported and domestic products are directly competitive or substitutable.
>
> *[para 10.86]*

In the Panel Decision in *Chile – Taxes on Alcoholic Beverages*, the Panel reviewed the Japan case at both appellate and panel levels and considered a concept that had been used in domestic competition law, the principle of potential competition. As well as the test elements as set out above, the Chile Panel considered substitutability of end use from the perspective of goods having certain characteristics which consumers consider substitutable (even where the goods might be physically very different, such as butter and margarine). They relied on a study by Kelvin Lancaster.[30] In comparing the end uses of pisco and whisky, the Panel noted that even though the products were produced from grapes and barley, they shared a number of physical characteristics. The Panel also relied on a ruling of the Chilean Competition agency, which found that the relevant market that contained pisco was the market for alcoholic beverages, including beer, wine and liquor. Since the antitrust market was generally narrower than the Article III.2, second sentence market for reasons stated above, the Panel found that this was good evidence of a broad Article III market as well.

Directly Competitive and Substitutable: Potential Competition

In the *Chile case*, the EC submitted that Article III should deal not only with products that were actually competitive but also with products that are potentially competitive. They argued that this should include not only competition that would exist for the tax measures at issue, but also competition that could reasonably be expected to develop in the near future.

The Panel noted that because Article III protects competitive opportunity and not export volumes, it cited with approval the Korea Panel when it stated that:

> We will not attempt to speculate on what could happen in the distant future, but we will consider evidence pertaining to what could reasonably be expected to occur in the near future based on the evidence presented. How much weight we will give to such evidence must be decided on a case-by-case in light of the market structure and other factors, including the quality of the evidence and the scope of the inferences to be drawn. If one is dealing with products that are experience based consumer items, then trends are particularly important and it would be unrealistic and, indeed, analytically unhelpful to attempt to separate every piece of evidence and disregard that which discusses implications for market structure in the near future.
>
> *[para 10.50]*

The Chile Panel took a dynamic view of the directly competitive or substitutable test, in part to accommodate the fact that in that case, the level of actual competition between pisco and whiskey was much less than it would have been had the tax system not been in place. The tax system that was the subject of the complaint in fact inhibited consumers from choosing the imported product. The Chile Panel also noted that the built-in preferences could affect not only the dynamic interpretation of the directly competitive or substitutable test but could also have an impact on product end uses. For example, if the products had common end uses in another market but not in the one at issue, then that could be evidence that it was the government action that in fact locked in that consumer preference. In other words, the products are not actually competitive in the market at issue but could very well be potentially competitive and the evidence of a different market (where the governmental behaviour that caused the locked-in preference in the market at issue did not take place) might be helpful to the analysis.

The Panel in the Korea case looked at this issue in considerable detail. The Korea Panel at para 10.45 accepted that evidence of competition from markets outside Korea could be analysed and could be helpful in establishing "potential competition" in addition to looking at cross-price elasticity. The Panel in discussing potential competition said at para 10.47:

> We, indeed, are not in the business of speculation...[but] we do not agree that any assessment of potential competition with a temporal aspect is speculation...Panels should look at evidence of trends and changes in consumption patterns and make an assessment as to whether such trends and patterns lead to the conclusion that the products in question are either directly competitive now or can reasonably be expected to become directly competitive in the near future.

The Panel explicitly applied a dynamic view of market analysis that could take into account potential or future competition.

It should be noted that this kind of analysis goes very considerably beyond a conventional product market analysis in antitrust, although antitrust has developed a doctrine which expressly allows potential competition to be taken into account.

Potential Competition Theory

Potential competition has been widely accepted under the US antitrust principles for some time. However, under the US antitrust law, its application is rigidly circumscribed. The doctrine was first developed in a series of cases, stemming from *US v. Falstaff Brewing Corp.*[31] The doctrine holds that if a potential acquirer in a concentrated market is not already a competitor in that market, the acquisition may nevertheless violate the antitrust laws. The violation would occur if:

a the acquirer had viable alternative means of entering the market either de novo or via a small "toe-hold" acquisition, thereby providing more vigorous competition, or

b the acquiring firm was perceived by market participants as being a potential entrant whose presence served as a competitive constraint disciplining the market. In either case, the merger removes the acquirer as a potential entrant and potential source of competition.[32]

The theory was initially introduced to deal with cases where behaviour occurred that prevented entry into a particular market. Potential competition theory is really two theories – actual potential entry theory and perceived potential entry theory.[33] Most recently, potential competition theory has found its modern-day expression in the notion of innovation markets.

We submit that there are good reasons why the Article III test should be broader than the antitrust version of potential competition theory. Essentially, the potential competition theory antitrust test should be broadened in the trade context to deal with the fact that we are dealing with government and not private behaviour, and that imports may have had a historical disadvantage caused by a history of high tariffs, difficulties at customs and so forth. The import of competition concepts into trade theory must take into account the fact that it is government distorting the market and therefore competition concepts may need to be broadened to deal with government as opposed to purely private behaviour. This reflects that the government is not a profit maximiser and can engage in activity based on non-economic concerns that impact the market. Finally, government has coercive power which the private sector does not share.

Reflections on Integration of Competition Concepts into Directly Competitive or Substitutable Test

A student might be forgiven for thinking that the test for directly competitive or substitutable goods is a far more discretionary test than is conducive to establishing a predictable business environment, and this is partially true. However, out of the many cases in this area, one can begin to distil a test that has some sound economic underpinnings, even if such a test has not been expressly set forth in the case law so far. The test would be based on an antitrust product market analysis, subject to the fact that it is the government that is engaged in the distortion and would account for the tariff, tax or other barriers. The price of a product, based on what would be competitive but for the trade barrier, would be implemented.

The Final Element: So as to Afford Protection to Domestic Products

The final element which has to be proved in order to establish an Article III.2, second sentence case is that the measure was introduced so as to afford protection to domestic products. Here, the law has changed over the years. The *Japan* Appellate Body case is clear that there is no issue of intent, and no need to second guess legislators (see *Japan* at pp. 27 et seq).

It is not necessary for a panel to sort through the many reasons legislators and regulators often have for what they do and weigh the relative significance of those reasons to establish legislative or regulatory intent….it is irrelevant that protectionism was not an intended objective if the particular tax measure in question is nevertheless, to echo Article III:1, "applied to imported or domestic products so as to afford protection to domestic production." This is an issue of how the measure in question is applied.

The Appellate Body, in considering whether a tax would violate Article III,2, second sentence, said (at p. 31):

> we believe that an examination in any case of whether dissimilar taxation has been applied so as to afford protection requires a comprehensive

> and objective analysis of the structure and application of the measure in question on domestic as compared to imported products.

The decision stands for the proposition that in order to establish protective application, one must look at the design, architecture and the revealing structure of a measure. The differential itself might be grounds for finding a protective effect.

The Panel Report in the case of the *Chile – Taxes on Alcoholic Beverages* case makes it completely clear that there is no longer any place for the old aim and effect test in establishing whether the tax has the effect of protecting domestic production. The foundation of the test is to protect the competitive opportunities between imports and domestic products (see para 7.124). The Chile Panel also cast out any version of a trade-weighted test by noting at para 7.158:

> First of all, it does not save a measure from running afoul of Article III:2, second sentence, merely because there are domestic products taxed at the same level as the imported products.

De Minimis

The 1987 *Japan – Alcohol* case was the first case that opened the door to the possibility that *de minimis* differences in effective taxation would not necessarily give rise to a GATT violation. Note that the *de minimis* rules only apply to a case involving directly competitive or substitutable products. In the case, at para 5.11:

> The panel was of the view that also small tax differences could influence the competitive relationship between directly competing distilled liquors, but the existence of protective taxation could be established only in the light of the particular circumstances of each case and there could be a *de minimis* level below which a tax difference ceased to have the protective effect prohibited by Article III:2, second sentence.

Finally, the GATT allows under Article III.3 that any tax that discriminates would violate Article III.2, but which was sanctioned prior to the GATT, is legal notwithstanding the provisions of the GATT.

Non-Tax Discriminatory Regulations: GATT Article III.4

Article III fundamentally impacts a WTO members policy space as it reaches into domestic regulations if they discriminate between imported and local goods. Article III.4 provides that:

> The products of the territory of any contracting party imported into the territory of any other contracting party shall be accorded treatment no less favourable than that accorded to like products of national origin in respect

> of all laws, regulations and requirements affecting their internal sale, offering for sale, purchase, transportation, distribution or use. The provisions of this paragraph shall not prevent the application of differential internal transportation charges which are based exclusively on the economic operation of the means of transport and not on the nationality of the product.

Note that Article III.4 only applies to "like products."

Like Product Analysis under Article III.4

In the *European Communities – Asbestos*[34] case the Panel cited with approval Article III.2 cases such as *Japan – Alcohol Beverages* in order to analyse what products constituted like products. The Panel agreed with the general definition used to identify like products, such as end use, tariff classification, consumers' tastes, product quality and so forth. The asbestos case arguably broadens the like product definition (a broader view of like products is taken than in the *EEC – Measures on Animal Feed Proteins*[35]). The Panel reviewed whether asbestos fibres were like products with other substitutable fibres that did not contain asbestos. The EU requested that the Panel consider the different chemical composition of the fibres but the Panel found that to do so would mean that products that had the same end uses would frequently not be regarded as like products, whereas products that had very different uses might be like. They rejected a chemical composition test in the case, noting that the case-by-case analysis meant that all the different factors to be considered should be mutually supportive.

Foreclosure

The *Canada Periodicals*[36] case (Appellate Body decision) also settled the question of whether there could be concurrent jurisdiction of GATT and GATS. The Canada periodicals case turned on whether a provision of Canada's Excise Tax Act could be a measure that affected trade in services, as well as a measure that applies to trade in goods. The Appellate Body responding to Canada's argument that the measure applied only to trade in services said that since the measure imposed an excise tax on split-run periodicals, it was a tax on a good and was therefore susceptible to GATT. The periodical contains advertising content and editorial content, both of which had services attributes but they combine to form a physical product. In addition, since the tax had to be paid by the publisher (and not the advertiser), this was clearly a tax aimed at a product. The Appellate Body affirmed the Panel statement, which said:

> The ordinary meaning of the texts of GATT 1994 and GATS, as well as Article II:2 of the WTO agreement, taken together, indicate that obligations under GATT 1994 and GATS can co-exist and that one does not override the other.
>
> *[Panel Report para 5.17]*

However, the issue was not fully decided by the Appellate Body as it was not necessary for the appeal.

Affording Protection: No Less Favourable Treatment

Under Article III.4, there must be a law, regulation or requirement affecting the internal sale, offering for sale or distribution of the product in question. Article III.4 is informed by Article III.1 as described above. As early as the 1989 decision in *US – Section 337*, panels had analysed the no less favourable treatment standard to call for "effective equality of opportunities for imported products" (para 5.11, *US – Section 337*). The Panel further noted that this standard set a minimum permissible standard as a base. The Panel said that it was incumbent on the party applying differential treatment to show that the treatment is no less favourable, nonetheless. The Panel found that in order to establish the standard, it was necessary to assess whether or not Section 337 in itself "may lead to the application to imported products of treatment less favourable than that accorded to products of US origin" (see 5.13). In other words, the test protected expectations and did not seek to look at actual case-by-case results. Implicitly, the Panel recognised potential impact of regulations, which has important implications for the way in which the like product analysis might include products potentially competitive with domestic products. The Panel expressly rejected any notion of balancing more favourable treatment of some imported products against less favourable treatment of other imported products. The Panel noted that:

> Such an interpretation would lead to great uncertainty about the conditions between imported and domestic products and thus defeat the purposes of Article III.

This does not mean that elements of more favourable treatment are ignored. It simply means that they are relevant only if they would always accompany and offset an element of differential treatment causing the less favourable treatment – i.e. these would form part of the architecture of the regulation itself and could be seen without reference to cases.

The Japan – Measures Affecting Photographic Film decision notes that therefore Article III.4 must be interpreted by reviewing whether there is equality of competitive conditions for imported products in relation to domestic products. However, the case notes that there is a difference between Articles III.2 and III.4 in this respect. Under the *EC – Bananas III* case, Article III.4 differs from Article III.2, particularly because a finding of an Article III.4 violation does not require a separate consideration of whether a measure affords protection to domestic production. This is a key difference between the two provisions. The *Japan-Photographic Film* Panel applied this difference by stating the following (at 10.371):

Accordingly, and in line with the Appellate Body's most recent stipulation in Bananas III, we shall use the general principle articulated in Article III.1 as a guide to interpreting Article III.4 but shall not give separate consideration to whether measures cited by the US "afford protection to domestic production."

The central question of whether there is an impact on the equality of competitive opportunity is the standard for not only Article III.2 but also for Article III.4 (para 10.379, *Japan – Measures Affecting Photographic Film).* The *US – Section 337* case set out the test for "no less favourable treatment" as follows, at 10.379:

> the "no less favourable" treatment requirement set out in Article III.4 is unqualified. These words are to be found throughout the General Agreement.... as an expression of the underlying principle of equality of treatment of imported products as compared to the treatment given either to other foreign products, under the most favoured nation standard, or to domestic products under the national treatment standard of Article III. The words "treatment no less favourable" in paragraph 4 call for effective equality of opportunities for imported products in respect of the application of laws, regulations and requirements affecting the internal sale, offering for sale, purchase transportation, distribution or use of products. This clearly sets a minimum permissible standard as a basis.

In the *EC – Asbestos* case, the Panel reviewed a French decree which prevented the sale and use of asbestos in France. The Decree also contained an import ban. *Ad* Article III provides as follows:

> Any internal tax or other internal charge, or any law, regulation or requirement of the kind referred to in paragraph 1 which applies to an imported product and to the like domestic product and is collected or enforced in the case of the imported product at the time or point of importation, is nevertheless to be regarded as an internal tax or other internal charge, or a law, regulation or requirement of the kind referred to in paragraph 1, and is accordingly subject to the provisions of Article III.

In this case, even though the restrictions on the sale of product were applied at the time of importation, this still counted as an internal regulation. The Panel decision also notes that if the decree has led to the fact that there is no like domestic product (as opposed to there being no like domestic product for other reasons), then an Article III claim still holds. In the asbestos case, because the Decree prohibited the manufacturing and sale of asbestos-containing products in France, there were no domestic like products.

The *Japan II* case provides that "less favourable treatment" means anything that upsets the competitive balance between imported products and like products. In the EC-Aasbestos case, the terms of the Decree on their face satisfied this standard.

In the Section 337 case, it was noted that in order to establish whether there was less favourable treatment, one had to consider whether the regulation "may lead to the application to imported products of treatment less favourable than that accorded to [domestic products]..."

The issue was also dealt with in the Appellate Body decision in *EC – Bananas III*,[37] at p. 89, where the EC's practice of issuing hurricane licences was considered to be less favourable treatment under Article III.4. Hurricane licences allow for additional imports of third country (and non-traditional ACP) bananas at the lower in-quota rate. Although the licences are issued to EC producers, they lead to an increase in exports from those countries. The hurricane licences therefore act as an incentive to operators to market ACP or EC bananas, and therefore skews competitive conditions in favour of EC bananas. The Appellate Body said: we do not dispute the right of WTO members to mitigate or remedy the consequences of natural disasters. However, Members should do so in a manner consistent with their obligations under the GATT 1994 and the other covered agreements.

The Appellate Body also made it clear (overruling the Panel decision on this point) that for the purposes of Article III.4, since Article III.4 does not refer to Article III.1, there is no need to show that the measure affords protection to domestic production.

Article III.4 was also analysed under less favourable treatment in the context of the *US – Standards for Reformulated and Conventional Gasoline* case.[38] The rule which was being reviewed was the Gasoline Rule in the Clean Air Act (CAA). The allegation made by Venezuela and Brazil was that foreign gasoline, which was "like" domestic gasoline, was subject to more demanding quality requirements than gasoline of US origin. The analysis of whether the US rule accorded less favourable treatment turned on the application of Section 211 of the CAA. This statutory provision established certain compositional and performance specifications for reformulated gasoline. The oxygen content had to be at least 2.0% by weight and the benzene content less than 1% by volume. Reformulated gasoline also had to be free of heavy metals such as Manganese and Lead. The performance requirements called for a 15% reduction in the emissions of both volatile organic compounds and toxic air pollutants, and no increase in the reduction of nitrous oxides. This is calculated by comparing the performance of reformulated gasoline in baseline vehicles (1990 model year) with baseline gasoline.

Under the CAA, the EPA determines the quality of 1990 gasoline, to which reformulated and conventional gasoline would be compared in the future. The EPA was instructed to determine the quality of the 1990 gasoline – these determinations are baselines. In addition to the historical baselines set for certain entities, certain entities were assigned to the statutory baseline. Importers were assigned the statutory baseline where they could not establish a baseline based on its actual 1990 gasoline. Although domestic importers could use one of three methods for calculating a baseline, foreign importers, if they could not show content based on method one, were forced to resort to a statutory baseline. Brazil and Venezuela succeeded in showing that in practice this meant that they had to produce higher standard gasoline than did domestic importers. The US argued that overall, the individual and statutory baselines meant that overall treatment was the same. This was because the statutory baseline and the average of the sum of the individual baselines was the same. However, the Panel noted that prevailing law meant that there should not be any balancing of benefits and losses in an Article III.4 analysis. The only test was whether foreign products could be treated less well under the regulation.

The case therefore again firmly rejects any attempt to apply a balancing test in Article III.4 analysis. All that matters is that foreign products may receive less favourable treatment under the regulation being considered. The Panel also ruled that if an Article III.4 violation was made out, there was no need to examine the impact of the Article III.1 language. This makes the analysis different from Article III.2 analysis.

Both the Panel and the Appellate Body in *Korea – Various Measures on Beef* further clarified the steps in an Article III.4 analysis. The measure at question was Korea's "dual retail system" for beef, which obliged stores and supermarkets authorised to sell imported beef to hold a separate display, forced small retailers to choose between selling either domestic or foreign beef, and obliged foreign beef shops to display a sign stating, "Specialised Imported Beef Store." The Panel had found, among other things, that the "dual retail system" was a violation of Article III.4 of the GATS 1994. Korea appealed this decision but the Appellate Body upheld the Panel decision, although the AB offered some important criticism on the Panel's reasoning.

The AB began by outlining the key ingredients in establishing an Article III.4 violation: the imported and domestic products concerned are "like products"; the measure in question is a "law, regulation, or requirement affecting their internal sale, offering for sale, purchase, transportation, distribution, or use"; and the imported products must be found to receive "less favourable" treatment than the domestic like products (AB, para 133).

This case concerned only the last element, "less favourable" treatment. In the context of Article III.4, the Panel had interpreted "treatment no less favourable" to mean that imported products are accorded "effective equality of opportunities" with like domestic products. The Panel then continued to say that

> Any regulatory distinction that is based exclusively on criteria relating to the nationality or the origin of the products is incompatible with Article III and this conclusion can be reached even in the absences of any imports... confirming that there is no need to demonstrate the actual and specific trade effects of a measure for it to be found in violation of Article III.

The AB disagreed, saying that different treatment is not necessarily a violation of Article III.4, as long as the different treatment does not impose conditions of competition that are less favourable to the imported products that the like domestic product. The AB had made this same point earlier in *US – Section 327*:

> On the one hand, contracting parties may apply to imported products different formal legal requirements if doing so would accord imported products more favourable treatment. On the other hand, it also has to be recognised that there may be cases where the application of formally identical legal provisions would in practice accord less favourable treatment to imported products and a contracting party might thus have to apply different legal provisions to imported products to ensure that the treatment accorded them is in fact no less favourable. For these reasons, the mere fact that imported products are subject under Section 337 to legal provisions that are different from those applying to products of national origin is in itself not conclusive in establishing inconsistency with Article III:4.
>
> *(US-327, para 5.11)*

The AB added that the Panel had gone on to examine the manner in which the measure modified the conditions of competition so as to disadvantage foreign beef. Essentially, when Korea instituted the dual retail system in 1990, the government-mandated measure had cut off access to the previously existing distribution outlets for imported beef, while leaving domestic beef unaffected. It was this government intervention that had adversely affected the ability of imported beef to compete with domestic beef, thereby violating Article III.4.

Summary of Other WTO Provisions Which Could Implicate Conditions of Competition

Other provisions of the WTO implicate conditions of competition. We are seeing an increase in the use of a number of sanitary and phytosanitary (SPS) measures which are used to protect animal or plan health. While the WTO obviously does not prevent Parties from protecting human or plant health, it does create some restrictions on how Parties can implement SPS rules and remain WTO compliant.

Approach of Trade Agreements to Labour and Environmental Issues

The inclusion of labour and environmental issues in trade agreements has been considered from the beginning of the GATT system, but substantive approaches are a relatively new introduction (given the 75-year history of the GATT/WTO system). There was an aborted attempt in 1947 with the aim of introducing legally binding provisions in the International Trade Organization. However, the ITO was still born, as the US Congress never approved the arrangements that included it. Instead, the world was left only with a contract between contracting parties called the General Agreement on Tariffs and Trade (GATT). It took another 50 years before these issues were again introduced this time via side letters in trade agreements such as the NAFTA. The reason they were in side letters and not in the agreement was because it was not clear at the time whether these were indeed trade-related issues and there was concern that their inclusion (while worthy objectives in and of themselves) would damage the goals of the trade agreement which was to increase import competition and thereby increase choice and lower price, leading to more efficient outcomes and ultimately more economic output. Chapters in FTAs followed in the case, for example, of the US-Jordan agreement. Since then most trade agreements have included labour and environmental chapters, although without the same types of enforcement mechanisms that typically applied to violations of the trade rules on discrimination and National Treatment.

Some complained that these provisions were not enforceable and so were merely hortatory in nature. The trade world has looked at ways of enforcing them but doing so in ways that did not undercut the purpose of the trade agreement. Most trade agreements now include sustainable development chapters which include labour and environmental issues, the US tends to have standalone chapters for these subjects and the EU tends to lump them together in an overall sustainability chapter approach. In neither case does full dispute resolution apply to these subjects.

By way of example, the CPTPP which the UK aspires to accede to contains a chapter on environmental issues. The CPTPP is worthy of study not just because it is an agreement which the UK aspires to accede to, so if the UK adopts a very different approach, this will be hard to reconcile with its potential CPTPP partners. It is also worthy of study because four of the CPTPP countries (Australia, Malaysia, Mexico and Peru) are in the 17 "mega diverse" countries supporting 70% of the world's biodiversity. The CPTPP countries also export and trade and consume very high levels of natural resources. The CPTPP chapter does three things. First, it ensures that the CPTPP members properly enforce their own laws in the environmental space (by allowing interested parties to request national level investigations and so forth). Second, it provides that CPTPP members will have high standards of transparency in their environmental laws, and consultation in respect of these laws. Third, it provides frameworks for CPTPP members to work together on a host of environmental challenges, such as protecting the ozone layer, protecting the marine environment from ship pollution, combatting illegal wildlife trade, and combatting over-fishing and illegal fishing.

Explanation of How the WTO Analyses Technical Regulations

It is perfectly permissible for countries to enact technical regulation for prudential reasons, but there are some limitations which prevent them from discriminating against other WTO members in so doing. The major agreements that deal with these regulations are the Technical Barriers to Trade Agreement ("TBT Agreement") and, in the case of protection of animal, human or plant health, the Sanitary and Phyto-Sanitary Agreement (the "SPS Agreement"). The first question to ask is whether the agreement relates to the protection of human, animal or plant health in which case it will be analysed under the SPS Agreement. If it does not apply to these, it will be analysed under the TBT Agreement. If the rule does not constitute a "technical regulation" within the meaning of the TBT Agreement, it will be analysed under the GATT. The TBT and SPS Agreements are mutually exclusive, the SPS Agreement applying only to measures that are intended to protect plant, animal or human health (typically from food-borne pathogens or pests). The TBT scope applies to both technical regulations and standards (which are not compulsory). The TBT Agreement allows members to have a greater flexibility than the SPS Agreement on their technical regulation (which is subject only to a legitimate objective test).

We first review how the SPS Agreement applies to regulations designed to protect animal, human and plant health.

Approach of WTO Trading System on SPS Issues and Mutual Recognition/Equivalence

The WTO trading system has looked at issues related to the protection of animal or plant health through the SPS Agreement. The SPS Agreement provides for a system of rules that allow countries to maintain these measures subject to some basic requirements. First, the measures must be proportionate relative to the regulatory goal they are seeking to achieve. Second, they must be based on sound science. Third, they must be necessary for the particular goal, and they must not constitute an unnecessary burden on international trade.

The SPS Agreement encourages members to grant equivalence in respect of each other's SPS rules (underlying product regulation). Under the SPS Agreement, members should grant each other equivalence if their ultimate objectives remain the same, and the Parties' regulatory system objectively achieves those goals. The objective standard means that countries cannot simply self-certify that their regulatory frameworks satisfy particular health and safety goals, but a reasonable observer would have to agree that they were. This importation of an objective standard is a high bar that allows countries to only declare equivalence where there is a sound basis for doing so.

Precisely what this objective standard is and how it applies is worthy of further discussion. The WTO Decision on the Implementation of Article 4 of the SPS Agreement (the "Equivalence Decision") provides that it specifically does not require "sameness" of measures but expressly contemplates that measures may achieve goals in alternative ways. The overall thrust of the Equivalence Decision is that the policy is towards granting equivalence where possible. On request of the exporting member, the onus is on the importing member to explain what its goals are in terms of SPS protections and clearly identify the risks that the regime is intended to address. The importing party shall respond to equivalence requests in a timely manner (within six months).

It is important that developing country requests for technical assistance are properly and expeditiously dealt with by developing countries. Members should also actively participate in equivalence work going on in the OIE, Codex and IPPC.

The Codex has developed these ideas more fully in its Guidelines on the Judgement of Equivalence (CAC/GL 53–2003). These Guidelines look at what is covered by food inspection and certification systems. These cover infrastructure, programme design and specific requirements.

The importing country is able to implement its ALOP (Appropriate Level of Protection), and the exporter needs to show that it can satisfy the importer's ALOP. This it can do by a mixture of documentary checks as well as on-site inspections and so forth.

The IPPC deals with equivalence in the case of plants. Most equivalence decisions in the plant sector are based on approach to pest control (which affect crops). The same principles as set forth above apply here also.

SPS Equivalence regimes are most developed in the food sector. An understanding of how equivalence regimes work in these more well-developed areas is useful in exploring what is possible in newer areas.

Examples of Equivalence Arrangements

There have been a number of successful equivalence deals that have been agreed including those on underlying product regulation.

a Australia-New Zealand CER

The Australia-NZ arrangements are probably the most advanced equivalence arrangements that exist around the world. Building on the Trans Tasman Mutual Recognition Agreement (1998), the principle that any good that may be legally sold in one market can be legally sold in the other is enshrined into the CER. The agreement also laid the groundwork for the Joint Australia New Zealand Food Standards Code (2002).

b NZ-EU Veterinary Agreement

In the area of meat products, the EU and NZ have agreed to the equivalence of their SPS regimes. Because of this equivalence, only 2% physical inspections are required for NZ meat exports to the EU.

c CETA

The EU and Canada have agreed equivalence measures in the CETA which are to be taken forward by the SPS Joint Management Committee. In the area of food safety, this includes Canadian recognition of EU member state meat inspection systems, simplified certificates for the export of Canadian meat and meat products into the EU. In an area of interest to the UK, CETA has an animal welfare technical working group. Countries historically have adopted specific rules that relate to food hygiene, food standards and the protection of crops.

It is also clear that where the level of protection in an importing country exceeds what is implied as its ALOP, then equivalence does not mean that the exporting country has to match the importing country's higher level of protection. It means that the exporting country must show that it meets the importers' ALOP. Clearly where an importing countries' regulations or standards are not necessary to protect animal or plant health (because, for example, they are not based on sound science), they cannot be said to be a legitimate ALOP. Particular emphasis will be paid in equivalence decision-making on ensuring that there is no discrimination between the products of WTO members.

Understanding International Trade Rules and their Application: TBT Agreement

If the regulation does not cover animal, human or plant health, it could be analysed under the TBT Agreement. The TBT Agreement consists of a specialised legal regime for a set of applicable technical regulations. First, the regulation must be within the scope of the TBT Agreement itself for the TBT to apply. These regulations apply to product characteristics or related processes or production methods and may be in a positive or negative form.

Where international standards exist, or where they are imminent, the technical regulation should be based on those standards. The TBT rules on standards are to be found in Annex 3 of the TBT Agreement.

a Is it a Technical Regulation within the meaning of the TBT Agreement?

The first question to answer is whether a particular regulation is even a measure to which the TBT Agreement applies. This issue was considered in *European Communities – Measures Prohibiting the Importation and Marketing of Seal Products* – AB-2014-1–AB-2014-2 (the "Seals case").[39] The case considered the question of whether a ban on all products containing seal products was a technical regulation (to which the TBT Agreement applied). The test of whether a regulation is a technical regulation for the purposes of the TBT Agreement turns on the precise meaning of Annex 1.1 of the TBT Agreement which states that the TBT applies to:

> Document(s) which lays down product characteristics or their related processes and production methods, including the applicable administrative provisions, with which compliance is mandatory. It may also include or deal exclusively with terminology, symbols, packaging, marking or labelling requirements as they apply to a product, process or production method.

In the Seals case, the ban on seal products was subject to an exception for seal products on certain Inuit and traveller groups. At issue in the Seals case was whether the measure banning seal products bans certain objective characteristics from all products (like the ruling that the ban was on any product containing seal products, or was akin to the ban on products containing asbestos fibres as in EC-Asbestos).[40] The fact that the set of regulations, which must be looked at holistically, contained permissive elements as well as prohibitions did not by itself prevent the regulation from being a technical regulation for the purpose of the TBT Agreement. In the Seals case, the AB concluded that the fact that there were exceptions to the ban for Inuit hunters and certain other groups which did not relate to product characteristics, meant that the measure did not have permissive and prohibitive provisions which related to product characteristics and therefore was not a technical regulation to which the TBT applied. Norway had further alleged in the Seals case that a technical regulation would also apply not only to one that covered product characteristics but also one that dealt with processes and production methods (PPMs). But the AB dismissed this argument stating that in order to be found a technical regulation, the regulation could either relate to product characteristics or it could relate to PPMs *which are related* to specific product characteristics.

Unlike GATT Article III.4 which requires equality of competitive opportunity between directly competitive or substitutable products, the TBT Agreement does allow such changes in competitive opportunity for cases of legitimate regulatory distinctions. (See below.)

Once a regulation is established as a technical regulation for the purposes of the TBT Agreement, we must then consider whether it violates the TBT Agreement by providing less favourable treatment for like products of the domestic producer or like products of other members, pursuant to Article 2.1 of the TBT Agreement. Article 2.1 of the TBT Agreement provides that:

> Members shall ensure that in respect of technical regulations, products imported from the territory of any Member shall be accorded treatment no less favourable than that accorded to like products of national origin and to like products originating in any other country.

The first question that needs to be answered is whether the products are indeed "like products."

b Like Products

The provisions in the TBT Agreement on non-discrimination apply to like domestic products and like products of other members. The *US-Clove Cigarettes* case (see post) examined what "like products" meant. The case was very clear that the concept of like products does not apply to distinctions between products which are based on the regulatory objectives of the measure itself. Such an interpretation would defeat the entire purpose of Article 2.1 of the TBT Agreement. When analysing the TBT Agreement, the AB disagreed with the Panel's narrow interpretation and relied on the directly competitive or substitutable test of GATT Article III.2, which it said informed the test in both Article III.4 and in Article 2.1 of the TBT

Agreement. This test is broader than a test that determines like products solely from physical characteristics, end uses, and consumer tastes and habits. In summary, likeness is determined by the competitive relationship between the products in question for TBT purposes.

One of the leading cases on the application of Article 2.1 of the TBT Agreement is the *United States – Measures Concerning the Importation, Marketing and Sale of Tuna and Tuna Products* ("Tuna II") case.[42]

In Tuna II, the US used a labelling scheme whereby only tuna caught in a prescribed manner would be allowed to be marketed in the US under its "Dolphin-safe" label. While product could be marketed in the US without this label, the US regulations set out that there could be no other way of satisfying the "Dolphin-safe" labelling requirement outside of the US proscribed mechanism. Mexico complained that it subscribed to a labelling standard for Dolphin safe products that was outside the US mechanism but it claimed that its dolphin safe standard was an international standard and that the US's rules violated the TBT Agreement, or in default violated the GATT as it discriminated against Mexican products.

Discriminating on the Basis of Production Methods

From a trade perspective, discriminating on the basis of production methods as opposed to the ultimate product itself has potentially very serious impacts on trade. This is why such discrimination has long violated international law principles, as particularly espoused by the WTO.

When countries promulgate laws that impede trade flows based on laws that relate to production methods, they go much further than is ordinarily acceptable in international trade. Generally, WTO law frowns on attempts to discriminate based on production methods for the very good reason that such provisions could become a protectionists' charter. It is too easy for an incumbent, protected interest to claim that a particular production method is unacceptable so that it does not have to compete against that particular product. This is a long-standing concern and dates back to the original ITO Charter in 1947. At that time, one delegation stated that

> Indirect protection is an undesirable and dangerous phenomenon. ... Many times, the stipulations 'to protect animal or plant life or health' are misused for indirect protection. It is recommended to insert a clause which prohibits expressly [the use of] such measures [to] constitute an indirect protection ....[41]

There are a very limited number of cases where discrimination on the basis of production methods has been found to be WTO-consistent but these are usually based on international standards.

c Article 2.1, TBT Agreement

In Tuna II, there was an enquiry as to what constituted a technical regulation (and whether a labelling requirement constituted a technical regulation which would then be subject to the labelling requirement of the TBT Agreement. The Appellate Body ("AB") also considered what constituted an Article 2.1 violation, specifically whether the technical regulation could lead to treatment no less favourable for imported products or like products from other countries. The AB noted that Article 2.1 did not mean that distinctions between product characteristics, or processes or production methods would automatically mean less favourable treatment under Article 2.1. As noted in US-Clove Cigarettes, Tuna II and US-COOL, some regulatory distinctions were legitimate.[43] The TBT preamble provides an important context and allows countries to enact regulations to protect animal or plant life or health at the levels it thinks appropriate provided that these measures are "not applied in a manner which would constitute a means of arbitrary or unjustifiable discrimination" or a "disguised restriction on international trade."

The AB supported previous AB decisions that required the Panel to:

> seek to ascertain whether the technical regulation at issue modifies the conditions of competition in the relevant market to the detriment of the group of imported products vis-à-vis the group of like domestic products or like products originating in any other countries.

The AB pointed out that measures which were origin-neutral on their face could nevertheless be de facto inconsistent with Article 2.1. Simply because the measure on its face did not make a distinction based on origin did not mean that it could not alter the conditions of competition between like imported products and products of other countries. A major point that the AB considered was whether the technical regulation was "even-handed." The AB also considered that less favourable treatment could be inferred if the technical regulation was a way for one member to exert pressure on another to modify its practices. The AB found that even if consumers would have made different choices in the absence of the measure, the measure itself did distort the competitions of competition for Mexican products. In assessing whether this distortion had a detrimental impact on Mexican products, the AB approved the Panel's conclusion that the US had not shown that the detrimental impact on Mexican trade stems exclusively from a legitimate regulatory distinction. The AB said that the US had failed to demonstrate that it was even-handed in the relevant respects. The AB then reversed the Panel's decision and found the US labelling system was covered by the TBT Agreement and violated it, because it provided less favourable treatment to Mexican producers, and was inconsistent with Article 2.1 of the TBT Agreement.

The AB also examined the Panel's decision under Article 2.2 of the TBT Agreement (was the measure more restrictive than necessary to fulfil the legitimate objectives pursued by the US). Article 2.2 of the TBT Agreement provides that:

> Members shall ensure that technical regulations are not prepared, adopted or applied with a view to or with the effect of creating unnecessary obstacles to international trade. For this purpose, technical regulations shall not be more trade- restrictive than necessary to fulfil a legitimate objective, taking account of the risks non-fulfilment would create. Such legitimate objectives are, inter alia: national security requirements; the prevention of deceptive practices; protection of human health or safety, animal or plant life or health, or the environment. In assessing such risks, relevant elements of consideration are, inter alia: available scientific and technical information, related processing technology or intended end-uses of products.

The first test was whether the objective was legitimate. Here, the AB reviewed the Panel's conclusion that there was a legitimate objective. Mexico alleged to the AB that the US' objective could not be legitimate because it coerced another WTO member to change its practices to comply with a unilateral policy of the US. But the AB found that this was irrelevant to the issue of whether the objective was itself legitimate.

Article III.4 must be read differently than the TBT Agreement, and the more general prescription of Article III.4 is balanced by the Article XX exceptions. The AB in the Seals case was clear that the concept of legitimate regulatory distinction ("LRD") does not apply to Article I or III, only to the TBT Agreement. As Canada argued in the Seals case, and the AB agreed, the LRD defence to a technical regulation that would otherwise violate Article 2.1 of the TBT Agreement does not apply to Articles I and III of the GATT but that LRD should be read consistently with Article XX of the GATT, and not vice versa.

The Panel had said that it was possible to envisage risks to dolphins that were outside the US mechanism to control risks, and so the US measure was not able to contribute to the protection of dolphins in all cases. In analysing Article 2.2, the AB said that a panel should consider the following factors:

i The degree of contribution made by the measure to the legitimate objective at issue.

ii The trade restrictiveness of the measure.

iii The nature of the risks at issue and the gravity of the consequences that would arise from non-fulfilment of the objective pursued by the Member through the measure.

In most cases, a comparison of the challenged measure and the possible alternative measures should be undertaken. Any alternative measure should be considered in terms of whether it is less trade-restrictive, whether it would make an equivalent contribution to the relevant legitimate objective (taking into account the risks non-fulfilment would create), and whether it is reasonably available. The AB found that allowing the Mexican labelling system to co-exist with the US labelling system would involve no reduction in the protection afforded to dolphins.

d Reliance on Labelling Requirements

Rather than impose legal bans, some countries have investigated using labelling requirements which specific a "safe" product. Since this might also be considered by DEFRA in respect of deforestation initiatives, it is important to point out that any proposed labelling requirements must be analysed under the TBT Agreement also. A mandatory labelling requirement may be deemed to be a technical regulation under Annex 1 of the TBT Agreement.

> It [technical regulation] may also include or deal exclusively with terminology, symbols, packaging, marking or labelling requirements as they apply to a product, process or production method.

In the Tuna II case, the AB found that the US regulations set out a very specific labelling requirement to sell tuna with a "dolphin safe" label. Any other labelling features which did not comport with the US legislation on what specifically constituted how tuna were to be caught in a dolphin safe manner were prohibited. This was deemed by the AB to be a "single and legally mandated set of requirements for making any statement with respect to the broad category for 'dolphin safety'."[44] No claim in respect of dolphin safety was allowed except for the one that was set out in the US laws and regulations. The US measure also provided for specific enforcement mechanisms. In the Tuna case, the US maintained that a labelling requirement could only be a technical regulation if it was mandatory to use that label in order to place a product on the market. Since suppliers could place products on the market (albeit without any dolphin safety label, no matter what dolphin safety provisions they included). The AB rejected this view and said that this did not preclude a finding that a labelling requirement was a technical regulation.

e The Role of International Standards

Under the TBT Agreement, parties can promulgate technical regulations that have a legitimate objective if they are based on international standards (or even international standards that are imminent). The issue is whether the standard is in fact an "international standard." In order to be an international standard, the Tuna II decision laid down some ground rules as to what constitutes an international standard.

Article 2.4 TBT Agreement sets out:

> Where technical regulations are required and relevant international standards exist or their completion is imminent, Members shall use them, or the relevant parts of them, as a basis for their technical regulations except when such international standards or relevant parts would be an ineffective or inappropriate means for the fulfilment of

> the legitimate objectives pursued, for instance because of fundamental climatic or geographical factors or fundamental technological problems.

Annex 1.2 of the TBT Agreement defines a standard as follows:

> Document approved by a recognized body, that provides, for common and repeated use, rules, guidelines or characteristics for products or related processes and production methods, with which compliance is not mandatory. It may also include or deal exclusively with terminology, symbols, packaging, marking or labelling requirements as they apply to a product, process or production method.

In terms of Article 2.4, there is a three-stage analysis which needs to be undertaken as follows:

i the existence or imminent completion of a relevant international standard;
ii whether the international standard has been used as a basis for the technical regulation and
iii whether the international standard is an ineffective or inappropriate means for the fulfilment of the legitimate objectives pursued, taking into account fundamental climatic or geographical factors or fundamental technological problems.

f What is a Relevant International Standard?

The Tuna II case analysed this issue and found that the ISO/IEC Guide 2 that a standard is one "adopted by an international standardizing/standards organisation and made available to the public" was not the final word. It is envisaged that Annex 1 of the TBT Agreement goes beyond the ISO/IEC Guide 2. The relevant standard must emanate from a "body that is based on the membership of other bodies or individuals and has an established constitution and its own administration." Annex 1.2 refers to a "body" not an "organisation," and therefore the AB in Tuna II found that in order to constitute an international standard, it must be adopted by an international standardising body. The international body must have its membership open to at least all Members (Annex 1.5, TBT). The body must have recognised activities in standardisation, which means that WTO members must be aware that the international body in question is engaged in standardisation activities. They must also be open at all stages of the development of a standard to the relevant standardising bodies of at least all WTO members. The determination of whether a body is a recognised standards setting body is determined, according to the AB in Tuna II by "adherence to the six principles set out in the Principles for the Development of International Standards, Guides and Recommendations with Relation to Articles 2, 5 and Annex 3 of the Agreement."[45] The AB found compliance with the six TBT principles enunciated by the TBT Committee in 2000 that were determinative of whether a body was a recognised standardisation body.[46] The six principles relate to transparency, openness, impartiality and consensus, effectiveness and relevance, coherence and development. If a body does not comply with these six principles, that is evidence that the body is not "recognized" by other WTO members as a standardising body.

The AB also said that an international standardising body should not privilege any particular interests in the development of a standard. In Tuna II, the AB found that Mexico's standard setting body was not open to at least all WTO members and so could not be an international standard setting body consistent with the TBT Agreement.

Interconnection with GATT and Its Article XX Exceptions

In the event that the TBT or SPS Agreements do not apply to a particular measure at issue, it may still fall foul of WTO rules if it violates the GATT itself, especially its provisions on MFN (Article I) and National Treatment (Article III). However, it can be defended if it falls into one of the Article XX exemptions.

Article XX contains a list of exceptions to the ordinary MFN and National Treatment provisions of the GATT but makes these exceptions subject to its "chapeau."

Article XX exceptions are as follows (subject to the chapeau below):

> nothing in this Agreement shall be construed to prevent the adoption or enforcement by any contracting party of measures:
>
> *i* *necessary to protect public morals;*
>
> *ii* *necessary to protect human, animal or plant life or health;*
>
> *iii* *relating to the importations or exportations of gold or silver;*
>
> *iv* *necessary to secure compliance with laws or regulations which are not inconsistent with the provisions of this Agreement, including those relating to customs enforcement, the enforcement of monopolies operated under paragraph 4 of Article II and Article XVII, the protection of patents, trademarks and copyrights, and the prevention of deceptive practices;*
>
> *v* *relating to the products of prison labour;*
>
> *vi* *imposed for the protection of national treasures of artistic, historic or archaeological value;*
>
> *vii* *relating to the conservation of exhaustible natural resources if such measures are made effective in conjunction with restrictions on domestic production or consumption;*
>
> *viii* *undertaken in pursuance of obligations under any intergovernmental commodity agreement which conforms to criteria submitted to the* CONTRACTING PARTIES *and not disapproved by them or which is itself so submitted and not so disapproved;**
>
> *ix* *involving restrictions on exports of domestic materials necessary to ensure essential quantities of such materials to a domestic processing industry during periods when the domestic price of such materials is held below the world price as part of a governmental stabilization plan; Provided that such restrictions shall not operate*

> *to increase the exports of or the protection afforded to such domestic industry, and shall not depart from the provisions of this Agreement relating to non-discrimination; (j) essential to the acquisition or distribution of products in general or local short supply; Provided that any such measures shall be consistent with the principle that all contracting parties are entitled to an equitable share of the international supply of such products, and that any such measures, which are inconsistent with the other provisions of the Agreement shall be discontinued as soon as the conditions giving rise to them have ceased to exist. The CONTRACTING PARTIES shall review the need for this sub-paragraph not later than 30 June 1960.*

The chapeau of Article XX provides that:

> Subject to the requirement that such measures are not applied in a manner which would constitute a means of arbitrary or unjustifiable discrimination between countries where the same conditions prevail, or a disguised restriction on international trade, nothing in this Agreement shall be construed to prevent the adoption or enforcement by any Member of measures…

The analysis requires us to first see if a particular measure falls into one of the Article XX exceptions. If it does, then the Panel must determine if that exception is applied in such a way that conforms to the Article XX chapeau. Only if both are satisfied can the measure pass muster under WTO law. In the original Tuna case, the US-Restrictions on Tuna (1991 Panel Report (unadopted), the Panel recalled that:

> previous panels had established that Article XX is a limited and conditional exception from obligations under other provisions of the General Agreement, and not a positive rule establishing obligations in itself.[47] Therefore, the practice of panels has been to interpret Article XX narrowly, to place the burden on the party invoking Article XX to justify its invocation, and not to examine Article XX exceptions unless invoked.[48]

In the Shrimp-Turtle case,[49] the Appellate Body considered the impact of an Article XI violating import ban for shrimp caught without turtle excluder devices. The case turned on whether such an import ban based on the PPM, not the characteristics of the final product (shrimp) was legal under one of the Article XX exceptions. The AB ultimately found it was not because the ban was applied in a manner that violated the chapeau of Article XX and discriminated between like fisherman in Malaysia, India and the Philippines (as opposed to fisherman in the Caribbean who received exceptions, implementation periods and technical assistance). The implication was that if such discrimination did not exist, the ban could have been legal. The AB also found that for the chapeau's test to be met, it was highly relevant to examine the manner in which the particular measures were applied and the fundamental enquiry is whether they are being applied in a manner which suggests an abuse of the exception.

The Shrimp-Turtle case analysed the applicability of Article XX(g) which relates to "exhaustible natural resources." It found that these were not limited to minerals or non-living things as the appellants suggested, but also covered such items as sea turtles and endangered species. The next requirement of the Article XX(g) exception is that the measure must be even-handed (and apply equally to domestic production as well as imports). In then doing the analysis under the chapeau, it is clear that the policy goal of the measure cannot be relevant to the analysis of whether the measure constitutes an unjustified trade restriction in countries where the same conditions apply; otherwise, the chapeau would be meaningless. The AB noted that the exceptions in Article XX were limited and conditional exceptions, and that the purpose of the exceptions and the chapeau was to enable members to be able to rely on an exception, while balancing this against the duty to preserve the rights of other party's under the GATT system itself. But the exceptions should not be regarded as members' rights in the way that other GATT provisions are. Tellingly, the AB reviewing the US regulations said:

> However, it is not acceptable, in international trade relations, for one WTO Member to use an economic embargo to require other Members to adopt essentially the same comprehensive regulatory program, to achieve a certain policy goal, as that in force within that Member's territory, without taking into consideration different conditions which may occur in the territories of those other Members.

Another important element in discussing whether the application of the measure violated the chapeau's injunction against arbitrary or unjustifiable trade restrictions was to what extent the member seeking to rely on the exception had engaged other WTO members in negotiations related to the measure. In the Shrimp-Turtle case, the US had not so engaged with other members and this counted against it. The AB cited approvingly Principle 12 of the Rio Declaration on Environment and Development which stated:

> Unilateral actions to deal with environmental challenges outside the jurisdiction of the importing country should be avoided. Environmental measures addressing transboundary or global environmental problems should, as far as possible, be based on international consensus (emphasis added).

In almost identical language, paragraph 2.22(i) of Agenda 21 provides:

> Governments should encourage GATT, UNCTAD and other relevant international and regional economic institutions to examine, in accordance with their respective mandates and competences, the following propositions and principles:
>
> … (i) Avoid unilateral action to deal with environmental challenges outside the jurisdiction of the importing country. Environmental measures

addressing transborder problems should, as far as possible, be based on an international consensus (emphasis added).

Other environmental agreements also strongly push the idea of cooperation among nations to resolve global problems and seek to avoid unilateral actions. The CPTPP language cited to it at the beginning of this comment is designed to adopt a joint as opposed to a unilateral approach. Where parties engage in unilateral actions, WTO Panels will enquire as to whether there was a reasonable alternative action that would have been more cooperative. The need for an alternative is greatest where there is an import prohibition which is deemed to be the "heaviest weapon" in a country's "armoury of trade measures."[50]

(a) Reliance on the Public Morals Exemption

The UK has considered using GATT exemptions in order to support unilateral domestic policies in the areas of deforestation and animal welfare. It is therefore important to consider how the relevant GATT exemption (Article XX(a)) has been used in the past and how it can be used in the future. It is also important to understand the limitations on the GATT exemptions and the wider context in which they can be deployed.

Both in the case of animal welfare, and in the case of deforestation, an argument has been made that these could be based on the WTO's public morals exemption. The public morals exemption has been rarely tested.

The leading case on the public morals exception is the Seals case.[51] As noted above, the case related to the ban on importation of seal products in the EU, which was subject to certain exceptions for Inuit communities in Greenland, and travellers. Having found that the measure was not within the scope of the TBT Agreement as it was not a technical regulation, defence of the measure relied on citing to the Article XX(a) exemption in the GATT.

At issue in the case was the question of whether a public morals defence had to be the sole objective of the legislation, and what was the precise role of other objectives that might be inconsistent with the public morals objection (as was the case for Inuit and traveller exceptions which can hardly be consistent with the seal welfare argument). This is an important issue otherwise the public morals exemption could allow any regulatory barriers to trade as long as it could be said that there was some public morals aspect to the legislation or regulation. In the case, the AB agreed with the Panel that the EU had a single public morals objective which led to a regulation the effect of which it mitigated on certain communities who it also had an interest in. Article XX(a) also specifically says that the measure must be necessary to protect public morals (therefore must be proportionate). As we have noted, Article XX(a) requires a two-tier analysis where a measure is first reviewed to see if it was necessary and then a separate enquiry is made into whether the measure satisfies the chapeau of Article XX, i.e.

> Subject to the requirement that such measures are not applied in a manner which would constitute a means of arbitrary or unjustifiable discrimination between countries where the same conditions prevail, or a disguised restriction on international trade, nothing in this Agreement shall be construed to prevent the adoption or enforcement by any Member of measures...

This will be relevant to any measure a WTO member might apply in this area – the rule cannot apply differentially as between trading partners where the same conditions prevail. There must be a sufficient nexus between the measure and the public morals being protected, and the particular measure must actually make a contribution to the public morals objective that is being claimed.

The debate in the UK, the EU and the US about animal welfare and pathogen reduction treatments (PRTs) is instructive for any attempt to rely on GATT Article XX exemptions. In the case of animal welfare and PRTs, there is a question as to whether the purpose of PRTs is to protect human health or to allow animals to be mistreated (and then the resultant diseases to be eradicated by PRTs). It is highly relevant here that the US requires PRTs for any import of products for human health reasons, and that PRTs are demonstrably proved to be helpful in combatting campylobacter and other food-borne pathogens. In the animal welfare debate, there is a danger that food hygiene issues and animal welfare issues become conflated. Regarding food hygiene issues, given that incidence of food-borne disease is much higher in the EU than it is in the US, it is likely that any barrier the US might erect to the UK products based on the fact that they are *not* treated with PRTs would be based on the SPS Agreement. There would then be two competing objectives that would have to be considered in the analysis, the food hygiene issues where PRTs protect human health and the separate animal welfare issue.

As noted in a recent piece for CAPX:

> As for food-borne pathogens, incidents of Campylobacter and Salmonella are much higher in the EU than in the US despite the fact that the US consumer eats twice as much poultry as the average EU citizen per capita. Whereas 20 cases of campylobacter are diagnosed each year in the US per 100,000 people, 94.8 cases per 100,000 people are diagnosed in the UK. The reason why the US requires pathogen reduction treatments is not, as the conventional wisdom in the UK goes, because they want to mistreat animals, but rather because they want to keep people safe, and they do a much better job of it than the UK.
>
> In any event, these same chlorine rinses are already used in this country in salads, fish and our drinking water. The real reason it is not used for poultry has nothing to do with safety and everything to

> do with keeping out US imports. In any case, about 90% of American poultry is washed not in chlorine, but in peracetic acid (which is more like vinegar), which was certified by the European Food Safety Agency as safe more than five years ago. Nor is this brand of protectionism anything new – the poultry wars of the 1960s were a direct result of French and German protectionism against American chicken...[52]

With respect to the quite separate animal welfare issue, the question would be whether the ban on PRTs actually contributes to the goal of protecting animal welfare, and whether the ban satisfies the chapeau of Article XX. Even though the science on animal welfare is less "hard" than that developed regarding human health and food hygiene, there is still a requirement for some scientific basis for any proposed ban. The question is what is the animal welfare issue that must be considered. If it is a concern about stocking density (for example, where the allegation is that chickens are kept in crowded conditions leading to disease), then the actual stocking densities in different markets are important (see Box 2). Box 2 considers the different packing densities as between the UK and the US.

The UK maximum packing density for chickens is 39 kg/square metre.

US maximum densities depend on the size of the bird and range from 6.5 lbs (2.948 kg) per square foot for smaller birds to 9 lbs (4.08 kg) per square foot for larger birds, thus:

the US maximum packing density ranges between **31.7 kg/square metre** to **43.9 kg/square metre**.

US maximum densities are thus somewhat stricter than the UK (7 kg below the UK limits) for younger birds and a little less than 5 kg above the UK limits for larger birds.

https://www.nationalchickencouncil.org/about-ncc/overview/

The National Chicken Council (NCC) member companies include chicken producer/processors, poultry distributors and allied industry firms, accounting for approximately 95% of the chickens produced in the US.

https://www.nationalchickencouncil.org/wp-content/uploads/2021/02/NCC-Animal-Welfare-Guidelines_Broilers_Sept2020.pdf#:~:text=The%20NCC%20Animal%20Welfare%20Guidelines%20have%20been%20developed,types%20of%20poultry%20as%20management%20practices%20may%20differ.NATIONAL CHICKEN COUNCIL ANIMAL WELFARE GUIDELINES AND AUDIT CHECKLIST FOR BROILERS

US Flock Husbandry Guidelines

i Birds should have space to express normal behaviours such as dust bathing, preening, eating, drinking, etc. Upon entering a broiler house, most of the birds should be sitting and relatively quiet, with background chirping or clucking. Evaluated flock husbandry practices, including, but not limited to, stocking density, lighting and gait scoring, are important to assess normal behaviour.

ii Stocking density must allow all birds to access feeders and drinkers, and will depend on the target market weight, type of housing, ventilation system, feeder/drinker equipment, litter management and husbandry. Stocking density is typically determined at the end of the flock based on target market weight, by adjusting the initial placement numbers with the average mortality and must not exceed the following:

Maximum Bird Weight Range	***Maximum Stocking Density***
Below 4.5 lbs liveweight	6.5 lbs per square foot
4.5–5.5 lbs liveweight	7.5 lbs per square foot
5.6–7 lbs liveweight	8.5 lbs per square foot
More than 7 lbs liveweight	9 lbs per square foot

No Broiler chickens are raised in cages: https://www.chickencheck.in/farm-to-table/are- broiler-chickens-raised-in-cages/

UK: https://www.gov.uk/government/publications/poultry-on-farm-welfare/broiler-meat- chickens-welfare-recommendations

Stocking density in UK

If you have 500 or more conventionally reared meat chickens on your holding you can stock birds at up to 33 kg per square metre. You can increase this up to 39 kg birds per square metre but there are extra requirements.

When stocking above 33 kg per square metre, you must keep documents in the housing with technical details and information on equipment, including:

- a plan that shows the dimensions of the surfaces the chickens occupy
- a ventilation plan and target air quality levels (including airflow, air speed and temperature) and details of cooling and heating systems and their location
- the location and nature of feeding and watering systems (e.g. automatic or manual, how many feeders and how each is operated)
- alarm and backup systems if any equipment essential for the chickens' health and well-being fails
- floor type and litter normally used
- records of technical inspections of the ventilation and alarm systems
- if you plan to stock above 33 kg per square metre you must tell the Animal and Plant Health Agency (APHA) and state what your planned stocking density is.

You must give at least 15 working days' notice before changing the stocking density.

What other countries do will also be relevant. Here since the UK admits poultry from Poland and other EU member states which have higher stocking densities than the UK or the US, (sometimes as high as 43 kg/m^2), a ban on PRT-treated product will be seen as not passing muster under the chapeau, as it is not even-handed. For it to be satisfactory, it will be at least necessary to ban product coming from EU member states as well as from other countries. The UK would have to additionally prove that the ban actually contributed to the objective of improving animal welfare. The animal welfare/PRT issue highlights how difficult the complexities involved are when a WTO member seeks to rely on Article XX exemptions

Approach to EU Timber Regulation

Another analogous measure to the one being contemplated by the UK government is the EU's Timber Regulation ("EUTR"). The EUTR requires timber importers, inter alia, to assess the risk that their imports contained illegally produced commodities. Conditioning entry into the UK market solely on whether products were produced and harvested legally raises similar issues under the WTO Agreement as discussed herein. One of the fundamental problems with such an approach is that it imposes penalties or barriers that are based on the legality of a method under which the commodities were produced, and has little to do with the "environmental friendliness" of the production. So, the same commodity from two different countries could be produced in exactly the same way, but because their domestic laws are different, one might be considered legal for import, and the other illegal. Because such a law does not specify product characteristics, nor process and production methods, it will likely not be a technical regulation under the TBT Agreement. It could therefore be considered to result in arbitrary or unjustifiable discrimination between the like products from different countries. This could not be justified under the GATT Article I:1 or Article III, if the measure creates an advantage for products from some countries, unless it is saved by one of the Article XX exemptions we refer to. The EUTR has not been challenged by another WTO member yet. The EU has been careful to consult with large timber exporting countries to mitigate this possibility. However, that does not mean that a challenge would not be successful.[53]

In the Seals case, Canada sought to bring an argument that there had to be an identifiable risk to public morals that the measure was protecting (and was a proportionate response). Canada also claimed that the EU had to show that this public moral risk was consistent with the EU's risk appetite in similar cases (i.e. wildlife hunts and animal conditions in abattoirs). The argument was that the EU tolerated this risk in other areas. These arguments were rejected by the AB noting that it was up to members to determine how to develop measures to deal with specific public morals issues. The degree of trade restrictiveness of the measure is relevant to the consideration of whether it was necessary.

The AB cited to the Brazil-Retreaded Tyres case[54] and noted that:

> In Brazil – Retreaded Tyres, the Appellate Body identified certain principles in evaluating the contribution of a measure in the context of a necessity analysis under Article XX: The selection of a methodology to assess a measure's contribution is a function of the nature of the risk, the objective pursued, and the level of protection sought. It ultimately also depends on the nature, quantity, and quality of evidence existing at the time the analysis is made.
>
> Because the Panel, as the trier of the facts, is in a position to evaluate these circumstances, it should enjoy a certain latitude in designing the appropriate methodology to use and deciding how to structure or organize the analysis of the contribution of the measure at issue to the realization of the ends pursued by it. This latitude is not, however, boundless. Indeed, a panel must analyse the contribution of the measure at issue to the realization of the ends pursued.

Canada had argued that it was important to assess the contribution of the measure to the satisfaction of the public morals objective. The AB in the Seals case did find that material contribution was one (but certainly not the only factor) which was relevant in a necessity analysis, but there was no specific standard of materiality which the Panel had to apply.

In the Seals case, the AB did enquire into the evidence considered by the Panel about whether the measure actually achieved the public morals objective stated (and did not take a position, since this was an issue of fact on which the Panel had decided based on the evidence before it).

In assessing the measure, the Panel in the Seals case had also assessed whether a reasonable alternative method was available. Considering this the AB said that it is legitimate for panels to examine alternative measures presented by other parties, and to bear in mind that the contours of alternative measures were affected by the non-specific nature of the public morals concerns in the first place. In the Seals case, a certification system was considered but the complexities of monitoring and compliance were found to be problematic. The AB concluded that the certification system would be beset by difficulties (whether it was stringent or more relaxed) and therefore could not be said to be a viable alternative.

The AB emphasised that the analysis of the Article XX exemptions is a two-stage analysis. The second stage is to apply the chapeau, specifically stating:

> The function of the chapeau of Article XX of the GATT 1994 is to prevent the abuse or misuse of a Member's right to invoke the exceptions contained in the subparagraphs of that Article.1497 In that way, the chapeau operates to preserve the balance between a Member's right to invoke the exceptions of Article XX, and the rights of other

> Members to be protected from conduct proscribed under the GATT 1994. Achieving this equilibrium is called for "so that neither of the competing rights will cancel out the other and thereby distort and nullify or impair the balance of rights and obligations constructed by the Members themselves". As the Appellate Body stated in US – Gasoline, the burden of demonstrating that a measure provisionally justified under one of the exceptions of Article XX does not constitute an abuse of such an exception under the chapeau rests with the party invoking the exception. The Appellate Body explained that this is "a heavier task than that involved in showing that an exception ... encompasses the measure at issue.

The chapeau specifically refers to ensuring that the exceptions are not used to ground arbitrary or unjustifiable restrictions on trade which must mean something more than the Article I and III provisions. The chapeau refers to whether the conditions in other countries also apply – in other words, if the standard applies to one country but not others where the same conditions apply, there will be a problem. We submit that a relevant question would be is there a negative impact on the competitive opportunities between other members. In the case of an animal welfare rule that discriminated between the US and the EU, where stocking densities were found to be the same or similar would almost certainly violate these principles. It should be noted that the justification for such measures is handled very differently in the TBT Agreement than in the chapeau of Article XX. In the TBT Agreement, the measure can be justified by legitimate regulatory distinctions (according to the AB in US-Tuna II). In the chapeau, the test is to balance a member's right to rely on these exceptions and the interests of other GATT members which should not be nullified or impaired by the reliance on the exception.

The AB concluded that the EU seal ban was covered by Article XX(a) but violated the chapeau of Article XX. This was because it discriminated between similar conditions which prevailed in Inuit communities in Canada and Greenland (the Inuits in Greenland benefiting from an exception to the rule, whereas the Inuits in Canada could not so benefit because the exception had been specifically written for the Greenland Inuits. This was similar (though not legally identical) to the finding in Tuna II.

Economic Considerations of Equivalence and International Consensus Building

There is another important element why an equivalence/recognition approach based on developing an international consensus which emerges as an international standard is preferable to a unilateral approach. There is a significant economic benefit to regulatory competition because it is through the give and take of managing regulatory competition (and different ideas that countries have about how to solve big emerging problems) that we are more likely to reach the goals enshrined in Good Regulatory Practice (GRP). These are, broadly speaking to regulate in a way that is least restrictive of trade and least damaging to overall market competition, consistent with a legitimate, publicly stated regulatory goal. It is through this process, clunky and frustratingly slow as it may appear to some, that the legitimate expectations of all WTO members, including developing countries, can be frustrated as little as possible. This is precisely why unilateral action is eschewed. The net result of such a cooperative approach is to maximise the overall potential for wealth creation across the whole of the global economy, ensuring that poverty can be alleviated in as comprehensive a manner as possible.

Specific application of international trade rules in the case of deforestation; potential trade- consistent approaches

The UK and the EU have deforestation initiatives under way which could have WTO implications. It is likely that any document which relates to production methods with which compliance is mandatory may count as a technical regulation to which the TBT Agreement applies. The particular technical regulation must then pass muster under the TBT Agreement (see, for example, US-Tuna II case). If the labelling requirement is such that it can only be satisfied by adherence to the UK legislation or regulation, then the labelling requirement will be a technical regulation to which the TBT Agreement also applies.

a TBT Analysis

Article 2.1 of the TBT Agreement provides that members must enact technical regulation that is no less favourable to the products of other WTO members and like domestic products, and like products from other countries (which means being placed at a disadvantage). All forestry products from all WTO members would have to be treated the same way even where there is no advantage being given to domestic producers as would be the case for the forestry regulation. The issue is that the regulation should not alter the conditions of competition of like products as between domestic producer and foreign producer as well as like products from other WTO members, and it would be difficult to craft a unilateral measure that achieves this given that the nature of production varies considerably around the world. A measure that is deemed to be an attempt by one member to force another to modify its practices would be especially vulnerable under Article 2.1 of the TBT Agreement. Under Article 2.2 of the TBT Agreement, the measure would have to have a legitimate objective as set out in Article 2.2. Protecting the environment is one such category (note that animal welfare often discussed in the UK context is not). The requirements for non-discrimination and even- handedness as well as a rigorous review of potential alternatives is also required under Article 2.2.

In the alternative, if the UK were to approach this issue by setting up a labelling mechanism to indicate where products were "Deforestation Safe" in an analogous manner to tuna products that were "Dolphin Safe," this would not insulate the labelling mechanism from WTO challenge. As was noted in the Tuna II case, the UK would have to ensure that it was being even-handed in its regulatory approach and was not discriminating against a particular group of countries. Given the potentially unbalanced application of this labelling requirement to certain WTO members, for example, forestry product producers in developing countries close to the equator, it would be difficult for the UK's scheme to pass muster under the TBT Agreement.

International standards play an important role here as well. This is because once an international standard is imminent, then it is permissible for a party to pass a technical regulation based on that standard and for it to pass muster under the TBT Agreement. However, the caveat is that the standard must be truly international, in other words it must be set by a recognised body that is normally engaged in standard setting processes. So the UK could not invent or create a standard setting body as this would fall foul of the rules set out in Tuna II on what are appropriate international standards. Such a standard setting body must be truly open to at least all WTO members and must be recognised by them (which it cannot be unless it satisfies the six TBT principles set out in the TBT Committee Decision (2000)).

b GATT Analysis

If a regulation is found not to be covered by the SPS or TBT Agreements, it could still violate GATT Article I (MFN) and III (non-discrimination). The regulating Party would have to rely on a GATT exception (if the applicable law is outside the scope of the TBT Agreement).

This will have significant application for environmental initiatives that are outside the scope of the TBT Agreement because they do not relate to product characteristics. In this case, there are two potentially applicable exceptions, Article XX(a) (public morals) and Article XX(g) (conservation of exhaustible natural resources). In both cases, any panel reviewing a challenge to this regulation would look to see whether the UK was relying on this in a limited and conditional manner, and whether the measure was truly necessary. In performing the necessity analysis, the Panel would look at the methodology laid out in the Brazil-Retreaded Tyres case under which the following factors would be considered:

i Nature of the risk
ii Objective pursued
iii Level of protection sought

The question of whether the measure actually contributed to the goal would be an important consideration, especially in the comparison of alternative measures. Here, it is extremely relevant that unilateral action by the UK would not contribute to the goal of a reduction in deforestation if it was not followed by other countries, or worse, if other countries rejected the unilateral approach and this compromised more international, consensus-based methods.

These exceptions would be subject to the chapeau of Article XX, and the UK would have to be able to show that it was acting in an even-handed manner, and the regulations were not being applied in a manner that was an arbitrary or unjustified restriction on trade. In satisfying the Chapeau obligations, the UK would have to show it had consulted with the WTO members affected by its ban (in a manner that the US had failed to do in the Shrimp-Turtle case) and sought to reach a negotiated solution. If the suggestion is a unilateral ban, then the UK would have to be guided by the language of the Appellate Body which stated:

> However, it is not acceptable, in international trade relations, for one WTO Member to use an economic embargo to require other Members to adopt essentially the same comprehensive regulatory program, to achieve a certain policy goal, as that in force within that Member's territory, without taking into consideration different conditions which may occur in the territories of those other Members.

Given that an import ban is the most devastating in the armoury of trade restrictions, any future Panel would look at what alternative measures were available to the UK, either through negotiated agreement or international standards. They would also look at Principle 12 of the Rio Declaration which sets out that unilateral solutions to global environmental problems should be avoided.

The WTO and Trade Facilitation

Trade facilitations and customs processes are often the stepchild in international trade law and economics terms. Trade professionals immerse themselves in the details of border barriers and behind the border barriers, neglecting that much of the economic benefit that is realisable and which the economic models set out in Chapter 4 show us is significant arises from trade facilitation. It is also the one area in the last 28 years where the WTO has made reasonable progress.

Introduction to Trade Facilitation

The SRB economic model reveals one counterintuitive point which is that within the international trade pillar, trade facilitation is a bigger contributor to economic development than traditional market access issues such as tariffs. This means that an emphasis on how trade can be facilitated and how borders can be made more efficient is an essential part of the way a country can develop economically.

There has been some emphasis in the WTO on trade facilitation recently (in the absence of anything more substantive), but these WTO Trade Facilitation provisions are most useful for countries that have very poor border management systems. It will make little or no difference to countries that are more advanced.

This is not say that there advanced, developed countries cannot improve border management systems. They can. This is also not limited to goods but the provision of services does also require efficient border management systems for people also.

There are a number of key areas which need to be singled out for special attention.

The Border Is a Series of Transactions

The modern-day border is no longer just a line on a map for the movement of goods and people, but instead a series of transactions which can occur away from the physical border. The days of a customs official in a tri-cornered hat testing the brandy as it passed by are over. Modern customs processes must catch up to the reality of 21st-century trade. The more physical checks and controls are limited in intensity based on risking the more trade will flow. Increasingly, the focus is on the traders that buy and sell goods not the goods themselves. For people, the more we know about the traveller, the more easily can their border crossing be made. The idea is to ensure that traders and people that are verified or trusted can flow easily across borders while processes are reserved for the unknown traders or people who present much higher degrees of risk.

Single Window

The single window (SW) is often regarded as the holy grail of customs and trade administration. Under an SW, traders should have to provide relevant data to government officials only once. The SW should then be able to ensure that all the relevant government departments and agencies are able to receive data relevant to their processes so that goods can flow freely across the border. While there are no doubt barriers between different government departments because of different government systems and the like, often the biggest barriers to cooperation are the turf battles between departments and the desire by certain departments to protect their territory. It is of course valid that different government departments have different equities in border management as they do in other aspects of trade and competition, and there does need to be a forum for allowing those equities to be balanced, this should not impede the ability of the government as a whole to ingest data from traders in a manner most efficient for the trader so that free flow of goods can be preserved.

Trusted Trader Schemes

One way that trust can be used to simplify the flow of goods is through trusted trader schemes. The concept behind trusted trader schemes is that depending on the level of trust that the government has in the trader, based on evidence about the trader, greater levels of customs simplifications can be granted. In order to access customs simplifications, the trader needs to demonstrate that they have the human resources department, finance department and overall view of their supply chains which would justify not requiring them to make a customs declaration (for example) every time one of their goods crosses a border. There are many potential simplifications which can make life easier for a trader. Some simplifications include:

Periodic Declarations

Trusted traders might be able to make declarations on a period basis as opposed to each time a good crosses a border. By aggregating the declarations by quarter or even longer, the customs declaration has been moved from a transaction-based system to something that looks more like a tax return.

Simplified Frontier Declarations

A simple declaration with a much reduced data requirement could be made. There are many such simplifications possible. Under the EU and UK systems, an authorised trader can do a very straightforward simplified frontier declaration with no need for import commodity codes and other data, limited to goods descriptions and volumes, subject to doing a supplementary (final) declaration within four days of the month following the month of the movement. Even the supplementary declaration could benefit from a reduced set of data fields necessary for the supplementary declaration.

Aggregation and Bulking

Many traders move a large number of consignments in one truck or container and these would ordinarily attract the requirement for a declaration for each consignment in the load. Aggregation and bulking allow loads to be consolidated in certain circumstances and this provides a significant simplification for trusted traders.

Many of the above simplifications are already part of most countries' laws. In the EU, the Union Customs Code expressly allows these simplifications, as does the US Customs law. However there are a range of other simplifications and easements which would not only simplify the process but also would follow the grain of treating the border as a series of transactions and not just a line on a map. These include moving checks and controls away from the border. Provided there is security so that goods can be shown to be under customs control between the check and the physical border, in facility checks in particular for regulatory controls such as those for SPS rules should be possible away from the border. Some very advanced customs agencies such as the Dutch do allow mobile inspections in certain cases. In particular, the Dutch customs authorities allow authorised consignee locations for the purposes of closing transit journeys to be deemed at a location which the trader or haulier can call in after the transit journey has started. This is possible because the Dutch have mobile transit inspection units so interventions can be made. This allows a very easy transit journey where the haulier can simply go to the place where the goods are to be delivered and close the transit journey there (with any physical inspection if necessary being made at that place).

A systems-based approach to customs will inevitably be required with the rise in e-commerce trade which has been exponentially increasing even before the COVID-19 pandemic. The volume of customs declarations required for this trade is also exponentially increasing with the Dutch Agency reporting it was expecting an increase from 250 m declarations in 2018 to 800 m in 2021. Ordinary goods-based customs declarations systems cannot survive such an increase without curbing the flow of this vital trade.

Facilitating Trade through Increased Use of Special Economic Zones/Prosperity Zones

The last 30 years or so has seen a market increase in the number of free trade zones, special economic zones, freeports and other zones where customs and trade facilitations, and some regulatory easements are applied. As tariffs have been reduced over time, an increasing amount of trade is intra-company as opposed to inter-company trade. This means that it is global supply chains that compete with each other and there is a premium on efficiency. Increasingly, we are seeing the development of these special economic zones which we have termed Prosperity Zones to function as nodes on global supply chains.[55] Global capital ever more desperate for cost reductions is seeking these nodes as places where customs and trade facilitations as well as regulatory easements deliver a better operating environment. We are also seeing the development of specific trade corridors emerging between nodes on this supply chain. Karlsson, Singham, and Gottschald's article in the World Customs Journal outlines how these developments are necessary to power international trade as we emerge out of the COVID-19 pandemic.[56]

Modern special economic zones sit on a spectrum from a more basic free trade zone on one end of the spectrum to an advanced Prosperity Zone with customs, trade and regulatory simplifications on the other. There are some 5,000 different zones of one type or the other in about 140 countries worldwide at the moment. Freeports were originally established over 200 years ago, and an argument can be made that the old Hanseatic League consisted of a number of "freeports" such as Hamburg which are even older. The idea of a zone or subnational entity having a different set of laws from the surrounding country is not new either. Indeed, the ancient privileges of the City of London Corporation date back well before Magna Carta in 1215, and even before the Norman conquest of Britain in

1066, as William the Conqueror had to accept the ancient privileges of the City of London written into the City of London charter, a document now lost in the mists of time, but certainly referred to for a 1,000 years or more.

In more recent years, the freeport concept consisted of a free trade zone with tariff benefits as the main benefit. Goods could enter the free trade zone and not pay a tariff, but could be processed into other goods which could then enter into free circulation (and pay the tariff for the finished product) or be exported to other markets. This tariff advantage underpinned many free trade zones such as the maquiladoras in Mexico which produced primarily textile products. Then, recognising that customs process simplifications constituted a significant benefit for traders, more customs simplifications were introduced. These included simplifying the data that needs to be included for customs declarations and simplifying the frequency of such customs declarations. However to do this, a level of trust is required, and it is possible for the freezone operators themselves to benefit from this level of trust, such as the World Customs Organization (WCO) Authorised Economic Operator (AEO) programme.

Concerns began to be raised by customs agencies around the world and government departments that they did not have high visibility into what was being traded inside these free trade zones. As a result, the OECD Clean Zone programme was initiated in order to address these issues.[57] There was also concern expressed by governments about the potential for violations of intellectual property inside free zones, and this issue has been dealt with by the OECD and the European Observatory on Infringements of Intellectual Property Rights among others.[58] Other government departments grew concerned about illicit flows of funds into these zones and whether they would become sites for money laundering. These risks have been identified by the Financial Action Task Force (FATF).[59] The WCO has developed its SAFE framework partly in response to these concerns.[60] The OECD's Clean Zone programme is a partial response to the concerns expressed.[61] Other private sector organisations have come up with their own assurance schemes such as the World Free Zone Organization Safe Zone certification programme.[62]

Many modern free trade zones apply these mechanisms to prove that they are clean and safe. These support the many simplifications in customs and trade processes. But there is another element of modern special economic zones which can make a big difference to the amount of economic activity which can be created in them, and the decision of global capital to invest. These are regulatory easements. Some of the most advanced special economic zones, which Karlsson, Singham and Gottschald have called Prosperity Zones, are that they allow different rules to apply inside the zone from the national regulations. Examples include Panama Pacific which has different immigration rules from the rest of Panama to capitalise on its position as a financial services hub. The Special Economic Zone in Duqm, Oman makes a number of changes to domestic law which apply only in the zone. These include a change to the domestic Omanisation requirement of 35% (which drops to 10% in the zone) as well as the suspension of the law that provides significant protection to local distributors of foreign products which has been a long-standing trade irritant. The significance of these two changes is that they constitute very important domestic legal changes which would be almost impossible to achieve on a national basis because of the power of vested interest groups that benefit from the status quo, but which nevertheless damage competition and trade. The Prosperity Zone hence becomes an alternative delivery mechanism for regulatory reform (and could be a laboratory for seeing how regulatory reform can deliver economic growth).

The UK, leaving the EU, has announced an important freeport programme which could take advantage of these changes as well as serving as a test bed for its regulatory reform agenda. In order for the freeport programme to be effective in delivering its goals, it will be necessary for it to encompass the highest levels of customs and trade facilitations as well as relevant regulatory easements.

Economic Impact of Customs and Trade Facilitations

As we have noted in Chapter 4, trade facilitations have a tendency to have a disproportionate effect on economic growth in the overall trade liberalisation pillar of the SRB economic model. Hence agreeing maximal trade facilitations is crucial for the freeport. In order to secure these, we would expect freeport operators to satisfy the following criteria:

1. Compliance with revised Kyoto Convention.
2. Certification under an internationally recognised compliance programme. This includes AEO, WFZO Safe Zone, OECD Clean Zone and so on.
3. Fully electronic operating environment.
4. Integration with customs to ensure on-site customs presence, data sharing, and in general ensuring that customs offices have visibility of goods in movement.
5. Integration with customs to ensure on-site customs presence, data sharing and in general ensuring that customs offices have visibility of goods in movement.
6. Fully electronic SW.
7. Mutual recognition of trusted trader and other applicable provisions by to ensure the full development of trade superhighways.

Clearly, it needs to be clear that these zones do not operate above or outside the law. They will continue to apply criminal law (including for fraud and financial fraud), intellectual property law (unless the Prosperity Zone applies an intellectual property law that is more protective of property rights than national law) and are only outside the customs territory in which they are hosted for tariff and some economic regulation purposes.

The GATT Regime and Competition Policy: An Emerging Trend?

There has traditionally been notable opposition to discussing competition policy within the framework of the WTO. However, there are a number of cases where WTO jurisprudence has already started to reflect formative competition analysis.

We have discussed some of the cases above where competition principles have aided interpretation of WTO rules. The important point to emerge out of the analysis of Article III is the notion of the "equality of competitive opportunity." At least as it applies to Article III cases, this has meant that producers should have equality of competitive opportunity. This test is not without innate difficulty as it could lead to the disciplining of behaviour where there is no impact on consumer welfare at all. This could become a tool to promote competitor welfare at the expense of global consumers unless it is carefully applied. If we recall the discussion on the development of competition policy in the US and the EU, we saw the debate that raged for over 75 years in the case of the US between those who advocated competitor welfare and those who advocated for competitor welfare. Although this debate has largely been settled in the case of antitrust and competition at least in the economic literature if not in very recent US pronouncements, it is far from settled among practitioners in the trade area. The same area where competition concepts can spread values into the trade world that will help trade liberalisation deliver benefits to consumers. We will now look at some of the newer areas of jurisprudence where these issues have been considered also. We will examine State Trading Enterprises more specifically in the subsequent chapters.

Notes

1 *Report of the Appellate Body* on *Turkey – Restrictions on Imports of Textile and Clothing Product,* AB-1999-5, WT/DS34/AB/R (99-4546), World Trade Organization (22 October 1999), at para. 48.

2 For a global perspective on how the provision has been understood and applied within existing Rats, *see Liberalisation Process and Transitional Provisions in Regional Trade Agreements,* WT/REG/W/46 (02-1776), World Trade Organization (5 April 2002). Recent submissions within current negotiations within the Negotiation Group on Rules are the documents entitled: *Submission on Regional Trade Agreements – Australia,* TN/RL/W/15 (02-3820), World Trade Organization (9 July 2002) and *Submission on Regional Trade Agreements – Turkey,* TN/RL/W/32 (02-6502), World Trade Organization (25 November 2002), para 4.

3 World Trade Organisation, "Regional Trade Agreements: Facts and Figures," www.wto.org/english/tratop_e/region_e/regfac_e.htm (last visited May 2004).

4 Organisation for Economic Cooperation and Development (OECD), *Regional Trade Agreements and the Multilateral Trading System* (Rohini Acharya ed., OECD 2002), p. 12.

5 *Report of the Appellate Body* on *European Communities – Conditions For The Granting Of Tariff Preferences To Developing Countries,* AB-2004-1, WT/DS246/AB/R (04-1556), World Trade Organization (7 April 2004).

6 *Report of the Panel* on *European Communities – Conditions For The Granting Of Tariff Preferences To Developing Countries,* WT/DS246/R (03-6284), World Trade Organization (1 December 2003).

7 *Report of the Appellate Body*, *supra* note 5, paras. 160 *et seq.*
8 Council Regulation 2501/2001 *applying a scheme of generalised tariff preferences for the period from 1 January 2002 to 31 December 2004*, 2001 O.J. (L 346) (EC), at 1; extended for an additional year until 31 December 2005, by Council Regulation 2211/2003, 2003 O.J. (L 332), at 1.
9 *Report of the Panel* on *Canada - Administration of the Foreign Investment Review Act (FIRA)*, L/5504 - 30S/140, World Trade Organization (7 Feb 1984), para. 4.4.
10 *Report of the Panel* on *EEC - Regulation on Imports of Parts and Components*, L/6657 - 37S/132, World Trade Organization (16 May 1990), para. 5.21.
11 *Report of the Panel* on *Japan - Measures Affecting Consumer Photographic Film and Paper*, WT/DS44/R (98-0886), World Trade Organization (31 Mar 1998).
12 *Report of the Panel* on *United States - Section 337 of the Tariff Act of 1930*, L/6439 - 36S/345, World Trade Organization (7 Nov 1989).
13 *Report of the Panel* on *Italian Discrimination Against Imported Agricultural Machinery*, L/833 - 7S/60, World Trade Organization (23 Oct. 1958), para. 12.
14 *Appellate Body Reports* on *Japan – Taxes on Alcoholic Beverages*, AB-1996-2, WT/DS8/AB/R, WT/DS10/AB/R, WT/DS11/AB/R (96-3951), World Trade Organization (4 October 1996); *Report of the Panel* on *Japan – Taxes on Alcoholic Beverages*, WT/DS8/R, WT/DS10/R, WT/DS11/R (96-2651), World Trade Organization (11 Jul 1996).
15 The WCO harmonised system is at the six-digit level but countries classify products up to ten digits with additional product codes to reflect whether certain products are restricted or controlled. Only the WCO harmonised tariffs are implicated here.
16 *Appellate Body Report* on *Korea – Taxes on Alcoholic Beverages,* AB-1998-7, WT/DS75/AB/R, WT/DS84/AB/R (99-0100) World Trade Organization (18 Jan 1999); *Report of the Panel* in *Korea – Taxes on Alcoholic Beverages*, WT/DS75/R, WT/DS84/R (98-3471), World Trade Organization (17 Sep 1998).
17 *Id.* para 118.
18 *Report of the Panel* on *United States - Measures Affecting Alcoholic and Malt Beverages,* DS23/R - 39S/206, World Trade Organization (19 Jun 1992).
19 *Report of the Panel* on *Canada – Measures Relating to Exports of Wheat and Treatment of Imported Grain,* WT/DS276/R (04-1443), World Trade Organization (6 Apr 2004); appears on appeal as *Report of the Appellate body* on *Canada – Measures Relating to Exports of Wheat and Treatment of Imported Grain*, AB-2004-3, WT/DS276/AB/R (04-3592), World Trade Organization (2004).
20 *Report of the Panel* on *United States - Taxes On Petroleum and Certain Imported Substances*, L/6175 - 34S/136, World Trade Organization (17 Jun 1987).
21 *Report of the Panel* on *Chile - Taxes on Alcoholic Beverages*, WT/DS87/R, WT/DS110/R (99-2313), World Trade Organization (15 Jun 1999).
22 Commission Notice 372/03 *on the definition of relevant market for the purposes of Community competition law*, 2003 O.J. (C 372), at 5, para. 20.
23 US Department of Justice and Federal Trade Commission, *Horizontal Merger Guidelines* (2010), Sec. 4.1.3.
24 Nonetheless, the Agencies often define markets for groups of targeted customers, i.e., by type of customer, rather than by individual customer. By so doing, the Agencies are able to rely on aggregated market shares that can be more helpful in predicting the competitive effects of the merger.
25 Federal Trade Commission, *Analysis to Aid Public Comment on The Provisionally Accepted Consent Order*, File No. 011 0057, Docket No. C-4032, In the Matter of Diageo PLC and Vivendi Universal S.A (2001).
26 See Annex I GATT, *Notes and Supplementary Provisions, Ad* Article III, http://www.wto.org/english/docs_e/legal_e/gatt47_03_e.htm# annex (last visited Feb 2022).
27 United States v. E. I. du Pont de Nemours & Co., 351 US 377 (1956).
28 US Department of Justice and Federal Trade Commission, *Horizontal Merger Guidelines* (1992, rev'd 1997).

29 *Report of the Panel* on *Japan - Customs Duties, Taxes and Labelling Practices on Imported Wines and Alcoholic Beverages*, L/6216 - 34S/83, World Trade Organization (1 Nov 1987), para 5.9.
30 Kelvin J. Lancaster, *A New Approach to Consumer Theory*, 74 J. of Pol. Econ. 132 (1966).
31 United States v. Falstaff Brewing Corp., 410 US 526 (1973).
32 *See* Sumanth Addanki, *Antitrust Analysis of High Technology Mergers: The Role of Potential Competition*, testimony before the FTC's Hearings on Global and Innovation-Based Competition (25 Oct 1995).
33 Herbert Hovenkamp, *Federal Antitrust Policy: The Law of Competition and its Practice* (6th ed., West Academic Publishing 2020), at 717–722.
34 *Appellate Body Report* on *European Communities - Measures Affecting Asbestos and Asbestos-Containing Products*, AB-2000-11, WT/DS135/AB/R (01-1157), World Trade Organization (4 May 2001); *Report of the Panel* on *European Communities - Measures Affecting Asbestos and Asbestos-Containing Products,* WT/DS135/R, World Trade Organization (18 Sep 2000).
35 *Report of the Panel* on *European Communities - Measures on Animal Feed Proteins,* L/4599 - 25S/49, World Trade Organization (14 Mar, 1978).
36 *Appellate Body Report* on *Canada - Certain Measures Concerning Periodicals*, AB-1997-2, WT/DS31/AB/R (97-2653), World Trade Organization (30 Jul 1997); *Report of the Panel* in *Canada - Certain Measures Concerning Periodicals,* WT/DS31/R (97-0939), World Trade Organization (14 Mar 1997).
37 *Appellate Body Report* on *European Communities - Regime for the Importation, Sale and Distribution of Bananas*, AB-2008-08, WT/DS27/AB/RW2/ECU, WT/DS27/AB/RW/USA (08-5797), World Trade Organization (9 Sep 1997).
38 *Report of the Panel* on *US - Standards for Reformulated and Conventional Gasoline*, WT/DS2/R (96-0326), World Trade Organization (29 Jan 1996).
39 *Reports of the Appellate Body* on *European Communities – Measures Prohibiting the Importation and Marketing of Seal Products,* AB-2014-1, AB-2014-2, WT/DS400/AB/R, WT/DS401/AB/R (14-3051), World Trade Organization (2014).
40 *See Appellate Body Report, supra* note 34.
41 7 EPCT/C. II/32, *Note of the Netherlands and the Belgo-Luxembourg Economic Union* (30 October 1946).
42 *Report of the Appellate Body* on *United States - Measures Concerning the Importation, Marketing and Sale of Tuna and Tuna Products*, AB- 2012-2, WT/DS381/AB/R (12-2620), World Trade Organization (2012) ("Tuna II").
43 *Report of the Appellate Body* on *United States - Measures Affecting the Production and Sale of Clove Cigarette*, AB-2012-1, WT/DS406/AB/R (12-1741); *Report of the Appellate Body* on *United States – Certain Country of Origin Labelling (COOL) Requirements*, AB-2012-3, WT/DS384/AB/R, WT/DS386/AB/R (12-3450); Tuna II, *id.*
44 Tuna II, *suprsa* note 43, at 77-78.
45 For further analysis, *see* "The TBT Committee's Six Principles for the Development of International Standards: Are they still Relevant?," World Trade Organization (2020), https://www.wto.org/english/tratop_e/tbt_e/tbt_six_principles_e.htm.
46 *Id.*
47 *Report by the Panel* on *United States - Section 337 of the Tariff Act of 1930*, L/6304 - 36S/345, World Trade Organization (1989), at 385, para. 5.9.
48 *Report by the Panel* on *EEC - Regulation of Parts and Components*, L/6657 - 37S/132, World Trade Organization (1990), para. 5.11.
49 *Report of the Appellate Body* on *United States — Import Prohibition of Certain Shrimp and Shrimp Products*, AB-1998-4, WT/DS58/AB/R (98-3899), World Trade Organizaiton (1998).
50 *Id.*, at 12, para 172.
51 *Reports of the Appellate Body, supra* note 40.

52 "The Mail on Sunday's Campaign against US Food Imports is a New Low," CapX (15 Jun 2020), https://capx.co/the-mail-on-sundays-campaign-against-us-food-imports-is-a-new-low/.
53 Council Regulation (EU) No. 995/2010, 2010 O.J. (L 295/23); *see* also Andrew D. Mitchell and Glyn Ayres, *Out of Crooked Timber: The Consistency of Australia's Illegal Logging Prohibition Bill with the WTO Agreement,* 29 Env't. & Plan. L. J. 462 (2012).
54 *Report of the Appellate Body* on *Brazil – Measures Affecting Imports of Retreaded Tyres,* AB-2007-4, WT/DS332/AB/R (07-5290), World Trade Organization (2007).
55 *See,* in particular, Lars Karlsson, Shanker A. Singham, and Daniel A Gottschald, *The Global Zone Network: A Safe Pathway to Prosperity in the post Coronavirus Era,* 15 World Customs J. 51 (2021), https://worldcustomsjournal.org/Archives/Volume%2015%2C%20Number%201%20(Apr%202021)/1910%2001%20WCJ%20v15n1%20Karlsson%20et%20al.pdf.
56 *Id.*
57 *See,* for example, *Recommendations of the Council on Countering Illicit Trade: Enhancing Transparency in Free Trade Zones,* Organization for Economic Co-operating and Development (2019), http://legalinstruments.oecd.org/en/instruments/OECD-LEGAL-0454.
58 *Trade in Counterfeit Goods and Free Trade Zones: Evidence from Recent Trends,* Organization for Economic Co-operating and Development and European Union Intellectual Property Office (2018). http://dx.doi.org/10.1787/9789264289550-en.
59 *Money Laundering Vulnerabilities of Free Trade Zones,* Financial Action Task Force (2010).
60 *SAFE Framework of Standards,* World Customs Organization (2021), http://www.wcoomd.org/-/media/wco/public/global/pdf/topics/facilitation/instruments-and-tools/tools/safe-package/safe-framework-of-standards.pdf?la=en
61 *See Recommendations of the Council on Countering Illicit Trade, supra* note 57.
62 *See Safe Zone: an Izdihar Free Zone Certification Program,* Proposal, World Free Zones Organization (n.d.), https://www.worldfzo.org/Portals/0/OpenContent/Files/664/World_FZO_Safe_Zone_Manual.pdf.

7

TRADE AND COMPETITION IN AGRICULTURE

A Trade Negotiation and Sugar Case Study

As a precursor to our discussion of the impact on trade negotiations of the mercantilist rhetoric that we have seen in other areas, we will use the way in which trade in agriculture came to be negotiated to indicate the negotiating dynamics in this area and identify the potential interfaces between trade and competition. We will illustrate how market distortions in this sector damage competition and impact trade flows.

Agriculture has long been the bugbear of trade negotiations since trade negotiations began. The subject was considered so difficult that it was not even included in the trade agenda until the Uruguay Round concluded in 1994. Even then, the expectations were limited and the Agriculture Agreement left many holes to be plugged by subsequent negotiation. The major sticking points can be classified in the following broad headings:

i Very high tariffs protecting a number of specific sectors.
ii Export subsidies which incentivise farmers to produce more than demand would require.
iii Domestic programmes which tend to insulate farmers from the effects of failure.

Prior to the Uruguay Round, quotas played a significant part in agricultural trade. The impact of the Uruguay Round Agreement on Agriculture (URAA) was to tarifficate many of these quotas. Countries then agreed to reduce their tariffs by significant amounts (by an average of 36%). These reductions were to be phased in gradually over a six-year period from the conclusion of the Uruguay Round in 1995. Countries commitments are set out in the URAA market access schedules of each of the WTO members. Special safeguards were allowed for

DOI: 10.4324/9780429323331-7

products that made the transition from quotas to tariffs. URAA also establishes rules to deal with export subsidies. URAA targeted certain types of export subsidies for reduction. These are the most direct export subsidies such as those that are contingent on export performance, government export sales below market price, payments on the export of agricultural products that are financed by governments, subsidies on certain kinds of agricultural products that are contingent on their being included within products to be exported, subsidies affecting marketing. Although not specifically reduced, WTO members agreed to work towards agreement on export credits, export credit guarantee and also insurance programmes.

Domestic programmes have proven much harder to get WTO discipline on, but precisely for that reason careful attention needs to be paid to them. Domestic programmes can contain just as pernicious trade measures as an open tariff or export subsidy. The structure of what is allowed under the URAA falls into categories of green, amber and blue boxes. Green box subsidies are allowed and generally are assumed to have little or no impact on trade. Amber box subsidies are trade distorting and consequently must be reduced. Blue box subsidies are those that would be amber but also require farmers to limit production. In order for a particular subsidy to be regarded as a green box subsidy, it must not involve a transfer of wealth from consumers to producers and producers must not receive any kind of price support as a result. Furthermore under the URAA, WTO members will retain the right to provide domestic food aid and to undertake adjustment assistance or disaster relief. They can even pay producers directly as long as such payments are "decoupled" from production.

Having laid the groundwork, we should note that the purpose of this chapter is not to provide a detailed account of agricultural trade negotiations, but to highlight the type of trade distorting arrangement in one particular sector (sugar) that exists in a particular market which has now been subject to WTO dispute resolution and draw some inferences from the transition of this programme through domestic (pro-competitive) reform. Some of the points that we will discuss will have specific impacts for other sectors and may illustrate the interface between trade and competition in this most difficult of sectors. As with other parts of the book, it is hoped that by focusing on a specific case study, we will be able to develop some themes and ideas that will help advance these issues.

Historical Perspective

So how then did trade in agriculture come to be included in the Uruguay Round and what was the political history of these negotiations? The background of the Uruguay Round was very high budget deficits in the US and in some other countries brought about in part because of cold war spending. These high deficits put pressure on government spending, including government spending on agricultural programmes. Under this pressure, the Reagan administration even contemplated a unilateral agricultural reform in the mid-1980s. This went the way of most unilateral reform programmes amidst the backdrop of fierce opposition from a number of domestic agricultural groups. As a result reform-minded members of the European Union (EU), Japan and US governments sought to use the multilateral agenda to increase the pace of domestic reform.[1] The budget costs to the US had reached $26 bn by 1986. Commentators have noted that the GATT negotiation dynamics lessened the discipline that budgetary consideration usually imparted to a discussion of agricultural programmes, thus weakening the process of using the multilateral negotiations as a way of providing support for domestic reform movements.[2]

There has been some recent movement on the need to address trade distorting domestic payments. In particular, Australia has set up a group in the WTO to look at domestic support. While this initiative is in its very early stages, many WTO members, especially the big agricultural exporters such as the Cairns group, will seek to apply some downward pressure on the Aggregate Measure of Support (AMS) allowed under the WTO. WTO members have agreed AMS ceilings but they vary quite dramatically as the graphs below show, and they are generally increasing, not decreasing (Figures 7.1 and 7.2):

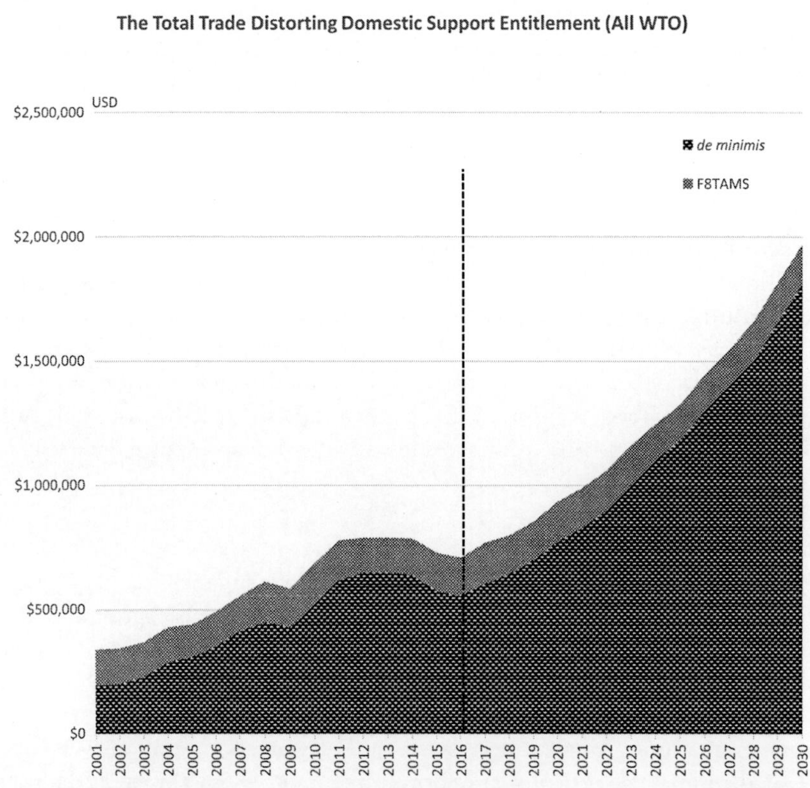

FIGURE 7.1 The Total Trade Distorting Domestic Support Entitlement (All WTO)[3]

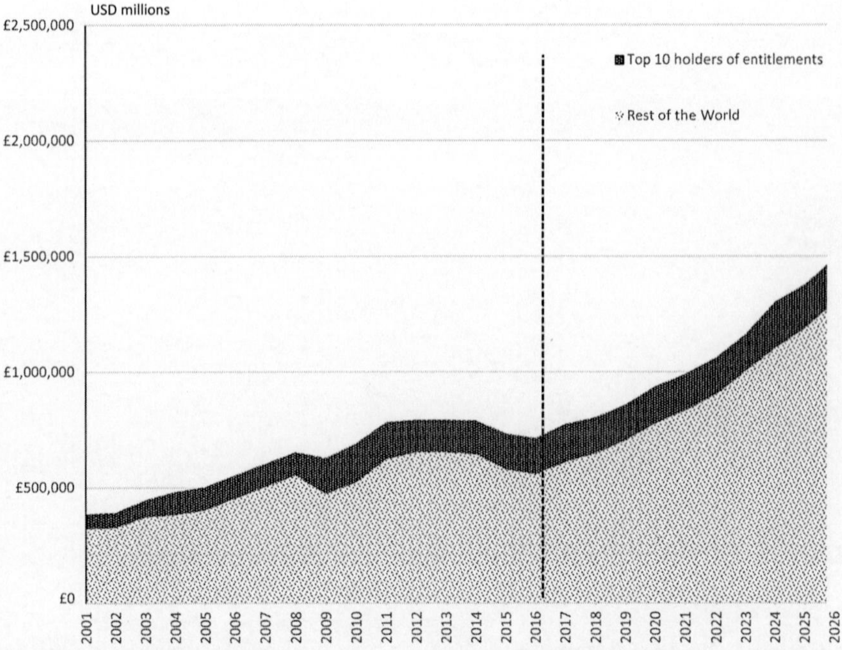

FIGURE 7.2 Total Trade-Distorting Domestic Support Entitlements (Top Ten WTO Members (2016) versus Rest of the Membership)

The graph above shows the extent to which AMS is increasing for all WTO members, in particular the extent to which the largest members contribute to overall AMS levels.

We can see from the graph below that the Chinese production support for agriculture is increasing dramatically, and now represents almost as much as the OECD in totality (which includes significant support from the EU, Japan and Korea). This is a troubling trend and one that is counter the general trends which we can see from the other countries in the chart. It is also consistent with the general trend of massively increasing Chinese distortion of a number of sectors. We also see that the overall production support from OECD countries has declined by only 40m or so Euro (from €250 m to €208 m) in the last 20 years. European support has also actually increased in the last 20 years, which is important because it starts from a very high base. It is easy to see why both developing countries and the big agricultural exporters are upset about the lack of progress in this area (Figure 7.3).

The graphs above shows that production subsidies, far from decreasing, are on a dramatic rise. It also shows that while the EU has historically been one of the biggest distorters in this area, now China is among the biggest (with China ranking as the biggest and India the third biggest). These supports can have a profound effect on competition.

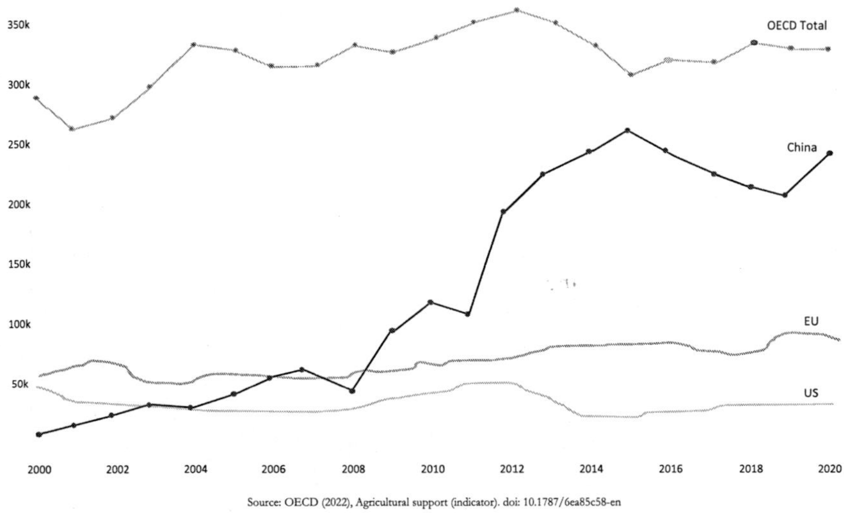

FIGURE 7.3 Comparison of OECD Total Support versus Chinese Total Support
Source: OECD (2022), Agricultural support (indicator). doi: 10.1787/6ea85c58-en

However these are systemic issues. There may well be specific sectors where there are market distortions beyond price supports. In particular, we do see regulations being crafted to specifically allow trade from a certain other country, and this may give ruse to a specific policy response. Usually, it is the combination of different supports, and regulations which gives rise to a complex web of distortions which combine to damage market competition and trade. It is useful to examine a particular case study where we can show a highly distorted sector as well as efforts to reform it and their effects.

Trade and Competition in Agriculture: The EU Sugar Programme Case Study

A particularly interesting example, both because it has been the subject of a WTO case and because it has gone through a process of reform already, is the EU sugar programme. It is interesting to track this process from the pre-reform elements of EU sugar policy to post-reform elements and the interface with the WTO case. The case is a good one for analysis since the way that the policy was changed and its interface with competition was a significant driver for a more pro-competitive and market-based policy.

EU Sugar Programme

Overview of the EU Sugar System Prior to Reforms and WTO Case

EU sugar is concentrated in a very small percentage of land and small number of producers. Sugar beet growing in the EU covered 1.8 million hectares before the expansion of the EU ("EU 15") to include Central and Eastern Europe. It is grown in every country of the EU 15 except Luxembourg. Sugar amounts to 1.2% of EU-utilised agricultural area. Sugar amounted to only 1.6%–1.8% of EU agricultural production prior to reform.[4] Because of the small size of sugar production and the concentration of producers, there may be anti-competitive activity in the sugar market that hurts consumers. The Staff Working Paper noted:

> Sugar production in the Community of 15 varies between 15 and 18 million tonnes. It is in the hands of 30 firms owning 135 sugar-mills and 6 refineries scattered throughout sugar beet growing regions (sugar mills) or near port areas (refineries).[5]

Two countries, Germany and France, accounted for over half of EU 15 sugar production. The next two largest producers, the UK and Italy, each produced 8% of EU sugar. Among the ten new Member States ("New EU 10"), seven manufacture sugar. This totals an additional 3 million tons. Poland accounts for two-thirds of this total. The Commission estimated, prior to the expansion, that as a result of the New EU 10, the total area under sugar beet production was likely to increase by 30%, while sugar production itself would increase by 15%.[6] Because of the generous EU sugar supports, there was a concern that the New EU 10 would increase production and exports. It is equally important to note that if consumption in the New EU 10 did not match production, the EU would have either absorbed the surplus or exported it and thereby further decreased world sugar prices. At the same time, EU 15 sugar producers were increasing their purchases of sugar processing plants in the New EU 10. Because the purchase of a processing plant is equivalent to the purchase of a quota, and prices are sold at higher than the subsidised intervention price for domestic EU consumption, it is not surprising that one buyer of a sugar plant remarked, "It is like buying a money printing machine."[7]

CMO

The EEC (predecessor to the EU) created the common market organisation ("CMO") in 1968. At the time, the purposes of the CMO were to guarantee sugar producers a "fair" income and to supply the EEC market from domestic sugar production. The CMO created import levies which gave protection from non-EEC countries sugar. The Staff Working Paper noted that EU consumers pay for EU sugar subsidies. However, the EU has long made the claim that the CAP system for sugar pays for itself. EU production was offered guaranteed quotas for sugar production. Any sugar in excess of the quotas was given export refunds subsidies.

Elements of the CMO supported the Common Agricultural Policy ("CAP") policy. These were:

Institutional support prices. Constituent elements include the intervention price, the basic sugar price and the minimum sugar price. The purpose of institutional support prices is to guarantee a certain level of income for the sugar growers and industry. The 2003 minimum price was set at €46.72 per ton for A-sugar and €32.42 per ton for B-sugar.[8] The intervention price was set at €631.90 per ton for white sugar and €523.70 per ton for raw sugar. As the Staff Working Paper suggests, "The intervention price, kept high, is a barrier to a competitive prices policy; the arrangements applying to relations with third countries to a large degree protect the Community market from external competition."[9]

Intervention purchases. The purchases are made either by the Member States' intervention agencies or by the EU Commission at a certain price to ensure a certain level price in case of a price drop of sugar.

Production quotas and levies. These regulate both the total quantity of sugar production in the EU and each Member State. As the EU explains:

- The basic levy on all A and B quota production is a maximum of 2% of the intervention price, i.e. €12.76/t of sugar; the amount generated from this is always insufficient;
- The B levy is imposed solely on B quota production at a maximum rate of 37.5% of the intervention price, i.e. €224.21/t;
- The additional levy, imposed if the amount generated is still insufficient, is a flat rate percentage of the amounts due by each enterprise under the above two levies; this (no maximum) is set so as to achieve the sum required. Since 1990 the additional levy has had to be applied one year out of two. The maximum rate has been 18.5% and the average payment €13/t on A-sugar and €246/t on B-sugar. As a weighted average of total production under the A and B quotas the levy works out at €55 per tonne of sugar, €23 (42%) charged to the sugar refiners and €32 (i.e. €4.1/t of beet) to the growers.[10]

Production quotas limit the ability of the most efficient EU sugar producers to develop. Thus, production quotas impose limits on the production of competing products. This serves to limit new entrants and to keep production concentrated and therefore more likely to engage in tacit collusion.

Export refunds. These subsidies ensure that sugar producers will receive a guaranteed price for exported sugar even if the world market sugar price is lower than the EU intervention price. At the time of the programme, the average export price for EU white sugar was €280 per ton.[11] Three types of export refunds were granted. The primary method of refunds was granted under a standing invitation to tender for an annual quantity of between 2.5 and 2.6 million tons of white sugar.[12] These refunds occurred weekly or every other week. Refunds of this sort can be significant. They totalled €443 per ton for 2001/2002 and €485 per ton for 2002/2003. The second form of refund is for refunds fixed at regular intervals for marginal quantities of white sugar outside invitations to tender and for other types of sugar. Approximately, 90,000 tons of sugar receive export refunds. The refund is fixed at regular intervals at the level of the best tender less

€30 per ton. The third form of export refund was for sugar contained in products not listed in Annex I to the Treaty, primarily foodstuffs. These refunds were fixed each month on the basis of the average refund resulting from the invitation to tender less €30 per ton.[13]

Import duties and preferential imports. These duties prevented low-cost sugar from being supplied to the EU but granted preferential status to some countries for importation of sugar. There are a number of at the border controls that the EU places to protect its sugar industry from competition. These include rules of origin requirements, safeguards, tariffs, country-specific tariff quotas and country-specific suspensions from eligibility for tariff concessions. Moreover, Article 5 of the WTO Agriculture Agreement special safeguards provisions guarantees that sugar cannot be imported except under the country-specific concessional arrangements. The barriers for providing imports other than those imports under concessional arrangements were immense. Such imports faced barriers estimated at more than €700 per ton.[14] The various tariffs and special safeguards ("SSG") on sugar imports into the EU were as follows as of the 2003 report:

230 €/ton duty plus SSG applies to dried or powdered sugar beet (HS1212.91.20);
67 €/ton duty plus SSG to other sugar beet (HS1212.91.90);
46 €/ton duty plus SSG to sugar cane (HS 1212.92.00); and
507 €/ton duty plus SSG applies to isoglucose (HFCS) (HS 1702.40.10)

ACP

The CMO first changed in 1975, as a result of the UK's accession to the EEC. The CMO took over British commitments to purchase sugar from its former colonies, the African, Caribbean and Pacific ("ACP") countries. The Sugar Protocol opened the EEC to a cane sugar quota from 19 ACP countries and India. These countries benefited from preferential access at EEC internal prices. The Agreement stated, that "the [European] Community undertakes for an indefinite period to purchase and import, at guaranteed prices, specific quantities of cane sugar, raw or white, which originate in the ACP states and which these States undertake to deliver to it."[15] In large part, these ACP privileges were shielded from EU commitments to reform the CMO unless there was consent from the ACP beneficiaries. "Subject to Article 7, these quantities may not be reduced without the consent of the individual states concerned."[16] Indeed, EU CMO regulation (No. 2038/1999) ensured that the ACP/EU Sugar Protocol quantities were irreducible even in cases where the EU had to reduce A- and B-sugar production quotas (as described *infra*) as a result of EU WTO commitments.

The 19 ACP sugar preference recipients (plus India) were Barbados, Belize, Congo, Côte d'Ivoire, Fiji, Guyana, India, Jamaica, Kenya, Madagascar, Malawi, Mauritius, St Kitts, Nevis, Swaziland, Tanzania, Trinidad & Tobago, Uganda, Zambia and Zimbabwe.[17]

WTO

As a consequence of the Uruguay Round of trade negotiations, the EU undertook amendments to the CMO sugar policy. The new commitments placed restrictions on export refunds. Consequently, if imports to the EU increased, the EU would re-establish the market equilibrium for sugar by a reduction mechanism to reduce sugar quotas. The EU presently regulates the CMO with Regulation (EC) No 1260/2001, which expired in June 2006.

Everything but Arms

The EU CMO policy is affected by the Everything but Arms ("EBA") initiative. The EBA suspends all common customs tariff duties of products from the 46 least developed countries. This group includes six ACP countries. The EBA was introduced gradually from 2001 by increasing preferential quotas. The EBA will have a significant impact from 2009, when there will be free access to the EU market but even at present, EBA sugar has begun to impact Balkan, ACP and India sugar.

Balkan Sugar

As a consequence of the Balkan wars, the EU has granted access to a number of Balkan countries. Imports under the Balkan programme totalled about 100,000 tons in 2001/2002.

Sugar Quota System

The EU sugar system established quotas for A-sugar and B-sugar for five-year periods.

A-Sugar

A-sugar is designated by quota from sugar grown in the EU. A-sugar quotas are allocated to each Member State. These quotas are only tradable within a Member State but not between Member States. Such A-sugar is eligible for EU market supports and export subsidies. The A-sugar quota holders who process the sugar must pay fixed minimum prices to A-sugar growers. A production levy, up to 2% of the intervention price, is payable as a contribution to the cost of direct export subsidies. Some of the levy costs are recoverable from A-sugar growers.

B-Sugar

B-sugar is designated by quota from sugar grown in the EU. The B-sugar system works similarly to the A-sugar system except that the fixed price for B-sugar quota holders is lower than that of A-sugar. A production levy is payable, ranging from 30 to 37.5% of the intervention price. Levy costs are recoverable from B-sugar growers. The role of B-sugar was originally to serve for the export market. However, as B-sugar could obtain higher prices within the EU, it was not exported, creating the C-sugar for export purposes.

C-Sugar

C-sugar was all sugar produced in excess of A- and B-sugars. There was no limit on total production of C-sugar. However, all such sugar must be exported unless it gets a "carry-over." The carry-over is for the sugar plant that produced beyond its quota. If it is stored for over 12 months, it is treated as A-sugar produced by the plant as part of that year's production. Unlike domestic sugar, which has a guaranteed price and direct subsidies, C-sugar lacks such direct subsidies. An export licence for C-sugar is granted only when A-sugar and B-sugar quotas have been filled.[18] C-sugar used to average around 2.6 million tons, which equals approximately 20% of sugar production under quota.[19]

Problems of the System

The EU has itself noted the problem of the CMO. While there is price stability in the EU as a result of the CMO, this comes at a very high price for consumers. As the EU Staff Report states, "The CMO's contribution to price stability is also acknowledged even though protection from the volatility of world market prices is bought at a very much higher internal price and an uncompetitive commercial environment."[20] The EBA initiative itself concludes that if EBA-eligible countries could export sugar to the EU without quantitative restrictions, this would result in an additional EU budgetary outlay of €439 per ton.[21]

Dumped World Market Sugar

The EU is not a low-cost producer. Moreover, because of the nature of the CMO, it has clearly encouraged a surplus of sugar production. This surplus is then exported, which adds to world supply and serves to depress world sugar prices.

There are two different types of direct export subsidies – the 1.6 million tons of sugar equivalent to the ACP and India sugar that is imported. There are no budgetary limitations on the 1.6 million tons. There may be export subsidies for up to an additional tonnage of 1.273 million. This budgetary outlay cannot be more than €499.1 million.[22]

When the EU set the rate for export subsidies, the relationship between costs of production and world prices was not factored in (except in relation to the element of costs associated with the requirement to purchase beet for quota sugar production at minimum guaranteed prices). The tender process also lacked price competition. The EU adjusted the intervention price to arrive at an artificial internal price. Because the methodology and calculation base are known in advance, tenderers know the exact level of maximum export subsidy that would be accepted by the EU. This prevents any real competition in tendering. As the EU Court of Auditors states:

> Given that the method and elements of the procedure to set the maximum refund [export subsidy] are public knowledge and that the sugar market is dominated by a very small number of large companies, the tendering system, designed to set export refunds in the most economical way for the Community budget, does not function as a real tendering system in the sense that the traders are in meaningful competition with each other...
>
> The level of the refund for sugar is significant. For the samples audited the accepted refunds were in the range of 40 to 50 euro per 100kg, which is about double the level of the world price. 'C' sugar has to be exported without the benefit of export refund, so it would be expected that the production of this type of (over quota) sugar would be small. Over the past years, however, the production of 'C' sugar has varied between 11% and 21% of quota production, which equals in some years the quantities of sugar that is exported with the aid of export refund. This calls into question the substantial level of aid granted to the export of sugar, bearing in mind that export refunds should only be granted to the extent necessary to enable the product to be exported.[23]

As such, the tendering process system was clearly abused.

Cross-subsidisation came into play to allow for otherwise non-competitive EU sugar to be exported. Preferential sugar was imported into the EU (such as the ACP and India sugar) and was consumed within the EU. An equivalent amount of EU quota sugar was then used for export.[24] This allowed EU sugar, which is high-cost sugar, to be exported abroad at below marginal cost pricing.

There is a second element to the cross-subsidisation claim. This conclusion was borne out by the EU Court of Auditors:

> EU sugar is clearly not competitive on the world market. Subsidies of the order of 75% of the EU intervention price are currently needed to enable the quota surplus to be sold. 'C' sugar (production in excess of quotas), which receives no export refunds, can only be sold profitably because the prices obtained for quota sugar are sufficient to cover all the fixed costs of the processing companies.[25]

Hence, high EU sugar prices allows for the production of otherwise inefficient EU sugar. Because the A-sugar and B-sugar quotas are subsidised to cover the fixed costs, a system was put into place to artificially lower the variable cost of additional C-sugar. Therefore, quota sugar subsidises C-sugar.[26]

Indeed, quota holders have added incentives to over-produce sugar to create C-sugar. Because of the attractive rate of return of both A-sugar and B-sugar and because underused quotas would be reassigned to other farmers, EU farmers have every incentive to over produce sugar. This leads to a greater abundance of C-sugar, all of which must be exported, which then depresses world prices because it is sugar that is effectively produced under its true costs. The Australian submission in the WTO case on EU sugar drew this link clearly:

> The same growers and processors produce quota sugar and 'C' sugar. 'C' sugar exports have averaged 17% of the combined 'A' and 'B' quota over the decade to 2001–2002. It is evident that 'C' sugar is not a mere spill over from quota production, but that 'C' production is directly related to quota production, in regard to annual production in excess of quota to guard against yield variability (which was the original purpose of the 'B' quota) and protection of high value quotas against redistribution by Member State agencies.[27]

The impact of EU enlargement is that four sugar surplus countries have been introduced into the picture, Czech Republic, Hungary, Lithuania and Poland. Here, the A quota is set at the level of domestic consumption, and B quota is the sum of the WTO-permitted export refunded sugar exports. One of the problems is that excess C-sugar is used to service export markets, thus further lowering the global sugar price. For the three deficit countries (Latvia, Slovakia, Slovenia): the A quota is set at the level of production and the B quota at 10% of the A quota. Under this system, the total quota may not exceed the level of consumption. For other countries of the EU 10 that do not produce sugar, there is no quota.

The EU has also used food aid as a means to dump its excess sugar into the world market. The EU accounts for 80% of sugar sent as food aid.[28]

Developing World Preferences

The EU grants some countries preferential access to the EU sugar market. The EU has WTO-bound tariff quotas on 1.389 million tons of sugar. These quotas comprised two parts. The first is 1.304 million tons of sugar, which are allocated to certain ACP countries and India. The second is a quota of 85,463 tonnes of raw cane sugar for refining from designated countries.[29] Additional tariff preferences are granted under

> (a) fixed annual quotas under the 'Everything But Arms' (EBA) arrangement involving duty free access for least developed countries within quota limits; (b) variable quotas at reduced duties for suppliers of raw cane sugar for refining from the ACP and India under the 'Special Preferential System' (SPS); and (c) duty free access for designated Balkans sugar exporters.[30]

The EBA sugar quota began at 74,185 tons and has increased by 15% a year. The ACP plus India quantities are not fixed. Instead, this amount is determined by the maximum supply needs of refineries. This amount is linked to domestic supply and imports.[31] There has been a decline in ACP and India sugar as a result of EBA sugar. Moreover, Balkan sugar imports started to decline (imports peaked at 320,000 tons in the 2002/2003 marketing year) as controls (including special rules of origin) have been instituted to reduce quantities.[32] Any of these imported sugars count as part of EU domestic supply and enjoy free circulation in the internal market.

Behind the Border Anti-Competitive Restraints

The Staff Working Paper noted certain indirect anti-competitive effects of the CMO. The CMO encouraged tacit collusion in the EU sugar industry itself. This allows market prices to be set at a much higher level than would otherwise be the case. Anti-competitive critiques have emerged as well from the Commission itself, certain national authorities (such as the Swedish Competition Agency), the Court of Justice, the Court of Auditors, the OECD, sugar-user industries and consumer bodies complain of the lack of competition on the European market. The OECD states, "Changes in the structure of the world sugar market suggest little respite from historically low world sugar prices and price volatility over the medium term."[33]

An early case in the history of the EU sugar programme before the European Court of Justice ("ECJ") emphasises that the sugar system was by its nature anti-competitive. In *Suiker Unie v Commission* [1975] ECR 1663, the ECJ had reduced fines imposed by the Commission because it argued that common organisation of the sugar market was essential for a minimum price for sugar beet. In *Suiker Unie* the relevant market concerned a product that was subject to the CAP in the framework of a system of national production quotas allocated among the main producers. One element to the case involved tacit collusion of sugar companies. The companies argued that there would be no difference in the economic effect between an exchange of trading information between a group of traders and the results of an individual trader reacting to public information about his nearest rivals. The ECJ ruled that if a party were to share price information with his competitors, this would lead to inefficiencies and cartel-like behaviour. The ECJ also decided that import and export bans not only restricted competition between brands but also threatened the integration of the single market. A relevant market could be defined as "a pattern and volume of the production and consumption of the said product as well as the habits and economic opportunities of vendors and purchasers...." This suggests that a number of sub-EU markets could be identified as the proper geographic markets. In the actual case, the Court ruled that the Belgo-Luxemburg market and southern Germany were considered substantial for market definition purposes. Therefore, the ECJ found that pressure that an undertaking applied not to export to customers in Belgium was an abuse under Article 82 of the Treaty of Rome. The importance of this decision is not merely that it highlights that sugar markets may be cartelised but that there are a number of sub-regional sugar markets, each of which may result in monopolisation through anti-competitive conduct by sugar companies.

A report by the Swedish Competition Commission bore out that there are a number of sub-regional sugar monopolies. The Swedish Report notes that sugar trade among Member States is very small and that firms seem to have successfully carved up the EU market into smaller geographically separate markets. The Swedish Reports suggested, "Were it not for the CMO it cannot be excluded that the EU would constitute one market for sugar or even that the European Union would be part of a market larger than the Union."[34] This is not surprising, given that the EU sugar industry is highly concentrated, with only one producer in seven of fourteen sugar producing Member States holding the Member States' entire sugar production quota. In the other Member States, the sugar industry is highly concentrated with only a few large firms.

The Swedish Report suggested that EU prices were so high in part because firms can engage in tacit collusion. Tacit collusion has been aided by a concentrated number of sugar producers, a lack of competition from non-EU sugar and a lack of competition from sugar substitutes such as HFCS. Moreover, since the CMO assigned fixed production quotas nationally, the CMO has helped to consolidate national markets, which facilitates firms to divide sugar markets geographically. Moreover, the CMO sets up a relation system to enforce tacit collusion within the EU sugar market. Because the CMO leads to subsidisation of excess sugar production and exports, firms could use the threat of shifting quantities from exports to sales within the EU.[35]

CAP policy seems to override competition policy at the EU level. Old Articles 81 and 82 (now Articles 101 and 102) of the Treaty of Rome prohibit anti-competitive coordinated and individual firm conduct. Agriculture is governed by different sections of the Treaty. While Article 32(1) provides for the extension of the competition rules to the agricultural sector, Article 36 limits these provisions by providing that the competition rules of the Treaty shall apply to agricultural products only to the extent determined by the Council, account being taken of the objectives set out in Article 33. Article 33 lays out the purposes of the CAP.

- *to increase agricultural productivity by promoting technical progress and by ensuring the rational development of agricultural production and the optimum utilisation of the factors of production, in particular labour;*
- *thus to ensure a fair standard of living for the agricultural community, in particular by increasing the individual earnings of persons engaged in agriculture;*
- *to stabilise markets;*
- *to assure the availability of supplies;*
- *to ensure that supplies reach consumers at reasonable prices.*

Hence, CAP objectives may to some extent override the competition rules as these goals are not necessarily the same as those of competition policy, where the goals are those of efficiency and consumer welfare. The CJEU (European Court of Justice) has recognised that competition policy must be enforced in agriculture through Agriculture provisions of the Treaty of Rome.[36] In this sense, it is important to note that in Council Regulation 26/625,[37] the Council of Ministers of Agriculture has established that both (now) Articles 101 and 102 (old Articles 81 and 82) are fully applicable in the agricultural sector. However, Article 2 of Regulation 26/625 exempted certain agricultural agreements from the application of old Article 81(1), particularly those agreements which form an integral part of a national market organisation or are necessary for attainment of the objectives of the CAP. Therefore, change must occur within CAP to allow for a more competitive sugar sector.

Production quotas limit the ability of the most efficient producers to develop, impose limitations on the production of competing products or create barriers to entry of new producers. Moreover, production quotas may be transferred within a Member State but not among Member States. This continues to limit efficient use of sugar quotas within the EU by having high-cost producers not be able to trade quotas to more productive regions. The outcome would lead to greater economic efficiency within the EU and concentrate sugar production within lower cost areas. A further outcome would be more intra-EU trade in sugar. It would then make geographic division of EU sugar markets more difficult to sustain and make tacit collusion less likely. The Swedish Report concluded that a reduction of import tariffs or the implementation tradability of sugar quotas would make tacit collusion among sugar producers harder to sustain.

National quotas naturally encouraged market partition. Note also that Italy, Portugal, and Spain have been allowed to pay national aid to sugar producers. This only encourages further un-economic production.[38] Specifically, the national aids are authorised to Italy, Spain and Portugal until the end of the 2005/2006 marketing year. In Italy, the aid is restricted to €54.3/t of sugar. The aid in Spain is restricted to maximum of €72.5/t of sugar, while in Portugal aid of €31.1/t of sugar may be granted.[39]

Two merger cases and two recent studies illustrate that domestic sugar prices are higher than the intervention price, which suggests that there was no price competition within the EU sub-markets in the period before reform. A merger case before the German Competition Authority that analysed the merger between Nordzucker and Union Zucker suggested that the average price of industrial sugar in Germany in 2001 was 14% higher than the EU intervention price, which it concluded was based on a lack of competition in the German market.[40] In the second merger case, Südzucker and Saint Louis Sucre, the EC found that sugar prices in the EU were 10%–20% higher than the intervention price.[41] Similarly, the Swedish Competition Agency has also found that competition was lacking in EU sugar markets and that there was tacit collusion among sugar producers. Finally, the European Court of Auditors stated that because of export refunds, sugar is not offered for intervention within the domestic market. The Auditors conclude:

> This has contributed to the situation where competitive forces are not functioning effectively and there is no real 'common market' for sugar. In discussions with the various stakeholders it became apparent that processors have little interest in competing with processors in other countries and remain largely in their home markets.[42]

In addition to the basic programme, many Member States applied state aids that have been authorised under EU state aids laws.

Cost of Production

The EU is a high-cost producer of sugar, and a full liberalisation of its sugar system would immediately lower its production to a third of present levels and in the long run to the elimination of EU sugar production completely.[43] Because of its shorter growing season of only three months, beet sugar is generally not as cost effective as cane sugar which has a nine-month growing season. As such, cane sugar yield is 65 t/ha, while beet sugar yield is merely 40 t/ha.[44] According to the World Bank:

> The average cost of producing raw cane sugar by major exporters, was 10.39 US cents per pound during 1994/95–1998/99, and the average cost of refined cane sugar was 14.25 cents per pound. The raw-to-white spread averaged 3.86 cents per pound. Refined sugar from beets cost an average of 25.31 cents per pound -78 percent more than refined cane sugar. Among low-cost producers, the difference between refined cane and beet sugar was even wider. The average production cost for low-cost producers of refined cane sugar was 11.44 cents per pound compared to 22.29 cents per pound for refined beet sugar—a difference of 95 per cent. Based on this comparison, sugar from beets was not competitive with sugar from cane by either major exporters or low-cost producers.[45]

EU's WTO Commitment

The EU is in excess of its WTO commitments. In 2002, the EU exported over 4 million tons of sugar, far in excess of the EU's export subsidy reduction commitment of 1.2753 million tons in the EU's WTO Schedule.[46] The export subsidies applied to sugar exports also exceed the €499.1 million commitment level in the EU sugar schedule. This can be best illustrated through the following (Table 7.1):

TABLE 7.1 EU export subsidies

Year	*Export subsidies (mio ECU)*	*Quantities (kt)*
1986	878.4	1645.0
1987	712.0	1859.0
1988	794.5	1615.0
1989	453.3	989.0
1990	692.9	1187.0[47]

Possible Reforms

The Staff Working Paper offered four different options: (a) status quo; (b) fixed quotas; (c) fall in prices or (d) liberalisation. It is worth looking at these four proposals and discussing how each would impact competition and then assess how reform actually impacted competition.

Status Quo

Under the status quo, a system similar to the present one was suggested in 2006, when the system expired. The status quo would be affected by a number of factors. Since the WTO case brought by Australia, Brazil and Thailand found against the EU, even under the status quo option there would be a significant reduction in EU sugar production. Indeed, such an option would probably hurt the more efficient EU producers more because the quotas would be reduced for all EU members proportionately. Because profit margins would continue to be guaranteed by set prices regardless of the actual costs of production, this could potentially mean even higher sugar prices in the EU for consumers. However, subsidised exports would be abolished, which would increase the world market share of the EU's competitors, especially Brazil.

Fixed Quotas

The advantage of fixed quotas is that the sugar situation would be more predictable. However, it would have required the EU to renege on its international commitments made under the EBA initiative. This would have even more deleterious effects at the WTO level generally for further attempts at general liberalisation. The Staff Working Paper suggests that a return to fixed quotas would entail considerably lower productions quotas than under the current system. Under the fixed quota system, internal EU prices would remain high.

Fall in Prices

This is the option that the Staff Working Paper considered would be the most feasible. The supposition of this model is that domestic prices would be supported by a certain amount of tariff protection. The EU intervention mechanism would protect EU sugar farmers against a sharp fall in domestic prices. Should there be an increase in non-quota sugar, the market would adjust to the lower price. Under this model, production quotas would be abolished. High-cost producers both among the ACP and within the EU would be negatively impacted under this proposal.

The Staff Working Paper noted that:

> Calculations of overall economic welfare, although sometimes rather theoretical, show that the 'liberalisation' and 'price fall' sets of options would provide the greatest boost because they reduce the expenditure of users and budget expenditure much more than the profits of the sugar sector.[48]

The price fall option proposal includes some core elements: (1) reduction of EU sugar price €600 per ton, (2) abolition of the intervention price; (3) preference price for ACP sugar and (4) reduction of EU sugar price to €435 per ton.

Liberalisation

Under liberalisation, domestic price supports would be abolished. Low-cost producers would replace both domestic and most ACP sugar. Most of EU sugar production would be drastically reduced and Brazil and other low-cost producers would bring lower prices to the EU and take a significant market share. Consumers would benefit from this system.

The Results of Sugar Reform in the EU

EU sugar reform has had significant consequences for both the EU and countries outside.

Critically, market distortions generally have the impact of increasing exports from countries that distort their markets. The Brazil Pro-Alcool programme is a good example of this. The EU sugar reform did lead to a drastic reduction in the amount of sugar exported from the EU and also led to a significant cut in the amount of sugar which was produced in the EU.

Pre-reform, annual production was 20 m tonnes. Post-reform it was 14–15.5 m tonnes. The number of sugar beet producers also fell dramatically from 285,000 growers cultivating 2.1 m ha to 164,000 cultivating 1.4 m ha. The number of workers declined from 50k to 30k (40% reduction) and the number of factories went from 189 to 114. Refiners increased from 7 to 26 full-time refiners. Very importantly, exports plummeted from 7.5 m tonnes to 1.37 m tonnes, a fall of 82%. This all occurred against a backdrop of increasing EU sugar consumption from 15 m tonnes to 17 m tonnes. The export refunds mechanism, while not abolished, has declined in use, and this means that the incentive to produce more and therefore have more to export has diminished considerably. Diversification funds were also introduced to facilitate the movement away from beet sugar production which will also contribute to lower excess export numbers (amount of sugar exported above the level that would have been dictated by ordinary competition). The ECA also analysed the differences in profitability of the sugar sector in multiple Member States, and the UK is in the group that is the most competitive and profitable. This suggests that the excess exports arising from distortions are lower for competitive industries such as the UK, rather than other members states which are much less competitive such as Ireland, Greece, Italy and Portugal. The Economic Partnership Agreement (EPA) also notes that both the EU domestic price and the reference and intervention prices have all fallen, while global market prices have increased lowering the excess exports from the EU.

Exports from the EU experienced a step change downwards in 2006 and 2007 after the reforms. Production has also decreased or levelled off after a period of sustained increase from 1961 until the reforms of 2006. By contrast, Brazil's exports have steadily increased (Figure 7.4).

It is certainly true that the sugar sector was one of the most distorted from 1961 but the data does show a significant decline of the exports from the EU as a result of distortions. The reforms put into place in 2006 culminated in the end of sugar quotas in 2017 and since that time, global sugar prices have reduced considerably (Figure 7.5).

This statistic depicts the average annual prices for sugar from 2014 through 2025. In 2020, the average price for sugar stood at 0.28 nominal US dollars per kilogram.

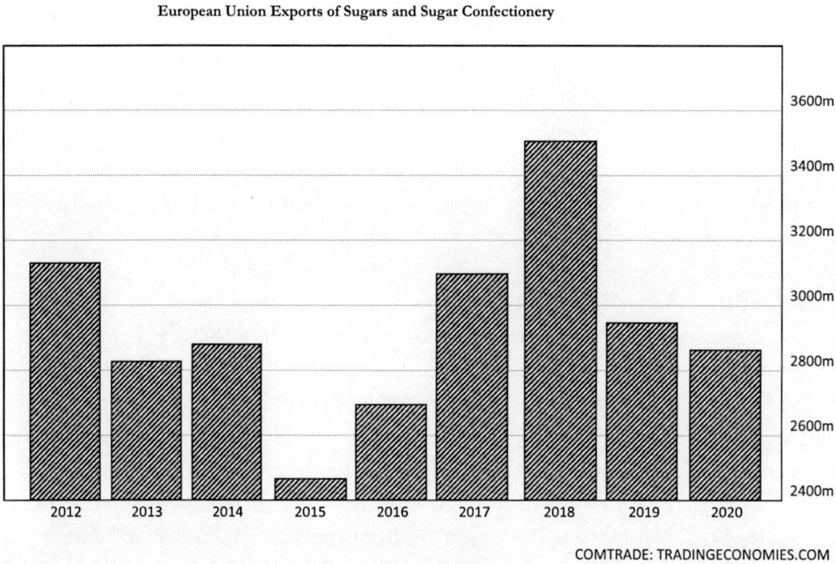

FIGURE 7.4 European Union Exports of Sugars and Sugar Confectionery[49]

See also chart on following page for production, import and export data (Figure 7.6):

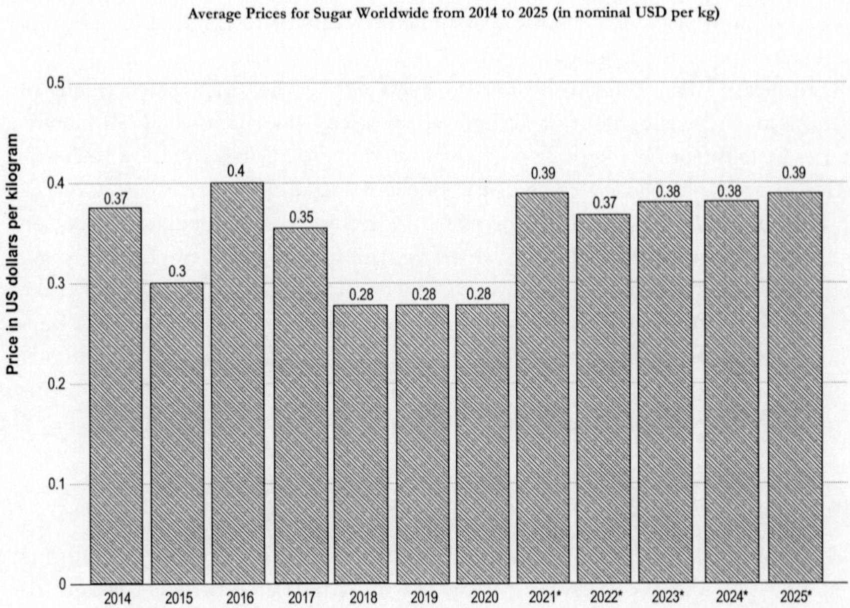

FIGURE 7.5 Average Prices for Sugar Worldwide from 2014 to 2025 (in nominal USD per kg[50])

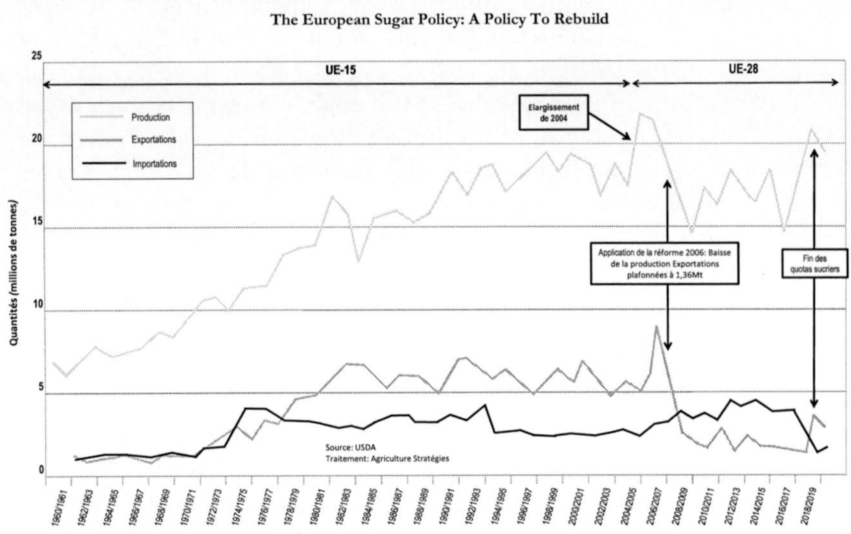

FIGURE 7.6 The European Sugar Policy: A Policy to Rebuild[51]

This shows that excess exports have reduced – the price incentive to produce and export more has significantly reduced in recent years also. The EU and Brazil continue however continue to price significantly lower than other countries. Brazil's price is often referred to as the international price, but in fact it is not an equilibrium price in the sense that an equilibrium price is the intersection of aggregate supply and aggregate demand.

European Sugar reforms were also analysed by the UK's Department of International Development in an analysis by LMC International. GSP beneficiaries benefit from being price takers of high domestic prices and they are negatively impacted by the lowering of EU prices as a result of the reforms.[52]

Further evidence that the reforms in the EU had an immediate impact on price is an analysis of vertical price transmission as a result of the EU sugar reforms.[53] This suggests that there is evidence that the sugar reforms did make a significant difference (but did not lead to a completely efficient market). Other data shows that the elimination of the quotas in 2016/2017 had a much bigger effect than the original announced reforms did in 2006, thus illustrating the differential impact of policy reforms.

Impact of European Sugar Reforms on Developing Countries

Many countries have historically benefited from sugar preference programmes and clearly the higher the EU tariff and the more restricted the EU market, the greater the preference for these countries. With respect to ACP countries, there was a substantial effect. For example, this would include Caribbean countries and the Dominican Republic, as well as India and countries in the Asia Pacific region. The majority of ACP sugar comes from countries that are not competitive. Therefore, any developing country which is more competitive in sugar production (such as the Dominican Republic, for example) would benefit from this change.

The EU's EBA programme also has had an implication on sugar trade as the EBA programme is an automatic zero tariff for the poorest LDCs. However, the EU has also started to negotiate EPAs from September 2002. Under these EPAs, all ACP countries are to be provided the same access provided to the 48 least developed countries. The Commission initially estimated that this access would create the diversion of 3.5 million tons to the EU and the diversion of the entire production of the ACP could reach 6 million tons.[54] The EU has negotiated an EPA with the CARIFORUM countries, which includes the Caribbean and the Dominican Republic. It has also a range of EPAs with other developing countries, and this has seen sugar imports increase. However, the initial predictions of massive increases in sugar imports have not materialised. EBA/EPA countries have not seen significant increases in exports to the EU (at least along the lines predicted) because the ending of the quota system and the reform of the EU system meant that the price differential between different sources of sugar was not so great as it had been in the past.

The EBA imports would need to be offset in the EU by a 17% lower production quota for domestic producers or the increased use of sugar for non-food products such as ethanol to comply with ACP/EU Sugar Protocol and WTO commitments. EBA and ACP combined could supply 60% of current EU sugar production. The current EU system is therefore not sustainable unless the EU was to switch this extra production to ethanol production. Moreover, under Article 20 of the basic Regulation sugar syrup that is processed into alcohol, including fuel alcohol, the EU treats such alcohol as having been produced outside the scope of the CMO.[55]

Actual EU Reform and the Impact of the WTO Case

With the above internal EU discussions as the backdrop, in 2004, Brazil, Australia and Thailand brought a WTO case against the EU sugar programme. The final ruling was issued by the WTO panel on 8 September 2004. The final report confirmed the ruling in favour of the complainants. As a result of the ruling, 2.7 million tons of exported EC surplus sugar (C sugar) was found to be cross-subsidised by the high guaranteed prices paid for in-quota sugar (A- and B-sugar). The panel also held that an additional 1.6 million tons of refined sugar, which the EC exported to the world market, corresponded to the amount of raw sugar it had imported from India and the ACP. Partially as a result of the case, and partially as a result of its own internal reform process, the EU came up with a reform proposal that would deal with many of the issues raised in the case. Interestingly, the opening paragraph of the EU reform proposal emphasised the linkage between the impact of the sugar programme on international trade and competition and the link between the two:

> The present sugar regime is often subject to fierce criticism for a lack of competition, distortions in the market, high prices for the consumers and users, and its effect on the world market, particularly in relation to developing countries.[56]

The timing of the communication is indicative of the process of government-to-government consultations as the WTO process worked its way through the system. In its Communication, the Commission proposed that there should be a significant reduction of the support price of sugar (by eliminating the intervention mechanism and introducing a reference price). Farmers would receive a decoupled payment to partially compensate them for the reduction in the support price (amounting to about 64% of the price cut). A and B quotas were to be merged into one and reduced to reflect internal consumption. The idea is to promote a more market-oriented sugar sector. The reference price was to be one third lower than the intervention price, steadily dropping until 2008. It is estimated that the world sugar price would double (to 302 EUR/ton in 2015 compared with 154.9 EUR/ton in 2007).

These changes are both a unilateral desire by the EU to move towards a more market-based system and a response to the WTO case filed by the three countries cited above. It therefore represents a combination of trade and competition restrictions that taken together distort trade and distort markets delivering consumer welfare damage.

We have endeavoured to demonstrate through an analysis of an evolving agricultural programme which has seen some reform the many different elements that together illustrate its anti-competitive and trade distorting effects. The EU sugar programme is but one example of agricultural programmes around the world that have this distorting impact. We use this to illustrate a broader point about the intersection of trade and competition policy in agriculture.

Ongoing Competition Distortions in the Sugar Sector: Legacy Effects of Distortions

Different distortions have different effects in real time and in terms of legacy effect. Some distortions lock in a pattern of behaviour which substantially lowers or increases costs for certain operations even after the distortion is ended. An example of a continuing lowering of costs would be a distortion which permanently increases production. The Brazilian government's Pro-Alcool Programme had the effect of permanently increasing the arable land deployed to the production of sugar by incentivising a product from which it is made (ethanol). Any government intervention which lowered the cost or indeed created a market for ethanol would inevitably have an impact on the production of the ethanol stockfeed, which is raw sugar cane. The Pro-Alcool Programme led to a massive increase in production of raw sugar cane, beyond levels that would have been used in the normal food supply. This created an overabundance of sugar which when the programme ended continued to be produced. However this led to a surge in Brazilian production which the domestic market demand could not absorb and led directly a very high level of excess exports produced by the distortion. These excess exports continued long after the legal provisions which gave rise to the distortion were ended.

Brazil continues to manipulate this downstream market by, for example, recently imposing a 20% tariff on ethanol. The US's access to the Brazilian market has been curtailed, creating a gap in the market which must be filled by overproduction of Brazilian sugar. The US ethanol industry has complained that when the tariff is lifted, the extra production of sugar in Brazil will have to be exported once more. This type of practice occurs because of the underlying programme which continues to have effects to this day. The lingering effect of the original distortion creates a latent capacity in the market that can relatively easily be switched on.

This is in sharp contrast to other market distortions which do not have such lingering effects. These would apply in cases where the initial distortion does not involve the creation of a downstream market, for example. We will look at below at one example of this which is the increase in consumption of sugar by the introduction of a government owned buying and marketing entity (see post). Such a distortion does not create a downstream market different from sugar. Once that entity is removed, the market quickly subsides to less distorted production levels. If a temporary bar on imports is then introduced through a tariff or other regulatory means, because of prevailing WTO rules, such a barrier is unlikely to be permanent, and would also have to apply to the sugar sector itself and not a downstream market. However, if a tariff such as the Brazilian ethanol tariff were to be increased, there would not necessarily be a domestic demand which could fill the need during the likely duration of the tariff absent these lingering effects of the distortion in the first place. In essence, the original Brazilian distortion created a new market for sugar production that can be intensified by the application of other trade barriers in Brazil in that product market.

Examples of Distortion with Significantly Fewer Legacy Effects

An example of distortions which have considerably fewer legacy effects includes the creation of state-owned buying entities, such as the Queensland Sugar Corporation. When these entities cease to exist or become mere private entities, the market demand they create disappears relatively quickly. This is because they do not create new market demand for a product that requires sugar as an input. We have noted that the creation of new market demand for sugar as a feedstock has significantly different competition effects.

The impact of legacy effects will depend on how much the particular law, policy or administrative action locks in a particular pattern of behaviour that lasts much longer than the ACMD action itself. If the ACMD action is related to a government buyer that is inserted into the market and then removed, we can expect the market to correct any over production relatively quickly. Other examples of this would be a tax holiday given to a trader that upon removal creates an immediate tax liability that only diminishes if the trader lowers production. Direct subsidies tend not to outlast their removal in terms of effects. When the direct payment is removed, the production level re-orients to a market-based amount.

Once the QSC was eliminated, there was no lingering effect of the distortion. Hence, a short-term tariff or even import ban would not lead to a domestic overproduction. In fact, the signal from ending the QSC would be to immediately lessen the market for sugar as producers would know that there was no captive/government buyer. This would incentivise them to lower production levels as there was no permanent change in the market. A temporary ban or tariff would only have an effect if the market then believed it was permanent. However, given WTO rules, it is extremely unlikely that the market would perceive this to be permanent, and the producers would have to evaluate the costs of ramping up production. Because of the cyclical nature of the harvest, it would not be possible to plan the type of production increase based on a likely short-term measure. In essence, the QSC did not create a new market for sugar production. As such, any trader barrier would have to apply to the sugar market itself.

Legacy Effects of EU Distortions

It has reasonably been suggested that in order to properly evaluate the impact of distortions on a global basis, it is necessary to look at the impact of distortions on the sugar sector in the UK as well, in order to understand how they compare with distortions in the rest of the world.

The UK distortions in this sector emanate from the legacy impact of the EU's CAP. These distortions are primarily in the area of subsidies.

We have outlined the significant changes to the EU's CAP AMS, and the way that the EU's subsidy programme works. The major change is the ending of the "C" sugar programme, under which low priced sugar (C Sugar) was exported onto global markets thereby depressing global prices.

Regulations that Increase Cost of Sugar Production in Other Countries

There are many examples of regulations that increase the costs of producers who are exporting into a particular market. We include some examples in the agricultural sector below. These regulations very often have anti-competitive effects. These regulations apply an extraterritorial approach to international trade in that regulations in the country of import may ban the products of another country if they don't satisfy the particular regulatory preferences of the country of import. Clearly if there was no bar at all to doing this, then any country could ban any product from another country on any grounds and this would have a profoundly negative impact on trade. However as noted in Chapter 5 on WTO issues, the general exemption under GATT Article XX does impose some limitations on what countries can do and still be WTO-compliant.

EU Neonicotinoid Ban

The EU has a neonicotinoid ban which increases the costs base of European sugar producers where the ban is in place. This ban includes the UK. This increase in costs for the UK producers does make them less competitive than producers where the ban is not in place. This certainly has a big impact on sugar producers in the UK and changes the competitive landscape between producers in the UK and elsewhere where the ban is not in place.

Conclusion on Competitive Impact of EU Sugar Programme including Reforms

The EU sugar programme has already had significant impacts on the net "excess" exports of EU sugar around the world, substantially reducing them. This shows the type of distortion which can be switched off with almost immediate effect. These are very different from the impact of the Brazilian distortion which fundamentally changed the nature of the Brazilian sugar market and increased production on a long-term basis. However, the EU programme and its reforms cannot be looked at in a vacuum and conditions of competition are affected by what occurs in other countries. We have shown the impact of distortions in Brazil. The Brazil distortion permanently increased production because they led to the creation of a new market for sugar which had a lingering effect. The EU distortion did not have such a lingering effect as it did not create a new market in the same way the Brazilian distortion did, and even within it, the UK application of the EU programme had even less of an impact on competition.

Conclusion on Dealing with Distortions in the Agricultural Sector

Attempts to deal with distortions in the agricultural sector have been very unsuccessful thus far. We have instead adopted a regulatory approach in trade policy that is focused on what the countries are doing rather than the outcomes and effects of such actions. This led to the green, red and amber box approaches for production supports as opposed to an evaluation of the impact of these subsidies on competition. A more competition-based approach would enable policy makers to separate out practices that actually damage competition and have an unnecessarily distortive effect on trade.

Similarly little effort has been made to discipline regulatory practices that artificially increase (or lower) costs to gain competitive or trade advantage. As noted in Chapter 6, there are specific exemptions which apply under GATT Article XX which enable countries to have significant flexibility to engage in anti-competitive market distortions subject to regulating in ways that are based on sound science (in the case of SPS regulation) and in a non-discriminatory fashion (in the case of TBT and SPS regulation). The precautionary principle gives added policy flexibility to countries. The net result is a series of anti-competitive regulations which are designed to inflate the costs of competitors and protect domestic incumbents.

Instead, agriculture should be treated as other sectors of the economy are. Regulations in this sector should be measured in terms of their trade and competition effect. As in all cases, as we go on to explain in Chapter 7, this does not mean that countries should only regulate in cases where the legitimate regulatory goal benefits exceed the costs in financial terms. But it does mean that these regulatory goals, including goals like animal welfare and the safety of food, should have both benefits and costs made explicit so policymakers can make informed decisions and inform publics properly in political debate.

Notes

1 For a detailed historical treatment, see Robert L. Paarlberg, *The Uruguay Round and Agriculture: International Path to Domestic Policy Reform?,* Working Paper No. 96-1, 30, Weatherhead Centre for International Affairs at Harvard University (1996).

2 *See id.*

3 Source: Higher and Higher – HIGHER AND HIGHER – GROWTH IN DOMESTIC SUPPORT ENTITLEMENTS SINCE 2001, Submission from Australia and New Zealand, JOB/AG/171 (22 Nov 2019), https://docs.wto.org/dol2fe/Pages/SS/directdoc.aspx?filename=q:/Jobs/AG/171.pdf&Open=Tru.
4 EC Commission Staff Working Paper, *Reforming the European Union's Sugar Policy*, SEC (2003) ("Staff Working Paper").
5 Staff Working Paper at 7.
6 EU Agriculture Commission, *Sugar: International analysis - Production Structures Within the EU* (2003) ("Agriculture Commission").
7 Swedish Competition Authority, *Sweet Fifteen: The Competition on the EU Sugar Markets* (2002) ("Swedish Report"), at 65.
8 European Commission, Agricultural Directorate-General, *Common Organization of the Market in Sugar* (2004) ("Common Organization"), at 5.
9 Staff Working Paper at 13.
10 Common Organization at 13–14.
11 Agriculture Commission at 20.
12 *Id.*
13 *Id.*
14 Common Organisation at 15.
15 Article 1 of the ACP/EU Sugar Protocol.
16 Article 3(2) of the ACP/EU Sugar Protocol.
17 *See* the official ACP sugar website, https://acpsugar.org. More detailed statistics, *see* https://acpsugar.org/dataexplorer. Note: not all countries currently receive such preferences but have in the past.
18 Regulation 1464/95, art. 5.
19 Common Organisation at 11.
20 Staff Working Paper at 11.
21 European Commission, *EU Trade Concession to Least Developed Countries, Everything but Arms Proposal: Possible Impacts on the Agriculture Sector* (2002).
22 Australian submission citing EC Notifications to the WTO Committee on Agriculture: G/AG/N/EEC/5, 11, 20, 23, 32, 36, 44; EU Court of Auditors (ECA) Special Report 9/2003, at 13.
23 ECA special report No 9/2003, at 36–38.
24 Australian submission citing ECA special report No 9/2003, at 9; Report of the Pannel, *European Communities – Refunds on Exports of Sugar,* L/4833-26S/290, General Agreement on Tariffs and Trade (1979), para. 2.19 ("GATT Sugar Panel report").
25 ECA Special Report No 20/2000, at 35, 96.
26 Note also that a number of marginal lands are supported by the current sugar system. As a result, there is an intensification of farming methods that would not be necessary if the most productive land was used for sugar farming.
27 Australia submission, *supra* note 23, at 49.
28 *See* ECA Special Report No. 20/2000, *supra* note 24.
29 EC WTO (CXL) Schedule, Section I-B, at 12.
30 European Communities, *Export Subsidies on Sugar*, WT/DS 265, Australia Summary of First Written Submission, at 19.
31 Regulation (EC) No 1260/2001, art. 39.
32 *Supra* note 29, at 20.
33 OECD, *Agricultural Outlook 2003–2008*, Highlights 2003, at 8.
34 Swedish Report at 9.
35 Swedish Report at 11.
36 Case 139/79, Maizena [1980] ECR 3393, at 23–24.
37 Council Regulation No 26 applying certain rules of competition to production of and trade in agricultural products. OJ [1959–62], at 129.

38 Donald Mitchell, *Sugar Policies: Opportunity for Change*, World Bank Policy Research Working Paper 3222, World Bank (2004) ("World Bank"), at 28.
39 Regulation (EC) No 1260/2001, art. 46.
40 Swedish Report at 65.
41 European Commission, Competition Policy M.2530 (2001).
42 ECA Special Report No. 20/2000, *supra* note 24.
43 Staff Working Paper at 33.
44 Sugar International Analysis Production Structures within the EU, 22/09/03, at 8.
45 World Bank at 13–14.
46 Commission of the European Communities, *Financial statement concerning the European Agricultural Guidance and Guarantee Fund (EAGGF) – Guarantee Section Financial Year 2002* (Com(2003)680), at 17.
47 Australian submission citing WTO document G/AG/AGST/EEC, Table 11.
48 The European sugar policy: a policy to rebuild/Agriculture Strategies (agriculture-strategies.eu), 19 June 2022.
49 Staff Working Paper at 35.
50 LMC International and Overseas Development Institute, *The Impact of EU Sugar Policy Reform on Developing Countries,* Department for International Development (2012).
51 European Union Exports of sugars and sugar confectionery – 2022 Data 2023 Forecast 2000–2020 Historical (tradingeconomics.com) Trading Economics, European Union Exports of sugars and sugar confectionery was US$2.86 Billion during 2020, according to the United Nations COMTRADE database on international trade. European Union Exports of sugars and sugar confectionery – data, historical chart and statistics – was last updated on March of 2022.
52 https://www.statista.com/statistics/675828/average-prices-sugar-worldwide/, Average prices for sugar worldwide from 2014 to 2025, Published by Aaron O'Neill, 22 February 2022.
53 Maurizio Aragrande, Mauro Bruni, Alberico Loi, and Roberto Esposti, *The Effect of EU 2006 Sugar Regime Reform on Vertical Price Transmission,* 5 Agric. and Food Econ. (2007), no. 1.
54 Staff Working Paper at 10.
55 Commission Regulation (EC) No 314/2002, OJ L 50, 21.2.2002, Article 1(2)(f).
56 *See Communication from the Commission to the Council and the European Parliament accomplishing a sustainable agricultural model for Europe through the reformed CAP-sugar sector reform*, COM (2004) 499 final (Brussels 14 Jul 2004).

8

STATE TRADING ENTERPRISES AND STATE-SUPPORTED MONOPOLIES

Beginnings of a Consumer Welfare Test

We can see the beginnings of a consumer welfare test in some aspects of WTO and European Union (EU) jurisprudence, as we have noted. Article XVII of the GATT imposes competition law disciplines on a commercial activity by state trading enterprises (STEs). Various provisions of the EU Treaty have a far broader application than Article XVII in curbing anti-competitive actions that are condoned or authorised by EU member governments and their instrumentalities. A review of these GATT and EU authorities sheds valuable light on the extent to which two major treaties – one global in state (GATT) and one regional (the EU Treaty) – may be effective in constraining anti-competitive behaviour that constrains trade and harms consumer welfare. We begin with an important GATT Article XVII case study and then turn to an overview of EU law in this area.

GATT Article XVII

GATT Article XVII applies to STEs, which are state-owned companies that buy and/or sell products produced by local producers. They frequently exist, particularly in the agricultural sector to give local farmers a greater market power when they come to sell their products on global markets. While the law in this area is far from settled, and what little of it appears to foreclose the use of competition arguments in arguing an Article XVII case, it is worth looking more closely at the leading case on the issue, involving the Canada Wheat Board (CWB).

Article XVII provides disciplines on what STEs are allowed to do when it comes to purchasing goods for commercial or their own use. These disciplines get close to a consistent and competition-based series of disciplines which limit what STEs can and cannot do.

DOI: 10.4324/9780429323331-8

Article XVII provides that:

1 a Each contracting party undertakes that if it establishes or maintains a state enterprise, wherever located, or grants to any enterprise, formally or in effect, exclusive or special privileges, * such enterprise shall, in its purchases or sales involving either imports or exports, act in a manner consistent with the general principles of non-discriminatory treatment prescribed in this Agreement for governmental measures affecting imports or exports by private traders.

b The provisions of subparagraph (a) of this paragraph shall be understood to require that such enterprises shall, having due regard to the other provisions of this Agreement, make any such purchases or sales solely in accordance with commercial considerations, including price, quality, availability, marketability, transportation and other conditions of purchase or sale, and shall afford the enterprises of the other contracting parties adequate opportunity, in accordance with customary business practice, to compete for participation in such purchases or sales.

c No contracting party shall prevent any enterprise (whether or not an enterprise described in subparagraph (a) of this paragraph) under its jurisdiction from acting in accordance with the principles of subparagraphs (a) and (b) of this paragraph.

2 The provisions of paragraph 1 of this Article shall not apply to imports of products for immediate or ultimate consumption in governmental use and not otherwise for resale or use in the production of goods* for sale. With respect to such imports, each contracting party shall accord to the trade of the other contracting parties' fair and equitable treatment.

3 The contracting parties recognise that enterprises of the kind described in paragraph 1 (a) of this Article might be operated so as to create serious obstacles to trade; thus negotiations on a reciprocal and mutually advantageous basis designed to limit or reduce such obstacles are of importance to the expansion of international trade.*

4 a Contracting parties shall notify the CONTRACTING PARTIES of the products which are imported into or exported from their territories by enterprises of the kind described in paragraph 1 (a) of this Article.

b A contracting party establishing, maintaining or authorising an import monopoly of a product, which is not the subject of a concession under Article II, shall, on the request of another contracting party having a substantial trade in the product concerned, inform the CONTRACTING PARTIES of the import mark-up on the product during a recent representative period, or, when it is not possible to do so, of the price charged on the resale of the product.

c The CONTRACTING PARTIES may, at the request of a contracting party which has reason to believe that its interest under this Agreement are being adversely affected by the operations of an enterprise of the kind described in paragraph 1 (a), request the contracting party establishing, maintaining or authorising such enterprise to supply information about its operations related to the carrying out of the provisions of this Agreement.

d The provisions of this paragraph shall not require any contracting party to disclose confidential information which would impede law enforcement or otherwise be contrary to the public interest or would prejudice the legitimate commercial interests of particular enterprises.

Broadly, Article XVII sets up two different standards. Where the STE is buying products for resale or other commercial use, it is subject to "commercial considerations." When the STE is buying products for its own use, it is subject merely to "fair and equitable standards." These different standards have been analysed in a number of WTO cases.

The CWB case[1] dealt with Canada's state-owned buying entity that purchased wheat from Canadian farmers and sold it in global markets. Wheat farmers in the US and the EU complained about the fact that the Canada Wheat Board had a monopoly of purchases and sales, and was not subject to the requisite "commercial considerations." The case turned on what "commercial considerations" meant. The CWB case is worthy of further study, as it contains the seeds of the debate about the role of competition policy as it applies to public sector companies, in this case state trading companies. As such, it is highly contentious and serves to illustrate the fact that not all WTO members have accepted the basic notion that private actors are better at managing the means of production than governments.

In 2003, the US challenged Canada's treatment of grain and filed a claim on its export scheme in the WTO. Specifically, the US alleged that the set-up and operation of the CWB, a marketing board that Canada notified as an STE, were inconsistent with Article XVII of the GATT 1994 [PR[2] 4.170, 4.172].

The CWB handles wheat from over 85,000 Western Canadian farmers and markets, sells, finances and supplies the wheat in domestic and international markets.[3] In 2003, the CWB was governed by a 15-person Board of Directors, 10 of whom were elected by Western Canadian grain producers and 5 of whom were appointed by the Canadian government. Except for the president, each CWB director's term consisted of a maximum four years and each director was eligible to serve up to three terms.[4] The statutory mandate of the CWB, as alleged by the US, was the "marketing in an orderly manner, in inter-provincial and export trade, of grain grown in Canada."[5] In pursuit of this objective, Canada granted the CWB monopoly rights of purchase and sale of wheat, a government guarantee of CWB's borrowing and certain CWB credit export sales, the right to set an annual initial rate paid to producers upon purchase and to distribute remaining income in "pool" payments, and a government guarantee of the initial payment.[6] The *CWB Act* provides in Section 7(1) that the CWB shall determine pricing "as it considers reasonable with the object of promoting the sales of grain produced in Canada in world markets."[7]

The US alleged that the CWB paid premiums to domestic producers for high-quality wheat that resulted in production of such wheat that exceeded demand by 32%.[8] The US speculated that the CWB dealt with the above excess by discounting the high-quality wheat to prices of lower quality wheat in different markets, resulting in a quality giveaway.[9] The CWB does not publish any information regarding the terms of its sales and for the purposes of this dispute, did not disclose any information regarding its export sales.[10] In the course of the proceedings, Canada admitted that it does not participate in the day-to-day operations of the CWB.[11]

US's Article XVII:1 Challenge

Citing the Panel's decision in *Korea – Various Measures on Beef*, the US argued that Article XVII: 1 of the GATT 1994 imposes three distinct legal obligations on a Member who establishes and operates an STE and that a breach of any of these obligations constitutes a violation of Article XVII.[12] According to the US, Canada had an affirmative duty to guarantee:

1 that the CWB would "act in a manner consistent with [the] general principles of non-discriminatory treatment,"
2 that the CWB's sales and purchases would be "solely in accordance with commercial considerations" and
3 that the CWB would "afford the enterprises of the other contracting parties adequate opportunity…to compete for participation in" the CWB's sales.[13]

Without identifying particular instances or transactions where Canada breached the above duties, the US argued that Canada failed to meet its Article XVII:1 obligations because the "CWB Export Regime," encompassing the CWB's governance structure and statutory mandate, the "unchecked exercise" of CWB's exclusive privileges and Canada's alleged failure to monitor or control CWB's activities, of itself, necessarily encourages CWB to make export sales that are discriminatory, non-commercial and anti-competitive.[14]

In launching this argument, the US advanced a broad interpretation of the coverage of Article XVII:1. First, the US read the "general principles of non-discriminatory treatment…for governmental measures affecting imports or exports by private traders" to prohibit both discrimination between different export markets (most-favoured-nation principle) and discrimination between export markets and the domestic market of the STE (national treatment principle). The Panel accepted that Article XVII:1(a) embraces the most-favoured-nation principle but left open the question of whether the US was correct in its assertion that Article XVII:1(a) embraces the discrimination between sales in domestic and export markets.[15] Relying on the Ad Note to Article XI barring Members from imposing restrictions on exports through the use of STEs, the US reasoned that the Article XVII principle of non-discrimination extends to sales between domestic and export markets.[16] The Panel characterised the US's allegation of discriminatory sales as a "consequential allegation" resulting from its allegation that the CWB sales failed to comply with Article XVII:1(b) requirements.[17]

The US's construction of Article XVII:1(b) flows from normative competition principles. As such, it is a competition policy-based reading of Article XVII of GATT 1994. Interpreting Article XVII:1(b), the US claimed that Canada and the CWB must afford competing wheat sellers as well as potential wheat buyers an "adequate opportunity...to compete for *participation in*...[the CWB's]...sales." Noting that competing sellers would seek to "prevent...and win for themselves" an export STE's sales rather than seek to "participate in" such sales, the Panel rejected the US's reading. [6.69][18] The US stated that this obligation, "in addition to the first obligation under Article XVII:1(b) to act in accordance with commercial considerations, obliges a Member to ensure that its STEs with special and exclusive benefits and privileges act as commercial actors."[19]

The US argued that the first clause of Article XVII:1(b) is intended to prevent anti-competitive practices: "the 'commercial considerations' requirement... ensure[s] that STEs do not use their special privileges to the disadvantage of commercial actors."[20]

The US interpreted action "solely in accordance with commercial considerations" as not only rational profit-maximising behaviour but also as commercial behaviour that takes into account a STE's obligation to provide enterprises from other Members an opportunity to compete.[21] Such a reading of Article XVII:1 implies that a Member must ensure that despite the privileges a Member confers on its STE, the STE behaves as a commercial actor operating under similar market constraints as a private commercial actor. Since the *CWB Act* conferred special privileges on the CWB and only restricted its pricing to a reasonable level, the US reasoned that the CWB's statutory mandate to promote *sales* instead of profits necessarily leads it to take unfair advantage of its privileges.[22] In other words, the US advanced the proposition that Article XVII's "commercial considerations" test included profit maximising, but not revenue-maximising behaviour. This is as close to a consumer-welfare-enhancing competition test as one is likely to find.

EC's Reading of Article XVII:1

The European Commission (EC), like the US, expressed concern that the *CWB Act* only constrains the CWB to price reasonably and to conduct marketing in "an orderly manner" without compelling the CWB to transact business "in accordance with commercial considerations" or principles of non-discrimination.[23] Though the EC agreed that the CWB's exercise of its special privileges in the context of trade-related activity potentially endangers competitive opportunity and results in non-commercial action, the EC did not agree with the US's view that the use of these advantages *per se* prevents the CWB from acting "in accordance with commercial considerations."[24] The EC believed that the Panel needed to analyse CWB's prices on export sales to determine if it was acting consistently with that obligation.[25] So what analysis did the EC offer?

The Panel's Ruling on the US's Article XVII:1 Claim

As an initial matter, the Panel stated that it was not necessary to its determination of the dispute to decide whether Article XVII:1(b) sets out obligations which are independent of those in subparagraph (a). The Panel "proceed[ed] on the assumption that an inconsistency with Article XVII:1 can be established merely by demonstrating that an STE is acting contrary to the principles of subparagraph (b)."[26] In its analysis, the Panel took a sharply different view of Article XVII:1's requirements than the US interpretation. Citing the definition of "commercial" as "[i]nterested in financial return rather than artistry; likely to make a profit; regarded as a mere matter of business,"[27] the Panel adopted the view that the "commercial considerations" requirement obliges STEs to transact business "on terms which are economically advantageous for themselves and/or their owners, members, beneficiaries."[28]

The Panel also stated that this requirement prohibits STEs from behaving as "political actors"[29] and suggested that transactions based on considerations of a party's nationality, government policy or national economic or political interest could violate Article XVII:1.[30] However, the Panel rejected the US's contention that Article XVII:1 requires export STEs to provide competing sellers with an adequate opportunity to compete in the marketplace.[31] Further, the Panel found no support for the US's claim that Article XVII:1(b)'s "commercial considerations" language requires STEs to act like "commercial actors" unable to use their special or exclusive privileges to the disadvantage of competing sellers.[32] In contrast, the Panel suggested that an export STE might "in accordance with commercial considerations" reduce their prices so as to deter competitors from entering the market.[33] The question of how low that price could be was not analysed.

Declining to adopt the US's interpretation of Article XVII:1(b), the Panel found that the US failed to establish that the structure of the CWB Export Regime "necessarily results" in sales inconsistent with the requirements of Article XVII:1 and determined that the US's allegations of non-conforming sales involving quality giveaways were unsubstantiated. The Panel characterised the US's *per se* challenge to the CWB Export Regime as dependent upon four broad assertions:

1 the CWB derives more flexibility in setting prices and sales terms than private traders because of its exclusive purchase rights, its ability to acquire wheat with an initial purchase price at 65%–70% of its market value which remains fixed for a year, and its access to government guaranteed financing[34];

2 the flexibility derived from such privileges allows the CWB to makes sales based on non-commercial considerations, suppress competitive opportunity, and target markets in a discriminatory fashion[35];
3 the CWB's statutory mandate to maximise sales quantity or revenue instead of profit and its governance structure offer incentives for the CWB to use its flexibility to undersell "commercial actors" who are unable to compete with the low prices CWB's privileges enable it to set[36]; and
4 Canada has failed to oversee the CWB and guarantee that its sales conform to Article XVII:1(a) and (b).[37]

After noting that the US needed to establish each assertion to prevail, the Panel found no merit in the US's third assertion. Taking up the US's argument that the elected CWB directors who seek re-election by Canadian producers have incentives to satisfy the maximum amount of producers with the maximum amount of sales, the Panel, *inter alia*, argued that the CWB directors satisfy such producers by maximising their returns on those sales and therefore, the governance structure does not provide incentives to transact business in a non-commercial manner.[38] The Panel noted that the CWB's governance structure ensures that the Canadian producers control the CWB and that the Canadian government's non-interference in the CWB's sales activities strengthens the Panel's conclusions that the governance structure encourages CWB's transactions that are driven solely by the commercial interests of the Canadian producers.[39] The Panel found that the CWB's legal mandate or objective to promote the sale of Western Wheat was a commercial objective, was not a *per se* incentive to make sales based on non-commercial considerations, and in light of statements by the CWB's CEO and evidence that the CWB deferred sales to maximise producers' returns, does not support the proposition that the CWB has an incentive to sacrifice profit for sales revenue.[40] Further, the Panel found that the "reasonable pricing" standard contained in Section 7(1) of the *CWB Act* does not encourage the CWB to sell below the best price it could obtain in any given market.[41] Rejecting the US's argument that Article XVII:1 requires the CWB to act like a private grain trader, the Panel also found no support for the US's assertion that the Article XVII:1 "commercial consideration" obligation requires STEs to function as profit-maximisers as opposed to revenue-maximisers.[42]

The Panel concluded that neither the statutory mandate nor the governance structure *per se* encourages the CWB to exercise its privileges to conduct sales based on other than commercial considerations. In the absence of such evidence, the Panel further concluded that the CWB has no incentive to engage in non-commercial discrimination between markets.[43] Having disposed of the US's claim that Article XVII:1(b)'s "adequate opportunity" requirement applies to an export STE's sales competitors, the Panel concluded that the US failed to establish that CWB Export Regime "necessarily results in non-conforming CWB export sales; and … that Canada breached its obligations under Article XVII:1 of the GATT 1994."[44]

Appellate Body Arguments and Findings

The Parties' Arguments on Appeal

On appeal, Canada asserted that the Panel erred in its interpretation of the relationship between the obligations set out in Articles XVII:1(a) and (b). Canada argued that the Panel's statement that a finding of a breach of the obligations in subparagraph (b) is sufficient to establish a violation of Article XVII:1 is an incorrect reading.[45] In Canada's view, an Article XVII:1 violation can be established only after it is determined that an action violates the principles of non-discriminatory treatment under subparagraph (a) *and* fails to conform with the criteria in subparagraph (b).[46] Therefore, the Panel erred in assessing the CWB Export Regime's compliance with subparagraph (b) independently and before it determined whether it complied with the principles of non-discriminatory treatment.[47] In support of its position, Canada cited a statement by the *Canada – FIRA* Panel that it claimed was later endorsed by the Panel in *Korea – Various Measures on Beef*: "the 'commercial considerations criterion becomes relevant only after it has been determined that the governmental action at issue falls within the scope of the general principles of non-discriminatory treatment.'"[48]

On appeal, the US argued that the Panel incorrectly interpreted "solely in accordance with commercial considerations" and "enterprises" within second clause of Article XVII:1(b).[49] Specifically, the US challenged the Panel's statement that the "commercial considerations" requirement was "simply intended to prevent STEs from behaving like 'political actors.'"[50] The US urged that "'commercial considerations' are those 'experienced by commercial actors…interested in financial return'…act[ing] within the limits of their cost constraints…sell[ing] at prices that, at a minimum, would equal the replacement value of a good."[51] Disagreeing with the Panel's textual reading of subparagraph (b), the US renewed its argument that the enterprises to which a STE must provide competitive opportunity include not only those enterprises who wish to buy from the STE but also those who wish to compete for its sales.[52] The US argued that these interpretive errors led the Panel to undertake only a partial analysis of the challenged measure.[53]

Statements of Third Parties on Appeal

Australia supported Canada's argument that the fundamental obligation of Article XVII:1 is of non-discriminatory treatment and that in order to establish a violation of this provision, it is necessary to find a violation of subparagraphs (a) *and* (b).[54] China took an indeterminate position, stating that if an STE complied with the criteria of subparagraph (b), then the Member fulfilled the non-discrimination requirement under (a).[55] The EC argued that subparagraph (b) defines the scope of the non-discrimination requirement under (a), and thus, a violation of (b) would necessarily result in a violation of (a). The EC rejected the US's view that subparagraphs (a) and (b) establish independent obligations.[56]

Australia and China supported the Panel's interpretations of "commercial considerations" and "enterprises" within subparagraph (a).[57] China added that gaining market share is a better indicator of commercial considerations than replacement value which may not be met in certain situations, specifically when a commercial actor attempts to penetrate a market.[58] The EC expressed agreement with the Panel's interpretation of "commercial considerations" but in the interests of clarification, stated that "the sole benchmark for interpreting the term…is to determine whether the market behaviour of an STE is in accordance with normal private behaviour."[59] The EC, however, stated that the Panel erred in excluding sellers from the "enterprises" to which an STE must afford an opportunity to compete. The EC argued that their position is supported by the language "to compete" and by the need to compensate for the market advantage STEs derive from their special privileges.[60]

Findings of the Appellate Body

Relationship between Subparagraphs (a) and (b) of Article XVII:1 – Appellate Body

Disagreeing with the US's position that subparagraphs (a) and (b) of Article XVII:1 contain separate and independent obligations, the Appellate Body concluded that subparagraph (a) of Article XVII:1 is the "general and principle provision" that imposes an obligation of non-discrimination and subparagraph (b) elucidates the scope of that obligation by "identifying types of differential treatment in commercial transactions."[61] The Appellate Body contextualised the isolated language in the *Korea – Various Measures on Beef* panel report that the US relied on for the proposition that Article XVII:1 set out three distinct legal obligations and in doing so, supported its contention that the *Korea – Various Measures on Beef* and *Canada – FIRA* panels' interpretations of Article XVII:1 obligations were in harmony with their own.[62]

With regard to Canada's claim that the Panel erred in the order of its analysis, the Appellate Body stated:

> we are of the view that a failure to identify *any* conduct alleged to constitute discrimination…*before* undertaking an analysis of the consistency of an STE's conduct with subparagraph (b) of Article XVII:1 would constitute an error of law. Had the Panel in this case simply *ignored* the issue of possible discrimination…and passed immediately to its analysis under subparagraph (b), we would have no difficulty….concluding that that Panel erred…[y]et this does not appear to be what the Panel did.

Tracing the Panel's discussion and analysis of discrimination, the Appellate Body concluded that the Panel did not err in its mode of analysis.[63]

Interpretation of "Commercial Considerations" in Subparagraph (b) of Article XVII:1

As an initial matter, the Appellate Body noted that the US's sole challenge on this issue was the Panel's statement regarding "political actors."[64] The Appellate Body commented that the US's assertion that the Panel equated the obligation to act in accordance with "commercial considerations" with an "obligation to make "non-political" decision" was a decontextualised mischaracterisation of the Panel's interpretation of "commercial considerations."[65] Dismissing the appeal, the Appellate Body concluded that the Panel's statement did not intend to equate "non-commercial" actors with "political actors" but only served to indicate that political considerations were one of several possible non-commercial considerations.[66] The Appellate Body identified the Panel's interpretation of "commercial considerations" "as encompassing a range of different considerations that are defined in any given case by the type of 'business' involved (purchases or sales), and by the economic considerations that motivate actors engaged in business in the relevant market(s)."[67]

The Appellate Body added, in light of its conclusion that the scope of enquiry into "commercial considerations" is governed by the principle of non-discriminatory behaviour under subparagraph (a), that a panel does not have the authority to engage in a speculative enquiry as to whether STEs are "acting 'commercially'" but must tie the enquiry to discriminatory behaviour. It chided the US: "[w]e see no basis for interpreting that provision as imposing comprehensive competition-law-type obligations on STEs, as the United States would have us do."[68] The Appellate Body also rejected anew the US's argument that STEs could not utilise their special privileges to the competitive disadvantage of private enterprises: "STEs, like private enterprises, are entitled to exploit the advantages they enjoy to their economic benefit."[69] The Appellate Body supported the Panel's reasoning that "commercial considerations" are assessed by a "market-based analysis" not by whether STEs function as "*virtuous* commercial actors" and that Article VI of the GATT 1994 and other WTO agreements also discipline the activities of STEs.[70]

Interpretation of "Enterprises" in Subparagraph (b) of Article XVII:1

The Appellate Body concurred with the Panel's assessment that in this case "enterprises" encompassed only potential wheat buyers and excluded sellers who sought to compete with an export STE for its sales.[71] The Appellate Body extrapolated that finding into a more coherent principle:

> the requirement to afford an adequate opportunity to compete for participation…in import or export transactions involving an STE must refer to the opportunity to become the STE's counterpart in the transaction, *not* to

> an opportunity to replace the STE as a participant in the transaction. If it were otherwise, the transaction would no longer be the type of transaction described by the phrase "*such* purchases or sales" in the second clause of Article XVII:1(b), because it would not involve an STE as a party.[72]

Agreeing with the US's argument that "enterprises" encompasses buyers and sellers, the Appellate Body found that its application depended on the role of the STE in the particular transaction involved.

The US attempted to insert competition into Article XVII:1, a measure designed to ensure that as STEs engage in commercial trade, they operate in conformity with the principle of non-discriminatory treatment. While the Panel rebuffed the US's attempt, the Appellate Body expressly foreclosed the use of Article XVII:1 as grounds to challenge the anti-competitive conduct of STEs if such conduct is divorced from evidence of discrimination.

However, in ruling as it did, the Appellate Body may have opened the door to precisely the kind of consumer-welfare-enhancing test that the Panel had initially tried to block. By restricting the "adequate opportunity to compete" test to consumers of the CWB (and not competitors) – the Appellate Body was in effect saying that if consumers were damaged, then a claim might be held. New in practice, any behaviour which would harm consumers of the CWB would also damage CWB competitors but the opposite would not always be the case. By analogy, in competition cases brought by private parties, one of the pre-requisites to bringing a case is that the plaintiff must first establish antitrust standing by showing evidence of consumer injury.[73] While competitors may be "damaged" by behaviour that has no impact on consumer welfare, they may be harmed if there is consumer harm.

The US could have pursued a different line of attack in the CWB case by focusing on the precise type of behaviour that gave rise to problematic consequences. By focusing on the precise behaviour, the US could have argued that certain types of behaviour by the CWB violated the "commercial considerations" standard, which was applicable to the situations where the STE was buying in order to sell on international markets. By so arguing, the alleged predatory conduct by CWB could have been highlighted, and the specific problematic behaviour exposed. The behaviour consisted of the following (Figure 8.1):

It is important to note that in both cases, CWB is pricing below *real* cost, because of its monopolistic position. In other words the reason that $P_i = C_i - \Delta x$, as opposed to $C_i + \Delta x$ as it would be in a normal competitive market scenario is because of the monopoly power which is conferred on the CWB by statute. There is no other reason that Canadian farmers could sell below cost to the CWB.

Now the CWB does get preferential credit treatment from the Canadian government; hence, the actual cost for CWB in its sales is really $[C_i - \Delta x/z]$ to reflect the government-granted preferential credit terms.

P_j which equals $(P_i + \Delta y)$ becomes $[C_i - \Delta x/z] + \Delta y$. These are all substantially below cost, and therefore have negative impacts. But by holding P_j constant,

Where $P_i = C_i - \Delta x$,

Where C_i = cost of production of wheat crop, $_i$

And Δx represents the monopoly rent of the CWB

$P_j = (C_i - \Delta x + \Delta y)$, where $\Delta y < \Delta x$, and represents a "profit" element that can be passed back to Canadian farmers.

FIGURE 8.1 Schematic for Canadian Wheat Production

CWB can increase its profit by $P_i - P_j = [C_i - \Delta x] - [C_i - \Delta x/z]$. As z increases, CWB's profit margin increases while not affecting the profit element, Δy that can be returned to the farmer. This is a classic problem for competition. The producers (farmers, the CWB) are happy because they are all seeing some kind of profit, but the money is being taken from consumers.

It is interesting that Canadian farmers are prepared to sell at $P_i = C_i - \Delta x$, whereas competing farmers would be forced to sell at $P_i = C_i + \Delta x$, where x represents their profit element. The difference in price (a multiple of Δx) could be significant and could lead to significant market share erosion for competing farmers. Canadian farmers would only tolerate selling to CWB at P_i if they knew that the profit element returned to them Δy exceeded their loss, Δx. Even taking into account the preferential credit terms, the profit element that can be returned is $(C_i - \Delta x) - (C_i - \Delta x/z) + \Delta y$. Unless z is very large (i.e. the credit term extremely preferential), this is unlikely to be a significant profit. Farmers must either get another loan from the government to cover their loss or CWB must get a highly preferential credit rate.

Lack of Transparency of Regulation

In either case, farmers are made whole and/or given a profit element. The question is where does that profit element come from? If it is paid to farmers in the form of loans/subventions or even in preferential credit which is obtained by government privilege and not by economies of scale, then it is the taxpayer who pays. The length of time that the taxpayer is prepared to underwrite this, Δt, is inversely proportional to the transparency of the regulations in question. If transparency of regulation is denoted by R_t then $\Delta t = k/R_t$, where k is a constant.

Consumer Welfare Test

If CWB is competing with other producers, P_n where n represents producers from country, n, and these producers must charge a price of $(C_i + \Delta x^1)$ where C_i is their cost of production, and Δx^1 is the profit element which they charge then if these producers can establish harm to consumers of the CWB – by demonstrating that purchase of wheat on global markets are receiving below-cost prices, an Article XVII violation might be established. Both the Panel and AB were at pains to point out that the existence of a producer-controlled monopoly was not by itself GATT inconsistent. The only area that implicated the GATT was if the monopoly had a distortive impact on trade. The problem with this logic is that by definition a producer-controlled monopoly will have an impact on trade. Such a fact pattern is more likely to ground a violation of Article XVII as the AB conceived it in the CWB case. It is ironic that the AB and Panel in trying to prevent the introduction of competition concepts opened the door for a real antitrust argument to establish an Article XVII violation.

The case illustrates the tension inherent in GATT provisions between underlying competition principles – those that the fundamental economics on which trade liberalisation is based suggest, and the strictly legalistic application of the pillars of the GATT which we have discussed earlier in this book, non-discrimination and MFN. The appellate body resolves this tension by effectively reading non-discrimination into Article XVII. However the presence of STEs like the CWB will continue to distort markets and thwart the very agricultural market openings that trade negotiators are presently working towards. The case offered an opportunity to enshrine the economic underpinnings of global trade agreements into the interpretation of those agreements themselves, but it is clear that the Panel and the AB missed an important opportunity. It is useful to look carefully at the US arguments as it is likely that these types of arguments will keep recurring in the WTO not only as regards STEs but also in other areas.

The central point of contention was the precise definition of "commercial considerations" in the context of activity where the state was buying as a market participant. Here widely different views were expressed by Canada, which argued that anything not overtly political was "commercial," the US which argued that only behaviour that was profit maximising satisfied the test, and the EU middle path. Stepping from the minutiae of the GATT rule itself, and considering the role that STEs play in the global economy where they regularly compete with private companies, it is quite clear that any rule of international law which gives them treatment different from those private companies with whom they compete does indeed distort the playing field. Applying the theory of trade and competition that we have expressed in this book, it seems obvious that where STEs engage in behaviour that moves away from the consumer-welfare-enhancing market equilibrium, this is an unwarranted distortion which should be disciplined. Note that this does not mean that every benefit that the STE gains from its government ownership is necessarily problematic, only if used to negatively impact consumer welfare. This rule would allow governments to assist their STEs and would allow STEs to continue to operate. It also explicitly recognises the fact that STEs can be beneficial to consumer welfare and are not harmful per se a point that the Panel and AB in *CWB* were most anxious to express. The question is what is the precise impact of their activity on the market and this is fairly clearly a competition question. This also ties in the issue of transparency of regulation and accounting clarity which we discuss in other chapters. As we have noted both the length of time that taxpayers will tolerate subventions to producers and the length of time that STEs can engage in below-cost pricing is inversely proportional to the transparency of regulation. This is an important dynamic, as in order to establish Article XVII violations, plaintiffs will need substantial data from the STEs and their governments about how costs are allocated and precisely what privileges accrue to the STE. Claims may be very difficult to bring without this data, so GATT Article XI's transparency obligations become far more than just a hortatory measure.

WTO Members' Positions on State Trading Enterprises

WTO members have reacted to the potential for cases to be brought under Article XVII by generally taking a more limited position and a restrictive reading of Article XVII. There has been some discussion of agricultural reform in the state trading sector in the agricultural negotiations. A summary of those negotiations which have been very limited is discussed below. The starting point for the discussion is the State Trading Enterprises (GATT Article XVII) Understanding. This provides that Members must notify such enterprises to the WTO (and Article 1 further defines STEs to include market boards as well as governmental and non-governmental enterprises which have been granted exclusive or special rights or privileges, including statutory or constitutional powers. Under the Understanding (Article 5) the Council for Trade in Goods to review notifications and counter-notifications. This provides an avenue for parties to complain about the activities of other parties. The most recently released minutes of the working party (22 Feb 2006) illustrates that the New Zealand Dairy Board, the US Commodity Credit Corporation, as well as the antitrust exemption for agricultural co-operatives under the Capper-Volstead Act (Australia asserted that the said antitrust exemption was a special privilege within the meaning of the Understanding or STEs.

However, it should be noted that these discussions are somewhat in their infancy. The working party did not meet in 2005 and only twice in 2006.

The essential collapse of the Doha Development Agenda in the early 21st century has done little to take forward the important discussions on the precise meaning of Article XVII. However, in the area of the interface between trade and competition, the way STEs can be disciplined is key to the development of trade and competition concepts and also key to the competition between private companies and STEs. Interestingly, largely as a result of the consumer damage caused by these STEs, both in Canada and in Australia, there are significant parliamentary pressures to at least eliminate the state-granted monopoly.

In addition, there have been a number of cases on "state bodies" since the CWB case. Clearly the role of government enterprises in the global economy has changed over the last couple of decades in ways that increase their impact, as well as their scope. These problems are not confined to traditional definitions of STEs. This has created a number of problems in the WTO, including the most recent impasse on the Appellate Body. The US has refused to authorise new members of the Appellate Body, and thus prevented it from sitting largely because of their concern about the direction of travel of various decisions regarding state bodies. Some of the US's concerns here relate to judicial activism in the areas of subsidies, trade remedies and technical standards, where the AB has actually issued rulings that clarify obligations under the WTO agreements especially the TBT, and agreements relating to trade remedies. There is an additional US complaint where the AB has restricted the interpretation of what constitutes a "state body." Both of these complaints are somewhat inconsistent, as in the area of "state bodies" the US is asking for a wider interpretation than the strict letter of the WTO agreements (which China among others opposes).

The definition of "public body" is subject to the interpretation of the Agreement on Subsidies and Countervailing Measures (SCM Agreement). Under the SCM Agreement, a market-distorting subsidy can be alleged if the financial contribution is made not only by the government, but also by a "public body." Hence, the "public body" definition is very important. The US opposed the AB ruling that in order to qualify as a public body, the entity must possess or exercise governmental authority.[74] Of course, many Chinese SOEs do not have such powers but do use their government funds to distort markets. The US there argued that a better test was if the body could use the state resources as if they were its own. The US opposed to imposition of a new test that was not consistent with the problem that the WTO agreement itself was trying to solve. In some ways, this is part of an ongoing clash between civil and common law interpretations. The USTR interpretation flows directly from the purpose of the SCM Agreement – to lower the level of funds given by the state to private firms, whereas the AB test sought to limit the fulfilment of that purpose by taking out certain funds from the scope of the agreement simply because of the design of the public body itself. The AB also said that you do not need to compare prices with prevailing market prices to find a distortion and could use other benchmarks especially where the market was affected by government activity. This illogical approach suggested that you could not use the benchmark of market prices because market prices were not useful in markets where prices are distorted by government intervention.[75]

We now turn to EU rules governing anti-competitive activities fostered by EU member governments.

EU Treaty Articles (Other than State Aids) Designed to Curb Government Restraints on Competition

The EU Treaty contains various articles designed to curb anti-competitive activities facilitated or authorised by EU member states.[76] These provisions promote the Treaty's broad aim of facilitating economic integration and the creation of a single market within the EU. At the same time, they seek to achieve a balance by advancing procompetitive market integration goals in a manner that takes into account legitimate sovereign member state interests in overseeing their national economies. Article 107 of the Treaty, which we addressed previously in Chapter 3, deals directly with "state aids," trade-distorting financial subsidies. Below, we discuss those Treaty measures aimed at other methods by which EU member state governments may undermine competition and free trade within Europe. Properly applied, Article 107 and the other articles we highlight below are complementary means for promoting competition and free trade within the EU, and, thus, for enhancing consumer welfare. (The US constitutional structure imposes far greater constraints on the reining in of anti-competitive governmental action. In marked contrast to the EU, the US states are not barred from conferring subsidies on favoured companies, from creating or operating state monopolies, or even from displacing competition in particular defined sectors, as long as such displacement affirmatively expresses state policy and is actively supervised by the state.)

In particular, EU Treaty Article 4(3) (*effect utile* doctrine), Article 36 (state monopolies) and Article 106 (public undertakings) have been invoked to combat state-facilitated anti-competitive actions that run afoul of the substantive antitrust prohibitions found in Articles 101 and 102. Articles 4(3), 36 and 106 have been invoked in legal actions brought by the EC and in private actions brought in EU member states courts. The judicial holdings in this area are rife with ambiguities and exceptions, but overall they reflect a serious effort to rein in state-sanctioned anti-competitive abuses, albeit imperfectly (reflecting at least in part the need to accommodate legitimate state sovereign interests).

Article 4(3) (*effet utile*)

Article 4(3) requires that member states not adopt or maintain in force measures that would "jeopardise the attainment of the Union's objectives" (*effet utile*), including of course the objectives of the Articles 101 and 102 competition clauses. As one leading scholar explains, "[t]he *effet utile* doctrine provides the EU with a powerful instrument to police member state economic activity. National competition authorities and member state courts also play an important role."[77] Thus, for example, on multiple occasions a national EU competition agency that has found national laws undermined competition has invoked the support of the European Court of Justice, pursuant to Article 4(3).

In *Italian Matches*,[78] the Italian competition authority found that Italian legislation conferring monopoly power on a consortium of Italian match producers violated EU competition law, and requested the views of the ECJ. Invoking Article 4(3), the court held that a national competition authority must disregard a national law that legitimises or reinforces the effects of private conduct that the national law facilitates.

Various cases have dealt with state delegations to private undertakings responsibility for taking decisions that affect markets.[79] The decisions have been inconsistent. In one matter (*Commission v. Italy*),[80] an Italian law setting prices for the hiring of private customs agents was held to violate Articles 4(3) and 101. In a later judgement (*Arduino*),[81] however, the court upheld an Italian law authorising the Italian Justice Minister to fix minimum and maximum lawyers' fees, based on a proposal prepared by a lawyers' committee. The not entirely convincing reasoning of the court emphasised that the Minister was not bound by the committee's recommendation, and that Italian courts could deviate from the fee schedule in exceptional cases.

The courts have held that, in certain areas implicating traditional sovereign exercises of authority, member states maintain substantial scope for state action affecting the operation of markets, without violating Article 4(3). Thus, the Court of Justice has generally rejected challenges to member state action to maintain national price controls, impose taxes or collect levies.[82]

Article 37 (State Monopolies)

Article 37 is a non-discrimination provision that seeks to limit obstacles to the free movement of trade

> except for those inherent in the existence of the [state-granted] monopoly. Article 37 has been applied to alcohol and tobacco monopolies, monopolies for the retail sale of medicines, and monopolies for the import and sale of natural gas and electricity.[83]

It states in pertinent part:

1 Member states shall adjust any State monopolies of a commercial character so as to ensure that no discrimination regarding the conditions under which goods are procured and marketed exists between nationals of member states.
   The provisions of this Article shall apply to any body through which a member state, in law or in fact, either directly or indirectly supervises, determines or appreciably influences imports or exports between member states. These provisions shall likewise apply to monopolies delegated by the State to others.
2 Member states shall refrain from introducing any new measure which is contrary to the principles laid down in paragraph 1 or which restricts the scope of the articles dealing with the prohibition of customs duties and quantitative restrictions between member states.

For example, in *Franzen*,[84] the court dealt with a Swedish state-owned liquor retail monopoly (Systembolaget), combined with a complex system of state-imposed licences for import, export, production, and wholesaling that favoured another state-owned company, V&S. The court found that the licencing scheme violated Article 34 (the prior number for Article 37), in that it constituted an obstacle to the importation of alcoholic beverages from other EU states and imposed additional costs on such beverages. The court rejected Sweden's justification of the licencing scheme as necessary to maintaining public health by restraining alcoholism (under Article 36 of the EU Treaty, which authorises "public policy" exceptions to Article 37 if they do not involve "arbitrary discrimination or a disguised restriction on trade"). The court stressed that Sweden had not established that the alcohol licencing system was proportionate to the public health system being pursued or could not have been obtained by means that are less trade restrictive.

Article 106 (Public Undertakings)

Article 106 deals with public undertakings, including state-owned and -controlled enterprises. It states:

1 In the case of public undertakings and undertakings to which member states grant special or exclusive rights, member states shall neither enact nor maintain in force any measure contrary to the rules contained in the Treaties, in particular to those rules provided for in Article 18 and Articles 101 to 109.
2 Undertakings entrusted with the operation of services of general economic interest or having the character of a revenue-producing monopoly shall be subject to the rules contained in the Treaties, in particular to the rules on competition, in so far as the application of such rules does not obstruct the performance, in law or in fact, of the particular tasks assigned to them. The development of trade must not be affected to such an extent as would be contrary to the interests of the Union.
3 The Commission shall ensure the application of the provisions of this Article and shall, where necessary, address appropriate directives or decisions to member states.

Public undertakings are entities over which public authorities may exercise a direct or indirect dominant interest through ownership, financial participation, or public rules. Public undertakings that receive favourable or discriminatory treatment are deemed to have been granted special or exclusive rights in derogation of Article 106. Article 106 may be directly invoked in member state courts by private individuals. In addition, the EU can issue general directives and decisions to member states in order to ensure that they comply with their Article 106 obligations. Thus, for example, in 2006 the Commission issued the Transparency Directive to verify that public undertakings are not unlawfully receiving public funds.[85] And the Commission has issued quasi-legislative sector-specific directives to liberalise or deregulate markets previously reserved for state-owned companies.

As indicated by its language, Article 106(2) exempts from Article 101 and Article 102 liability undertakings that have been assigned "services of public economic interest" (SGEI), to the extent a 106 prohibition would obstruct the performance of particular public tasks, if certain conditions are met. The Commission has explained that SGEI include "economic activities which deliver outcomes in the overall public good that would not be supplied (or would be supplied under different conditions in terms of quality, safety, affordability, equal treatment or universal access) by the market without public intervention."[86] A key limitation, however, is that "[t]he exclusive or special rights must be proportionate and not go beyond what is necessary to achieve the public interest objective."[87] Member states do have broad discretion to define SGEIs, which include such service as public broadcasting, telephone systems, basic postal services, and operation of necessary but commercially non-viable air routes.[88] Banks and copyright societies are examples of non-SGEIs that do not receive Article 106 exemptions.[89]

EU competition scholars Whish and Bailey have drawn three major principles from the extensive Section 106 case law: (1) for a violation, there must be a causal link between legislative or administrative intervention and the undertaking's infringing conduct; (2) mere creation of a dominant position by the grant of exclusive rights does not infringe Article 106(1); and (3) an infringement of Article 106(1) does not require abuse of a dominant position, merely the risk of an abuse.[90]

A brief view of some well-known Article 106 cases provides a practical perspective on the breadth of application of this important provision.

A number of cases have involved state-owned ports that were gateways to international trade. States typically enacted measures to strengthen those ports' ability to exclude and discriminate against competitors.

In *Port of Rødby*,[91] DSB, a Danish public undertaking operated by the transport ministry, held exclusive rights to operate railroad traffic in Denmark, owned the Port of Rødby, and operated ferry services between Denmark and neighbouring countries. Stena was a Swedish shipping group that specialised in ferry services and wished to operate between Denmark and Germany (Puttgarden), which effectively links eastern Denmark with Germany and the rest of western Europe. Stena requested Danish Government permission to use the Rodby port facilities or build a nearby port, the Government refused, and Stena complained to the EC. In light of the case law, the Commission concluded that

> an undertaking that owns or manages an essential port facility from which it provides a maritime transport service may not, without objective justification, refuse to grant a shipowner wishing to operate on the same maritime route access to that facility without infringing Article [102].

Furthermore, case law indicated that Article 106(1)

> prohibits Member States from placing, by law, regulation or administrative provision, public undertakings and undertakings to which they grant exclusive rights in a position in which those undertakings could not place themselves by their own conduct without infringing Article [102]. [W]here the extension of the dominant position of a public undertaking or an undertaking to which the State has granted exclusive rights resulted from a State measure, such a measure constituted an infringement of Article [106], read in conjunction with Article [102] of the Treaty.

Applying this precedential reasoning, the Commission held that DSB's refusal of access to Stena violated Articles 102 and 106. The Commission found no evidence that granting such access would saturate or exceed Rødby's port capacity. Moreover, even on a saturated market, the Commission concluded that

> an improvement in the quality of products or services offered or a reduction in prices as a result of competition is a definite advantage for consumers; this could also lead to an increase in demand which, in the present case, could be met by expanding the port.

Merci Convenzionali Port di Genova v. Siderurgica Gabrielle SpA (Case C-179/90)[92] involved a government-imposed port hiring scheme that discriminated against non-Italian workers. The Italian Navigation Code established an exclusive right to organise dock work needed by third parties, and mandated retention of dock work companies that employed only registered workers who were Italian nationals. In addition, carriers coming to port were barred from using their crews to load and unload, and the port authority controlled the organisation of dock work. Merci, holder of the exclusive right to organise dock work in the Port of Genoa, delayed unloading Siderurgica Gabrielli's goods, thereby imposing damages on Siderurgica, which sought compensation. An Italian Court asked the European Court of Justice whether the Italian rules violated Articles 4(3), 102 and 106 (plus other EU Constitution Italian articles dealing with the free movement of goods and workers). The Court held that the Italian rules induced undertakings granted exclusive rights: (1) to demand payments for services that had not been requested; (2) to charge disproportionate prices; (3) to refuse to use modern technology (causing delays and prices increases) or (4) to grant reductions to certain consumers and at the same time to offset such reductions by an increase in the charges to other customers. These effects amounted to an abuse of a dominant position under Article 102 and were capable of affecting trade between EU member states. As such, Article 106 was violated.

Another interesting case involves competition in employment services. In *Hofner v. Macrotron GmbH*,[93] a German national court referred to the European Court of Justice a private employment agency's challenge to a German law that conferred an exclusive right of job placement on the German Federal Employment Office (allegedly aimed at achieving a high level of employment and at improving the distribution of jobs). The agency claimed that the law excluded competition in violation of Article 102 and thereby violated Article 106. The court agreed with the agency, finding that the German Employment Office "is manifestly not in a position to satisfy the demand prevailing on the market for activities of that kind and when the effective pursuit of such activities by private parties companies is rendered impossible."

In *Greek Lignite*,[94] in connection with electricity market liberalisation, Greece granted an exclusive licence to explore and exploit lignite to DEI, the former electricity monopoly still majority owned by the Greek government. Lignite (brown coal) was the cheapest source of electricity in Greece. The EC found an Article 102 abuse of a dominant position and a violation of Article 106. The European Court of Justice backed the Commission (and overturned a General Court determination) in finding a violation. The Court of Justice found that DEI's exercise of exclusive lignite exploitation rights had the effect of extending its dominant position from the lignite supply market to the wholesale electricity market, in breach of Article 102. Importantly, the Court held that it is not necessary for the Commission to show, in every case, that the undertaking concerned enjoys a monopoly, or that the state measure at issue awards it exclusive rights over a neighbouring or separate market, or that it has any regulatory powers. Furthermore, the Court emphasised that the Commission has no duty to show the actual impact of the Article 102 and Article 106 infringement on the interests of consumers.

Even that most traditional of state-owned monopolies, the national postal service, may violate Article 106 by abusing its dominant position in derogation of Article 102. For example, Deutsche Post, which owns a monopoly over postal service in Germany, was fined in 2001 by the EC for granting rebates, in addition to engaging in predatory pricing for its parcel services.[95] These abusive prices undermined competition. Deutsche Post also was required to establish a new separate entity for business parcel services, and to sell goods and services, under the same prices (market prices) and conditions, to both the new entity and the new entity's competitors.

The European Court of Justice, however, declined to condemn a Dutch law granting to a specified state-endorsed fund an exclusive right to manage supplementary textile pensions, in the *Albany International BV and Textile Industry Pension Funds*[96] case. Albany International, a textile firm that sought to provide pensions for its workers through an insurer of its choice, challenged the law. The Court stated (citing *Hofner*) that the mere creation of a dominant position (conferred on the pension fund by Dutch law) is not incompatible with Article 102. Here, the Court opined that a particular social task of general interest had been assigned to the state-favoured fund, making it an Article 106(2) SGEI. The Court noted that the state-supported fund "fulfils an essential social function within the Netherlands pension system." Specifically, the fund was required to manage the supplementary pension scheme for all workers in the textile sector, without regard to risk. Because this feature rendered the service provided by the favoured fund less competitive than a comparable service provided by insurance companies, the fund required exclusivity in order to carry out its assigned public function, according to the Court. Although it declined to find an Article 106 violation, the Court did, however, suggest that the Dutch Government could have chosen an economically efficient more efficient means to provide supplementary pensions for textile workers:

> Finally, as regards Albany's argument that an adequate level of pension for workers could be assured by laying down minimum requirements to be met by pensions offered by insurance companies, it must be emphasised

> that, in view of the social function of supplementary pension schemes and the margin of appreciation enjoyed, according to settled case-law, by the Member States in organising their social security systems, it is incumbent on each Member State to consider whether, in view of the particular features of its international pension system, laying down minimum requirements would still enable it to ensure the level of pension where it seeks to guarantee in a sector by compulsory affiliation to a pension fund.

EU Oversight of Anti-Competitive State Activity

Considered as a whole, Articles 4(3), 37 and 106 of the EU Treaty give EC competition enforcers and private parties substantial power to root out and challenge state-owned and state-supported monopolies and business consortia whose activities harm competition. This power is not unlimited; the Articles in question have sufficiently flexible language (and contain limited public policy exceptions, in the case of Article 106) to restrain enforcers and the courts from challenging all material competitive harms fostered by state actors. Nevertheless, as documented by individual enforcement actions and case holdings, these EU Treaty provisions have achieved significant successes in blocking particularly abusive conduct and in reining in member state government favouritism. As such, Articles 4(3), 37 and 106 helpfully complement Articles 107–109 of the European Treaty, that seek to rein in anti-competitive state subsidies (state aids).

Five broad points regarding the power of EU constitutional constraints on state-imposed harm to competition emerge from the case law.

First, both the EC and national competition authorities have vigorously challenged (and, in the case of national authorities, requested supportive rulings from European federal courts) national government actions (including legislation) that undermine competition through state-backed entities. This record underscores the remarkable degree of political independence possessed by competition agencies in Europe and their willingness to take on politically sensitive interests.

Second, successful challenges to anti-competitive state schemes have been particularly noteworthy in the case of state monopolies that clearly distort international trade. Successful challenges to discrimination by international ports and by the Swedish alcohol trade monopoly (among other cases) illustrate that point. In such cases involving substantial cross-border effects, the EU's interest in promoting a single market and preventing trade distortions within Europe is paramount. Because such matters involve substantial distortive cross-border effects, they possess the essential nature of ACMDs – but for the fact that unlike ACMDs, they fall within the ambit of competition law prohibitions.

Third, when state competition-restrictive rules have purely (or almost purely) domestic effects, as in the cases of the Dutch supplementary pension scheme and Italian state-sponsored lawyer price fixing, the European single market goal is far less implicated and national public policy interests not surprisingly will be accorded greater deference. Thus, EU law challenges to schemes of purely national anti-competitive impact are not very likely to succeed. In such instances, challenges under national competition law by national competition authorities may offer far better prospects for success.

Fourth, by commendably empowering both private parties and state enforcers to combat many (though not all) anti-competitive state monopoly abuses, the European Treaty provides a powerful disincentive to rent-seeking activities within the EU that are aimed at obtaining or retaining state monopoly privileges. As such, the EU constitutional constraints on anti-competitive state action may provide a useful model for other jurisdictions that are considering statutory and constitutional refinements to enhance competition policy.

Fifth, taking action against government-fostered monopolies and related competitive constraints is an excellent investment of scarce resources by competition authorities. Because naked imposition of monopoly schemes by governments almost never has credible efficiency justifications, successful enforcement endeavours in this area almost unequivocally enhance consumer welfare. Error costs are close to nil. In contrast, competition law challenges to purely private business restrictions often raise difficult questions about whether the behaviour under scrutiny has efficiency justifications that outweigh alleged anti-competitive harm (except for cases of plainly harmful hard core cartel behaviour). As such, they are rife with error costs, and thus the social return on combating private non-cartel competitive constraints may be relatively smaller than on combating hard core cartels and government-imposed monopoly abuses. (Of course, political constraints of various sorts may well preclude a reallocation of enforcement resources suggested by this analysis.)

The EU's approach gives us an indication of what can be expected from a more multilateral approach to the problem. The EU's jurisprudence is quite developed largely because the EU single market is much more integrated than the global market. However as global trade integrates global markets more, there is learning from the EU's approach which could be helpful for trade agreements and for the multilateral approach.

Nevertheless, progress on the multilateral agenda has been very slow. Part of the problem has been that there are significant concerns being expressed by some countries that any attempt to deal with a behind the border barrier of any kind is an unjustified reach into their domestic sovereignty. This has been most strongly expressed by the Chinese government in respect of their state-owned enterprises and government distortions, although it is by no means limited to China. Many big emerging markets distort their economies in anti-competitive ways. The WTO Appellate Body's decisions regarding "public bodies" have led to the situation where the US had blocked the establishment of the Appellate Body itself, creating a crisis in the WTO. A solution clearly needs to be found. Some of that work is being in the market distortions agenda (through the work of the trilateral group (see Chapter 2)).

The UK is currently negotiating FTAs with key WTO members and is in a position to push this agenda. Given the slow progress in the trilateral group on market distortions in the WTO, an opportunity exists for a group of countries who are particularly adversely affected by distortions to push for their resolution. Such a group of countries could include the UK, the US and Australia. Japan is certainly exposed to China market distortions but has its own distortions supported by powerful domestic interests.

Having surveyed GATT and EU Treaty provisions that limit anti-competitive government-sponsored initiatives, we now consider recent initiatives to limit market distortions in the state-owned sector.

Recent Initiatives to Deal with State-Owned Enterprises and Other Market Distortions

Since the CWB case led to an Appellate Body ruling which did not find that a deviation from profit maximisation could ground a violation of Article XVII,[97] various attempts have been made in free trade agreements and in plurilateral initiatives to discipline anti-competitive market distortions especially those carried out by State-Owned Enterprises. Most modern FTAs now have chapters on State-Owned Enterprises although these are quite limited in scope and do not significantly build a competition test into the interpretation of SOE behaviour. A sample chapter which does include competition-based disciplines on SOEs is included as Annex 1.

The 2019 Trilateral on Market Distortions launched by the US, the EU and Japan is a positive contribution to solving the market distortion problem. However the focus of the trilateral that has emerged over the last two years is very much about building on the existing anti-subsidy regime, and therefore does not deal with the heart of the problem of market distortions which is their anti-competitive effect. Of all the recently concluded FTAs, the CPTPP contains the most significant disciplines on SOEs. IT is therefore worth considering this agreement in detail. The CPTPP's chapter on SOEs builds on language that can be found in the US-Singapore FTA.

Evolution of FTA Language on SOEs

There have been two primary ways of dealing with the SOE problem. The way that the US-Singapore FTA suggests is a classification route – to identify what an SOE is before applying specific rules to it. Chapter 12 of the Agreement deals with Anticompetitive Conduct, Designated Monopolies and Government Enterprises of the NAFTA had similar restrictions on designated monopolies. The provisions echo the requirement in Article XVII regarding "commercial considerations" in purchase or sale of a monopoly good or service. Critically there are disciplines on the monopoly engaging in anti-competitive cross subsidisation into a non-monopoly market. Similar restrictions apply to government enterprises, except that the test for anti-competitive practices being covered is limited preventing the government entity from engaging in agreements that restrain competition or engaging in exclusionary practices that substantially lessen competition. In the definitions section (at Article 12.8), an attempt was made to define what would be a covered entity, including by specific reference to Temasek Holdings (which is excluded). Annex 12A contained a very specific flow diagram showing how the government could exert influence through its company holdings. This was an early effort to define what was a level of government control or influence that could make an entity a covered entity. Subsequent FTAs moved away from attempting to define SOEs in this manner. The CPTPP added some novel concepts to the principle that SOEs should apply their buying and selling practices subject to commercial considerations. Article 17.6 of CPTPP provides that Parties should not cause adverse effects to the interests of another Party through the use of non-commercial assistance it provides to an SOE directly or indirectly. This concept of not causing adverse effects is the beginning of something that looks more like a competition type test, and is more consistent with the approaches laid out in this book.

Despite these developments, it is clear that countries have struggled to introduce these concepts in any meaningful manner which can lead to a reduction of anti-competitive market distortions around the world. The chapter in Annex 1 achieves this objective in the following ways:

1 Creating an affirmative commitment on behalf of countries not to distort their markets in ways that damage trade and competition (through a substantial or significant lessening of competition).
2 Allowing a WTO consistent mechanism for countries to tarifficate distortions that are damaging to trade and competition, where the complaining party can show causation and damage, as part of an extension of trade remedies.

In reality the actions of SOEs are just a subcategory of ACMDs. Simply because an entity is an SOE does not necessarily mean it will have an adverse impact on trade or that it will act in market distortionary ways. What matters is whether the actions of the SOE (or indeed a private firm acting on government privilege) distort markets in anti-competitive ways. The Annex 1 language does achieve this goal.

Notes

1 Reports of the Panel, *Canada – Measures Relating to Exports of Wheat and Grain,* WT/DS276/R (04–1443), World Trade Organization (2004) ("PR"); *Report of the Appellate Body* in *Canada – Measures Relating to Exports of Wheat and Grain,* AB-2004-3, WT/DS276/AB/R (04–3592), World Trade Organization (2004) ("ABR").
2 PR 4.170, 4.172.
3 PR 4.105.
4 PR 6.122.
5 STE Notification, quoted in PR 4.172, 6.125.
6 PR 4.172–4.175, 4.405–4.408, 6.15.
7 Quoted in PR 4.192, 6.125.

8 PR 4.447.
9 PR 4.447.
10 PR 4.173.
11 PR 4.190; *Responses of Canada to Questions Posed in the Context of the First Substantive Meeting of the Panel*, *in* PR, para. 118, *Responses of Canada to Questions Posed in the Context of the First Substantive Meeting of the Panel*, para. 77.
12 *Responses of the United States to Questions Posed in the Context of the First Substantive Meeting of the Panel*, *in* PR, Question No. 20; PR 4.443.
13 PR 4.443, 4.444.
14 *Responses of the United States to Questions Posed in the Context of the First Substantive Meeting of the Panel*, *in* PR, Question No.1; PR 6.12, 6.21, 6.27.
15 *Responses of the United States to Questions Posed in the Context of the First Substantive Meeting of the Panel*, *in* PR, Question No.25; PR 6.45.
16 *Responses of the United States to Questions Posed in the Context of the First Substantive Meeting of the Panel*, *in* PR, Question No.25; PR 6.45.
17 PR 6.58.
18 Article XVII:1(b) emphasis added; *Responses of the United States to Questions Posed in the Context of the First Substantive Meeting of the Panel*, *in* PR, Question No. 21(b).
19 *Responses of the United States to Questions Posed in the Context of the First Substantive Meeting of the Panel*, *in* PR, Question No. 21(b).
20 *Responses of the United States to Questions Posed in the Context of the First Substantive Meeting of the Panel*, *in* PR, Question No. 23.
21 *Id.*
22 *Responses of the United States to Questions Posed in the Context of the First Substantive Meeting of the Panel*, *in* PR, Question No. 26.
23 PR 4.629.
24 PR 4.627.
25 PR 4.631.
26 PR 6.59.
27 PR 6.84, quoting *The New Shorter Oxford English Dictionary*, L. Brown (ed.) (Clarendon Press, 1993), Vol. I, at 451.
28 PR 6.87.
29 PR 6.94.
30 PR 6.88, F.N. 170.
31 PR 6.69.
32 PR 6.92, 6.98, 6.101.
33 PR 6.102, FN183.
34 PR 6.110.
35 PR 6.111.
36 PR 6.112.
37 PR 6.114.
38 PR 6.123.
39 PR 6.124.
40 PR 6.127.
41 PR 6.131.
42 PR 6.134.
43 PR 6.134.
44 PR 6.151.
45 ABR 14.
46 ABR 15.
47 ABR 17, 19.
48 ABR 17.
49 ABR 29, 32.
50 ABR 29, quoting PR 6.94.
51 ABR 29.

52 ABR 31–33.
53 ABR 35.
54 ABR 59.
55 ABR 64.
56 ABR 70.
57 ABR 60–61, 65–67.
58 ABR 65.
59 ABR 71.
60 ABR 72.
61 ABR 99–100.
62 ABR 103–106.
63 ABR 130.
64 ABR 139.
65 ABR 139–140.
66 ABR 141–143.
67 ABR 140, footnote omitted.
68 ABR 145.
69 ABR 149.
70 ABR 149–150.
71 ABR 159.
72 ABR 157.
73 *See*, for example, from US jurisprudence, Atlantic Richfield Co. v. USA Petroleum Co., 495 US 328, 334 (1990).
74 *Report of the Appellate Body* in *United States - Countervailing Measures on Certain Hot Rolled Carbon Steel Flat Products from India,* AB-2014–7, WT/DS436/AB/R (14–7136), World Trade Organization (2014).
75 *See* especially, *Report of the Appellate Body* in *United States-Countervailing Duty Measures on Certain Products from China,* AB-2014–8, WT/DS437/AB/R (14–7329), World Trade Organization (2014).
76 For a good concise overview of these articles and their application, see Barry E. Hawk, *Antitrust and Competition Laws* (Juris Publishing 2020), 215–218; A more detailed exposition may be found in Elanor M. Fox and Damien Gerard, *EU Competition Law* (Elgar, 2017), 274–311. The following discussion draws on these sources.
77 *Id.*, at 216.
78 Case C-198/01, Consorzio Industrie Fiammiferi v. Autorità Garante della Concorrenza e del Mercato, 2003 E.C.R. I-8055.
79 Case C-338/09, Yellow Cab Verkehrsbetriebs v. Landeshauptmann von Wien, 2010 E.C.R. I-13927, EU: C:2010:814.
80 Case 35/96, Commission v. Italy, 1998 E.C.R. I-3851, EU:C:1998:30.
81 Case C-35/99, Arduino, 2002 E.C.R. I-1529, EU:C:2002:97.
82 *Bellamy & Child: European Union Law of Competition* (David Bailey and Laura Elizabeth John, eds., Oxford University Press, 2018), at 993.
83 *Antitrust and Competition Laws, supra* note 76, at 217 (citation omitted).
84 Case C-189/95 *Franzen* [1997] ECR 1–5909, EU:C:1997:504.
85 Transparency Dir., Dir. 2006/111 OJ 2006 L 318/17.
86 *See Communication from the Commission to the European Parliament, the Council, the European Economic and Social Committee and the Committee of the Regions, A Quality Framework for Services of General Interest in Europe 3* (COM 2011) 900 (final), adopted on 20 December 2011.
87 *Antitrust and Competition Laws, supra* note 76, at 218.
88 *Bellamy & Child, supra* note 82, at 1003.
89 *Id.*, at 1004–1005.
90 Richard Whish and David Bailey, *Competition Law* (9th ed., Oxford University Press, 2018), at 237.

91 Commission Decision 94/119/EC of 21 December 1993 [1994] *O.J.* L 55/52.
92 Case C-179/90, Merci convenzionali porto di Genova SpA v Siderurgica Gabrielli SpA., 1991 E.C.R. I-5889, EU:C::1991:464.
93 Case C-41/90 Klaus Höfner and Fritz Elser v Macrotron GmbH., 1991 E.C.R. I-1979, EU:C:1991:161.
94 Case C-552/12 P European Commission v Dimosia Epicheirisi Ilektrismou AE, 2014 ECLI: EU: C:2014 2083.
95 Commission Decision 2001/354/EC, 2001 O.J. (L125/27). In marked contrast, the US Postal Service is exempt by statute from antitrust law scrutiny.
96 Case C-67/97 Albany International BV v Stichting Bedrijfspensioenfonds Textielindustrie, 1999 ECR I-5751, EU:C:1999:430. [1999] ECR I-5751, EU:C:1999:430.
97 *Report of the Appellate Body* in *Canada – Measures Relating to Exports of Wheat and Treatment of Imported Grain,* AB-2004-3, WT/DS276/AB/R (04–3592), World Trade Organization (2004).

9

DOMESTIC REGULATORY REFORM

One aspect of reducing ACMDs worldwide is for individual countries to engage in meaningful regulatory reform domestically. As noted elsewhere, the OECD has already made recommendations on this in its competition assessment and regulatory toolkit (see below).

Reduction of Anti-Competitive Market Distortions

Many countries, including the European Union (EU), the US and the CPTPP members have embraced competition on the business merits as the organising economic principle, which is key to a productive and innovative economy. This principle is also embedded in the OECD (specifically in its regulatory toolkit and competition assessment). Competition on the merits relies on regulation and legislation being as pro-competitive as possible, consistent with regulatory goals. Pro-competitive regulation and legislation tend to maximise economic welfare (measured by consumers' plus producers' surplus) and the rate of economic growth.[1] When anti-competitive regulation and legislation are allowed to fester, deadweight losses (pure net reductions in net economic surplus) are imposed on the economy. Such losses are generally associated with lower rates of economic growth and innovation. Accordingly, it is vital to better align regulatory promulgation mechanisms in all the UK's trade agreements between the UK and its trading partners.

If competition assessments are used to evaluate from a market standpoint the welfare losses generated by regulations (both present and future), this will help ensure that regulation is as pro-competitive as possible. The appropriate measure or metric by which these assessments should be made is their impact on consumers' and producers' surplus. It should be noted that regulatory barriers that serve

DOI: 10.4324/9780429323331-9

as trade barriers as well have consumers' and producers' surplus effects in the markets where they appear, as well as producers' surplus impacts in other markets. Furthermore, in order for assessments of this type to actually be workable, early public release of proposed regulations is key, and so transparency is a vital part of the generation of pro-competitive regulation. The goal is to produce a regulatory climate designed to grow economies based on non-zero sum, mutually beneficial economic transactions among firms.[2]

1 Anti-Competitive Market Distortions ("ACMDs")

As we have noted elsewhere, anti-competitive market distortions are the "behind the border" barriers that adversely affect both trade and domestic markets. Various attempts have been made to deal with them, but none have proved very successful because (1) trade methods tend to focus on whether the measures are discriminatory, as opposed to anti-competitive; and (2) domestic competition agencies typically lack the political power and tools to ensure pro-competitive regulation. We believe that the UK's external trade policy represents a great opportunity to make progress on the systematic reduction of ACMDs. Since many if not all the UK's key partners prioritised for FTAs profess to be states whose economies are based on competition on the merits as a normative economic organising principle, they ought to be in favour of attempts to promote pro-competitive regulation and eliminate ACMDs where possible. We thus advocate an agreement to eliminate ACMDs between both jurisdictions in any UK FTA, as well as through domestic regulatory reform.

Anti-competitive market distortions are typically government regulations, or legislation which impedes competition, or distorts a competitive market. Examples fall into categories which are as follows (non-exhaustive list[3]):

2 Restrictions that raise barriers to entry or expansion in a market

Increased barriers to entry reduce competitive pressures on existing firms in the market, potentially resulting in higher prices, lower quality of goods and reduced innovation. Barriers to exit should also be considered, as they turn investments into sunk costs, thus increasing the risk associated with entry.

Restrictions that increase barriers to entry can take several forms, including (but not limited to) those below:

i Restrictions that give monopoly rights to a firm
  a Only one firm or a limited set of firms are permitted to provide certain goods. The effect may be to reduce competitive pressure and facilitate collusion among these firms.
  b Common in agricultural marketing boards, industries seem as natural monopolies. In addition, historically, government-owned companies have often enjoyed monopolies in their respective market(s).
  c Exclusive rights may be given to encourage infrastructure investments or research. The idea is that the guaranteed revenues that

come from the granted market power encourage the firm to make investments in infrastructure that it would otherwise not have made.

- d Exclusive rights may also be intended to achieve social goals, such as narrower control and monitoring of the consumption of certain substances (e.g. alcohol).
- e May also be used as a means of subsidising some sort of universal service – the monopoly creates the profits to ensure expanded service (e.g. postal service, where profitable routes are used to subsidise mail delivery to remote locations).

ii Restrictions on which firms are permitted to compete in the market

- a Even where the regulation does not grant an exclusive right, it may unnecessarily limit which firms can compete in a market.
- b Firms may be required to conform to certain business models (e.g. must be structured as a partnership; clinic cannot be co-owned by non-practitioners)
- c Foreign ownership restrictions.
- d Minimum mandatory set of services must be offered.
- e "Set-asides," allocating a portion of supply to a particular type or class of suppliers.

iii Restrictions that limit access to essential infrastructure, resources or facilities

- a Often related to exclusive rights, discussed above.
- b May take the form of access to facilities such as airports (particularly slots) or towers for antenna, infrastructure such as electricity cables, pipelines, resources such as natural resources (e.g. fishing rights) or regulated resources (e.g. agricultural quotas). May also include rights-of-way, e.g. access to underground below city streets to install cables.
- c Incumbent firms (especially traditional government-sanctioned monopolies) may enjoy preferential access to infrastructure, resources or facilities that are needed to effectively compete in a market.
- d May be mitigated by mandating access at a regulated price. However, such regulated prices may also lead to margin squeezing and other anti-competitive behaviours.

iv Restrictions which stop the free flow of goods and capital across borders

- a May take the form of prohibitions or taxes on the import of goods from other jurisdictions.
- b Such restrictions may also take the form of unnecessary regional standards, e.g. requiring that products be packaged or presented in a certain way (e.g. requiring margarine to be coloured white).
- c Business location requirements or requirements to have local establishments or facilities.

d Reduces the number of firms in a given geographic area, giving them more market power.

e Licencing or educational requirements.

f Professions may require minimum educational standards or practical experience.

These restrictions are often stricter than what is needed to protect consumers and serve instead to exclude some practitioners from the market. For example, professionals from other jurisdictions with equivalent expertise to domestic practitioners may be nevertheless forced to retrain.

g Regulatory standards that impose a significant cost for compliance, e.g. rigorous product testing requirements or forced adoption of certain technologies.

h Financing constraints – firms often need to rely on external financing to start up a business. Thus, any significant restrictions on the free flow of investment capital can become a barrier to entry.

3 Restrictions that control how firms are allowed to compete in a market

i Market regulations that favour certain firms over others.

a Government-owned companies and/or traditional monopolies may be given preferential treatment, e.g. rights of first refusal on contracts or sales, more generous terms of sale, preferential access to restricted facilities or infrastructure, etc.

b Standards for product quality can be set in such a way as to favour some firms over others, e.g. requiring a particular technology or strict standards that require investments beyond the reach of small competitors.

c Where new restrictions are being implemented in a market, regulation may allow existing firms or practitioners to have a permanent or temporary break from the new restrictions. The so-called "grandfather clauses" can unfairly favour incumbents over new entrants. Generally, these are more problematic where the relief for incumbents is long-term, although it will depend on circumstances of each market.

ii Price controls

a Regulations may set specific prices or otherwise influence how prices can be set in the market. Often put in place for natural monopolies, such as utilities, telecom and transport. Often used in conjunction with government-granted monopolies, to help control high prices that would otherwise result from market power.

b When maximum prices are set, firms' incentives to innovate by providing new and/or high-quality products can be substantially reduced. Also, suppliers may be able to coordinate their prices around the maximum price.

- c Minimum prices may be set to discourage consumption of certain goods, e.g. alcohol and gasoline. They may also be used as a means of protecting small suppliers from "unfair" competition by larger firms that can achieve better economies of scale.
- d When minimum prices are set, low-cost suppliers are prevented from winning market share by undercutting their rivals.

iii Control of non-price terms of sale
- a Non-price terms of sale, such as contract lengths, warranties, servicing and inducements, can also be an important part of a product offering. They may also be an important part of promoting products.
- b Regulations that restrict such terms can eliminate a viable avenue of competition and reduce choices available to consumers.

iv Restrictions on quantity
- a Regulations may also control the amount of quantity of a good that can be produced by each firm (e.g. quotas). Measures restricting supply below competitive levels will either increase prices to consumers or lead to the undersupply of products. If instead supply is set above competitive levels, this can result in oversupply of products and inefficiency.

v Restrictions on advertising
- a Advertising restrictions are common in regulated professions, often seem as essential to maintaining the dignity of the profession and consumer confidence.
- b Restrictions on advertising for undesirable products or to vulnerable groups may also be implemented.
- c Restrictions on false or misleading advertising not usually a problem – if anything, such restrictions provide consumers with the ability to make better choices and improve competition.
- d May be restrictions on comparative advertising (where firms explicitly compare their price, quality, etc., against their competitors' offerings) or non-comparative advertising (general statements about the firm's products, without comparisons to others'). Restrictions may also be imposed on the medium and channels used for advertising, e.g. can only advertise to wholesalers, not directly to retailers.
- e May restrict advertising of many items of significant value to consumers, including prices, hours of operation, technical specifications, etc.
- f May have a disproportionate impact on new entrants, as they prevent the firm's ability to tell consumers about their presence in the market and price and quality of their products.

4 Restrictions that shield firms from competitive pressure

i Regulations that exempt the activity of a particular industry or group of suppliers from the operation of general competition law a Particular sectors may be exempt from the general competition law, especially government-owned companies. Such companies are free to engage in a number of anti-competitive acts – cartels, abuse of dominance, etc.

b They may or may not be subject to sector-specific legislation. Where such sector-specific legislation contains industry-specific limits on anti-competitive behaviour, concerns may be reduced.

ii Regulations that permit firms or practitioners to exchange information or communicate each other's intentions, which may reduce their incentives to compete. Such regulations may inadvertently facilitate cartels between firms.

a Regulations that create self-regulated professions can be problematic. On the one hand, professionals can ensure that sufficient standards are put in place to protect the public and adapt to new technologies and social policies. On the other hand, self-regulated professions often adopt rules that reduce incentives or opportunities for members to compete, e.g. price restrictions and advertising restrictions. Unduly strict qualification requirements may restrict entry, especially from professionals trained in other jurisdictions. Self-regulated professions may also jealously guard their scopes of practice from practitioners in related fields.

Voluntary standards and suggested guides can be less problematic than required restrictions but can still be used by members to collude.

Powers may be delegated to a single entity that operates as both the regulatory body and an industry association advocating for its members, creating a conflict of interest. It is preferable for regulatory functions to be given to an independent body where possible.

b Regulations that require firms to publish information on their outputs, prices, sales or costs. Such publications can significantly aid in the formation and maintenance of cartels – facilitates monitoring for defections.

iii Restrictions that limit the amount of profits that a firm may collect, or the market share it may accumulate. Such restrictions (e.g. rate-of-return regulation) prevent firms from benefiting from achieving efficiencies, taking risks and innovating, reducing their incentives to do so.

iv Restrictions that control the choices available to consumers.

a Limitations on which firms' consumers may buy from discourage entry into the market by other firms. Remaining firms have less incentive to vigorously compete, as consumers have effectively become a captive market.

b Limiting information available to consumers means that they may mistakenly choose firms that do not provide optimal price or quality. This enables sub-optimal firms to stay in the market. Often related to advertising restrictions, previously discussed above.

5 Regulatory Promulgation and Cost-Benefit/Impact Analysis

i Systems of Review

While external trade policy is an opportunity to craft a set of regulatory promulgation principles that bind trading partners to meaningful competition assessment of new regulations, countries should work to ensure meaningful cost-benefit analyses since pro-competitive regulatory reform is a good thing to do solely for domestic reasons. The US cost-benefit analysis, European impact assessment and OECD competition assessment recommend taking into account the effects of proposed new regulation on competition and markets. This is not to say that there should not be any regulation where competition is harmed but rather that there should be a process whereby such competition costs are made explicit, so regulators and legislators can render better-informed decisions. We believe that this process should contain the following elements, which, if missing, could be subject to binding dispute settlement.

The Executive Orders that set up the US federal regulatory review process, coordinated by the Office of Information and Regulatory Affairs ("OIRA") within the Office of Management and Budget, specifically reference the need to assess the impact of new regulation on competition. Those orders must be read in light of the Congressional Review Act ("CRA"), which defines a "major rule" as one that will result in at least one of (1) an annual effect on the economy of $100 million or more; (2) a major increase in costs or prices for consumers, individual industries, federal, state or local government agencies or geographic regions; or (3) significant adverse effects on competition, employment, investment, productivity, innovation or on the ability of US-based enterprises to compete with foreign-based enterprises in domestic and export markets.[4] Executive Order 12866 provides that a major rule is a rule that may

> have an annual effect on the economy of $100 million or more or adversely affect in a material way the economy, a sector of the economy, productivity, competition, jobs, the environment, public health or safety, or State, local, or tribal governments or communities.

In both cases, the role of the rule's impact on competition is a very important factor to consider.

In the CRA, each one of the relevant categories can be interpreted as a competition assessment test of sorts. Although these have largely been interpreted in terms of compliance costs, their impacts on competition are potentially far more significant. Yet, despite this emphasis on competition, competition assessment in the US system is a comparative rarity.

There are other examples of legislation requiring impact assessments that can be seen to be competition assessments in fact. Section 654 of the Treasury and General Government Appropriations Act, 1999 (P.L. 105–277, 5 US C. § 601 note) requires federal agencies (other than GAO) to assess their pending regulations that "may affect family well-being" to determine whether the proposed benefits of the action justify the financial impact on the family. Family well-being includes many other social issues to be sure (such as whether legislation impacts the marital bond, the strength of the family, etc.) but it is clear that financial impact on the family of particular regulation must mean some measure of consumers' surplus loss. As noted in Regulatory Analysis Requirements: A Review and Recommendations for Reform (Christopher Copeland, April 23, 2012):

> Section 1022(b)(2)(A) of the Dodd-Frank Wall Street Reform Act (12 US C. § 5512) establishes certain "standards of rulemaking" for the newly established Consumer Financial Protection Bureau (CFPB). Specifically, it states that the Bureau "shall consider—(i) the potential benefits and costs to consumers and covered persons, including the potential reduction of access by consumers to consumer financial products or services resulting from such rule; and (ii) the impact of proposed rules on covered persons, as described in section 1026, and the impact on consumers in rural areas."

This section illustrates once again a competition test associated with regulations under Dodd-Frank, which would evaluate the impact of those regulations on consumers. Section 15(a) of the Commodity Exchange Act (7 US C. § 19(a)) requires the Commodity Futures Trading Commission (CFTC) to consider costs and benefits before issuing certain regulations and states that those costs and benefits

> shall be evaluated in light of - (A) considerations of protection of market participants and the public; (B) considerations of the efficiency, competitiveness, and financial integrity of futures markets; (C) considerations of price discovery; (D) considerations of sound risk management practices; and (E) other public interest considerations.

This focus on competitiveness and efficiency (in particular the latter) is once more an assessment based on consumers' and producers' surplus.

ii The Importance of Transparency

Transparency is often regarded as an optional extra – a nice thing to have in the regulatory promulgation process to ensure that the public's views are being heard. However, transparency is not an extra, but rather a vital part of the regulatory promulgation process. Without it, the proper regulatory assessments cannot be done. In the US, the Administrative Procedures Act of 1946 requires agencies to publish Notices of Proposed Rulemaking and give interested persons an opportunity to comment for at least a 30-day period. Internally, there are a number of statutes that require agencies to alert other members of the government to their proposals early in the process. These include the Negotiated Rulemaking Act of 1990 and the CRA, which requires major rules to be delayed for 60 days pending a review by GAO and the Congress. Executive Order 12889 requires agencies to provide a 75-day comment period for technical regulations or SPS measures (applied to the NAFTA, now USMCA). Transparency is necessary in the case of competition assessments, in particular because competition agencies will need to collect some survey evidence from market participants in order to determine the competitive effects of the proposed regulation.

It is therefore important that in the context of any trade negotiations, there be transparency in comment periods and adequate periods during which the public can review proposed regulations so that their comments can meaningfully contribute to the regulatory promulgation process.

iii Competition Assessment of New and Existing Regulations

The domestic regulatory review process cannot be looked at in isolation as it does have an impact on external trade policy. The UK goal should be to lower anti-competitive market distortions whether they are found in trading partners' markets or domestically. We have noted that there is ample authority in a number of US Executive Orders and legislation in specific areas that suggests that competition assessment of new regulation has always been a part of the process there.

Unfortunately, this has rarely been done as a practical matter, and when it has only on an ad hoc basis. The UK, emerging from the EU with an opportunity to craft a new regulatory framework, therefore has an opportunity to be world leading in this area and advocate competition assessment as part of the regulatory process. We note that in the EU, various member states have competition assessment as a mandatory part of the regulatory promulgation process. Essentially, competition assessment evaluates the harm to the competitive market as measured in producers' and consumers' surplus losses, which result from particular proposed regulations or legislation. These losses are particularly destructive to a nation's economy because they are deadweight losses which result in wealth being destroyed (not merely transferred). Successful competition assessment requires a process that allows early input based on real drafts of regulation and legislation. While the fact of the assessment should be mandatory, other regulators and legislators should be free to follow its recommendations or not. Where they choose not to follow the recommendations of a competition assessment, they should explain their reasons for so doing in writing. We recommend that the sectoral regulator or relevant legislative committee must either accept the competition assessment and attempt to re-regulate in ways that are less anti-competitive, or must give a rational justification for continuing on the regulatory pathway that is damaging to competition. We anticipate that a simple statement that the view of the regulator is that the benefits outweigh the costs with some reasonable justification would be sufficient to satisfy this requirement. We believe that such a statement, by itself, will over time have domestic impacts that will ultimately lead to better and less anti-competitive regulation.

iv Legislation

Competition agencies should be involved in the legislative process as well as the regulatory process. In the case of legislative committees, the competition agency should be asked to testify before the committee to explain the anti-competitive harms of legislative proposals. Failure to invite the competition agency to give public testimony would be a violation of these core principles.

v Sectoral Regulation

In the case of sectoral regulators, the regulator should have met with the competition agency and engaged in a sufficient dialogue to ensure that a reasonable regulator would be informed of the competition assessment and be in a position to weigh it against the alleged benefits. We believe that the advantage of this approach is that it will force the kind of discussions that must ultimately lead to more, rather than less, pro-competitive regulation and thus will start turning deadweight losses into surpluses. We are hopeful that this process will lead to a virtuous circle as regulators and competition agencies work more seamlessly together.

6 Assessing Legitimate Regulatory Goal

The proposed regulatory goal should not be a general carve-out for any sort of prudential regulation but should itself be public, and transparent, and should be tested against the harm it is intended to correct. If the importance of the regulatory measure is x, the question is whether x is the least restrictive regulatory measure possible to achieve the goal. An example helps us understand how this would work in practice. Suppose the harm relates to the quality of air. An appropriate regulatory response would be to limit the air particulates emitted by producers. That response's effect on the harm can be measured and will be very fact-specific based on which producers the ban applies to and the differentia impact of different kinds of particulates. We can construct a matrix which illustrates the different harms and impacts that are thus relevant (Table 9.1):

This matrix can be used by policymakers to determine regulatory choices within each area. It should be noted that the impact on trade and impact on competition are not the same thing. The impact on property rights protection is also different. The productivity simulator which is outlined in Chapter 4 enables us to separate out impacts on trade, competition and property rights.

There is no simple balancing of each of these values but it will help policymakers to come to right decisions by using this matrix approach. Harms can be measured in a number of ways, including loss of human life,

TABLE 9.1 Regulatory impact assessment

Impact of regulation, $R(1)$ on harm = $\alpha(1)$	Impact of regulation $R(1)$ on competition = $\beta(1)$	Impact of regulation $R(1)$ on trade = $\gamma(1)$	Impact of regulation, $R(1)$ on property rights = $\delta(1)$
Impact of regulation, $R(2)$ on harm = $\alpha(2)$	Impact of regulation R(2) on competition = $\beta(2)$	Impact of regulation $R(1)$ on trade = $\gamma(2)$	Impact of regulation, $R(2)$ on property rights = $\delta(2)$
Impact of regulation, $R(3)$ on harm = $\alpha(3)$	Impact of regulation $R(3)$ on competition = $\beta(3)$	Impact of regulation $R(1)$ on trade = $\gamma(3)$	Impact of regulation $R(3)$ on property rights = $\delta(3)$

hospitalisation and loss of wealth-creating activities by human beings. Some harms may be weighted differently from others. This would be a policy decision. For example, a decision would have to be made about the cost to human life or hospitalisation versus damage to ecosystems, loss of endangered species or animal welfare.

Comment on Climate Change, Energy Policy and International Trade

As the governments of the world turn their attention to net-zero policies, the impact of regulations designed to correct the harm caused by anthropogenic climate change on international trade and competition brings various government objectives into conflict. Imposition of trade restrictions such as an ex-ante tariff as is the case in the EU border tax adjustment measures (CBAM) or those contemplated by other countries contravenes a fundamental WTO principle that there should not be trade discrimination on the basis of the manner in which products are produced rather than the products themselves. There is a good reason for this principle as different trade treatment based on how products are produced risks serious damage to international trade flows as countries take issue with particular production methods that might be lower cost than they themselves are capable of. Furthermore, incumbents who would benefit from such a tariff can easily manipulate the process so that their competitors are placed at a disadvantage. We should therefore embrace such discrimination only as a very last resort.

We discuss the CBAM also in the chapter on electricity and gas. For the purposes of domestic regulatory approach that have an impact on trade, the question is whether there is another mechanism that could be employed which deals with the harm being caused by irreversible, anthropogenic climate change. In order to understand this, it is first crucial to understand the harm that we are seeking to mitigate.

It is important to base the regulatory response on a legitimate and justifiable, publicly stated regulatory goal. In this case, it is harmful emissions of a particular country that must be set to a level at which the negative impacts of climate change are (a) no longer irreversible and (b) limited to a level that is deemed acceptable to society. With regard to (b), the analogy is with clean air and clean water where a certain tolerance to harmful substances is acceptable because there is a diminishing return associated with going from minor to zero concentration but there is an equivalent exponentially increasing cost imposed on society of this transition.

i Harm Caused by Anthropogenic, Irreversible Climate Change

Irreversible, anthropogenic climate change can cause great damage to ecosystems and to the loss of human habitats, leading to considerable economic damage not all of which can be mitigated against through movement of these systems. To the extent harm is caused, the quantum of harm can be correlated with the total volume of harmful emissions in the atmosphere.

ii Does the Policy Proposed Reduce the Harm?

Not all policy proposals would actually reduce the stated harm and some would reduce it in different ways to others. For example, one policy proposed is for an ex-ante border tax adjustment. Such a mechanism would only lower the overall level of emissions if the result of the border tax is to reduce production on a global basis. If the mechanism simply displaces trade from countries that impose the mechanism to others (for example, developing countries), it is unlikely to lead to a lower volume of emissions globally. If, as is the case, countries differ substantially in the intensity and volume of their emissions, then a more appropriate policy response would be a targeted ex-post tariff applied to countries which can be demonstrably proven to have violated existing environmental agreements in this area, or who are otherwise systematically distorting their markets for trade advantage.

iii Is there a less trade-restrictive measure?

If we assume a border tax adjustment to be the policy choice most likely to be adopted, even though we have shown that it is unlikely to significantly reduce the harm it is intended to address, the relevant question is whether there is a less trade-restrictive way to achieve the regulatory goal. An ex-post facto tariff in cases of countries that can be shown to seek trade advantage by derogating from an agreed environmental standard is a less trade-restrictive way to achieve the emission-reducing goal.

iv Is there a less anti-competitive way of reducing the harm?

A negative effect on trade and a negative effect on competition are two different but related things. It is likely that regulations that damage competition also distort trade but this is not always the case. It is therefore important to have a separate analysis to determine impact on competition in the relevant market. The first question to ask is what is the relevant product and geographic market for the regulation proposed. We can answer this question by adopting the Small but Significant Non Transitory Price Apply (SSNIP) test adapted from an antitrust analysis. If an SSNIP (which would typically be a 10% increase in price) were to be applied as a result of the regulation to a particular product would consumer source a different product. In the cases of an ex-ante or an ex-post tariff, the question would be if the price increase would cause consumers to source domestic product (which is likely) or whether they would use a product from a different market (equally likely). If they would, the relevant market should be reclassified to include those other products. Hence, the market is likely to be the global market for the particular product and its available substitutes. The regulatory approach is less likely to have an anti-competitive effect for products where there are many available substitutes, and where there is availability of those substitutes in multiple markets. This suggests the potential for exemptions and waivers in case of anti-competitive effect for particular products. An analogy here would be with the waivers under the Buy America Act from the 1930s in the US where if the application of the provisions leads to an increase in price, then it can be set aside by the federal government. This mechanism could also be deployed in the case of any climate change mitigation policies.

v What is the Clearly Stated, Legitimate Regulatory Goal

The European Green Deal provides that the goal of the border adjustment tax (CBAM) is to prevent carbon leakage in a WTO-compliant manner. The EU acknowledges that it is increasing its climate ambition and has expressly stated that they seek to ensure through the CBAM that producers do not start producing in other countries and exporting into the EU (the so-called carbon leakage). These goals do seem to be different from a policy goal to reduce emissions globally which is the higher-level climate policy goal. This combination of goals together forms the "Policy Goal."

vi Would the Policy Achieve the Policy Goal?

The Policy Goal, even if achieved, would not appear to have any impact on overall global emissions, as it has no effect on production and trade that occurs outside the EU, something the EU acknowledges in its paper.

vii Are there less anti-competitive ways of achieving the policy goal?

One alternative is that proposed in the Trade and Agriculture Commission report to DIT on import policy.[5] This proposal, which commanded the full support of all the Commissioners, suggested that where the parties to a trade agreement had agreed a particular set of environmental standards, and one party derogated from these for trade advantage that would constitute an anti-competitive market distortion enabling the aggrieved party to impose a tariff.

Interaction with External Trade Policy: Reconciling the EU and US Approaches

As noted elsewhere, domestic regulatory choices have a powerful impact on international trade policy and cannot be readily separated. This is particularly true in areas like standards policy. Since the UK has a trade agreement with the EU and is negotiating one with the US, it is important that its approaches in the area of regulation and standards are consistent. This is also an opportunity to test how different regulatory systems can be reconciled in an equivalence framework as opposed to a harmonisation framework because this will benefit traders and minimise disruptions but will also allow regulatory competition to ensure that the most pro-competitive regulatory framework is more likely to be arrived at. The overall governing principle which we set out in this book is that both parties' laws, regulations and standards should be set in the most pro-competitive manner possible consistent with a legitimate and publicly stated regulatory goal. That said, we recognise that different standards could have negative impacts on businesses trading across the wider transatlantic area (US-UK-EU). We submit that it is more pro-competitive for the UK to adopt a regulatory recognition approach, as opposed to the EU's regulatory harmonisation approach.

i Regulatory Promulgation

Both the UK and the EU have agreed to a Good Regulatory Practice chapter in the EU- UK TCA which broadly encompasses much of what is discussed here. Similar provisions in the US-UK FTA would not be inconsistent with this approach.

ii Standards

There is more scope for inconsistency in the standards area. The EU standard setting approach consists of membership of the key standard setting institutions, the European Committee for Standardisation (CEN), the European Committee for Electrotechnical Standardisation (CENELEC) and the European Telecommunications Standards Institute (ETSI). By contrast, the US generally adopts a less centralised approach which can lead to better regulatory outcomes because of regulatory competition but is also difficult to understand for exporters into the US market. It is often said that these approaches are mutually irreconcilable. The challenge will be to see if there is a possibility of equivalence across the US-UK-EU regions. This has to be done at a sectoral level and by way of example, we look at how this might work in the electrical goods sector.

Electrical Goods Sector as an Example

Different sectors vary significantly but we have highlighted a sector where regulatory promulgation in the EU is closest to the pro-competitive regulatory framework we advocate (in our view), and therefore where there is the greatest scope for a mutually consistent agreement across the US-UK-EU zone.

A fundamental challenge is the fact that the US regards its standards as international because the TBT 6 Principles apply to them and regards the EU's as regional and not international standards because the TBT 6 Principles do not apply to them. The UK negotiators will be looking for a sweet spot where the UK standards can be interoperable with US standards in some way, as well as ensuring minimal barriers between the UK and the EU. In order to reduce barriers with the EU, some in the electrical goods sector will want the UK to remain members of CENELEC, the European Standard Setting Organisation ("SSO") for electrical goods, but the US and UK negotiators will be mindful of the fact that the US will want divergence where possible. It is possible that the US could seek in the UK-US FTA some mechanism whereby it could obtain some input into CENELEC for US (non-EU companies).

The UK would like the EU to recognise not only conformity assessment but also its product standards, and where possible its underlying regulation. The UK will ground these issues in the WTO TBT Agreement. The TBT Agreement covers technical regulation, standards and conformity assessment. The WTO TBT Agreement is designed to balance the need for members to regulate in the health and safety space for products, as well as to avoid unnecessary trade barriers. Under the TBT Agreement, countries may not implement their technical regulations in a way that violates the non-discrimination principle and shall be no more trade-restrictive than necessary to support a legitimate regulatory objective. Members should also use relevant international standards where they exist or are imminent as a basis for their technical regulation. On conformity assessment, the TBT encourages parties to recognise each other's conformity assessment where possible.

The UK's goals in the TBT area are unlikely to change from the EU's goals in terms of safety of products. The UK's underlying regulation and TBT standards must objectively deliver these goals. Under the WTO TBT Agreement, members should seek to recognise these standards and even underlying regulations in this case.

This would also be true for the US-UK relationship.

This is the only way of simultaneously interoperating between US and EU standards. This requires the UK not to be a promoter of EU (or for that matter US) standards around the rest of the world. Mutual recognition should be based on an existing international standard. If both countries are basing their standards on international standards, there should be mutual recognition.

Both the UK and the US will want to ensure as pro-competitive a set of standards and underlying technical regulation as possible. The US achieves this by relying on voluntary standards that compete with each other. Regulatory competition is more likely to lead to welfare-enhancing outcomes than regulatory harmonisation. The EU relies on more of a top-down standards setting system where standards are agreed by the SSOs and any inconsistent standards are withdrawn. This makes for greater administrative simplicity but not necessarily for a more pro-competitive solution.

Potential Solution

A potential solution may lie in using a potential UK-US FTA to allow the US to work with the UK to correct what it regards as deficiencies in the EU system with respect to the TBT Six Principles. The UK could remain a member of the EU standards bodies but agrees with the US in the UK-US FTA to rectify the EU's deficiencies under the six principles by:

- a Allowing any US body to be a member of the UK representative in the European SSOsCEN/CENELEC and ETSI.
- b Providing longer notice periods to the US of European SSO activities, plus comment periods so the UK and the US can take a common position.
- c Ensuring that membership of UK SSOs which are participants in the European SSOs is on a non-discriminatory basis.
- d Ensuring that the EU processes do not privilege the EU undertakings.
- e Ensuring that the EU SSOs produce relevant standards which are performance (and not production) based.
- f Ensuring that the US SSOs participate more fully in the ISO/IEC process.

In the electrical goods sector, this would enable the UK to demonstrate to the US bodies that it did have a meaningful impact on the development of EU technical standards (which it maintains it does not do now). The US is also concerned about the Dresden and Vienna Agreements under which there is fast track IEC adoption of CENELEC standards on the basis that this "limits opportunities for non-EU stakeholders to contribute to the development of standards at an early stage."[5] This concern could be assuaged by allowing access to the EU bodies through the UK-US FTA.

The US also has concerns regarding the EU's conformity assessment programme, where each member state has a single national accreditation body, specifically at Regulation (EC) 765/2008 and Decision 768/2008. The US accreditation bodies have long complained about the stifling of competition at the accreditation level and how this bars the US bodies from market access in the EU. The UK-US FTA could allow participation of US bodies in the UK's accreditation system. The US would like the ability to test and certify products for the EU market outside the EU, and it may be possible to also use the UK-US FTA to allow the US bodies to do that testing in the UK or using the UK-US bodies to lower time to market for the US entities. The US is also concerned that the EU's FTAs include provisions where the other partner agrees to apply only standards that have been generated by bodies in which the EU plays what the US would characterise as an outsize role.[6] Here again, the UK-US FTA could be more open as to which standards generated by which bodies could be applicable in both the UK and US markets. The way to handle this issue is to lower the "outsize role" by enabling the US bodies to play a role, if they wish to play it and to allow the UK-US FTA to enable this more, as opposed to seeking to change the institutional bodies that are engaged in these issues.

Dual Regulatory Proposal for Resolution of the Northern Ireland Protocol Dispute between the UK and the EU

The UK has suggested the potential for dual regulatory approaches in a number of different settings (most recently in the Northern Ireland Command Paper).[7] This was the UK government's position regarding the renegotiation of the Northern Ireland Protocol ("NIP"). A dual regulatory regime could work in the following manner:

- i Goods may be produced to two different regulatory regimes' requirements.
- ii A mutual recognition agreement is agreed between both parties for recognition of conformity assessment (testing), market surveillance and also underlying product regulation.
- iii Goods may then be produced to the requirement of either regime, as long as it satisfies the rules of either, with ordinary customs controls and a minimum of physical checks. Any mark that is required to enable products to be placed in the market can be given.
- iv Goods may be placed in the market from either party for onward export to a third country provided that they can be proved to satisfy the requirements of that third country regime in the party where the product is produced.

Looking to the specific flows in the jurisdictions of the US, the EU and the UK, as well as considering how these flows implicate Northern Ireland, we can assume the following:

- i Assume three different applicable regulatory environments in the US, the EU and the UK.

ii Goods manufactured compliant with R1 can be put in the market in the US, R2 for the UK and R3 for the EU.

iii Parties may negotiate Mutual Recognition Agreements (MRAs) to cover conformity assessment, market surveillance and underlying product regulation. The UK is likely to seek maximal MRAs with the US starting with the 11 areas which were prioritised in the US-EC MRA, 1998 (of which only 2.5 have been covered). It is also likely to do the same with the EU, understanding that the EU has indicated that it is much less likely to grant MRAs to the UK.

iv Assuming maximal MRAs covering all three dimensions, products could be manufactured in the UK to UK regulations which could then be accepted in the US with documentary checks and minimal physical checks. Products could also be manufactured to comply with R1 which could be tested in the UK, and which could then be placed in the market in the US upon proof of UK compliance.

v Assuming no MRAs between the UK and the EU, then products satisfying R3, and tested in the EU could be produced in the UK and placed in the market in the EU.

vi Regulatory proposal would require a substantial change to the NIP, in line with the suggestions in the NI Command Paper.

vii Assuming no MRA products satisfying R2 could be placed in the market in NI provided they were "not at risk."

If the negotiated solution between the UK and the EU under the NI Command Paper negotiations was more in line with the NIP as it currently stands, then goods entering NI would have to satisfy R3, but how you prove that compliance would potentially differ as between "at risk" (goods at risk of moving into the EU) and "not at risk" (goods remaining within the UK customs territory movements). In that case, evidence-based systems to prove compliance would become more critical.

While regulatory authorities on both sides of the Atlantic and around the world have paid lip service to the concept of competition assessment, it is critical that countries adopt these measures to ensure that domestic pro-competitive regulation can contribute to more efficient outcomes, lower costs and higher rates of growth around the world.

The UK has just announced a new regulatory reform agenda post-Brexit which seems to incorporate these key principles.[8] In particular, the UK government paper does suggest that impact on trade, market competition and innovation should be considered in the decision to promulgate regulations. This is the clearest statement so far from any country of how it intends to apply the OECD regulatory toolkit and competition assessment.

Certainly, the UK could use its regulatory reform agenda to be a market leader in the area of good regulatory practice and ensure that regulations damage competition and trade as little as possible. By doing this, deadweight losses in its economy that result from anti-competitive market distortions created by regulation and legislation can be eliminated and new wealth can be injected into the economy at a time of great need. By joining up regulatory goals in trade negotiations and regulatory reform at home, we can better ensure good regulatory results.

Dispute settlement in trade agreements will also be a key lever. Holding countries to account in the manner in which competition assessment is included in regulatory and legislative analyses will go a long way to ensuring that pro-competitive legislation and regulation consistent with regulatory goals is more likely in the future.

Notes

1 Existing empirical research is consistent with the proposition that more pro-competitive regulatory environments and robust competition law are associated with higher economic growth, *ceteris paribus. See, e.g.,* Alessandro Diego Spoliti, *Competition and Economic Growth: An Empirical Analysis for a Panel of 20 OECD Countries*, MPRA Paper No. 20127, MPRA (2009) (product market liberalisation and labour market deregulation associated with an increase in total factor productivity, and reduction of market rigidities is associated with enhanced innovation); Steven J. Nickell, *Competition and Corporate Performance*, 104 J. of Pol. Econ 724 (1996) (stronger competition is associated with a significantly higher rate of total factor productivity growth); Niels Petersen, *Antitrust Law and the Promotion of Democracy and Economic Growth*, Max Planck Institute for Research on Collective Goods (2011) (antitrust law has a strongly positive effect on the level of GDP per capita and economic growth).

2 We note that a number of EU member states (including, for example, Bulgaria, Romania and Croatia) already have mandatory competition assessments as part of their regulatory reform processes. Such mechanisms (in these and other jurisdictions) might help inform the development of future competition-based regulatory and legislative review processes.

3 This list is drawn from the work of the International Competition Network's project on competition assessment, and is available at www.internationalcompetitionnetwork.org.

4 5 US C. § 804 (2).

5 *See Final Report,* Trade and Agriculture Commission (2021), https://assets.publishing.service.gov.uk/government/uploads/system/uploads/attachment_data/file/969045/Trade-and-Agriculture-Commission-final-report.pdf.

6 See, for example, EU-Japan FTA, Article 7.6.

7 *See Northern Ireland Protocol: The Way Forward,* Secretary of State for Northern Ireland by the Command of Her Majesty (2021), https://assets.publishing.service.gov.uk/government/uploads/system/uploads/attachment_data/file/1008451/CCS207_CCS0721914902-005_Northern_Ireland_Protocol_Web_Accessible__1_.pdf.

8 *See The Benefits of Brexit: How the UK is Taking Advantage of Leaving the EU,* HM Government (2022), https://assets.publishing.service.gov.uk/government/uploads/system/uploads/attachment_data/file/1052148/benefits-of-brexit-document.pdf

10

THE ROLE OF PROPERTY RIGHTS IN BUILDING A COMPETITIVE MARKET

Property rights are an indivisible part of the market economy whole – they are a leg of the three-legged stool that is required for a market economy to properly function. Working together, all of these elements – trade liberalisation, competitive markets and property right protections – can lift the poor out of poverty. A useful analogy, in terms of poverty reduction, is with a net which is used to catch fish. If one of these core elements is missing, this is akin to the fisherman fishing with a net with holes. In that case, any attempt by a government to lift its people out of poverty fails, as people are lost through the holes of the net. These issues are also foundational pillars on which a functioning market economy rests. A defect in one of the pillars will bring the structure down.

The reason property rights are so important to a functioning economy is that they lead to a higher level of consumer welfare optimisation as property rights are the foundation upon which firms compete. Property rights can therefore be said to support the many different platforms which are the basis of competition. These rights therefore underpin the process of market competition.

We have noted that property rights play a fundamental role in building a competitive market economy. However, property rights are much deeper even than this. Property rights have long been regarded as one of the essential rights of man. As such, the property right is an economic right, one of the rafts of economic rights in a bundle of so-called basic human rights. The right to the peaceful enjoyment of one's property and the right to exclude others from it is one of the most fundamental of these basic rights. As early as moral philosophers Locke, Grotius and Pufendorf, the notion that the property right was a fundamental economic right has been enshrined as a basic tenet of moral and

DOI: 10.4324/9780429323331-10

international laws. John Locke (in his Second Treatise of Government (1689)) noted that

> every man has a property in his own person. This nobody has a right to but himself. The labour of his body, and the works of his hands, we may say, are properly his. Whatsoever then he removes out of the realm of nature [and] mixes his labour with it makes it his property.

Locke believed that the major purpose of man's putting himself under government was for the preservation of property.[1]

In England, the Magna Carta was the foundation of English constitutional democracy. Magna Carta (10 June 1215) provides that "no freeman shall be … disseised [dispossessed of his property] … except by the lawful judgment of his peers and by the law of the land."

John Locke had essentially established a theory where the governor and the governed had a compact. If the governor deviated from this by abusing the governed's property rights, the governor forfeits his governing privilege. Locke argued that the property right was a natural right. Locke's views were fundamental to the development of the common law. Blackstone's Commentaries stated that the property right was so important to the law that "it will not authorise the least violation of it." Property and liberty had become two sides of the same coin.[2]

The founding fathers of the US similarly recognised that their economic freedoms depended on property rights.[3] Perhaps the most eloquent expression of the basic and fundamental nature of the right to property is from Arthur Lee of Virginia who said that it was "the guardian of every other right, and to deprive people of this, is in fact to deprive them of their liberty."

One of the US's founding fathers, Thomas Jefferson noted that "if we can prevent the government from wasting the labours of the people under the pretence of taking care of them, they must become happy."[4] This very pointedly attacks the notion of removing property from people "for the public good."

From these treatments and others, it can be seen that the key elements of property rights are the right to own property, and the right to transfer it. As long as the two rights are applied without vitiation, then prices will properly and efficiently be allocated for goods and services, leading to the smooth and efficient functioning of a competitive market economy.

Early Ideas on Property Rights and their Importance

It is worth reviewing the early literature which discusses property rights as this will give a better understanding of how it was analysed, even in the earliest years of legal scholarship.

In his seminal work, the Rights of War and Peace, Hugo Grotius, writing in the 16th century, examines the nature of rights carefully. Much of Grotius' thinking is formed by how property rights and rights over persons are affected by war between nations.

Foreshadowing the civil law limitation on property rights, Grotius in his first book suggests that the rights of man can be divided into inferior rights of individuals and eminent rights of the sovereign. This division was to find echoes in the future where the rights of government in property were to be declared pre-eminent over certain individual rights.

Pufendorf, writing in the 17th century in his "Of the Law of Nature and Nations," Book IV, Chapter IV, noted that one of the key benefits of a property right was "the exclusion of others from [one's property]"[5] Earlier in Chapter IV of Book IV, Pufendorf notes that there is a bundle of rights which accompany the property right itself which, if taken away, make that property right less valuable. These include being "bound to allow another some particular use of them, by way of service."

Interestingly, this hints at the debate over compulsory licencing that we will discuss in detail in Chapter 9 (intellectual property rights). The critical point that Pufendorf sets out is the notion that the bundle of uses that together make up property rights cannot be eroded, for to do so is to erode the property right itself. Understanding the very basic nature of how the free market operates, Pufendorf notes,[6] "But now, upon the introducing of Property…everyone grows more industrious in improving his peculiar portion…." This expressly recognises the fundamental notion that the property right itself acts as an incentive to greater industry and innovation, and gives to property rights their proper place in the underlying architecture of the market economy.

In the 20th century, von Mises argued[7] that private property rights lead to long-run objectives for individuals and firms. It is the acquisitiveness of more property protected by defined and well-understood property rights that leads to the best arrangement of production activities.

The contrary view is expressed by Hobbes and Austin and essentially focuses on the state's ability to grant rights. This is because we have given this power to the State on the basis that it is necessary in order to prevent anarchy.[8]

In von Mises' view, the State is "an apparatus of compulsion and coercion … with human nature as it is the state is a necessary and indispensable institution."[9]

Under von Mises' construction, private property rights and the rights of individuals are the most important rights even when those rights are pitted against each other. Unlike Locke, von Mises did not subscribe to the view that property rights arise out of natural law even suggesting that this is merely a new type of theology or superstition.

Von Mises adopts a generally pragmatic view of the market, shying away from the almost "magical" approach of some commentators.

> There is nothing inhuman or mystical with regard to the market. The market process is entirely a result of human actions. Every market phenomenon can be traced back to definite choices of the members of the market society.[10]

When von Mises expressed reservations about natural law, it is important to note that he was expressing concern about the notion that law could be handed down by the state (and the state could use its military power or its power of coercion to enforce such laws). He was criticising the so-called "worship of the state." However, this does not mean that ordinary market processes can lead to property rights protection. Some commentators, such as Rothbard,[11] suggest that market processes will define and allocate property rights: "Any other allocation or definition would be completely arbitrary and contrary to the principles of a free society." Benson has suggested the notion of "customary law" evolving naturally (analogous to the invisible hand of the market).[12]

Benson suggests that self-interest motivations will lead to the clear definition of property rights because it is in the interests of the parties in their interactions with each other to do so. As that group becomes larger (and its members less well-known to each other), there is a need to impose institutions on the individuals because reputation and trust may not lead to enforceable rights between the constituent members of the group.

However, whether you regard property rights as emanating out of natural law or as a result of the complex interplay of market forces, the net effect is broadly the same – the property right is brought into being by forces that are not promulgated by the State. If these rights emanate outside of the State, then the State has no power to interfere with them (or at least must pay a price for doing so). Such interference would then have the same effect as if any other actor interfered with those rights.

The Nature of the Property Right as a Derivative of the Actions of the Rights Holder

Grotius examines the notion of the property right as a right resulting from some activity by the purported rights holder. He seems to accept the notion that the property right can arise as a reward for the actions of the rights holder, and the investment he makes in the property itself. This is an important notion as it is this that is central to the importance of property rights to a functioning market economy. In Book II, Chapter II of The Rights of War and Peace, Grotius notes that the reason for property rights was because men were no longer content with what was readily available from the land but recognised that "Labour and Industry" were required to transform basic things into things of value which made for a more commodious existence for mankind. In concluding that the sand cannot be property to which a right attaches, Grotius noted that sand cannot be exhausted, and cannot be cultured.[13] This suggests the two most important aspects of property rights.

- i The fact that the property right is designed as an incentive to the labour and industry that is required to develop something out of property.
- ii The fact that rarity value of certain kinds of property also affects whether a right should attach to it.

In noting that property rights include acquisitions from man's own deeds, Grotius says that kings cannot alienate the property of their subjects.[14] Even where the king has the right to certain income from the property, it is important to understand that this does not mean that the king has any right to the property itself. This is a fundamental point. Grotius distinguishes between the property and the income to be generated from the property.

These are very important concepts that underpin our understanding of property rights, and everything that flows from them. Property that has potential for development is valuable to the person who can develop something out of it. To the person incapable of such development, the property does not have the same value. Therefore some part of the intrinsic value of the property comes from the potential for development and the ability of the market for that property to develop. Property can become more valuable as the market develops the ability to develop something from it. For example, suppose you have a piece of land that contains an ore of a very valuable element, but there is no process for deriving the element from the ore. If such a process were then discovered, the value of the land would increase dramatically. Clearly here the property and what was on it has not changed, and no new products have been discovered. However the value of the land was locked up in the potential for extracting the element, and realised when a process was discovered for extracting the element. The difference between the value of the land before and after the discovery is potentially vast. But the property only becomes valuable when the process for producing the valuable element is discovered.

Study of the early authors, such as Grotius and Pufendorf, is important, as much can be learned and applied from their description of what was important in their world. This also illustrates that the protection of property rights, a fundamental pillar of the market economy is a very old concept, and one that was well understood many centuries ago.

This analysis helps us also understand the central role that all aspects of property rights have in the market economy, including intangible property rights, such as intellectual property rights. As we will explore in the next chapter on intellectual property, intellectual property rights form a subset of property rights, and require no less protection as part of the bedrock of the market economy.[15] This is in contrast to the notion that intellectual property and competition policy are in tension. We will demonstrate in the following chapter that far from being in tension, both policies have the same innovation-enhancing goals.

The Notion of Common Property

However, even in these early days, the notion of community property was an important one. Grotius noted that men have a right to use certain property even if it is owned by others as long as that use is not detrimental to the true owner of the property. He uses the example of the right to extract water from the sides of a river, where technically the owners of the land abutting the river would own the right to the water. This hints at the beginnings of a doctrine of public or common goods. However, the key words here are Grotius' statement that use of another's property must not so deprive that other of any of the benefits of his right. Hence, the owners of the river are not disadvantaged by the drawing of water from the river by others because the river water is an inexhaustible supply (at least it was for the purpose of Grotius' analysis). Grotius would have had a very different approach to the property right if he had thought that water was not an inexhaustible supply.[16]

The notion of common property, which had been discussed by the Roman writers, was accepted by Grotius, and built on. It is important to look at where common property applies because this illustrates what the restrictions are to using property rights as an anchor of the competitive market economy. The notion of common property applies when there is "necessity." Necessity includes cases where a man must take something from another's land in order to survive. However, Grotius set out this doctrine under the strict principle that "necessity" must not be extended too far. He also states that:

> all other possible Means should be first used, by which such a Necessity may be avoided; either, for Instance, by applying to a Magistrate, to see how far he would relieve us, or by entreating the Owner to supply us with what we stand in Need of.[17]

For example, as Plato had said, you cannot draw water from another's well, unless you have truly exhausted your own by digging to the point where there is no longer any hope or expectation of water. However, even where necessity forced one to take the property of another, restitution had to be paid.

This is an important discussion because it foreshadows the discussion about compulsory licencing, and even the modern doctrine of eminent domain, discussed in this chapter.

We discuss the doctrine of compulsory licencing specifically in the chapter on intellectual property laws. As we demonstrate in that chapter, compulsory licencing is a remedy drawn from antitrust which is drawn from the same philosophical wellspring as the notion of common property.

Eminent domain laws are laws that allow property to be taken from private parties in order to satisfy some "public good" (such as the laying of electricity or phone lines). The notion that in certain cases, private rights are trumped by the public good is again drawn from this notion of common property. Precisely how far this notion is delineated is an important element in working out the scope of the public good exemption to the general principles of property right protection.

The common property doctrine also underpins exceptions to property rights protection that are made on the basis of the public or universal service obligations which apply to providers of telecommunications, postal and other services which we discuss at length in Part III.

Prescription and Abandonment

Another issue that can affect the property right itself is the doctrine of prescription/abandonment. These doctrines arise from the notion that an owner can, by his actions, allow his property to fall into the hands of another. They suggest that in these cases, property title can pass from the original owner to another person. Arguing for prescription and abandonment, Tacitus noted that it was impertinence to revive old pretensions. Cicero, in De Offic., Lib. II, Cap. XXII, asked if there "was any reason why Lands that a man has been possessed of for many years, or even many Ages should be taken from him."

Grotius notes that property can be abandoned. However, at the same time, he notes that abandonment cannot be inferred if the owner does it "Through the necessity of Time, and with the Intention to recover it if he can."[18] Grotius goes on to say that,

> Thus again, should a Man knowingly suffer another to enjoy what is his for a considerable Time, without demanding it, it might be concluded from his Forbearance that he designed to part with it altogether, and looked upon it no longer as his Property; unless there was any other Reason, that manifestly hindered him from making opposition.[19]

Grotius sets up two exceptions to the above general rule. The first is where one does not know that one's property is being used by another. The second is where one is not able to speak, or where one "does not have full liberty to speak." Grotius' exception regarding someone who does not speak because he does not have full liberty to speak is very widely drawn. He notes that "if there appears any other Reason that hinders him from acting, the Conjecture drawn from silence can have no Place."

Grotius, in Chapter IX deals with when jurisdiction and property cease. He notes that they can cease when the holder himself (or itself when it is a state) ceases to exist. He also notes the previous discussion of how rights can be terminated if they are abandoned.

Pufendorf also considers usucaption and prescription in Chapter XII of Book IV, Of the Law of Nature and Nations. In analysing these two methods for acquiring property, Pufendorf cites approvingly the Laws of the Twelve Tables,[20] "Let the Claim against Things stolen hold good everlastingly...." Once again, this limits the possibility of prescription in cases where the true owners parted with property unwillingly and follows from Grotius' treatment of the same issues. While the thief cannot claim possession because of the initial crime, the honest possessor is also limited in what he can claim, "because of the unjust means by which it was acquired." Pufendorf explicitly notes that thieves are in the habit of putting stolen property in the hands of others (laundering it) because of the doctrine of prescription, and he warns that no one "should be the Gainer from his Wickedness." This is an important notion as well, as it undercuts the idea that a bona fide purchaser without notice can take good title.

Pufendorf claims that prescription is based in part on the negligence of the owner in going after his "lost" property. He notes that in the case of theft, this reason cannot be used against true owners because stolen goods are always carefully concealed. He goes on to comment on the law then in place that gave prescriptive rights even in these cases after 40 years of use. Moveable property, he notes, can pass into prescriptive use more quickly than immoveable property. In analysing prescription, he notes:

> the Assertion is not true, that those who suffer their goods to be withheld from them by prescription, are really offenders against the Commonwealth.

Persons who abuse or squander their goods do damage the public. Similarly, damage is done when the proprietor "sits over it...and is a proprietor only in name, let[ting] it grow useless for want of application."[21]

Increasingly, we see that scholars have not countenanced a situation when prescription easily trumps property rights.

In Book IV, Chapter XII, Pufendorf describes the right of prescription. He notes that even the Roman authors, such as Cujacius, said that the prescriptive rights violate the principles of the law of nations because it takes a man's property without his consent. This is not to say that prescription should never apply; it merely notes that the benefit to the community must be substantial, outweighing the property right that has the force of international law behind it. Cujacius had noted that:

> No man can constitute another as the Proprietor of a thing, unless he were himself so before.[22]

While Pufendorf accepts that a man can renounce his right to a thing, but then the acquisition of property does not arise through prescription, but rather because the right has been renounced. However, if a man is silent as to his rights, then his negligence cannot be used as a basis for taking away his right because that right attaches to the property or thing and is inviolable. Only if you take the view that property rights are rights granted by the State (a civil law/positive law concept), can it be material that a man has "slept on his rights." In this case, the reason for this is that when the right was granted by the state, it was accompanied by the obligation to restate the right, so if a man did not assert his rights, he was somehow affecting the two-way bargain between himself and the state. This view treats property rights just as other contractual rights, except that the contract is with the State and not an individual.

However, even those who hold to a positive law view of prescription accept that a man may appear to relinquish his right for a time with the intention of taking it up again in the future. Pufendorf also notes that if we are ignorant of the taking, we should not be penalised, nor should we be penalised if our silence was occasioned through fear. He noted instead that:

> Even a long, continued silence does not always give us sufficient ground to suppose a tacit dereliction…

If there is a claim brought in the future after a supposed abandonment, then the abandonment was not a real abandonment. Pufendorf rejects Grotius' view that a long silence might lead to dereliction because men would not act uncharitably towards one another, on the basis that what men might do to each other was irrelevant to the actual property right itself.

Instead in his Chapter XIII of Book IV, Pufendorf attacks prescription by listing the obligations that arise from property:

> He who is in possession of what belongs to us ought to [e]mploy his utmost ability towards putting it again under our command.

Importantly, this obligation arises when the party in possession knows that the thing is ours. He also notes that the party in possession when he knows that the thing belongs to someone else "will be no hindrance to the Owner in the recovery of them."

The important element of Pufendorf's analysis is that this obligation is the same however the possessor came by the property, whether by honest or dishonest means. The obligation, like the property right on which it is based, arises from the property itself and not from any default by any party. There is no difference in the obligation to restitute between the guilty and the honest possessor. However, the guilty possessor may be responsible in damages or some other penalty in addition to having to make restitution. Section VIII of Chapter XIII notes the obligation on the possessor to restitute property. Here there is another difference between the thinking of Grotius and that of Pufendorf. In making restitution, Grotius was of the view that the property and the fruits that flowed naturally from the property should be restituted, but not fruits that were the result of the hard work of the possessor (but would not have been possible without the property). Pufendorf took the view that both should be restituted, less the expenses incurred by the possessor and some measure of his profit. This again illustrates that property rights are completely different in nature from other kinds of rights and elicit very different policy responses. Pufendorf's view of the property more closely approximates the Cochran view, whereas Grotius is closer to Hobbes and this is what explains the different approaches to restitution.

Indeed, Pufendorf thinks of property rights so differently from other kinds of rights that he even suggests (foreshadowing the remedy of self-help) that

> those who live in a state of natural liberty, may as fairly seize by violence the price of what has been stolen from them, as the thing itself…

In Section XIV, he notes that the moment that a possessor is aware that he has goods belonging to another, "[he] should be at the same time obliged to discover to the Owner, upon his demand, where his goods are lodged, that he may have an opportunity of regaining them."

These are obligations which we submit are different in kind from the ordinary obligations which flow from other kinds of rights based in contract, or granted by the state.

State Confiscation of Property

We will now examine property rights and how they interface with governments that seize that property. We will look at both initial taking and what governments do with the property they have taken.

Governments that engage in the confiscation of property tend to believe that confiscation of property will not have an impact on the productive use of that property. The motivation for confiscation is to then redistribute the property usually, though not always, to the poor. However, to do this misses the fundamental point that the confiscation itself changes the incentives and thus reduces the yield that will come from the property itself. The lower yield arises from the lack of efficiency. This lower yield ultimately results in higher prices which have a negative impact on the very group that the change was intended to help. The result of confiscation is therefore consumer-welfare-damaging. There are many ways that governments effect expropriations, but one of the most difficult to deal with is the confiscatory tax, where the tax rate is so high that it effectively takes the property away from the owner.[23] In addition, very onerous environmental regulation can also take property away from property owners.

It is useful to look at what national laws say about property rights and government confiscations. The US Constitution provides in the Fifth Amendment that private property cannot be taken for public use by the government without compensation. Building on this and notions of the importance of property rights, a number of trade agreements have included protection for property rights of foreign investors. Perhaps the best-known example is Chapter 11 of the North American Free Trade Agreement (NAFTA). NAFTA Chapter 11 provided that:

> No Party may directly or indirectly nationalise or expropriate an investment of an investor of another Party in its territory or take a measure tantamount to expropriation of such an investment...except [for a public purpose, in accordance with due process, on a non-discriminatory basis and on payment of compensation.[24]

Article 14.8 of the USMCA, NAFTA's successor agreement, imposed the same four conditions on expropriations of property.[25] These provisions drive at what is at the heart of property rights and how they are to be protected. The US view of what constitutes a regulatory taking under its constitutional law has impacted the way that US trade negotiators have negotiated trade agreements. Generally, they have imported concepts of trade into their discussions. The question under US law usually turns on the boundaries of what constitutes police power, and what constitutes an action tantamount to expropriation. This interface determines what constitutes a regulatory taking. Some commentators believe that some recent NAFTA decisions, notably the Metalclad and Methanex decisions, substantially extend the US takings doctrine.[26] We will discuss these cases specifically later in the chapter. However, proper analysis of this subject depends on a full understanding of how the takings clause has developed over the years and precisely how NAFTA Article 1110 has been interpreted by the cases.

A Brief History of the Takings Clause of the US Constitution

It is clearly beyond our present scope to analyse the US Constitution's takings clause in its entirety but it is worth doing some analysis of the key points. The takings clause received much attention during the 1970s as the US environmental laws meant that property owners became more restricted in what they could do with their property. An example of this related to the activities of the Army Corps of Engineers under the authority of the Federal Water Pollution Control Acts Amendments of 1972 (the Clean Water Act) under which the emission of pollutants into the US waters could be regulated by the federal government. One of the largest claims paid by the federal government as a result of a takings claim was *Whitney Benefits, Inc v United States.*[27] In that case, Whitney had a coal mining lease on land where coal mining was subsequently made illegal as a result of the application of the Surface Mining Control and Reclamation Act of 1977. In this case, the entire value of the coal mining lease was rendered valueless. There have been a number of applications of the takings clause where the value of the investment was limited. These applications are listed below and are extracted from a Report prepared for the Congressional Budget Office:

The Diversity of Government Actions that Have Led to Successful Takings Claims[28]

The following are examples of successful takings cases decided against the federal government:

Noise from Military Aircraft – *Branning v. United States.*[29] The court held that noise from low-flying Marine Corps aircraft caused a taking, despite the fact that the aircraft were above the 500-foot aerial easement typically granted to landowners.

Forfeiture of a House to the United States – *Shelden v. United States.*[30] The owner of a second mortgage on property forfeited to the US (because of the borrower's criminal conviction on racketeering charges) prevailed in a taking claim against the federal government for "destruction" of its mortgage.

Installation of Groundwater Monitoring Wells – *Hendler v. United States.*[31] The circuit court found that the installation of wells by the Environmental Protection Agency to monitor a plume of contaminated groundwater was a taking by physical occupation. On remand, the US Court of Federal Claims awarded no compensation, holding that the benefits of the wells to the landowner outweighed any damages from the occupation.

Denial of an Oil and Gas Drilling Permit – *Bass Enterprises Production Co. v. United States, Rev'd.*[32] The owner of a federal lease was denied a permit to drill for oil and gas by the Bureau of Land Management pending a determination by the Environmental Protection Agency of whether drilling would be consistent with the Waste Isolation Pilot Plant Land Withdrawal Act of 1992. The US Court of Federal Claims held that the denial was a permanent taking. The Court of Appeals reviewed the case and remanded it for trial on the issue of temporary taking.

Statutory Cancellation of Coal Exploration Permits – *NRG Co. v. United States.*[33]

In accordance with the Act of 9 October 1980 (the Cancellation Act), the Bureau of Indian Affairs cancelled permits authorising mineral prospectors to explore for coal on Indian lands. The court held that the cancellation was a taking.

A Poultry Quarantine – *Yancey v. United States.*[34] A quarantine that the US Department of Agriculture imposed on uninfected turkeys to control the spread of avian influenza was held to be a taking.

A Statute Limiting the Division of Indian Land – *Babbitt v. Youpee.*[35] The Supreme Court, affirming the decision of the lower court, found the federal statute that treated the division of Indian land ownership to be a taking. The statute, Section 207 of the Indian Land Consolidation Act, attempted to prevent the fractionalisation of Indian land. Under the law, the owner of an allotment was precluded from bequeathing his or her property to multiple heirs if the resulting parcels did not meet certain acreage and income standards.

Use of a Patented Mining Process – *Dow Chemical Co. v. United States.*[36] The court held that the use of a patented process for injecting slurry into mine voids without securing a licence from the patent holder constituted a taking of the licence. This was particularly interesting because it demonstrated that in order to show a taking under the fifth amendment, it was not necessary for the entire entity to be rendered valueless, only the relevant separable business line. In addition, this taking was of a company's intellectual property, and therefore has important implications for the next chapter's discussion of compulsory licencing.

Making a Company Responsible for an Underfunded Health Plan – *Eastern Enterprises v. Apfel.*[37] Claimants challenged reach-back provisions in the Coal Industry Retiree Health Benefit Act of 1992 that made them responsible for underfunded miner retiree health plans and sought injunctive and declaratory relief. The District Court granted a summary judgement for the government, ruling against the claimant, and the First Circuit Court affirmed the decision. The Supreme Court reversed the decision, sending the case back to the lower court to be decided consistent with the finding that the act constituted a taking. Enforcement of the act was suspended as applied to Eastern Enterprises.

It can be seen from the above set of examples that the takings clause has been broadly interpreted. The cases illustrate that courts evaluate the following factors:

a the nature of the government action;
b whether the action interferes with reasonable, investor-backed expectations and
c the action's economic impact.

Nature of Government Action

The nature of government action is also tied to the nature of the property right that is being excluded. In most cases, if the government physically dispossesses a property owner, this is more likely to be a taking. The right to pass property is also considered a fundamental property right and where it is interfered with, there is also likely to be a taking.[38]

Interference with Reasonable, Investment-Backed Expectations

This essentially means that the government should not take steps that harm the reasonable expectations of property owners that their property will increase in value as its development potential is realised. The higher the level of investment, the more this expectation should be protected.

Impact of Government Action

The question is what proportion of the total value of the property has been destroyed by the government action. Most courts have said that the parcel of property has a whole should be considered, not severable parts of it, but it is not always easy to estimate what constitutes the property as a whole. One question which will be asked is what is the economically viable use of the property?[39] If the economically viable use of the property is severely curtailed then a taking is likely to be found. It is certainly arguable, and the CBO report does suggest, some alternative methodologies that might be used whereby some level of compensation would be paid even where the government action has not completely destroyed the value of the property.

Continuing Tension between Property Rights and Expropriation Schools

The Cordell Hull formula of "prompt, adequate and effective" compensation arose out of the expropriations of US-citizen-owned oil and agrarian properties by the Mexican government prior to the Second World War.[40] There were at this time two competing views – the first was the notion of the primacy of national sovereignty as asserted by doctrines like the Calvo doctrine. The second was the notion of the primacy of property rights and the inviolability of those rights. These two principles clash head on in restitution cases.

Bilateral investment treaties (BITs) are an expression of the primacy of the property rights school of thought. The notion that property rights were in some way primally important was carried by the so-called traditional school in the US. While the Hull formulation encapsulated this view, there were changes underway as countries that supported the Calvo doctrine increased their power over international organisations.

In 1962, the UN General Assembly adopted Resolution 1803 which was still suggestive of the traditional school. Resolution 1803 provided that countries could only expropriate or nationalise property in cases of public need, and there should be appropriate compensation. The word "appropriate" was chosen as a compromise with the US delegate stating that it meant the Hull formulation, and other delegates suggesting that it included the country's ability to pay and other factors.

Calvo Doctrine-type proponents won a significant victory in the 1974 Charter of Economic Rights and Duties of States which provided that nations had the right to expropriate and limited the role of international law in evaluating what appropriate compensation meant. Limiting appropriate compensation to whatever prevailing national law said would effectively gut the traditional school in countries where it was not the ascendant view.

Negotiation of Free Trade Agreements/Bilateral Investment Treaties

Many countries have a history of signing BITs. The US has the longest history of including investment provisions in trade agreements, although it is relatively commonplace now. Analysis of these early provisions in the US agreements is therefore constructive.

The US has pushed back on threats to investor and property rights protection through the negotiation of a number of BITs and Free Trade Agreements with Investment chapters, such as the old NAFTA agreement (Article 1110 discussed above) and its successor USMCA (Article 14.8, noted above, which reiterates the requirements of Article 1110). These negotiations form a single approach to the protection of property rights and stand on the opposite side of the developments occurring in the United Nations.

The case of *Metalclad v Mexico* (2000) examined the application of Article 1110 of NAFTA, as well as NAFTA Article 1105, which required fair and equitable treatment of investments. The US company, Metalclad, had acquired a Mexican company that owned and operated a hazardous waste landfill site in Mexico. Metalclad had acquired all the operating licences that it thought were required in order to run the site, and indeed was told so by the Mexican National Ecological

Institute (the body that issued the federal permit). As a result of local pressure, Metalclad was subsequently denied municipal operating permits. Metalclad claimed that the actions of these sub-divisions (San Luis Potosi and Guadalcazar). The NAFTA panel essentially found that because the federal system had already granted Metalclad the permits it needed to operate the site, the refusal to grant municipal licences was an expropriation since it was evidently not being done to satisfy the environmental requirements set out in Mexico's law. Interpreting Article 1110, the Panel said that expropriating activity included:

> covert or incidental interference with the use of property which has the effect of depriving the owner, in whole or in significant part, of the use or reasonably-to-be-expected economic benefit of property even if not necessarily to the obvious benefit of the host State.

A different approach was taken in the Methanex case. This involved the claim by a Canadian company, Methanex, that California's ban on MTBE in fuel was an action tantamount to expropriation contrary to NAFTA Article 1110. Methanex claimed that California's regulatory goal was to deal with the detection of MTBE in water resources caused by leaking gasoline. Methanex argued that such a regulatory goal could be accomplished in other ways that were less damaging to its investments. Methanex, citing studies that suggested that MTBE was not necessarily as much of a health risk as the gasoline itself (MTBE displaced Benzene in gasoline and Benzene was a known cancer-causing agent). Instead Methanex believed that the real environmental problem was the leaking of gasoline from storage tanks which could have been dealt with in other ways. Although Methanex did not produce ethanol or MTBE (fuel additives), it produced methanol which was one of the raw materials that was used to produce MTBE. What is interesting about the Methanex case is that Methanex had alleged that ADM, an ethanol producer was expressly pursuing a strategy of lobbying against the MTBE additive in order to increase consumption of ethanol. Methanex alleged that this was part of ADM's general business strategy, and that in effect their property was being expropriated by the lobbying activities of a rival firm. This is particularly interesting in the context of our analysis of the interface of trade and competition, because this activity (if the allegations were true) would have been a classic application of producer or competitor welfare at the expense of consumers (because its net impact would have been to remove a rival fuel additive from the additive mix, and leave the field to ethanol, where ADM had approximately 70% market share). The taking resulting from the MTBE ban was therefore an application of straightforward producer welfare economics. ADM wanted the ban to protect its product from competition (MTBE produced from methanol by a Canadian firm). Methanex was the leading producer of methanol for MTBE in the state of California. Hence, at least on a de facto basis, all the methanol and MTBE in California was foreign, and all the ethanol domestic. Viewed in this context, NAFTA Article 1110 acts as a bulwark against this type of protectionist activity and therefore leads to consumer welfare gains by protecting property. In other words, the protection of the property right in the context of this case delivers consumer welfare gains, and the MTBE ban, the taking of property under the terms of Article 1110 delivers competitor welfare or producer welfare gains.[41] In the end the final panel ruling dismissed all of Methanex's claims, and found for the US.

The panel said that a non-discriminatory regulation for a public purpose was unlikely to ground an expropriation or action tantamount to expropriation claim under USMCA Article 1110 unless specific commitments had been given to the foreign investor by the regulating government that the government would refrain from such regulation.[42] The panel further suggested that there had to be some sort of reliance on the government commitments in order for this element to be satisfied.[43] From a consumer welfare perspective, this is a backward step as it suggests that absent direct discrimination, then a regulatory taking will not be found, even where it can be shown that a firm had deliberately sought an anti-competitive regulation through the regulatory process that harmed a rival and delivered benefits to itself (and that firm had a very high market share of the competing product). Such activity is specifically what former FTC Chairman Tim Muris had in mind when he talked about the abuse of the regulatory process under the cover of the Noerr-Pennington doctrine to secure competitive advantage.[44]

In addition to free trade agreements with investment chapters, the US has also provided for explicit restitution remedies in cases where the property rights of US investors in foreign countries have been abused by governments or others. The most well-known example of this kind of legislation is the Helms-Burton Act which is aimed at disincentivising people from dealing in the US citizen's property that was expropriated by the Cuban Government. The Act is an extension of other attempts by the US to ensure that the traditional approach to property rights protection was the one that prevailed.

Multilateral Agreement on Investment

Attempts to protect investment have not solely been entered into by countries unilaterally and in their bilateral trade agreements and BITs. The OECD had initiated an attempt to create a Multilateral Agreement on Investment (the "MAI"), but due to resistance primarily from developing countries this attempt failed. The MAI would have contained many of the investment protections that are enshrined in the USMCA[45] and other US-FTAs at the bilateral and regional level. Like USMCA, MAI would have given private investors rights of actions against states, and this has proved to be a very controversial area. The MAI sought to take the most advanced "technologies" from existing investor protection agreements. It had a number of innovative features First, the MAI sought to protect a much wider class of investments. The OECD's drafters attempted to pick up the full range of investments that were presently available not just the more conventional investments. The MAI would have included intellectual property in its definition of investment. This is very consistent with this book's hypothesis that intellectual property is really a type of property right. In addition, the ambitious agreement was intended to cover privatisations (imposing MFN and National Treatment obligations on them), state monopolies, and state enterprises or enterprises that had substantial government involvement.

The MAI, as a whole, tracked WTO precedent by enshrining MFN and National Treatment into the obligations of governments when dealing with private investments. In many ways the MAI would have been a powerful agreement that dealt with investment barriers as well as anti-competitive regulation.

BITs contain provisions which relate to investor protection. They provide that where foreign investors have their property rights taken away by governmental action, then those foreign investors can sue the offending governments through dispute resolution in the World Bank under the ICSID[46] rules. There is a rich history of ICSID arbitration under a number of BITs. Most recently, the Government of Argentina has been sued in ICSID by property rights owners that lost their property either through direct expropriation or through the impact of the currency devaluation brought about by the Argentinean default on its IMF loans.

Advocates of strict national sovereignty have argued that this limits the policy space of governments, which is tantamount to suggesting that national sovereignty should protect governments from actions taken in the international arena, or the arena where the rights holder is located, to prevent them from abusing their own people. As well as having little foundation in law, this approach is morally bankrupt. It misses the wider point, which is enshrined in international law, that there is a contract between governor and governed, with duties and obligations on both sides. In any event, countries regularly limit their effective national sovereignty through commitments to agreements such as WTO, regional and bilateral free trade agreements and so on. Provisions in these agreements do not force a government's hand to be sure, but they do require a country to pay for violating a particular commitment through trade sanctions and the payment of tariffs.

Protection of Property: From GATT 1947 to Extraterritoriality and Helms-Burton

We have seen how property rights protection has developed over the history of man's productive labour. We have reviewed the modern history of property rights protection in the global context. We will now discuss the global rules which have covered property rights production in the GATT and its progeny. The US took this to another level in the 1990s by enacting what its trading partners have referred to disparagingly as extraterritorial legislation. These include the Helms-Burton and Helms-Gonzales Acts. The question is whether these are a difference in kind from the old GATT/WTO approach or whether this is a different in degree. A frequent criticism levelled at the Helms-Burton and Helms-Gonzales laws is that they are extraterritorial in nature. However, the

Helms-Burton law is not extraterritorial when viewed from the perspective of where the property owner is located after its property has been illegally taken, and not where the property happens to be located. Indeed as we review the international laws that protect property, we see a common thread that runs through all, including the Helms-Burton law. This common thread stems from the recognition that a functioning market economy is built on three central planks. These central planks are (i) free trade and removal of border trade barriers, (ii) competitive market inside the borders and (iii) protection of property rights, including intangible property rights. If the protection of property rights is eroded in any way, then this central plank fails and the market economy will fail to develop benefits for the economy, and for consumers in the market. Central to this is that the right of property is attached to the owner of that property, and is not a grant by the government of the country where the property is.

This central theme is the reason that the rules that have underpinned the global economy have had the protection of property as their major objective. We can see in the history of the developments of international trade law that this principle has been fundamental to developments to ensure the promotion of trade.

The General Agreement on Tariffs and Trade included as one of its key agreements the Trade-Related Investment Measures Agreement. This agreement provides protection to investment, and ensures that any measures that provide different rules for foreign investment or impose conditions on foreign investment such as a local working requirement or local content rules violate international trade law.

The TRIMS agreement is a fairly limited investment protection agreement, certainly much more limited than the MAI would have been. During its negotiations, a wider array of rules that were generally applied to investments in WTO members and which could be seen to be damaging to overall trade were discussed, but in the end only those measures which were already inconsistent with the GATT made it into the final agreement. These two GATT rules were Article III (national treatment) and Article XI (quantitative restrictions). The Annex to the TRIMS provides an illustrative, though not exhaustive, list. TRIMS is significant because the measures it is intended to apply to are not only measures that condition the investment itself – for example, rules that say that without a certain percentage of local content in the investment itself, it will be barred, but also measures with which it is necessary to comply in order to gain an advantage (such as a preferred position in a government procurement or a tax break or subsidy). This substantially expands the TRIMS into a number of areas of domestic law and policy and reaches into the way that the domestic market operates. In general, Article III violating principles refer to local content requirements, whereas Article XI violating principles would include import restrictions, limitations of foreign exchange access or restrictions on exports.

We have already discussed the fact that USMCA Chapter 14 provides that investments are protected. USMCA members commit not to nationalise, expropriate or take any action tantamount to expropriation. The bar on actions tantamount to expropriation is interesting – as it opens the door to disciplining many behaviours that, while they are not technically confiscatory, may be confiscatory in effect – such as environmental or tax regulations. These get to the heart of what is the value of the property. Most of the US and EU bilateral free trade agreements currently include some measure of investment protection, recognising the powerful role that property rights protection plays in ensuring a functioning market economy. Indeed, many of these agreements provide protection for property rights that goes beyond the level of protection generally conferred in international trade agreements. These include investor-state dispute resolution provisions. Investor-state dispute resolution is a very powerful tool as it means that individual investors have the right to sue governments and win money damages awards. This is a powerful incentive and discipline on the actions of governments and their decisions with respect to expropriation of the property of private persons. This is one way that investors have sought to ensure that their property is protected. This level of protection arises from the fact that the nature of property rights protection is different from rights that arise merely from contracts which means that individuals can enforce the rights against foreign governments that are seeking to abrogate them.

There are many ways of ensuring that property should be properly protected, and the role of property restitution in that process is key. We have highlighted some of the ways that international law protects property. There are some methods where novel approaches can ensure that property that is particularly prone to being smuggled does not end up underground. We focus in this next section particularly on art and antiquities. We focus on this both because art can be used to hold large amounts of money in easily transportable and moveable objects, and also because in many countries around the world, art and antiquities have been relatively recently stolen. These include Iraq, Afghanistan and China. In addition, the example of how the art world has dealt with Holocaust art is also noteworthy, in particular in Central and Eastern Europe.

Recent Developments between the UK and the EU; the UK-EU Trade and Co-operation Agreement 2020

When the UK left the EU in January 2020, it was necessary to negotiate a free trade agreement between the UK and the EU. This agreement included provisions that tackled the issue of investor protection. In addition to the usual type of investment protection, there was a new concept introduced which links investment provisions more closely to market distortion principles.

In the negotiation process, the EU was very concerned about suggestions that there is a nonlevel-playing field between the UK and the EU, and argued successfully for a "Rebalancing Mechanism" which specifically allows tariff retaliation in cases of "trade" or "investment" distortion. It is unclear at this time how these provisions will be interpreted and evidence of this will only be forthcoming once litigation under the Rebalancing Mechanism is initiated. Based on the negotiating history, the EU's fear was that the UK would use its tax policy to make investment in the UK more attractive than investment in the EU, but this is only one interpretation of the provisions. It could equally be involved in the case of an investment distortion, i.e. where investors rights are being damaged in market-distorting ways. The use of the tariff is then not intended to stop a particular government policy, but instead is used to discipline a government engaged in damaging investor rights. It is quite likely that these two opposing interpretations will clash as the UK and EU's regulations in this area start to diverge over time.

The EU and UK address issues of investment distortions in the subsidy control mechanism and the Rebalancing Mechanism.

The Subsidy Control mechanism is in Title XI on fair competition (thus recognising the link between competition, trade and market distortion). With regard to the investment distortion test, Article 358(1) of the EU-UK TCA provides that:

> The Parties recognise the importance of free and undistorted competition in their trade and investment relations. The Parties acknowledge that anticompetitive business practices may distort the proper functioning of markets and undermine the benefits of trade liberalisation. The definition of subsidy does extend to certain areas of taxation, but exempts general taxation. Article 366 lays down certain new principles designed to ensure that subsidies are proportionate and do not have a "material effect on trade and investment."

The parties have also agreed that they will not lower current standards in labour and environment in a manner affecting trade or investment.

Both in the case of subsidy control, labour and environmental issues, the parties can suspend concessions given under the agreement (i.e. impose tariffs). This foreshadows the possibility of a tariffication of the market distortion.

Article 441 of the TCA provides that:

> If material impacts on trade or investment between the Parties are arising as a result of significant divergences between the Parties in the areas referred to in paragraph 1, either Party may take appropriate rebalancing measures to address the situation. Such measures shall be restricted with respect to their scope and duration to what is strictly necessary and proportionate in order to remedy the situation. Priority shall be given to such measures as will least disturb the functioning of this Agreement. A Party's assessment of those impacts shall be based on reliable evidence and not merely on conjecture or remote possibility.

The fact that the rebalancing measures must be strictly necessary and proportionate opens the door to the notion at they are designed only to correct the distortion brought about by the divergence as opposed to being punitive. One question which the litigation under this measure will clarify is whether the impact is based on an economic distortion in the sense we have outlined in this book, or whether it will be based on how divergent one party is from the other *having no regard to internationally agreed benchmarks*. For example, the EU is currently in violation of various WTO agreements in the SPS area. If the UK's compliance with WTO gave rise to a divergence (as it would), surely that would not be regarded as distortionary. Indeed, the distortion would be the EU's violation of SPS rules (even though that distortion was actually increasing and not reducing producer costs to which the measure applied, although it certainly would impede the UK's access to the EU market in a manner which could be quantified).

Logically, and in order to ensure WTO consistency of the underlying agreement, you would certainly have to read in WTO compliance into this provision. This would include the WTO's TBT Agreement which is violated if there are technical regulations which are applied in a discriminatory manner. Any standards and technical regulations in the agreement must comply with the TBT Agreement (see Chapter 6). However where the agreement is silent and one party imposes a requirement, or exempts a requirement for the other party only, such a measure would likely violate the TBT Agreement. A fortiori, we would argue that if the measure subject to rebalancing is based on a regulation that is not in compliance with international agreements or indeed violates those agreements, it cannot be a distortion for the purpose of this article. Indeed, such violations may themselves be distortions allowing the other Party to use the Rebalancing Mechanism. Such a result might not be the intention of the EU which was the key demander for these provisions when they sought to negotiate the Rebalancing Mechanism itself. Ultimately, it will require litigation to clarify when a particular rule or regulation constitutes a distortion.

Multilateral Conventions on Property Rights Protection

There are a number of global conventions that have protected individual rights. Reviewing the changing climate for property rights protection is instructive and demonstrates the importance of a global consensus on these points. The initial focus emanated from the natural rights vision of property rights, and the Lockean view that those who work the property are entitled to a high degree of protection.

The 10 December 1948 General Assembly of the United Nations adopted the Universal Declaration of Human Rights. Article 17 states that:

> Everyone has the right to own property alone as well as in association with others … No one shall be arbitrarily deprived of his property.

The Convention for the Protection of Human Rights and Fundamental Freedoms (Rome, 1950) focused on the right of everyone to "respect for his private and family life, his home …"[47] The American Convention on Human Rights (San Jose, Costa Rica, 1969) continued this trend. In Africa, countries agreed the Africa Charter on Human Rights and Fundamental Freedoms. The European Convention for the Protection of Human Rights and Fundamental Freedoms, 1952 states that: .

> Every natural or legal person is entitled to the peaceful enjoyment of his own possessions. No-one shall be deprived of his possessions except in the public interest…

In November 1990, the Conference on Security and Cooperation in Europe (CSCE) adopted the Charter of Paris, which designates the right to own property and to exercise individual enterprise as one of the most fundamental of human rights.

The Spitzbergen Archipelago Problem

We can see in some of these Conventions the fundamental tension which we described from the earliest scholars in the area. The common underlying theme of these conventions and treaties is the notion that property rights are fundamentally independent of state sovereignty, and so the actions of state governments do not affect them. Even where there is a lack of a government, property rights can be present. However, some international treaties and conventions appear to come from the notion that property rights emanate from governments and are given to the citizens by the state. The simple example of the Sptizbergen Archipelago Problem demonstrates the difference between these two views.

Barren islands off the coast of Norway were mined by US companies before any country asserted any right to them. After the initial investment and working of the land by the US mining companies, the Government of Norway asserted jurisdiction over the islands. The question was then who had the right to the property. A state-conferred view would mean that there was no property right at all until a State had asserted jurisdiction. The school of thought that property rights were generated by the work done on the land (a Lockean view) would conclude that the US companies owned the property and their rights were consolidated by the labour that they had already applied to the land. Similarly, a "natural rights" view would hold that the property rights were vested in the US companies because there was no need for the State to exist to confer the property rights.

Transfer of Property

We have seen how state action in confiscating private property has been challenged under constitutional principles. We will now consider another area where property is treated very differently from other rights – the manner in which it can be transferred. The ways in which property can be transferred help us to understand the particular importance of property, and why it is different in nature from other choses that can be transferred, such as personality. Pufendorf noted in Chapter IX, Book VI of "Of the Law of Nature and Nations," that:

> the chief point usually controverted on this subject is, whether or not in the transferring of property the law of nature requires Delivery...

While Grotius was of the opinion that property could be transferred by bare covenant, Pufendorf differentiated between two types of property. He drew a distinction between the possession of property and what he described as the dominion over property. While Pufendorf accepted that the mere covenanting of a property did confer some useful right, he also admitted of the possibility that there was an extra step required to complete the rights transferred to the new owner. This, therefore, distinguished property from other kinds of objects that could be more easily transferred.

When property is passed by will, there are equivalent additional steps that must be taken. The English law of property which followed from the writings of Pufendorf and John Locke also differentiates between real and personal properties. For transfers of real property, more needs to be done in order to properly convey such property.

However, this is where there is a sharp divergence in the works of Grotius from the other authors we have discussed. Grotius (Book II, Chapter III) notes that:

> When [private property] depends on the general Property of the State, ... that which has no particular owner does not therefore belong to the first occupant, but returns to the whole society...

This lays the foundation for the civil law concept of property rights as emanations of the state, which is very different from the common law concepts that Locke and others pioneered.

Grotius (book II, ch X) provides that where someone comes by a Thing honestly, he is not obliged to make restitution if the Thing is gone. But he must restitute the fruits or produce of the Thing that he has derived, even if he has lost those. So began a line of legal concepts that ultimately resulted in the notion that a bona fide purchaser without notice can take good title to even stolen property.

The Role of Property Restitution in the Market Economy

One of the most difficult issues in the area of property rights is the idea of property restitution. This is a contentious issue because it brings into conflict two classes of property rights owners. The first class is the foreign investor whose present rights in a new investment clash with the property rights of the original owners of that property which was taken from them through some confiscation or other act where property was taken without due compensation being paid.

These issues have become particularly important in the way that privatisation has played out in newly privatising markets.

Introduction to Restitution and Unjust Enrichment

The study of restitution used to be a major field of activity especially in US academic circles. It has become far less important now and this is a symptom of the difficulty in ensuring satisfactory outcomes in restitution cases. This is a wider problem. As Hanoch Dagan, a leading restitution scholar, has noted, restitution is a window into a larger project of social understanding. Dagan has also noted that restitution is a vital part of nation-building. Restitution has links to all aspects of property rights and indeed is one of the key central pillars that underpins the foundations of the market economy. This is particular when countries are in the process of understanding their approach to privatisation.[48]

Importance of Property Rights to a Free and Prosperous Society

As we note elsewhere that an economically free society rests on three pillars:

- competitive markets
- free trade and market liberalisation
- protection of property rights

If any of these pillars is missing, the ability of the market economy to deliver benefits to consumers is much more limited.

Viable property restitution principles must be accepted in order to support the protection of property rights themselves.

General Principles of Property Rights and Restitution

The general principle of restitution relies on the fact that the more property that implicates an owner's personhood, the more likely the legal system will be to restore the property as opposed to giving damages to the person who has lost the property.

One key element is that there is a connection between property and personhood. Dagan notes that the closer property implicates personhood, the more important restitution becomes as a remedy. Dagan posits that there is a spectrum of interests starting with one's personal integrity and land that require a very high degree of protection that would require remedies such as restitution if that property had been stolen, through property that is less connected to personhood such as contractual relationships and information. Where the particular asset being discussed is on this spectrum largely determines the appropriateness of restitution as a remedy.

Dagan helpfully sets out, in tabular form,[49] the types of remedies that should be available for different kinds of property when it is stolen. The table notes that land and chattels at a minimum merit the greater of fair market value and profits, and that the rationale for this is the need to ensure the well-being of the right-holder.

Historical Basis for Restitution

The history of restitution as a remedy actually dates back to the beginnings of legal development itself. The importance of property rights can be seen from the Roman law. Tacitus discussed the important of property rights and restitution.[50] In particular, Tacitus' account of the German tribes in Germania[51] suggests that a notional concept of property rights existed among them. Roman law was originally set out in the Twelve Tables.[52] Table VII involved rights in land and was the early Roman recognition of property rights. Roman law set out the ownership rights that people had in land. Tenants had the right to use the land. Apart from slaves that had no rights, Rome did not take the land of its citizens, except rarely and with some compensation. In slightly more recent history, the argument between Pope John XXII and William of Ockham about whether the Franciscans owned property highlighted the central issue in how one looks at property and the property right. These lessons are very important today. Early theologians had argued that property was introduced by human positive law, as opposed to being based on natural law. Ockham argued that property did not emerge immediately, but only arose when the power to appropriate a thing was exercised by man. The central theme of property protection was that a thing could be mine in a way that it could not be yours.

In the previous section, we analysed the two scholars who set the framework for property rights protection, Grotius and Pufendorf. Both men came out of the civil law tradition. Grotius suggested that property rights came out of human agreement, and hence that property rights emanated from man's pact or agreement with other men. They appear to reject the notion that property rights emanate from natural law. John Locke, by contrast, held that occupation of land by labour (i.e. working of the property) gave rise to the property right, and that this was a result of natural or positive law and not human convention.

Modern Basis for Restitution

More recently, the aspect of unjust enrichment has become a major driver in restitution theory and practice. Particularly with respect to land, there is much more of an appreciation that the major reason for restitution is to give due reparation for the unjust and forcible removal of property rights. It is important to recognise that we are really talking about the principles that underpin the law of unjust enrichment when we are dealing with property restitution.

History of Moderns Restitution Programmes

There are good examples in the restitution programmes of Lithuania and Nicaragua which have been studied in some detail by the World Bank and others.[53] In the case of Lithuania, a major motivation was to delegitimise the deeply unpopular Soviet occupation. A World Bank study contrasts this where the fact that the land was held prior to the Sandinista expropriations by persons connected to the Somoza administration complicated the question as to whether a simple reversion to the status quo ante was desirable in that case.[54] This leads to a question in the case of restitution which focuses on the nature of the original expropriation. Restitution becomes a more desirable remedy when the original expropriation was reprehensible or otherwise unjustified.

The two programmes suggest that sometimes the recognition of former property rights owners can put an end to competing property claims, and therefore increase tenure security. The two programmes also suggest that a mechanism that makes property claims more certain is vital to ensuring a system that increases tenure security. In the US, the Foreign Claims Settlement Commission (FCSC) has functioned in this way since 1967. However, one must recognise some economic disadvantages from restitution resulting in the fragmentation of land. Indeed in Nicaragua small-holders protested the potential loss of their lands, and found a politically powerful voice. Some argue that dealing with this complexity alone is a reason not to proceed with land restitution. However if the view is that land rights come from natural law or the original working of the land by its true owners, and not mere convention or agreement, this argument holds no water.

In order to ensure that property expropriated from the US citizens is properly protected, the US has engaged in some novel methods to incentivise protective regimes, and to disincentivise the elimination of property rights. In the case of Nicaragua, the Helms-Gonzales Act provided that the US could deny financial aid to states that expropriate property of US citizens.

The Helms-Gonzales Act sets out the manner in which the State Department must apply the law to a country that had expropriated the assets of US citizens. In the case of Nicaragua, the law provides that US citizens that have had their properties expropriated can establish claims against the Nicaraguan government. The law also provides that the US can obstruct the approval of loans to countries that have expropriated the assets of US citizens when such loans are provided by intergovernmental lending institutions of which the US is a member. In the case of Nicaragua, the US even established a claims office in Nicaragua itself to process these claims. The US also tied the issue of property restitution to the economic reforms that the Nicaraguans were being asked to make in order to obtain IMF and World Bank funding, a nod to the importance of property rights protection in the panoply of the economic policies needed to deliver growth and economic development to the country.

Property tribunals were also created in the country to deal with the many US claims. These property tribunals have been important ways of ensuring a rapid processing of property claims. The country has a National Confiscation Review Commission to deal with the list of confiscations and policymakers regard the NCRC as a necessary step along the way towards restitution.

Property Restitution in Post-Communist Europe

On 10 September 2003, the Helsinki Commission, a body set up by the US Congress, reported that there had been mixed progress on restitution issues involving the former communist countries of Central and Eastern Europe, as well as the former Soviet Union. Recognising the difficulty of enforcing claims through the courts, then Senator Clinton noted that:

"[We must be] constantly creating an atmosphere in which these claims are viewed as appropriate, legitimate and justiciable."[55]

She went on to note that it was vital to establish the entitlement to these claims that should exist. The point she was seeking to make was that these claims are often treated as if they were in some way frivolous or without merit. This occurs because the new owners of property cite the fact that the illegal expropriation act was a long time ago, or that the old owners are motivated by greed, or that the property should not be restored for economic development reasons, since the new owner is an important investor in the country. It is this last issue that is particularly difficult because newly opening or transition economies are in need of foreign investment and foreign investors need some certainty in the rights that they are acquiring.

Privatisation and Restitution

Opinions differ on whether restitution can be a benefit or a hindrance to privatisation. One school of thought suggests that restitution can complicate privatisation processes, by making land claims for newly privatising assets uncertain. Foreign investors may be more reluctant to make investments where there is fear that there will be restitution to former owners of land. For this school, the original expropriating act must be legitimised for the government to have good title to assets to be privatised. Another school of thought suggests that restitution can enhance privatisation because it sends a signal to foreign investors that the government's original expropriation was wrongful, and that wrong is being corrected. Such actions underscore a government's commitment to property rights protection. A government that is prepared to adopt that attitude is unlikely to erode property rights that the foreign investor might acquire. The fundamental driver of this school is the sanctity of the bond between the property and its true owner.

In addition to the two theories set out above, restitution can sometimes be a bulwark against the abuses that frequently occur in privatisation processes. Frequently, privatisation processes can result in power grabs by officials who happen to understand the licencing and concessions process. A classic example of this is what happened in Russia when that country embarked on a privatisation programme. In that case, many of the state assets were effectively given (through knock-down pricing) to officials in the communist party and others that proceeded to use them to unjustly enrich themselves at the expense of consumers. These purchasers were essentially buying the monopoly rents that came with these assets that were becoming private monopoly without regulation. The lack of entrepreneurship in Russia is perhaps symptomatic of a lack of property rights protection. This lack of entrepreneurship is not altogether surprising. If contacts and knowledge of the licencing process are what are incentivised, it should come as no surprise that the business world will define itself by those attributes. The ability to influence the government for private gain and the ability to obtain certain governmental licences will be the activities that are prized. By contrast, the ability to take risks, to innovate and to manage a business efficiently will not be so highly valued. This is one of the reasons why property rights protection is so integral to developing a sound market-based economy. Property restitution which hardly occurred at all in post-Soviet Russia could have prevented or at least slowed down some of the abuses in the privatisation processes and their aftermath.

By contrast, there was much more property restitution in Eastern Germany, and a fair degree of restitution in the Czech Republic. This signalling mechanism has arguably led to a greater proportion of entrepreneurialism in these countries compared with that found in Russia. The country that has engaged in the most significant property restitution among the Central and Eastern European countries is Estonia, and it is no coincidence that Estonia's market has been for a number of years ranked very highly in the index of Economic Freedom published by the Cato Institute.[56]

The case for restitution is also strengthened by the fact that restitution delegitimises the original expropriations. It essentially draws a veil over what happened in the communist or state controlled period, and acknowledges that these activities were wrong. It does not allow the thief to profit from his acts, and disincentivises future expropriations. It therefore has profound implications for the protection of future investments and the operation of a system of justice that investors can rely on. Most importantly, countries that have strong property restitution programmes do so, not because they are looking for an immediate gain from the restitution programme, but rather because that is reflective of their overall perspective on how economic freedom is achieved. The notion that we have expressed in earlier chapters that economic freedom is built on a three-legged stool of trade liberalisation, competitive markets and property right protection requires that each of these legs is fully functional. Property restitution is an integral part of property rights protection and therefore results from an overall cohesive approach to economic issues in general.

There are various kinds of restitution models:

Pure Restitution

One model is to give back the property that was illegally confiscated. This is the model that the Czech Republic and Slovakia have adopted in its purest form.[57]

However for the restitution model to work, the laws must deal with commercial property, former owners must satisfy certain basic conditions and there must be clear limitations.

Compensation Model

This model recognises the difficulty of providing pure restitution. In some cases, it is necessary to have both restitution and compensation, in order to accommodate the concerns of foreign investors. The danger of compensation is the financial burden imposed on countries.

Under the former East German system, owners would have to pay compensation to contribute to a compensation fund. Expropriated enterprises had to be reconveyed (in certain limited cases). In these cases, the former owner must be compensated for reduction in value of property while held by the state and must pay for any improvements which have been made through public funds.

Recognising that property claims can be obstacles to necessary privatisation of enterprises, German law specifically provided that allowed the privatisation agency to sell or lease any property even if a former owner has filed a reconveyance claims.

In the Czech Republic, the First and Second Restitution Acts[58] provided that property confiscated by the communist government between 1955 and 1959, and 1968 and 1989, respectively. These was a substantial alternate compensation fund (in cases where restitution was not possible) of $750 m. Under the Second Restitution Act, only individuals could have property returned. Restitution was not limited to Czech citizens, but was applied broadly to citizens and non-citizens alike.

By contrast, Poland's approach was only to restore property or compensate owners whose land was taken between 1944 and 1960 in contravention of laws then in force. Even where a case could be made out (which was difficult), compensation was preferred to restitution. Most problematic in the Polish programme was the notion that required former owners of real estate to pay the case value of the confiscated real estate.

Direct restitution of, at least, real property which has commercial use has been noted by some commentators to be the best way of rapidly ensuring long-term funding for the development of these resources. In the case of former East Germany, the Treuhandstalt does actually weigh the plans of foreign companies with the original owners to assess who should be given the land. In general, unless the former owner has some plan for developing the property, he will receive compensation not restitution.

The key elements that emerge from these various plans are as follows:

i Time limit on filing claims.
ii Intention of former to do something intensive with the property.
iii If there is a significant exile community that could re-invest restitution is a good way to vesting them into the process of reconstruction and building a private sector.

US Experience: Role of Foreign Claims Settlement Commission

The FCSC is an independent agency within the US Department of Justice that adjudicates the claims of US nationals against foreign governments. It was officially established in 1954 as the successor agency to the War Claims Commission and the International Claims Commission. It has 43 claims programmes that have resulted in the transfer of billions of dollars. These have included claims involving the Soviet takeover of Central and Eastern Europe, Cuba, China, Vietnam, Panama and other countries.

One of the most important elements of the Commission's work is that it is final and conclusive on all questions of fact and law and is not subject to any review by a court or agency. The FCSC reports on an annual basis the impact of its claims programmes for different countries. It reports on whether Congress has set up funds, or whether the government of the country concerned has paid monies which will then be used to partially settle claims.

The FCSC has had varying degrees of success. The success rate tends to be determined by the relationships that different countries have with the US. For example, in the case of Cuba, where there are no diplomatic relations between the countries, there is no Congressional funding, nor has Cuba committed monies to settlement funds for the properties that have been expropriated and are covered by the FCSC, whereas Cuba has settled restitution claims without countries, notably Spain.

Establishing the Right to a Claim

The context for claiming private property has changed dramatically in the last few decades, but especially in the aftermath of the Second World War and the Holocaust. We will start this summary with a quote from former United States Secretary of State Colin Powell:

> The hidden architecture of sustainable development is the law, the law. The rule of law that permits wonderful things to happen. The rule of law permits people to be free, and to pursue their God-given destiny, and to reach and to search and to try harder for their country and their family.
>
> The rule of law that attracts investments. The rule of law that makes investments safe. The rule of law that will make sure that there is no corruption, that will make sure there is justice in a nation that is trying to develop.[59]

The recent period of retrenchment which unfortunately stressed the rights of the state over the individual (and led to communist and authoritarian rules in the first place) was very different from original conceptions of property rights protection which we describe in this book. The rights of victims of state expropriations eroded as a newfound respect for the rights of government started to assert itself on the global stage. It is necessary to understand this assertion of the rights of the state over the rights of the individual in modern history.

The end of the 19th century saw the beginnings of the intellectual basis for an assertion of the state into the economy. The writings of Karl Marx and others were a reaction to the perceived failures of capitalism. Capitalism according to these authors had led to an increase in inequality that was somehow intrinsically unfair. However, the failure that these authors had detected was the lack of a competitive market which enabled rent-seeking behaviour to occur. In the US, the reaction to this was not to throw capitalism out altogether, but rather to make it work better by the introduction of competition concepts such as those enshrined in the Sherman Antitrust Act, 1890 which we discuss at length in Chapter 3. We can classify this as a positive response, as opposed to the negative responses of Marx and Engels.

The first half of the 20th century then saw the application of these negative responses into practice in a number of different guises. All of these negative responses, it should be noted drew from the producer welfare side of the economic ledger that we discussed in the early chapters of this book. The US response, by contrast was drawn from the consumer welfare side of the ledger (although, as we note in Chapter 3, it was incorrectly applied in the first half-century or so of its implementation). The resultant emphasis on the state's role in the economy, protectionism, mercantilism and the increased importance of borders led directly to the greatest conflict and loss of life in the history of mankind – not only during both world wars, but also internally in Hitler's Germany and Stalin's Soviet Union.

It took the unprecedented atrocities of the Second World War to cause a rethinking of this trend, at least insofar as it related to property affected by the Holocaust. Even in this case however, restitution was not effective because the difficulties thrown up by the legal systems in the countries where property had been wrongfully taken. The Helsinki Commission meetings commented very specifically on the number of cases where restitution claims had fallen on the sword of national court systems, which is ironic given the legal basis of the property right as we have demonstrated. We will discuss the major legal theories that have blocked restitution at the end of this chapter.

Steps Taken by US Congress to Date

The House has passed a resolution, House Resolution 562, and the Senate passed a resolution in 1996 (S.73, 104th Congress (1996)) which condemned private property takings by communist and other totalitarian regimes. However beyond this and the enactment of a number of laws, such as the Helms-Gonzales and Helms-Burton laws, very little has been done at the legislative level by the Congress.

Steps Taken by European Union

The European Union has approached the issue in a very different manner, starting with the European Convention on Human Rights which we have discussed above. Supporting the Convention, the European Court of Human Rights acts not unlike the FCSC in the US to adjudicate claims brought by European citizens that their rights have been violated by a government action. Restitution claims have been brought before the European Court of Human Rights. An example of this is the claim of Titina Loizidou for property she owned but to which she was denied access by the Turkish government. Loizidou was a person displaced from Northern Cyprus when the Turks invaded it in 1974. Another example is the 23 November 2000 ruling by the ECHR that Greece had wrongfully confiscated the property of the former Greek royal family. These were two very different cases, one involving the rights of a refugee, the other involving the rights of the former Royal family who estimated their loss as GRD 168 bn. Both cases stand for the proposition that the right to property arises because of the bond between the property and its owner, regardless of who that owner is, and regardless of the manner or alleged merits of the confiscation itself.

Moveable Property: A Modern Example of Restitution Safeguards

Governments have expropriated all manner of property and these actions are not limited to land. In the case of moveable property, paintings and art collections have been particular targets for governmental expropriations. These properties present very real problems because they are small and moveable properties with very high values. As such, they can be used to transfer large amounts of wealth from private persons to governments and then through their trade to other persons. They have been used to aid counterfeiting, narco-trafficking and terrorism through money laundering schemes. Initially, those who dealt in such property, or who benefited from this trade, were supportive of doctrines, such as the act of state doctrine, which made it very difficult to restitute these properties through legal process. However, partly because so much art was taken during the Holocaust by the German government and its representatives, and partly because of the active engagement of groups like the Helsinki Commission, the tide has somewhat turned. We look now at one example of how the art world is reacting to this issue.

A Case Study: Sotheby's Art Guidelines

International art auction house, Sotheby's, has entered into a number of ground-breaking Guidelines that serve to protect property and ensure that appropriate restitution can take place. In the case of Holocaust art, Sotheby's operate guidelines that ensure restitution is given a high priority. As a result of these guidelines,

Sotheby's have created a new position, Director of Restitution. Sotheby's have also agreed to override their duty of confidentiality to a consignor, by holding stolen art and putting the true owner in touch with the consignor to determine issues of title inter se. Sotheby's will additionally sua sponte request a title ruling from a court if the parties do not agree. These are significant achievements but do not solve the problem altogether. The reason they do not completely solve the problem is that the reaction of a court proceeding to resolve title will be determined largely by the geographical location of the court itself. Depending on where precisely the court is located, the prevailing act of state doctrine may defeat any claim of ownership by property owners. Where the property happens to be located in a jurisdiction where there is an act of state doctrine that is very narrowly limited, so that it gives the maximum latitude to the expropriating state, it is unlikely that the true owner of property will gain meaningful redress from the courts. We deal with this issue in more detail in the Act of State section below.

However, given this start, it is important that the art industry as a whole adopt these guidelines in order to ensure that the market for stolen art is curtailed. However, curtailing the market for stolen art through Guidelines of this nature will not be enough by itself.

Judicial Remedies: The Act of State Doctrine

The Helsinki Commission has noted that judicial remedies have failed to deliver meaningful restitution. In part, this is because of the length of time that court proceedings take, and their unsuitableness for property that is easily moveable (particularly true in the case of paintings). In part, the problem arises from the application of the Act of State doctrine. The Act of State doctrine is a doctrine that appears in the jurisprudence of most legal systems and provides generally that the courts of a particular country will not look behind the acts of a recognised state. For example, if State A expropriated property from citizen X and that property ended up in State B in the possession of citizen Y, if citizen X sought recovery, the courts in State B would say that since State A expropriated the property and State A could give a valid title to citizen Y, citizen X had no claim. This would apply even in cases where the expropriation was without compensation, and was unjust, even where it was accomplished by violence. The main point was that the government of the expropriating state had to be recognised by the other state.

Countries differ on how they apply the Act of State doctrine, and much depends on how courts have interpreted this. Courts in the UK and the US have historically taken an approach which would allow citizen X in the example quoted above to cite the fact that the original expropriation violated international law or was otherwise defective in order to vitiate the Act of State doctrine. Indeed some US legislation expressly rules out the application of the Act of State doctrine, for example, after the *US v. Sabbatino*[60] case, Congress enacted the *Second Hickenlooper Amendment* which provided that courts could not apply the Act of State doctrine to Cuban confiscations that were carried out by the Castro administration. There is also a process where the State Department may intervene in legal proceedings to state that it is not in the US national security interest to apply the Act of State doctrine in particular cases. This is known as the Bernstein Letter exemption,[61] and recognises that there may be other foreign policy reasons why the Act of State doctrine should not be applied. However, the Act of State doctrine itself was designed to promote international comity. The Bernstein letter exception was intended to support the notion that international comity, which was the goal of the Act of State doctrine, would not be served in certain cases by allowing the Act of State doctrine. This meant that the drive in determining whether the Act of State should apply was whether its application promoted international comity. If it did not, the State Department could say it did not, and thereby prevent its erroneous application (since the State Department was the branch of the US government most likely to know what furthered international comity).

However, it should be noted that the Bernstein letter process is rarely successfully invoked and the State Department tends to give deference to the actions of other sovereign states. Most civil law jurisdictions tend to give considerable deference to the actions of other states. The reason that, arguably, the US and the UK tend to show less deference to the actions of the acts of other states is because of the common law system. Gradually over the years, jurisprudence has weakened the scope of the act of state doctrine in the US.

The situation in civil law jurisdictions is very different. In these jurisdictions, the Act of State doctrine is much more protective of the acts of recognised states. The reason for this difference can be found in the very different approach to property rights protection in civil law jurisdictions than in common law jurisdictions. This difference stemmed from the issue that we have highlighted in this document, namely whether property rights come from a positive natural law relationship between the property owner and the right, and the view that property rights stem from a government grant. This difference is highlighted in the Spitzbergen archipelago problem which we referenced above. This, in turn, stems from the Lockean view that it is the labour that is applied to the land that grounds the property right, and not any government-conferred licence.

Modern Property Rights Issues

In a more modern setting, the issue of private property rights clashes with the role of government in the area of eminent domain where governments can exercise the right to take property from citizens (for example, to run power lines) where it serves the public good. Very recently as a result of a recent US Supreme Court judgement, *Kelo v. New London*,[62] which found that a government taking of private property for use by a developer for economic development did not violate the US Constitution (particularly the takings clause). The decision resulted in a firestorm of criticism, as it seemed to undercut well-understood principles of property rights protection. In the case, the Supreme Court found that when the government takes property for the promotion of economic development, this is a public use pursuant to the Fifth Amendment of the US Constitution even if that economic development is to be undertaken by private parties. The court paid attention to the fact that the area was depressed, and the City of New London had an economic plan for the area (thus, the *Kelo* taking should not be viewed in isolation).[63] It was also relevant that the benefit was not going to particular identified persons.

However, Alan Greenspan noted the importance of property rights in a market economy in a speech on Market Economics and Rule of Law.[64] Indeed, his remarks bear repetition:

> Market economics require a rule of law. A society without State protection of individual rights, especially the right to own property, would not build private long-term assets, a lay ingredient of a growing modern economy.

In the last two decades, more and more trade agreements have dealt specifically with investment issues. Indeed, investment is featured not only bilaterally but also in regional, platform agreements. The most obvious example of this is the Comprehensive and Progressive Trans Pacific Partnership ("CPTPP"). The investment chapter in CPTPP is built on the deep investment chapter in NAFTA (now USMCA). Under CPTPP, investors and their investment cannot be subject to discrimination. Investments can only be expropriated for a public purpose and on prompt payment of market value compensation. CPTPP clarifies that non-discriminatory regulatory actions designed to safeguard public welfare do not constitute expropriations (but these cannot contain elements of discrimination) If an action has an adverse impact on the economic value of an investment, this without more does not constitute an expropriation. This last provision changes the emphasis from some of the NAFTA cases discussed above. Indeed, the presence of this language is in some ways a response to those cases which were perceived by many to go too far in terms of the limitations imposed on governments to regulate in the areas of health, safety and the environment. However, the danger with this approach is that if developed countries adopt this approach, then developing countries will seek a complete exemption themselves and they are less likely to have robust mechanisms to protect property rights. Prudential regulation tends to always trump trade and investment protection. Instead, it would be more protective of property rights if an appropriate balance was struck between prudential regulation, and the need for any regulation to be implemented in the least trade and investment distorting manner, consistent with a clear, publicly stated and measurable legislative and regulatory goal. Even prudential regulation should be implemented on the basis of necessity and proportionality. The regulatory tests set out in Chapter 8 should ensure that such regulations are implemented in such a manner. It is more likely that like-minded countries will be able to enact such disciplines in their trade agreements (such as the UK and the US).

Foreign investors and their investments are afforded a minimum standard of treatment. This minimum standard comprises an obligation to (i) treat investors fairly, including due process in courts, and (ii) provide protection to investments, including police protection for physical assets. Foreign transfers can also be made freely and without delay. The only areas where transfers can be delayed or limited would be good faith applications of the law (in areas like bankruptcy or securities trading, or as a result of judicial orders (subject to due process requirements). There may also be limitations in cases of a balance of payments crisis or in cases of serious macro-economic difficulty.

There are other significant protections where CPTPP represents an advanced agreement. Some of these include:

- i There is a prohibition on the imposition of any performance requirements in connection with the establishment, acquisition or operation of an investment. These include requirements to buy only domestic goods, use of a particular technology or adoption of a specific royalty in a licenced contract.
- ii Prohibition on obliging foreign investors to appoint people of specific nationality to senior management position.
- iii Protection for an agreement occurring natural resources, public utilities and infrastructure.
- iv Protection for an alleged breach of an authorisation granted by a CPTPP member to an investor seeking to invest in the other CPTPP member.

> Critically and importantly the investment chapter also has a mechanism for dispute resolution between investors and states directly (so called Investor State Dispute Resolution or "ISDS").

The ISDS mechanism has attracted a lot of negative attention recently a certain groups have criticised it as a way for private companies to force governments to adopt particular policies that do not damage those companies' interests. This assertion that the policy space of government is negatively impacted by property rights protection is a deeply flawed one. As we have noted property rights are a key part of delivery of economic growth. As such, they play a critical role in lifting people out of poverty. This is a major governmental objective for any government. Since property rights are what firms compete with they are foundational in nature and underpin competition (international and domestic). If property rights owners are having to rely on their governments to bring cases for violations, then some will be at a disadvantage simply because of the competence and willingness to engage of their host governments. If the affected firm can bring a case, however, this will constrain government from damaging property rights, or if they do so, to ensure that there is a valid justification for such actions.

Conclusion

We can see from the modern history that even countries that appear to be proponents of property rights protection have statutory systems that weaken property in the teeth of government demands. The *Kelo* case was important because it applied to government action to take a home in order for a private construction (not for a state end, such as running electricity pylons). The purpose of the taking was to further economic development. What is particularly troubling about the case, also, is the Supreme Court's acceptance that public use included the redevelopment of property by private companies. Justice O'Connor, dissenting noted that "any property may now be taken for the benefit of another private party … the decision eliminates (the) distinction between private and public use of property."

We have discussed the importance of property rights as a vital leg of the three-legged stool that delivers economic growth and is the capacity to life people out of poverty. We have seen that property is intrinsically different from other kinds of rights, and must be protected adequately.

We have demonstrated that private property rights are among the oldest rights that have been recognised by man. These rights are fundamental to the establishment of a market economy because these rights support the goods and services that are tradeable in a free and competitive market. Once these rights are protected, the value of these tradeable properties is increased and the competition between them unlocks greater value. Realising full value for these tradeable assets also ensures that investment flows are maximised which will, in turn, boost internal competition in the market, creating a virtuous circle of growth and development. Finally, we have demonstrated how these rights can be protected in international trade agreements and how regulatory disciplines in these agreements also go some way to protecting investor and private property rights. Next, we turn to a particularly important type of property right – the intellectual property right.

Notes

1 John Locke, Two Treatises of Government (1689), Second Treatise, Chapter IX, Section 123–126.
2 William Blackstone, *Commentaries on the Laws of England: A Facsimile of the First Edition of* 1765–1769 (University of Chicago Press, 1979), vol. 1, at 139.
3 *See* John Adams, *Property Must be Secure or Liberty Cannot Exist*, in *The Works of John Adams* (Charles Francis Adams ed., Little and Brown 1850), Vol. 1, at 280.
4 "From Thomas Jefferson to Thomas Cooper, 29 November 1802," Founders Online, National Archives, https://founders.archives.gov/documents/Jefferson/01-39-02-0070, [Original source: *The Papers of Thomas Jefferson, vol.* 39, 13 November 1802–3 March 1803 (Barbara B. Oberg ed., Princeton University Press 2012).
5 Samuel Pufendorf, *Of the Law of Nature and Nations* (William Percivale, Jean Barbeyrac, and Basil Kennett trans., L. Lichfield 1710) (1672), Book IV, Chapter IV.
6 *See Id.*

7 *See generally* Ludwig von Mises, *Human Action*: A *Treatise on Economics* (Yale University Press, 1949).
8 *See* Thomas Hobbes, *Leviathan or The Matter, Forme and Power of a Commonwealth Ecclesiasticall and Civil* (Alfred R. Waller ed., University Press, 1904) (1651).
9 *Human Action*: A *Treatise on Economics, supra* note 7, ch. 2.
10 *Human Action*: A *Treatise on Economics, supra* note 7, at 258.
11 Murray N. Rothbard, *Power and Market*: *Government and the Economy* (Institute for Humane Studies, 1970), at 3.
12 Bruce Benson, *The Impetus for Recognizing Private Property and Adopting Ethical Behaviour in a Market Economy: Natural Law, Government Law, or Evolving Self-Interest*, 6 Rev. Austrian Econ. no. 2 (1993), at 43.
13 Hugo Grotius, *The Rights of War and Peace* (Archibald C. Campbell trans., M. Walter Dunne 1901) (1625); Grotius used sand as an example of something of which he thought there is an inexhaustible supply, and which could not be used as a base material from which human industry – an interesting example given the rise, at about the same time as Grotius was writing, of the Venetian glass industry. But the point is well made. He admits property that does not have an intrinsic value because it cannot be turned into something of value by human industry. Grotius goes quite far in even suggesting that this property might not even be capable of being referred to as property.
14 *Id.,* Sec. XI, ch. VI.
15 For a discussion of the US constitutional foundations of intellectual property rights as property and recognition as such by the courts, *see* Adam Mossoff, *The Constitutional Protection of Intellectual Property*, Heritage Foundation (2021).
16 *See* The *Rights of* War *and* Peace, *supra* note 13, Book II, ch. II, para. XII.
17 The *Rights of* War *and* Peace, *supra* note 13.
18 *Id.*, Book II, ch. IV, para. IV.1.
19 *Id.*, Book II, ch. IV, para. V.I.
20 The Law of the Twelve Tables (c. 451 B.C.E) was the initial Roman law.
21 *See Of the* Law *of* Nature *and* Nations, *supra* note 5, Book IV, ch. XII.
22 *Id.*, Book IV, ch. XII.
23 *See Human Action*: A *Treatise on Economics*, *supra* note 7.
24 North American Free Trade Agreement (NAFTA), U.S.-Can.-Mex., 2008, art. 1110.
25 United States-Mexico-Canada Agreement (USMCA), U.S.-Mex.-Can., 2020, ch. 14.
26 *See* Denise Grab and Larry Karp, *Expropriation Clauses: A Natural Extension of Domestic Takings Law or Much More?* EEP 131, U. of Calif. Berkley (2004).
27 Whitney Benefits, Inc. v. U.S., 926 F.2d 1169 (Fed. Cir 1991), *cert. denied.*
28 *Regulatory Takings and Proposals for Change*, Congressional Budget Office (1998). The CBO Report usefully sets out the scope of the takings clause and we set it out here in full.
29 Branning v. United States, 654 F.2d 88 (Ct. Cl., 1981). 654 F.2d 88 (Ct. Cl., 1981).
30 Shelden v. United States, 7 F.3d 1022 (Fed. Cir., 1993).
31 Hendler v. United States, 952 F.2d 1364 (Fed. Cir., 1991); 36 Fed. Cl. 574 (1996).
32 Bass Enterprises Production Co. v. United States, 133 F.3d 893 (Fed. Cir., 1988).
33 NRG Co. v. United States, 24 Cl. Ct. 51 (1991).
34 Yancey v. United States, 915 F.2d 1534 (Fed. Cir., 1990).
35 Babbitt v. Youpee, 519 US 234 (1997).
36 Dow Chemical Co. v. United States, 32 Fed. Cl. 11 (1994).
37 Eastern Enterprises v. Apfel., 118 S. Ct. 2131 (1998).
38 Hodel v. Irving, 481 US 704 (1987).
39 Agins v. City of Tiburon, 447 US 255 (1980); Lucas v. South Carolina Coastal Council, 505 US 1003 (1992).

40 US Secretary of State, Cordell Hall used this language in the context of Mexican expropriations. For an analysis, *see* Henry Steiner, Detlow Vagts, and Harold H. Koh, *Transnational Legal Problems: Materials and Text* (4th ed., Foundation Press, 1994), at 456–457; also, for notes exchanged during the US -Mexico dispute, *see* Green H. Hackfoorth, *Digest of International Law* (Cambridge University Press, 1942), § 228, at 655–665.

41 For an explanation of Methanex' claim, *see* the Methanex Corp. v. United States, First Partial Award, 7 August 2002.

42 *See* Methanex Corp. v. United States, the Final Award of the Tribunal on Jurisdiction and Merits, 3 August 2005, pt. IV, ch. D, para 41 See above at para 8 et seq.

43 *Id.*, para 8 et seq.

44 *See* Timothy J. Muris, *Clarifying the State Action and Noerr Exemptions*, 27 Harv. J. L. & Pub. Pol'y 443 (2004).

45 For a summary description of the USMCA, *see* Office of the United States Trade Representative,"United States-Mexico-Canada Agreement" (n.d.), https://ustr.gov/trade-agreements/free-trade-agreements/united-states-mexico-canada-agreement.

46 The rules of investor-state dispute resolution are governed by the International Centre for Settlement of Investment Disputes ("ICSID") of the World Bank.

47 European Convention on Human Rights (1950), art. 8.

48 Hanoch Dagan, *Unjust Enrichment: A Study of Private Law and Public Values* (Cambridge University Press, 1997).

49 *See id.*, at 107.

50 *See The Complete Works of Tacitus: The Annals* (Alfred John Church and William Jackson Brodribb eds., Modern Library 1942).

51 Tacitus, *Germania* (98 C.E.).

52 *Supra* note 20. The original code was inscribed on tin, and subsequently 12 bronze tablets.

53 For an extensive treatment, see Frances H. Foster, *Restitution of Expropriated Property: Post-Soviet Lesson for Cuba*, 36 Colum. J. Transnat'l L. 623 (1995).

54 *Id.*

55 *Property Restitution and Compensation in Prost-Communist Europe: A Status Update*, Commission on Security and Cooperation in Europe ("Helsinki Commission") (2003).

56 *See*, for example, James Gwartney and Robert Lawson, with Eric Gartzke, *Economic Freedom of the World: 2005 Annual Report*, Frasier Institute (2005) (where Estonia is seen as having a competitive advantage).

57 G. Douglas Harper, *Restitution of Property in Cuba: Lessons Learned from Eastern Europe*, Association for the Study of the Cuban Economy (ASCE) (1999), https://www.ascecuba.org/asce_proceedings/restitution-of-property-in-cuba-lessons-learned-from-east-europe/.

58 First Restitution Act, 2 Oct 1990; Second Restitution Act, 21 Feb 1991.

59 Secretary Colin Powell, *Making Sustainable Development Work: Governance, Finance, and Public-Private Cooperation*, Remarks at State Department Conference, Meridian International Centre, U.S. Department of State (12 Jul 2002).

60 Banco Nacional de Cuba v. Sabbatino, 376 US 398 (1964).

61 The Bernstein letter exemption was first articulated in the Bernstein v. N.V. Nederlandsche Americaansche StoomvartMaatscheapij, 210 F.2d 375 (2nd Cir. 1951).

62 Kelo v. City of New London, 545 US 469 (2005).

63 Kelo v. City of New London, 268 Conn. 1, 865 A.2d 500, *aff'd.*

64 Chairman Alan Greenspan, *Market Econonmies and the Rule of Law,* Remarks at the 2003 Financial Markets Conference of the Federal Reserve Bank of Atlanta, Sea Island, Georgia (4 Apr 2003).

11

PROTECTING PROPERTY RIGHTS

The Triple Interface between Intellectual Property, Competition and Trade[1]

The interface between intellectual property (IP), competition and trade has proved to be one of the most difficult areas of trade negotiations and domestic policy. It has proved to be a front-page news story when it affects healthcare, and increasingly the vital tool of today's internet economy, software. The notion that IP is in tension with competition policy – that the world of IP is governed by law (focused on providing rigid and legalistic protections), and the world of competition is governed by economics (which is focused on ensuring that knowledge is disseminated) – is deeply held by many analysts and commentators. However, our contention is that IP laws and competition laws are not in tension at all but rather have the same fundamental goal which is to ensure the stimulation of innovation by consumer-welfare-enhancing competition.

The interface with trade rests on the notion that the protection of IP rights is a subset of the protection of property rights, which are fundamental to the idea of consumer-welfare-enhancing markets that is the fundamental underlying principle of this book. Since IP protection is a fundamental right, in the nature of any property right, the kind of right that is appropriate to exercise government power to protect, trade rules that tend to lead to the protection of IP will move markets to more consumer-welfare-enhancing outcomes. For example, by protecting IP rights, monopolistic competition can lead to better outcomes for consumers in a number of different sectors. This occurs by stimulating competition between different competitive products that are each protected by IP.

Connection with Property Rights

We discussed property rights at some length in a previous chapter. Most commentators have acknowledged the link between rights in physical property and rights in IP.[2] Many commentators divide themselves into a pro-IP camp that talks about the

DOI: 10.4324/9780429323331-11

need to provide incentives for further research and innovation, and an anti-IP camp which talks about access to knowledge. This dichotomy misunderstands the nature of the issue. In the case of real property, it is clear that the enclosure movement (which provided greater protection of property) made substantial contributions to agricultural productivity. Similarly, mining rights made a significant difference in encouraging prospectors to mine land. It is equally clear that it is the dynamic benefit of the property right which is the incentive that leads directly to the creation and improvement of a resource (enabling people to "reap where they have sown").[3]

However, there are differences between property and IP that should not be understated. The most significant difference is that IP contains public goods characteristics, where consumption of the IP by one person does not reduce its availability to others. However, this difference is also a reason why from an economic standpoint, there is an even greater need for IP protection. If a piece of property (real or personal) is stolen, then it can be returned with its value undiminished. However, if IP is similarly stolen, then its value declines to zero (you can't put the toothpaste back in the tube). This is one difference which points towards the need to even greater IP protection that might be accorded to property rights protection.

Another difference is that IP can have multiple ownerships (through licencing and cross-licencing). In other words, IP can be enjoyed by many users without destroying its value as long as the owner of the property controls its use.

Very different concepts apply as between abandonment of property and abandonment of IP. The doctrine of adverse possession applies to abandoned property (as we describe in detail in the chapter discussing property rights), and this means that this property can pass into the hands of the adverse possessor. However, abandoned IP passes to the public domain. There are provisions in law which allow IP to be taken deliberately and without compensation (see, below, section on compulsory licencing).

With the negotiation of the Trade-Related Intellectual Property agreement ("TRIPS") provisions in the Uruguay Round Agreement, IP was included in a trade agreement. However, IP had long been discussed in international fora. Indeed, the key treaties that have underpinned international IP rules date back to the 19th century.

As many countries embrace competition policies and enact competition laws, the interface between IP policy and competition policy has come into sharp focus. Many believe that these policies are in tension. Others claim that the policies are not in tension but have the same global goal. Since economic development depends critically on a three-legged stool of trade liberalisation, competitive markets delivered through competition policy and protection of property rights, this tension needs to be carefully examined.

The Birth of Notions to Protect Intellectual Property[4]

The need to protect innovation and to incentivise technological development is not a new one. Aristotle wrote about such protection in *The Politics*.[5] Though ideas on the protection of IP stem from ancient times, government protection of IP has been traced back to the early Italian Renaissance, particularly to 13th-century Venice, where patents were given for particular types of glassmaking. Patents were used primarily as tools for technology transfer until the 18th century, at which point patents became engines of innovation in Europe and the American colonies.[6] The right to patent was viewed with such importance that the only time the word "right" is mentioned in the US Constitution is in this context. Article I, Section 8 of the Constitution states, "to promote the Progress of Science and useful Arts, by securing for limited Times to Authors and Inventors the exclusive Right to their respective Writings and Discoveries."[7] The economic theory behind patent protection echoes the belief of the founders for the protection of this right. Patents provide important public goods.[8] Goods that result from patents can be consumed by multiple economic actors, at a very low marginal cost, because the cost of replication of the creation of an invention is significantly smaller than the cost of invention of a new product. A patent introduces a static distortion in the form of knowledge being sold at above its marginal cost. This distortion, however, is a necessary way to foster the dynamic benefits associated with innovation.[9] If pricing were to occur at the marginal cost to maximise consumer welfare, there would be a chilling effect on innovation since the incentives to create would be diminished by economic actors who would free ride on the efforts of others, given that the marginal cost of reproducing the innovation is far below that of the average total cost. As noted professor and judge Frank Easterbrook notes, "Curtail the top returns, and the whole structure of rewards changes for the worse."[10] Therefore, by granting temporary exclusive rights to new inventions, the IP law allows the inventor to recoup the cost of investment for the innovation.

However, IP protection is not without its social costs, and not all IP is the same. While IP protection certainly encourages the searcher for information (and, in the case of patents, generates a market that facilitates the spread of innovation), it also incentivises people who acquire a property right in order to engage in rent-seeking, which does have a social cost. The process for the protection of IP is itself costly from a social cost standpoint. There are also societal costs for fencing off IP so it cannot be used. Costs of this sort, however, are common to all forms of property. They are an unavoidable feature of the legal system that is required to generate valuable property rights in general, and IP rights in particular. In the case of IP, there is a good reason to believe that the costs are trivially small, compared to the huge dynamic welfare gains that IP creates.

The Myth of IP as a State-Granted Monopoly

While some commentators have regarded the IP right as a state-granted monopoly, it is more accurately a temporary property right[11] but does not necessarily confer a monopoly in the ordinary sense of that term. Under antitrust principles, monopoly occurs when there is market power in a particular defined product market. The defined product market is one that stands up to antitrust analysis. The product market is defined by looking at supposedly competitive products, ones that might be in the same product market and asking the question whether if a small but significant price increase occurred, consumers would switch from one to the other. Generally, if they would, both products are in the same product market.[12] However, the IP right applies to one particular product or process. There might therefore be, in any one field of activity, many types of protected products that each competes within the same product market but which are separately protected by IP rights. Here, there is no monopoly conferred by the IP right itself, and indeed the increased competition between different protected products will increase consumer welfare.

There could still be cases (for example, if a new drug is discovered to treat a disease, and it is the only treatment currently known) where the IP right is conferred on a product where there are no present substitutes. However, it is worth pointing out that the pricing decisions in this case that are made by the monopolist are made because it is a monopolist and not because it has an IP right. Here, it is possible for the grant of IP rights to prevent new entrants from breaking into the market, at least during the term covered by the grant. But that lack of entry is a function of the defence of a property right (akin to the right of a landowner to invoke his right to deny trespassers access to his property), not an example of abusive business behaviour that may raise antitrust issues. Indeed, far from raising antitrust issues here, the patent grant incentivises risky research that drives innovation and actually enhances competition in markets for new products and processes that benefit consumers. As a leading economist of innovation, Professor Daniel Spulber, has explained:

> Protection of IP and antitrust policy are complements, because protecting IP promotes competition in the market for inventions and in markets for goods and services that embody or are manufactured with patented inventions. Conversely, antitrust policy that favors competition in the market for inventions and in product markets will increase incentives to innovate. This implies that both patent policy and antitrust policy should favor stronger IP rights. Patent policy and antitrust policy should avoid making exceptions to protections of IP rights. Policymakers should thus avoid restrictions of IP rights for arbitrarily selected cutting-edge technologies such as software, business methods, or biotechnology.[13]

Accordingly, it would seem that a different approach is required for products that compete with each other in a defined antitrust market, where the IP right does not confer a monopoly, and those rarer examples where it does. While current IP law does not make any such distinction, this does not mean that radically new concepts or ideas must be applied. It merely means that competition law needs to be property applied.

Early patent cases certainly did confuse the notion of monopoly under the antitrust law with the right conferred in the patent context. Posner and Landes note that:

> At one level it is a confusion of a property right with a monopoly. One does not say that the owner of a parcel of land has a monopoly because he has the right to exclude others from using the land. But a patent or a copyright is a monopoly in the same sense. It excludes other people from using some piece of intellectual property without consent. That in itself has no antitrust significance…Talk of patent and copyright "monopolies" is conventional…The usage is harmless as long as it is understood to be different from how the word is used in antitrust analysis.[14]

The point is that many patents confer no monopoly at all in the antitrust sense, as recognised by the US Supreme Court in the 2006 Illinois Tool[15] case and by the US federal antitrust agencies in their 2017 *Antitrust Guidelines for the Licensing of Intellectual Property*.[16] Nor is the presence of price discrimination (charging different customers different prices) necessarily evidence that consumer welfare is being harmed – indeed, it may efficiently increase output and raise welfare.[17] What's more, exclusion of other competitors from a certain type of property may be procompetitive even if the result is a reduction in the number of competitors or a move away from the perfectly competitive equilibrium. Simply because the number of competitors is higher does not mean that we are closer to a consumer-welfare-enhancing equilibrium – such an equilibrium occurs when society's resources are being exploited as efficiently as possible, and this may occur when there are fewer rather than more competitors. In many cases, consumer welfare may be gained where an IP right confers an increased level of market power but that same right increases the size of (or makes possible the creation of) the market itself. In other words, a strong IP right may spur the dynamic creation of huge economic gains for consumers and producers (consumers' and producers' surplus) that dwarfs short-term static effects.

The Myth that IPR and Competition Are in Tension

Just as there is a myth that IP rights automatically confer monopolies, there is also a myth that the purposes of IP and competition policy are always in tension. Our prior discussion indicates, however, that properly understood, the two doctrines basically share the common goal of promoting innovation and enhancing consumer welfare.[18] Indeed, many commentators have noted that the benefits of competition are dwarfed by the benefits of innovation-enhancing IP (see below).

Impact of New Technology and the New Media Environment

The significant impact of new technology is that the cost of copying has declined dramatically at least for work that has traditionally been protected by copyright.

This would include books, software and so forth. This would therefore appear to have increased the need for copyright protection in this area. One aspect of the new technologically different economy is that non-price competition becomes a greater source of changes in behaviour. Some incentives offered by strong IP protection will stimulate higher quality and thus enhance this non-price competition.

The Trade Context

It has long been recognised that there is a trade interface to the protection of IP. If an exporter's IP rights are not protected when they enter foreign markets, they will be unable to capture the profits that they would have legitimately obtained if those rights were in fact protected because their market share may be eroded by counterfeit products. Indeed, it could be argued that the failure to protect IP is an artificial cost reduction strategy for a country's businesses and a trade barrier. An example of this is the historic lack of software protection in some countries. If a government tolerates this lack of protection, then the government is directly contributing to an artificially low cost for the business which uses this software as an input (which is any business in the 21st century). In 2005, the Business Software Alliance estimated that 90% of all software in Chinese computers was pirated. It is estimated that a significant percentage of copied software is used in Chinese factories. This leads to a dramatic change in costs for the production of products from these factories, where the local producers do not have to pay for the cost of the IP-protected product or a licence fee.

So the failure to protect IP leads to a loss of market share from direct copies (a harm visited on producers of the products themselves) as well as a separate consumer harm that is more systemic from the illegal reduction in costs brought about by pirated inputs (be they software or other products).

For these reasons, it is important that trade agreements deal with these kinds of issues, and indeed they have been on the trade agenda since its inception in 1947 agreements that were to give rise to the International Trade Organization ("ITO"). The original ITO was to have a chapter on IP rules but this development failed when as we note elsewhere, the ITO did not pass the US Congress. This failure meant that the issue of IP, like many issues that formed part of the trade agenda, was not addressed by governments until the Uruguay Round of negotiations. This meant that the TRIPS agreement became the first trade agreement that was part of the WTO arrangements to include IP. However, there were many agreements that covered IP and had multiple signatories that predated the TRIPS agreement, and that the TRIPS agreement actually included by specific reference.

The provisions that the TRIPS agreement covered by specific reference are intended to ensure that the compliance mechanisms which apply to trade agreements will be available to those who wish to ensure that their IP rights are not violated in countries where they export. TRIPS provides minimum standards whereby (a) countries must have IP-protective laws on their books, and (b) governments may not turn a blind eye to situations where those laws are being ignored by the courts or by enforcement agencies. The TRIPS provisions therefore, in addition to incorporating the Berne and Paris Conventions on the scope of IP protection, also include specific provisions at Article 50 et ff. which provide for the "proper and adequate" enforcement of preliminary measures, such as injunctive relief. Where the provisional measure is not being enforced in an adequate fashion as the TRIPS agreement sets out, there are sanctions.

What Does TRIPS Say about the Scope of Intellectual Property Protection?

The scope of the major categories of IP protection differs. On copyright, in addition to the Berne Convention, TRIPS provides that computer programs can be protected as literary works and gives authors of computer programs[19] and films the right to authorise or prohibit commercial rental of copyright works.[20] On trademarks, as well as protection for well-known marks, TRIPS reiterates the Paris Convention's provisions that any sign or combination of signs which is capable of distinguishing the goods or services of one undertaking from those of other undertakings must be eligible for registration as a trademark, provided that it is visually perceptible.[21] TRIPS provides that at least ten years' protection must be given to independently create industrial designs that are new or original.[22]

TRIPS, by integrating the Paris Convention, emphasises that for an invention to be patentable, it must be new, involve an inventive step (i.e., be non-obvious) and be capable of industrial application.

What Does TRIPS Say about Well-Known Marks

One pernicious problem in particular for the owners of well-known trademarks is the fact that in the many countries that operate first-to-file registration systems, these well-known marks are deliberately registered in order to then hold the true owner to ransom when it actually enters the market. The Paris Convention for the Protection of Industrial Property, 20 March 1883,[23] provides that well-known marks may not be used by non-owners even in the event of a first-to-file system. Article 6b provides that:

> [The countries of the Union undertake, ... to refuse or to cancel the registration, and to prohibit the use, of a trademark which constitutes a reproduction... liable to create confusion, of a mark considered by the competent authority of the country of registration or use to be wellknown in that country as being already the mark of a person entitled to the benefits of this Convention and used for identical or similar goods.][24]

This is an important provision because many products which are traded across borders are very well-known brands. Trade in these products would be substantially impaired if their trademark could only be protected by a trademark registration in every market in which they are traded. Many countries have first-to-file rather than first-to-use trademark systems, and therefore there has been a history through the 1990s with the rise in international trade that pirates have registered the trademarks of goods in particular markets in order to extract a payment from the "true" owner of the trademark.

What Does TRIPS Say about Injunctive Relief and Provisional Measures

It is a fundamental difference between IP and other property rights that once the IP has been copied, there is little that can be done to restore its value to the owner. IP differs from real property because in the case of real property or even personal property, the property can be returned. If I steal your television set, and then some months later return it in good working order, it still works and it is still valuable to you (at least you will be able to use it for the time that you have it). If I take your land, it still has value if I am forced to return it to you. However, if I appropriate your brand name which you affix to, say clothing, and then return it to you some months later (return here means I stop using it for my own personal gain), you have lost the entire value of the brand. The brand is no longer associated with you in the minds of consumers, who are now confused as to whether the brand means your high-end style of clothing or my less high-quality line.

Furthermore, your reputation is sullied by mine if I produce an inferior or weak product. In this respect, the case for protecting IP rights is even stronger than the case for protecting real or physical property.

It is because of this dynamic that it is so important for provisional measures to be properly applied. Provisional measures recognise that "you cannot get the toothpaste back in the tube." They provide a way for the alleged owner of a mark to protect himself by preventing the copying of his mark. If, subsequently, it turns out that there was no infringement (for example, where the marks are not confusingly similar), then the party that alleged that there was and claimed protection is liable in damages to the aggrieved party. This system ensures that a potentially damaging event does not take place. All that the claimant must do is show that there is at least the likelihood of irreparable harm to his reputation (the toothpaste cannot be put back inside the tube).

Under the TRIPS agreement, Article 50 provides that:

> The judicial authorities shall have the authority to order prompt and effective provisional measures;
>
> a To prevent an infringement of any IP right from occurring, and in particular to prevent the entry into the channels of commerce in their jurisdiction of goods.
>
> b To preserve relevant evidence in regard to the alleged infringement.

The ability to rely on provisional measures is also a key element in ensuring that IP is protected and hence that trade frictions are minimised. How well these measures lead to a reduction in these barriers will have a direct impact on trade flows.

Copyright

Scope

Copyright's purpose is to protect the expression of ideas. Historically where the cost of copying has been high, and the time lag between production and copy was significant, a certain level of protection was accorded to authors and producers. Now, the dynamics are changing and the cost of copying has been significantly reduced. Indeed in order to correct this, authors and producers are spending, ever-greater sums of money on encryption techniques, leading to rents sucked out of the economy as would-be copiers seek to find ways of overcoming the encryption techniques. This argues for potentially greater (or at least a different form of) protection in this new environment.

Cost of Production

There is no question that the IP attached to a particular property increases the cost of production of new works. Here, copyright and patent must be treated differently. In the case of copyright, copyright does increase the cost of producing new works, because in the case of literature and art in particular, new works frequently rely on old works for sources of inspiration. In many cases (listed by Posner and Landes[25]), famous works of art have been lifted from previous authors directly – such as Shakespeare's Romeo and Juliet, or indeed the Pyramus and Thisbe sub-play in Shakespeare's A Midsummer Night's Dream, which was lifted directly from Ovid's Pyramus and Thisbe. If copyright protection had prevailed in these cases, innovative new works that were actually building incrementally on existing knowledge would not have been produced. This is to be directly contrasted with the patent situation, where the filing of the patent actually triggers dissemination of knowledge into the public domain, through the patent application itself. The dichotomy that most commentators consider when looking at these issues is the dichotomy between access to information on the one hand and knowledge on the other. However, as Posner and Landes note, there is another consideration, the dichotomy between innovation and the cost of expression, a term they coin to mean the cost of producing expressive works, which may be increased in the short term by copyright protection.[26] However, it should be noted that while the cost of expression can lead to lower supply, it can also lead to higher supply of the protected work. While some commentators[27] believe that copyright protection might lead to an increased (or "excessive") production (citing wheat as an example), there are significant differences between commodities and products that are derived from innovation. First of all, it is not a trivial exercise to produce IP, and second, while excess commodities may be wasted, "excess" IP may have all manner of beneficial effects. IP-based products are different because of the very high failure rate that is associated with their development. IP protection in general exists to incentivise risk-taking (which naturally leads to a high degree of failure).

Difference between Ideas and Expression

It is generally understood that copyright protects the expression of ideas and not the underlying ideas themselves. The difficult area is where the expression and idea cannot readily be separated, because to copyright the expression leads to a situation where there are no other ways of expressing the same idea. However, even for cases where a particular expression of an idea would appear to convey the idea itself, it is rare to find an example where there are no alternatives of expressing the idea. For example, the first inventor of a clock might seek to copyright the "face and hands" method of telling the time. However, there are other ways of representing the time (digitally, or through a "sand in the hour-glass" method). An overly broad application of copyright could limit innovation and act as a barrier to trade in itself.

Importance of Encouraging Derivative Works

It is an important economic development issue that derivative works are encouraged and so the overall knowledge base is built on. In order to promote a more innovation-enhancing approach, it is necessary to grant the copyright in these derivative works to the owner of the original work. This ensures efficiency and consumer welfare optimisation. Otherwise, the rights to works will be fragmented and the rights of the owner to the original work will be dissipated.

Benefits to Copyright Owner in Case of Copying

There are benefits associated with copying that must be considered. These include the fact that copying can potentially strengthen a network: value increases with installed-based proportional to the square of the number of users, according to Metcalf's law. Additionally if consumers of certain products cannot afford the original, but can afford the copy, then the owner of the copied work still obtains a benefit. The flip-side of these public goods characteristics of IP is that if the consumer cannot afford the original, then the fact that a copy exist does not reduce the producer's inventory. In some ways, the producer of the original loses nothing if the person consuming the copy could not pay for the original. However, the diminution in value of the original is a real issue for the producer.

An interesting aspect of the importance of encouraging derivative works is the development of BMI and ASCAP. These are two companies that hold the performers' copyrights and exist to lower transaction costs, so people who play music can negotiate more easily with broadcasters. This is because they can negotiate as a group. The benefit of organisations like BMI and ASCAP is that they avoid having to extend the fair use doctrine into areas which limit innovation.

The Economic Function of Trademarks

Trademarks are a shorthand way of identifying a particular brand that has an association in the mind of a consumer. As such, it plays a vital role in the economics of buying and selling. Unlike copyrights, and especially unlike patents, trademark theory falls more within the legal area of unfair competition and less within the realm of property law. This is important as trademarks lose their value if they become generic. This would be impossible if they were simply property rights. Property rights do not lose their value because they become well-known or generic. Trademarks therefore have a value which is entirely dependent on what the consumer thinks of them, and the association that he or she draws when faced with them. Trademarks do have some aspects of property rights, however. These include the fact that they may be bought and sold, that there is a system of registration of these rights so that they can be protected, among other attributes.

Like property rights, trademarks can be diluted or tarnished depending on how they are used. In this way, they are like pure property rights. Non-owners may not appropriate the trademark for their own use in the traditional sense – i.e., they may not try and use the trademark to deceive or confuse consumers, but they are also prevented in appropriating the mark where to do so causes no consumer confusion but merely leads to the dilution of its value. This occurs when another party with no intent to deceive appropriates some of the investment that has gone into the use of the mark. For example, where a company has spent vast resources on developing a mark that connotes luxury and quality, such as Gucci, someone else should not be able to use that mark, even if it is applied to products that are clearly outside the fashion industry, for example, tractors. The purchaser of fashion products will have the Gucci tractor in its mind when it makes buying decisions, thus diluting the elite and fashionable connotations associated with the word, Gucci.

Trademarks are a crucial aspect of ensuring strong inter-brand competition (a very important element of the new technological/media economy, as we see in the chapter on media). But this protection must be secured without taking too many words out of regular usage. The registration process of the trademark system lends itself to potential rent-seeking activity. Thus, the TRIPS agreement (and the trade treaties before that) provided that certain well-known marks could not be registered without proof of use, and first-to-use systems (as opposed to first-to-file) were preferred.

Duration of Copyright and Trademark Protection

Copyrights and trademarks generally have very long lifetimes. In the case of trademark protection, this lifetime is infinite (although they must be renewed)

– in the case of copyright, the protected lifetime, that is the period when the right may not be violated, is very long – 70 years plus lifetime of author.

Posner and Landes have suggested that the copyright term could be changed to reflect the life of the author, plus 25-year periods which are renewable, perhaps for a renewal fee. This would ensure a better defining of when the need to stimulate innovation is counterbalanced by the need to get certain information into the public domain. The fact that the owner would have to pay a fee would force him to consider what benefits are being accrued as a result of the copyright and take account of the fact that the value of the copyright does appear to decline quite rapidly well before the expiry of the standard life plus 70-year term.[28] The advantage of the Landes and Posner approach is that the precise length of the original term, the length of the renewal term and the renewal fee can all be varied in order to deliver the most socially optimal length of copyright term, taking into account the need to stimulate innovation and yet keep a large number of works in the public domain. Clearly, this calculation is different for different products and sectors, and so a sensible copyright policy ought to take this into account.

Copyright, as well as trademark creation, can be an ongoing process, where the initial act of creation can be continuously added to during the lifetime of the copyright itself. For example, extra investments can be made in the marketing of the work protected by copyright (for example, where a book which has not been particularly well read at the time of its creation suddenly becomes more valuable when it is picked up by policymakers, such as Friedrich von Hayek's 1944 Road to Serfdom, which attracted much greater readership when it became the economic manifesto of Margaret Thatcher in the mid-1970s). Similarly, the branding of a product can greatly increase the value of the trademark. Here, it is important to note that only the fact of IP protection makes these subsequent investments likely, as the investor chases what he perceives to be the reward that could accrue to him. This fact suggests that in determining the gains to innovation and commerce of the copyright or trademark term, one has to also consider this type of post-creation activity.

In evaluating an appropriate discretion for protection, one interesting factor is the renewal rate for books, music and graphic art. These differ significantly.[29] Books in particular can depreciate rapidly if linked to a particular moment in history or event. Commentators have argued that this makes a case for indefinite renewal.

Covering the Cost of Failure

We will say much more about this in the pharmaceutical patent case study which we set out below. Even in the copyright area, there are significant costs associated with the possibility of failure. A publisher of books may see his first seven or eight forays into a particular literary genre fail, only to find the next one a success for reasons which could not really have been knowable in advance. While many children's fantasy books have been written on the subjects of dragons, wizards and so forth, none happened to capture the market in the way that JK Rowling's Harry Potter series has. This cost of failure must also be incorporated into the overall calculation of the balance between dissemination of knowledge and the incentivisation of the development and commercial application of that knowledge. That said, we must also note that the IP laws do not protect (and therefore prevent the dissemination of) knowledge per se. They protect that actual commercial application of that knowledge and it is this that the IP laws incentivise.

In addition, copyrights and trademarks are of limited duration. This limited duration restricts the likelihood of rent-seeking by effectively capping the patent's expected value.

Patent Protection

Patent protection deserves a separate mention as it operates in a slightly different way economically from copyrights and trademarks. One of the most significant differences is how the patent system contributes to increasing the stock of knowledge by requiring the inventor, in order to obtain a patent to disclose the invention, by placing in the public domain information regarding the patented technology. But just as with copyright laws, fundamental ideas are not patentable. The idea of the patent system is to incentivise the process of applying knowledge, not the process of knowledge accumulation per se. The patent law is intended to protect the fruits of man's labour, as is the case for real property. Thus, it is not intended that the patent law should protect the discovery of physical laws (for example) that already existed. This is to be distinguished from cases where the invention is something that has not existed before.

We will spend more time discussing the trade/competition interface for patents as this has become a somewhat controversial and not well understood area.

Patents, Innovation and Growth

There exists an important relationship between a strong patent regime and Research and Development (R&D). R&D plays an important role in the world economy. The amount spent on R&D in the developed world slightly exceeds 2% of GDP.[30] The US spends an even greater percentage of its GDP on R&D, 2.8%, or approximately $552 billion in 2018.[31] This is to be expected, given the US pre-eminence in advanced research in the world. Not surprisingly, R&D is particularly important in the pharmaceutical sector. Firms in the pharmaceutical industry typically invest, at the very least, 10% of their sales into R&D. In the US, this percentage is even higher and is estimated to be between 16% and 20.8% of revenue.[32] This makes the cost of research for the discovery of a single drug exceptionally high. Drug research in particular is risky, time-consuming and expensive. Only five out of every 4,000 chemical compounds that pharmaceutical research discovers demonstrate a level of effectiveness sufficient to warrant trial testing on humans.[33] In all, only one of 4,000 new chemical compounds discovered in the laboratory is ever marketed.[34] A recent study estimated the cost of a single new drug to be $500 million.[35] Therefore, the need for patent protection in the pharmaceutical industry is significantly higher than in other industries spending far less on such costs. A 1994 study by Grabowski and Vernon found that only 30% of drug products introduced from 1980 to 1984 generated returns higher than their average after-tax R&D costs.[36] Their work revealed that the 20% of products with the highest revenues generated 70% of returns during this time period.[37] Another study found that 55% of industry profits came from just 10% of drugs.[38] As one study notes, "Patent protection of pharmaceutical and chemical products and processes is critical to justify high R&D expenditure in these sectors."[39] Thus, given the high costs and risks associated with drug research, companies must rely on a limited number of highly successful products to finance their continuing R&D.[40]

Copycat pharmaceutical companies threaten the future ability of innovative pharmaceutical firms to undertake R&D for new drugs. If companies can easily copy the products of drug research, the economic incentive to conduct new drug research is greatly diminished. One study suggests that 65% of medicines would not have been commercially introduced or developed if patent protection was not available, a much higher percentage than in other industries.[41] The implication is clear. Without strong patent protection in developing countries, we risk making future research into lifesaving drugs financially unattractive. The loss of a possible AIDS vaccine or drug that would ameliorate the effects of malaria seems unconscionable. Yet, this very possibility results from making drug research unviable due to overly high costs that cannot be recouped without sufficient patent protection.[42] Notably, the existence of patents played a key role in the development of various COVID-19 vaccines in 2020. A number of highly successful COVID-19 vaccines (including the Moderna and Pfizer vaccines) came about due to earlier innovative mRNA research that was spurred by patents.[43]

It is important to note that the costs of R&D have increased dramatically. Annual global R&D expenditures (in current purchasing power dollars) more than tripled between 2000 and 2018, from $722 billion to $2.153 trillion.[44] One aspect of ensuring efficient use of R&D spending is through the use of patent pools to stimulate multiple industry participant joint research projects. A patent pool promotes efficiency "by enabling the formation of a market in disembodied informational assets" linking large numbers of licensors and licences, and by facilitating lower costs of access to key technology inputs.[45]

The Specific Case of Pharmaceutical Patent Protection and TRIPS

Patent Rights, Pharmaceutical Case Study[46]

One way to understand the patent system is through an analogy to the mineral rights claims of the 19th-century American West.[47] During this period, the US government had two competing objectives: to retain government ownership of public land and to make it possible for private firms to find and extract minerals contained in that land.[48] In the mineral claim system, priority was given to those who were the first to discover, stake and file a claim. The claimant had the exclusive right to mine a particular piece of land. As in the patent system, the mineral claim system required claimants to strictly limit their claims both in what they sought and how it differed from the public domain. One of the functions of the mineral claim system was to create incentives for the prospectors (inventors) to search for minerals (innovations). If the risk in R&D is high, then the reward for discovery must compensate for the high level of risk. In the mineral case, it is easy to see the potential for output-increasing effects (as opposed to output restriction). It is the same with the patent system.

A patent increases the efficiency with which investment in innovation can be managed. The patent owner is incentivised to coordinate the search for technological and market enhancement of the patent's value which allows information to be exchanged among searchers and ensures that duplicative investments are not made. It facilitates the channelling of development into the most efficient invention for achieving a goal. ("A" can also coordinate work on the production of product, "P" avoiding wasteful expenditure on product, "Q," which is a substitute for "P," which must be independently invented and developed). These efficiency-creating, output-expanding aspects of the patent system counteract part or all of the output-restricting consequences of creating an exclusive property right. The patent owner also has an incentive to make investments to maximise the value of the patent, without fear that this effort will lead to unpatentable information, which may be directly appropriated by competitors. Incentivisation is needed to achieve a more efficient allocation of incentives. Strong patent rights reduce the risk to investors to create new projects. As one economist suggests:

> In this context, patents can be understood as a second-best solution to the problems created by the public-good characteristics of knowledge. In theory, the term of patent protection could be set such that it would stimulate the development of new products and production processes at a socially optimal rate....[49]

Thus, a lack of patent protection leads to sub-optimal behaviour. Some take a particularly stark view of the deleterious effect of patent copying. Former Deputy US Trade Representative Richard Fisher has stated that, "The result of [copying] would be the erosion of America's comparative advantage in high technology; and ultimately loss of the benefits of new advances in health, public safety, education, defence and freedom of information for the entire world."[50] Fisher likened IP to a warehouse of ideas and the unauthorised copying of such patents as analogous to theft of goods from a warehouse.

Another effect of the patent right is its promotion of innovation both within the same field, because advances from innovation can be extended, and its extension of innovation to other areas in which innovators can apply for patents of their own, thereby "inventing around" the patent. Moreover, because of patent rights, inventors have an incentive to disclose knowledge to the public that they might otherwise try to keep a secret. This dissemination of information has the effect of accelerating the R&D of others. As information from patents is disclosed in patent applications, information about new technologies becomes more readily available to other inventors as an input into their own R&D.

One can increase the efficiency of the production of new drugs through a patent system because a patent right allows for contracting between two firms. The innovative firm can sub-contract parts of the development and manufacturing work to other firms at a lower cost if its right to its innovation is protected.[51] As one study notes, the movement of knowledge through the contracting for the transfer of information associated with innovations plays an important role for developing country firms.[52] Moreover, the opportunity to compete in the market with a strong patent regime remains. Just because one company has produced a cancer treatment medication does not mean that other companies cannot create better cancer-fighting medications. Stated differently, therapeutic alternatives create pressure to keep the price of patented drugs down. The year after Recombinate was released to treat haemophilia, Kogenate was introduced onto the market to treat the same symptoms. Similarly, in the case of Invirase, a protease inhibitor for AIDS/HIV, Norvir was introduced just three months later.[53] Thus, the possibility that patent holders would use their exclusive right to engage in monopolistic practices is limited because the patent holder seldom in fact possesses substantial power over price. One writer points to the fact that statistical studies prove that in the overwhelming number of patents, there is very little monopoly power.[54] Competition laws that prevent predatory pricing and other monopolistic practices also serve to keep any monopolistic impulse by patent holders in check.

What Is the Nature of the Patent Right?

At first blush, it might appear that the patent system is designed solely to strike a balance between granting a permanent and absolute monopoly to an inventor for a particular innovation (which would discourage other inventors from engaging in further research within the field covered by the monopoly), and giving the inventor exclusive rights for so short a period of time that they could not possibly recoup their initial investment, serving as a disincentive for invention. It is important to point out that, from an economics perspective, it is difficult if not impossible to make a judgement as to where the balance is properly drawn. Anything done is at best merely an estimate. The size of the monopoly profit has more to do with elasticity of demand and marginal cost of production than it does with amounts invested in R&D. However, it remains the best method that we currently know of for incentivising R&D.

The patent system is, however, far more than a particular legal regime designed to incentivise inventions. Indeed, the most profound benefit of the patent system, which is too often ignored, is its role in creating and facilitating a market for inventions that is key to the dissemination of new technologies throughout the economy. In this manner, the patent system increases the rate and dispersion of innovation, thereby driving dynamic economic growth.[55] The patent system does this in several ways. First, key patent system features – exclusion, transferability, disclosure, certification, standardisation and divisibility – generate efficiencies and drive competition in the market for inventions. Second, this market benefits society by determining the value for inventions, selecting the best inventions, and allocating inventions to the highest-value users. Third, by serving as intangible real assets, patents facilitate contracts that finance inventions. In short, the patent system is a forward-looking institution that is key to bringing forth the market mechanisms that drive innovation and, thus, economic advancement. As a leading commentator explains, this feature dwarfs in economic significance the "rewards for inventors" feature of patents.[56]

As summarised above, the key benefit of the exclusive patent right is that it allows a free market to operate for the licencing of the right, and it avoids having a government institution or a court decide what the royalty rate should be. In this context, it is important to draw a distinction between the monopoly right in the product, which is itself the subject of the patent right, and a monopoly in the treatment of a particular disease in the case of pharmaceutical product patents. In the case of patent protection for a particular pharmaceutical product, there is no monopoly conferred for the treatment which that drug is intended to provide, as a substitute could be found which does not operate in the same way that the patented product operates in treating the same disease.

Today, antitrust enforcers in the US fully acknowledge that a patent right is indeed a property right, and should be treated as such in the context of antitrust analysis. The 2017 DOJ-FTC *Antitrust Guidelines for the Licensing of Intellectual Property* state:

> Intellectual property law bestows on the owners of intellectual property certain rights to exclude others. These rights help the owners to profit from the use of their property. An intellectual property owner's rights to exclude are similar to the rights enjoyed by owners of other forms of private property. The antitrust laws generally do not impose liability upon a firm for a unilateral refusal to assist its competitors, in part because doing so may undermine incentives for investment and innovation. As with other forms of private property, certain types of conduct with respect to intellectual property may have anticompetitive effects against which the antitrust laws can and do protect. The exercise of intellectual property rights is thus neither particularly free from scrutiny under the antitrust laws, nor particularly suspect under them.[57]

Understanding that a patent is a property right, not a grant of monopoly, will determine its role in the context of competition policy. It is a fundamental matter, and one that too often has been glossed over. It is fundamental in the sense that the global economic architecture referred to and relied on in this work depends on the proper protection of property rights. The economic role of patents as property rights can be understood in the context of relevant market assessment as a part of antitrust analysis. From a competition policy standpoint, the starting point is to determine the size of the relevant market. In the case of drugs, or more accurately treatments, the key question is, "What is the product market?" Is it, for example, all drugs that treat a particular disease? Or is it one particular drug for the treatment of that disease which is protected by patent? Patents protect particular drugs or processes, not the treatment itself. Hence, if the relevant market is the treatment of a disease, then the patent cannot confer long-term monopoly power in the antitrust sense, because it does not confer long-term power over price. The price of the drug may be lowered by other therapeutic substitutes.[58] Zantac and Tagamet are both patented pharmaceuticals that can be substituted for each other for the treatment of ulcers. Because of substitutes, the price of ulcer medication is lower than it would be if there was only one drug for ulcers. Only in cases where there are no substitutes can the potential power over price be found.[59] Even so, the calculation is identical to the first fact pattern. In neither case does the patent grant in and of itself give the patentee power over price.

The question posed above is answered in antitrust analysis by posing a further question. We assume the smallest possible market – that of only one patented drug – and ask would, if the price of that drug increased, consumers shift to cheaper substitutes. The answer is of course yes, as long as such substitutes exist. In other words, the relevant product market only will be the single patented drug *where no other products are substitutable*. So, the monopoly issue is only relevant when there is only one treatment for a particular disease. Indeed, not only are there different chemical entities which can treat a disease, these different chemical entities actually can be delivered by different brands, and the prescribing doctor has a choice of chemical entities and brands (such as in the case where there is a patented brand and a series of generics). The choices possible equal the number of chemical entities multiplied by the number of brands, which rapidly becomes a large array of possibilities. Each of these permutations offers competition to the patented product, and the possibility of independently reducing its price through competition. To put it simply, the presence of other available or potentially available substitutes is a price discipline on the behaviour of the patentee. The greater the cross-elasticity of demand, the greater the effect of price substitution. However, studies suggest that this is not a constant. In some cases, a smaller number of brands may sometimes lead to a smaller price increase in a post-patent world, where the cross-elasticity of substitution between chemical entities actually exceeds the overall cross-elasticity of demand. Hence, stronger therapeutic competition does not necessarily lessen the profit-maximising potential of patentees. Frequently, as patent protection raises price, as is so under more intense therapeutic competition, all of the competitors increase price too, weakening the disciplining effect of competition. The key criterion appears to be the number and weight of off-patent chemical entities. If this is high, then a high degree of therapeutic competition will lead to lower profits (and hence prices). However, where elasticity is low, greater competition will have less of an effect on profits and price. In this context, it should be borne in mind that elasticity will increase the less developed a country actually is, as price factors will become more important to a poorer population. Hence, the disciplining effect on pharmaceutical profits is actually the greatest in countries with the poorest people. It is also important to note that in antitrust, market power alone is not enough to violate antitrust laws. It is only when a company with market power uses its power unreasonably with respect to its patent right that antitrust laws may be triggered, such as when a merger in a field risks harm to competing new goods and services.

As previously noted, in their Intellectual Property Licensing Guidelines,[60] the US antitrust agencies emphasise that IP does not necessarily create market power in the antitrust context. The Guidelines make the point that although the patent right may confer the power to exclude with respect to a specific product or process, there will often be sufficient actual or potential close substitutes for such products, processes or works to prevent the exercise of market power.[61]

Defining the market is critical in evaluating whether patentees actually have market power in relevant antitrust markets, and not solely over a particular patented product. One of the most significant questions in determining the relevant market is, "What are the potential substitutes?" Traditionally, a legal antitrust analysis has focused exclusively on product and geographic market definitions. One important aspect of the market is time, which is often considered in potential competition theory. Is there a separate technology or innovation market for certain pharmaceutical products? Potential competition theory was "resurrected" in the 1990s to deal with the issue of technology.[62] Broadly, potential competition theory was formerly used to challenge mergers or acquisitions where the acquiror might have entered the market independently (so that the acquisition removed the future benefits of new entry), or that the perceived new entry by the acquiror may have disciplined the behaviour of those already in the market. The FTC began to rely on the doctrine once again in the early nineties, after it had laid largely dormant during the Reagan era.[63] The doctrine then shed its antique name, and re-emerged as the modern-sounding theory of "innovation markets,"[64] in cases involving R&D.

More recently, the FTC has distinguished between potential competition theory and innovation market theory in classifying its prior antitrust challenges to pharmaceutical mergers, with innovation market analysis centred on IP rights related to R&D, and potential competition focused on potentially competing drugs that are in the regulatory approval pipeline.[65]

Thus, for example, in an innovation market case settled in 1997, the FTC alleged that the merger of Ciba-Geigy and Sandoz would result in an anticompetitive impact on the innovation of gene therapies.[66] The firms' combined position in gene therapy research was so dominant that other firms doing research in this area needed to enter into joint ventures or contract with either Ciba-Geigy or Sandoz in order to have any hope of commercialising their own research efforts. Without competition, the combined entity could appropriate much of the value of other firms' research, leading to a substantial decrease in such research. In addition, there was direct competition between the two companies with respect to specific therapeutic products. At the time of the merger, no gene therapy product was in the market but potential treatments were in clinical trials. As a remedy, the new merged firm, Novartis, was required to grant to all requesters a non-exclusive licence to certain patented technologies essential for development and commercialisation of gene therapy products. Depending on the patent, Novartis was also required to grant a non-exclusive licence of certain technology and patent rights related to specific therapies for cancer, GVHD and haemophilia to an FTC-approved licensee.

In a representative potential competition merger settled in 2020, the FTC alleged that the acquisition by Bristol-Myers Squibb of Celgene would harm consumers in the US market for oral products to treat moderate-to-severe psoriasis.[67] BMS had a pipeline product under development that was considered the most advanced oral treatment for moderate-to-severe psoriasis. According to the complaint, BMS's pipeline product will likely be the next entrant into the market and would compete directly with Celgene's Otezla product. The FTC settlement allowing the merger required Bristol-Myers Squibb to divest to Amgen, Inc., Celgene's Otezla, the most popular oral treatment in the US for moderate-to-severe psoriasis. The FTC determined that Amgen, a California-based pharmaceutical and biologic company, had the expertise, the US sales infrastructure and resources to restore the competition that otherwise would have been lost due to the challenged acquisition.

Scope of TRIPS Coverage

TRIPS has an additional non-discrimination rule in addition to the fundamental WTO principles that prevent discrimination against foreign suppliers. Article 27.1 TRIPS provides that patent laws should not discriminate between technologies or products. This is an important concept since it goes beyond the standard GATT jurisprudential history which tends not to find violations of foreign and local suppliers are equally harmed.

One concern in the case was that pharmaceutical products were treated differently from other products. Under Article 27.1 TRIPS agreement, no technology should be treated differently in terms of IP protection. The purpose of this provision is to ensure that differential patent treatment does not skew the incentives for inventiveness and the capital that supports this inventiveness. This principle of technology neutrality we shall see underpins not just patent protection under TRIPS but other areas where government regulations interface with inventions.

In the Canada case, the Panel considered whether exceptions to core patent rights might violate the non-discrimination rule.

In the Canada case,[68] provisions which allowed generics to manufacture and stockpile patented products were challenged by the European Union (EU) and others as violating TRIPS since it curtailed the duration of the patent and applied only to pharmaceutical products. This would be de facto discrimination, which the Panel noted (at p. 174, para 7.101) was

> a general term describing the legal conclusion that an ostensibly neutral measure transgresses a non-discrimination norm because its actual effect is to impose differentially disadvantageous consequences on certain parties, and because those differential effects are found to be wrong or unjustifiable.

Although the legislative history made it clear that the primary reason for passing the law was to impact the pharmaceutical industry, the Panel was not persuaded of a discriminatory purpose because this could be a situation where a particular problem which the legislature was trying to fix could be the catalyst for legislation which had a broader purpose. Since the legal scope could have been beyond the pharmaceutical industry, the Panel found neither de jure, nor de factor discrimination.[69]

There is a question as to whether the provisions of Article 27.1 can be applied more widely to other industries beyond the pharmaceutical industry. One industry that has hoped to avail itself of this provision is the software industry. However, this has attracted some criticism from commentators. Some commentators (Kahin) argue that the principle of non-discrimination is solely designed for the pharmaceutical industry and should not be applicable to different industries.[70]

Scope of Patent Protection: Allowable Exemptions or Limitations to Patent Protection

In the Canada case, the Panel looked at both the regulatory review exception (explain) and the stockpiling exception. Article 30, TRIPS contains exceptions to the exclusionary patent rights laid down in Article 28. Article 30 refers to "limited exceptions."

Specifically, Article 30, TRIPS provides that:

> Members may provide limited exceptions to the exclusive rights conferred by a patent, provided that such exceptions do not unreasonably conflict with the normal exploitation of the patent and do not unreasonably prejudice the legitimate interests of the patent owner, taking account of the legitimate interests of third parties.

These three conditions are cumulative. The Panel said that limited was to be interpreted with respect to how the exclusive rights of the patent owner were actually curtailed. Canada argued that there was no such curtailment of rights because the exception preserved the exclusive right to sell to the ultimate consumer during the patent term. The Panel rejected any attempt to classify certain rights associated with the patent as being more important than others. To determine whether there was a limited exception, the extent to which the patent owner's rights have been curtailed should be measured. One of the rights was the right to a period of extended market exclusivity after the patent expired. This market effect could be predicted and must have been in the mind of legislators because the patent law had been repeatedly enacted to allow it to exist. The stockpiling exception constituted a substantial curtailment of rights. Canada asserted that the regulatory review exception was limited because it did not interfere with the right to sell to the ultimate consumer. The Panel found that the Canadian regulatory review exemption was a limited exemption. It was limited because of the narrow scope of its curtailment of Article 28.1 rights. Anything that was limited to what was necessary to comply with the requirements of the regulatory approval process would be small and narrow (and therefore limited). The Canada case showed that the Panel interpreted Article 28 very narrowly.

Article 30 also prevents exceptions that unreasonably conflict with the normal exploitation of the patent. Canada took the position that exploitation of the patent meant that commercial value had to be extracted by working the patent. Working meant either selling or licencing the product to others. Again, the case turned on what actually constituted the patent right. Analogising with property rights, any diminution in the way property is held or used diminishes the property right, and so it is with IP rights. Canada made an assertion that was rejected by the Panel that patents constituted a bundle of divisible rights, some of which were more important or relevant than others. The Panel said that the post-expiration market exclusivity created by the exercise of the patent conferred a bundle of rights.

The Panel concluded that "normal exploitation" in the context of Article 30 meant both what was common within a relevant community, and that it conformed to a normal standard of entitlement. Normal practice of patent owners was to exclude all forms of competition that could detract significantly from the economic returns anticipated from a patent's grant of market exclusivity. This is in common with owners of any other form of IP. The Panel noted that patent laws carefully establish a defined period of market exclusivity and contemplate in that period, the issues faced by would-be competitors in terms of establishing the requisite inventory. In dealing with the regulatory exception, the Panel said that the regulatory issue as it concerned product approvals and its preclusion until the expiry of the patent was not a normal patent right, but was the result of an accidental conflation of patent and pharmaceutical regulatory laws. Most patent owners did not in fact use the patent right to block the commencement of the regulatory process. Here, the carefully defined period of patent protection was being extended through the regulatory delay. Hence, the regulatory review exception of Section 55.2(1) did not conflict with the normal exploitation of the patent.

"Legitimate interests of the patent owner" under Article 30, TRIPS must also not be unreasonably prejudiced by the exception. The Panel's view was that "legitimate interests" could be evaluated by looking at the negotiating history of Article 9(2) of the Berne Convention on which it was based (even though this applied strictly to copyright). In the Article 30 negotiation history, a specific list of exceptions, such as private use, scientific use, prior use, an exception for pharmacists gave way to a general authorisation for limited exceptions. The Panel took the view that legitimate interests must be those that are widely recognised as such in the country concerned.

The appellate body looked at a related issue in another TRIPS case involving Canadian patents for pharmaceutical products.[71] In the case, the appellate body considered Article 33, TRIPS which provided that the 20-year patent term must be "available." In order to be available, the 20-year patent term must be "readily discernible and a specific right," and it must be clearly seen as such by the patent applicants. It is the patent grant that must be sufficient in itself to obtain the minimum term mandated by Article 33. The Canadian law was challenged in this case because the regulatory process for drug appraisals was such as to substantially erode the 20-year patent term. The EC advanced an important point both in this case and in the *Canada-Patent Term* case, which was that the patent owners suffered from regulatory delays that could be as much as 8–12 years after the patent is filed. This meant that patent owners would only get exclusivity for a period that was 40%–60% of what was society's bargain between the patent owner and society (20 years). Since the research-based pharmaceutical companies had to suffer this regulatory hurdle, their competitors should not be given an early opportunity to start to make and market their competitive products. In the *Canada-Patent Production of Pharmaceutical Products* case, the Panel examined whether this was an assertion of a legitimate interest within the meaning of Article 30. The Panel looked at the practice of different countries and found that countries legislation reflected both sides of the debate with some countries enacting regulatory review exceptions like the Canadian law. The Panel concluded that this interest was neither compelling nor widely recognised (apparently drawing on the fact that many countries had similar legislation to Canada's). This highlights the potential problems in taking the widely accepted normative standard because it subjects what should be a legal expectation (of patent owners) to the changing whims of countries. This could have profound consequences on innovation incentives. Since the Canadian regulatory review exception did not activate all three of the cumulative conditions of Article 30, so was not inconsistent with Canada's obligations under the TRIPS agreement.

There was a dispute as to whether the principle of non-discrimination should apply to both the core patent right itself and exemptions and limitations to those rights. Canada was forced to argue with somewhat tortured logic that the non-discriminatory rule should apply to the Article 31 limitation on compulsory licencing, but not to the neighbouring Article 30 provision. The Panel quickly found that the non-discrimination rule should be applied both to the scope of patent rights as well as to the limited exceptions to those rights, stating at p. 171, para 7.90 that "A discriminatory exception that takes away enjoyment of a patent right is discrimination as much as is discrimination in the basic rights themselves."

Drug Prices under a Patent Protection Regime

Drug prices will not necessarily increase if countries shift to a patent-enforcing system.[72] New patents only will apply to new products unless pipeline protection is available, not to those that already exist. Hence, there will be no effect on price and any future effect on new products will take some time to percolate through to the market. A number of critics of a strong patent regime argue that prices will increase if patent rights are recognised. This is not necessarily true. In Italy, price increases were lower than the general increase in prices after the patent regime was strengthened.[73] Additionally, prices eventually go down after the patent expires. Numerous studies conclude that generic competition after the expiration of a patent brings prices of a drug close to its marginal production cost.[74] The market thereby makes the pricing more competitive as competition from other pharmaceutical companies forces the original holder of the patent to reduce price or accept a loss of market share.[75] Another common argument is that the price of drugs will rise because of the displacement of copycat firms from the market because of patent protection. The displacement of copycat firms does not lead to a net social loss. A study by MacLaughlin, Richard and Kenny notes, "[the] transfer of sales or royalty payments to other nationals would represent merely a transfer of income from one member of society to another and therefore, from the nation's perspective, would represent no net loss at all."[76] Likewise, much is made by critics of patent protection regarding the payment of royalties for patented products that copycat companies had previously utilised without such payment. Yet, a developing country that purchases technology is not disadvantaged by the purchase. Over the long term, it will result in gain due to the incentive to build up its own imitative R&D capacity for when the drug patent expires.[77] The payment for patented technology has an offset that can prove to be advantageous. Japan saw its high technology sector increase as the flow of new technologies stimulated domestic technological growth.[78]

At the consumer level, the introduction of strong patent protection will not have a large effect on consumer welfare. If the new rate of product innovation is stable over time, the introduction of new patented drugs will be matched by those going off patent. While Lanjouw's study on the Indian market was inconclusive as to whether introducing a stronger patent regime would speed up or slow down the availability of drugs to Indian customers, Lanjouw notes that if the domestic market is already competitive, as in India, then the ability of the drug innovator to extract higher prices from consumers is limited.[79] The availability of other drug therapies that are off patent also reduces the price of drugs under a strong patent system because firms will compete in price for sales, thereby reducing price to a level slightly above that of marginal cost.[80] By the end of 1996, only eight of the drugs on the World Health Organization's 7th Model List of Essential Drugs were still under patent in Europe.[81] This suggests that switching to lower priced alternative drugs is an available option for all but 10% of drugs on the WHO list.[82] The availability of therapeutic substitutes serves to restrain prices and limit the amount of welfare loss that consumers would suffer.

Another reason that patent protection will not affect the welfare of most consumers is a sad but true fact. Many people are priced out of drugs once the price of drugs reaches a certain level. It does not matter if the cost of a drug is $100 or $180 a year if the average salary in a particular country is $560 a year. Both drugs are equally unaffordable. As Lanjouw notes, "for the 70% or so of the population who currently do not have access to pharmaceuticals, the introduction of patent protection, and any price effects that may follow are irrelevant."[83]

Weak patent regimes, however, encourage anti-competitive and exclusionary behaviour that permits the abuse of monopoly power in defending home markets or in penetrating foreign markets. This manifests itself in a number of different ways: export cartels, predatory dumping in the export of copied drugs and collusive agreements among firms to divide markets in the internal sale and distribution of copied drugs.[84] Such firms may behave in an oligopolistic manner in which each copycat firm is assigned a particular part of the domestic market. The firms could then enforce their pricing scheme through the threat of disciplining a member of the oligopoly through predatory pricing that would attempt to increase its market share.[85]

Do Copycats Compete?

An important element of overall drug pricing is the extent to which copycat industry is competitive. Copycats frequently collude to fix prices[86] and engage in other forms of anti-competitive conduct which leads to higher, and not lower, prices. Indeed, the evidence from Argentina, where the average imitation product is actually more expensive than the patented product, strongly suggests price fixing or other anticompetitive behaviour by copycat firms.[87] Why else would the products be *more* expensive? If there is a lack of competition in the market for copied products as evidence suggests, then weakening the patent system will serve only to enrich the copycats at the expense of local consumers (who do not see material price reduction), the patentees (whose potential R&D investment is significantly diminished), and global welfare generally, measured by fewer new drugs being developed.

The off-patent market where generics are still 30%–40% less than branded drugs is interesting for comparison purposes.[88] The reason could be a perception of higher quality among branded products. This price difference cannot be explained by the patent system.

R&D costs are not, though they should be, calculated by many critics into the price of drugs since the R&D costs make up a significant portion of the price that pharmaceutical firms charge for products. As a result, those scholars that have noted lower costs in some countries that have low patent protection have flawed analyses since they never factor into consideration the lost drugs that companies do not produce because of the increased development costs from copying.[89] The overall loss in terms of the increased cost of R&D and the loss to companies in revenue because of copying explains how the extra cost of R&D makes some drugs untenable. When this is factored into the cost of the purchase of a copied drug, the cost of that drug rises. The cost of the copied drug also fails to take into consideration the cost of nontariff barrier and higher distribution costs that affect only imported, legitimate drugs.

The Role of Distribution Laws in Inflating Profit Margins

Many countries maintain distribution laws which are uncompetitive and provide large protection for local distributors at the expense of foreign suppliers (but not local suppliers). These laws, known as dealer protection laws, are leftovers from days of import substitution and usually provide for very high termination indemnities which must be paid by foreign suppliers upon terminating local distributors. Such indemnities do not arise for purely local relationships. Hence, these laws certainly violate GATS article XVII, and arguably also GATT article III.4 (the GATT provisions on non-discrimination between foreign and local entities).[90] The result is that, for products which are distributed by foreign suppliers, distributors can, without fear of recourse, extract very high profit margins from local suppliers. In some cases, these can be as much as 80%. Clearly, this represents a substantial part, if not all the difference between foreign pharmaceuticals prices for patented products and those of copycats in some markets.

At present, in the Latin American and Caribbean regions alone, these laws apply in the Dominican Republic, Costa Rica, Honduras, Guatemala, El Salvador, Haiti and to a lesser extent, in Brazil and Colombia. These laws also apply in the Middle East and in some Asian countries.

Government Pressure to Purchase Price

Compulsory Licencing Convergence or Clash between Antitrust and Patent Protection

A compulsory licence arrangement is one in which a government mandates that a patent holder release her patented right to a government institution or licensee in return for a set fee. Put differently, "[a] compulsory license is an involuntary contract between a willing buyer and an unwilling seller imposed and enforced by the state."[91] Compulsory licencing is a particularly damaging way that some countries use to weaken patent rights, even if patent rights are recognised in that country. Developing countries fear that without compulsory licences, they will not get the drugs needed by their populations. They also believe that the licences prevent overpricing of drugs by multinationals. Yet, compulsory licencing serves to make the patent right less secure because it allows for the free-riding of other companies that, after the expensive R&D is completed by the innovative firm, can apply for a licence to sell the drug and make considerable profit from doing so.[92] As Robert Sherwood explains:

> A compulsory licensing system is a policy contradiction. In effect, the state, having bestowed an exclusive property right for an innovation in order to serve the public good, then exercises its discretion to reduce the value of that right through compelled sharing of the property right under defined circumstances, also to serve a public good.[93]

In fact, compulsory licences do not necessarily lead to significantly lower prices in developing countries. Copied products through compulsory licences often sell at high prices even though the R&D costs are minimal.[94] Prices, therefore, should be even lower than they tend to be in the developing world.

As a result, a high social rate of return is sacrificed in favour of a high private rate of return to the few beneficiaries of compulsory licences.[95] Since compulsory licencing weakens the patent right, it diminishes foreign investment into a country's economy. This, in turn, limits the opportunity for increased growth.[96] Canada, for example, repealed significant portions of its compulsory licencing statute because of the near demise of the Canadian R&D-based pharmaceutical industry.[97] Compulsory licencing is anti-competitive because it encourages free-riding, thereby increasing societal economic cost. Further, it destroys the "prospect function" of a patent right, as analogised earlier in this article,[98] because the patent owner loses the ability to control who uses the patent.[99] Third parties can find ways of increasing the value of the patent and then force the owner to licence the patent at a regulated rate. There are also serious questions as to who regulates the rate for a compulsory licence and what basis the regulator uses for doing so. It is very difficult to measure the putative future value of a given patent and a government may do a poor job in estimating such value.

In the developing world, compulsory licences have been identified as a way to increase competition and reduce prices for poor consumers. Manot Tshabalala-Msimang, South African Minister of Health, stated that he believes compulsory licencing to be a crucial tool to make HIV/AIDS drugs more widely available.[100] Many nongovernmental organisations ("NGOs") have also stated that compulsory licencing holds the key to the world's health problems.[101] Many of those that support compulsory licencing do so based on the possibility of greater access to generic products. Joelle Tanguy, Executive Director of the NGO Doctors Without Borders, has advocated that long-term strategies, such as "generic production," be undertaken to make medicines affordable to the developing world.[102] In fact, Tanguy does not mean generic production as it is commonly known – production of drugs by companies after the patent right has expired.[103] Rather, Tanguy and many NGOs conflate the practice of producing generics, which involves respecting a system of patent rights and rewarding innovation on the one hand, with the use of copied drugs through a system of compulsory licencing and parallel trading that weakens the ability of firms to innovate on the other hand. This misguided conflation becomes more apparent in the HIV/AIDS Pricing Report that Doctors Without Borders produced in connection with the 13th International AIDS Conference in July 2000.[104] In its report, Doctors Without Borders explicitly states that compulsory licencing and parallel trading are ways to mitigate the "negative consequences" of patent rights.[105]

A review of publications by Doctors Without Borders sheds light on why the group, as representative of a number of NGOs, takes this view. In one document, the group states, "Millions of poor people die every year from infectious diseases because medicines that could cure them are too expensive. For other diseases there is no treatment: no effective medicine exists and nobody is looking for a cure."[106] Surprisingly, the group never asks why it is that pharmaceutical companies do not research diseases for which there are no effective treatments. In order for companies to do so, there needs to be an economic incentive to pay for the process of innovation. As noted earlier, this innovation can only occur in countries which protect the patent right. The fact that anti-malarial medications in India are only now being developed is due to the fact that the developing world did not respect patent rights and thereby removed the incentives to create such a drug.[107] In an attempt to lower prices for drugs through a weak patent system, developing countries actually served to increase the price for new drug development to a level that made R&D into these drugs economically unfeasible. Doctors Without Borders therefore seriously underestimates the disincentivising effect that a compulsory licencing and parallel trading system would have on the world's ability to come up with new treatments for diseases, and by doing so undermines the position of its own constituency.

Another problem that Doctors Without Borders notes in its publications is the prohibitive cost of medicines in developing countries that spend as much as half of their total health budgets on medicines.[108] The answer here lies not so much in the hands of innovative companies, but rather in the use of procurement methods which can dramatically reduce the cost of healthcare on a nation's budget. This means that many countries need to create better programmes in which procurement problems can be mitigated through mass purchases of medicines through transparent agencies. As one World Bank report notes, "Experience has demonstrated that when procurement is executed well… significant savings are possible—resulting in the maximisation of pharmaceutical budgets."[109] These savings can be significant and immediate. For example, Nicaragua spent $21 million of its health budget, 17% of the total health budget, on pharmaceutical procurement.[110] Nicaragua established a transparent procurement agency and accompanied the creation of this agency with the implementation of an essential drug list.[111] Within one year, the pharmaceutical budget shrank to $13 million.[112]

The Demise of Compulsory Licencing as an Antitrust Remedy

Proponents of strong compulsory licencing statutes argue that they are a solution to the problem of patent exclusivity because they are a remedy that is sometimes used in patent cases under the US law. In order for compulsory licencing to be a remedy, there must be some right that is violated; it is in antitrust cases that these remedies are most often fashioned. The basis of antitrust jurisprudence is to distinguish between lawful and unlawful acquisition and maintenance of monopoly power in order to promote greater competition, yield an efficient allocation of resources and benefit consumers.[113] When a patented product represents one of many products that compete in the market, few antitrust problems will arise. In the case where a patented product is so successful that it either evolves into its own market or engulfs a large percentage of the pre-existing market, there is potential for tension between the antitrust and patent laws.[114] However, the US Supreme Court has found that, "Compulsory licensing is a rarity in our patent system...."[115] The types of cases in which compulsory licences have been granted are a small group in which the "intellectual property has been wrongfully acquired or pooled and cross-licensed with competitors and only if one of these acts is accompanied by other predatory conduct."[116] As a major treatise on antitrust notes, compulsory licencing may be used as a remedy for certain antitrust violations involving patents but "it must be used sparingly."[117]

Even where there has been an antitrust violation, compulsory licencing is not favoured as a remedy because any advantages are outweighed by administrative difficulties. The courts would have to supervise it and there is no way of determining what a "reasonable" royalty rate would be. The royalty rate will depend on the value of the patent but the value is almost impossible to determine until the product has been in the market for some time.[118] In the US, compulsory licencing has not been adopted as a statutory requirement but is part of the relief which petitioners may receive if there has been a demonstrated patent misuse or antitrust violation. It has also been used on a few occasions by the Federal Trade Commission in settling antitrust suits.[119] Nevertheless, in the US, there are very few cases where the use of compulsory licencing as a remedy resulted from the non-use of a patent.[120] Importantly, compulsory licencing as a remedy for non-use is inapplicable to the pharmaceutical sector in which companies would want to bring new drugs to market to earn back the high cost of R&D.

In short, the status of those rare situations under the US law in which compulsory licencing may be granted may be summarised as follows:

> A patent owner may be compelled to license its patent in various situations: (1) the US federal government practices the patent; (2) in the case of federally-funded inventions [under the Bayh-Dole Act], the US federal government "marches in" and licenses the patent to a third party; or (3) a private party practices the patent, and a court in a typical infringement case finds that an injunction would not serve the public interest.[121]

Compulsory Licencing and the Patent Misuse Doctrine

Arguments that support compulsory licencing are also sometimes based on some variant of the patent misuse doctrine. The US Federal Circuit has construed the patent misuse precedent narrowly.[122] Thus, for example, the Federal Circuit found no misuse in an alleged concerted failure to licence an essentially unused patent.[123] As a general rule, the patent misuse doctrine has a broader scope than that of antitrust laws; though there is a large amount of overlap between the two as long as antitrust concerns such as market structure, intent and anticompetitive effect can be met.[124] "All that a successful defence of patent misuse means is that a court of equity will not lend its support to enforcement of a mis-user's patent."[125] The patent misuse doctrine is a court-made doctrine that is intended to prevent a patent holder from extending the power of the patent beyond the grant defined by the patent statute.[126] The doctrine is most frequently raised as a defence in infringement suits and breach of contract actions to pay royalties.[127] If a patent holder is found guilty under the misuse doctrine, the patent is rendered unenforceable until the patent holder remedies the misuse.[128] However, patent misuse may limit the validity of a patent for behaviour that does not rise to the level of an antitrust violation. With the exception of non-economic reasons why the doctrine should apply (e.g., fraud on the patent office), this represents a serious flaw in the doctrine itself. Indeed, though the doctrine regrettably still survives (albeit in weakened form), it represents bad public policy. As the leading American antitrust treatise writer has stated:

> [T]he patent misuse doctrine seems precisely wrong. The clear implication was that patents were a kind of 'suspect class,' and that arrangements involving patents were to be treated with greater hostility than would be applied to similar practices not involving patents. In fact, the opposite is generally true. Patent licensing is most generally efficient and should be encouraged.[129]

The lack of enforceability of a patent has the same *de facto* effect as a compulsory licence. The patent misuse doctrine differs from antitrust violations. The US Supreme Court has noted that a patentee's act may constitute patent misuse without rising to the level of an antitrust violation.[130]

The patent misuse doctrine applies the "clean hands" equitable doctrine as a vehicle for enforcing good faith requirements.[131] Unclean hands alone will not render a patent right unenforceable, as the unclean conduct must have a relation to the patent in question.[132] Yet, the doctrine has been applied to cases in which the patent holder has attempted to "tie" the sale of goods not covered by the patent.[133] The test the Federal Circuit uses in its patent misuse jurisprudence examines whether "the patentee has impermissibly broadened the 'physical or temporal scope' of the patent with anti-competitive effect."[134] A patent holder's behaviour can be a misuse on its face in the case of *per se* antitrust violations such as a tie-in (in which the purchase of two products is tied together) or price fixing.[135] The rule of reason serves as the basis for judging the legality of a potential anti-competitive effect. In *Mallinckrodt, Inc. v. Medipart, Inc.*, the Federal Circuit held that, "where an anticompetitive effect is asserted, the rule of reason under *35 USCA § 154* is the basis of determining the legality of the provision."[136] If, under the rule of reason, there has been a violation, then the misuse doctrine will apply. The patent misuse doctrine seems ill equipped as a remedy in the pharmaceutical setting. The patent right makes it possible for pharmaceutical firms to get out products, which they are incentivised to do. Others are equally incentivised to come up with therapeutic alternatives if a large market exists for the drug. If there were *per se* violations, then the patent misuse doctrine as well as antitrust legislation would apply. However, these types of *per se* violations are not common in the drug industry. Problems in the pharmaceutical industry are those of pricing – a result of copycats.[137] It is not a patent misuse problem. It is a problem of the use of patented property without the right to do so.

Compulsory Licencing and WTO Cases

In the Canada patent case, Canada arguing against the principle that the limitations allowed under Article 30, TRIPS should be non-discriminatory acknowledged that the non-discrimination rule was to ensure that:

> two types of discrimination that had been practiced against pharmaceuticals and certain other products - either a denial of patentability for such products, or, if patents were granted, automatic compulsory licenses permitting others to manufacture such products for a fee.[138]

Hence, even countries seeking to limit patent protection in WTO cases accepted the general principle that compulsory licencing laws that dealt only with pharmaceutical products as a concept were innately discriminatory against pharmaceutical products.

How Must a Patentee Treat Rivals?

Compulsory licencing's popularity has arisen largely because of the perception that it is a legitimate way of lowering price. Intellectually, and philosophically, it comes from the same place as the view that property rights are granted by the state and therefore do not relate to the individual owner in the same binding sense. In order to examine this notion, it is necessary to look at what obligations a patentee has to deal with its rivals. In particular, does the public's interest in cheaper medicines trump the rights of the property owner and confer on him the positive requirement to deal with others?

The patentee's obligation with respect to how it treats rivals is a significant issue, and one that is becoming more serious for patentees every day. Some have suggested that patentees might be deemed to have some kind of obligation to deal with others. The apparent basis for this suggestion is public concern with the purported monopoly nature of the patent right. There appears to be a view that, since the patent confers a monopoly on the patentee, one has to be very concerned about the behaviour of the monopolist. Furthermore, on occasion, it may be appropriate to use government intervention to force a monopolist to licence his products. However, this characterisation is deeply misleading. First, patentees are not necessarily monopolists. Whether they are or not depends on the range of substitutable products available to treat a particular disease. Second, even if the patentee is a monopolist, forcing the patentee to licence his product may not necessarily lead to positive results for consumers, for reasons detailed below. However, requiring a firm with market power to deal with rivals could have significant deterrent effects on innovation and could lead to a decline in overall R&D spent by innovators. Some have also sought to use the patent misuse doctrine to discipline the patentee's decision to licence or not licence his patented product.

The US experience is instructive here also. In the US, refusal to licence is not a basis for the patent misuse doctrine.[139] According to the Xerox litigation, it will not be grounds for any kind of antitrust violation either if the patentee is merely exercising his right under the patent. In 2020, in *FTC v. Qualcomm*,[140] the US Court of Appeals for the 9th Circuit decisively rejected the assertion that Qualcomm's refusal to licence its patents to rival chipmakers violated the antitrust laws, citing the US Supreme Court's holding in *Trinko*[141] that a firm generally has no antitrust duty to deal (subject to a very limited possible exception).

Compulsory Licencing as a Remedy for Refusals to Deal

Compulsory licencing has had changing fortune in the US litigation, principally as a remedy for antitrust violations, such as refusal to deal. However, recent US learning in this area is very important. The increasing protection of patent rights in the US in recent history has done much to boost innovation, and provides a model for other countries intent on building economic growth.

The compulsory licencing doctrine has not been significantly relied upon in the US. In general, it has only substantively been applied where IP has been wrongfully acquired or pooled and cross-licenced with competitors, and only if one of these acts is accompanied by some predatory conduct.[142] The use has been more typically limited to consent decrees in merger cases. There is now a rebuttable presumption that a monopolist's desire to exclude others from its protected work is a pre-emptively valid legal business justification for any immediate harm to consumers.[143] Originally a copyright test, this has now been extended to patents also.[144] In the *Image Technical* case, the court held that this presumption could be rebutted by evidence of pretext.[145] The Xerox litigation makes it clear that the courts will not enquire into the subjective motivation for exercising statutory rights granted under the patent laws, "even though [the] refusal to sell or license [a] patented invention may have an anti-competitive effect, so long as the anti-competitive effect is not illegally extended beyond the statutory patent grant."[146] A US patentee that refuses to licence may, however, find itself relegated to damages when third parties infringe its patent and utilise its technology, in light of the Supreme Court's *eBay* decision,[147] holding that there is no automatic entitlement to an injunction in a patent suit.

US FTC Enforcement Action and the Imposition of a Duty to Deal

In *Intergraph Corp. v. Intel Corp.*,[148] the district court imposed significant obligations on Intel by imposing an affirmative duty to continue to deal with a competitor. The court so held even though Intel was effectively being asked to reveal its trade secrets to one of its rivals.[149] The decision caused some consternation among antitrust practitioners. Intergraph was a manufacturer of graphical interface workstations, and had acquired the Clipper computer technology but abandoned it in favour of a relationship with Intel. Intergraph threatened to sue Intel for patent violations relating to its chip technology. In response, Intel demanded that it enter into a cross licence agreement.[150] When Intergraph refused, Intel allegedly retaliated by denying access to chips and technical product development information which it had previously furnished to Intergraph.[151] The district enjoined Intel from refusing to deal with Intergraph.[152] The Federal Circuit, however, rejected the district court's assertion that Intel's microprocessor technology was an essential facility, with respect to which Intel had "affirmative duties to refrain from acting in a manner that unreasonably harms competition."[153] Indeed, the Federal Circuit was careful to make sure that the essential facility doctrine was confined to competition with the controller of the essential facility, and not to competition in derivative markets. The Federal Circuit stated that:

> [the] courts have well understood that the essential facility theory is not an invitation to demand access to the property or privileges of another, on pain of antitrust penalties and compulsion; thus the courts have required anti-competitive action by a monopolist that is intended to 'eliminate competition in the downstream market.'[154]

As we will see below, however, even this limiting holding is dated. The essential facilities doctrine is close to being a dead letter today in the US. As a practical matter, the Supreme Court has effectively left it on jurisprudential life support and may extinguish it entirely when presented the opportunity.

The Exception to the Right to Refuse to Deal Essential Facilities Doctrine

The seminal definition of the essential facilities doctrine in the US can be found in *MCI Communications Corp. v. American Tel. and Tel. Co.*, in which the Court held

> A monopolist's refusal to deal under these circumstances is governed by the so-called essential facilities doctrine. Such a refusal may be unlawful because a monopolist's control of an essential facility (sometimes called a 'bottleneck') can extend monopoly power from one stage of production to another, and from one market into another. Thus, the antitrust laws have imposed on firms controlling an essential facility the obligation to make the facility available on non-discriminatory terms.[155]

Under *MCI*, four elements must be met to establish liability under the essential facilities doctrine: (1) control of the essential facility by a monopolist; (2) a competitor's inability practically or reasonably to duplicate the essential facility; (3) the denial of the use of the facility to a competitor and (4) the feasibility of providing the facility.[156] It should be stressed, however, that the essential facilities doctrine appears to be close to moribund under the current US case law, in light of the statement in *Verizon Communications, Inc. v. Trinko*[157] that the doctrine has never formally been adopted by the Supreme Court. Moreover, the leading US antitrust treatise writer has stated that "the essential facilities doctrine is manifestly hostile toward the general goal of the antitrust laws. The doctrine can serve to undermine rather than encourage rivals to develop alternative inputs of their own."[158]

Even assuming that the essential facilities concept still exists in some form under the US law, it is not readily applicable to pharmaceuticals. In the pharmaceutical setting, the patented drug itself does not create a bottleneck. Indeed, it could be regarded as the opposite of a bottleneck since new innovations can be derived as a result of the patented product. To the extent that there are bottlenecks in the pharmaceutical sector in the developing world, they are distribution bottlenecks. Solving these bottleneck problems would only lower prices because it would reduce vertical monopolistic restraints on price imposed by a number of the copycat producers.

The Global Context: Compulsory Licencing under TRIPS

The TRIPS agreement allows for compulsory licencing under Articles 27(1), 31 and 65(4), but limits these circumstances to cases of antitrust violation, national emergency and public non-commercial use.[159] The damaging effect of compulsory licences was recognised by the WTO, and hence, where WTO Members insist on maintaining such provisions, the WTO rules strictly regulate what can be used as a basis for compulsory licencing. Indeed, laws can be TRIPS-compliant with no provision for compulsory licencing at all. TRIPS, Article 31 states that, "Where the law of a Member allows for [compulsory licensing]... the following provisions shall be respected."[160] In other words, even if Members have compulsory licencing provisions, they must respect certain basic provisions.[161]

Article 31 of TRIPS lists, conjunctively, the criteria which must be met before a compulsory licencing regime is deemed to be TRIPS-compliant. These include:

- a each case must be considered on its merits;
- b the grant is conditional on the purported licensee having attempted to obtain authorisation by the patentee on commercial terms, and failure to achieve it in a reasonable period of time;
- c the use of compulsory licencing is limited to the purpose for which it was initially authorised;
- d the licence may not be exclusive;
- e the licence cannot be assigned;
- f that licence should be predominantly (note earlier drafts stated "solely" or "exclusively" for domestic market use;
- g compulsory licencing is allowed only during the time that the circumstances which gave rise to the licence still prevail, and provided that a competent authority has the power to review the continuation of the licence;
- h requires proper compensation to the patent holder;
- i provides that the procedure in deciding compensation;
- j provides that the decision itself must be subject to higher judicial review; and
- k enables countries to bypass (b) through (h) in cases of anti-competitive actions by patentees.[162]

Although much has been made of the fact that Article 31 of TRIPS is ambiguous, this should not cloud those aspects of the article which are clear and unambiguous. Compulsory licencing is subject to very strict conditions, which must all apply (except in cases of anti-competitive conduct by the patentee). The references to a reason behind the need for the licence grant, and the fact that the licence only will be granted while that reason prevails, are strongly suggestive that the compulsory licencing regime should be used as a remedy for some form of market failure only, and, therefore, should not be universally applicable. The foregoing addresses what constitutes anticompetitive behaviour, and what might further constitute patent misuse. However, many countries' submissions to the WTO trade and competition group help to further clarify this issue.

Applying TRIPS, anti-competitive practices must be strictly construed. Article 40 of TRIPS gives a clue as to what should be considered anti-competitive for these purposes.[163] Article 40 provides that some licencing practices "may have adverse effects on trade and may impede the transfer and dissemination of technology."[164] Article 40(2) gives examples of how abuses of IP rights which might have an adverse effect on the market can be corrected.[165]

In its submission to the WTO Trade and Competition group, the EU offers useful examples of what may or may not constitute anti-competitive practices, possibly justifying the imposition of a compulsory licence:

"The core rationale for their [IPR] protection is that they tend to create a dynamic efficiency that is pro-competitive and outweighs any short term allocative efficiency gains that might exist in the absence of such protection…."[166] The EU notes that the exclusive right given to the patentee will, in and of itself, not give rise to an abuse of market power. This depends on the availability and market share of substitutable products. The practices that might give grounds for anti-competitive abuse of a monopoly right are:

1 If competitors grant licences to each other for the purposes of dividing up markets, then there may be a market division problem. But transfers in and of themselves do not present a problem. Competition problems only arise if the transfer is the subject, the means or the consequence of an anti-competitive arrangement.
2 The patentee may not try and impose a fixed margin on licensees. If he does so, that may constitute a competitive problem.
3 The exclusive right conferred by the patent is not in and of itself sufficient to determine the existence of a dominant position. The price of goods is not necessarily an abuse of dominant position. Indeed, the EU submission states that "only in exceptional circumstances, should abnormally high prices be considered as an abuse in themselves."[167]
4 A refusal to grant a licence, even for a reasonable royalty, does not in itself constitute an abuse of a dominant position. Additional requirements are required, such as where the patentee is not working the patent itself, withholding important technical information from the public against the public's interests, engaging in unfair sales prices, or engaging in discriminatory sales practices (e.g., unfairly refusing to supply certain parts of the market).[168]

All of these points are directed towards practices by patentees which tend to impede trade and prevent the invention being fully exploited in the domestic market. Many of the US cases also illustrate the type of anti-competitive practices, which are outside the limited antitrust immunity that the patent itself provides. In *Twin Labs, Inc v. Weider Health & Fitness*,[169] the Second Circuit relied on the authority of the leading antitrust treatise, stating that "facilities that are natural monopoly, facilities whose duplication is forbidden by law, and perhaps those that are publicly subsidised and thus could not practicably be built privately."[170] It is clear from the case law and commentary that patent owners risk compulsory licencing of their property only if they are a monopolist for a particular treatment, have some intent to foreclose competitors from that particular treatment or are otherwise engaging in anticompetitive activity. Generally, the patent right itself will be a legitimate business justification for refusing to licence a patent in the absence of other anti-competitive factors as set out above. As if further clarification was necessary, the IP Guidelines state that the agencies will not require a patent owner to create competition in its own technology.

The FTC Action against Intel considered the issue of a patent holder's duty to licence to customers who were not direct competitors with Intel (the OEMs).[171] The FTC's case alleged Intel's practices stifled competition in microprocessor-related technology.[172] But even in this case, the consent order permits Intel to restrict use of its advanced technical information to the production of computer systems that incorporate the microprocessor to which the information applies, not to the creation of rival microprocessors.[173] Bill Baer, former director of the FTC's Bureau of Competition (and subsequently Assistant Attorney General for Antitrust during the Obama Administration), said:

> A... concern some have expressed is that the Commission's action seeks to force compulsory licensing of Intel's patents to its competitors. Even a cursory reading of the Commission's complaint and proposed order shows that suggestion to be seriously misleading... Where however, Intel had a legitimate business reason - such as evidence of misuse or misappropriation of its inventions, the company would be free to protect its rights.[174]

By analogy, where pharmaceutical patent holders know that their property is being misused or misappropriated, as in the case of copycats, there is simply no antitrust issue in their refusal to licence, and no antitrust remedy (such as compulsory licencing) is appropriate. Any other approach could lead to serious economic erosion of the very fabric of the patent right itself.

In the words of one commentator, "allowing competition policy to trump property rights is, in all but the most egregious of situations, an extraordinary result."[175] The essential facility doctrine applies more in the area of regulated utilities, such as the *MCI* case itself.[176] It is a departure to try to apply such a doctrine to the ordinary business of patent holders where such considerations do not apply. The Xerox litigation and the *Intergraph* case seem to finally put out of court the suggestion that patent property ever can be subject to the essential facility doctrine. Indeed, the freedom to licence or not licence is one of those integral bundles of rights conferred by the patent system itself.[177]

The Effect of Compulsory Licencing on Pharmaceutical Companies

Compulsory licencing could have dramatic effects on pharmaceutical companies. The compulsory licence will lead to a reduction of price for patented products. That loss will have to be somehow absorbed by pharmaceutical companies. There are various possibilities:

1 *Raising revenue by increasing other products' price.* This cannot occur where drugs are sold in a competitive environment and may be capped by countries which have price controls. In other words, prices of the non-compulsory licenced patented drugs would likely increase in more competitive,

non-price-controlled markets, such as the US, which would be politically unpalatable.

2 *Reduction of expenditure.* The major expense that pharmaceutical companies incur is the cost of R&D. Other expenses include advertising and returns on investment. If returns on investment are lowered, share price could decline and might lead to further consolidation in the industry. Lowering advertising revenues would have a little impact on the losses that would result from compulsory licencing. The most significant reductions would have to come from R&D budgets. Companies might elect to engage in lower risk activity, such as generic production. In any event, a lower R&D budget will lead to fewer new pharmaceutical products being developed.
3 *Reduce costs by merging with rivals.* Pharmaceutical companies may be faced with no other alternative but to merge with rivals in order to reduce costs. The result of this could be an overall reduction in innovation as competition in innovation is reduced and the incentive to invest substantially in R&D declines.

Parallel Trading

Parallel trading in the pharmaceutical setting occurs when a product in one market is exported to another country. Parallel traders seek to take advantage of the arbitrage possibilities available in the pricing of drugs due to different economic and regulatory practices between countries.[178] The practice has attracted international attention because of the perception that use of parallel importation regimes results in cheaper drugs prices in the developing world.

Although empirical evidence on the implications of parallel trading is scant, a number of theoretical works show the negative implications of a parallel trading system.[179] Parallel trading undermines the patent right and therefore creates an economic loss to both innovators and consumers, thereby creating an anticompetitive practice. Barfield and Groombridge note four types of market settings in which parallel trade has particularly pernicious effects to the pharmaceutical industry.[180] Such settings include:

1 where parallel imports would inhibit the ability of pharmaceutical firms to recoup R&D and other fixed costs and chill further innovation;
2 where price discrimination would enhance welfare by facilitating entry of pharmaceutical firms into new, low-priced markets and thus expanding output;
3 where government-created monopolies create price distortions and drive price down below marginal cost of the production of a pharmaceutical product; and
4 where parallel imports could freeze out authorised distributors through lower prices.[181]

To extract the lowest possible price for pharmaceutical products, consumers need a strong competition policy that encourages trade liberalisation, protection against monopolisation power and the encouragement of FDI, rather than a system of parallel trading. This strong competition policy will let the market determine a pareto-enhancing allocation of resources in the economy. It will also create proper regulatory supervision to prevent monopolisation or exploitation of market power, since businessmen have an incentive to pursue anti-competitive behaviour. This will prevent any abuse of the patent right.

In contrast to the appeals made on behalf of parallel trading, the economics of such trading does not significantly help consumers. Burstall and Senior note, "Doctors and patients may not profit from parallel trade but the distributors - the wholesalers, the dispensers in the high street or in hospitals, and, of course, the traders themselves - very definitely do."[182] Likewise, the National Economic Research Associates found similarly that,

> the major beneficiaries of parallel trade are the parallel traders who, on average, claim about 70 percent of the price difference between a parallel import product and the local price. Other direct beneficiaries are pharmacists and, to a much lesser extent, payors. The consumer hardly benefits at all.[183]

Such studies prove that parallel trading serves to benefit a few private individuals at the expense of society at large. It raises R&D costs and makes financially infeasible R&D into some necessary drugs.

Advocates of parallel trading often claim that parallel trading is in reality no different than the doctrine of international exhaustion of rights. Exhaustion occurs when a patent holder, or other IP rights holder, has sold a product and can thereafter not prevent its authorised entry into a different market. The patent holder cannot prohibit the subsequent resale of the product because their rights to a particular item have been exhausted by the act of selling it. Such a definition requires a particular geographic area. For example, once a product enters the US market, it is exhausted anywhere within the US market.[184] This is quite different from international exhaustion of rights, which is what parallel traders seek. A study by the National Economic Research Association on the consequences of an international exhaustion regime on trademarks in Europe extends this theory to other IP rights, such as patents.[185] It notes that an international exhaustion of rights doctrine would have significant negative economic consequences.[186] The report argues against an international exhaustion of rights system noting that pareto-efficient outcomes will occur when patent holders are allowed the freedom to exploit their rights through price discrimination in different national markets.[187] Exploitation of the property right creates incentives to innovate and develop new products. International exhaustion of rights disadvantages consumers by making patents less effective in protecting the consumer by maintaining quality through safety or technical standards and identifying the origin of a product.[188] It would also make it difficult for the patent holder to control the distribution chain and conditions under which products are sold.[189] In the absence of a strong competition policy, an exhaustion doctrine and exclusive distributorship agreements would have a detrimental effect on welfare, since domestic brands may be part of a single *de facto* cartel that would conspire to keep prices high through the exclusive distributor relationships – vertical arrangements between upstream and downstream sellers. This type of vertical restraint was deemed untenable in the US 60 years ago.[190] National exhaustion, in contrast, is permissible since traders are given the right to move goods within a national border, in the case of the US, or regional borders, in the case of the EU. The situation of international exhaustion where one country allows for parallel imports from another unrelated country does not fit within this national exhaustion policy. The only reason why the doctrine might have some vitality in Europe is because of the drive towards a single European market. It has no application in free trade areas or among countries where market conditions are significantly different. Moreover, in Europe, the doctrine of exhaustion of rights is a bifurcated one. Recognising the drive to retain and develop Europe's single market, exhaustion of rights applies to trademarks in Europe, but outside Europe the doctrine has no application.[191] However, even in Europe, there are significant problems with the application of the doctrine in the case of pharmaceutical products where price controls exist in some countries, but not in others, and where pricing is not set in a uniform manner.

Some who believe in parallel trading and an international exhaustion system argue that such a system favours free trade, whereas systems that limit parallel trading reduce free trade and are thereby anti-competitive. This reveals a certain confusion. Followed to its logical conclusion, it would eliminate all forms of IP because it fails to recognise that the IP right is not merely tolerated by competition law, but encouraged.[192] In addition, it also fails to take into account that efficient pricing may depend on a certain level of international price discrimination as described above. This is because the world is not yet a single, uniform market and different prices have to be charged for different products. If companies cannot rely on the integrity of their pricing structures (because parallel traders are arbitraging the price differences), this efficiency would be lost. Further, the argument for parallel trading does not take into account the fact that patents restrict market forces for a period of time in order for the patent holder to recoup the cost of innovation. This is based upon the assumption that the dynamic effects of the patent right will produce greater societal economic welfare gains than would occur without the patent right. The exhaustion doctrine is not so much a question of free trade as much as it is one of which form of patent policy to pursue. As one scholar notes, there are two serious problems with the exhaustion as free trade argument rather than as one of patent policy.

> First, the conditions surround parallel trade do not fit into the assumptions on which standard static trade models supporting the case for laissez-faire trade are built. Second, a static analysis with regard to IPRs... would require the removal of all rights to intellectual property.[193]

The economic reality is that price discrimination in the setting of drug prices in different markets, through market segmentation, can have significant positive effects for both producers and consumers. Because of the possibility of arbitrage, parallel importation also has a disciplining effect on the ability of companies to offer discounts for drugs in poorer countries' markets. Any discounted drug simply would be the subject of an arbitrage action by a parallel trader, which would treat the drug like a discounted foreign currency. This would lead to dampened innovation and less of a likelihood that companies will lower price in less developed nations' markets.

Under Ramsey pricing, companies base pricing on how much a particular consumer will be willing to pay for a particular good, above the marginal cost of producing such a good, because of different price elasticities for pharmaceuticals.[194] The ability to discriminate based on price is a common and economically justified practice.[195] Examples include offering volume discounts or discounts to initial customers.[196] Price discrimination is permitted in the case of movie tickets, where matinees and evenings shows are priced differently, as are tickets for youth and senior citizens, or advanced purchases over the phone, or prices for a large group.[197] Price discrimination has ill effects when it is used to gain or enhance monopoly power. Without a differentiation of markets, pharmaceutical companies will not be able to recoup the cost of innovation during the life of their patent right.

Another significant problem with allowing parallel trading is that the arbitrage it offers is a significant incentive for traders to cartelise their operations, and even for patentees to collude on price. This erosion of the incentive to charge a national market-based price will ultimately lead to problems in efficient allocation or resources.

Within the borders of the US, price discrimination is permitted in some circumstances, although § 2(a) of the Robinson-Patman Act and § 2 of the Sherman Act prohibit price discrimination in other circumstances.[198] The standards for each Act differ slightly. Price discrimination violates the Robinson-Patman Act if it involves (1) two sales to different person; (2) in interstate commerce; of (3) goods that are of like grade and quality; (3) at different prices; (4) where the effect of the discrimination may be to lessen competition substantially among the sellers of the product (primary-line injury), the buyers of the product (secondary-line injury) or the customers of the buyers (third-line injury).[199] The prima facie case can be rebutted with several defences, such as meeting competition or volume discount.[200]

The Sherman Act § 2 offence of monopolisation has two elements: (1) the possession of monopoly power in the relevant market and (2) the wilful acquisition or maintenance of that power as distinguished from growth or development as a consequence of a superior product, business acumen or historic accident.[201] The essence of a § 2 monopolisation or attempted monopolisation claim is that a single firm with a great deal of market power has engaged in conduct designed to exclude and foreclose competition in a relevant market. It may be the market in which the party already has market power or the market into which it would like to extend that market power (although the latter case, to the extent it is viewed as "monopoly leveraging," is now highly disfavoured under the US antitrust case law).[202]

TRIPS-Based Solutions for Developing Countries?

A modern patent law would allow for compulsory licencing only in very specific cases, as specified in the TRIPS agreement itself. The law would be focused on sound patent protection (including enforcement of patent rights) that would stimulate innovation in the country. Adherence to TRIPS should be seen as a minimum requirement but should not be seen as the maximum amount of patent protection. The law should give patentees the right to discipline parallel traders by enforcing their patent rights against them.

However, provisions also need to be made for procurement of patented drugs. International financial institutions could contribute to procurement programmes based on competitive bidding, not dissimilar to the programmes which already exist in the World Bank for the procurement of generic drugs.[203] In order to avail itself of such a programme, the country concerned would have to demonstrate TRIPS compliance and show that compulsory licencing and parallel trading regimes were not present in its law and that proper enforcement steps were being taken against violators. For patented drugs, any bidder, if not the actual patentee, would have to be licenced by them.

Given the key, and often understated role that distribution difficulties play in these countries in ensuring that drugs are delivered throughout the country, distribution issues should also be a central element in the certification process. Indeed, countries that maintain distribution laws of the type described herein should not be eligible for these new procedures because of the significant profit margins that local distributors could charge and effectively block proper distribution of the drugs once purchased.

The COVID-19 pandemic sparked a controversy over the possible justification for the relinquishment of TRIPS-covered patent and other IP rights by the makers of COVID-19 vaccines.[204] In October 2020, India and South Africa submitted to the WTO's TRIPS Council a request for a waiver of IP rights protections covering vaccines and medicines, related to the prevention, containment and treatment of COVID-19. The proposal subsequently was co-sponsored by the delegations of Kenya, Eswatini, Mozambique, Pakistan, Bolivia, Venezuela, Mongolia, Zimbabwe, Egypt, the African Group, the LDC Group, the Maldives, Fiji, Namibia, Vanuatu, Indonesia and Jordan.[205] This led to a discussion among WTO delegations on the fundamental question of whether a waiver was the appropriate and most effective way to address the shortage and inequitable distribution of and access to vaccines and other COVID-related products. Several developed and developing members that cautioned that equitable access and distribution could be attained while maintaining IP as the basis for incentivising investment in innovation, and for licencing technology transfer, so that members could effectively fight new strains of COVID-19 and any future diseases and pandemics. Some were particularly concerned that waiving IP rights might undermine the existing efforts and arrangements for large-scale production of vaccines that rely, in part, on the IP system. Moreover, certain leading experts, including former Directors of the US Patent and Trade Office, argued that a TRIPS waiver would severely disincentivise future investments in and developments of future drugs and vaccines, while doing nothing to solve the problem of distribution to poorer countries.[206] As of November 2022, the WTO had issued a partial waiver covering COVID-19 vaccines and was considering whether considering an extension of this partial waiver to COVID-19 diagnostics and therapeutics.[207]

The above discussion demonstrates that real innovation losses can occur if inventors are not able to patent their inventions and have those patents respected on a global basis. These losses can mean that new products will not be invented in the future to cover our future needs. This illustrates the linkage both with competition and with trade. It also illustrates the zero-sum approach taken by some analysts who have hinted that if patent protection was not available, then the losses visited on the producers would be compensated by net consumer welfare. This mistakes the notion that consumer welfare will increase as a result of the lack of IP protection in a given sector. In many cases, consumer welfare (specifically the welfare of future consumers) is actually enhanced by the IP right. This enables the different holders of IP rights to compete more effectively against each other, thus rapidly increasing overall consumer welfare. The importance of monopolistic competition, competition between different products that are each protected by IP rights, will become ever more important in the future.

Impact of the New Economy

As we note elsewhere in the book, the impact of the new economy must be considered in evaluating the appropriate policy response to the interface between IP, competition and trade. In the new economy, a much higher percentage of output is likely to be the kind of property to which IP rights attach. Hence, the theory of monopolistic competition that we describe in these pages becomes much more important as an operating theory. In addition, the impact of rapidly evolving technology changes the way that product and geographic markets are defined. The chances that a firm with market power in a particular product market will then be supplanted by a firm that radically changes the market for the particular product or service is ever-increasing. An old economy example of this is the impact of the cellular telephone on the basic telephony market. These kinds of changes are now commonplace, making market power a much less firm indicator of a potential competition problem. Also the barriers to entry that have existed in many traditional markets are changing as a result of new technology. To draw on the telecommunications example, the higher barriers to entry in making the necessary investments to compete with the operator of the Public Switched Telephone Network (PSTN) are rendered less relevant, if I can invent around the wireline system by inventing the cell phone. However, the network externalities that are associated with these new technologies (software is an example) may increase barriers to entry (so-called path dependence, where an inferior technology wins because the existing technology is less costly). Network externalities may mean that social benefits of the new technology are thwarted because in order for the new technology to realise its full potential, many consumers must all use the same technology. Simply put, if the world is using software A, and I invent software B which is better, B will only take off if a significant number of people switch to it, so we can all communicate using B. If that does not happen, then B will never really catch on (even though it may be empirically better). The precise balance between consumer welfare enhancement and innovation delaying activity depends on a case-by-case analysis.

Property Rights as a Central Pillar of a Functioning Market Economy

We have argued that property rights are a fundamental pillar of a market economy. IP rights are also a fundamental pillar of that market economy. We have illustrated however that while IP rights have many of the characteristics normally associated with property rights, there are differences. This does not mean that IP rights should be extended without discussion but it does mean that innovation-enhancing aspects of them must be considered in trade agreements or in any attempt to evaluate how their protection impacts trade flows. In order to encourage trade flows and to stimulate the very kind of import competition that will enhance consumer welfare as we have described elsewhere in the book, it is imperative that property rights and IP rights are protected. Failure to protect these rights in trade agreements will lead to an erosion in the very trade that would lead to more consumer-welfare-optimising outcomes. Failure to protect intellectual properties in trade agreements therefore amounts to a trade barrier. Now, that said, the precise manner in which those rights should be protected depends on the discussion above, and on the precise balance of innovation-enhancing activity, and on ensuring that the market power conferred (if any) is not abused. This certainly impacts the scope and duration of the IP right, and different products will not always attract the same duration of IP protection.

A Strong Intellectual Property Regime Leads to Greater Prosperity

Linkage between IP protection to economic growth has been longstanding, at least in the developed world. Robert Solow's seminal work over 40 years ago on the relationship between technology to growth demonstrated that 87.5% of the growth of American economic output between 1904 and 1949 was related to technological factors.[208] Other studies have also shown the strong correlation that the injection of new technology into the economy produces, and the resulting significant expansion of public wealth and social welfare that it achieves. Charles Jones argues that in the period between 1965 and 1990, over 40% of US growth can be attributed to the rise in research intensity.[209] A strong IP system allows for the growth of new technologies. Industrial studies suggest evidence that the social returns to R&D exceed private returns, i.e., countries benefit more from R&D undertaken than the companies that pursue the R&D.[210] More generally, a significant body of research suggests that strong patent systems promote innovation, which, in turn, is a crucial driver of economic growth.[211]

Though less research exists in the impact of R&D in the developing world, Edwin Mansfield's work illustrates that the IP protection afforded by a country directly relates to the amount of technical development and transfer into the developing country.[212] This factor significantly influences the composition of Foreign Direct Investment ("FDI"). Countries with strong IP protection tend to experience a continuing flow of new high technology firms entering the industrial base. One World Bank study concludes that patent protection is an important ingredient in any package to support domestic R&D.[213] The higher the IP protection, the greater the amount of investment. This investment in technology has important secondary effects on the economy of a developing country. Because of the competition, older firms adapt to the new technology. As more FDI penetrates the economy, the benefits permeate to human capital investment since workers need to be trained in the new technologies. As the amount of high technology investment grows – once the development reaches a certain threshold level – remaining in the country to pursue high technology work, rather than moving to the US or Europe, becomes an option for developing highly educated workers. Once there are more high skilled workers that remain in a developing country as a result of stronger IP laws, private capital investment, such as venture capital, increases because of the increased investment opportunities. This, in turn, creates more employment opportunities as more technology businesses are developed, thereby creating a net social economic gain for the developing country.

Another area in which developing countries benefit from the impact of greater patent protection is FDI in technology. Significant FDI occurs in countries with stronger patent regimes since a legal regime that protects IP is one of the factors that foreign investors use in order to decide where to place their investments. FDI is an important way for knowledge to be diffused from one country to another as a multinational firm will externalise proprietary knowledge with its local partners. Even in the case of wholly owned local subsidiaries of multinationals, knowledge is still transferred because local employees are hired by and receive training from the multinationals. The relationships of these subsidiaries also produce an externalisation of knowledge with the local firms with which it has business relationships.[214] Evidence shows that the US firms that invest in foreign production in developing countries are more R&D-intensive than similar US firms that invest in developed countries.[215]

Surveys have found the strength of the IP rights regime of a country to be of particular importance to firms making R&D decisions regarding investment in the manufacturing stage of development, and in licencing of technology to unrelated firms.[216] It follows that the stronger the IP regime, the stronger the patent protection will be (and the greater the FDI will be). This is particularly true in the case of the pharmaceutical industry, which is sensitive to patent protection. In an examination of the Indian pharmaceutical market, Lanjouw argues that there may be economic reasons why an IP regime matters in decisions regarding the location of an R&D facility in a country.[217] This may have spillover effects of R&D into neighbouring firms. Just as important, a country's level of IP protection may be used as a signalling mechanism for investors indicating the general business climate in a particular country: where the stronger the IP regime, the more favourable the general business climate. The effect of trade barriers on technology transfers is linked to FDI when based on the level of IP rights. Parente and Prescott argue that the extent of barriers to trade plays a key role in per capita income across countries since trade may affect growth by lowering the barriers to technology adoption.[218] Therefore, as free trade increases, so too will the impact of FDI on increasing per capita income. These findings are supported by Gould and Gruben's work in which they determine that the importance of patent protection is a key determinant of economic growth. Moreover, they note that there is a stronger effect from a robust patent system in open economies than in closed economies.[219] Augmenting this point is a recent study that suggests that weak patent protection is itself a barrier to trade.[220]

Increased patent rights stimulate investors and businesses inside and outside of a country to undertake activity beneficial to the country.[221] Because patents protect innovation, even smaller developing countries can benefit from a strong patent regime since such a regime will help to establish a pro-invention culture in the domestic industry of such a country.[222] A study of developing countries on the higher end of the development spectrum, such as the Philippines, Argentina and Turkey, suggests that such countries must protect IP in order to encourage the rapid development of long-term innovative abilities.[223] In the 13 years since the publication of the study, the countries in the surveyed group that have seen the greatest technological innovation are the very ones that created strong patent systems, for example, Mexico and South Korea.[224]

In contrast to a strong patent system, a weak patent system, or one that fails to protect patents at all, will have a chilling effect on local scientific and technological capabilities. Scientists and engineers may abandon their home countries in search of stronger IP systems so as to pursue their innovations in more hospitable settings. There is no incentive to innovate in countries where innovators cannot protect their work product from copycats. Copycat companies keep these countries from developing a robust technology-related sector in their country. One author notes that highly educated graduates in developing countries often do not have technologically sophisticated businesses, universities or other research institutes in which to continue innovative high technology work that one can more easily find in the developed world.[225] Establishing such institutions is costly.[226] Perhaps a quicker means to establishing such institutions is to attract high technology firms to a developing country. Since the only way that a high technology company will share its technology with a developing country is if a strong IP (and particularly patent) system is in place, this will affect the business decision to transfer technology to the country.[227] Moreover, a weak patent system has a chilling effect on the return of technologically skilled nationals who have studied or worked abroad in the developed world.[228] Information from India suggests that despite the fact that about 2%–3% of the world total of scientific papers originate in India, the number of scientists engaged in industrial research there is low and did not increase between 1977 and 1982 – a period when industrial research was expanding globally.[229]

Another benefit of heightened patent protection is the incentive it provides to public-private partnerships in university-based research. Private companies tend only to invest the sums needed to spur research in universities when they can gain the exclusive rights to the research. This insight has been borne out in practice in the US.[230] By 1992, some $3–$5 billion of US GDP originated from university licenced products. Canada, Europe and Japan also have shown that a more robust patent system increases the number of technology transfers from universities to private companies that exploit the research to the benefit of national economies.[231] In contrast, too often in developing countries, potentially useful research contributes only to the university library and not to the economy of the country.[232] The key to facilitating this type of technology transfer is, again, a robust patent protection system.

Creation of Venture Capital Opportunities

Venture capital is an area that is encouraged by a strong patent regime. Venture capital is financing that comes from firms that invest in young and rapidly growing companies. Venture capitalism is particularly important as a source of funding for start-up companies.[233] In the US, private equity funds, which include firms specialising in venture capital, have expanded from $150 billion in 2012, to roughly $281 billion in 2022.[234] "Private equity-led bids for listed companies in Europe hit a record $73 billion in the first six months of this year [2022] to date, more than double volumes of $35 billion in the same period last year and representing 37% of overall private equity buyouts in the region, according to Dealogic data." .[235] In the US, venture capital alone accounted for $135.65 billion of private equity in 2019, up from $26.59 billion in 2009.[236]

In the developing world, the amount of venture capital available is smaller. In part, this is a result of a weak IP system. A strong IP system is crucial to the success of venture capital and encourages the creation of venture capital investment in fledgling technology industries. Venture capital fills a void that larger institutions cannot fill, as it serves as an intermediary between investors searching for high returns and entrepreneurs seeking funding. Consequently, venture capitalists require a higher return than other investments because of the more risky nature of the endeavour. Venture capitalists therefore structure their deals to minimise risk and maximise returns.[237] Private funds only will seek out new technologies and innovations if the risk of that creation being copied is very low. Otherwise, the risk on a return will be too great to make the venture viable, given that many enterprises can list their innovation as their only significant asset. If the innovation cannot be protected, there is little chance that a venture capital firm would incur the risk of investment since the collateral for the investment could be easily copied, and thereby rendered worthless. The theory is born out in figures from countries that have stronger IP regimes. For example, as of 2021 there are 166 venture capital firms in South Korea operating over 1,800 venture capital funds with nearly 7.7 trillion won ($5.6 billion; €5.5 billion; £4.8 billion) invested.[238]

The Case for a Strong Patent Regime in Developing Countries

Developing countries have traditionally argued in favour of a weak patent regime.[239] Previously, one could explain the level of patent protection in relation to the economic development of a country. The greater the level of economic development, the higher the protection a country afforded to its patent regime.[240] However, since the early 1980s, this traditional understanding has not held up as patent protection in the aggregate has increased worldwide, even with regard to developing countries.[241] Moreover, the TRIPS agreement, when put into effect, raised the level of patent protection in many developing countries.[242] Perhaps it is therefore not surprising that since the 1980s, IP rights have grown with regard to a country's output in international transactions of goods and services. Between 1980 and 1994, the amount of knowledge-intensive or high technology products as a percentage of the trade in goods worldwide has doubled from 12% to 24%.[243] As patent rights increase the range of traded goods through innovation, this may stimulate the development of technological capabilities in developing countries.[244] One recent study finds that the impact of patent protection enhances growth the more open a country is to trade.[245] Therefore, developing countries removing their trade barriers and creating stronger patent regimes generate greater economic growth.

Some developing countries have argued that strong patent regimes only have helped developed countries because foreign companies displace domestic producers of pharmaceuticals. The evidence does not seem to support this position. In 1978, Italy adopted a system of full patent protection, replacing a system without any patent protection. A study undertaken ten years later revealed that local manufacturers actually increased their market share by 5%.[246] One factor that changed in Italy, however, was the size of the surviving local firms. Thirty per cent of the companies that existed in 1978 had disappeared by 1988. Interestingly, while employment in the rest of the industry declined, employment within the pharmaceutical sector rose by 2.7%. This increase could be traced to the significant growth within R&D during this period equalling 22.8% of revenue, an almost 20% growth annually in real terms.[247] This data suggests a strong correlation that the new robust patent regime played a vital role in the growth of the pharmaceutical sector. Further, anecdotal evidence from South Korea and Mexico supports the conclusion that stronger patent systems lead to greater local R&D and greater growth within the pharmaceutical sector.[248] In Mexico, US R&D into the Mexican pharmaceutical market has doubled since the adoption of a strong Mexican patent law.[249]

One recent study by Lanjouw and Cockburn sheds light on some of the empirical issues in this debate.[250] They suggest that more important than legal change itself is whether or not firms believe that legal changes will be implemented and how effective the new system will be.[251] In this way, some international investment into countries with low patent rights can be explained as a belief by firms that these countries were serious about the future enforcement of laws they were in the process of enacting. They offer India as an example of where patent applications doubled in 1995, the year before the TRIPS agreement was signed, strengthening protections there.[252]

Investment and Technology in the Developing World

Local capital seems even more dependent than foreign capital on a strong IP system because of the greater mobility of foreign capital to invest in projects that have a higher return and less risk. As one study notes, local capital has fewer options than its foreign counterpart especially in areas where R&D is necessary for originating its products or services, either through local R&D or through the acquisition of foreign R&D.[253] Certain types of diseases are less profitable for drug manufacturers to research because they affect either a smaller group of people or the group cannot afford the drug even if it were to go on the market. Many of such drugs would combat tropical diseases which disproportionately affect the developing world.

These diseases could be treated by the so-called orphan drugs,[254] but only if there is an incentive to innovate and develop these drugs. In the US, the incentives for companies to develop these drugs were increased by passage of the Orphan Drug Act.[255] Before 1983, there were only ten drugs for rare diseases approved by the US FDA. In the decade after passage of the Orphan Drug Act, 99 drugs were approved, and 189 were reported to be under clinical testing.[256] The Orphan Drug Act allowed seven years of market exclusivity for drugs where the target population was fewer than 200,000 patients.[257] Perhaps the most well-known drug that would not have been developed for market but for the Orphan Drug Act is the anti-AIDS treatment AZT.[258]

If drug manufacturers have no economic incentive to work on the R&D of tropical disease remedies, then it is the poor of the developing world who will suffer. The weak IP regime that creates disincentives for R&D further creates an important negative externality upon world health.[259] Lanjouw notes that the strengthening of IP rights appeared to be stimulating domestic R&D in countries that previously had weak protections.[260] Lanjouw demonstrates the belief that TRIPS would be taken seriously led firms to take greater interest in tropical disease research.[261] This was a departure from previous firm practice of doing very little research into tropical diseases because, in India, for example, the weak patent system would not have allowed firms to recoup the cost of their investments.[262] As the study concludes in the case of malaria research, "it is hard to avoid the conclusion that the historical absence of IPRs played an important role in retarding the development for this important disease."[263]

In the past, many in developing countries have argued that a weak patent regime was necessary to create and increase the size of domestic pharmaceutical firms.[264] This policy may have worked in some countries such as Argentina and India.[265] In Brazil, the absence of controls was not in itself sufficient to boost the market share of Brazilian pharmaceutical companies.[266] Even if in general this is true, there are two important responses. First, the growth of domestic industries did not necessarily help consumers, which will be addressed later in the chapter.[267] Second, even if it helped infant industries in the past, these domestic industries are strong enough to compete in the world today and many do so by exporting abroad. India and Argentina provide examples. At their current stage of development, in the long term, both companies and their home countries in the developing world will be hurt by programmes that protect these industries since they retard high technology growth in the home country. If anything, IP rights should be seen as a tool for development in countries because of the increase in the technology base from funding, local research and the introduction of technology that produces economic growth.[268] Copying the work of others makes it more difficult for firms to innovate on their own since they too will merely copy the work of others. This means that they are generally not first movers in science and technology. Should technology become more difficult to copy as it gets more complex, it would further set back the domestic industry from the world leaders. Jeffrey Sachs notes:

> In the poorest countries, it is possible to have economic growth without much innovation because they can borrow or import technology. However in a country like Argentina, that has a high level of revenues, progress really requires a much larger community of innovation.[269]

In countries where innovation could lead to great results because of an educated workforce, a lack of patent protection is therefore particularly damaging.

Excluding IP Violating Imports: Section 337 and the Trade/IP/Antitrust Interface[270]

There is one provision of US law, Section 337 of the Tariff Act of 1930, administered by the US International Trade Commission (ITC), that is directed at anticompetitive and other harmful business conduct affecting American imports. Section 337 condemns as illegal imports that violate US IP rights related to a US industry or involve "unfair methods of competition and unfair acts" that cause harm to a US industry. In recent decades, almost all Section 337 cases have involved violations of US IP rights, especially patents. Section 337 authorises (subject to certain public policy exceptions) the exclusion of imports that violate the US IP rights, including patents. In light of this, aggrieved US patent holders, who fear that they will not be granted an injunction by a US court,[271] have been flocking more and more to the ITC, in the hope of obtaining exclusion orders against infringing imports. Although Section 337 has very seldom been used to attack anticompetitive conduct, there were some signs in 2021 of a heightened interest in invoking its "unfair methods of competition" language to bring antitrust charges against foreign producers that export to the US.[272]

Section 337 has an accepted role in protecting the interests of US IP holders from infringing imports. Its expansion into a quasi-antitrust statute could, however, raise real substantive problems for free trade. By its terms, Section 337 focuses on harms to the US industries, not to consumers, an approach at odds with the consumer welfare focus of contemporary American antitrust law. Thus, there is a risk that the ITC could apply its "unfair method of competition" provision in a manner favouring producer, not consumer, welfare. This could, in turn, lead to ITC exclusion orders that effectively condemned efficiency-promoting, cost-reducing foreign business practices, thereby interfering with beneficial trade – an undesirable protectionist outcome, which could spark international trade frictions. It is to be hoped that Section 337 will not be applied in such a welfare-reducing manner.[273]

The argument that the protection of IP rights is crucial as it is a subcategory of property rights still needs to be remade. As a result of the COVID-19 crisis, many have called for compulsory licencing of the patents for COVID vaccines. Although this has been limited to COVID vaccines in the case of many of its advocates, there is an undercurrent that it is the underlying IP system that is preventing the release of these products especially into developing country markets. However as noted above, the reasons for the lack of progress in this area are more related to with issues that have nothing to do with IP such as ACMDs at the distribution level, or transportation monopolies or restrictions. Indeed set against the fact that diluting IP protection would have a negligible impact on distribution of vaccines, the cost of such an action on the development of future pharmaceuticals and indeed COVID-19 or other similar zoonotic disease vaccines would be significant.

The Rise of Geographical Indications

Recently, the EU in particular has pushed for geographical indications to be recognised and protected in trade agreements. Geographical indications give protection to certain products which are produced in particular locations, for example, Champagne from the Champagne region of France or Parma ham from Parma, and so on. They are different from IP because the indication comes from a geography not a particular act of labour or work as in the case of other IP where it is the work done that grounds the right. Indeed, the same work can be done in other locations (such as Swiss-style cheese manufacturers in Wisconsin whose families are descended from regions of Switzerland and use the same techniques which those farmers used to produce an "Emmental" cheese, for example). This has understandably become a battle between farmers in the "old world" (Europe) and the "new world" (the US, Australia, New Zealand and South Africa for wine, for example). The EU is now including a range of geographical indications in its trade agreements, which will be opposed by the "new world" countries. Interestingly in the UK-EU withdrawal agreement, geographical indications were included by the EU (and not in the FTA which would have been more expected), so that the notion of protection of GIs is embedded in the EU-UK relationship. This will make the UK negotiation of trade agreements with other countries especially CPTPP accession and any FTA with the US more complicated.

Conclusion

We have demonstrated in Chapter 9 the vital link between trade, competition and property rights. In Chapter 10, we have focused our attention on an aspect of those property rights, IP. IP has taken an even greater significance now than it had in the past because of the volume of tradable goods whose value is dependent on IP rights. The protection in IPRs is a vital way of ensuring a competitive market with consumer-welfare-enhancing outcomes.

Notes

1 I draw in this chapter on a number of articles that I have written, in particular, Shanker A. Singham, *Competition Policy and the Stimulation of Transaction: TRIPS and the Interface between Competition and Patent Protection in the Pharmaceutical Industry*, 26 Brook Int'l L. J. 363 (2001).
2 Richard Posner and William Landes, *The Economic Structure of Intellectual Property Law* (Belknap Press, 2003), at 11.
3 *See Competition Policy and the Stimulation of Transaction, supra* note 1, at 1.
4 The next section is drawn from *Competition Policy and the Stimulation of Transaction, supra* note 1.
5 Aristotle, *The Politics, Book II* (Carnes Lord trans., 1985) (c. 350 B.C.E), at 72.
6 Wolfgang E. Siebeck et al., *Strengthening Protection of Intellectual Property in Developing Countries: A Survey of the Literature* WDP-112, World Bank (1990), at 77.
7 US Const. art. I, §8.
8 *See* Kenneth W. Dam, *Economic Underpinnings of Patent Law*, 23 J. L. Stud. 247 (1994).
9 Seminal work in this area was conducted by Kenneth Arrow. *See generally* Kenneth W. Arrow, *Economic Welfare and the Allocation of Resources for Invention*, in The Rate and Direction of Inventive Activity: Economic and Social Factors (Richard R. Nelson ed., Princeton University Press, 2015), at 609.
10 Frank Easterbrook, *Cyberspace versus Property Law*, 4 Tex. Rev. L. Pol. 103, 106 (1999).
11 Trademarks are a partial exception to this statement. If a trademark is properly asserted and protected, and if it retains its distinctive role as an indication of source, it may have an indefinite life.
12 United States v. E. I. du Pont de Nemours & Co., 351 U.S. 377 (1956).

13 Daniel Spulber, *The Case for Patents* (World Scientific, 2021), at 39.
14 *The Economic Structure of Intellectual Property Law, supra* note 2, at 374; *see* also Maureen K. Ohlhausen, *Patent Rights in a Climate of Intellectual Property Skepticism*, 30 Harv J. L. Tech. 103 (1976) (describing empirical work suggesting that a strong patent system spurs innovation and economic welfare).
15 Illinois Tool Works Inc. v. Independent Ink, Inc., 547 U.S. 28 (2006), 45–46. ("Congress, the antitrust enforcement agencies, and most economists have all reached the conclusion that a patent does not necessarily confer market power upon the patentee. Today, we reach the same conclusion.")
16 *Antitrust Guidelines for the Licensing of Intellectual Property*, US Department of Justice and the Federal Trade Commission (2017).
17 *Competition and Monopoly: Single-Firm Conduct Under Section 2 of the Sherman Act*, US Department of Justice (2008), at 86. ("The ability to price-discriminate often allows firms to increase output. More consumers can be served when firms charge higher prices for customers that value a product highly and lower prices for those that value the product less.")
18 Atari Games Corp. v. Nintendo of Am., Inc., 897 F.2d 1572 (Fed. Cir. 1990), 1576 ("[T]he aims and objectives of patent and antitrust laws may seem, at first glance, wholly at odds. However, the two bodies of law are actually complementary, as both are aimed at encouraging innovation, industry and competition"); *see* also Intergraph Corp. v. Intel Corp., 195 F.3d 1346 (Fed. Cir. 1999), 1362. ("The patent and antitrust laws are complementary, the patent system serving to encourage invention and the bringing of new products to market by adjusting investment-based risk, and the antitrust laws serving to foster industrial competition.")
19 Marrakesh Agreement Establishing the World Trade Organization, 1994, Annex 1C – Agreement on Trade-Related Aspects of Intellectual Property Rights, art. 10.
20 *Id.*, art. 14.
21 *Id.*, art. 15(a).
22 *Id.*, art. 26(3).
23 Paris Convention for the Protection of Industrial Property, as amended 28 Sep 1979.
24 *Id.*
25 For a fuller list, *see The Economic Structure of Intellectual Property Law, supra* note 2.
26 *Id.*, at 66.
27 *Id.*, at 55.
28 *Id.*, at 216.
29 *Id.*, at 242–243.
30 *See* Matt Hourihan, AAAS, *A Snapshot of US R&D Competitiveness: 2020 Update* (2 Oct 2020), https://www.aaas.org/news/snapshot-us-rd-competitiveness-2020-update.
31 *Id.*
32 *See Research and Development in the Pharmaceutical Industry,* Congressional Budget Office (2021).
33 *See* Alan M. Fisch, *Compulsory Licensing of Pharmaceutical Patents: An Unreasonable Solution to an Unfortunate Problem*, 34 Jurimetrics 295, 302–303 (1994).
34 *See id.* at 303.
35 *See* Boston Consulting Group, *Sustaining Innovation, in US Pharmaceuticals Intellectual Property Protection and The Role of Patents* (1996), Mimeo. A study by the Office of Technology Assessment estimated that cost of a new drug was $359 million in pre-tax 1990 dollars for drugs that first entered human testing in the period 1970–1982, when drugs were less complex than they are today. *See Pharmaceutical R&D: Costs, Risks, Rewards*, Office of Technology Assessment (Feb 1993).
36 Henry G. Grabowski and John M. Vernon, *Returns to R&D on New Drug Introductions in the 1980s*, 13 J. Health Econ. 238 (1994).
37 *Id.*
38 Frederic M. Scherer, *Pricing, Profits, and Technological Progress in the Pharmaceutical Industry*, 7 J. Econ. Persp J. ECON PERSP. 86, 97 (1993).

39 *See Strengthening Protection of Intellectual Property in Developing Countries*, *supra* note 6, at 103.
40 *See Returns to R&D on New Drug Introductions in the 1980s*, *supra* note 36. Earlier studies show how the pharmaceutical industry is particularly dependent on the protection of patent rights. *See also* Christopher T. Taylor and Z. Aubrey Silberston, *The Economic Impact of the Patent System* (Cambridge University Press, 1973); Frederic M. Scherer, *The Economic Effect of Compulsory Patent Licensing* (New York University, 1977); Edwin Mansfield, *Patents and Innovation: An Empirical Study*, 32 Mgmt. Sci. 173 (1986); Richard C. Levin et al., *Appropriating the Returns from Industrial R&D*, 3 Brookings Pap. Econ. Act. 783 (1987); *See* generally Martin N. Baily, *Research and Development Costs and Returns: The US Pharmaceutical Industry*, 6 J. Pol. Econ. 232 (Feb 1972) (Baily was among the first to show the relationship that the profit of pharmaceutical companies was linked to the number of patents issued to it because of the correlation between the returns on profits based on the patented drugs).
41 *See Patents and Innovation: An Empirical Study, id.* (Mansfield used a random sample of 100 firms from 12 industries in the US, and reports that 65% of the innovations generated by pharmaceutical firms from 1981 to 1983 would not have been marketed, and 60% would not have been developed, if patent protection had not been available. The corresponding figures for companies in the next two highest industries were considerably lower. In the chemical industry, 30% of the innovations would not have been marketed and 38% would not have been developed. The petroleum industry ranked a distant third with 18% and 25%, respectively.)
42 A McKinsey study on the pharmaceutical industry in India notes that multinational corporations limited their involvement in the Indian drug market after the adoption of the weak patent system in 1970. Some stopped selling drugs that were priced too low, while many multinationals limited the portfolio of products they sold in India to only patent expired products. *See* Rajesh Garg et al., *Four Opportunities in India's Pharmaceutical Market*, 4 McKinsey Q. 132 (1996).
43 *See, e.g.*, "Moderna's Patent Estate: Messenger RNA Technologies (mRNA) & Delivery Technologies," moderna (2021), https://www.modernatx.com/mrna-technology/modernas-intellectual-property; Daniel Shores et al., "The mRNA IP and Competitive Landscape, A Three Part Series," Rothwell Figg (11 Apr 2021).
44 *Research and Development: US Trends and International Comparisons*, National Science Board, National Science Foundation (2020), at 7.
45 Jonathan M. Barnett, Innovators, Firms, and Markets: The Organizational Logic of Intellectual Property (2021), at 135–136. (Barnett notes the criticism that patent pools are merely responses to transaction cost-increasing patent thickets but he explains that those critics implicitly support weaker patent protection, which would threaten dynamic innovation.)
46 Pulled from *Competition Policy and the Stimulation of Transaction*, *supra* note 1.
47 *See* Edmund Kitch, *The Nature and Function of the Patent System*, 20 J. L. ECON. 265 (1977).
48 *See id.*
49 *See* Carlos A. Primo Braga, Carsten Fink and Claudia Paz Sepulveda, *Intellectual Property Rights and Economic Development*, TechNet Working Paper, Institute for Agriculture & Trade Policy (2000).
50 *Violations of Intellectual Property Rights: How Do We Protect American Ingenuity?: Hearing before the H. Comm. on Int'l Rel.*, 106th Cong. 5–11 (testimony of Hon. Richard Fisher, Deputy US Trade Representative).
51 *See* Jean O. Lanjouw and Iain Cockburn, *Do Patents Matter?: Empirical Evidence after GATT*, Working Paper 7495 National Bureau of Economic Research (January 2000), at 5.
52 *See* Ashish Arora, *Contracting for Tacit Knowledge: The Provision of Technical Services in Technology Licensing Contracts*, 50 J. Dev. Econ. 233 (1996).

53 *See* Claude E. Barfield and Mark A. Groomberg, *Parallel Trade in the Pharmaceutical Industry: Implications for Innovation, Consumer Welfare and Health Policy*, 10 Fordham Intell. Prop. Media Eng. L. J. 185, 203 (1999).
54 *See* F. M. Scherer, *The Value of Patents and Other Legally Protected Commercial Rights: Panel Discussion*, 53 Antitrust L. J. 535, 547 (1985).
55 The following summary of the patent system's benefits is drawn from the seminal work, The Case for Patents, *supra* note 13, at 3–4.
56 *Id.*, at 4–5.
57 US Department of Justice and the Federal Trade Commission, "Antitrust Guidelines for the Licensing of Intellectual Property," supra (12 Jan 2017), https://www.justice.gov/atr/IPguidelines/download.
58 *See Do Patents Matter?, supra* note at 51, at 10.
59 *Id.*
60 *Antitrust Guidelines for the Licensing of Intellectual Property, supra* note 16.
61 *Id.*, at 4 ("The Agencies will not presume that a patent, copyright, or trade secret necessarily confers market power upon its owner. Although the intellectual property right confers the power to exclude with respect to the specific product, process, or work in question, there will often be sufficient actual or potential close substitutes for such product, process, or work to prevent the exercise of market power.") (citation omitted).
62 *See* Mark Whitener, *Potential Competition Theory - Forgotten but Not Gone*, 5 Antitrust 17 (1991).
63 *Id.*
64 *See id.*
65 *See Overview of FTC Actions in Pharmaceutical Products and Distribution*, Federal Trade Commission (2020), at 62–72.
66 Ciba-Geigy, Ltd./Sandoz, C-3725, FTC File No. 9610055 (final order issued March 24, 1997).
67 Bristol-Myers Squibb Company/Celgene Corporation, C-4690, FTC File No. 191-0061, (final order issued January 13, 2020).
68 *Report of the Panel* in *Canada – Patent Production of Pharmaceutical Products*, WT/DS114/R (00–1012), World Trade Organization (2000).
69 For counter-view of non-discrimination principle, *see* Brian Kahin, *Through The Lens of Intangibles: What Patents on Software and Services Reveal About the System*, Proceedings of the OECD Conference on Patents, Innovation and Economic Performance, 28–29 August 2003, Organization of Economic Co-operation and Development (2003).
70 *See* Dan L. Burk and Mark A. Lemley, *Policy Levers in Patent Law*, 89 Va. L. Rev. 1576 (2003).
71 *Report of the Appellate Body* in *Canada – Term of Patent Protection*, AB-2000–7, WT/DS170/AB/R (00–3564), World Trade Organization (2000).
72 *See* Robert M. Sherwood, *The TRIPS Agreement: Implications for Developing Countries*, 37 IDEA 491 (1997), at 498.
73 *See* G. Jori, *The Impact of Pharmaceutical Patents – The Italian Experience,* in Protection of Intellectual Property Rights: The Case of the Pharmaceutical Industry in Argentina (Fundacion de Investigaciones Economicas Latinamericana 1990), at 62.
74 *See* Julia Nogues, *Patents and Pharmaceutical Drugs: Understanding the Pressures on Developing Countries,* WPS Paper 18, World Bank (1990); The Economic Impact of the Patent System, *supra* note 40; Henry Grabowski and John Vernon, *Longer Patents for Lower Imitation Barriers: The 1984 Drug Act*, 2 Am. Econ. Rev. 76, 195–198 (1986) (examining the U.B. drug market).
75 *See Patents and Pharmaceutical Drugs, id.*
76 *See* Janet H. MacLaughlin et al., *The Economic Significance of Piracy, in* Intellectual Property Rights: Global Consensus, Global Conflict (R. Michael Gadbaw and Timothy J. Richards eds., 1988), at 89.

77 *See Strengthening Protection of Intellectual Property in Developing Countries, supra* note 6, at 56.
78 *See* Guntram Rahn, *The Role of Industrial Property in Economic Development: The Japanese Experience*, 14 Int'l Rev. Ind. Prop. Copyright L. 449 (1983).
79 Jean O. Lanjouw, *The Introduction of Pharmaceutical Product Patents in India: "Heartless Exploitation of the Poor and Suffering?,"* Working Paper 6366, National Bureau of Economic Research (1998), at 9. jouw, *supra* note 84, at 9.
80 *See id.*
81 *See id.*
82 *See id.*, at 10.
83 *See id.*, at 30.
84 *See* Keith E. Maskus, *Regulatory Standards in the WTO: Comparing Intellectual Property Rights with Competition Policy, Environmental Protection and Core Labour Standards*, 1 World Trade Rev. 135 (2002), at 5; *The TRIPS Agreement: Implications for Developing Countries, supra* note 72, at 500 (noting that copycat drag companies have been known to fix prices among themselves).
85 On the destructive potential of oligopolies, *see* George Stigler, *A Theory of Oligopoly*, in The Organization of Industry (George J. Stigler, ed., 1968), at 39.
86 In 2021, the US Department of Justice Antitrust Division reported having assessed hundreds of millions of dollars in fines in price-fixing cases brought against multiple producers of essential drugs used by millions of American consumers. Division Update Spring 2021, Generic Drugs Investigation Targets Anticompetitive Schemes, 24 March, 2021, https://www.justice.gov/atr/division-operations/division-update-spring-2021/generic-drugs-investigation-targets-anticompetitive-schemes.
87 *See Compulsory Licensing of Pharmaceutical Patents, supra* note 33.
88 *See id.*
89 *See, e.g.*, Robert Weissman, *Long, Strange Trips: The Pharmaceutical Industry Drive to Harmonize Global Intellectual Property Rules, and the Remaining WTO Legal Alternatives Available to Third World Countries*, 17 U. Pa. J. Int'l L. 1069 (1996); A. Samuel Oddi, *TRIPS-Natural Rights and a "Polite Form of Economic Imperialism,"* 29 Vand. J. Transnat'l L. 415 (1996).
90 *See* Marrakesh Agreement Establishing the World Trade Organization, 15 Apr 1994, General Agreement on Trade in Services, art. 17 ("GATS Agreement"); General Agreement on Tariffs and Trade, 30 Oct 1947, 61 Stat. A-11, T.I.A.S. 1700, art, 3, para. 4 ("GATT Agreement").
91 Paul K. Gorecki, *Regulating the Price of Prescription Drugs in Canada: Compulsory Licensing, Product Selection, and Governmental Reimbursement Programs*, Economic Council of Canada (1981), as cited *in* Gianna Julian-Arnold, *International Compulsory Licensing: The Rationales and Reality*, 33 IDEA 349 (1993), at 349.
92 *See Id.*, at 357.
93 *The TRIPS Agreement: Implications for Developing Countries, supra* note 72, at 276-7
94 *See International Compulsory Licensing: The Rationales and Reality, supra* note 91, at 364; *See also* Juan Aznarez, "Los medicamentos nacionales, más caros," La Nacion (28 May 1999), (Argentina) (offering evidence that copied products in Argentina sell at a higher price than even the products of the multinational pharmaceutical firms that have patented the product elsewhere).
95 *International Compulsory Licensing: The Rationales and Reality, supra* note 91, at 362.
96 *See id.*, at 363.
97 *See* Pub. No. 332-302, *Global Competitiveness of US Advanced Technology Manufacturing Industries: Pharmaceuticals*, Pub. No. 332-302, US Int'l Trade Comm'n (1991), at 3–15, as cited *in Compulsory Licensing of Pharmaceutical Patents, supra* note 33, at 315).
98 *Id.*

99 *Id.*
100 *See* "The Crippled Continent," Medecins Sans Frontieres (2 Dec 2000), https://www.msf.org/crippled-continent.
101 *See* Joelie Tanguy, "Treating AIDS," NY Times (6 Jul 2000), https://www.nytimes.com/2000/07/06/opinion/l-treating-aids-081515.html.
102 *Id.*
103 *Id.*
104 *See* Carmen Pérez-Casas et al., *HIV/AIDS Medicines Pricing Report – Setting Objections: Is There A Political Will?*, Medecins Sans Frontieres (2000).
105 *Id.*
106 *International Activities Report*, Medecins Sans Frontieres (1999).
107 *See Do Patents Matter?, supra* note 51, at 29.
108 *See Do Patents Matter?, supra* note 51, at 29.
109 Jillian Clare Cohen, *The LAC Pharmaceutical Sector,* World Bank (2000).
110 *See id.*
111 *See id.*
112 *See id.* A more in-depth study of the type of policies that will reduce costs through better administration and procurement can be found in Jillian Claire Cohen, *Public Policies in the Pharmaceutical Sector: A Case Study of Brazil,* LCSHD Paper Series No. 54, World Bank (2000).
113 *See* Wynne S. Carvill and Douglas D. Leeds, *Antitrust Issues in Management of Intellectual Property*, 483 PLI/Pat 59.
114 See SCM Corp. v. Xerox Corp., 645 F2d 1195, 1203 (2d Cir. 1981); Eastman Kodak v. Image Tech. Srvs., Inc., 504 US 451 (1992).
115 Dawson Chem. Co. v. Rohm & Haas Co., 448 US 176, 215 (1980).
116 James B. Koback, Jr., Antitrust Treatment of Refusals to License Intellectual Property, 566 PLI/Pat 517, 533. As the Court stated in Eastman Kodak Co. v. Image Technical Services, Inc., 504 US 451, 479 (1992), "The Court has held many times that power gained through some natural and legal advantage such as a patent, copyright, or business acumen can give rise to liability if 'a seller exploits his dominant position in one market to expand his empire into the next'" (Citing Times Picayune Pubrg Co. v. US , 345 US 594, 611 (1953)). It is important to note that on its own, dominating a market is not punishable. In fact, it is rewarded. See US v. Grinell Corp., 384 US 563, 570 (1966) (noting that it is not unlawful for a competitor to become a monopolist by virtue of a superior product, business acumen or historical accident).
117 Areeda and Hovenkamp, Antitrust Law (rev. 1996), vol. III, §705.
118 *See id.* Vol. III, §704.
119 *See* Alden F. Abbott, General Council, Federal Trade Commission, *The IP-Antitrust Interface: An FTC Perspective,* Keynote Address, IP Watchdog CON 2020 Virtual Conference (17 Sep 2020), https://www.ftc.gov/system/files/documents/public_statements/1581598/abbott_ip_watchdog_speech_09-17-20.pdf.
120 *See* Jack Kaufmann, *Symposium: Antitrust and the Suppression of Technology in the United States and Europe: Is There a Remedy?*, 66 Antitrust L. J. 527, 529 (1998).
121 Brain Coggio, Sushil Lyer, and Cheryl Wang, "Overview of Approaches to Compulsory Licensing," JDSUPRA (20 May 2020), https://www.jdsupra.com/legalnews/overview-of-approaches-to-compulsory-69989/.
122 *See* Patricia A Martone et al., *The Patent Misuse Defense - Does it Still have Vitality?*, 566 PLI/Pat 547 (2000), at 552.
123 Princo Corp. v. Internationl Trade Com'n., 616 F,3d 1318 (Fed. Cir. 2010), cert. denied, 131 S.Ct. 2480 (2011).
124 *See Antitrust Issues in Management of Intellectual Property, supra* note 113, at 89.
125 Senga-Gel Corp. v. Seiffhart, 803 F.2d 661, 668 (Fed. Cir. 1986).
126 *See Antitrust Issues in Management of Intellectual Property, supra* note 113, at 88.
127 *See id.*

128 *See id.*
129 Herbert Hovenkamp, *Federal Antitrust Policy: The Law of Competition and its Practice* (6th ed., 2020), at 308.
130 Zenith Radio Corp. v. Hazeltine Research, Inc., 395 US 100, 140 (1969).
131 See *The Patent Misuse Defense - Does it Still have Vitality?*, *supra* note 122, at 554.
132 *See id.*
133 *See id.*, at 555.
134 Windsurfing Int'1 Inc. v. AMP, Inc., 782 F.2d 995, 1001–02 (Fed. Cir. 1986).
135 See Mallinckrodt, Inc. v. Medipart, Inc., 976 F.2d 700, 708 (Fed. Cir. 1992).
136 *Id.*, at 706.
137 *See* discussion, *infra* Section IX.
138 *Report of the Panel*, *supra* note 68, at 171.
139 See Patent Reform Act, 1988 S271(d); In re Indep. Serv. Orgs. Antitrust Litig., 203 F.3d 1322 (Fed. Cir. 2000) (hereinafter Xerox litigation).
140 Federal Trade Commission v. Qualcomm Inc., No. 19–16122, (9th Cir., 11 Aug 2020).
141 Verizon Communications, Inc. v. Law Office of Curtis v. Trinko, LLP, 540 US 398 (2004).
142 *See* S. Pac. Communications Co. v. AT&T Co., 740 F.2d 980 (D.C. Cir.1984). The FTC has, however, imposed de facto compulsory licencing terms in a handful of consent decrees involving controls over standard essential patents by a monopolist. *Strengthening Protection of Intellectual Property in Developing Countries, supra* note 6.
143 *See* Data Gen. Corp. v. Grumman Sys. Support Corp., 36 F.3d 1147 (1st Cir. 1994).
144 *See* Image Technical Servs., Inc. v. Eastman Kodak Co., 125 F.3d 1195 (9th Cir. 1997).
145 *Id.*
146 Xerox Litigation, *supra* note 159.
147 eBay Inc. v. MercExchange, L.L.C., 547 US 388 (2006).
148 Intergraph Corp. v. Intel Corp., 3 F. Supp. 2d 1255 (N.D. Ala. 1998).
149 *Id.*, at 1289.
150 *Id.*, at 1267.
151 *Id.*, at 1267–1268.
152 *Id.*, at 1259.
153 *Id.*, at 1277.
154 Intergraph Corp. v. Intel Corp., 195 F.3d 1346, 1358 (9th Cir. 1999).
155 MCI Communications Corp. v. Am. Tel. and Tel. Co., 708 F.2d 1081, 1132 (7th Cir. 1983).
156 *Id.*, at 1132–1133.
157 Verizon Communications, Inc. v. Law Office of Curtis v. Trinko, LLP, 540 US 398 (2004).
158 Federal Antitrust Policy, *supra* note 129, at 406.
159 Marrakesh Agreement Establishing the World Trade Organization, 15 Apr 1994, Agreement on Trade-Related Aspects of Intellectual Property Rights, Annex IC, (*hereinafter* "TRIPS Agreement").
160 *Id.* Art. 31.
161 *See id.* Art. 31(a)–(i).
162 *Id.* Art. 31.
163 *Id.* Art. 40.
164 *Id.*
165 *Id.* Art. 40, para. 2.
166 *See Communication from the European Community and its Member States on the Relationship between the Trade-Related Aspects of Intellectual Property Rights and Competition Policy, and between Investment and Competition Policy*, WT/WGTCP/W/99 (98–3720), World Trade Organization (1998).
167 *Id.*
168 *Id.*

169 Twin Labs, Inc. v. Weider Health & Fitness, 900 F.2d 566 (2d Cir. 1990).
170 *See* Antitrust Law, *supra* note 117, (Supp. 1988), §736.2.
171 Decision and Order, In the Matter of Intel Corp., Docket No. 9341, Federal Trade Commission (2010).
172 *See id.*
173 *See id.*
174 William J. Baer, *Antitrust Enforcement and High Technology Markets*, Remarks before the American Bar Association Sections of Business Law, Litigation, and Tort and Insurance Practice, San Francisco, California, American Bar Association (12 Nov 1998).
175 Robert P. Taylor, *Intellectual Property As "Essential Facility,"* Address at the American Bar Association Practicing Law Institute Seminar on Intellectual Property and Antitrust, San Francisco, California, American Bar Association (20–21 July 2000).
176 MCI Communications Corp. v. AT&T Co., 708 F.2d 1081, at 1132.
177 *See* Dawson Chem. Co. v. Rohm & Haas Co., 948 US 176, 215 (1980).
178 *See Parallel Trade in the Pharmaceutical Industry, supra* note 53, at 185.
179 *See id. See also* National Economic Research Associates, *The Economic Consequences of the Choice of Regime of Exhaustion in the Area of Trademarks* (8 Feb 1999).
180 *Parallel Trade in the Pharmaceutical Industry, supra* note 53, at 187.
181 *Id.*
182 M. L. Burstall and Ian S. T. Senior, *Undermining Innovation: Parallel Trade in Prescription Medicines* (1992), at 22, as cited *in Parallel Trade in the Pharmaceutical Industry, supra* note 53, at 251.
183 *Survey of Parallel Trade*, National Economic Research Associates (NERA) (1997), at 25, as cited *in Parallel Trade in the Pharmaceutical Industry, supra* note 53, at 251.
184 US v. Univis Lens Co., 316 US 241, 249 (1942) (noting, "[b]ut merely because the licensee takes the final step in the manufacture of the patented product, by doing work on the blank which he has purchased from the patentee's licensee, it does not follow that the patentee can control the price at which the finished lens is sold").
185 *The Economic Consequences of the Choice of Regime in the Area of Trademarks*, National Economic Research Associates (NERA) (1999), Executive Summary at 3.
186 *Id.*
187 *Id.*
188 *Id.*, at 6–7. (The problem of counterfeit and poor quality medicines that Doctors Without Borders notes is only exacerbated by parallel trading.)
189 *See id.*
190 *See* Ethyl Gasoline Corp. v. *US*, 309 US 436 (1940).
191 *See* Case C-355/96, Silhouette International Schmied GmbH & Co v. Harlauer Handelsgesellschaft mbH, 1998 E.C.R I-4799.
192 *See Parallel Trade in the Pharmaceutical Industry, supra* note 53, at 191–193.
193 *Id.*, at 193 (citing Carsten Fink, *Does National Exhaustion of Intellectual Property Contradict the Principle of Free Trade?* 3–4, Draft Paper for Conference on Exhaustion of Intellectual Property rights and Parallel Importation in World Trade, Geneva, Switzerland (6–7 Nov 1998)).
194 *See Parallel Trade in the Pharmaceutical Industry, supra* note 53, at 224.
195 *See id.*
196 *See id.*
197 *See id.*
198 Robinson-Patman Act, 15 US G. §§13a, 13b, 21a; Sherman Act, 15 US C. §§I-6, 6a, 7.
199 Robinson-Patman Act, 15 US C. §§13a, 13b, 21a.
200 *See id.*
201 Sherman Act, 15 US C. §2.
202 *See* Federal Antitrust Policy, *supra* note 129, at 415–416. *See* Herbert Hovenkamp, Federal Antitrust Law, supra, at 415–416.
203 *See id.*

204 The COVID-19 discussion is based on "WTO, Trade and Health: WTO Response to the COVID-19 Pandemic," World Trade Organization (6 Jan 2022), https://www.wto.org/english/thewto_e/minist_e/mc12_e/briefing_notes_e/bftrade_and_health_e.htm.

205 In a surprise to most observers, the US Trade representative supported the waiver proposal, although the European Union did not.

206 *See* Gary Locke, Andrei Iancu, and David J. Kappos, *The Shot Heard Round the World: The Strategic Imperative of U.S. Covid-19 Vaccine Diplomacy*, Center for Strategic & International Studies (2021).

207 Tom Lee, American Action Forum, *Another TRIPS Waiver for COVID-19?*, Nov 14, 2022, https://www.americanactionforum.org/insight/another-trips-waiver-for-covid-19/.

208 Robert Solow, *Technical Change and the Aggregate Production Function*, 39 REV. ECON. & STAT. 312 (1957).

209 Charles Jones, *Sources of US Growth in a World of Ideas*, STAN. FAC. WORKSHOP PAPER (Sept 1999).

210 *See Strengthening Protection of Intellectual Property in Developing Countries, supra* note 6, at 56.

211 *See, e.g.*, Maureen K. Ohlhausen, *Patent Rights in a Climate of Intellectual Property Skepticism*, 30 Harv. J. L. & Tech. 103 (2016); Viju Raghupathi and Wullianallur Raghupathi, *Innovation at Country-level: Association between Economic Development and Patents*, 6 J. Innovation Entrepreneurship no. 4 (2017).

212 Edwin Mansfield, *Intellectual Property Protection, Foreign Direct Investment, and Technology Transfer: Germany, Japan and the United States* (1995) (*hereinafter* "Mansfield – Foreign Direct Investment").

213 *See Strengthening Protection of Intellectual Property in Developing Countries, supra* note 6, at 103.

214 *See* Frances Stewart, *Technology Transfer for Development*, in Science and Technology: Lessons for Development Policy (Robert E. Evenson and Gustav Ranis eds., Routledge 1990), at 301; Robert E. Lipsey, Magnus Blomström, and Irving B. Kravis, *R&D by Multinational Firms and Host Country Exports*, in Science and Technology: Lessons for Development Policy (Robert E. Evenson and Gustav Ranis eds., Routledge 1990), at 271.

215 *See Technology Transfer for Development, Id.*

216 *See* Edwin Mansfield, *Intellectual Property Protection, Foreign Direct Investment, and Technology Transfer*, International Finance Corporation Discussion Paper 19, World Bank (1994) (The study bases evidence on surveys of American, Japanese and German multinational corporations which suggests that intellectual property protection affects FDI decisions.) *See also* Kamal Saggi, *Trade Foreign Investment, and International Technology Transfer: A Survey*, Policy Research Working Paper No. 2349, World Bank (2000).

217 *Do Patents Matter?*, *supra* note 51, at 7.

218 Stephen L. Parente and Edward C. Prescott, *Barriers to Technology Adoption and Development*, 142 J. POL. ECON. 298 (1994).

219 David M. Gould and William C. Gruben, *The Role of Intellectual Property Rights in Economic Growth*, 48 J. Dev. Econ. 323 (1996); Jeffrey Sachs and Andrew M. Warner, *Economic Reform and the Process of Global Integration*, 1 Brookings Pap. Econ. Activity (1995) (An open economy also has significant general benefits. Developing countries' open economies grew on average at 4.5% per year in the 1970s–1980s while those with closed economies grew by only .07%.).

220 *See* Pamela J. Smith, *Are Weak Patent Rights a Barrier to US Exports?* 48 J. Int'l Econ. 151 (1999), corrected citation *from Parallel Trade in the Pharmaceutical Industry, supra* note 53, at 220.

221 *See The TRIPS Agreement: Implications for Developing Countries, supra* note 72.

222 *See id.*, at 276.

223 *See* J. Davidson Frame, *National Commitment to Intellectual Property Protection: An Empirical Investigation*, 2 J.L. TECH. 209, 217 (1987).

224 *See The TRIPS Agreement: Implications for Developing Countries, supra* note 72. (The volume of applications following the adoption of Mexico's strong patent regime was a 46% increase and steady increases thereafter.)

225 *See* Edmund W. Kitch, *Policy Consideration: The Patent Policy of Developing Countries*, 13 UCLA Pac. Basin. L. J. 166, 173–175 (1994)).

226 *See id.*

227 *See id.*, at 175.

228 *See National Commitment to Intellectual Property Protection, supra* note 222, at 224.

229 *See 1986 Statistical Yearbook,* United Nations (1986), at V-37.

230 *See The TRIPS Agreement: Implications for Developing Countries, supra* note 72, at 509. *ee* Sherwood, *supra* note 53, at 509.

231 *See id.*

232 *See id.*

233 *See* Adam Hayes, Investopedia, *Venture Capital: What Is VC and How Does It Work?* https://www.investopedia.com/terms/v/venturecapital.asp#:~:text=Venture%20capital%20provides%20funding%20to,gain%20equity%20in%20promising%20companies.(updated May 31, 2022, last visited 20 Nov 2022). According to the National Venture Capital Association, "75% of the largest U.S. VC backed companies would not even exist or [have] achieved their current scale without an active VC industry." *See* National Venture Capital Association Web-site at https://nvca.org/ (last visited 20 Nov 2022).

234 IBISWorld, *Private Equity, Hedge Funds & Investment Vehicles in the US - Market Size 2003–2028* (updated 31 Oct 2022), https://www.ibisworld.com/industry-statistics/market-size/private-equity-hedge-funds-investment-vehicles-united-states/.

235 *See* Joyce Alves, Reuters, *Analysis: Private equity's swoop on listed European firms runs into rising execution risks*, June 28, 2022, https://www.reuters.com/markets/europe/private-equitys-swoop-listed-european-firms-runs-into-rising-execution-risks-2022-06-28/ (last visited 20 Nov 2022).

236 *See* OECD, "Venture Capital Investments," https://stats.oecd.org/Index.aspx?DataSetCode=VC_INVEST (last visited 20 Nov 2022).

237 *See, e.g.*, Alejandro Cremades, "How Venture Capital Works," Forbes (2 Aug 2018), https://www.forbes.com/sites/alejandrocremades/2018/08/02/how-venture-capital-works/?sh=389265e71b14.

238 *See* "Current Investment — 2021 4Q," Disclosure Information of Venture Capital Analysis, http://ediva.kvca.or.kr/die/did/DivEngRecentInvstInq.

239 *See Intellectual Property Rights and Economic Development*, *supra* note 49, at 19.

240 *See id.*

241 *See id.*

242 One area of concern is that developing countries will see the TRIPS Agreement as an upper limit to patent protection rather than as a minimum threshold. Since the TRIPS Agreement is a compromise agreement, a country must create stronger patent protection than merely under TRIPS to maximise the effect of a strong patent system.

243 *See Intellectual Property Rights and Economic Development*, *supra* note 49, at 28.

244 *See id.*, at 44.

245 *See* Carlos A. Prima Braga and Carsten Fink, *International Transaction in Intellectual Property and Developing Countries*, 19 J. Int'l. Tech. Mgmt. (2000).

246 *See The Impact of Pharmaceutical Patents - The Italian Experience, supra* note 73.

247 *See id.*

248 *See The TRIPS Agreement: Implications for Developing Countries, supra* note 72, at 357–358, 497.

249 *The TRIPS Agreement: Implications for Developing Countries, supra* note 72.

250 *See Do Patents Matter?*, *supra* note 51.
251 *Id.*, at 7.
252 *Id.*, at 9.
253 *See* Robert M. Sherwood, *Intellectual Property Systems and Investment Stimulation: The Ratings of Systems in Eighteen Developing Countries*, 37 IDEA 261 (1997), at 275.
254 *See* The Orphan Drug Act, Pub. L. 97–414 (1983).
255 *See id.*
256 *See The Introduction of Pharmaceutical Product Patents in India, supra* note 79.
257 *See id.*
258 *See id.*
259 *See Regulatory Standards in the WTO, supra* note 84.
260 *Do Patents Matter?*, *supra* note 51, at 20.
261 *Id.*
262 *Id.*
263 *Id.*, at 29.
264 *See* Flavio Grynszpan, *Case Studies in Brazilian Intellectual Property Rights*, in Intellectual Property Rights In Science, Technology, And Economic Performance: International Comparisons (Francis W. Rushing and Carole G. Brown, eds., Routledge 1990), at 99; Claudio R. Frischtak, *The Protection of Intellectual Property Rights and Industrial Technology Development in Brazil*, in Intellectual Property Rights In Science, Technology, And Economic Performance: International Comparisons (Francis W. Rushing and Carole G. Brown, eds., 1990), at 61.
265 *See The Protection of Intellectual Property Rights and Industrial Technology Development in Brazil*, *id.*, at 13.
266 *See id.*
267 *See id.*
268 *See* Gianna Julian-Arnold, *International Compulsory Licensing: The Rationales and Reality*, 33 IDEA 349 (1993), at 360.
269 242 Margalit Edelman, *Treading on Toes in US-Argentine Trade Tango*, 2 J. Com. 419 (1999).
270 *See* generally Alden Abbott, *Section 337 of the Tariff Act: Fighting Distortionary Import Trade and Strengthening American Intellectual Property Rights*, Heritage Foundation (2016). *ff.*
271 As previously noted, the US Supreme Court's *eBay* decision made it far more difficult for patentees to obtain an injunction against patent infringers, *see* eBay Inc. v. MercExchange, L.L.C., 547 US 388 (2006).
272 *See* Barry Pupkin, "Beyond IP Rights: Pursuing Antitrust Claims Under Section 337 of the Tariff Act," Global IP and Technology Law Blog (13 Apr 2020), https://www.iptechblog.com/2020/04/beyond-ip-rights-pursuing-antitrust-claims-under-section-337-of-the-tariff-act/.
273 This might, of course, require appropriate amendments to the Section 337 statute, either to conform it fully to the US antitrust principles or to limit its application only to imports that violate the US IP rights.

12

TRADE IN SERVICES

General Introduction

Services have not historically formed part of the negotiation of trade agreements. The first time that services appeared on the agenda was the Uruguay Round negotiations. This introduction was a recognition of the increasing role that services were playing in global trade flows, and also a recognition that there were particular problems associated with the regulation of trade in services. Services unlike goods could not be easily pointed to, could not be stopped at borders so easily and so a whole raft of protectionist legislation had sprung up to prevent market access in services. This has come to be known as regulatory protection, i.e. a network of regulations that limited the ability of foreign service providers to properly access markets. In many cases, these regulations protected a competing domestic industry – in some cases, they simply forestalled entry from foreign and local new entrants alike.

Growth of Services as a Sector

Global trade in services has been increasing significantly. As a percentage of GDP, services trade has been dramatically increasing (until a collapse during the COVID-19 pandemic lockdowns).

Services as a sector has grown dramatically over the last half-century. Services now comprise the lion's share of tradeables in the global trading system. Services share of trade as a percentage of GDP has grown dramatically in recent years as illustrated by Fig 12.1(Figure 12.1).

We can see that global trade in goods has increased since 2001, but at nothing like the dramatic rate that services trade has increased See Figure 12.2). This demonstrates the importance of ensuring that services trade is covered by global rules and the barriers to such trade are properly eliminated.

DOI: 10.4324/9780429323331-12

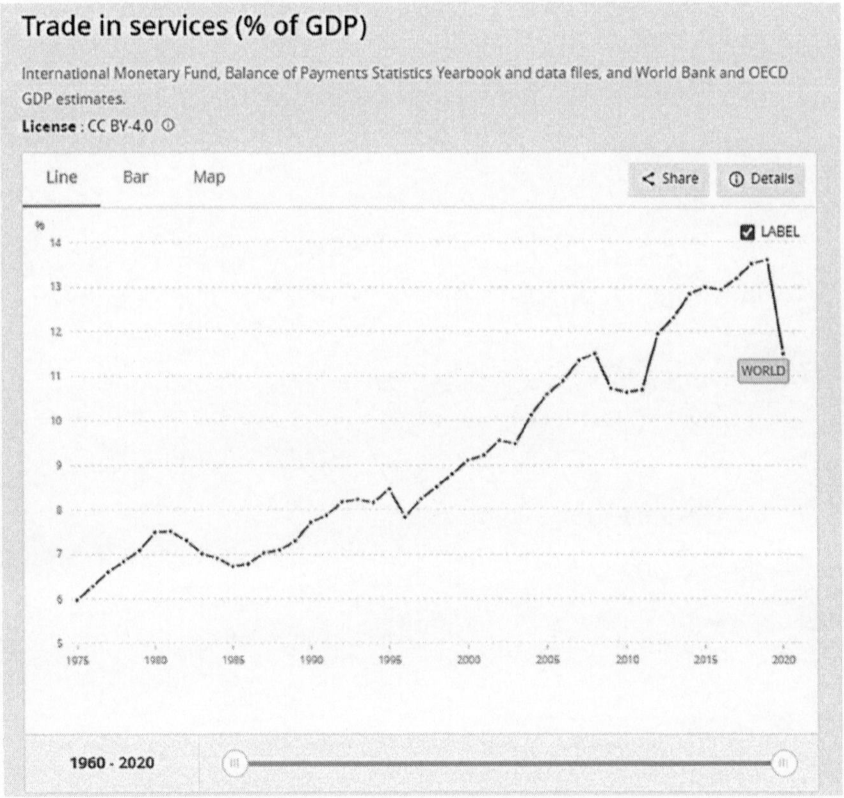

FIGURE 12.1 Trade in Services (Percentage of GDP)

Global trade in e-commerce has similarly exponentially increased in the last 20 years, and if anything the COVID-19 pandemic has accelerated this pre-existing trend. Global trade in e-commerce stats is as follows (Figure 12.3):

E-commerce trade will soon be more economically significant than global merchandise trade.

Another trend is the increase in products that are both goods and services (sometimes clumsily referred to as servitised goods). Examples include goods whose value is dependent on the services that are usually bought with them, such as computer products. Modern cars, especially electric vehicles, have become almost entirely computers on wheels. But it is not just high goods to which Mode 5 might apply. Even traditional agriculture can implicate services as the services that support high-tech wine production demonstrate.[1]

In fact, the General Agreement on Trade in Services ("GATS") was developed to respond to these challenges and the vastly increased role of services in the global economy. The GATS thus mirrors the GATT's general exhortations against discrimination and includes requirements for MFN treatment, with one

FIGURE 12.2 Services Trade Figures

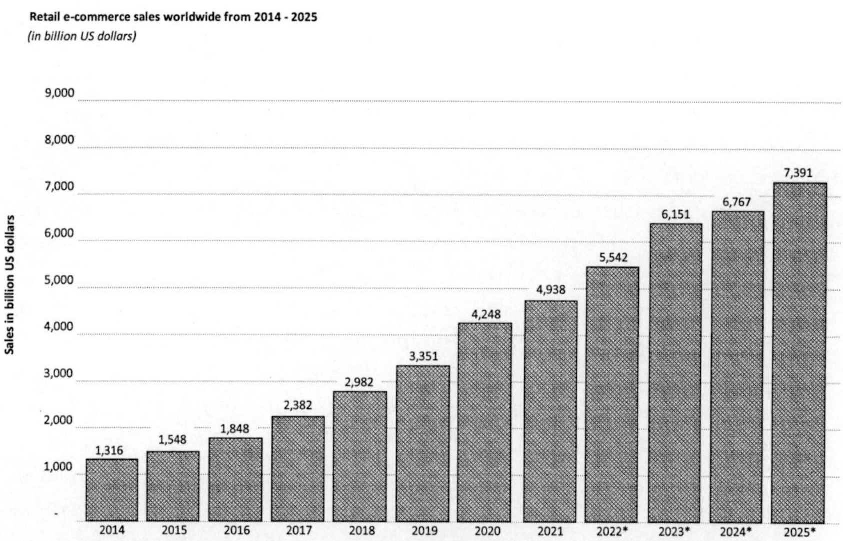

FIGURE 12.3 Retail E-commerce Sales Worldwide 2014–2025/Billions USD

important difference. Because the notion of services coverage in the WTO was a difficult one for many countries to accept (by its very nature, such an agreement would impact domestic regulations far more than a goods agreement would), the scope of coverage of the agreement was much less. The GATS operates under a dual framework. This involves a range of general provisions in what has come to be known as the basic agreement, and then specific commitments for particular sectors in an approach that is known as the positive list approach. The positive list approach is derived from the principle that only those sectors that countries affirmatively state they are making commitments in are covered (a negative list approach has been used in some other trade agreements, notably the NAFTA where all services sectors are covered unless specifically exempted). Only for these covered sectors, the general principles of the GATS apply.

One does not therefore get a sense of how deep liberalisation is in a particular WTO member unless one has a clear sense of what the particular commitments that a country has made actually are, and how they have been incorporated into actual laws and regulations affecting specific sectors.

GATS: General Provisions

The general provisions of the GATS, as we have noted, mirror the provisions of the GATT. The agreement itself covers the following broad areas:

i Scope – all services are covered, except those that are provided in the exercise of government authority (which means those not supplied on a commercial basis, nor those that are in competition with other service suppliers).

ii Definition of what constitutes services – since services unlike goods are difficult to track and trace, the GATS provides a way of looking at how services are supplied so that countries can make commitments in relation to these different methods of supply. Services, according to the GATS, can be supplied in the following ways:

(Mode 1) Cross-border supply. Services are provided by a service supplier in country A and consumer by a buyer in country B.

(Mode 2) Consumption abroad. This covers when a buyer in B goes to country A to purchase a service in A.

(Mode 3) Commercial presence. This applies to situations when a supplier of a service in country A sets up a subsidiary or other operation in country B to serve customers in B.

(Mode 4) Temporary movement of natural persons. This covers situations where personnel from the service provider travel to different countries to provide the services in those countries.

iii The GATS sets out threshold obligations, such as non-discrimination (GATS Article (Article XVII) and MFN (GATS Article II). Specific exemptions are allowed for regional trade areas as under GATT Article

XXIV (GATS V). Article V provides that if any of the modes of service provision are excluded, then the agreement will not pass muster under Article V. Otherwise, the exemption tracks Article XIV's injunctions to be trade creating rather than trade diverting and cover substantially all trade (all sectors in the language of Article V).

iv The GATS, like the GATT, provides for rules on transparency. These rules are particularly important to service providers because domestic regulations are key to their ability to operate in foreign markets.

v The GATS also provides that benefits given by the GATS should not be taken away by domestic regulation. These measures are directed towards the raft of technical and licencing standards that are applied in many services sectors, especially professional service providers.

vi Like GATT's provisions with respect to state trading, Article VIII provides that a monopoly provider of a service must not act inconsistently with a member's MFN obligations or commitments. Additionally, if a country grants monopoly rights after making specific commitments, then it will have to pay compensation.

vii The GATS has exceptions that are similar to the GATT exceptions, for national security and other reasons, subject to the general exhortation that measures that are covered under the exemptions should not be unjustified or disguised trade restrictions. As in the GATT, the general exemption list allows trade measures that violate WTO rules but which are in place to protect public morals, or human, animal or plant life, or for conservation purposes. There is also a national security exemption as there is with the GATT.

viii There is an ongoing GATS agenda which includes discussions of the following subjects:

a Safeguards
b Subsidies
c Domestic Regulation
d State-Owned Companies.

These discussions have been moving at a glacial pace since the launch of the Doha Development Agenda, and are not anticipated to deliver much progress in the near term.

ix Article IX of the GATS is worthy of special mention – in particular because it is a new development for the WTO. Article IX provides disciplines on anti-competitive business practices by service suppliers. However, full dispute resolution does not follow a violation of this article, merely an agreement for consultation, and exchange of information leading to the potential elimination of anti-competitive practices. Article IX is important because it supports the notion that the trade and competition interface already finds expression in the WTO. We have specifically discussed the national treatment provisions of GATT Article III, the State-Owned Enterprise provisions of GATT Article XVII which contain competition, or competition-like provisions. Article IX is a mere recognition that these issues can have major impacts on trade in services and that a market that does not maximise consumer welfare can distort services trade.

Specific Commitments

Article XVI of the GATS provides the equivalent national treatment provisions that can be found in GATT Article III. These provisions set out the minimum standards which must be applied to foreign suppliers. There are certain provisions which may not be applied to foreign service providers, such as limitations on the number of service suppliers, limitations on the total value of services transactions or assets, limitations on the service operations or quantity of service output, limitations on the number of people that may be employed in a particular sector, measures that restrict the supply of the service, percentage limitations on the participation of foreign capital. These national treatment provisions only apply to those services sectors where countries have made commitments, a significant departure from the twin pillar approach of GATT.

Annexes

Services are liberalised by reference to specific sectors in the form of annexes to the GATS. These annexes cover topics like air transport (strictly speaking on aircraft repair and maintenance services, as well as computer reservation systems),[2] financial services, telecommunications and maritime transport. We deal expressly and in detail with financial services and telecommunications in separate chapters, given their importance to international trade flows. In the case of financial services, the interplay is between liberalised services markets and domestic rules on prudential regulation to ensure that service providers have the backing to make good on their commitments to consumers. While it is understood that such provisions are necessary in the proper regulation of the financial sector, it is equally clear that they should not be abused in order to unduly protect domestic incumbents' providers. Telecommunications is particularly interesting and important as we discuss in detail later because of the provisions that specifically deal with competition issues as well as Reference Paper on Competition Safeguards, the first of its kind.

GATS Schedules

As we have pointed out, commitments are made specifically by countries. The result of these commitments together forms the GATS schedule for a particular country. The schedules relate to a number of sectors, including:

- i Business, professional and computing services;
- ii Communications Services;

iii Construction and Related Engineering services;
iv Distribution services;
v Educational services;
vii Environmental services;
viii Financial (insurance and banking) services;
ix Health-related and social services;
x Recreational, cultural and sporting services;
xi Transport Services;
xii Other.

For each of these sectors, countries make commitments, including MFN and national treatment obligations across the different modes of supply. If the entry in a particular mode of supply under MFN or national treatment is none, this means that the member has undertaken not to limit MFN or national treatment for that mode of service in that particular sector. Unbound means the member makes no such commitment and mirrors the GATT bindings (unbound indicating that there are no bindings and therefore no threshold minimum requirements). Within the schedule, there are horizontal commitments as well as sector-specific commitments framed in the same way.

The scope of the commitments actually made in the Uruguay Round varies significantly from country to country. Of the 149 possible services sectors, for example, the developing world has made commitments in only 16 of them. Even developed countries have made commitments in only 64.[3] At the time of the GATS, audiovisual, telecoms, postal and transportation were exempted because they were to be dealt with in separate annexes. It should be noted that even where a country has actually made commitments, this is an imperfect picture because that country may have made very limited commitments with respect to national treatment and MFN. Country schedules also provide for an extensive list of MFN exemptions in various sectors.

Since the end of the Uruguay Round, countries had agreed a programme of ongoing services negotiations to continue the work that had begun in the Uruguay Round. However, this work has not been very successful and the offers that WTO members have made in the services context have been pretty spartan. This is particularly true for developing countries, including advanced developing countries where the barriers to services trade are the greatest. Indeed the last decade does represent a missed opportunity by these countries to bolster economic reform which some have embarked on and others have not.

The question is why has it been so difficult to have more meaningful services commitments from countries and more meaningful services liberalisation. The answer is twofold. First, the manner of WTO negotiations which we have discussed in Chapters 1, 2 and 4 has been highly mercantilist in nature and has encouraged countries not to make unilateral concession (to use the mercantilist WTO rhetoric) until they see concessions from the developed countries which favour them, even where such concessions are actually beneficial to their own economies. This game of waiting to see who blinks first has as we have explained led to a considerable slowdown in trade negotiations. But there is another and a deeper problem which is the fact that trade liberalisation in the services sector is largely about domestic regulatory policy, and policymakers have jealously guarded their right to their own "policy flexibility." Where this "policy flexibility" involves the continuance of anti-competitive regulation that visits consumer harm, it is basically the flexibility to damage one's own citizens. The reality is that, as we point out elsewhere, competition/regulatory policy and trade in goods and in particular services are now intimately connected and cannot be as easily separated as these policymakers would like.

The bottom line has become that if you believe that international trade and competitive markets are a way of improving your economy and lifting your people out of poverty, you must accept all that this entails and not just pick only those measures that your producer lobbies allow you to discuss. To do otherwise would merely lead to the direct transition of tariff and border measures into regulatory protection. Nowhere is this seen more clearly than in the services discussion. This is precisely the reason why provisions like GATS Article IX exist, and why the annexes deal so specifically with competition issues.

We have discussed the different annexes that have been negotiated under the GATS. We will in the next few chapters focus particular attention on telecoms, financial services and some other sectors which are ripe for the kinds of sectoral annexes that the WTO has initiated. We will look at the energy sector where there have been privatisations without the move to competitive markets. We will look in detail at the services commitments that have been made in the trade context and then place these in the context of domestic developments, highlighting in particular areas where trade commitments appear to be vitiated by anti-competitive public sector restraints or regulations. This will by no means be an exhaustive list, but as elsewhere by looking at specific case studies we endeavour to draw up some general themes that can assist us in determining how best to approach these problems in the future. We will look not only at what makes economic sense in the context of the mathematical relationship between trade and competition but also at political realities. We must not forget that we are dealing with powerful political forces, as well as in some areas highly emotive forces. Once again by focusing on specific case studies, we hope to diffuse some of the emotion out of the issues and generate support for workable approaches going forward.

At the WTO level, this area is in its infancy and is only beginning to be mapped out. The infantile period has been regrettably long (and is now almost 30 years old). We will include each sectoral chapter by some recommendations that foreshadow what that map might look like. There has been more progress made at the level of trade agreements and we now turn to concrete achievements there.

As early as 1994, the NAFTA agreement did deal with services and did so from a negative list approach, meaning that all services were covered unless expressly excluded from coverage by positive statements by the party. The European Union's agreements by contrast adopted the positive list approach of the WTO where only those services expressly included by the parties were actually covered. Most recently, the Comprehensive and Progressive Trans Pacific Partnership does include more disciplines in the areas of services and much greater coverage. However, even trade agreements have not got to the heart of the types of barriers which particularly affect services negotiations – which is regulatory barriers. Certainly, many prudential carve-outs still exist in the area of services which are full protections from any kind of discipline. We see this in financial services, for example. However, not every restriction merits being protected entirely by the prudential carve-out. Certainly, some restrictions are justified but this needs to be tested. Even the most advanced trade agreements are some way from that now.

Services Domestic Regulation Negotiations

While little progress has been made in a number of the areas above, negotiations on domestic regulation have inched towards a conclusion in the WTO and an agreement was reached in 2021 (see below). Initially, these negotiations were felt by developing countries to be exercises in protecting their own domestic regulatory space and not genuine attempts to lower market distortions. The original Basic Telecommunications Agreement which accompanied the GATS agreement included a Reference Paper on Competition Safeguards. When the Reference Paper approach was first suggested in the Basic Telecoms Agreement, it was anticipated that many sectors would follow (especially financial services), but there was no progress at a sectoral level and for over 20 years, the Basic Telecoms Agreement stood alone.

However, the Reference Paper approach has now been followed in the domestic regulation negotiations. The Reference Paper agreed in MC12 provides for the following key disciplines:

1 Transparency
   a Publishing and maintaining information required to comply with requirements and procedures.
2 Ensuring stakeholders can participate in the process through comment periods and proper consideration of comments received.
3 Non-Discrimination
   a One new area here is the requirement that authorisation measures do not discriminate between men and women.
4 Good regulatory practice
   a Only one competent authority for authorisation.
   b Independence of competent authorities from service suppliers.
   c Develop technical standards through open and competitive processes.

While these are significant (and the first serious services agreement in the WTO for 24 years), the agreement still does not touch on what is probably the most damaging aspect of regulation which is its anti-competitive effect. This applies not only to services but to goods trade also.

Attempts to Deal with Services Regulatory Issues in Trade Agreements

It was hoped (and anticipated in some quarters), given the interconnected nature of their economies, that the UK and EU would develop services liberalisation much further in their own FTA. However, while the UK-EU TCA contains many innovations, in some areas it is lacking in the depth of its services coverage. The UK's new trade agreements particularly with Japan, Australia and New Zealand do include new services-related innovations. This is particularly true in data. The key areas of disciplines on data localisation, provisions relating to data flow, are included in all these agreements.

It is disappointing that the early ambition of the GATS in terms of countries putting their own sectors forward for liberalisation has not materialised, but perhaps we should not be too surprised. The entire GATS construction of positive list commitments lends itself to a country's defensive interests overriding its offensive interests. Modern FTAs have for some time adopted negative list approaches (where everything is on the table for liberalisation unless specifically exempted), such as the NAFTA from as long ago as 1994. Most recent EU agreements such as the EU-Japan FTA also adopt a negative list approach. This is an important development as it requires a sector to make public its arguments as to why it should be protected from competition.

There has been progress at the plurilateral level (as noted in Chapter 2) with agreements like the CPTPP containing more robust services chapters. But as we will see in later chapters, the primary barriers in services remain domestic regulatory barriers, and this is where there is comparatively little progress. The services domestic regulatory agreement just concluded in the WTO is a step forward, as we note above, but comes on the back of developing countries using the negotiations as a way of protecting their policy space.

There are initiatives underway to develop a more pro-competitive standards process, as the standards process itself can be a way of raising barriers to new entrants by incumbent companies. These normally take place in standards setting bodies themselves and through the work of domestic regulators. However having a regulatory process in place that promotes competitive regulation as set out in Chapter 8 coupled with real trade disciplines on domestic regulatory choices that damage trade and competition could, acting in tandem, lead to positive choices by governments who are subject to enormous pressure in these areas.

Notes

1 *See* Alessandro Antimiani and Lucian Cernat, "Liberalising Trade in Mode 5 Global Services: How Much Is it Worth?" DG Trade, European Commission (2017), https://trade.ec.europa.eu/doclib/docs/2017/july/tradoc_155844.pdf.ff.

2 Importantly, the provisions of the Annex do not cover the actual pricing of services which are covered separately by the International Air Services Agreement, Chicago, 7 December 1944. However, the Annex allows for an extension of the GATS Annex into other areas of air transportation services by review every five years.

3 Guideto the Uruguay Round Agreements (1999).

13
FINANCIAL SERVICES

In this chapter, we examine the role of pro-competitive sectoral regulation, its impact on consumer welfare optimisation, and discuss the competitiveness of a country's national economy by considering how competitive the financial services sector is. The case studies are in the insurance and banking areas and draw on the Japanese government's unique (and subsequently much delayed and hobbled) attempt to privatise the Japan Post, which contains the largest retail bank and largest insurance company in the world by far. Additionally, we present a case study from the privatisation of state-run financial and insurance institutions in Australia. While the postal privatisation planned by the Koizumi government was much delayed, the privatisation wave in Australia led to successful economic outcomes and the discussion of these cases contains valuable and useful lessons for the way that distortions operate in the financial services sector.

Trade agreements have struggled to deal effectively with financial services and the sector has generally been carved out of trade negotiations (except in the loosest way possible) on the basis that it is different in kind from other services. The suggestion (strengthened after the fiscal crisis of 2008 ("GFC 2008")) is that the prudential requirements around financial services are so vital and so important that the sector cannot be treated as a mere tradeable services sector.

This has led to the prudential carve-out in trade agreements where there is a complete exemption for all financial services regulations that may have negative effects on trade and competition on the basis that failure to protect the financial services sector could have consequences so devastating that they cannot be tolerated. The problem with this logic is that it seriously underestimates the consequences of barriers in financial services trade, especially for

DOI: 10.4324/9780429323331-13

developing countries. These are felt particularly in sectors like banking and insurance as opposed to more sophisticated financial services offerings, important though those are.

There are regulations that impact financial services that are sources of capital particularly to developing countries. Ensuring pro-competitive regulation in these sectors is important because the insurance and banking sectors form the financial services infrastructure for the modern-day business world. Lowering the costs and rendering these structures more efficient will lead to cost savings for businesses, which will lead to better performance on the global stage and better outcomes for domestic consumers.

The pro-competitive regulation of financial services, and the consumer-welfare-enhancing benefits it delivers, will have a direct impact on the competitiveness of the national economy. In the case of products like life insurance and savings banks, these services are key to managing consumer assets. These assets can then be deployed into the economy to generate consumer-led growth, a key aspect of economic development.

Increasingly, there are multiple ways for firms to attract the financing needed to succeed domestically and in international markets. For example, the activities of equity funds, venture capital funds and others can release capital that these firms simply would not have access to. Therefore, regulations that block this access could have market-distorting impacts. We analyse all of this in the broad context of its impact on international trade in services.

Like many of the sectors we have analysed, financial services seem to present problems for a purely market-based prescription. The reason for this is that financial services concern sectors like banking and insurance where there is considerable asymmetry of information between consumers and providers. There are also prudential concerns about the solvency and security of the institutions that are holding deposits of citizens or providing insurance services to them. While many sectors have concerns regarding consumer protection, the perceived disparity of strength and knowledge between consumers on the one hand, and the banks and insurance companies on the other means that these consumer protection concerns need to be dealt with in the context of a market economy approach to the financial services sector. The regulatory framework should avoid the temptation to use consumer protection concerns now to set up a regulatory environment that damages future consumers. In many countries, there is significant government involvement in these sectors either through regulatory interference or because of direct government control of the entities providing the products and services. Equally, many countries are seeking to transition to more market-based systems (see our later example Japan Postal privatisation). The transition from a distorted market to a more market-based system is a difficult one to manage. The difficulties are compounded by the fact that in many countries, parts of the sector are owned by governments or were recently owned by governments. In addition, even in countries where there was considerable private ownership, there are usually restrictions on what foreign market entrants can do in the country, and this serves to further stifle economic development. Many of these restrictions are being gradually lifted as a result of the WTO Annex and Understanding on Financial Services. It is during this transition period for financial services that we should be particularly concerned because market power during the transition can forestall true competition beyond the transition phase, as can occur in other areas that we also examine. Many sectors undergoing this type of transition have a similarly strong legacy of state interventionism in the economy, including state ownership of regulated industries. Some of these industries have been fully or partially privatised, while others remain under state ownership. In a number of countries, the privatisations have not been accompanied by market liberalisation that would ensure that incumbents could not engage in anti-competitive practices. In markets that continue to have state-owned enterprises (SOEs), new entrants are faced with a situation where a government serves as both regulator and market participants.

Trade Barriers in Financial Services

Trade Barriers in financial services are being lifted largely through the General Agreement on Trade in Services (GATS), Annex on Financial Services (AFS). GATS broadly provides that countries must treat trading partners equally in terms of the commitments they make in market access as well as in any limitations which they provide in market access. This is the application of ordinary MFN principles. The second major pillar of the WTO is the principle of national treatment. The GATS framework provides that countries make certain commitments in the context of financial services to all WTO members. As with other GATS provisions which we have described elsewhere, these commitments apply to the four modes of supply of the service:

- i Cross-border supply (Mode 1)
- ii Consumption abroad (Mode 2)
- iii Commercial presence in the consuming country (Mode 3)
- iv Temporary movement of natural persons (Mode 4).

For each of these modes of service, countries make specific commitments on MFN and national treatment. These commitments can be:

- i Bound commitment where country agrees to national treatment or MFN in a particular sector.
- ii Unbound – where a country does not make any commitments in a particular area under MFN or national treatment.

iii Bound, except for [...]. Here a country makes a bound commitment, but subject to certain narrow limitations or exceptions.

In addition, and particularly important for financial services is the GATS requirement for publication of all relevant measures of general application. This transparency requirement is very important as it is in other sectors. Transparency is a very important and sometimes neglected element of ensuring competitive markets. The less transparent the regulatory environment actually is, the more likely that anti-competitive markets will remain, since consumers have less information about the regulatory environment than the regulated entities do and are therefore less likely to complain about a practice that reduces consumer welfare.

Sector-specific limitations on financial services sectors are moderate. The table below shows the scope of sector-specific commitments and indicates where financial services fall into the overall picture, as of 1999.[1] These have not significantly improved in the multilateral system.

Sector-Specific Limitations by Service Sector

(Percentages in each category)

We can see from the attached table that in the area of Mode 4, 75% of commitments are unlimited and only 25% have limitations or are unbound. Mode 4 commitments in services are usually the most difficult to make. We can also see that the major restrictions apply in the commercial presence category, where only 31% of commitments include no limitation on commercial presence. Hence, the main barriers are in the regulatory structure that applies to foreign investment, once it is made. Much of this restriction emanates from prudential sources.

Typical limitations on MFN include the licencing requirements for the establishment of foreign service providers on the basis of reciprocity. Most countries stated that any change in this restriction would be conditional upon the level of commitments and exemptions made by other participants in the final results of the negotiations on financial services. Typical national treatment violations include requiring foreign financial institutions to have a representative office in the country or state before they can be licenced.

The number of countries that have made financial services commitments is increasing (for example, 38 developing countries and four transition economies have made commitments in the life insurance sector). In this context, it is more likely that there will be greater friction arising out of the domestic regulatory environment as out of other more traditional border measures.

Sector	*Cross-border*			*Consumption abroad*			*Commercial presence*			*Natural persons*		
	No limits	*Limits*	*Unbound*	*No limits*	*Limits*	*Unbound*	*No limits*	*Limits*	*Unbound*	*No limits*	*Limits*	*Unbound*
Business	72	3	25	88	1	11	86	11	4	86	8	7
Communication	73	10	16	84	2	14	73	20	7	89	2	10
Construction	17	1	82	83	0	17	80	15	5	91	6	3
Distribution	69	3	28	93	0	7	87	12	1	92	5	3
Education	81	9	10	92	3	6	77	18	5	90	6	5
Environment	20	0	80	6	0	4	6	5	0	94	4	2
Financial	51	19	30	57	17	26	39	56	5	75	15	10
Health	20	0	80	89	2	9	76	16	8	89	6	6
Tourism	51	4	45	88	1	11	78	17	5	82	8	10
Recreation	68	0	31	94	1	5	86	9	5	89	5	6
Transport	48	3	49	94	0	5	74	13	13	91	3	6

Notes:

1 Limitations include both market access and national treatment. "No limits" indicates the absence of sector-specific limitations. "Unbound" means that a mode of supply is excluded. Percentages may not add up to 100 due to rounding.

2 Cross-border supply is unbound where it is technically infeasible (construction, health, education and environment).

The Role of Competition and Structural Restraints

Normative competition principles play an important role, particularly in transitioning economies, in financial services liberalisation. Policymakers must focus on preventing anti-competitive behaviour in liberalising insurance and banking sectors. As we discuss in other areas, what we mean by competition is a consumer-welfare-enhancing market equilibrium. This does not necessarily mean that more competition is automatically pro-competitive in the sense of whether it moves the market towards this equilibrium. By relying on a consumer-welfare-enhancing paradigm, it is possible to focus on efficiencies that are derived from industries with economies of scale or network effects which are often present in the case of financial services. An act that reduces consumer welfare or economic efficiency from this optimised equilibrium therefore is anti-competitive within our meaning. In the case of banking, a competitive banking sector is a basic pre-requisite for a successful economy as competition in the banking sector determines several things such as the availability of banking products and the available interest rate for credit. A higher than market interest rate leads to a lack of incentivisation of innovative activity and a focus on business strategies that are perceived to be safe. These might include servicing domestic markets and not looking for export opportunities. Since exports have higher growth rates than merely servicing domestic markets, this lack of innovation limits that growth.

Similarly, insurance is a key element in the overall business risk climate. With risk comes opportunity, but anything which limits risk can lead to lost opportunities and stunted growth. If the insurance sector is not competitive, then firms will have less access to the types of products that can help to defray risk. If these products are less available, firms will undertake a less risky activity, and this will lead to less innovation, and ultimately less economic development.

As noted in Walter,[2] in financial services, the presence of controls over the establishment and operation of foreign affiliates will determine the actual market access. As Walter goes on to note:

> ... because financial institutions provide a board range of services..., it is possible that such controls can have quite selective effects, protecting certain domestic financial institutions... by distorting market conditions.

Importance of Competition in Financial Services

Competition in the financial services sector is a fundamental building block of a competitive economy. Banks, insurance companies and other financial services providers are the lifeblood of the economy and are of particular importance to small businesses as a key generator of economic development. There are also significant synergies between the banking and insurance sectors that together lead to increased economic growth.

An uncompetitive banking sector can lead to upward pressure on the interest rate and a higher cost of capital. In an increasingly competitive global market, such factors can be the difference between success and failure. The higher interest rate also contributes to an irritant in the global supply chain. In extreme cases, this can also act to prevent a country's insertion in the global supply chain itself. This can lead to grave consequences for the country concerned. Insurance contributes to the following key aspects of economic growth and development:

1 *Financial Stability.* Insurance promotes financial stability among businesses and individuals, in part by mitigating and sharing the risks of catastrophic losses.
2 *Promotion of Commerce.* Insurance promotes commerce because products and services often must be ensured in order to be sold. High-risk and innovative activities would often not be undertaken but for insurance, and insurance plays a role in ensuring that innovative activity takes place. The development of new business also relies on the adequacy of insurance provision.
3 *Reduction of transaction costs.* Insurance can lower transaction costs by using premiums to invest in businesses. This is a key intermediation function which is much more efficient than direct investments by policy holders. Efficiencies arise primarily from greater liquidity and more economies of scale.
4 *Management of risk.* Risk management is one of the key ways that businesses can make the right investment decisions and grow. This business growth is an important driver for the economy. Insurance allows businesses to transform their own risk profiles, and also allows overall levels of risk to be reduced through pooling arrangements.
5 *Improved Efficiency.* Because insurers tend to support more efficient firms to minimise their own risk profiles, insurers in their intermediation role are part of the incentive structure to support efficient businesses.

Building competitive banking and insurance markets is a vital part of economic development. Critics of the role of competitive markets in the insurance industry as opposed to highly regulated markets often say that competitive markets do not adequately ensure that the market is solvent and that insurance claims can be met, and this could have adverse effects on consumers. Clearly, it is important that markets be solvent. Solvency, however, is best addressed by capital adequacy requirements (as in banking) and by a focus on the entity that is providing the insurance, as opposed to by anti-competitive practices or regulation that limits new entry, on the erroneous basis that new entrants are less well known to the regulator and therefore are somehow inherently risky. As markets become more competitive, prudential regulation becomes increasingly important. The key point is that prudential regulation and competitive markets are not mutually exclusive.

The banking sector, however, has certain built-in difficulties associated with a lack of transparency and other governmental restrictions. In addition, because bank failure is seen as so destructive to consumers, governments tend to put in place guarantee mechanisms (both explicit and implicit) that have a tendency to lead to further market distortions. In Japan, for example, these market distortions have resulted from various payment and settlement incentives which lessen the selection incentives for depositors.[3]

The most significant recent change in financial services has been the rapid technological progress that has led to increased competition from substitute financial products, greater sophistication among consumers (by diminishing consumer information asymmetry), and the introduction of newer, innovative products. Increasingly, the market for risk management is the market in which different financial services entities compete. Even traditional banking products such as derivatives can be regarded as hedging or insurance products that are designed to manage risk. This changing environment also means that the economies of scope that exist as between banking and insurance companies can be better leveraged and special care needs to be taken in countries where there is joint ownership by governments, and thus these government-owned companies have access to a market dynamic denied to private sector participants. A good example of this is the Japanese Postal Network, where Yucho and Kanpo are the savings bank and insurance provider. Even under privatisation, both Yucho and Kanpo would remain substantially in government hands until 2017, and the overall Postal Holding company would have the ability to buy back shares in both entities. We deal with Japanese postal privatisation and its impact on financial services markets in greater detail later in this chapter.

We have discussed in other contexts the possibility that in certain sectors a consumer-welfare-enhancing equilibrium can only be achieved by having low concentration in the market. These situations historically have been referred to as "natural monopolies." In "natural monopolies," competition would require the installation of redundant systems which would be an inefficient outcome. We have noted that in some sectors, such as energy, telecoms and postal, governments elect to impose a regulatory structure on the marketplace because of this reality. In other instances, the government creates a monopoly in such areas by its own accord because of political ideologies such as nationalisation or import substitution. We have seen that government-created or -owned monopolies create numerous competition problems that limit consumer welfare enhancement. This also applies in the financial services sector for reasons which we will demonstrate.

The banking environment is characterised by a historic lack of innovation, because in order to compete banks must do routine tasks perfectly. Risk-taking in the banking industry is frowned on, as it comes with high costs. Instead, the incentive is towards efficiency in tasks that are already established, with less of a focus on developing innovative products. However, new technological changes (if unrestrained by anti-competitive regulation) render old systems obsolete and can lead to more innovation. Hence it is even more important that new innovation is encouraged by ensuring that regulatory barriers do not forestall innovation.[4]

Privatisation Process

Many financial services sectors are being opened up around the world as a result of privatisation processes. However, as we have noted elsewhere, governments must be careful that the privatisation process actually unleashes the forces of competition and leads to the consumer-welfare-enhancing outcomes, as opposed to outcomes that lead to the strengthening of now private monopolies with little regulatory oversight. When the aim of reform is to increase competition, public sector restraints leading to private monopoly will result in the failure of that aim.

In order to understand how competitiveness of the market impacts financial services, we will look at two case studies. The first will be a discussion of the privatisation process of the Japanese postal service, which includes both banking and insurance services. Second, we will discuss the economic benefits and performance gains from privatisation seen in Australian banking markets.

Privatisation Case Study: Japanese Postal Privatisation

In 2005, the Koizumi administration won its hard-fought campaign to privatise the Japanese Post Office. Japan Post is one of the largest post offices in the world and encompasses the largest savings bank, the Yucho bank as well as the largest insurance company, the Kampo insurance company as well. Japan Post has historically also been very politically powerful and has used its large number of post office counters throughout Japan to ensure a connection to the ruling LDP party. It has become part of the fabric of Japanese society in a way that few other companies have. The decision of the Koizumi administration was predictably met with strong opposition in the Diet by both parties, and initially the vote was lost in the upper house. Only when Prime Minister Koizumi made this a general election issue, an election he won by a landslide, was the road to privatisation cleared. The decision to privatise Japan Post's insurance and banking services is a very positive and interesting step. Unlocking the forces and benefits of competition will lead to major opportunities for Japanese consumers and businesses alike. The insurance and banking sectors comprise the financial services infrastructure of the modern business world. If these are efficient and low-cost, business costs will decrease and lead to more competitive businesses. However, the precise manner in which the privatisation occurred determines whether the benefits of competition will be successfully unlocked. The Japanese postal privatisation is a good example of many of the threshold issues that affect privatisations throughout the world, particularly the privatisations of the 1990s which were too often focused on generating sales revenues for treasuries, and not on unleashing consumer welfare. The privatisation itself was significantly delayed and the holding company was still in government hands as recently as September 2021 despite the mandate for reform in the general election of 2005 which Koizumi won in a landslide.

Moreover, the process is complicated by the presence of SOEs and the fact that even after privatisation, a significant government ownership has remained over all the Japan postal entities, including the banking and insurance arms. A significant problem with respect to SOEs in particular is that they are not profit-maximising entities. The guarantee of an SOE's monopoly power and its regulation by a governmental agency changes its behaviour from economic to political – it must influence and manipulate the regulatory agency for its own gain. In addition to attempts to increase costs or hide profits in cost to allow it to earn excessive profits, the monopolist may also try to curry favour with influential figures. This can take the form of creating pricing schemes to appeal to political allies or paying its employees inflated salaries to mobilise a constituency base highly interested in influencing the regulatory agency.[5] The power of the regulatory agency over its functions leaves the monopoly with little if any incentive to respond to actual consumer demands or market conditions.[6]

Regulatory Reform in Japan: A Case Study

The role of regulatory reform in Japan's economic growth has been a subject for analysis by the Organisation for Economic Cooperation and Development ("OECD") from the OECD's initial report on the subject in 1999[7] through its 2004 progress report.[8] The consistent principle throughout the OECD's analysis is the notion of competition as an organising principle, rather than as simply another species of regulation. The OECD has encouraged the competition agency – the Fair Trade Commission of Japan ("JFTC") – to take a more proactive role in shifting Japanese economic development goals to a consumer welfare orientation.[9] The OECD Report recognises that the following are the goals of competition policy in Japan, with the last two as the most important:

1. Free competitive processes;
2. Fair market outcomes;
3. Private Innovation;
4. Economic Growth (including business expansion);
5. Political Democracy and
6. Consumer welfare.

This is a long list and contains some inherent dangers. The fact that competition policy is assumed to have so many goals can be very damaging for the economy. In particular, many of these goals are not consistent. Business expansion, for its own sake, for example, does not necessarily lead to consumer welfare enhancement (although it might). It is much more likely that many of these goals will lead to the building of national champions at the expense of consumers. This is to be avoided and should not be a goal of a country's general economic policy, let alone its competition policy. It is important to note that it is not just the fact that competition policy is introduced into the regulatory reform agenda that matters; it is also the precise meaning of competition and how it enforces the regulatory process. In this context, the OECD has noted that regulations can contradict, replace or even reproduce competition policy, depending on the way that competition is defined.[10] The long history of the US with respect to the implementation of competition policy has demonstrated that economically positive outcomes occur when consumer welfare is the primary goal of competition policy.[11] The OECD has further noted that regulation can use competition policy methods – such as instruments designed to take advantage of market incentives and competitive dynamics – and that coordination between regulator and competition agency may be required to accomplish this.[12]

Japan's Anti-Monopoly Act (the "AMA") does provide the tools to discipline private monopolisation, and does foresee a role for the JFTC in newly deregulated or deregulating industries. The JFTC thus could use the AMA to further competition in financial services markets in cases of overtly exclusionary or controlling conduct.[13] This would include cases involving, for example, conduct by a series of firms that systematically exclude new entrants to certain types of markets. It is important, however, that in evaluating regulatory systems or in looking at potentially anti-competitive practices, the JFTC does not fall into the trap of protecting competitors, rather than protecting the competitive process.

The 1999 OECD report noted the importance of the JFTC consulting and working with other ministries of government so that it would have the potential to be a "core economic policy agency."[14] The report further noted that the JFTC does have the power to veto legislation and regulatory proposals that violate the AMA but has never done so, and that it also could make its views known in the regulatory process (through the Cabinet Secretary) but again has rarely done so.[15] It is clear that the AMA directly reaches public entities where they operate in the commercial space. For example, a 1989 Supreme Court case found that a municipal slaughterhouse competing with a private one could be reached by the AMA.[16] The 1999 OECD Report encouraged the JFTC to use this authority to take a leadership role in regulatory reform.[17] In 2004, the OECD observed that the JFTC's move to the Cabinet Office implies a potentially stronger role for the agency in government-wide reform, while also noting that this promise has not yet been realised and therefore reiterated its previous call for JFTC to increase the visibility and impact of its participation in policymaking.[18]

We have seen from International Competition Network ("ICN") reports that it is very difficult for competition agencies to advocate successfully and early engagement is vital to the process.[19] Where agencies wait until after the regulatory framework of a privatisation, for example, has already been established, it becomes very difficult to impact that regulatory structure in a pro-competitive fashion. At the ICN meeting in Bonn in 2005, many of the participants discussing the role of competition advocacy noted that the key was to advocate early. The reason this was specifically mentioned is because there are many examples where a failure to advocate early has resulted in an inability to effectively make the case for competition after the regulatory structure has been put in place. Applying this in the Japanese context, if the competition agency does not react prior to the completed process of postal privatisation, assuming this happens, it will find it extremely difficult to change the behaviour of the postal company itself, post privatisation. There have been many examples of privatisations involving telecoms and other sectors that we discuss in detail elsewhere, where competition has not been successfully introduced into the privatisation programme. Frequently, this happens because once the privatisation process is complete, it is very difficult to apply competition disciplines if competition was not the normative framework of the privatisation itself. Privatisation, in this case, merely creates a powerful market participant, unshackled by competition constraints. Like King Kong, such a monster cannot be easily contained, and is liable to break through any constraints that the competition agency subsequently attempts.

As we have noted, a common way to institutionalise competition advocacy is for the competition agency to intervene in regulatory proceedings. Only the competition agency has the institutional capacity to best understand the economic impact of regulation on competition and therefore is best suited to provide such guidance to other agencies. The issues raised in regulatory proceedings tend to involve the same types of questions that the competition agency has to deal with, e.g., whether competition is feasible; whether an industry is naturally monopolistic; whether cross-subsidies impact consumer welfare in a negative way; whether economies of scale are substantial; and whether particular regulations are likely to accomplish their stated objectives.

The Cross-Subsidisation Problem in Financial Services

As noted above, the goal of competition policy is to enhance consumer welfare. Competition laws particularly are required to restrict anti-competitive business practices and prevent cross-subsidisation. We have examined in the chapters on telecom and postal the nature of the cross-subsidisation problem. We noted there that cross-subsidies occur when a regulated part of a business subsidises its competitive affiliates by shifting affiliate costs to the regulated portion of the business. When some of the affiliate's costs are paid by the regulated side (and built in to the cost structure for the regulated price through the use of accounting methods that do not accurately allocate costs), consumers will have subsidised the competitive affiliate and the affiliate will have a cost advantage relative to its competitors. In the case of the financial services arms of Japan Post, the particular issue which we analyse, the major problem applies in the access these entities have to funds from government sources, or from government privileges which can then be used to cross-subsidise. The other issue is the fact that if these government-owned entities are subject to a different regulatory structure than private competitors, this is an additional way for them to artificially lower their costs and gain an advantage that does not result from efficiency but rather from government grant.

When financial services entities are subject to a particular regulatory environment, they must incur substantial compliance costs. Often firms will staff large compliance departments whose sole function is to ensure compliance with this regulatory environment. If some firms are exempt from the application of this regulatory environment, then they are saved the costs that would be incurred by supporting those large compliance departments. They are therefore subject to lower costs in producing their portfolio of financial services products. Critically, this means that what would be a predatory price in the case of the higher cost product appears not to be predatory (at least based on its declared cost) for the product produced by the unregulated firm, and this gives the unregulated firm a competitive advantage. The solution to this problem is to either put both firms on the same regulatory footing or increase the cost base of the unregulated firm when evaluating and subsequently disciplining predatory behaviour. Naturally putting both firms on the same regulatory footing is a better way of achieving these goals since otherwise one would have to rely on antitrust enforcement which may be delayed from the point in time that behaviour takes place and is also uncertain in its enforcement.

Japan's WTO Commitments in the Financial Services Sector

The interface with trade is to be found in how the WTO deals with financial services in Japan, and attempts to enshrine a level playing field as between foreign and domestic providers. However, the disciplines on Japan in the WTO will also serve to help (indirectly) Japan's domestic but not state-owned providers of financial services. Japan's commitments pursuant to the World Trade Organization ("WTO") Uruguay Round Agreements mandate that Japan's insurance and banking sectors be subject to the very competition principles that are needed to ensure Japan's economic growth and stability. Japan has made commitments, under the GATS AFS, both for the delivery of insurance products and for banking products. This includes, importantly, the commitment to accord national treatment to the financial services providers of other members, meaning that foreign service providers must receive treatment no less favourable than that accorded to the most favoured domestic providers. Here there is a distinction between the domestic providers of financial services which are private entities and Japan Post entities Yucho and Kampo, where a government holding has persisted long after the original 2017 deadline.

Japan's commitments with regard to market access for financial services providers are not, however, without limitations. In its schedule of commitments Japan has noted, for example, that for prudential reasons it can apply discriminatory limitations on new financial products. In this context, securities firms may deal in certain types of securities products, while banks may not deal in those products. For insurance and insurance-related services, commercial presence is required for insurance for goods transported within Japan and for domestic registered shipping inside Japan. Additionally, 60% of the reinsurance required for compulsory automobile third-party insurance is subject to compulsory coverage by the government, and insurance services may not be provided through an intermediary in Japan. In the mode of cross-border supply, Japan requires commercial presence for the insurance business set forth above, and so they have market access barriers in this mode of supply.

Japan has undertaken further commitments – relating to both market access and national treatment – in accordance with the Understanding on Commitments in Financial Services, which imposes more detailed commitments on members than those set forth in the GATS and its AFS. With regard to market access, the Understanding provides that, in addition to the monopoly rights commitments set forth in Article VIII of the GATS, Japan must list certain monopoly rights and then must work towards their elimination or reduction in scope.[20] The Understanding further requires that, notwithstanding Article XIII of the GATS, Japan must accord Most-Favoured-Nation treatment as well as national treatment for foreign service providers in the provision of financial services to public entities.[21]

On Cross-Border Trade, the Understanding requires Japan to permit non-resident providers to provide, under terms and conditions that accord national treatment, insurance services pertaining to maritime shipping, commercial aviation, space launching/freight activities and goods in international transit; reinsurance, retrocession and services auxiliary to insurance; and the provision and transfer of certain financial information.[22] Additionally, Japan must permit its residents to purchase in the territory of any other member the following financial services:

- Insurance services pertaining to maritime shipping, commercial aviation, space launching/freight activities, goods in international transit, reinsurance and retrocession, as well as services auxiliary to insurance.
- Acceptance of deposits and other repayable funds from the public.
- Lending of all types.
- Financial leasing.
- All payment and money transmission services.
- Guarantees and commitments.
- Trading for own account or for account of customers of money market instruments, foreign exchange, derivatives, exchange rate and interest rate instruments, transferable securities, and other negotiable instruments and assets.
- Participation in all kinds of securities.
- Money broking.
- Asset management.
- Settlement and clearing services for financial assets.
- Provision and transfer of financial information.
- Advisory, intermediary and other auxiliary financial services.[23]

On commercial presence, the Understanding requires Japan to permit financial services providers of any other member to establish or expand its presence within Japan, including through the acquisition of existing enterprises.[24] The Understanding further requires Japan to endeavour to remove or limit the adverse effects of non-discriminatory measures or other measures adversely affecting the ability for foreign financial service providers to compete in Japan.[25] These requirements recognise that financial services providers of other members should be able to provide in Japan all the services that can be provided by Japanese financial services providers. The Understanding covers all measures that affect the ability of the provider of another member to adequately compete, even if such measures technically are allowed under the GATS.

With regard to national treatment, the Understanding requires Japan to provide to foreign financial services suppliers access to payment and clearing systems operated by public entities, as well as to official funding and refinancing facilities available in the course of ordinary business.[26] Foreign service providers similarly must be allowed access to any self-regulatory body, securities or futures exchange or market, clearing agency or any other organisation or association that is required to compete on an equal basis with Japanese financial services providers.[27]

These WTO commitments embrace many of the competition policy principles that should be applied in the privatisation of Japan Post, not only to advance international free trade but also to benefit Japanese businesses and consumers of financial services. These commitments, however, will not be incorporated automatically into the Japan Post privatisation. There is instead an important role to be played by the JFTC in promoting the implementation of competition principles to realise the full benefits of privatisation, as well as ensuring WTO compliance.

Case Study: Privatisation of the Commonwealth Bank of Australia

Following the deregulation of the Australian banking sector and changes to the capital adequacy requirements in the late 1980s which would have put an outsized pressure on the Government's budget, the Commonwealth Bank of Australia began the privatisation process in 1991. Between 1991 and 1997, various stages of privatisation were achieved, concluding with full privatisation for the 1997 financial year. Studies[28] have shown that during the time prior to privatisation, the bank was overstaffed, unprofitable and inefficient. Further, due to poor resource utilisation, the bank's growth was significantly smaller than any of its private sector rivals. As was the case in Japan, privatisation announcements and proceedings were met with pushback. Rival banks were understandably against the entrance of an additional competitor in the market, and the pressure it would place on them to innovate and adapt to the increased competition. Further, the newly privatised bank had the potential to cut costs and innovate at a rate not seen in its history under public management, leading it to pose a more significant competitive threat than a newly established bank.

Following regulatory reforms and full privatisation in 1997, the Commonwealth Bank of Australia has performed as well or better than its rivals on several metrics, such as loan portfolio efficiency, growth, and overall operational efficiency.[29] An aggressive reworking of its branch network and reduction in employees are a partial explanation for the increase in efficiency but it is not the whole story. Changes in management structure offered by privatisation have led to significant long-term outperformance and accelerated growth when compared to its rivals. This outperformance has come at the expense of increased risk on the company's balance sheet, however, indicating that the acceleration in growth is partially attributable to an increase in risk preference at the firm.[30] The firm, however, has one of the lowest capital adequacy ratios as compared to its rivals, indicating that it can maintain outperformance while facing less risk than its lower performing rivals.[31]

All told, the outperformance of the Commonwealth Bank of Australia only came about after the full privatisation was realised, leading to the conclusion that partial privatisation, at least in a regulatory environment like Australia's, has the potential to lead to lacklustre results. This follows similar thinking laid out earlier in this book, where complete revocation of SOE assets by the government is required to unleash the full competitive potential of newly privatised firms on the marketplace.

Regulatory Reforms in Australia[32]

The sale of the Commonwealth Bank of Australia came on the tail end of significant regulatory reform beginning in the early 1980s. A key tenet of such reforms was the reduction of public sector distortions in private markets by eliminating, where feasible, SOEs. Another key feature of the privatisation process was the use of revenue linked to the sale of government assets to pay down national debt, leading to a healthier national balance sheet. Below are some of the major reforms instituted by Australia:

- Trade Liberalisation
- Opening of Capital Markets
- Infrastructure Deregulation
- Labour Market Liberalisation
- Human Services Reforms
- Introduction of a National Competition Policy
- Macroeconomic Policy Shifts
- Tax Reform

Of particular importance for the discussion of privatisation are the opening of capital markets, infrastructure deregulation, and national competition policy reforms. First, the opening of capital markets allowed for increases in competition from foreign financial institutions for both commercial and retail customers. Second, the infrastructure reforms were the direct impetus for privatisation, attempting to structurally separate the government from private market distortions and remove barriers to competition posed by SOEs. Finally, the introduction of a national competition policy codified and clarified the conduct viewed as anti-competitive by the state, leading to an increase in certainty in the business community. A rather unique feature of these policy reforms to note is that they were brought about largely unilaterally, without corresponding concessions from other nations in the WTO (then GATT).

Current Obstacles to Competition in Japan

Under the current regulatory framework in which the two Japan Post financial services entities – the Yucho and the Kampo – will operate, there are a number of benefits which accrue to the Japanese companies from which foreign competitors cannot benefit. These include:

1 Preferential tax treatment.
2 Exemption from certain registration and licencing requirements.
3 A more favourable regulatory regime.

These benefits must be eliminated or substantially reduced as part of the privatisation process if the full benefits of competition are to be realised in the banking and insurance sectors.

In addition, under the current provisions of the postal privatisation law, Japan Postal Services Corporation – the holding company which was to have been created upon privatisation in October 2007 – would have been allowed to buy back shares of the privatised insurance and banking entities following their divestitures which were projected for October 2017. The holding company therefore could regain voting rights over the insurance and banking operations. This could open the door to government guarantees of deposits and insurance policies. The Postal Privatisation Committee ("PPC") was intended to recommend how the scope of financial entities' activities can be increased prior to their divestiture in October 2017, although this process has been substantially delayed. The PPC was intended to oversee, *inter alia*, banking services and will report to the Prime Minister every three years.

Another problem is raised by Japan Post's requested increase in the caps on life insurance and postal savings deposits. The problem with this request is that if the caps on these products are artificially high because of government guarantees, then this may erode the ability of private companies to compete with Yucho and Kampo. This will be particularly problematic in those cases when the private firms and the state-owned firms are on different regulatory and other footings.

Japan Post's financial services operations furthermore could benefit after privatisation from the Consolidated Taxation System introduced in 2002, under which corporate groups may pay corporate taxes on a consolidated basis. This system allows losses from one corporate entity to offset profits from other entities within the same corporate group for consolidated taxation purposes. The 2004 Tax Law Amendments abolished a 2% surtax for consolidated taxable income, thereby making the consolidated system more attractive to consolidated groups. Under this system, the Kampo and Yucho financial services entities benefited during the period 2007 to eventual sale of government stake in 2021 as members of the corporate group controlled by Japan Postal Services Corporation, which group also would include the Post Office Co. and the Postal Delivery Co. Losses incurred by the postal entities could reduce the tax burden on the financial services entities, thereby providing a cost advantage *vis-à-vis* competing financial services providers.

In addition, Japan Post is exempt from paying corporate tax under Section 4-3 of the Corporate Tax Law of Japan. Legislation also exempted Japan Post from registration/licencing tax and stamp tax during the transition period to full privatisation. Although Japan Post is subject to the National Treasury tax (under section 37 of the Japan Postal Law), and a local government tax (set at about one half of what private companies pay), the overall tax burden is less than the tax burden imposed on equivalent private companies.

Importance of Cross-Sectoral Approaches to Regulatory Reform

The European Union ("EU") in its regulatory dialogue with Japan has noted the importance of cross-sectoral responses to regulatory reform. Since 1995, the EU and Japan have engaged in bilateral consultations known as the "EU-Japan Regulatory Reform Dialogue." Through a series of reform proposals and high-level negotiations, the consultations aim to facilitate trade and economic growth, and in the case of Japan, provide much-needed economic stimulation.

Throughout the course of over a decade of this Reform Dialogue with Japan, the EU's message consistently has been underpinned by its calls for cross-sectoral approaches. The EU has noted that for Japan's attractiveness as an investment base to increase, investment opportunities must be expanded by vigorous deregulation across all sectors of the economy.[33] This would include stricter enforcement of competition laws and minimisation of sectoral restrictions on foreign investment, among other actions.[34] The EU also has reflected on its own experience in working towards its Single Market model in noting that a cross-sectoral approach is essential to ensure that progress made in one sector is not diluted by persistent inflexibility in another.[35] The EU further has consistently endorsed broadening the powers and scope of Japan's competition regulation as an indispensable element of its reforms.[36]

The OECD has likewise advocated cross-sectoral action in Japan's regulatory reforms. In its 1999 assessment of Japan's reforms, the OECD concluded that comprehensive, cross-sectoral reforms were essential to maximise and accelerate the overall effects within Japan's economy.[37] As noted in the review, historically, Japan's administrative systems were founded on consensus and accommodation and as a result produced item-by-item reforms that were slow to yield concrete economic responses. With comprehensive reforms, however, "benefits appear faster (which means that proreform interests are created sooner; affected parties have more warning of the need to adapt; vested interests have less opportunity to block change; and reform enjoys higher political profile and commitment."[38] The OECD also advised that comprehensive reforms help to balance multiple policy objectives and competing interests, furthering their overall effectiveness.[39]

EU-Japan EPA

Following the call for regulatory reform in Japan, the EU-Japan Economic Partnership Agreement (EPA) has instituted various measures that reduce barriers to entry and economic frictions significantly between the two economic areas in financial services sectors. Under this agreement, both economic areas allow unconditional access to public payment and clearing systems, as well as lending and refinancing facilities not including lender of last resort services.[40] Both parties will not take measures to prevent the transfer of information between parties in the normal course of business, and will not prefer one economic area's firms over the other when it comes to information transfer and access to self-regulatory organisations.[41] Requirements for licencing in the supply for financial services will be publicly available and transparent, requests for information will be made without delay, and self-regulatory organisations will publish rules of application for entry into the organisation.[42]

All of these stipulations are key to ensuring fair and open competition between domestic and foreign providers of financial services and the innovative potential of both economic zones. Following these guidelines, European companies will be able to enter the Japanese market and compete effectively without the fear of protectionist, consumer-welfare-inhibiting policies that relegate foreign forms to a lower status or subject them to more onerous capital requirements.

UK-Japan CEPA[43]

The UK-Japan Comprehensive Economic Partnership Agreement (CEPA) contains the same fundamental provisions as the EU-Japan EPA, with a few notable improvements from a trade facilitating standpoint. First, The CEPA clarified and strengthened the language in the provision allowing for the application of a licence and stipulated that the procedure must be completed "in a reasonable amount of time."[44] Second, the CEPA introduced a provision that disallows the obligation to store financial data within the country, allowing both Japanese and UK firms the ability to store financial data from all branches of their operations in a single location. This provision is notably absent from the EPA. Third, both governments committed to annual dialogues in order to further reduce barriers to entry, eliminate economic frictions and increase trade and investment in the financial services sector.

Interaction between JFTC and FSA

The interaction that the JFTC should have with the Financial Supervisory Agency ("FSA") should be similar to the interactions the JFTC currently has with other regulatory bodies. An independent regulator is a key part of ensuring a competitive market, especially in the case of a transition from a government-owned to a private participant, such as the case of the Kampo. FSA regulations should be pro-competitive whenever possible, and certainly should use the least anti-competitive regulation practicable to achieve public policy goals. The JFTC must work with FSA to ensure that FSA's sectoral regulations reflect appropriate competition principles and focus on consumer, as opposed to competitor, welfare.

The regulatory approval system in Japan for insurance products is based on a new product approval system conducted through the FSA. The key elements of the regulatory approval system include an evaluation of whether the premiums are reasonable and based on actuarial science.

Kampo is able to underwrite products much more effectively than private sector competitors because of its government-owned status. Method of regulation is based on financial stability of the entity. The financial stability of the Kampo is partly due to its government ownership.

As noted above, the difference between competition enforcement and sectoral regulation is that the former is generally *ex post*, and the latter is *ex ante*. As Japan moves towards a more competitive system, it will be necessary to rely more on competition enforcement in the area of new product regulation. It is a fundamental principle of the market economy that the market should define what products should be sold. To subject new product development to an onerous regulatory burden will stall innovation. Indeed as restrictions are systematically removed from the financial services products that can be sold and foreign firms can offer a greater range of those products, ensuring that the competitive playing field between those products is level takes on an even greater significance.

Competition in the Banking Sector

A competitive banking sector is a vibrant one. Competition in the banking sector moreover is vital because it acts as the transmission belt across a number of industrial sectors. For a competitive banking sector to emerge there must be certain indicia:

1 Strength must be incentivised. Many countries have historically operated a system which enables the weaker banks to survive. Bank failure is an ordinary part of business, and while recognising that some protections need to be in place for consumers, the concept that no bank will ever be allowed to fail has to be changed in order to ensure that right competitive incentives apply.
2 The market must not rely on implicit government protection of deposits. While deposit insurance is not per se an anti-competitive concept, the notion that banks will not fail because government will always bail them out is one that does severely distort markets and erode consumer welfare. Deposit insurance can also increase the potential for moral hazard, artificially increasing the risk appetite of banks.

Role of Competition in Regulation of Banks

The ICN has reported in its 2005 Annual meeting in Bonn on the importance of competition in bank regulation. The report noted that knowledge of the creditworthiness of customers was an important element in ensuring the development of a competitive market in retail banking. Without this, each individual bank has an informational advantage over other banks. This increases lock-in, the phenomenon where customers find it difficult to switch from one provider to another, and, in turn, leads to a less competitive market. The ICN report recommends that an open competitive banking environment should be promoted by competition agencies. Competition agencies should ensure that there is separation of prudential regulation and competition implementation. Agencies should advocate for the elimination of the exclusion of competition principles from the financial services sector. Competition agencies are also encouraged to advocate for lower switching costs by promoting an environment where knowledge of the debt exposure of potential borrowers is better known.

Indeed, Japan's history, in particular the *Jusen* problem,[45] is illustrative that banks with a substantial share of non-performing loans could also be a competitive problem as they operate as an informal, implicit deposit guarantee system that has market-distorting impacts. However, Japan's history of bank failure needs to be considered when advocating the importance of the market as a regulator.

Investment Advisory Companies ("IACs") could play a substantial role in the Japanese economy, but there is a limit on the access to funds managed by Yucho and Kampo. In both cases, the combined assets under management are in excess of $3.5 trillion (one third of the size of the entire US economy). Improved management of these massive assets obviously could have enormously beneficial effects throughout Japan's economy, sparking economic growth in all sectors.

The Japanese postal privatisation and its aftermath will be a very important indicator of whether the privatisation leads to a more competitive and vibrant banking and insurance sector or whether the lack of competitive focus leads to a very powerful market participant that simply erodes the ability of private firms to compete, with negative implications for consumers in the country. It is unclear at this point in which direction these actions will tend. Japanese consumers and businesses must hope that the political battle that was fought to agree privatisation in the first place is a precursor to ensuring that the true benefits of privatisation are captured in increased competition.

Issues for Liberalising Insurance Markets

We have already noted the major impact of competitive insurance systems around the world, and their importance to the private sector in growing economies. In the insurance, as in the banking sectors, there is an important and difficult issue, which is that much regulation appears to have a pro-consumer *raison d'être*. Under this theory, consumers are to be protected from rapacious insurance salesmen, or regulation is there to ensure that insurance levels are high enough to pay out claims. Certain social goals, of course, legitimately must be addressed by the insurance system. However, while all these goals can appear laudable to some, too often insurance regulation is used a shield for anti-competitive practices that serve to keep out new entrants. The result is to reduce consumer choice and to increase price – the opposite of the stated goal of the regulation.

EU Solvency II Directive[46]

A prime example of this is the EU's Solvency II directive, which came into full force in 2016. While claiming to provide a harmonised and structural framework based on the risk profile of each insurance provider, the costs of regulatory compliance place an outsized burden on small- and medium-sized insurance firms.

The three fundamental pillars of the directive are as follows:

1. Quantitative Requirements: This pillar sets out the basic rules for capital resource requirements and which forms of capital will fulfil said requirements. Included in this calculation are reserves in excess of those required to cover liabilities.
2. Supervisory Requirements: This pillar sets out the requirements for risk management and governance, and details the supervisory process that must be adhered to in order to maintain compliance.
3. Disclosure Requirements: This pillar sets out the specific requirements for disclosure to both the public and regulators, and is aimed at creating a uniform reporting system among insurers.

This system places an enormous emphasis on risk profiles and calibrates a firm's capital requirements to the level of risk that is borne by the firm. During its inception, the impetus behind updating the directive was to enhance and revise the principles surrounding risk management and bring them in line with more modern interpretations of risk. However, in its current form, the directive sets forth a rules-based approach to risk and dispels the idea that firms have flexibility in risk management. This methodology tends to make firms significantly more risk-averse than under prior regulatory regimes.

This has the potential to reduce both competition and innovation. Small- and medium-sized firms will have to reserve a significant portion of their portfolio for reserves, allowing for less innovation and growth in the short run. The guidelines purport to treat every business differently based on its risk profile, but this fundamentally misunderstands the developing markets for leaner, more technologically advanced insurance providers. Just like the fintech providers discussed later in this chapter, nascent insurance technology firms (insurtech) have been making headway into insurance markets by providing better services at lower costs.[47] These advances have the potential to bring large consumer welfare benefits but such lower cost structures may not be realised if regulatory capital and reporting burdens are imposed on such small companies. One estimate places the cost of compliance with the directive at over £200 million[48] for each firm, which is likely to price new firms out of the market before they are even able to enter.

Incumbent firms will be better able to swallow the cost of compliance and thrive in the new regulatory environment, but new firms may never have the chance. Without carve-outs for nascent firms, competition will decrease, innovation will slow and growth will likely decline as available capital in the market will be relegated to larger and more established firms.

UK Proposal to Diverge from Solvency II[49]

The UK, however, is taking a decidedly different approach to insurance capital requirements. While the Solvency II Directive primarily calculates capital holdings based on short-term risk sentiment, the UK is aiming to take a longer-term view of insurance markets and weight risk accordingly. In a speech on 22 February 2022, John Glen, Economic Secretary to the Treasury and City Minister, outlined a proposal to diverge from the EU in the following ways:

1 Risk Margin: "A reduction in the risk margin for long-term life insurers… in the order of 60 to 70 percent."
2 Matching Adjustment: Broaden the number and types of long-term assets that are eligible for lower capital requirements under a revised risk portfolio adjustment by
   a reassessing the calculation of fundamental spread to better reflect credit risk;
   b broadening the assets and liabilities which may be eligible, intending to incentivise long-term investment;
   c applying a more proportionate approach to breaches of the matching adjustment and revising the standard by which the whole portfolio is rendered ineligible and
   d streamlining the process for determining eligibility.
3 Simplifying Reporting Standards: Citing significant regulatory hurdles to compliance under the Solvency II framework, reporting would be simplified by
   a Revising processes for approval of internal risk models to calculate capital requirements.
   b Reforming reporting requirements to ease regulatory burdens on new insurers and reduce the frequency of reports.
   c Raising the threshold for size and complexity of insurance operations before a firm becomes subject to the revised Solvency II standards.

Glen noted that these reductions have the potential to reduce capital holds and expenditures by as much as 15%, allowing firms greater flexibility in investment strategy and long-term growth estimations. While the final proposal is yet to be drawn up, these changes provide for significant regulatory reform for both incumbent and nascent insurance providers alike. Not only does the UK have the potential to become a hub of innovation and growth adjacent to the European market, but Glen's remarks make clear the intention to place significantly fewer regulatory burdens on UK companies in the future, further cementing innovative potential.

The discussion around Solvency 2 and the likely UK proposal to diverge from it illustrates the difference between an EU harmonisation approach across the whole single market and the UK's developing approach based on necessity and proportionality. Not all companies should be required to do identical things, as they present very different levels of risk to the system.

Importance of Market Access and Contestability

Too often, efforts to open up markets do not lead to contestable ones. The result is that political capital that is spent to secure market opening (in the case of the privatisation of Japan Post the long political battle to agree to privatisation itself) is wasted because it is not accompanied by pro-competitive deregulation. However, in the insurance industry, there are issues that suggest that perfect competition will not be achievable. This includes the following:

1 Asymmetric information. Both buyers and sellers experience asymmetric information. Buyers do not know the financial health of the insurance company. Insurers do not have full information about their policyholders. Neither party can predict the future. The lack of information that policyholders have about the insurance companies as a whole leads to the bulk of insurance regulation.
2 Government policy can lead to monopolistic or oligopolistic markets. Discriminatory tax policies can also lead to market power in the hands of a few domestic companies at the expense of foreign companies.

Insurance regulation should correct market failures brought about because of government-induced market distortions. Abusive practices can be particularly damaging in markets that are in transition. In the case of the Japan Postal example, given the size of the Kampo business and its large share of Japan's overall insurance market, the market is certainly in transition as a result of the privatisation. There are many potential areas of existing distortions that need to be corrected through the kind of regulation that allows a competitive market to exist.

Information Access and Transparency

In the transition from a regulated to a competitive market, it will be necessary to ensure that customers have access to information as the burden will increasingly fall on consumers to make informed decisions. These decisions will relate to both the benefits and values of insurance products but also to an insurer's financial condition. This means that it is important that market access is applicable for rating agencies and other firms that provide this kind of information to consumers.

The regulatory system itself also must be transparent. GATS Article III recognises transparency as a fundamental principle, and thus requires transparency in the regulatory systems affecting market access and operation in the country. Where there is opaque regulation or a system that consumers find difficult to understand, this can increase the lifetime of poor regulation because consumers are unaware of the costs associated with the poor or anti-competitive regulation.

These issues are particularly important in the context of the marketing of insurance products to individual citizens, such as life insurance products. Problems of asymmetric information are much less significant in the case of the kinds of insurance products that businesses buy (such as insurance for industrial risks).

Information asymmetry is a major factor in the financial services sector. Information asymmetry is particularly prevalent in this area because consumers do not have the same access to information that the providers of these services have. However, the advent of the internet and high technology is changing the extent of this asymmetry. As more information about insurance companies' solvency, their product ranges and so forth are available to consumers through the internet and other sources, the problem of information asymmetry becomes more and more limited.

Prudential Concerns

The usual reasons given for allowing regulation to trump the competitive market in the case of insurance include the asymmetric information problem referred to above, and the ability of consumers to understand the terms of insurance contracts. This, in turn, has led to the notion that regulation is needed for prudential reasons to ensure that consumers are protected (which is a very different vision of consumer welfare than the economic one that underpins this book). But this is a straw man. It is possible to pay attention to prudential concerns without maintaining a complete prudential carve-out. Other sectors we have discussed that arguably have just as potential catastrophic risks such as food do not have blanket carve-outs. In the case of food and SPS goods generally, countries can adopt regulations to ban certain products provided that such SPS measures are based on sound science and are necessary to achieve a regulatory goal. There is no reason that concepts like the evidence-based nature of regulation and necessity should not be used in this sector also.

Pricing concerns have led to the use of market access and new product barriers, as well as price floors and, in many countries, the explicit toleration of private anti-competitive practices. The privatisation process and competition concerns cannot ignore the fact that there is significant vertical foreclosure where domestic firms deal solely with their captive insurance companies, and thus refuse to deal with foreign (or more accurately any other) companies. This type of refusal to deal is quantifiably different from a refusal to deal in a purely domestic scenario, because when the refusal to deal is with a foreign provider, that foreign provider must overcome a number of border barriers in addition to the anti-competition barriers it faces in the home market.

Control of licencing procedures is one of the key ways that new insurance products can be slowed or prevented altogether. Because the licencing procedure contains competitive risks, it is imperative that, where the private sector competes against government-owned companies, the same licencing procedure applies to both.

Differential licencing procedures are likely to quickly become preferential procedures for domestic, government-owned companies and therefore barriers to market access for new entrants as well as new products.

Financial Sector Convergence

There is a tendency, as with telecoms, for technology and other developments to result in convergence across sectors. In the context of financial services, convergence means that many different financial products can be offered by the same company, whereas in the past these products would have been offered separately by different companies, such as banks, insurance companies, and investment firms. To continue with the Japanese example, although Japan has taken important steps towards liberalisation of these sectors to allow greater convergence, significant impediments to full convergence remain. For example, as of December 2005, banks in Japan now are authorised to sell such insurance products as single premium endowment/single premium whole life policies, personal non-life insurance other than automobile insurance, and maturity-refund-type personal accident policies.[50] This expansion, however, affects only a few premium savings products that are similar to products banks previously were authorised to sell. The remaining restrictions on the sale of insurance products by banks provides a competitive advantage to Yucho and Kampo, which were commonly owned by the government, and which continued to operate under the common ownership of Japan Postal Services Corporation following privatisation from 2007 to 2021.

The Rise of Digital Financial Services

Along with convergence among product markets for different financial services, there has also been a trend of technological integration within the financial services sector. Often labelled as "fintech" firms, new companies entering the financial services space use nascent and emerging technologies to make financial markets more diverse, inclusive, competitive and efficient. Providing mobile banking services without the need for a physical storefront, online low-fee or fee-free equity trading, high-speed online money transfer services, and applying for loans through a mobile device have brought forth banking services to a significantly wider array of individuals, some of whom were in traditionally underserved populations.

Low-Income Utilisation of Fintech Services

Particularly important has been the introduction of these services into developing economies. With the rise of online-only banks, low-cost traditional accounts and expanding payment networks around the globe, consumers who had been exclusively cash-only are now able to access financial services on mobile devices. "Mobile money" services, such as M-Pesa in Kenya,[51] allow consumers to store and transfer money for low-fees from their mobile devices. They are also able to "Cash-In, Cash-Out" via local shops serving as financial agents, so that they may still participate in the cash-only economy. Following its introduction, M-Pesa uptake was slow, sitting at less than 20% of non-urban Kenyans.[52] However, by 2011 that share had risen as high as 72%, and as of 2020, as many as 21% of the Sub-Saharan population utilised mobile money accounts.[53]

Following the success of M-Pesa, Safaricom, M-Pesa's parent company, introduced M-Shwari as a collaboration with the Commercial Bank of Africa to bring savings and loan products to customers through the familiar mobile money platform. Expanding from the simple store and transfer of money, M-Shwari allows consumers access to deposit insurance, interest on deposits, and credit to further manage and build financial resources.[54] Key among the offerings pulling individuals towards such services is cess to credit markets and obtaining and improving credit scores.

While these loans are not generally used for large capital purchases, they are critical in maintaining financial stability for low-income populations. Based on survey data, a significant number of respondents reported using the loans for short-term economic stability and smoothing out fluctuations in income over time.[55]

Further, as the case of Safaricom illustrates, these services have the capability to be modular. Beginning with mobile money and bridging into savings and loan services, utilising an existing network is the key to maintaining low costs and high efficiency. Not only does this modularity allow fintech firms to remain nimble and innovative but can increase competition in financial services markets.[56] Traditional financial services firms are often slow to adapt, rolling out new services months or years after their fintech competitors.

This lag in innovation from incumbent players can give fintech firms the foothold necessary to make significant advances in financial markets and pique the interest of regulators at the same time. In 2019, following fierce competition from fintech firms offering reliable and near-instant payments and transfers to and from customers in Mexico, the Mexican Banking Association announced the removal of fees from digital accounts.[57] This move came after significant pressure from the legislature, which sought to institute the same change through regulation.

Traditional Firms Embrace New Technology

While the embrace of technology at large financial institutions has been more reactive than proactive, entrenched incumbents are steadily embracing the shift to a more dynamic approach to financial services. Mobile payments and person-to-person transfers were cemented with the emergence of Paypal in the late 1990s, and today nearly all mobile banking applications have similar features. Mobile-only banks, those without a physical presence, have been on the rise as well, offering lower fees and better rates in exchange for giving up access to a local brand. Large banks are following this trend and closing a significant number of branches. By 2025, Citi predicts it will operate with 30% fewer employees.[58]

One of the most discussed and controversial among recent changes to operations at traditional financial institutions is, however, the elimination of commissions on equity trades. Bowing to pressure from investing platform start-ups like Robinhood, who in 2015 began offering equity trading for free, incumbent brokerage firms have followed suit. In 2019, nearly all the large brokerage platforms eliminated fees associated with trades and reported revenue cuts between 8% and 16%.[59]

What has made the emergence of zero-fee trading is not its mere existence. It is the potential power that brokerage firms have in the face of rapid trading by their clients. In the past, general consumers who choose to invest relatively small amounts of money into the stock market have been dissuaded from making multiple trades in a single day due to the commission fees associated with those trades. When the fees were eliminated, however, traders could buy and sell stocks without regard to the number of transactions completed in a day.

This came to a head in 2021 when Robinhood suspended trading of some highly volatile stocks on its platform.[60] Citing regulatory capital requirements to complete trades through their clearinghouse, Robinhood suspended trading because the capital requirements for that single day of trades were in excess of capital they had raised in the past seven years of their existence. Capital adequacy requirements will be discussed later in this chapter, but it is clear that, in times of above average volatility, regulatory capital requirements placed on firms have a trickle-down effect on consumers. Because Robinhood was unable to meet its capital requirements, due in part to its business model of reducing fees for consumers and not collecting commissions on traded stocks, incentivising increased trading volume, the firm was required to cease trading on high-risk stocks that required excess capital reserves.

While these requirements are in effect to protect consumers and maintain liquidity in both capital and traditional banking markets, it presents a significant hurdle for innovative fintech companies that are attempting to create a better consumer experience. With these capital requirements, firms like Robinhood are unable to provide both low-fee trading and access to potentially risky stock choices, should consumers wish to trade such stocks.

This limitation reduces consumer choice and inhibits consumer welfare growth. By imposing strict capital requirements on brokerage firms that are more than the amount necessary to cover their liabilities, and scaled according to short-term market fluctuations, firms must decide whether to be innovative and high-growth, or be compliant. Not only do the capital requirements disproportionately affect smaller firms,[61] they also require firms to leave large amounts of capital idle and uninvested in long-term projects that have the potential to increase consumer welfare in the future.

Additionally, especially in the US, the lack of uniformity in regulation across jurisdictions slows growth and inhibits development of new services.[62] While traditional, nationally chartered banks are regulated and insured by the federal government, allowing for uniformity in product offering, from the outset most fintech firms are not. They are subject to state-by-state regulation, often facing disparate regulatory environments when attempting to service similar consumers across different states. This means that, in the case of loans or lines of credit, fintech firms have to obtain licences in every state where they wish to do business, which increases their costs significantly. Additionally, this state-by-state regulatory treatment necessitates discrimination based not on credit history or assets available, but by interest rate laws in any given state. This means that two individuals, similarly situated in terms of credit history and available assets, may pay vastly different rates of interest based solely on the state in which they reside.

This additional barrier tends to further entrench incumbent financial institutions and insulate them from competition. Because of the forced consumer discrimination, and often duplication of costs associated with regulatory compliance at the state level, fintech firms are unable to offer truly competitive products compared to their traditional banking rivals. This leads to a situation where, in order to maintain regulatory compliance, fintech firms often must partner with traditional banks to offer certain products, significantly reducing the efficiency gains and nimble, innovative approach fintech provides.

Regulation of Insurance Intermediaries

In many countries, the activities of insurance intermediaries are regulated through occupational licences. The licencing of insurance intermediaries is an example of prudential regulation which is required in order to protect consumers. However, even regulation such as this is prone to potential abuse. If the licencing procedure is such that the ability of entrants to access intermediaries is hampered, then this can be an anti-competitive restriction. The key issue here is whether new entrants (which are typically foreign insurance companies) have access to the necessary quality and quantity of intermediaries they need in order to reach the wider market. If their access to these is hampered then financial services commitments made in the WTO by countries may be vitiated by these internal restraints.

In Japan, life insurance companies cannot use solicitors who work for other insurance companies (although these provisions can be set aside where the Cabinet Ordinance considers that there is no problem in protecting interests of policyholders). A large number of solicitors already working for existing insurance companies and therefore there is some degree of foreclosure.

Under Article 291 of the Business Insurance Law, insurance brokers are required to make cash deposits for their operations. This requirement has the potential to act as yet another barrier to entry to new brokers. Also, in the case of Kampo, over-the-counter agency services for banking and life insurance business will be allowed. The cross-ownership of shares among all four companies could enable the four entities to operate as one.

Efficiency-Enhancing Practices

There are a number of practices in the insurance sector that look on their surface to be anti-competitive but are actually efficiency enhancing. One example, the sharing of loss information, helps correct the market distortions arising from asymmetric information (where the insurer has incomplete information about an insured's loss profile). Insurers are better able to understand the risk profile by reference to the large volume of historical data compiled cooperatively by many firms, and therefore are better able to predict accurately their future costs and thereby determine appropriate rates.[63]

Capital Adequacy

Capital adequacy considerations are frequently used to keep certain banks out of the market. After HSBC acquired Anthony Gibbs, a small British investment bank in 1981, the Bank of England required the bank to withdraw from the trade association of UK merchant banks (the Accepting Houses Committee). In the same year, HSBC was blocked from acquiring Royal Bank of Scotland. The subsequent financial deregulation in the UK was the financial services equivalent of the lifting of the corn tariff. Deregulation in the UK in the 1980s led to Big Bang in 1986 and the rapid acquisition of UK banks by foreign banking institutions.

As Japan opened its banking sector in the 1980s, one anomaly allowed foreign banks to engage in securities business in Japan if it is done through the subsidiary of a foreign institution. This was one of the rare instances where the domestic restrictions that prevented Japanese banks from engaging in securities business actually were relaxed for foreign companies. For a period, foreign companies were actually at an advantage – however the consumer welfare damaging impact of the regulatory barrier on Japanese consumers remained. This is an admittedly rare example of anti-competitive regulation or restriction distorting the market to disfavour the domestic industry. This highlights a concern raised throughout this book – that the problem is with market distortions that harm consumers. These distortions generally have a negative impact on foreign producers trying to access these markets, but not always. The central problem is the harm caused to consumers, not necessarily the impact of that harm on foreign producers.

This situation existed for the US banking system as well, when the Glass-Steagall Act prevented US commercial banks from engaging in securities business. However foreign banks were able to engage in such business until the International Banking Act, 1978 prevented this. However existing institutions were grandfathered in and did start to make substantial inroads into the US banking sector.

Good examples include Sumitomo's acquisition of a 12.5% stake in Goldman Sachs, as well as Nomura and Daiwa Securities leading major US issues.[64]

Capital adequacy is an example of the kind of public service approach to banking that can often lead to restrictions over the foreign sector and benefits given to the domestic banking sector.

One of the major challenges in the Japanese postal privatisation will be how to ensure that capital adequacy is separately dealt with as between Yucho, Kampo and its private competitors. If capital adequacy regulation does not properly reflect the risk of the institution as a whole, competition may be distorted in favour of higher risk institutions. This distortion applies to products also.

When China started to open its market in the 1980s, it required foreign representative offices to maintain a $12.5 m capital requirement – it also limited the amount of China business that could be done. These two requirements have limited the success of foreign banks in China.

Foreign financial institutions are particularly vulnerable to allegations surrounding capital adequacy. Differences between capital adequacy requirements will have an impact on flows of financial services trade. Japanese banks have been reported to have benefited from capital adequacy requirement differences, because Japan has had very low capital adequacy requirements historically.

International Approaches to Capital Adequacy

Post-GFC 2008, the pressure has been on institutions to maintain high levels of capital adequacy for systemic risk reasons. In the US, and in other countries, the Basel III standards on liquidity and capital adequacy have increased the minimum required levels of capital, forcing banks to reduce lending and increase excess reserves to maintain regulatory compliance. The European Capital Requirements Directive and Requirements represent a slightly more tailored and less onerous version of the Basel III requirements, but still impose strict capital requirements and incentivise short-term risk over long-term holdings. These regulations taken together, however, have had an outsized impact on small- and medium-sized financial institutions, which will struggle to maintain competitiveness while reducing lending.

Basel III

The Basle Committee on Capital Adequacy is the international group that reviews capital adequacy requirements on a global basis. The Basle Committee looks at the following areas in order to determine capital adequacy:

1. Measurement of bank portfolio risk.
2. Measurement of bank capital.
3. Establishment of minimal standards for capital relative to risk.
4. The role of market discipline in influencing bank capital and risk choices.

The Basle Committee had been moving towards a more scientific measurement of bank portfolio risk, (see, for example, the 3 June 1999 Basle Committee on Banking Supervision Proposal for a new Capital Adequacy framework for internationally active banks). However this changed after the GFC 2008. Commentators have suggested that there should be a move towards more self-regulation and self-risk assessment by the entities being regulated.[65]

The Basel III standards follow the same general framework as the EU's Solvency II Directive.[66] The framework is seen below:

1 Pillar 1: Minimum Capital Requirements. This requires banks and financial institutions to maintain an enhanced level of capital based on credit risk, operational risk, and market risk. The goal is to model the "real" risk of economic loss the firm faces more closely.
2 Pillar 2: Supervisory Review. Through risk management best practices, supervisors evaluate whether the bank should hold higher levels of assets than required in Pillar 1, and what further actions are required to mitigate risk.
3 Pillar 3: Market Discipline. Enhances transparency and discipline by requiring additional reporting to shareholders and customers.

Just as in the section discussing Solvency II, the Basel III standards go above and beyond prior iterations of the regulations and mandate significant overhauls of the banking system to maintain regulatory compliance. Not only does the revision place outsized burdens on businesses that operate in perceivably risky categories, such as making business loans, it also classifies longer-term assets as inherently more risky than shorter term ones, and weights their capital requirements at a higher rate. According to McKinsey, the liquidity requirements alone would require US banks to raise $800 billion in short-term funding and $3.2 trillion in long-term funding to come into compliance.[67] The figure for the EU is an additional €1.3 trillion in short-term funding and €2.3 trillion in long-term funding. This additional funding is not able to be leveraged for investment or new products, however. It is money that must sit on the balance sheet in order to comply with increased liquidity regulations.

Large US banks are less likely to be negatively impacted by the capital and risk requirements of Basel III due to the existence of the Dodd-Frank Act, which requires banks over a certain size to adhere to the similar regulations surrounding risk and capital requirements.[68] The greatest impact for these US firms will be the duplication of regulatory filings and excessive reporting requirements under both systems. Small US banks and non-bank financial institutions not subject to Dodd-Frank, however, face significant changes due to the imposition of Basel III. One estimate,[69] looking primarily at large US banks, showed an increase in rates of 13 basis points and a decrease in loan offerings of 1.1%. The outlook for small banks is likely to be more dramatic. This increase in interest rates and a decrease in the amount of loans available will likely have a cooling effect on the economy, since the business community will have less access to funding for capital growth and innovation.

The outlook in Europe is likely worse than in the US. Since the Basel III requirements give the US leeway to seek external calculations of risk, the risk weight associated with assets is generally lower than in Europe. For example, investment grade risk assets carry a risk of approximately 65% in the US, but between 85% and 100% in Europe,[70] causing European banks to carry significantly more reserves on their balance sheet than similarly situated US banks. This means the increase in interest rates and decrease in loan availability will likely be worse in Europe across the size spectrum.

Capital Reserve Directive and Requirements[71]

Seen in the Capital Reserve Directive V (CRD) and Capital Reserve Requirements II (CRR) are general clarifications for European firms in implementing the Basel III pillars. The most significant change from the strict Basel III requirements comes in the reporting standards for small and less complex firms, allowing them less burdensome and less frequent reporting standards when compared to their larger rivals. Additionally, for small firms, long-term funding requirements are revised to present a smaller burden and make it easier for these firms to incorporate existing assets into long-term liquidity requirements.

One significant change applicable only to large non-EU banking groups is the requirement to restructure subsidiaries operating in the EU (if two or more, such as separate banking and investing operations) under an intermediate parent company in the EU. This company, according to CRD, can either be a subsidiary of a larger company or a parent company, but it must be a company registered in the EU and not an international branch of a third-country bank. While this stipulation is relatively mild compared to the other requirements under CRR, CRD and Basel III, it represents another trade barrier leading to an increased compliance cost for large banks that must be considered when weighing the total cost of the regulatory oversight.

New Business Undertaken by SOEs

In many cases, the government-owned company, prior to privatisation, has certain limits on the kinds of business that it can do. There is at least some understanding that the government's ownership puts other companies at a disadvantage in the marketplace. However, many of these limits are removed with privatisation as the leaders of the newly privatised entities demand the ability to compete against their private sector rivals. If the government retains ownership or some shareholding over the companies, this can pose real problems in the marketplace. These siren calls can also be hard to resist, couched as they are in the language of competition. Let us compete, cry the SOEs by offering as many products as the other private firms do. To continue to restrict us is anti-competitive. The problem with this logic is that one has to look at the impact on the market of loosening the restrictions on the SOEs, and whether it might actually lead to damage to consumer welfare. Whether the historic restrictions were carefully thought through or not is not relevant. Once again, a good example of this comes from Japanese postal privatisation.

Japan Post has talked about potential new business after privatisation, such as (a) syndicated loans, securitisation and home loans for the Postal Savings Bank, (b) expansion of the amount of insurance coverage for Postal Insurance Company and (c) entry into other sectors such as medical insurance and care insurance (comments of Chairman Ikuta, 24 February 2006). Given the concerns raised by its existing advantages in postal and financial services, it would be important to ensure that the playing field is levelled before Japan Post could extend such advantages into new product markets. This is a classic example of the language of competition being used to derive advantage to Japan Post entities, while these entities still operate with government benefits and privileges. The result (of lifting restrictions before governmental benefits and privileges are properly dealt with) will be to distort the market.

Restrictive Business Practices in the Insurance and Banking Sectors

There are many examples of anti-competitive practices in the insurance and banking sectors. Many of these practices violate domestic antitrust laws. We will examine some examples of these practices and their impact on domestic markets. Coupled with some of the public sector practices that have anti-competitive impacts, these practices can also compound market distortions. We will again look at the Japanese case study that we have been reviewing throughout this chapter.

The fact that Japan's largest corporations tend to favour their own captive insurance companies for the provision of insurance products limits the ability of foreign companies to meaningfully participate in the Japanese market. There are certainly foreclosure effects in this area that are worthy of investigation by JFTC. Additionally, any tacit understanding among the captive insurers that they do not compete for customers beyond their keiretsu allies could further undermine the competitiveness of insurance markets, with concomitant impacts on consumers. The introduction of a dominant Kampo, with all of its government-related advantages, might serve only to reinforce the coordinated effects felt in insurance markets.

Given the scale of the assets under management (some ¥335 trillion), and the fact that ¥328 trillion is channelled into the public sector through government bonds and public bonds and this symbiotic relationship will mean that Yucho and Kampo will continue to be very powerful, favoured players.

Restrictive Practices in the Banking Sector

The US had traditionally maintained a number of restrictions in its financial services markets in a manner that has harmed foreign entrants into the US market but also the US institutions themselves. Perhaps the most well-known example is the Glass-Steagall Act (also known as the Bank Act of 1933) which separated the businesses of commercial banks and securities and other non-banking business. The effect was to create a wall between commercial banking and investment banking. Interestingly, one of the major motivations of Carter Glass, one of the law's authors was his desire for banks to return to less innovative, more conservative practices. He considered investment in stocks to be risky, and used the malaise in the US banking system of the time (coming out of the great depression) to push through this agenda. The Bank Holding Company Act of 1956 was an attempt to prevent banks becoming too large and amassing too much power.

In a US Treasury paper issued in 1987, the US Treasury Department recognised that the Glass-Steagall Act meant that the US banks were not as competitive as their counterparts in Japan, and the UK because of the restrictions imposed by Glass-Steagall. The Glass-Steagall Act provided that commercial banks could not maintain ownership interest in non-banking sectors. The Bank Holding Company Act provided that there should be limitations on nationwide branching. This was an artificial restriction that distorted the banking sector. It artificially fragmented the banking market in the US and limited the ability of US banking companies to compete against their foreign counterparts. It is a classic example of competitor welfare enhancement which fragmented the market and left the US banking sector vulnerable to international competition.

The new banking Act, the Gramm-Leach-Bliley Act (signed into law on 12 November 1999)[72] loosens the Glass-Steagall restrictions considerably but does consider the question of who the regulator should be. The notion which underpins the new legislation is functional regulation, where the source of regulation is not determined by the entity but rather by what business the entity is engaged in. Under Gramm-Leach-Bliley, the Federal Reserve is the regulator of the Bank Holding companies, but does not involve itself in regulation of securities activities (for example). This function regulation stems from the fact that the nature of the regulatory concern is different as between securities firms and banks. Securities regulators are concerned with the orderliness of securities' markets, and protection of investors. For example, SEC Commissioner, Norman S. Johnson noted the following in a speech shortly after the introduction of Gramm-Leach-Bliley:

> Rather, the Commission's concerns go to the heart of our role as protector of investors and regulator of the nation's securities markets. As you all know, the Commission does not try to insulate securities firms or other market participants from risks they incur in their business activities. Nor does the Commission advise investors about which securities to purchase. Instead, the Commission tries to promote fair and orderly markets by requiring that

issuers make full disclosure to investors and by imposing specific capital, supervision, disclosure and antifraud requirements on securities firms.[73]

Banking regulators, however, are fixated on the safety and soundness of the banking system. Interestingly, notions of functional regulation increase the role that competition agencies and competition itself should play because of all the regulatory concerns, only the competition agency is concerned about future consumers. Hence, there is an increased role to ensure that regulatory oversight does not lead to an anti-competitive market effect. This is particularly true, for reasons that we have stated above for the type of prudential regulation that we have discussed.

US Regulatory Environment Post-GFC 2008[74]

In the aftermath of the Global Financial Crisis of 2008, the US Congress took up the task of creating a unified regulatory framework to ensure financial stability and reduce the "too big to fail" problem. Enacted in 2010, the Dodd-Frank Act[75] was seen as the solution, claiming to provide significant oversight, transparency and accountability for financial institutions across the economy, and seeking to ensure that the instability seen during the GFC is never seen again. In the period since its enactment, many Dodd-Frank implementing regulations have come into effect.

Dodd-Frank Act

The Dodd-Frank requirements for capital adequacy and reporting are similar to those under the Basel III regime, but were fully implemented earlier. While full finalisation of Basel III was completed in 2017 and its widespread implementation scheduled for 2023, the Dodd-Frank requirements have been largely in effect since 2013. These regulations apply to all banks with assets under management greater than $1 billion and impose strict requirements on capital holdings based fundamentally on risk. The riskier the asset class, the greater the excess holdings necessary to offset the perceived risk associated with that asset, and in some cases the required holdings are larger than the value of the asset. Systemically Important Financial Institutions (SIFIs) face additional capital requirements associated with their status as the underpinning of the global financial services sector. These include a capital surcharge requirement for being an SIFI, requirements to meet a total loss absorbing capacity threshold to ensure the SIFI can weather a certain amount of loss before the FDIC steps in to cover losses, and an additional 2% leverage buffer to ensure additional levels of liquidity are maintained in the long-term.

Additionally, and in the largest departure from prior regulatory regimes, banks are now required to report stress test projections that are more stringent than expected losses based on risk. Both the Dodd-Frank Act Stress Tests (DFAST) and the Comprehensive Capital Analysis and Review (CCAR) test a bank's ability to withstand varying degrees of financial downturn, denoted in a normal, worse-, and worst-case scenarios framework. These reports are made public for even non-publicly listed firms, and the largest banks are required to run the tests yearly.

Financial Stability Oversight Council

Primary responsibility for determining the status of banks and financial institutions as SIFI is held within the Financial Stability Oversight Council (FSOC), an entity created by Dodd-Frank that brings together top regulators from across federal agencies dealing with financial regulation. One goal of the FSOC is to ensure the market for financial services is disciplined and to eliminate the expectation that the US Government will step in to absorb losses in the face of another crisis. By imposing higher capital requirements, subjecting these firms to stress tests, and increasing the regulatory compliance burden, the FSOC attempts to shift risk onto the SIFI and away from the market as a whole.

This scheme of designating some firms as systematically important, however, has some significant downsides.[76] The designation of an institution as a SIFI can make a firm more risk seeking. Shareholders, competitors, and creditors associated with these SIFIs will work with the assumption that the government is backstopping the firm, and the federal regulators have a large incentive to follow through on this assumption. With the reputation of the FSOC and Federal Reserve on the line, the destabilising effects of the Lehman Brothers collapse in 2008,[77] and despite statutory limitations against bailing out banks should another crisis hit, the Government's hands are likely tied when it comes to the collapse of SIFIs in the future.

These institutions are so critically important to the financial system in the US, and the world to a great extent, the market cannot risk the destabilisation associated with the collapse of these firms, and the market knows this to be true. Even with the increased regulatory requirements and scrutiny placed on SIFIs, the broader market sees the continued stability of these firms as a foregone conclusion not afforded to other players in the market. Not only does this increase the risk for another crisis because of the risk associated with SIFIs, but it limits competition in the market, leading to increased concentration and even greater uncertainty. It is this backing of the firm by non-commercial factors that was a primary reason for the GFC 2008 in the first place.

Increased concentration in the market comes fundamentally from the outsized burden placed on small banks. While regulatory scrutiny is higher on SIFIs, just as with the Basel III regulations, the burden is disproportionately felt by small financial institutions. Based on one estimate, the total cost of regulatory compliance with Dodd-Frank regulations is nearly $60 billion annually, with over $7 billion falling on small banks with less than $10 billion in assets.[78] While small banks hold around 10% of the financial system's assets, they have shouldered over 12% of the increase in compliance costs. These regulatory burdens tend to force some competitors out of the market, and they act as barriers to entry keeping nascent competitors out as well. As of 2016, as many as 20% of banks in the US have exited the market, and while the remaining banks remain profitable, there have been strikingly few new banks entering the market since Dodd-Frank.[79]

Should another crisis hit, the number of small banks will drop even lower. Since these small, often community-based institutions are not designated as SIFIs, the Federal Reserve has no incentive to bail them out. Accordingly, a new crisis would generate even higher levels of concentration, lower levels of competition, and decreased overall stability of the financial services sector.

Consumer Financial Protection Bureau

The Dodd-Frank Act consolidated regulation of financial products into a newly created agency within, but independent from, the Federal Reserve called the Consumer Financial Protection Bureau (CFPB). The CFPB is granted incredibly broad authority to protect consumers in the financial marketplace by ensuring consumers are informed, ensuring financial product markets are working, enforcing consumer financial law, and reducing regulatory burdens for consumers. The agency, however, is not required to analyse the effectiveness or stability of its regulations. This leads to a significant accountability gap, whereby the CFPB can enact rules that sound good on paper but have vast unintended consequences in practice.

Principal among these ill-informed regulations has been price-controls on debit cards and mortgages. The Durbin Amendment to the Dodd-Frank Act was enacted to reduce the fees banks are able to charge retailers to process transactions. The hope was that the savings retailers saw would be passed on to consumers in the form of lower prices for products and services. This reduction in prices, however, was not realised. Prices stayed the same or rose across retailers, and revenue dropped by as much as 25% for banks, realising a loss in revenue as high as $6.5 billion a year.[80] The effect for consumers was elimination of both rewards programmes for debit cards[81] and free checking accounts.[82]

Additionally, there is evidence to suggest that banks that fall under the CFPB's supervision are reducing the number of loans and mortgages to low-income individuals. Federal Housing Administration (FHA) loans are housing loans insured by the FHA and administered by the individual banks. These are generally sought by low-income or first-time home buyers, since they have less strict credit requirements and require a low (or zero) down payment on the loan. While these loans are a good offering for low-income or low-credit individuals, based on the current formulation of capital requirements they are no longer a good offering for banks. Since there is so much risk involved with the loan, even while being insured by the FHA, capital requirements are significantly higher than other loans. This, coupled with the increased legal and regulatory risks associated with FHA loans, have caused many banks to completely stop such offerings, instead substituting for them higher value, lower risk loans.[83] This amounts to an estimated 6% drop in the number of banks willing to offer FHA loans since 2011,[84] pricing some individuals for home loans out of the market when they are only able to qualify for FHA loans.

Of note is the 2020 Supreme Court case *Seila Law v. CFPB.*[85] This decision increased the accountability of the agency by making the director of the CFPB removeable "at will" by the President. Prior to this decision, the director was only removeable for cause, leading to an independent body without accountability to the Executive Branch, under whose purview the CFPB resides.

Sarbanes-Oxley Act[86]

Distinctly different from the Dodd-Frank regulations laid out above, the Sarbanes-Oxley Act was passed in 2002 as a counter to the financial fraud seen in the late 1990s. Applying only to publicly listed companies, the law strengthens oversight and reporting standards, ensuring investors are protected against false or misleading financial documents that have not been audited by an independent third party.

The benefit of this regulation is an increase in the accountability and transparency of publicly listed companies, requiring independent verification of all financial documents before they are made public. Additionally, strict internal controls are required to ensure that continuity is maintained throughout the various levels of an organisation.

There are downsides, however. These compliance standards apply to all public companies equally, regardless of size, resources or sector. This means that smaller firms have to spend a larger share of their revenue on compliance, seriously hampering their growth and competitive prospects. One estimate places this burden at $6 million per year for the smallest, least complex firm, while the largest firms in the market pay as much as $39 million.[87] Additionally, it is estimated that profitability of firms across the size spectrum is significantly decreased for the first four years after public listing, due in large part to the increased regulatory burden and the large outlay of capital needed for compliance.[88]

Imposition of Conditions on Banking Operations

Many countries provide that entry of foreign banks is dependent on certain conditions. Conditionality may also impact the operational capability of foreign banks. These relate to restrictions that apply to the type of business that the bank or financial institution can engage in, or prevent certain business being done. Even where the regulatory system is de jure equivalent, its incidence may fall differently between foreign and domestic institutions. There are a number of types of operating restrictions which include:

1 Market separation – where the foreign bank is limited in terms of which clients should be served. Examples include when Brazil allowed foreign banks to open two offices in provincial cities for each one they closed in Rio or Sao Paolo. Certain types of lucrative government business can also be limited to

domestic banks. There may also be rules that allow a certain type of business but make it difficult, for example, if banks are allowed to enter into a type of business, but have to issue a "health warning" to their clients that deposit insurance is not available, or setting out the risks associated with the transaction in some detail. In this way, while the business is not actually precluded, it is rendered more difficult. In an increasingly competitive world, these fine differences can be the different between success and failure.

2 Growth limits on allowable size of foreign institution. An example of this is the 1980 Canadian Banking Act, which limited foreign banks to a share of 8% of total Canadian domestic assets. This kept foreign banks away from certain Canadian business.
3 Funding limits. If banks are limited in how much deposits they can take (if any), then foreign institutions must fund themselves from the interbank market, resulting in higher costs. Foreign banks are therefore somewhat beholden on the liability side to powerful domestic banks.
4 Various regulatory hurdles that artificially raise the cost for the foreign institution to do business in the market (for example, licencing or other restrictions). Most of these restrictions lead to an artificial increase in the costs of foreign institutions. These restrictions can include refusing to allow charge cards to be offered to foreign banks. Many of these restrictions lead to fragmentation of the market which leads to the foreign institutions not being able to maximise their market positions. Operating restrictions can limit the overall profitability of the foreign firm, and thus marginally tip the scales in favour of the domestic company.

Impact of International Trade Theories on Financial Services Sector

International trade theories do apply in a fairly conventional way to international financial services. Financial services do comprise certain factors of production that differ from country to country. Ingo Walter has noted that productive technologies differ from country to country.[89] The shifting of productive technology around countries does have an impact on the standard Ricardian model of free trade and comparative advantage in factor production. Walter noted, as long ago as 1988, that:

> It is the presence of controls over the establishment and operation of foreign affiliates that will, in large measure, determine the degree to which effective access to a national market is open to foreign competition…[4,90]

The key area for international financial services is the rules surrounding the establishment of foreign affiliates or branches, as well as the rules that govern their operation. This is the area that governs the interface between competition and international trade in the financial services area.

There is a significant impact of competitive distortions on the productive side of the economy. As banking costs increase (due to the lack of competition), then the productive sector of the economy is disadvantaged compared with other exporting companies from other sectors. In this way, we see that the banking and financial services sector acts as a transmission belt for the economy. Any lack of competition at this level is automatically transmitted to the rest of the economy.

Local financial services companies will often argue that restrictions are necessary as they seek to strengthen their own internal systems to allow them to compete against powerful foreign companies. The problem is that many of these local companies have been present in markets for some time, and there is a tendency for the "infant industry" argument to be used without adulthood ever being reached.

Competitive restrictions can also be caused by the application of prudential regulation. This type of regulation is particularly difficult to deal with, since it appears to be for sound fiscal reasons, and reasons that are furthermore designed to protect consumers. However, local institutions have been successful in using prudential regulation as a way of gaining further protection and further distorting markets. The difficulty in dealing with this kind of protection is that it is relatively difficult to detect, and once detected, it can be changed in a way that preserves its protectionist goals relatively easily. The licencing process, where foreign banks are licenced after the application of a number of factors, is particularly difficult to unpick, since it is hard to tell whether there is a genuinely open process or whether the licencing process is somehow selective.

In many cases the selectivity in dealing with foreign banks is linked to reciprocity considerations as we noted in our discussion of the GATS and the Financial Services Annex. This is in some ways the equivalent of mercantilism in goods negotiations. Governments may make selective reductions in barriers based on their desire to achieve access in another market (and hence may prefer providers from those specific markets). Historically, Brazil allowed one US bank for each Brazilian bank allowed in the US. There is a risk that such reciprocity concerns could also lead to the potential for retaliation depending on what happens in certain markets. The retaliation in the financial services sector could impact the retaliating market (for example, if the UK retaliated against a particular country it might imperil its financial capital status), but this is simply an application of trade and competition theory in a financial services context.

Key Areas Where Foreign Institutions Must Have Equality of Opportunity

There are a number of areas where foreign financial institutions should have market access. These areas include:

1 Institutions should have freedom to establish branches, agencies, subsidiaries and rep offices.
2 All institutions should be subject to the same regulatory framework. In the case of the ongoing Japanese privatisation described above, national firms,

including state-owned ones should have not operated under a different regulatory climate than certain domestic firms do. Another important area that needs to be considered is the application of antitrust arrangements. Different countries interpret antitrust differently and antitrust enforcement could be used to secure protectionist measure if it is interpreted from a competitor and not a consumer welfare standpoint. For example, domestic firms may complain that a particular practice by a foreign firm threatens them – many of these complaints tend to be based on behaviour that is in the interests of consumers (usually because it leads to lower prices). If domestic competition agencies respond to this kind of pressure by disciplining such behaviour, consumers as well as the foreign entrants into these markets will end up suffering.

3 Freedom to have access to import critical resources, such as moving of professional services.
4 Exchange controls should apply equally to foreign and domestic institutions.

Access to Capital

As we have noted, it has become increasingly important for businesses to have access to capital in order to compete globally. This capital can come from banks, but increasingly comes from venture capital funds or form the market in the form of private or publicly traded equities. In particular, the value of private equity funds which take positions in companies which are then traded can be a very important way of filling a market gap if access to capital is otherwise difficult to secure. This is particularly helpful for developing market economies with uncompetitive financial services sectors or under-developed markets.

There are many ways that countries can limit the success of private equity funds to achieve their liberating potential in country. Primarily, these involve making it difficult for funds to repatriate profits, limiting their ability to use competitive tax strategies, or discriminating against their internal structures through domestic regulation or tax laws.

Many of these barriers, as well as limiting the ability of these funds to provide much-needed capital into the system, operate also as anti-competitive restrictions that ultimately damage consumer welfare. Barriers can generally be drawn from the following issues:

- Limits on foreign equity ownership
- Restrictions on scope of business
- Restrictions on number of branches
- Restrictions on composition of local partners
- Restrictions on number of operating licences
- Discriminatory tax
- Government subsidy to local firms
- Restrictions on ownership of land
- Discriminatory licencing requirements

- State procurement policy
- Quotas on foreign service
- Local content rules
- Flexibility in hiring/dismissing workers
- Double-income taxation
- Burdensome domestic regulations
- E-commerce regulation
- Currency Controls or Restrictions
- Restrictions on profit repatriation

A couple of these areas require a specific mention with respect to venture capital and equity funds.

Repatriation of Profit

Funds need to repatriate the profit they make in order to be successful. Rules that require profits to be retained in the country can act as anti-competitive distortions of the market. The same effect can be achieved by having rules that limit the ability to repatriate, but do not altogether deny it. For example, this would include discriminatory or simply very onerous taxation on profits that are repatriated, for example.

Discriminatory Taxation

Taxation that discriminates against equity funds or VCs because of their structure prevents them from assisting companies in developing countries from integrating into the global supply chain. It is important to note that this can include not only de jure tax discrimination, but also de facto discrimination.

Conclusion

We have seen that many of the regulatory barriers that impact the financial services sector in the context of trade liberalisation are in common with the network industries we have discussed. As with other sectors we have analysed, the major issue is one of ensuring that the cost base of competitive firms is not distorted by governmental interference or public sector restraints on trade. In addition, because of the high degree of regulation, that regulation contains within it the possibility of market-distorting practices that also impede entry by foreign participants.

Notes

1 Guide to the Uruguay Round Agreements (1999), at 190.

2 Ingo Walter, *Global Competition in Financial Services: Market Structure, Protection, and Trade Liberalisation* (Harper Collins, 1988), at 111.

3 Kyotaru Tsuru, *Depositor's Selection of Banks and the Deposit Insurance System in Japan: Empirical Evidence and Its Policy Implications*, Discussion Paper Series 03-E-024, Research Institute of Economy, Trade and Industry (2003).
4 *See*, for example, Economic Policy Reforms: Going for Growth 2006 (2006).
5 Richard A. Posner, *The Effects of Deregulation on Competition: The Experience of the United States*, 23 Fordham Int'l L. J. 7 (2000).
6 David E. M. Sappington and J. Gregory Sidak, *Competition Law for State-Owned Enterprises*, 71 Antitrust L. J. 479 (2003).
7 OECD Reviews of Regulatory Reform, *Regulatory Reform in Japan*, Organization of Economic Co-operation and Development (1999) (*hereinafter* "OECD (1999)").
8 OECD Reviews of Regulatory Reform, *Japan: Progress in Implementing Regulatory Reform*, Organization of Economic Co-operation and Development (2004) (*hereinafter* "OECD (2004)").
9 *See* OECD (1999) at 67; OECD (2004), at 67, 77–79.
10 *See id.*, at 192 (*Background Report on the Role of Competition Policy in Regulatory Reform*) ("*Background Report*").
11 *See* Chapter 3 for a detailed analysis.
12 *See id.*; OECD (2004), at 77.
13 *See* OECD (2004), at 64.
14 OECD (1999), at 208 (*Background Report*).
15 OECD (1999), at 64–65.
16 OECD (1999), at 215 (*Background Report*); OECD (2004) at 74.
17 OECD (1999), at 66–67, 224–228 (*Background Report*).
18 OECD (2004), at 67.
19 Comments of Alberto Heimler at ICN Annual Meeting, Bonn, International Competition Network (2005).
20 Understanding on Commitments in Financial Services, §B.1 ("Understanding").
21 *Id.*, §B.2.
22 *Id.*, §B.3.
23 *Id.*, §B.4.
24 *Id.*, §B.5.
25 *Id.*, §B.10.
26 *Id.*, §C.1.
27 *Id.*, §C.2.
28 For a review of such studies, *see* Isaac Otchere and Janus Chan, *Intra-industry Effects of Bank Privatization: A Clinical Analysis of the Privatization of the Commonwealth Bank of Australia*, 27 J. Bank. Financ. 949 (2003), at 952.
29 *Id.*, at 966.
30 *Id.*, at 968.
31 *Id.*, at 964.
32 For a comprehensive look at regulatory reforms in Australia, *see* Gary Banks, Chairman, Productivity Commission, *Structural Reforms Australian-style: Lessons for Others?*, Organization of Economic Co-operation and Development (2005).
33 *List of EU Deregulation Proposals for Japan*, European Commission (1998), at 7. *See also* Ove Juul Jorgensen, Ambassador and Head of Delegation, *Presentation to the Hearing of the Regulatory Reform Committee* (7 Nov 2000) (urging the RRC to take a broad cross-sectoral approach to investment, focusing on a set of reforms to improve market entry conditions and reduce establishment and basic operation costs).
34 *List of EU Deregulation Proposals for Japan*, *id.*
35 *EU Priority Proposals for Regulatory Reform in Japan*, European Commission (2000), at 2.
36 *Id.*, at 6; *EU Proposals for Regulatory Reform in Japan*, European Commission (2005), at 4.
37 *See* OECD (1999), at 14.
38 *Id.*, at 51.
39 *Id.*

40 EU-Japan Economic Partnership Agreement, 2019, art 8.61.
41 *Id.*, art 8.62–8.63.
42 *Id.*, art 8.64.
43 *See The UK-Japan Comprehensive Economic Partnership: Benefits for the UK*, Department of International Trade (2020).
44 UK-Japan Comprehensive Economic Partnership Agreement, 2020, art. 8.61.
45 The *Jusen* were private housing-loan companies that extended their investment portfolios into the riskier commercial market during the "bubble era" speculative real estate boom of the 1980s. The subsequent collapse of real estate prices left banks and other financial institutions holding huge bad debts and led to a massive government bailout.
46 *See* "Solvency II Overview – Frequently Asked Questions," European Union (12 Jan 2015), https://ec.europa.eu/commission/presscorner/detail/en/MEMO_15_3120; Katherine Coates, Hilary Evenett, and Clare Swirski, *Solvency II – What Insurance Companies Need to Know about the New Regulatory Regime*, Clifford Chance (2011).
47 For an overview of insurtech firms, *see Technology and Innovation in the Insurance Sector,* Organization for Economic Co-operation and Development (2017).
48 *See* "Insurers Face Solvency II Costs Estimated to Exceed £200m," Actuarial Post (n.d.), https://www.actuarialpost.co.uk/article/insurers-face-solvency-ii-costs-estimated-to-exceed-£200m-1158.htm.
49 *See* Andrew Barton and Alexander Cibulskis, "Solvency II Reform: An Overview," Macfarlanes (24 Feb 2022), https://www.macfarlanes.com/what-we-think/in-depth/2022/solvency-ii-reform-an-overview/; John Glen MP, Economic Secretary to the Treasury, *Speech to the Association of British Insurers Annual Dinner,* HM Treasuty (21 Feb 2022).
50 *See* European Commission, *EU Proposals for Regulatory Reform in Japan* (2005), at 32.
51 Rob Matheson, "Study: Mobile-Money Services Lift Kenyans Out of Poverty," MIT News (8 Dec 2016), https://news.mit.edu/2016/mobile-money-kenyans-out-poverty-1208.
52 Tamara Cook and Claudia McKay, *How M-Shwari Works: The Story So Far,* CGAP and FSD Kenya (2015).
53 *How M-Shwari Works: The Story So Far, id.*; Ceyla Pazarbasioglu, et al., *Digital Financial Services*, World Bank (2020).
54 *How M-Shwari Works: The Story So Far, supra* note 38.
55 *Id.*
56 Suchanan Tambunlertchai, et al., *Can Fintech Foster Competition in the Banking System in Latin America and the Caribbean?,* Working Paper WP/21/114, International Monetary Fund (2021).
57 "Banks Announce Elimination of Commissions on Digital Accounts," Mexico News Daily (23 Mar 2019), https://mexiconewsdaily.com/news/elimination-of-commissions-on-digital-accounts/.
58 *Digital Disruption: How Fintech is Forcing Banking to a Tipping Point*, Citi (2016).
59 Maggie Fitzgerald, "The End of Commissions for Trading Is Near as TD Ameritrade Cuts to Zero, Matching Schwab," CNBC (2 Oct 2019), https://www.cnbc.com/2019/10/02/the-end-of-commissions-for-stock-trading-is-near-as-td-ameritrade-cuts-to-zero-matching-schwab.html.
60 *See* Oscar Gonzalez and David Priest, "Robinhood Backlash: What You Should Know about the GameStop Stock Controversy," cnet (17 Mar 2021), https://www.cnet.com/personal-finance/investing/robinhood-backlash-what-you-should-know-about-the-gamestop-stock-controversy/.
61 Robinhood was not public at the time, but based on its IPO valuation months later, the single-day capital requirement of $3 billion amounted to just under 10% of its valuation.

62 For a broad overview of the regulatory environment in the US regarding fintech development, *see Modernizing Regulation to Encourage Fintech Innovation, Examining Opportunities and Challenges in the Financial Technology ("Fintech") Marketplace, Hearing before the Sub. Comm. on Financial Institutions and Consumer Credit, H. Comm on Financial Services*, 115th Cong. (testimony of Brian Knight, Director, Program on Financial Regulation, Mercatus Center at George Mason University).
63 *See* D. T. Armentano, *Antitrust and Insurance: Should the McCarran Act Be Repealed?* 8 Cato J. 729 (1989), 736.
64 *See* Global Competition in Financial Services; Market Structure, Protection and Liberalization, *supra* note 2.
65 *See*, for example, Sub-Group of the Shadow Financial Regulatory Committees of Europe, Japan and the United States, Speech, New York City, 14 June 1999.
66 See *Regulation Guide: An Introduction*, Moody's Analytics (2011).
67 *Id.*
68 *Id.*
69 *See* Ohannes G. Paskelian and Stephen Bell, *The Tale of Two Regulations – Dodd-Frank and Basel III: A Review and Comparison of the Two Regulatory Frameworks*, 21 Rev. Future Mark. 7 (2013).
70 *See* Thomas Poppensieker, et al., *Basel III: The Final Regulatory Standard*, McKinsey (2018).
71 *See Time to prepare for finalised CRR2 and CRD 5*, PWC (2019).
72 The Gramm-Leach-Bliley Financial Services Modernization Act of 1999, Pub. L. 106–102 (1999).
73 Speech by Commissioner Norman S. Johnson, *Securities Regulation After Glass-Steagall Reform* at SEC Speaks in 2000, March 2000, Washington, DC.
74 For additional details on the regulatory environment of the financial sector in the US, *see Who Regulates Whom? An Overview of the U.S. Financial Regulatory Framework*, Report R44918, Congressional Research Service (2020); *Introduction to Financial Services: The Regulatory Framework*, Congressional Research Service (2022).
75 Dodd-Frank Act, Pub. L. 111–203 (2010).
76 For a deeper look at the downsides associated with the FSOC and Dodd-Frank as a whole, *see* Dodd-Frank: What It Does and Why It's Flawed (Hester Peirce and James Brougel eds., 2012).
77 "Lehman Brothers: The Rise and Fall of the US Investment Bank," Corporate Finance Institute (n.d.), https://corporatefinanceinstitute.com/resources/knowledge/finance/lehman-brothers/.
78 *See* Thomas L. Hogan, *Costs of Compliance with the Dodd-Frank Act*, Rice University's Baker Institute for Public Policy (2019).
79 Rob Nichols, "Yes, Community Banks Are Struggling under Dodd-Frank," Politico (6 Sep 2016), https://www.politico.com/agenda/story/2016/09/community-banks-dodd-frank-000197.
80 Vladimir Mukharlyamov and Natasha Sarin, *The Impact of the Durbin Amendment on Banks, Merchants, and Consumers,* Faculty Scholarship, U. Penn. L. School (2019).
81 Zhu Wang, *Debit Card Interchange Fee Regulation: Some Assessments and Considerations*, 98 Econ. Q. 159 (2012).
82 Mark D. Manuszak and Krzysztof Wozniak, *The Impact of Price Controls in Two-sided Markets: Evidence from US Debit Card Interchange Fee Regulation*, Finance and Economics Discussion Series 2017–074, Board of Governors of the Federal Reserve System (2017).
83 Diana Olick, "Chase Mortgage CEO Red Flags FHA Loans," CNBC (21 Sep 2015), https://www.cnbc.com/2015/09/21/chase-mortgage-ceo-red-flags-fha-loans.html; Michele Learner, "The Mortgage Market Is Now Dominated by Non-bank Lenders," Washington Post (23 Feb 2017), https://www.washingtonpost.com/realestate/the-mortgage-market-is-now-dominated-by-nonbank-lenders/2017/02/22/9c6bf5fc-d1f5–11e6-a783-cd3fa950f2fd_story.html?tid=ss_mail.

84 Andreas Fuster, Matthew Plosser, and James Vickery, "Analyzing the Effects of CFPB Oversight," Federal Reserve Bank of New York (9 Oct 2018), https://libertystreeteconomics.newyorkfed.org/2018/10/analyzing-the-effects-of-cfpb-oversight/.
85 Seila Law LLC v. Consumer Fin. Prot. Bureau - 140 S. Ct. 2183 (2020).
86 Sarbanes-Oxley Act, Pub. L. 107–204 (2002).
87 Anwer S. Ahmen, et al. *How Costly Is the Sarbanes Oxley Act? Evidence on the Effects of the Act on Corporate Profitability,* 16 J. Corp. Fin. 352 (2010).
88 *Id.*
89 Global Competition in Financial Services; Market Structure, Protection, and Trade Liberalization, *supra* note 2.
90 *Id.*, at 111.

14

IMPACT OF THE NEW MEDIA ECONOMY

Introduction

The world of media and information delivery has changed dramatically in the last three decades. The advent of new advances such as e-mail and the internet have transformed the ways that people process information in the 21st century. While the invention of the printing press led to cost reductions of the order of 1,000, the invention of the microprocessor led to cost reductions of the order of 10 million. All of this means that the last three decades have witnessed an information revolution that has transformed the world even more radically than the industrial revolution transformed the world before it. It is against this ever-changing backdrop that governments must view regulation of the media and other information delivery sectors.

Downward pressure on the costs of transmitting information is transforming the relative costs of transmission and content. Increasing competition in the wireless and wireline telecoms markets as well as competition between them has led to a substantial reduction in costs of transmission. Even as this occurs, content is becoming more important and hence driving costs much more than transmission. Simply put, while consumers of the past understood that most of the costs associated with the transmission of ideas was in the mode of transmission, consumers now are less concerned about the mode of transmission and more concerned about the content of the ideas themselves. A premium therefore attaches to the quality of the content. As the importance of content increases, so people are assembling themselves around ideas and communities of interest as opposed to communities defined purely by geography. In this new marketplace, countries that have unique or attractive cultures will have an advantage. Countries that have an attractive cultural tradition will do well in this environment. Since many of these countries are either developing or advanced developing countries,

DOI: 10.4324/9780429323331-14

this could have a positive impact on developing country economics. Countries that spring to mind include Brazil, with its rich cultural tradition which includes well-known cultural products such as music, Carnival, and soccer, but also an increasing presence in films, tele-novelas and literature. The reality is that most countries have some form of comparative advantage in certain cultural aspects as culture is such a deeply rooted human interest that a market for it will always exist and thrive. As long as the new media economy is allowed to function in a competitive, consumer welfare optimising matter, then these comparative advantages will be liberated.

The new world is a world of technology, where entire product categories can be bypassed by new developments rapidly. The importance of encouraging the type of investment necessary to stay ahead of or at least up to speed with technology is paramount. Most countries are in a transition phase prior to reaching this new world. Actions that countries take in the regulatory arena can have major impacts on the development of the kind of environment that will lead to this new world and its rich promise.

This chapter will review the development of this "New Media Economy," and what countries should do to ensure that it can maximise its position in this new world. We will also analyse the impact of a number of policy responses, including some that many countries are currently analysing to evaluate their impact on the NME itself. We will see that policy responses impact sectors well beyond what has traditionally been called the media sector, and that a number of sub-sectors, while different, are impacted by the kind of regulation which applies to the media sector.

In the course of this chapter, we look at the way the transition from an old media environment to a new environment can be managed. It is important to note that we are not asserting that countries are already in the NME. In reality, there is a spectrum between old media and the NME. Different countries are at different points on that spectrum. Even language has not really caught up with this reality. A good example of such reality is the difficulty to translate the concept of "media" as used in the English language into Portuguese for the Brazilian market, for example. Media in English includes the telecommunications, broadcasting and audiovisual sectors. In Portuguese "media" is much more often associated with the content itself than the transmission means and services used to deliver such content. In the European Union (EU), the audiovisual and media policy focuses on the convergence of media services and the way in which these services are consumed and delivered. For purposes of this chapter, we will refer to the "media sector" as including all telecommunications, broadcasting and audiovisual sectors.

The convergence required for the NME to exist requires a pro-competitive regulatory environment. Without that, or worse with regulations that distort or fragment the developing converged environment, countries will take longer to reach the NME than others, and this will be to their detriment. In the course of this chapter, we make policy recommendations that support rapid entry into the NME. Policies and regulations that fragment the developing NME, such as local content or foreign ownership restrictions should be avoided. For the NME to exist, producers of content must be able to reach the widest market possible, as we describe in the paper. In this context, it is important to note that avoiding fragmentation does not mean that all regulation for the developing NME needs to be the same. What matters is the effect of regulation across all the different sectors and sub-sectors that together will form the NME. The same regulation will actually have very different effects on these different sectors. Instead, policymakers should focus their efforts on ensuring that regulations are not imposed which could have the unintended consequence of making it more difficult for countries to reach and benefit from the NME. We discuss the regulatory environment that is most conducive to the development of the NME in this chapter. The precise regulatory environment of the media sector will have an impact on the ability of both domestic and foreign entrants to successfully enter the market and therefore there is a strong interface with international trade flaws.

The Rise of Dominant Digital Platforms

Before proceeding further into analysing NME, a brief discussion to consider new means for advancing the NME – big digital platforms – is in order. Over the last decade, an increasingly large share of cultural content has been transmitted or otherwise made available through very big online digital platforms, such as Google, Facebook, Amazon, Apple and Microsoft. Although successful smaller (often specialised) platforms exist, the big platforms have (at least for now) assumed market dominance in key segments of electronic services, including, in particular, web browsing (Google), social networking (Facebook) and online sales (Amazon). Very recently, the European Commission and individual countries have adopted regulatory oversight of these big dominant platforms, which will undoubtedly affect the terms under which much cultural content (plus a wide variety of other communications-based services, including social networking, telemedicine, among others) is delivered. The rise and legal oversight of platforms, which will substantially shape the future of cultural content delivery, is addressed briefly in the next section.

Big digital platforms that dominate different market segments exemplify "Schumpeterian competition"[1] in action. Under this innovation-driven form of competition, firms compete "for the market," and the winner assumes a dominant market share – until it is displaced by another firm that rides a new "wave of creative destruction." (For instance, Google displaced Yahoo as the market leader in general web browsing, and Facebook similarly displaced My Space.) Big digital platforms are "multi-sided" – they bring together disparate parties to transact by means of the platform (such as consumers and sellers, researchers and advertisers, social interactors sharing particular affinities). They also are characterised by huge network effects (a rise in the number of transactors on one side of the platform increases the platform's value to transactors on the other side) and economies of scale and scope, that may confer short (or long) term monopoly status.

Dominant digital platforms have faced a mounting number of legal challenges over the last decade. Some noted lawsuits have arisen in the area of consumer protection. For example, in 2019 the US Federal Trade Commission (FTC) fined Google $5 billion and imposed new business restrictions on the company, in settling a complaint that Google had violated a 2012 FTC order by deceiving users about their ability to control the privacy of their personal information.[2] Alleged antitrust violations have featured particularly prominently. In 2018, the European Commission fined Google approximately $5 billion for abusing its market dominance over the Android operating system.[3] Amazon, Facebook, Google, and Apple have faced and continue to face multiple competition investigations in the US, the EU and countries around the world.[4]

Furthermore, by 2021 it was apparent that, in additional to antitrust prosecution, public regulation will be utilised by many jurisdictions to rein in perceived big platform abuses. Most notably, as part of the "European Digital Strategy," the European Commission announced in December 2020 "a comprehensive set of new rules for all digital services, including social media, online marketplaces, and other online platforms that operate in the European Union: the Digital Services Act [DSA] and the Digital Markets Act [DMA]."[5] The DSA focuses largely on consumer protection, while the DMA's requirements centre on promoting competition.

The DSA will introduce a series of new, harmonised EU-wide obligations for digital services (graduated on the basis of those services' size and impact), such as removal of illegal goods, services or content online; safeguards for users whose content has been erroneously deleted by platforms; new obligations for very large platforms to take risk-based action to prevent abuse of their systems; wide-ranging transparency measures, including on online advertising and on the algorithms used to recommend content to users; new powers to scrutinise how platforms work, including by facilitating access by researchers to key platform data; new rules on traceability of business users in online market places, to help track down sellers of illegal goods or services; and an innovative cooperation process among public authorities to ensure effective enforcement across the single market.

The DMA will apply only to "gatekeepers" – major providers of the core platform services most prone to unfair practices, such as search engines, social networks or online intermediation services. The DMA will prohibit a number of practices that are "clearly unfair," such as blocking users from un-installing any pre-installed software or apps; require gatekeepers to proactively put in place targeted measures allowing the software of third parties to properly function and interoperate with their own services; impose sanctions for non-compliance, which could include fines of up to 10% of the gatekeeper's worldwide turnover, to ensure the effectiveness of the new rules (for recurrent infringers, these sanctions may also involve the obligation to take structural measures, potentially extending to divestiture of certain businesses, where no other equally effective alternative measure is available to ensure compliance); and allow the Commission to carry out targeted market investigations to assess whether new gatekeeper practices and services need to be added to these rules, in order to ensure that the new gatekeeper rules keep up with the fast pace of digital markets.

Prominent nations are also quickly implementing regulatory restrictions over big digital platforms. In January 2021, Germany adopted the Digitisation Act, which imposes rules on digital platforms that have "overwhelming importance for competition across multiple markets."[6] Those rules cover such practices as a platform's self-preferencing of its own products or services; use of bundling and tying of products or services; use of competitively sensitive data for competitive advantage; impeding interoperability with other services or data portability; provision of insufficient information to users to evaluate platform services; and making of "unjustified" demands from companies to sell their products or services. By early 2021, the UK, France, Japan, Australia and China, among other countries, had advanced platform regulatory initiatives as well, in the form of rules or guidelines (China).[7] And two distinguished American former senior government officials have called for "light-handed, industry specific" US regulation of digital platforms (encompassing interoperability, interconnection, data portability, among other requirements) in lieu of antitrust remedies.[8]

The rapid move towards regulation of big digital platforms is a significant development. As a general matter, unfortunately, there is no reason to think that this regulatory impetus will prove economically beneficial.

Big digital platforms unquestionably have conferred substantial economic benefits on society, reducing transactions costs (think of sales generated through Amazon and other platforms), generating instantaneous low-cost transfers of information, and promoting new market segments (consider telemedicine and other gains facilitated through platform improvements). Proposals to impose new far-reaching limitations on digital platform activities appear to ignore how regulation may diminish platforms' ability to continue to provide these benefits as effectively, let alone continue to generate the innovations for which the platforms are noted. Added to these costs must be the costs stemming from regulatory compliance; from reduced economic efficiency due to the regulation-induced propping up of unregulated enterprises; and from reduced competition when dominant platforms manipulate regulation to bolster their monopoly status by undermining rivals and potential entrants. These potential costs should be (but seemingly have not been) weighed by governments against the questionable benefits of the complex regulatory schemes being advanced. Broad-based regulation has had a disappointing track record in the US,[9] and empirical research does not build a strong general case for the success of regulation.[10] Furthermore, the greater the complexity of regulatory proposals, the greater the possibility that error will intrude and undermine the hoped-for benefits of the regulatory scheme. Based on these considerations, it seems unlikely that comprehensive big data platform regulation will advance economic welfare – instead, it may well reduce it.

The net costs (or benefits) of digital platform regulatory oversight will be manifested over time and may be taken as a given. The welfare effects of platform regulation may, however, be considered separately from the legal treatment of the new media that platforms help promote. We turn now to a variety of considerations affecting the treatment of NME. In the context of NME, under the right circumstances narrowly and precisely focused regulation may be more justifiable than the broad-based regulation being imposed on platforms.

Definitional Note

The broad media sector consists of telecommunications, broadcasting, audiovisual and related services. However, regulation in this sector does have an impact on other related sectors. Because of the fundamental nature of the telecommunications sector to other branches of the economy, regulation of any aspect of the broad media sector can impact on parts of the economy that rely on basic and value-added telecommunications services. For example, regulation that damages competition in the telecoms sector can lead to fewer citizens having access to internet-based services, and thus can contribute to the digital divide. While many of these sub-sectors of what will eventually be the NME are different, they will increasingly compete. When we talk about the NME or the broad media sector, we refer to that future market segment, which will consist of both content and infrastructure.

Interface with Existing WTO Rules

The rules of the WTO have a special exemption for audiovisual services. This exemption stems in large measure from the cultural significance of these services and the concern of countries such as France and Canada to promote a general exemption in this area. In this sector, trade negotiations have lagged behind actual commercial and technological developments. Often rules are put in place at the WTO level not to increase regulation, but rather to prevent an erosion of the competitive nature of the market or to limit potentially damaging regulations. In the event, WTO negotiations in this area have essentially been moribund for decades. According to the WTO:

> Audiovisual services is one of the sectors where the number of WTO members with specific commitments is among the lowest. Only 18 WTO members undertook commitments following the conclusion of the Uruguay Round, with some additional members doing so as part of their process of accession to the WTO. Countries with significant audiovisual markets that have undertaken commitments in the sector include China, India, the Republic of Korea, Japan, Mexico and the United States.[11]

Commitments tend to be more frequent in movie-related services than in TV and radio-related services. The sector also has a high number of exemptions to the obligation of MFN treatment. These relate, for example, to film co-productions.

Currently, there are rules that do apply broadly to a number of different sectors in the information/audiovisual space. These include the General Agreement on Trade in Services (GATS) and the Trade-Related Intellectual Property Agreement ("TRIPS"). The current definitions in the GATS, which were initially developed when the agreement was originally concluded in 1994, have also been left behind by developments in the high-technology area. Under the GATS the audiovisual sector is classified under the general heading of communication services. This has left some blurring between services that should be covered by telecommunication services or audiovisual sector services obligations. Under the GATS system, countries make specific commitments in certain sectors which include market access and national treatment commitments. Depending on the type of commitments they have made, they cannot then subvert those commitments by legislation or other regulations. These can include limitations on foreign capital, limitations on types of employees, or restrictions on the value of certain transactions. Many countries however do retain carve-outs to preserve cultural diversity. The TRIPS agreement provides a minimum level of intellectual property protection which is required in the areas of patent, trademark, and copyright.

In addition, the Trade-Related Investment Measures agreement ("TRIMS") prevents measures covering investment that violates the WTO's fundamental provisions requiring national treatment and prohibiting discriminatory laws and practices. This means that conditioning investment on such requiring that a minimum amount of local content or a minimum number of local employees be used is potentially a violation of the TRIMS agreement. This restriction imposes some disciplines on the types of market-distorting regulations that countries can use.

Relatively little headway was made in WTO negotiations over cultural diversity. Culture has always had some carve-out space in trade negotiations. As we have noted, in GATT there is a general exemption for measures designed to protect, inter alia, artistic national treasures and the AV sector is generally exempt.[12] Countries may also limit the screen time given to foreign films.[13] In GATS negotiations (as part of the Doha Development Agenda), some countries pushed for a more extensive cultural carve-out (Canada, France), while others recognised that the media sector generally could be both a commercial enterprise subject to international rules and a vector for culture (Switzerland). The Swiss proposed instead a cultural diversity safeguard. The Swiss proposal would allow regulations to preserve cultural diversity but would limit their ability to be abused. Other countries have suggested that the principle of technological neutrality should be observed (US).[14]

The unproductive services negotiations form the backdrop of the discussion on the impact of regulation on competitive markets. The essential failure of those negotiations actually may have been a good thing, since, as with many trade negotiations, producer interests often trump consumer interests.

Turning back to the domestic sphere, it is important for domestic regulators to bear in mind the importance of consumer welfare considerations. The choice is not, as some countries have starkly put it, between promoting and preserving a cultural identity or liberalising trade in media services. In the New Media Economy (see post), and applying the principle of convergence, it is possible to enhance one's cultural identity and make trade in media-type services more open and less subject to government regulation.

Convergence

The major development in this sector that needs to be fully understood is the phenomenon of convergence. Convergence is the process whereby a number of different technology platforms are used by consumers in an increasingly interrelated fashion. We turn now to the EU, whose treatment of audiovisual convergence has evolved in recent decades.[15]

Background on EU Treatment of Audiovisual Services

During the 1980s, new developments in broadcasting technologies led to an increase in the number of commercial TV stations in the EU and to their broadcasts being able to be received in several countries. This gave rise to a need for common minimum standards, which were first laid out in the so-called Television without Frontiers Directive in 1989 (89/552/EEC). Its first revision in 1997 put in place the "country of origin" principle, meaning that broadcasters are under the jurisdiction of the member state in which they are based. Provisions taking into account new services, such as "video on demand" (VOD), were added in the 2007 revision. The directive was codified in 2010 and renamed the Audiovisual Media Services Directive (AVMSD).

The Commission's 2012 report on the application of the AVMSD and its 2013 Green Paper entitled "Preparing for a Fully Converged Audiovisual World: Growth, Creation and Values" focus on the steady increase in the convergence of media services and the way in which these services are consumed and delivered. A few additional words on the Green Paper are in order.

The 2013 EU Green Paper on a Fully Converged Audiovisual World[16]

Nearly a decade ago the European Commission launched a public consultation on convergence in the audiovisual sector. The 2013 Green Paper described audiovisual convergence as follows:

> Convergence can be understood as the progressive merger of traditional broadcast services and the internet. This results in viewing possibilities extending from TV sets with added internet connectivity, through set-top boxes delivering video content 'over-the-top' (OTT) to audiovisual media services provided via PCs, laptops or tablets and other mobile devices.

Consumers use tablets or smartphones while simultaneously watching TV, for instance to find out more about what they are watching or to interact with friends or with the TV programme itself.

Lines are blurring quickly between the familiar twentieth-century consumption patterns of linear broadcasting received by TV sets versus on-demand services delivered to computers. Moreover, with every smartphone enabling converged production as well as consumption, there might be a future shift from 'lean-back' consumption to active participation....

As convergence will become gradually more tangible over the next decade, it might have an impact in future on a number of legal instruments including the Audiovisual Media Services Directive (AVMSD) – focus of this paper -, the E-Commerce Directive and the electronic communications framework. The consultation does not presuppose any specific outcome. Nonetheless, it may pave the way towards possible regulatory and other policy responses in the longer term, in particular linking up Commission initiatives such as the Better Internet for Kids Coalition, possible activities to follow up the report of the High Level Group on Media Freedom and Pluralism, as well as work on self-regulatory initiatives.

The Green Paper briefly "teed up" a variety of topics for the consultation, including growth and innovation, market considerations, financing models, interoperability of connected TV, infrastructure and spectrum, values, the regulatory framework, media freedom and pluralism, commercial communications, the protection of minors, accessibility for persons with disabilities and next steps.

Of particular note, the Green Paper emphasised the importance of ensuring that "the same services are regulated in the same manner irrespective of the device on which they are consumed." Thus, the convergence of "linear (television broadcasts) and non-linear (on demand) services" indicated a need to end the separate regulatory treatment of these services. Accordingly, consideration of regulatory reforms, including more industry self-regulation, was appropriate.

Post-Green Paper Developments

In order to keep pace with developments, in 2016 the European Commission proposed a further revision of the AVMSD. Interinstitutional negotiations on the text were concluded in mid-2018. Key elements of the text agreed included (1) changing the limit for commercial communications from 12 minutes per hour to 20% per day between 06.00 and 18.00; (2) protecting minors from content that "may impair" them, with the same regulation applying to traditional broadcasts and on-demand services; (3) extending the provisions on European works to on-demand services providers, which have to ensure that European works make up at least 30% of their catalogues and (4) bringing video-sharing platforms (VSPs) under the scope of the AVMSD for the purposes of combating hate speech and protecting minors from harmful content. The amended directive (Directive

(EU) 2018/1808) was adopted by the European Parliament and the Council on 14 November 2018.

So as to help EU member states to transpose the revised AVMSD into national law, the Commission adopted two sets of guidelines in 2020: (1) guidelines on VSPs; and (2) guidelines on European works. These guidelines are expected to contribute to the harmonised implementation and enforcement of the directive.

History of Regulation of the Media Sector

Having briefly surveyed European developments, we now turn to some more general considerations regarding the oversight of the media sector. In order to properly analyse the impact of a government's regulatory options and choices in the media and other related sectors it is important to first look at the historical development of media generally. By understanding how the media sector has developed, we can see where it is going and how best to ensure that regulatory environments favour the development of high-value services and do not unduly distort trade and competition. These services will benefit the economy of countries that stimulate their development.

Analysts have generally fallen into two distinct camps when looking at the media. The first group generally regards media as a vector for social ideas and cultural identity. According to these analysts, media has no commercial significance per se. Their policy responses therefore do not consider the impact of regulation on the market, on competition or on the stimulation of foreign investment, but rather focus on restricting or setting parameters for the content produced. If, as a result of content management regulation, there are adverse economic consequences for consumers, these are minimised or ignored.

In contrast, the second group of analysts consider the sector to be a pure and simple commercial service. According to these analysts, there is no role for public policy considerations that spring from the cultural aspect of media. Instead, these analysts argue that any cultural concerns are irrelevant to the treatment of media in the regulatory space. We argue that media can be both, and that the commercial impact of regulation should not be ignored. We will demonstrate that regulation that damages or distorts the market can have a profound and negative significance recognisable even to the media as cultural vector camp.

The variety of media platforms has increased dramatically over time. In the US, by way of example, the Federal Communications Commission (FCC) has analysed these developments in some detail in its Review of Regulatory Requirements for Incumbent LEC Broadband Telecommunications Services (the "Report").[17] We discuss the Report in some detail as it is one of the most comprehensive early reviews into a dynamically changing sector that has been conducted by any regulatory agency globally. As such its findings are valuable and interesting for policymakers in all countries. In reviewing what the approach should be to develop competition for broadband services, the FCC carefully reviewed the history of the entire media sector across a spectrum leading from the birth of the industry to the most modern technological developments. While the report applies to developments in the US, because of the nature of technology many countries have tracked these developments and the FCC analysis has proven very instructive to other nations. It is one of the few examples of such a careful analysis by any regulatory agency in the world and as such holds important insights and lessons.

The Report notes that new media platforms have always been viewed with suspicion by existing ones. When commercial radio licences were granted, commercial radio attracted opposition from vaudeville theatre owners and booking agents who discouraged their acts from performing over the radio. They feared that frequent airplay of their records would lead to the songs losing their value. Within 10 years there were 600 radio stations and 12 million radio users. Frequent airplay of songs, far from dissipating their value, actually enhanced it by broadening the market and bringing more people to theatres who might not otherwise have gone. This is an example of the new technology enhancing the old, not rendering it obsolete. The early opponents of radio thought of the world as a zero-sum world, where the success of the new medium necessarily meant the failure of the old. However, the world is actually a non-zero-sum world, where new technologies can be successful even as the old technology is enhanced.

The cycle was repeated in the case of television, with the first US commercial licence issued in 1941. Ten years later, there were 108 stations and more than 15 million households. The next major technologies to emerge were cable and PAY-TV. There was a slight delay before these channels became competitive with mainstream TV. The turning point for cable in general and CNN in particular was the Gulf War which acted as an exogenous event to spur the uptake of CNN by consumers.

However, in the 1980s and 1990s, consumers started to use a technology which effected a switch from simply being receivers of information to seekers of it and set the stage for the NME. The VCR, which became generally available in 1982, gave consumers the ability to determine when they would watch selected content, freeing them from scheduling imposed by broadcasters. While there have been new technologies and other innovations, such as TiVo, that have continued down this path and rendered the original VCR technology obsolete, what is important is that this new technology follows the path blazed by the VCR and reflects a change in the way that consumers process information which was previously passively delivered to them.

These developments paved the way for the development of the internet and how it is used today. Had this mind shift not occurred, it is questionable whether the internet would be used in the way that it is being used today. Consumers by becoming active seekers of information are able to treat the internet as a vast library of information and interactively search this library for information in ways that increased their productivity. The ability to have access to the single source of all this information without any barriers is the key to the development and value of the internet. Today, the internet is a mechanism that consumers use to literally seek out knowledge.

The coupling of the mass of information available on the internet, and the way that consumers process this information, are the twin pillars on which the NME is built.

Developments of the New Media Economy ("NME") since 2001 FCC Report

We are now in an environment where there are many different delivery systems for content and where the content itself is becoming more important than the way it is carried. This is occurring because carriage costs for this content have been, and are still being, greatly reduced as a result of developments in technology and competition among carriers. If the cost reductions brought about by the introduction of the printing press were of the order of 1,000, the costs reductions brought about by the microprocessor are more on the order of 10 million. These cost reductions have paved the way for a variety of different delivery systems for information. (For example, high-speed digital streaming of motion pictures and other video productions through digital platforms has enabled a wide variety of competing online entertainment services.) In this sense, these costs reductions have led to the new information age and are at the heart of the NME.

The new media economy "is built on a technological infrastructure that carries content. Because content is crucial to the NME it carries regulatory concerns about culture, information flows, and balance that defy purely economic calls for liberalisation."[18] However, in trying to deal with this, regulators frequently violate the fundamental regulatory principle of avoiding unintended consequences. Even as we recognise that regulation of content may apply in ways that are specific to culture, we must also recognise that these regulations can have impacts in related markets and that these impacts can slow down overall progress towards the NME. In order to speed up progress towards the NME, it is necessary to (i) recognise that there will be multiple platforms which will deliver content and (ii) ensure that these platforms can compete effectively with each other. It is through this type of competition (sometimes known as monopolistic competition) that the full benefits of the NME will be realised. Regulators must therefore be careful to ensure that regulatory actions do not limit the effectiveness of this competition by adversely affecting one or more of the platforms.

Importance of Bridging Digital Divide through NME

Much has been written about the importance of bridging the digital divide – of ensuring that the world does not comprise those who know and those who know not (as opposed to haves and have nots). The NME's power is that it has the capacity to increase the number of people who have access to the internet through a variety of different, competing platforms. If these platforms are allowed to compete properly without restrictions, then the benefits which will be delivered to consumers will be significant.

Content plays a very important part in education, particularly childhood foundation learning. Increasingly media sources provide important supplements to education (consider, for example, the work of the Sesame Workshop, an NGO that provides local language versions of the children's programme Sesame Street in multiple countries.) Much of this is available on the internet, and children can learn powerful messages from these sources. These messages can relate to health messages that foster positive habits, as well as learning about other cultures and so forth. The ability to access this content and for content providers to be able to access as wide a market as possible is very important. As a result of the COVID-19 pandemic and the lockdowns and school closures that followed, we have seen how important it is to develop and make available quality educational content.

Network industries have powerful positive feedback loops, derived from strong demand-side economies of scale. This amplifies any perceived weakness and can lead to small differences in the regulatory environment giving rise to significant regulatory effects. This is particularly true for information industries. This means that networks that are not restricted will grow much faster than networks where restrictions are put in place. Since in high-tech, network industries, there are both demand-side economies of scale and supply side economies of scale, this results in a situation which can lead to rapid changes. These changes mean that any restrictive regulation, such as local content or ownership restrictions, will have a greatly amplified effect, and greatly amplified damage. Metcalfe's law (more a rule of thumb than a law) suggests that the value of the network goes up as the square of the number of users. The name of the game, for the NME, is to reach the widest possible market as quickly as possible. Any restriction will have an amplified and negative impact, particularly when you consider that a country's local content will compete against other content in the NME globally.[19]

Digital TV Standards

Positive feedback effects may also be seen in the battle over digital television standards. Globally, competing technological standards govern the transmitting, receiving, and broadcasting of digital television signals. In 1982, a consortium of US entities formed the Advanced Television Systems Committee ("ATSC") which developed a uniform code of technical standards to govern the digital television medium (ATSC Standard A/53). The ATSC standard was adopted by the United States Federal Communication Commission in 1996, and subsequently by the governments of Canada, Mexico and South Korea. Argentina originally adopted the ATSC standard, but reversed its decision in November 2005, deciding instead to adopt the standard ultimately chosen by Brazil. In Europe, a group of over 200 companies established its own Digital Video Broadcasting ("DVB") standards, which prevail throughout Europe and parts of Asia. Finally, Japan developed competing standards known as the Integrated Services Digital Broadcasting ("ISDB") standards. As nations transition from analogue to digital broadcasting, their choices between these standards have widespread economic implications (particularly in the technology manufacturing, broadcasting, television programming and network operations industries) which accentuate positive feedback effects. For example, many countries are currently deciding what format to adopt. Brazil's deliberation over its own digital television standard evidences these positive feedback effects. Brazil's choice of digital television standard is widely projected to determine the standard chosen in all of South America.

These choices are very important because the standards chosen will have impacts on the ability of products that are supported by particular standards to have adequate market access opportunities around the world. Incorrectly (or unscientifically) determined standards can lead to market distortions and a negative impact on international trade.

Traditional Economic Theories Regarding Media and New Developments

Because media products have been regarded as vectors of culture as well as commercial products a number of economic theories have been used to justify some level of governmental involvement.

Some of these theories have suggested that competitive markets do not work in the media sector. The prime example is the case of the broadcasting sector, and the role of public broadcasting within that sector, where there is a component of public goods theory. Notwithstanding these beliefs, it is important to note that regulatory responses to this perceived problem can have negative effects on the other sub-sectors of the NME and can have damaging economic consequences.

As background, public goods theory applies to situations where one person's consumption of a good does not deprive anyone else of the good. Competition is essentially non-rivalrous. Under public goods theory, the marginal cost of production declines to zero as opposed to following a U-shaped curve as is the case for most commercial goods. The reason for this is that consumption does not impact demand. Since competitive pricing requires producers to price close to this marginal cost, in the case of public broadcasting, broadcasters would have to price at prices close to zero. The argument for governmental involvement is that the market alone would not sufficiently incentivise the development of new content in this scenario.

However, there are analogous industries, such as airlines or hotels, where marginal costs are close to zero until capacity is reached. In these cases producers are able to overcome the problem by price discriminating among consumers – for example, a more price sensitive consumer may be offered a lower price on an airline or for a hotel room than a less price sensitive consumer. These are examples where producers can deal with the problem of low marginal cost without having to resort to governmental interference are instructive and demonstrate the value of subscription-based systems. Several other possible solutions exist to the public goods (sometimes referred to as the "free rider") problem. These range from various governmental responses, such as direct regulation, imposition of subsidies, and the creation of intellectual property protections, to more "libertarian" solutions such as Coasian or other solutions driven by individual rather than governmental initiatives. For purposes of this chapter, we will concentrate on the governmental response to the public goods problem.

When regulations are imposed, particularly in the broadcasting sector, there is good evidence that in regulations imposed tend to favour local over national programming, incumbents over entrants, single-channel offerings over multiple channel bundles. Regulatory responses like foreign ownership restrictions can emphasise this problem. Even in countries where the competition principle is the prevalent economic theory, public interest regulation which stems from public goods theory tends to favour those with political power and incumbent interests.[20]

Public Goods Theory: Static versus Dynamic Regulation

One of the traditional theories that has applied to the broadcast sector but which needs to be revisited in light of changing technology is the application of public goods theory. While traditional theories consider regulation in a static environment, a more modern approach is to consider regulation in the context of a dynamic environment. This modern approach allows us to explore new solutions to the public goods problem, such as granting defined property rights rather than just resorting to government regulation.[21] In this case, the theory is that vigorous "monopolistic competition," accompanied by products differentiated by a system of enforceable intellectual property rights The reality is that the protection of intellectual property rights is a vital part of the NME, just as property rights are a vital part of the market economy. Adequate protection of intellectual property rights allows the different platforms of the NME to compete effectively. This, in turn, can lead to more dynamic and pro-competitive markets than conventional natural monopoly theory would otherwise dictate.

The major difference between a normal competitive analysis and the public goods analysis is in dealing with the problem of marginal cost declining to zero when consumption of goods does not affect supply and fixed costs are simply amortised over time. Since marginal cost declines to zero, and competitive pricing is close to marginal cost, the problem is that competitive pricing also declines to zero. This clearly is an unworkable situation and does not incentivise the production of the content to which the public goods theory applies. This is the genesis of the natural monopoly argument.

Industries characterised by this type of marginal cost curve are forced to seek out as wide a market as possible. This notion has important consequences as it means that any regulation that can lead to an artificial limiting of the market will lead to a lowering of production levels, and therefore increased prices.

In the case of the media sector, the emergence of the NME, combined with the phenomenon of convergence discussed above, provides an opportunity to vastly increase the size of the market available for these types of products. So in order to promote a more competitive market for products with "public goods" characteristics that does not automatically lead to a natural monopoly, we must ensure that a combination of inter-platform competition (the so-called monopolistic competition), property rights protection and regulatory policy exists that allows platforms to seek out the widest market possible for distribution of their product. As long as these policies are in place the market will not move towards natural monopoly because the rivalry among different platforms will act as a disciplining effect on price. In this way, there will be a virtuous circle of greater competition among an ever increasing number of platforms. Any regulation or regulatory design that has the effect of limiting the size of markets or artificially fragments them will limit the ability of public goods producers to seek out the widest natural market for their products and services.

The phenomenon of convergence will determine precisely how competitive the different platforms actually might be in the NME. This will clearly impact how effective the theory of monopolistic competition would actually be in preventing public goods economics from fully applying.

Impact of Convergence on the NME

Convergence and the NME have combined to radically change the way consumers process information. As we noted above, these developments have resulted in a framework where content is far more important to consumers than the way it is carried to them. This has changed two very important elements of how consumers related to information: the definition of what is "local" and the definition of what is "free."

Impact of Convergence on the Issue of Locality

Historically, the word "local" had one very precise meaning and that was geographical in nature. However, as a result of the developments we have discussed, the meaning of the word "local" is changing. When transmission costs were high, local was defined in terms of carriage (how far could a particular radio signal reach, for example). With carriage costs becoming a virtual non-factor in an NME environment, it is content that defines local communities. Communities are bound together by common interests and viewpoints rather than merely by the accident of geography. The development of the internet has provided consumers a rich variety of platforms that can compete with more traditional media, such as television, radio, and newspapers, to bind these communities of interest together.

One of the main impacts of the internet revolution that we have discussed is the importance of the electronic media in uniting geographically dissimilar groups with common interests. Groups such as this can be tremendously beneficial for all their members, because they enable groups of people who may not otherwise have access to the most up to date information available to have such access. This enables people from all over the world to climb steep learning curves in all kinds of different areas. The rapid global spread of broadband platform-enabled social networks such as Facebook in the first two decades of the 21st century has been a key means by which common interest groups have been developed.

As we have noted, the FCC issued a report in 2001 regarding broadband and internet access which dealt with how the internet was affecting communications.[22] While this report was issued by a US agency, as with the 2013 European Commission Green Paper, it also clearly has lessons for many jurisdictions and is being widely used and cited to in ongoing work in this area by many countries. While stressing the importance of inter-platform competition, the report also noted how increasing bandwidth capability was changing the definition of "local." Decades ago, radio was the only way of receiving real-time news and information, and radio was inherently geographically local. The report noted that higher bandwidth is a critical component of successful multi-platform competition, because media quality limits the effectiveness of the competitor platform until higher speeds of internet access are secured. Since the report was issued, internet speed has increased astronomically, at relatively low cost.

Over the last two decades, revolutionary advances in bandwidth capability have transformed the communications sector. Real-time communication of extremely complex data and streaming audiovisual services has become a reality with the adoption of 4G and 5G standardised transmission technologies. The incorporation of broadband digital communications capabilities into a host of goods and services (including transportation), enabling the "internet of things," has also transformed markets, and even more dramatic change will be generated through 6G and subsequent updated internet technology standards.

While it may be that media platforms, when looked at individually, may trend towards a concentrated market (or what is sometime termed natural monopoly), the effects of inter-platform competition can mitigate this problem and lead to overall benefits for consumers, downward pressure on costs across the board, and the stimulation of innovation in new technologies. One of the goals of media regulation is to ensure that consumers have access to a high volume of content and prices that are affordable. These twin goals are met when platforms are allowed to compete vigorously against each other. In this regard, the availability of low-cost vastly increased bandwidth will enable individual platforms to provide new offerings to consumers and to compete more effectively with each other. In short, greater bandwidth and improved transmission standards will translate to more vigorous competition over time among media platforms.

Impact of Convergence on the Issue of Free Content

We have explained the dynamics of public interest regulation which arises out of an attempt to correct or mitigate market problems associated with the application of the public goods theory. In the context of the media sector, a central component of such regulation is the notion that some types of broadcasting must be provided for free in order to satisfy certain universal service and "quality" goals. This includes goals such as promoting and enhancing cultural identity. Also these will be achieved and enhanced by the NME. The failure of the market to achieve these goals with respect to public goods has been the justification for governmental regulation of this sector. In the converged NME, market failure carries much less weight as market failure in one component sector can be compensated for by related sectors which are alternative means of disseminating the all-important content. In other words, in a pure NME scenario the ability of the internet sector to disseminate content on a *pari passu* basis with the traditional media sector mitigates the market failure inherent in the media sector. However, it is important to understand that the NME which is vital for the internet to deliver these benefits is not yet a reality, and regulatory responses such as ownership restrictions or other fragmenting regulation can impede the adoption of the NME and therefore prevent the internet from giving rise to these benefits. By extension, less regulation of the internet sector is needed to ensure that it can properly perform this mitigating function.

This debate played out in both the US and the EU in the context of free television. It is important to note that intrusive regulation of TV was initially promulgated because the electromagnetic spectrum available for broadcast services was a limited resource. This was a zero-sum environment, where certain kinds of public service broadcasting would be literally precluded if no spectrum was available. Simply put, enabling certain types of speech necessarily meant less speech in certain other areas.[23]

Public service broadcasting's main aims are to provide consumers with content with characteristics that the regulating authority does not believe the free market would otherwise provide, such as pluralism, diversity, independence and quality (including cultural content). However, the kind of regulation that achieves these goals does not come without costs. These costs are borne by consumers and can lead to greater levels of poverty, and a greater digital divide.

In addition, the constraints which gave rise for the alleged need for government regulation to support public sector broadcasting have become less and less important. The spectrum constraint is no longer as important, as methods of content delivery have shifted to rely less on the limited radio spectrum and increasingly on data access bandwidth which is available through several means. In the NME consumers can choose their content from cable news channels, newspapers, radio or the internet, and are far less reliant on public service channels. The fact that consumers today are not passive receivers of content but rather are active seekers with many potential sources of content, means that the availability of openTV and public sector channels no longer greatly affect consumer behaviour. This is part of the non-zero-sum environment of the NME where greater information benefits all efficient platforms.

Role of Regulatory Design in the Stimulation of Innovation

Regulators must consider what kind of regulatory environment best stimulates innovation in their jurisdiction and, more broadly, how this regulatory environment will interact with others to foster global innovation.

We note here that it is the commercialisation of knowledge, not merely the acquisition of knowledge for its own sake, that leads to economic development and is ultimately useful for society in an economic sense. Economists who have studied the phenomenon of technological innovation generally note that the role of the venture capitalist community is key.[24] The cycle that venture capitalists invest in has been described as a continuous feedback cycle of generation, application, verticalisation (responding to supply chain) and then diffusion. In particular, the last two steps are affected by the regulatory environment. While there have been comparatively few studies on the impact of venture capital on innovation, recent Australian studies do show a strong connection.[25] Studies demonstrate that venture capital does have a strong positive impact on innovation but also that there is a cyclicality in the venture capital business.[26] Under this cyclicality, the impact of venture capital on innovation declines in boom or hot economies. In Brazil, where access to capital in general is limited when compared to other global economies, the potential impact of venture capital as a positive factor for enhancing innovation is enhanced and therefore this is an area we will look at more closely.

The basic question is what type of regulatory environment favours venture capital formation and deployment. The type of regulatory policy that lends itself to achieving this goal tends to be a policy that allows the market to determine where venture capital money should flow, as opposed to one where regulatory distortions limit the ability of venture capitalists to accurately predict whether a particular innovation will be successful or not. The other aspect that venture capitalists certainly look towards is the property rights protection environment.[27] It is no accident that both of these basic conditions are important to the development of the NME as well.

Summary of Optimum Regulatory Design

A theoretical optimum regulatory environment can be developed by combining the NME, convergence and what we know about natural monopoly and public goods theory. As suggested above, we see the following key elements:

i A regulatory environment which allows platforms of information delivery to reach the widest possible market.
ii A regulatory environment that promotes strong inter-platform competition.
iii Property rights protection. This includes intellectual property rights in the traditional sense, but also means that domain names and other forms of creativity are also protected.

iv A deliberately light regulatory touch where regulation is limited to achieve the regulatory purpose and does not overreach.

v Ensuring that regulation that is designed to promote local cultural issues is not abused to benefit particular powerful local companies at the expense of consumers.

Ways of Getting to the Optimum Regulatory Design

It is not always easy to move to the optimum regulatory design. Frequently, powerful political forces that have benefited from the non-optimal design will work to ensure that this does not change or that it is further distorted to benefit them. It is not easy for governments to oppose these powerful forces. However, there are ways that different branches of government, working together, can deliver better, more pro-competitive regulation that benefits their consumers.

In many cases, changes in the regulatory design are made with the specific purpose of promoting "competition." In many cases, this occurs without much input from the agency whose primary function is to promote and protect competition, the competition agency itself. While we do not advocate that regulatory decision-making in the media sector or indeed in other sectors should be assumed by the competition agency, we do strongly promote the idea that the competition agency can play a very important role in helping other regulators understand the competitive process, and also make clear to them and the public in general the costs to consumers of uncompetitive regulatory design. If costs and benefits are made clear to all stakeholders, then they can determine whether or not to pay the costs in order to secure the benefits of a particular regulatory policy. In this way, a competition agency working together with regulators can help ensure movement towards an optimal regulatory design.

The question is not whether competition agencies should be involved in the regulatory process. This is clear. The question is how. While there are few examples of successful intra-governmental cooperation in this area, the UK's Better Regulation Task force has implemented one mechanism that is worthy of further study and which we believe could have more general applicability.[28] Under the authority of this task force, the UK government has instituted a Better Regulation Executive run out of the Cabinet Office, one of the more powerful branches of the UK's civil service. This is an important point as it demonstrates an understanding of the need for an arbiter that is both neutral and politically powerful in the interaction between the competition agency and other regulatory bodies.

Under this system, new regulations are required to go through a "competition filter," i.e. a process whereby the impact of new regulation on the market is assessed. In addition new regulations have to be accompanied by a Regulatory Impact Assessment which asks the following questions:

i In the market(s) affected by the new regulation, does any firm have more than 10% market share?

ii In the market(s) affected by the new regulation, does any firm have more than 20% market share?
iii In the market(s) affected by the new regulation, does any firm have more than 50% market share?
iv Would the costs of the regulation affect some firms more than others?
v Is the regulation likely to affect the market structure, changing the number or size of firms?
vi Would the regulation lead to higher set-up costs for new or potential firms that existing firms do not have to meet?
vii Would the regulation lead to higher ongoing costs for new or potential firms that existing firms do not have to meet?
viii Is the sector characterised by rapid technological change?
ix Would the regulation restrict the ability of firms to choose the price, quality, range and location of their products? [29]

An affirmative response to any of these questions triggers automatic involvement by applicable competition agencies. In the UK, for example, the Better Regulation Executive is run by the Cabinet Office which enables it to solicit input across a range of government departments, as well as external agencies such as the Competition and Markets Authority, especially as to the cost to consumer welfare of anti-competitive regulation. This tends to ensure that it will have greater credibility and persuasiveness in the overall process or regulatory design.

The advantage of this approach is that it forces the agency that is primarily responsible for consumer welfare to make the argument that a particular regulation has consumer welfare enhancement damaging characteristics. The problem this agency generally has is a lack of political credibility. If the agency is formally asked for its views, especially if it is by a powerful arm of government (in the case of the UK, the Cabinet Office is a politically powerful entity and the fact that it has made the requests vests the competition authority with external credibility).

Media Regulation in Different Markets

In the EU, considerable time has been spent grappling with the issue of how to ensure that cultural considerations are not lost while at the same time preserving a balance with commercial considerations. An underlying aspect of EU regulation is that regulation should be interpreted in the least restrictive way possible where there is ambiguity.[30]

The EU has taken the position (mirroring the Swiss position on media and culture referred to above) that one can have a fully functioning commercial sector and still preserve cultural ideals. Indeed, the EU position is that a vibrant commercial sector is one means of transmitting cultural content to markets around the world.

In 2000, the EU adopted a comprehensive agenda for the development of its information technology sector. This formed part of the Lisbon agenda, which was the European agenda for ensuring that the EU maximises technological advances for its economic growth.[31] The EU noted that it had fallen behind some its global competitors in this area and needed to focus on why this had occurred and how this process could be reversed. The process the EU went through in arriving at the Lisbon agenda is a very instructive one. It notes, for example:

> Most services are provided by the market. Developing new services needs significant investment, most of it from the private sector. But there is a problem: funding more advanced multi-media services depends on the availability of broadband...Action is needed to stimulate services and infrastructure to create the dynamic where one side develops from the growth of the other.[32]

It is noteworthy that the Lisbon strategy was not just about productivity and growth, but also about employment and social cohesion. As noted in Europe 2005:

> Europe 2005 puts users at the centre. It will improve participation, open up opportunities for everyone and enhance skills...One important tool to achieve this is to ensure multi-platform provision of services. It is generally accepted that not everyone will want to have a PC. Making sure that services, especially on-line public services, are available over the different terminals such as TV sets or mobile phones is crucial to ensuring the inclusion of all citizens...[33]

Beyond the Lisbon Agenda: Europe 2030

The Lisbon Agenda has been superseded by Europe 2030, an aspirational EU policy agenda that looks to promote economic and social improvements that will be realised by 2030. As part of this process, in March 2021 the European Commission announced the digital aspects of the 2030 initiative, the digital compass:

> The digital compass sets out objectives to achieve the EU's vision for the digital future. It uses the four points of the compass to identify the main goals to reach over the next decade:

- a digitally skilled population and highly skilled digital professionals
- secure and substantial digital infrastructures
- digital transformation of businesses
- digitisation of public sectors

Key policy areas to ensure these goals are met include cloud computing, artificial intelligence, digital identities, data, and connectivity.

The digital compass can also support the EU in meeting objectives in the European Green Deal, helping Europe to reach its goal of reducing greenhouse gas emissions by at least 55% by 2030. Digital technologies help to reduce environmental impact significantly. For example, the widespread use of videoconferencing plays a part in reducing flight emissions. And, digital technologies play a role in creating a greener approach to agriculture, energy use in buildings, and more sustainable city planning.[34]

The European Commission has been seeking input to implement its 2030 vision:

> On 12 May, the Commission launched a public consultation on the formulation of a set of digital principles. The consultation, open until 2 September 2021, seeks to gather views from citizens, non-governmental and civil society organisations, businesses, and all interested parties. These principles will guide the EU and Member States in designing digital rules and regulations that deliver the benefits of digitalisation for all citizens.[35]

The Commission already has enunciated several ambitious digital goals to be achieved by 2030. Key goals include (1) Skills (over 20 million ICT specialists, gender convergence, and at least 80% of the population possessing basic digital skills); (2) Secure and sustainable digital infrastructures, including connectivity (gigabit bandwidth for everyone, 5G everywhere); cutting edge semiconductors (double EU share in global production); data (edge & cloud: 10,000 climate neutral highly secure edge nodes); computing (first computer with quantum acceleration);

(3) Digital transformation of businesses, including tech take-up (75% of EU companies using Cloud/AI/Big Data); more innovators (grow scale ups & finance to double EU Unicorns); digital improvements for late adopters (over 90% of SMEs reach at least a basic level of digital intensity), and digitalisation of public services (100% of key public services online; comprehensive e-health, with 100% of citizens having access to medical records; and 80% of citizens using digital ID).[36] The European Commission proposes to advance these goals through multi-country projects and international public-private partnerships.[37]

Analysis of European Approaches to Public Service Obligation

An analysis of European approaches to public service obligations in broadcasting is difficult. The problem is, as we note earlier the widespread reliance by publics on public broadcasters and less of a reliance on commercial channels for this type of input. This kind of choice is made much more by European consumers than by consumers in the US or elsewhere, and reflects the power of European public broadcasters and their role in the minds of European publics for decades.

Recently, European commercial broadcasters have sought to use European state aids rules to discipline and rein in the aid being given to state-controlled broadcasters. After the European Court of First Instance had criticised the European Commission for failure to act on the complaints about state aids, particularly with respect to Spain and Portugal, the Commission issued a preliminary report on the financing mechanism for the broadcasters. Problems continued as state broadcasters continued to move into what had traditionally been the commercial market segment (for example, the BBC's 24-hour channel about which BSkyB had complained). The Commission had initially adopted a test that was similar to *Altmark* but even more simplistic – essentially saying that as long as the aid did not exceed public service costs, there would not be a problem with it.

The major potential issues that could give rise to market-distorting state financing are (i) licence fees, (ii) taxes, (iii) guarantees provided by the state, (iv) special tax arrangements and (v) debt cancellation.

One major difference in Europe between the treatment of broadcasting and other sectors is the Broadcasting Communication and the Amsterdam Protocol. The Amsterdam Protocol in particular highlights issues such as media pluralism and social and cultural needs as integral to the need for a system of public broadcasting.

The Commission requires member states to determine what is the scope of the public service function in accordance with the goals stated above. The Commission can only intervene if the goals set out by the member state are somehow manifestly wrong. One issue that does cause competition and trade problems is where the member state increases the scope of the Public Service Obligation by entrusting new services into the hands of the public undertaking. Where these are services that are provided by the private sector, new product entrustment can cause a number of difficulties and distort other related markets. We have seen similar issues played out in the postal and telecom chapter analysis. The BBC 24-Hour News Channel decision held that once a particular product was decided to be part of the PSO, then it did not matter how that product was delivered. The Commission found in that case that as long as the distribution of programmes through digital means addressed the same democratic, social and cultural needs, then the distribution mechanism did not affect the PSO decision. In the TV2 decision, which involved the Danish government's recapitalisation of TV2, a state-run broadcasting channel, the public service obligation was extended into the internet. The Commission held that the online presence of the service or an online reference to it could be within the PSO, but that online services that duplicated commercial services (such as games or chat rooms) would be manifest error if the country designated these as part of the expanding PSO. It certainly was relevant that European law differentiates between broadcasting services and information society services (perhaps an artificial distinction). The Commission's view was that while some online services could be covered under the Broadcasting Communication, not all new media services would be. It is particularly in the provision of these services that anti-competitive effects can result from an overbroad interpretation of what should be covered by public service obligations.

Adequate Supervision and Proportionality

Under the prevailing European law, member states are relied on to adequately supervise the fulfilment of the public service mission. This adequate supervision requirement mirrors the *Midcal* test for the US state action exemption doctrine (which we discussed in Chapter 3) which resembles more and more the "services in the general economic interest" exemption to European state aids law. Adequate supervision is required in order to ensure that there is downward pressure on costs at all times.

The measure must also be proportionate. The key question in answering this is to determine precisely how PSO costs are determined. Where a broadcaster is fulfilling a PSO as well as producing product that competes with commercial providers, the issue becomes one of accounting separation (as it is in other regulated sectors as described above). There are a number of models for calculating these costs. Some involve a stand-alone costs test (what are the costs of the PSO and commercial services standing alone, i.e. building into the cost of the commercial service the benefit derived from the PSO network), some an avoided cost test (which asks what the costs would have been if the non-public elements were removed). However, the grey area between these segments means that a rigid division will sometimes not be meaningful. In the RAI case, the Commission used a stand-alone costs test, using the cost base of the private competitor, Mediaset as a proxy for an efficient operator (under the Altmark test). In the case, the competitor was alleging that RAI was charging prices that would not allow the competitor to recoup cost if he charged them (i.e. an anti-competitive cross-subsidisation claim along the lines that we have discussed in telecom/postal).

There have been cases where there is a legal requirement to keep separate accounting, such as in the case involving the Italian broadcaster, RAI. Generally the Commission has rarely found that a broadcaster has been paid too much for its PSO. The only example is the TV2 case where the Commission found an overpayment of EUR84m.

In Singapore, the Minister of Communications and Information Technology noted the negative impact of maintaining, even for a short time, legislation that is less than pro-competitive. In a speech on 21 September 2001, the Minister noted that:

> The global info-communications industry relies heavily on telecommunications as a foundation for business. As such the openness of the telecommunications regulatory environment is a key factor in attracting new investments and players. Our phased liberalisation approach has now led key global info-communications players to perceive us to be less competitive and attractive…we cannot afford to maintain the two-year moratorium period [on further liberalisation] in this fast-paced info-communications industry, even a few months can make a substantial difference.

Importantly, the Minister noted that the right regulatory mix would mean that there would be more fierce competition and lower prices and the information technology industry would grow much faster than if the current market structure which was characterised by a lack of competition was maintained. Singapore, once it liberalised its market became far more successful due in part to the high degree of internet connectivity of its businesses and people. Unlike its approach in some other areas of political life, the Government of Singapore took an early decision not to over-regulate the internet and the resultant light touch regulation has led directly to economic growth.

Local Content Regulations as an Anti-Competitive Market Distortion

Local content regulations are regulations that provide that companies that invest in a certain country for production purposes must produce a minimum quantity of local content. While these kinds of regulations are designed to promote local culture and local content, they rarely have this effect. The United Nations Committee for Trade and Development Secretariat has prepared a note on Audio-Visual Service: Participation of Developing Countries (the "Note").[38] The Note stated that despite considerable state ownership of media channels and local content regulation, many developing countries simply had not produced much audiovisual product. An extreme example cited in the note is Africa, where the last 90 years have seen only 600 feature films (produced in Africa by African entities), resulting in only 2% of Africans, as of the date of the Note, having seen an African film. One explanation for the findings in the Note is that it is the creativity of content producers that leads to content, not the requirements set out in local content regulation.

The Note also makes the point that the barriers that developing countries face may be present in more developed countries, such as the local content regulations in Canada and France. There are also less well-known examples of restrictions on media distribution, such as the German Youth Protection Authority, an agency which rates DVDs under a special rating system and that requires local reproduction and distribution for compliance with such system. If a country provides local content regulation, then it runs the risk of retaliatory local content regulation by other countries. This encourages a "race to the bottom" of competing local content regulation that has a fracturing effect on the global market, and thus runs counter to the economics driving the NME.

In summary, local content regulation does not appear to lead to the stimulation of local content but rather seems to lead to the fragmentation of markets. This works against the interests of those countries that could benefit the most from the NME and the expanded markets it promises.

Local Working/Employment Regulation

Some countries adopt regulations that require foreign investors to employ a certain number of nationals. These regulations also distort markets and are violations of the TRIMS agreement. However, as in the case of local content, they have a tendency to restrict the ability of the different platforms for content delivery to compete against each other. The less competition among platforms occurs, the less likely consumers are to see the long run benefits of the NME.

The problem with these kinds of regulations is that, by distorting the economic calculus that companies engage in when making investment decisions, they lower both the type and scale of investment. Since countries are increasingly competing on a global scale, investors will look for opportunities where such regulations are not present and will increasingly eschew countries which restrict them in this way.

Ownership Restrictions

While ownership restrictions pose a number of problems, including whether they fully comply with a country's WTO obligations, most significantly they have a fracturing effect on the global markets that should be a feature of the NME. By fracturing the natural drive towards a global market, ownership restrictions tend to limit the value that the internet sector as a whole can provide to a country's economy, because as we have demonstrated above many of those gains require a global market for internet services. As we have demonstrated throughout this document, the negative impact of ownership restrictions would significantly impede the ability of Brazil to enter into the NME. This would have negative consequences both for the countries' economic development potential and with respect to an increasing digital divide.

Ownership restrictions can also prevent certain activities, such as pro-competitive and efficiency enhancing merger activity, that can lead to overall consumer welfare enhancement.[39] Today's media market is characterised by abundance and not by scarcity [of content], and the FCC has noted that relaxed US ownership rules would lead to greater levels of innovation. The case for allowing more merger activity in the media sector as a whole is based on the benefits that such mergers can give from the consumer welfare enhancement perspective. Ownership restrictions limit the efficient and consumer welfare enhancing activity. Like the other regulations referred to in this section, the fundamental problem with ownership restrictions is that they limit the calculus that businesses make when deciding how to deploy their limited resources. As a result of this, they forestall the possible benefits that could arise from the NME.

The US FCC still imposes a panoply of media-related ownership sets limits on the number of broadcast stations – radio and TV – an entity can own.[40] As required by Congress, the FCC reviews most of its media ownership rules every four years to determine whether the rules are in the public interest and to repeal or modify any regulation it determines does not meet these criteria. Supporters of these restrictions sometimes reference the importance to freedom of speech (a core American value) of having a plurality of independent media voices. Key features of the current FCC ownership rules as of 2021 include (1) a merger between any two of the big four US broadcast television networks, ABC, CBS,

Fox, and NBC, is effectively prohibited; (2) an entity is permitted to own up to two television stations in the same Designated Market Area (DMA), subject to certain conditions; (3) there are limitations on the number of radio stations a single entity may own in an area are based on a sliding scale that varies by the size of the market; (4) there is no limit on the number of television stations a single entity may own nationwide as long as the station group collectively reaches no more than 39% of all US TV households; and (5) there is no limitation on common ownership of a full-power broadcast station and a daily newspaper if the station's contour (defined separately by type of station) completely encompassed the newspaper's city of publication and the station and newspaper were in the same relevant media market (in 2017, the FCC eliminated a rule that prohibited such common ownership arrangements, and the Supreme Court upheld the FCC's action in 2021). It is questionable whether the FCC broadcast ownership restrictions have any real influence on the variety of information sources readily accessible to consumers in the internet age. Nevertheless, political realities suggest there is no reason to believe that existing restrictions are about to be lifted soon (indeed, the reimposition of old restrictions is just as possible, depending upon decisions by the FCC's political leadership, which changes over time).

In all of these cases, the fundamental problem with the applicable regulations is that they undercut the NME, which requires the strong inter-platform competition within the widest possible market. It is important to note in this context that most countries are in a transitional phase somewhere between the traditional approach to information delivery and the NME. It is important to restate that this transition is a market-driven transition. This market-driven transition is the direct result of the dramatic reduction in costs for transmission that have arisen in large part due to the introduction of the microprocessor (see discussion above) and the subsequent development of the global internet and information infrastructure. Government regulation can substantially interfere with this market-driven transition, and therefore regulatory design in this area can have far more wide-ranging consequences than regulators may have considered in framing the regulation itself. Regulation can reach other market segments, and other forms of information delivery (including suppressing some forms of information delivery not yet invented) which under a traditional scheme might have been completely independent from the subject area of regulation. As we approach the NME, regulators must be careful to ensure that regulation does not preclude or distort that market-driven process.

Beneficiaries of NME

It is cultures that will benefit from the NME. Cultures that have unique or positive attributes that make them attractive will attract a large audience not limited by geographical constraints. For example, interest groups will assemble on a global basis around a particular cultural component. This will serve as an even stronger carrier of the culture to these other groups, and serve to further strengthen the culture components themselves.

In this sense cultures that have a comparative advantage will do well, just as it might be said of any other tradable good or commodity. In this environment, strong and attractive cultures have nothing to fear and their representatives should be seeking to move them towards the NME, so that they can take full advantage of its benefits.

The internet and the NME are changing lives. The new environment offers significantly increased choice and better prospects for people everywhere. Strong cultures stand to gain significantly from the NME, provided that the regulatory environment is conducive to its development. It is very important that the regulatory system is pro-competitive in nature and facilitates the continued market transition towards the NME.

Given all of this, it is important that the kind of regulatory system that is in place for this space is pro-competitive and facilitates the flow of trade that will ensure the sector grows at a rapid pace. We have demonstrated that such growth is imperative for a dynamic market which has strong public goods characteristics, such as a marginal cost curve which is declining to zero. With marginal cost heading to zero, the only economic models that work are the dominant form, or monopolistic configuration where there are differentiated product markets (as there are in this case). Personalised pricing mechanisms (where there is considerable price discrimination) will help deal with declining marginal costs (*see also* hotels and airlines discriminating up to the point where capacity is reached). These are consumer welfare enhancing initiatives.

Product differentiation becomes very important in the NME. Again, product differentiation lends itself to maintaining a personal relationship with each consumer and lends itself to a monopolistic competition scenario. There may be additional competition concerns in the NME beyond price. Consumers are more likely to pay for premium service (especially since price discrimination will be the norm). Quality will therefore become a significant goal of consumers as well as low price. Market segmentation by product is complemented by geographical market breadth. Market segmentation of different products or versions of products works because if each segment has property protected by intellectual property, there can still be significant competition among the different segments with their segment counterpart in the other country. One can see that this drive for new versions and new segments stimulates new innovation.

Consumers increasingly demand customised bundles of information. This kind of bundling, which might have attracted antitrust concern in the past is, in the New Economy, precisely what customers want (how many customers would request a new computer with no software installed).

The NME coupled with the public goods nature of these products means that some of the product will likely have to be given away – this increases the need to ensure that money is made over those aspects of the product that are not given away.

The NME, we have seen, is also characterised by high rates of lock-in and high switching costs. By their very nature information systems tend to bind customer groups who are unwilling to change a familiar technology for another type of technology. Because lock-in will play a bigger role in the NME, we are more likely to see promotional programmes, loyalty programmes and so forth in the NME. We need to consider the impact of such programmes on competition. Lock-in is a significant problem not only for consumers who must pay high switching costs, but also for the companies that provide the technology to which customers might switch. Lock-in increases the effective market power of incumbent companies. Hence there are competing impacts on market power. Lock-in tends to increase it. New technologies that may revolutionise product markets tend to decrease it. Lock-in also means that there are significant first-mover effects. Companies that can build their installed base of customers by being first to market will likely retain these customers because of the lock-in effects we describe above.

The value of the network clearly depends in some part on the number of other people who are connected to it. These networks create positive feedback loops, which magnify both success and failure. Markets that are characterised by positive feedback tend to move rapidly to natural monopoly characteristics (see VHS versus Beta in the video recorder market). This type of market increases the effect of large market share, because these markets are characterised by a tipping point where once market share rises above a certain level it rapidly becomes total (the strong get stronger and the weak get weaker). But again the flipside of this is the propensity of new technologies to create entirely new product markets. This means that the NME is characterised by a sea of rapidly evolving monopolies that are swiftly replaced by new rapidly evolving but different monopolies. The NME is characterised by significant network externalities. Hence (according to Metcalfe's law), the value of the network to each of the network users is (n^2-n). Value increases much more rapidly than network size, exacerbating the effect of club size.

However, it is also important to note that even where these effects manifest themselves, lock-in and network externalities and positive feedback can be overcome if the new product is sufficiently differentiated and perceived to be very high quality.

More than in traditional markets, in network industries, there is a need to balance cooperation in order to enhance network effects, and to maximise pure competition based on property protected by intellectual property. The latter stimulates innovation, the former leverages positive network externalities. The balance, which is generally drawn by regulators and legislators, is key to determining whether the NME is moved forward or moved backward.

This has particularly strong impacts when it comes to standard setting. In network industries, standards have to be set and agreed among companies in the private sector. These companies have the knowledge and the ability to set standards that the regulator lacks. However, not all companies have the same interest in standard setting. Some companies may indeed want to see a new technology perish because no standard was ever set. Some of these companies may have inserted themselves in the standard setting process simply to thwart agreement. The regulator's role is to find ways of brokering these areas of potential disagreement.

This dynamic has led to a discussion of open standards, and to be sure, these may be able to leverage positive network externalities. However, one has to also consider the impact on technology development (the supply side question) of having an open standard. Similarly, proprietary rights can be used to block the emergence of a standard. Generally in the NME, the building of a market is at least as important as how competition affects that market. Companies operating in the NME will go to extraordinary lengths to build an installed base (or market) early on, perhaps even before the technology is launched. Such activity has to be incentivised in order to ensure that markets for new technologies will actually exist. This requires what some authors (notably Barry Nalebuff, *Co-opetition*, Shapiro and Varian, *Information Rules*)[41] have described as co-opetition.

Dangers of Openness to the Process of Competition

Many in the NME and new technology world accept as an article of faith that networks must be open. However, there are some dangers with respect to openness in terms of how innovation might be affected. A much better idea is to allow the individual platforms which are each protected by some form of intellectual property to compete with each other. This has been described as monopolistic competition, but this name is a little misleading. This is really competition among platforms that are each protected by some form of property rights protection. The danger with open standards and open technologies is that the same openness that enables interoperability and interconnectivity could also lead to a reduction in the incentive to, using the language of the old economy, "build a better mouse-trap."

There is also an efficiency argument with respect to the fragmentation that is possible with open standards. These frequently can be built on (which is their strength), but that same building can be their undoing if it leads to a multiplicity of "dialects." This is analogous to the argument that says that some vertical relationships are efficiency enhancing. Suppliers often want to preserve the integrity of their distribution channels. So it is in the interests of society not to have multiple technologies all speaking with slightly different languages. These efficiency arguments are really consumer welfare arguments, where the open access arguments come from a competitor welfare, or producer welfare vision. The precise treatment of open standards is therefore not dissimilar to the overall theme that runs through this book. That consumer welfare enhancement should be the touchstone not only of competition policy, but of domestic regulatory reform as well.

The key elements that will be required in order to succeed in this world were set out by Shapiro and Varian in *Information Rules*:

1 Control over an installed base of customers.
2 Intellectual property rights.
3 Ability to innovate, especially by making proprietary extensions.

4 First-mover advantages. The value of being first in information markets is very strong.
5 Complementary Technology.
6 Brand name.

The fact that positive feedback magnifies strengths means that there is a real premium in getting in front of your competitors and staying in front.

All of this increases the use of deep discounting and cross-subsidisation to lure and hold onto installed customer base. This kind of deep discounting could have anti-competitive effects. The question becomes who is actually engaged in the discounting and where does their source of revenue come from. Here internal market battles between two companies engaged in a price war for installed base could have an impact on global trade as these two companies duke it out around the world. Based on the propensity of companies in this sector to bring antitrust cases against each other, we may the see the global use of antitrust litigation to win business wars around the world. It is important in this context that the standard used to judge whether there is, indeed a problem is consumer welfare enhancement, as opposed to competitor welfare enhancement. Here the deep discounting might represent greater efficiency for reasons that are unique to the NME and hence have efficiency enhancing benefits.

Impact of Regulation of the Internet

One of the most challenging issues that is playing itself out today is the debate over "net neutrality" over the internet. This also has an impact for trade and competition policy. The internet is currently operated in such a way that there is equality of access for all applications and content. Any content provider can be assured that its content will have equivalent access or shelf space with other content providers in the internet supermarket.

One cannot talk about the net neutrality debate without considering the landscape for the provision of telephony and other related services. At the end of the day, this is an issue of the competitive environment. If there is a competitive environment for the provision of telecoms services – the service of the pipes, in internet language, then some of the concerns that have led to calls for net neutrality laws will abate.

Net Neutrality

Net neutrality refers to the concept that broadband internet access service providers should transmit all internet content equally, without discrimination based on user, content, website, platform, application, type of equipment, source address, destination address, or method of communication.[42] Given the cross-ownership that we have discussed in the sector, there may be competition issues associated with allowing parties that control access to determine whether certain content will appear on the net and how. A variety of jurisdictions have adopted net neutrality rules. Those enacted in the US and Europe merit special mention.

Over the last decade the US FCC has imposed "net neutrality" obligations on broadband providers governing the terms of transmission offered to different purveyors of online content (in 2015); repealed those obligations (2018); and is now likely to reimpose those obligations.[43] History suggests that, at least in the US, the much-hyped net neutrality issue was much ado about nothing. Evidence is lacking that the absence of a US net neutrality obligation prior to 2015 (and after 2018) had any influence on the rapid growth of the internet or the ubiquitous non-discriminatory access to internet transmission by internet content providers ("edge firms"). Thus, it is not terribly surprising that the three year period of US net neutrality regulation (2015–2018) did not usher in significant changes in the relationship between broadband providers and edge firms. The net neutrality experiment did, however, impose unnecessary regulatory costs on broadband providers and may have marginally reduced their incentive to invest in additional broadband capacity (the broadband investment effect, however, is a subject of debate among economists). The US example is a testament to the fact that market forces (in particular, consumer demand for varied online content) drove and continues to drive broadband providers to make their facilities widely available to edge players without the need for regulation (which, had it been pervasive, would have deterred growth and innovation in the internet economy).[44] Broadband providers do not act like uncontrolled monopolists, because, "the US broadband market is already healthy, and in most cases, competitive outcomes are close to optimal."[45] Thus the continued discussion of net neutrality in US policy circles is not due to economic substance. It appears to be more rooted in symbolism or in a philosophical attachment to regulation that is not grounded in economic realities.

The EU adopted a net neutrality law in 2015, the Open Internet Regulation (Regulation (EU) 2015/2120),[46] which is summarised by the Body of European Regulators for Electronic Communications (BEREC):

> Under the EU rules, ISPs are prohibited from blocking or slowing down of internet traffic, except where necessary. The exceptions are limited to: traffic management to comply with a legal order, to ensure network integrity and security, and to manage exceptional or temporary network congestion, provided that equivalent categories of traffic are treated equally. The provisions enshrine in EU law an end-user's right to be "free to access and distribute information and content, use and provide applications and services of their choice". Specific provisions ensure that national authorities can enforce this new right.
>
> The best effort internet is about the equal treatment of data traffic being transmitted over the internet, i.e. that the 'best efforts' are made to carry data, no matter what it contains, which application transmits the data (application-agnosticism), where it comes from or where it goes. The benefits of

> the best effort internet notably include the separation between application and network layers of the internet. This separation enables innovation of applications independent of the ISP, thereby enhancing end-user choice.[47]

Furthermore, individual EU countries have adopted additional net neutrality regulations that go beyond the requirements of the Open Internet Regulation.

Initial research on European net neutrality initiatives casts doubt as to its effectiveness and suggests that these efforts have been economically counterproductive. One study of the Open Internet Regulation and of national net neutrality initiatives in Europe[48] found that in key respects European net neutrality initiatives were counterproductive, and (in addition to the problematic imposition of substantial new regulatory costs) there were at least three unintended consequences. First, "[s]peed cannot be guaranteed without a quality-of-service guarantee or prioritisation, but these are unwittingly prohibited by most net neutrality rules." Second, regulatory surveillance required net neutrality rules could undermine internet users' privacy. Third, net neutrality did not stimulate innovation: "Europe continues to fall behind the US and East Asia. No European company has appeared on Mary Meeker's internet trends report for years, while Chinese internet companies gain an increasing foothold." Another study of over 50 countries found that hard net neutrality rules did a poorer job than voluntary efforts at promoting innovation at the edge of the network (including new mobile apps).[49] More generally, a 2019 compendium of economic analyses of net neutrality in the US and Europe displayed general scepticism about net neutrality initiatives, suggested they may have retarded innovation, and found no evidence of market failure sufficient to justify broad and far-reaching rules:

> Summarising, the existing peer-reviewed theoretical literature (as reviewed in this issue) shows that net neutrality is not unambiguously good; in contrast, only under specific market conditions could the policy be welfare enhancing. The related empirical literature (as reviewed in this issue) is very scant and points to negative effects of net neutrality regulations on network investment and innovation activities. One of the main economic findings in this special issue is that the presence or absence of net neutrality policy regulation makes either little difference for market outcomes, or certainly not enough positive impact on market outcomes to justify any strict, and arguably controversial, interventionist policies. The economic analysis indicates that net neutrality rules should be limited to prevent specific abusive behaviour in an ex-ante framework, if ex-post legislation is deemed insufficient. In any case, there is no evidence of apparent market failure and hence no justification for imposing strict and broad net neutrality rules.[50]

In addition to European nations, a number of economically significant jurisdictions, including, among others, India, Japan, Canada, Brazil, Chile, Mexico,

Israel, Russia and South Korea, have enforceable net neutrality policies, which vary significantly in their scope and impact.[51] (China is not involved in net neutrality, as the government uses ISPs to inspect and regulate the content that is available to their citizens, and blocks internet sites as it sees fit.)[52] These and other nations (particularly developing nations) that wish to expand their internet-based economies and participate in the NME should be mindful of the poor record of net neutrality regulation in promoting innovation.

The rather poor record of net neutrality in serving consumers and spurring high-tech innovation should be viewed in the broader context of government economic policy. Ex ante regulation should only be turned to when there is a clear market failure and there is reason to believe that government intervention will be less harmful than allowing the market to proceed unregulated.[53] Nations have adopted net neutrality rules without regard to this principle. Reliance on ex post antitrust law enforcement, guided by consumer welfare analysis, generally would be an economically far more economically beneficial means than net neutrality for dealing with anti-competitive market abuses caused by broadband providers.

Let us examine the antitrust question a bit more closely, in a multinational context. Suppose there is only one provider of broadband services in a jurisdiction. (The broadband provider may or may not also own or control its own ISP.) Edge providers of internet content and third-party ISPs must deal with this carrier in order that their customers can have access to their sites. Clearly, to the extent that those edge providers and ISPs are dealing across borders, which will be the case in most countries, then there will be a trade component to this discussion. A single broadband carrier may have an incentive to engage in anti-competitive practices around interconnection and generally in its agreements with edge content providers and third-party ISPs. The edge providers and ISPs will not have another option if they want to have a customer base in the country concerned. Recall that these services have public goods characteristics and that therefore the edge providers and third-party ISPs will be required to reach as wide an audience as quickly as possible (because of their generally declining marginal costs). Anything that limits this could have a severely distorting impact on their markets.

The solution is to ensure that the domestic competition agency is able to deal with anti-competitive practices by the broadband provider. That is the first order problem. The second order problem is where the broadband provider itself has an ISP and uses its monopoly position to favour its own ISP. This second order problem is a very real problem, particularly in countries that are developing or in transition. However, it is not isolated to those markets and the presence of cable and telecom companies with ISP units has meant that this is a serious issue in the US as well as in Europe. The first order and second order problems are really a new way of expressing the old problem that afflicted the opening up of the telecoms industry around the world, which we discussed at length in Chapter 12. The more competitive that the telecoms market actually is, the less likely that broadband providers can hold up the introduction of content onto the internet.

The key question then is, will competitive forces, backed up by the threat of ex post antitrust enforcement, be sufficient to enable a thriving internet with the growing provision of new and enhanced services demanded by consumers?

In the US, the answer to that question is an unequivocal yes. Two decades ago, some market participants complained that they would not be able to overcome structural competition problems and therefore needed regulation in order to prevent what they considered inevitable anti-competitive practices that would lead to a two (or multiple) speed internet, where the content provided by broadband carriers would be preferred to content provided by edge providers and other ISPs. In fact, fears of internet slowdowns and lack of access to consumers never materialised. This reflected (1) enhanced competition in broadband, and, (2) related to that, the rapid uptake of new and vastly improved mobile communications devices, fostered by an explosive growth in low-cost bandwidth and the rapid adoption of new mobile communications standards.[54] American consumers more and more substituted mobile computing for reliance on home computers. This led to a race to develop new mobile apps that were demanded by consumers, effectively thwarting any anti-competitive strategies that bandwidth providers might have considered devising.

This is not to say regulation is irrelevant to broadband provision in the US. The FCC is the primary telecommunications service regulator in the US The views of the FTC and Antitrust Division of the Department of Justice (DOJ), while they are sometimes sought, are certainly not final when it comes to questions of competition, although DOJ has a statutory role in reviewing mergers undertaking by telecommunications common carriers. In the US, as elsewhere, regulatory capture is more likely in the case of a sectoral regulator than in the case of a horizontal competition agency. There have been a number of anti-competitive restrictions in the case of the US telecoms sector which we have noted in this book in Chapter 3, Chapter 13, and in this chapter. These restraints historically impacted the ability of the US telecoms system to grow and develop. At the same time, decades of inefficient FCC regulation inefficiently retarded competition and the adoption of new welfare-enhancing technologies in telecommunications.

With respect to broadband provision and internet development, the FCC has long had a role to play, not all of it beneficial. As already noted, it regulated net neutrality for a three-year period (2015–2018) and may do so again, even though net neutrality rules were at best inconsequential and at worst a brake on innovation. Its more longstanding role in this regard, however, has been its assignment and licencing of scarce electromagnetic spectrum for private commercial uses. Successive mobile telecommunications standards, including 5G, have used spectrum more and more efficiently, but the explosion of new uses, including the internet of things and virtual online conferencing (critical during the COVID-19 pandemic), has placed a premium on the release of new spectrum to the private sector (with a high reliance now on spectrum auctions). Through its general regulatory role in facilitating commercial spectrum usage, the FCC will have an important (and hopefully positive) role to play in the further expansion of internet offerings, and in their extension to rural and underserved communities. The FCC's role, however, should focus on enabling new offerings through spectrum policies, not on regulating the competitive activities and new commercial initiatives of broadband entities. In the case of 5G-enabled services (and of future even more advanced standards), to maximise innovation-driven benefits, the FCC should work with DOJ to avoid unnecessary regulation and to allow competition to flourish. One scholarly commentator explained it succinctly:

> The benefits of the move to 5G can be sorted into two broad categories. The first benefits will come with direct and rapid increases in competition for broadband services. This growth in competition is set to invigorate the MNO, MVNO, and equipment manufacturing markets and move outward to service industries that rely on these network industries. The second category for benefits is those that flow from the indirect impacts of the new technologies. These benefits include those that come from increased competition (such as quality increases and price decreases), greater spread and densification of coverage, growth in IoT technologies, increased practicality of telehealth and online education opportunities.
>
> Prudent competition analyses by both antitrust enforcers and regulators will continue to include the potential impact of technological innovation in 5G. To do otherwise, to impose too much regulation or antitrust scrutiny too early about the progress of an underdeveloped technology, would discourage future innovation and the investment necessary to realise the full benefits of a 5G network.[55]

Put differently, the US experience indicates that while there will continue to be a role for some background ex ante regulation, it should be limited to overseeing the conditions needed (availability of broadband in particular) for internet-based services (mobile and non-mobile) to be offered effectively. Decisions governing the terms of commercial transactions among purveyors of broadband and other internet firms (including ISPs and edge services providers) should be subject to the unregulated competitive process, overseen solely by consumer-welfare-driven antitrust oversight.

Other jurisdictions may, of course, opt for somewhat more extensive oversight of broadband suppliers, based on local market conditions. Even if they consider ex ante regulation, however (say in the case of a monopoly broadband supplier with entry deemed infeasible in the foreseeable future), they would be well-advised to cabin the scope of regulatory oversight, so as to minimise disincentives to foreign investment in broadband and in ancillary internet services. Put simply, in a world characterised by vigorous global competition for capital, nations' ability to obtain financial backing for high-technology investments, including in particular investments that support NME development, will depend in no small part on avoiding unnecessary regulatory burdens that retard support for high-technology-enabled industries.

Conclusion

We have seen the impact that the move towards the NME is having around the globe. The major broadband platforms that play a major role in facilitating NME are subject to antitrust challenge and regulation, but the regulatory treatment of those platforms is distinct from (and may be considered separately from) the issues surrounding the legal treatment of the NME itself. In terms of regulatory policy, the NME means a move towards inter-platform competition where each of the platforms is protected by intellectual property. These platforms will be different ways of delivering information.

Concerns that these platforms would face competitive distortions potentially caused by broadband access providers led to calls for "net neutrality" rules in many countries. Although some forms of net neutrality regulation have been adopted by many jurisdictions, their effect has been inconsequential at best, and detrimental to innovation and dynamic markets at worst. As has often been the case throughout history, proponents of regulation ignored swift technological changes that have enabled a continuously improving and faster internet, affecting both traditional computing and new greatly enhanced mobile communications (the latter playing an ever more dominant role over the last two decades).

As new technical standards and improved artificial intelligence enable the build-out of the internet of things and drive even faster rates of technological enhancements, concerns about broadband monopolies being readily able to thwart internet improvements now appear quaint, if not totally absurd, to dispassionate observers. (Interventionist-minded politicians can always be counted upon to proclaim the need for new forms of government micromanagement, despite past failures.) Ex post consumer welfare-based antitrust, nevertheless, should remain a bulwark to deal with any harmful monopoly problems that may arise – firms with substantial market power will always have an incentive to enhance that power by undermining competition, if they can get away with it. However, populist "big is bad" antitrust attacks on high-technology companies, and new calls for regulation (this time directed at major digital platforms that include key edge providers, such as Google and Facebook), should be rejected as antithetical to innovation and dynamic economic growth. To the extent governments around the world keep this sound policy in mind, the global development of the NME, bestowing substantial economic and cultural benefits that promote domestic economic development and international trade, will proceed apace.

Notes

1 *See,* generally, Herbert J. Hovenkamp, *Schumpeterian Competition and Antitrust*, 4 Competition Pol'y. Int'l. no. 2 (2008), at 273.

2 "FTC Imposes $5 Billion Penalty and Sweeping New Privacy Restrictions on Facebook," Press Release, Federal Trade Commission (24 Jul 2019), https://www.ftc.gov/news-events/press-releases/2019/07/ftc-imposes-5-billion-penalty-sweeping-new-privacy-restrictions.

3 Foo Yun Chee, "Europe hits Google with record $5 billion antitrust fine, appeal ahead," Reuters (18 Jul 2018), https://www.reuters.com/article/us-eu-google-antitrust/europe-hits-google-with-record-5-billion-antitrust-fine-appeal-ahead-idUSKBN1K80U8.
4 For a compendium broken down by nations, see "Big Tech Antitrsut Investigations: Amazon, Apple, Facebook and Google Updates," CHANNELe2e (15 Apr 2021), https://www.channele2e.com/business/compliance/big-tech-antitrust-regulatory-breakup-updates/.
5 "Europe Fit for the Digital Age: Commission Proposes New Rules for Digital Platforms," European Commission Press Release (15 Dec 2020), https://ec.europa.eu/commission/presscorner/detail/en/ip_20_2347.
6 *See* "Germany Adopts New Competition Rules for Tech Platforms," Jones Day Insights (Jan 2021), https://www.jonesday.com/en/insights/2021/01/germany-adopts-new-competition-rules.
7 *See* "China Releases Anti-Monopoly Guidelines for Its Platform Economy," Dezan Shira & Associates China Briefing (16 Dec 2020), https://www.china-briefing.com/news/china-releases-anti-monopoly-guidelines-for-its-platform-economy/.
8 *See* William P. Rogerson and Howard Shelanski, *Antitrust Enforcement, Regulation, and Digital Platforms*, 168 U. Pa. L. Rev. 1911 (2020).
9 *See Regulatory Breakdown: The Crisis of Confidence in* U.S. *Regulation* (Gary Coglianese, ed., University of Pennsylvania Press, 2012).
10 David Parker and Colin Kirkpatrick, *The Economic Impact of Regulatory Policy: A Literature Review of Quantitative Evidence*, Expert Paper No. 3, Organization for Economic Co-operation and Development (2012).
11 "Audiovisual Services," World Trade Organization (n.d.), https://www.wto.org/english/tratop_e/serv_e/audiovisual_e/audiovisual_e.htm.
12 GATT Article IV, Article IV quotes that screen quotas are legal.
13 *Id*., art. III.10.
14 For country proposals, *see* generally www.wto.org.
15 The following discussion of European Union developments draws substantially on European Parliament, Fact Sheets on the European Union: Audiovisual and Media Policy (May 2021), https://www.europarl.europa.eu/factsheets/en/sheet/138/audiovisual-and-media-policy.
16 *See Preparing for a Fully Converged Audiovisual World: Growth, Creation and Values*, Green Paper, European Commission (2013), https://eur-lex.europa.eu/legal-content/EN/TXT/PDF/?uri=CELEX:52013DC0231&from=EN.
17 *Review of Regulatory Requirements for Incumbent LEC Broadband Telecomms. Servs*, 16 FCCR 22745 (2001).
18 Daniel Downes, "Telecom and the New Media Economy: Content versus Carriage Redux" (2000).
19 For a treatment of position feedback loops, *see* Carl Shapiro and Hal Varian, *Information Rules*: A *Strategic Guide to the* Network *Economy* (Harvard Business Review Press, 1998).
20 Thomas W. Hazlett, *Broadcast Regulation Politics are Local: A Response to Christopher Yoo's Model of Broadcast Regulation*, 53 Emory L. J. 233 (2004).
21 Garrett Hardin, *The Tragedy of the Commons*, 162 Sci. 1243, 1244 (1968); Ronald H. Coase, *The Problem of Social Cost*, 3 J. L. Econ. 1, at 2, 15 (1960).
22 *Review of Regulatory Requirements for Incumbent LEC Broadband Telecommunications Services, supra* note 18.
23 Christopher Yoo, *The Role of Politics and Policy in Television Regulation*, 53 Emory L.J. 255 (2004).
24 Henry Ergas, *Does Technology Policy Matter?*, in Technology and Global Industry: Companies and Nations in the World Economy (Bruce Guile and Harvey Books eds., 1987), at 191–245.

25 Joshua Gans and Scott Stern, *Assessing Australia's Innovative Capacity in the 21st Century*, Melbourne Business School (2003).
26 Shanker A. Singham, *Competition Policy and the Stimulation of Innovation: TRIPS and the Interface between Competition and Patent Protection in the Pharmaceutical Industry*, 26 Brooklyn J. Int'l L. 363, 380–381 (2000); *See also* Lerner, *Boom and Bust in the Venture Capital Industry*, Federal Reserve Bank of Atlanta Economic Review (Fourth Quarter 2002).
27 *Id.*
28 For more information, *see Better Regulation Framework: Interim Guidance,* Department for Business, Energy & Industrial Strategy (2020).
29 Office of the Deputy Prime Minister, Regulatory Impact Assessment: Local Government Act (2003).
30 Council Directive 89/552/EEC, 1989 O.J. (L 298) 23; *as amended by* Council Directive 97/36/EC, 1997 O.J. (L 202) 60.
31 The Lisbon Agenda describes a process initiated in March 2000, when the EU Heads of States and Governments agreed to make the EU "the most competitive and dynamic knowledge-driven economy by 2010." Although some progress was made on innovating Europe's economy, there is growing concern that the reform process is not going fast enough and that the ambitious targets will not be reached.
32 *eEurope 2005: An Information Society for All* (COM(2002) 263), Commission of the European Communities (2002); *See also Presidency Conclusions*, SN 100/1/02 REV 1, Barcelona, European Council (15–16 Mar 2000), at para. 40.
33 *eEurope 2005: An Information Society for All, Id.*
34 "The Digital Compass," European Commission (last updated 8 Jul 2021), https://digital-strategy.ec.europa.eu/en/policies/digital-compass.
35 "Public Consultation on a Set of European Digital Principles," European Commission (12 May 2021), https://digital-strategy.ec.europa.eu/en/consultations/public-consultation-set-european-digital-principles.
36 "Europe's Digital Decade: Digital Targets for 2030," European Commission (9 Mar 2021), https://ec.europa.eu/info/strategy/priorities-2019-2024/europe-fit-digital-age/europes-digital-decade-digital-targets-2030_en.
37 *See id.*
38 *Audiovisual Services: Improving Participation of Developing Countries*, TD/B/COM.1/EM.20/2, United Nations Conference on Trade and Development (30 Sept 2002).
39 Report and Order and Notice of Proposed Rulemaking, FCC 03–127, Federal Communications Commission (2003).
40 The following summary is based on Federal Communications Commission, FCC Broadcast Ownership Rules (updated as of 17 Jan 2020), https://www.fcc.gov/consumers/guides/fccs-review-broadcast-ownership-rules.
41 Adam M. Brandenburger and Barry J. Nalebuff, *Co-Opetition* (Currency Doubleday, 1996); *Information Rules, supra* note 19.
42 Angele A. Gilroy, *Access to Broadband Networks: The Net Neutrality Debate*, CRS Report R40616, Congressional Research Service (updated 10 Apr 2019), at 1.
43 *See* "The Road Ahead for Net Neutrality and the First Amendment," Jones Day Insights (Apr 2021), https://www.jonesday.com/en/insights/2021/04/net-neutrality-and-the-first-amendment.
44 See Thomas W. Hazlett, "Net Neutrality Is Far From Necessary," reason (August/September 2021), https://reason.com/2021/08/21/net-neutrality-is-far-from-necessary/.
45 Geoffrey A. Manne, Kristian Stout, and Ben Sperry, *A Dynamic Analysis of Broadband Competition: What Concentration Numbers Fail to Capture*, ICLE White Paper, International Center for Law & Economics (2021), at 2.ff.
46 Council Regulation (EU) 2015/2120, 2015 O. J. (L 310/1).
47 "All You Need to Know about the Open Internet Rules in the EU," Body of European Regulators for Electronic Communications (2015), https://berec.europa.eu/eng/open_internet/.

48 Roslyn Layton, "The Unintended Consequences of Europe's Net Neutrality Law after One Year," American Enterprise Institute (20 Oct 2017), https://www.aei.org/technology-and-innovation/telecommunications/the-unintended-consequences-of-europes-net-neutrality-law-after-one-year/. In particular, Denmark, which employed voluntary self-regulation, did better in generating new domestic mobile applications than the Netherlands, with the world's strictest net neutrality regime.

49 Roslyn Layton, *Does Net Neutrality Spur Internet Innovation?*, American Enterprise Institute (2017).

50 Wolfgang Briglauer, *Special Issue on "Recent Net Neutrality Polices in Europe and the US*," 17 Rev. Netw. Econ. no. 3 (2018), at 109.

51 "Net Neutrality by Country," Wikipedia (accessed 16 Mar 2022), https://en.wikipedia.org/wiki/Net_neutrality_by_country.

52 Henry L. Hu, *The Political Economy of Governing ISPs in China: Perspectives of Net Neutrality and Vertical Integration*, 207 The China Q. 523 (2011).

53 For a general discussion of regulation and methodologies, public officials should utilise to ensure that regulation is administered in the most economically efficient fashion, *see* Thomas A. Lambert, *How to Regulate: A Guide for Policymakers* (Cambridge University Press, 2017).

54 See Babette Boliek, *Competition, Regulation, and 5G*, in *Global Antitrust Institute Report on the Digital Economy* (Joshua D. Wright and Douglas H. Ginsburg eds., 2020).

55 *Id.*, at 863.

15
CONCLUSION

This book has attempted to illustrate the interface between trade and competition, and by extension the interaction between a country's external trade policy and its domestic regulatory environment. We have shown that there are anti-competitive distortions across all three dimensions of trade, competition and property rights protection, and that the theory of distortions stands above trade, competition and property rights protection policies.

We have shown that, in particular, as tariffs have come down, domestic regulatory barriers have become the most pernicious and difficult to remove trade barriers that face global firms, and increase price and lower choice for global consumers. We have made a number of recommendations for how this process can be addressed which we summarise in this conclusion, and we articulate what we consider to be an important set of workstreams that policymakers need to embark on now in order to solve the issue of anti-competitive market distortions which plague trade and domestic systems. First, there needs to be widespread acknowledgement of the problem. At the moment, the problem is only acknowledged by a handful of developed countries, such as the US, the UK, the EU and Japan. Many advanced developing countries have significantly distorted markets (such as China, Russia and others). There is a national security dimension to this problem as well as it is no coincidence that the countries that embrace a very different version of "capitalism" than one based on competition on the merits are also the ones most guilty of anti-competitive market distortions. This should be no surprise as it is ACMDs that carry cronyist economic policies as particular firms and friends of the government are favoured. The impact of these systems on global security cannot be understated.

Second, once the problem is acknowledged, solutions need to be found, at least among those countries that do acknowledge the problem. UK Foreign Secretary, Liz Truss, has talked about a "network of liberty" emerging from countries like

DOI: 10.4324/9780429323331-15

the UK, the US, Australia and others. These solutions must be both offensive (chapters on market distortions in trade agreements such as the one in Annex 1), and defensive as proposed in the trade remedies chapter of this book. They must be integrated. As we write, there is a new "great game" being played out on the global chessboard in which this work plays an important role. We face a great danger where market distorters like Russia and China divide up developing countries and plunder crucial resources from them using their cronyist market distortions as their economic basis for doing so, and one where religions authoritarians such as Isis, and other Islamic terrorists seek to run a belt of countries according to their profoundly non-market principles from Morocco in the west of Africa and Afghanistan and Pakistan and perhaps even as far east as Indonesia. In this world, a weakened West, distracted by a focus on issues not relevant to the new "great game," remains perpetually weakened, and unable to really resist the remaking of the world along these lines. This world will see a gradual decline in the West (including its historically high standard of living). This decline will be managed, to be sure, and consumers especially in the US will not see its effects for some time, and over this next 50-year period, the new axis countries of China (strengthened by the potential additions of Hong Kong and Taiwan) and a greater Russia (embracing many regions containing Slavic peoples) will start to dominate new technologies such as quantum computing, space and Artificial Intelligence. However, this is not inevitable if the West deals with these pressing problems now. It is outside the scope of this book to set forth all of the other ways in which such a world can be avoided, and that the network of liberty can be enhanced and extended. But reducing market distortions around the whole world will be an essential part of this agenda.

Third, these solutions, both offensive and most especially defensive, require that metrics to measure ACMDs are developed. We have noted some early and pioneering work in this area by the authors and their collaborators. This work is urgent and must be extended. There are many ways of arriving at a quantum for ACMDs. We have referred to econometric methods as well as an agency-based model based more on simulations to give an order of magnitude of the scale of the problem. These metrics should support a forensic tariffication of the ACMD which is allowed.

Fourth, political consensus globally and in countries themselves needs to be arrived at. The great difficulty here is the age-old problem of convincing publics that free trade or free markets are in their interest. The losses from competition can be very visible, whereas the gains from competition are very disparate and spread across the whole population. Individuals do not see the economic value generated, the efficiencies that are derived or the wealth that is created. But individuals who lose out from the creative destruction of competitive processes do see their standard of living decline. It is these individuals who are very persuasive in the political process, and who tend to lobby government successfully to maintain the status quo. Many of these individuals are large incumbent companies who benefit from the barriers that currently exist to new entrants. But governments should not respond only to these interests. They must also consider consumers of today and tomorrow, as well as businesses of today and tomorrow. Many consumers of today and tomorrow are themselves businesses as every business is a consumer of something. This political consensus will only be arrived at once the costs of ACMDs and their wealth-destructive effects can be made explicit (hence the need for a metric). It is only by showing to the public how much their standard of living will decline and what pain will be visited on the poor that the power of vested interest elites in developed and developing countries alike can be countervailed effectively. A metric is also important as it can help governments determine priorities for regulatory reform and in trade negotiations.

There are many issues which will impede the critical agenda outlined here, and explained in this book. The way governments are structured is one of them, and so there will also be a need to restructure the way governments operate. We have governments which are set up for a 19th-century world where products are produced in country A and sold into country B. The world has moved on. We now live in a world of competing global supply chains. It is therefore necessary to have a single mind covering a country's overall competitiveness, or a single department of competitiveness that contains within it elements of trade policy, regulatory reform and competition policy. There needs to be a member of the government who is constantly worrying about distortions whether they occur in other markets or in the home market as ultimately, they all have the same effect on global welfare. Similarly, trade negotiations need to include an element of negotiation between the export interests of country A and the consumer interests of country B. Some of these ideas were sketched out in a report for the Council on Foreign Relations in 2012.[1] While the Council on Foreign Relations report was written for the US, it is widely applicable to a number of jurisdictions.

That there is a critical interface between trade and competition cannot be seriously doubted. The interface has existed from the moment that man came out of the cave and bartered goods in voluntary exchange. As the national barriers to that voluntary exchange were first erected and then systematically reduced, the impact of these domestic distortions has had a bigger impact on trade but they have always had a big effect on the domestic market. These ACMDs impede the ordinary process of voluntary exchange and prevent human beings servicing human needs in the most efficient manner possible. As a result, they damage the incentives for innovation further holding up human progress. This is not a small and academically esoteric subject. Resolution or failure to resolve it will have profound consequences for humanity.

Note

1 *See* Shanker A. Singham, *Freeing the Global Market: How to Boost the Economy by Curbing Regulatory Distortions,* Council on Foreign Relations (2012), https://www.cfr.org/report/freeing-global-market.

ANNEX

ANTI-COMPETITIVE MARKET DISTORTIONS CHAPTER

Article x.1: Definitions

For the purposes of this chapter:

1 "**Arrangement**" means the Arrangement on Officially Supported Export Credits, developed within the framework of the Organisation for Economic Cooperation and Development (OECD), or a successor undertaking, whether developed within or outside of the OECD framework, that has been adopted by at least 12 original Members to the Arrangement that were members as of 1 January 1979;

2 "**commercial activities**" means activities the end result of which is the production of a good or supply of a service which will be sold to a consumer, including a state enterprise, state-owned enterprise or designated monopoly, in the relevant market in quantities and at prices determined by the enterprise and that are undertaken with an expectation of gain or profit[1];

3 "**commercial considerations**" means factors such as price, quality, availability, marketability, transportation and other terms and conditions of purchase or sale, or other factors that influence the commercial decisions of an enterprise in the relevant business or industry;

4 "**designate**" means, whether formally or in effect, to establish, name or authorise a monopoly, or to expand the scope of a monopoly to cover an additional good or service;

5 "**designated monopoly**" means a monopoly that a Party designates or has designated;

6 "**government monopoly**" means a monopoly that is owned or controlled by a Party or by another government monopoly;

7 "**injury**" means material injury to a domestic industry, threat of material injury to a domestic industry or material retardation of the establishment of a domestic industry;
8 "**market**" means the geographical and commercial market for a good or service;
9 "**monopoly**" means an entity or a group of entities that, in any relevant market in the territory of a Party, is the exclusive provider or purchaser of a good or service but does not include an entity that has been granted an exclusive intellectual property right solely by reason of such grant;
10 "**national competition laws**" shall mean the laws concerning the regulation of cartels and anti-competitive agreements or abuse of dominance/monopolisation;
11 "**non-commercial assistance**"[2] means the provision of:
   a grant or debt forgiveness;
   b a loan, equity infusion or capital, loan guarantee or other type of financing or loan satisfaction on terms more favourable than those commercially available to that enterprise; or
   c a subsidy within the meaning of Article 1 of the WTO Agreement on Subsidies and Countervailing Measures; or
   d a good or service, other than general infrastructure, on terms more favourable than those commercially available to that enterprise;

12 "**state enterprise**" means an enterprise that is owned or controlled through ownership interests, by a Party and
13 "**state-owned enterprise**" means an enterprise that is engaged in economic activities; and:
   a is owned, or controlled, by a Party's government; or
   b in which a Party's government appoints or has the power to appoint the majority of members of the board of directors or any equivalent management;
   c is controlled by a Party's government through a control person or control persons.

Article x.2: Competition Law and Anti-Competitive Practices

1 Each Party shall adopt or maintain national competition laws with the objective of promoting economic efficiency and consumer welfare, and shall take appropriate action with respect to that conduct. These laws should take into account the OECD Competition Assessment Toolkit (2007) (as revised from time to time), OECD Regulatory Toolkit and the APEC Principles to Enhance Competition and Regulatory Reform, done at Auckland, 13 September 1999.
2 Each Party shall endeavour to apply its national competition laws to all commercial activities in its territory,[3] including the activities of state-owned

enterprises both in their commercial sales and in their procurement activities. However, each Party may provide for certain exemptions from the application of its national competition laws provided that those exemptions are transparent and are based on public policy grounds or public interest grounds.

3 Each party shall maintain an authority or authorities responsible for the enforcement of its national competition laws (national competition authorities). Each Party shall provide that it is the enforcement policy of that authority or authorities to act in accordance with the objectives set out in Article x.2.1 and not to discriminate on the basis of nationality.

4 In modifying, enforcing, applying, amending, reviewing or issuing new national competition law, regulations or procedures, Parties shall conduct themselves consistently with the provisions of Chapter y (Regulatory Coherence).

Article x.3: Procedural Fairness in Competition Law Enforcement

1 Both parties shall ensure that before it imposes a sanction or remedy against any person for violating its national competition laws, it shall afford such person:

a information about the national competition authority's competition concerns;

b a reasonable opportunity to be represented by counsel and

c a reasonable opportunity to be heard and present evidence in its defence, except that a Party may provide for the person to be heard and present evidence within a reasonable time after it imposes an interim sanction or remedy.

2 In particular, each Party shall afford that person a reasonable opportunity to offer evidence or testimony in its defence, including if applicable, to offer the analysis of a properly qualified expert, to cross-examine any witness (if testifying before a court); and to review and rebut the evidence introduced in the enforcement proceeding,[4] subject to the confidentiality provisions of this chapter. Parties' competition authorities shall normally afford persons under investigation for possible violation of its competition laws reasonable opportunities to consult with such competition authorities with respect to significant legal, factual or procedural issues that arise during the course of investigation.

3 Parties shall adopt or maintain written procedures pursuant to which its national competition law investigations are conducted. If these investigations are not subject to definitive deadlines, each Party's national competition authorities shall endeavour to conduct their investigations within a reasonable time frame.

4 Each Party shall publish or otherwise make publicly available written rules of procedure and evidence that apply to enforcement proceedings concerning

alleged violations of its national competition laws and the determination of sanctions and remedies thereunder. These rules shall include procedures for introducing evidence, including expert evidence where applicable.

5 Each Party shall provide a person that is subject to the imposition of a sanction or remedy for violation of its national competition laws with the opportunity to seek review of the sanction or remedy, including review of alleged substantive or procedural errors, in a court or other independent tribunal established under that Party's laws.

6 Each Party shall authorise its national competition authorities to resolve alleged violations voluntarily by consent of the authority and the person subject to the enforcement action. A Party may provide for such voluntary resolution to be subject to judicial (or independent tribunal) approval or a public comment period before becoming final.

7 If a Party's national competition authority issues a public notice that reveals the existence of a pending or ongoing investigation, that authority shall avoid implying in that notice that the person referred to in that notice has engaged in the alleged conduct or violated the Party's national competition laws.

8 If a national competition authority of a Party alleges a violation of its national competition laws, that authority shall be responsible for establishing the legal and factual basis for the alleged violation in an enforcement proceeding.[5]

9 Each Party shall provide for the protection of confidential information and business secrets, and other information treated as confidential under its law, obtained by its national competition authorities during the investigative process. If a Party's national competition authority uses or intends to use that information in an enforcement proceeding, the Party shall, if it is permissible under its law and as appropriate, provide a procedure to allow the person under investigation timely access to information that is necessary to prepare an adequate defence to the national competition authority's allegations.

10 Both parties shall ensure that its national competition authorities afford a person under investigation for possible violation of the national competition laws of that Party reasonable opportunity to consult with those competition authorities with respect to significant legal, factual or procedural issues that arise during the investigation.

Article x.4: Private Rights of Action

1 For the purposes of this Article, "**private right of action**" means the right of a legal or natural person to seek redress, including injunctive, monetary or other remedies, from a court or other independent tribunal for injury to that person's business or property caused by a violation of national competition laws, either independently or following a finding of violation by a national competition authority.

2 Recognising that a private right of action is an important supplement to the public enforcement of national competition laws, each Party should adopt or

maintain laws or other measures that provide an independent private right of action.

3 If a Party does not adopt or maintain laws or other measures that provide an independent private right of action, the Party shall adopt or maintain laws or other measures that provide a right that allows a person:
   a to request that the national competition authority initiate an investigation into an alleged violation of national competition laws; and
   b to seek redress from a court or other independent tribunal following a finding of violation by the national competition authority.

4 Both Parties shall ensure that a right provided pursuant to Articles x.5.2 or x.5.3 is available to persons of the other party on terms that are no less favourable than those available to its own persons.

5 A Party may establish reasonable criteria for the exercise of any rights it creates or maintains in accordance with this Article.

Article x.5: Cooperation

1 The Parties recognise the importance of cooperation and coordination between their respective national competition authorities to foster effective competition law enforcement in the free trade area. Accordingly, both parties shall:
   a cooperate in the area of competition policy by exchanging information on the development of competition policy; and
   b cooperate, as appropriate, on issues of competition law enforcement, including through notification, consultation, and the exchange of information, including confidential information and business secrets.

2 A Party's national competition authorities may consider entering into a cooperation arrangement or agreement with the competition authorities of the other party that sets out mutually agreed terms of cooperation.

3 The Parties agree to cooperate in a manner compatible with their respective laws, regulations and important interests, and within their reasonably available resources.

4 The Parties commit to maintaining a high level of international cooperation and coordination. The Parties acknowledge the importance of cooperation and coordination internationally and the work of multilateral organisations in this area.

Article x.6: Consumer Protection

1 The Parties recognise the importance of consumer protection policy and enforcement to creating efficient and competitive markets and enhancing consumer welfare in the free trade area.

For the purposes of this Article, fraudulent and deceptive commercial activities refer to those fraudulent and deceptive commercial practices that cause actual harm to consumers or that pose an imminent threat of such harm if not prevented, for example:

- a a practice of making misrepresentations of material fact, including implied factual misrepresentations, that cause significant detriment to the interests of misled consumers;
- b a practice of failing to deliver products or provide services to consumers after the consumers are charged or
- c a practice of charging or debiting consumers' financial, telephone or other accounts without authorisation.

2 Both parties shall adopt or maintain consumer protection laws or other laws or regulations that proscribe fraudulent and deceptive commercial activities.[6]

3 The Parties recognise that fraudulent and deceptive commercial activities increasingly transcend national borders and that cooperation and coordination between the Parties are desirable to effectively address these activities.

4 Accordingly, the Parties shall promote, as appropriate, cooperation and coordination on matters of mutual interest related to fraudulent and deceptive commercial activities, including in the enforcement of their consumer protection laws.

5 The Parties shall endeavour to cooperate and coordinate on the matters set out in this Article through the relevant national public bodies or officials responsible for consumer protection policy, laws or enforcement, as determined by each Party and compatible with their respective laws, regulations and important interests and within their reasonably available resources.

Article x.7: Transparency of Policies and Practices

1 The Parties recognise the value of making their competition enforcement policies as transparent as possible.

2 On request of the other party, a Party shall make available to the requesting Party public information concerning:

- a its competition law enforcement policies and practices; and
- b exemptions and immunities to its national competition laws, provided that the request specifies the particular good or service and market of concern and includes information explaining how the exemption or immunity may hinder trade or investment between the Parties.

3 Each Party shall ensure that a final decision finding a violation of its national competition laws is made in writing and sets out, in non-criminal matters, findings of fact and the reasoning, including legal and, if applicable, economic analysis, on which the decision is based. Both parties shall further ensure that any such decisions and any orders implementing them are published, or where publication is not practicable, otherwise made available to the public in such a manner as to enable interested persons to become acquainted with them. The version of the decisions or orders that the Party makes available to the public shall omit confidential business information, as well as information that is treated as confidential under its laws.

Article x.8: Consultations

In order to foster understanding between the Parties or to address specific matters that arise under this chapter, on request of another Party, a Party shall enter into consultations with the requesting Party within a reasonable period of time regarding any matter arising under this chapter. In its request, the requesting Party shall specify the matter on which it seeks to consult and indicate, if relevant, how the matter affects trade or investment between the Parties. The Party addressed shall accord full and sympathetic consideration to the concerns of the requesting Party.

Article x.9: State-Owned Enterprises, State Enterprises and Designated Monopolies

1 This chapter applies with respect to the activities of state-owned enterprises, state enterprises and designated monopolies that affect trade or investment between the Parties.

2 Notwithstanding paragraph 1, this chapter does not apply to:

a a central bank or monetary authority of a Party;

b a financial regulatory body or a resolution authority of a Party;

c a financial institution or other entity owned or controlled by a Party that is established or operated temporarily solely for resolution purposes;

d government procurement;

e regulatory or supervisory activities of any non-governmental entity, including any securities or futures exchange or market, clearing agency, or other organisation or association, that exercises regulatory or supervisory authority over financial service suppliers or financial institutions, pursuant to direction or delegated authority of the Party;

f where the Party is exercising public power in their capacity as a public authority;

g where the Party is exercising powers of social solidarity, characteristics of schemes pursuing social solidarity include a compulsory scheme, which pursues an exclusively social purpose, is non-profit-making, where the benefits can be independent of the contribution made.

3 For greater certainty, nothing in this chapter shall be construed to prevent a Party from:

a establishing or maintaining a state enterprise or state-owned enterprise, or

b designating a monopoly.

4 Both parties shall ensure that when its state-owned enterprises, state enterprises and designated monopolies exercise any regulatory, administrative or other governmental authority[7] which the Party has directed or delegated to such an entity to carry out, such entity shall act in a manner that is not inconsistent with that Party's obligations under this Agreement.

5 Both parties shall ensure that its state-owned enterprises and designated monopolies, when engaging in economic activities:
   a act in accordance with commercial considerations in their purchases or sales of goods or services, except, in the case of a designated monopoly, to fulfil any terms of its designation that are not inconsistent with Articles x.9.5 (b) and x.9.7; and
   b accord to enterprises that are covered investments, goods of the other Party and services suppliers of the other Party, treatment no less favourable than they accord to, respectively, like enterprises that are investments of the Party's investors, like goods of the Party, and like service suppliers of the Party, with respect to their purchases or sales of goods or services.

6 Article x.9.5 does not preclude a state-owned enterprise or designated monopoly from:
   a purchasing or supplying goods or services on different terms or conditions, including those relating to price; or
   b refusing to purchase or supply goods or services, provided that such different terms or conditions or refusal are undertaken in accordance with commercial considerations and Article x.9.5 (b).

7 Both parties shall ensure that any designated monopoly that it establishes or maintains does not use its monopoly position to engage in, either directly or indirectly, including through its dealings with its parent, subsidiaries or other entities that the Party or the designated monopoly owns or controls, anti-competitive practices in a non-monopolised market in its territory that adversely affect covered investments or trade between the Parties.

Article x.10: Commercial Considerations

Except to fulfil the purpose[8] for which special or exclusive rights or privileges have been granted, or in the case of a state enterprise to fulfil its public mandate, and provided that the enterprise's conduct in fulfilling that purpose or mandate is consistent with the provisions in the chapter on Competition, both parties shall ensure that any enterprise referred to in Articles x.9.2 (d)–(f) acts in accordance with commercial considerations in the relevant territory in its purchases and sales of goods, including with regard to price, quality, availability, marketability, transportation and other terms and conditions of purchase or sale, as well as in its purchases or supply of services, including when these goods or services are supplied to or by an investment of an investor of the other Party.

Article x.11: Courts and Administrative Bodies

1 Both parties shall provide its courts with jurisdiction over civil claims against a foreign state-owned enterprise based on a commercial activity carried on its territory, except where a Party does not provide jurisdiction over similar claims against enterprises that are not state-owned enterprises.

2 Both parties shall ensure that anybody that it establishes or maintains, and that regulates a state-owned enterprise or designated monopoly, acts impartially with respect to all enterprises that it regulates, including enterprises that are not state-owned enterprises.

Article x.12: Adverse Effects

1 Neither party shall cause adverse effects to the interests of the other Party through the use of non-commercial assistance to enterprises active in markets open to trade.
2 Both parties shall ensure that no state enterprise or state-owned enterprise that it establishes or maintains causes adverse effects to the interests of the other Party through the use of non-commercial assistance that the state enterprise or state-owned enterprise provides to any of its state-owned enterprises, where the Party explicitly limits access to the non-commercial assistance provided by the state enterprise or state-owned enterprise to its state-owned enterprises, or where the state enterprise or state-owned enterprise provides non-commercial assistance which is predominately used by the Party's state-owned enterprises, provides a disproportionately large amount of the non-commercial assistance to the Party's state-owned enterprises, or otherwise favours the Party's state-owned enterprises in the provision of non-commercial assistance.
3 Adverse effects cannot be established on the basis of any act, omission or factual situation, to the extent that act, omission or factual situation took place before the date of entry into force of this Agreement.
4 For the purpose of Articles x.12.1 to x.12.3, adverse effects are effects that arise from the provision of a good or service by a Party's state-owned enterprise which has benefited from non-commercial assistance and:
   a displace or impede from the Party's market imports of a like product or service[9] that is an originating good of the other Party, or sales of a like product that is a good produced by an enterprise that is a covered investment;
   b consist of a significant price undercutting by a product of the Party's state-owned enterprise compared with the price in the same market of a like product that is an originating good of the other Party or a like product that is a good produced by an enterprise that is a covered investment, or significant price suppression, price depression or lost sales in the same market;
   c displace or impede from the Party's market a like service supplied by a service supplier of the other Party, or a like service supplied by an enterprise that is a covered investment, or
   d consist of a significant price undercutting by a service supplied by the Party's state-owned enterprise as compared with the price in the same market of a like service supplied by a service supplier of the other Party, or by an enterprise that is a covered investment, or significant price suppression, price depression or lost sales in the same market.

5 For the purposes of Articles x.12.4 (a) and x.12.4 (c), the displacing or impeding of a product or service includes any case in which there has been a significant change in relative share of the market to the disadvantage of the like product of the other Party or of a covered investment, or to the disadvantage of a like service supplied by a service supplier of the other Party or by a covered investment.

6 A significant change in relative shares of the market shall include any of the following situations:

- a there is an increase in the market share of the product or service of the Party's state-owned enterprise in the range of 5%–10%;
- b the market share of the product or service of the Party's state-owned enterprise remains constant in circumstances in which, in the absence of the non-commercial assistance, it would have declined significantly; or
- c the market share of the product or service of the Party's state-owned enterprise declines, but by a significantly lower amount or at a significantly slower rate than would have been the case in the absence of the non-commercial assistance.

7 Where the change manifests itself over an appropriately representative period sufficient to demonstrate clear trends in the development of the market for the product or service, which shall be at least one year unless exceptional circumstances apply.

8 For purposes of Articles x.12.4 (b) and x.12.4 (d), significant price undercutting shall include demonstration through a comparison of prices at the same level of trade and at comparable times within the same market as follows:

- a the prices of a product of the Party's state-owned enterprise benefiting from non-commercial assistance with the prices of a like product of the other Party or an enterprise that is a covered investment; or
- b the prices of a service of the Party's state-owned enterprise benefiting from non-commercial assistance with the prices of a like service supplied by a service supplier of the other Party or an enterprise that is a covered investment.

9 Due account shall be taken for factors affecting price comparability. If a direct comparison of transactions is not possible, the existence of the price undercutting may be demonstrated on some other reasonable basis, such as, in the case of goods, a comparison of unit values.

Article x.13: Injury

1 Neither party shall cause injury to a domestic industry of the other Party through the use of non-commercial assistance that it provides, either directly or indirectly, to any enterprises in the territory of the other Party and where:

- a the enterprise produces and sells a good in the territory of the other Party; and b a like good is produced and sold by a domestic industry of the other Party.

Article x.14: Requirements for Transparency and Corporate Governance

1 The Parties shall ensure that enterprises referred to in Articles x.9 (a) and (b) shall observe high standards of transparency and corporate governance in accordance with the OECD Guidelines on Corporate Governance of State-Owned Enterprises.

2 A Party which has reason to believe that its interests under this Agreement are being adversely affected by the operations of an enterprise or enterprises referred to in Articles x.13 (a) and (b) of the other Party may request that Party to supply information about the operations of its enterprise related to the carrying out of the provisions of this Agreement.

3 Both parties shall, at the request of the other Party, make available information concerning specific enterprises referred to in Articles x.9.1 (d)–(f) and which do not qualify as small- and medium-sized enterprises as defined in the relevant law of either Party. Requests for such information shall indicate the enterprise, the products/services and markets concerned, and include indicators that the enterprise is engaging in practices that hinder trade or investment between the Parties.

4 The information may include:

a the organisational structure of the enterprise, the composition of its board of directors or of an equivalent structure of any other executive organ exercising direct or indirect influence through an affiliated or related entity in such an enterprise; and cross holdings and other links with different enterprises or groups of enterprises referred to in Articles x.9.1 (d)–(f):

b the ownership and the voting structure of the enterprise, indicating the percentage of shares and percentage of voting rights that a Party and/or an enterprise referred to in Articles x.9.1 (d)–(f) cumulatively own;

c a description of any special shares or special voting or other rights that a Party and/or an enterprise referred to in Articles x.9.1 (d)–(f) hold, where such rights differ from the rights attached to the general common shares of such entity;

d the name and title(s) of any government official of a Party serving as an officer or member of the board of directors or of an equivalent structure or of any other executive organ exercising direct or indirect influence through an affiliated or related entity in the enterprise;

e details of the government departments or public bodies which monitor the enterprise and any reporting requirements;

f the role of the government or any public bodies in the appointment, dismissal or remuneration of managers; and

g annual revenue or total assets, or both; and
h exemptions, non-conforming measures, immunities and any other measures derogating from the application of a Party's laws or regulations or granting favourable treatment by a Party.

5 The provisions of Articles x.14.2 and x.14.3 shall not require any Party to disclose confidential information which would impede law enforcement or otherwise be contrary to the public interest or would prejudice the legitimate commercial interests of particular enterprises.
6 Both parties shall ensure that any regulatory body responsible for regulating any of the enterprises referred to in Articles x.9.1 (d)–(f) is independent from, and not accountable to, any of the enterprises referred to in Articles x.9.1 (d)–(f).
7 Both parties shall ensure the enforcement of laws and regulations in a consistent and non-discriminatory manner at all levels of government, be it central or local, and their application to enterprises referred to in Articles x.9.1 (d)–(f). Exemptions must be limited and transparent.
8 The provisions of this Article apply to enterprises operating in all sectors.

Article x.15: Provision of Information

1 Both parties shall provide to the other Party a list of its state-owned enterprises within 180 days of the date of entry into force of this Agreement, and thereafter shall provide an updated list annually.
2 Where a Party designates a monopoly or expands the scope of an existing designated monopoly, it shall promptly notify the other Party of the designation or expansion of scope and the conditions under which the monopoly shall operate.
3 On the written request of the other Party, a Party shall promptly provide the following information concerning a state-owned enterprise or a government monopoly:
   a the percentage of shares that the Party, its state-owned enterprises, state enterprises or designated monopolies cumulatively own, and the percentage of votes that they cumulatively hold in the entity;
   b a description of any special shares, or special voting or other rights, that the Party, its state-owned enterprises or designated monopolies hold, to the extent different from the rights attached to the general common shares of such entity;
   c the government titles, or former government titles, and decision-making ability of any official serving as a board member, officer, director, manager or other control person of such entity;
   d the entity's annual revenue and total assets over the most recent three-year period for which information is available;
   e any exemptions and immunities from which the entity benefits under the Party's law and

f any additional information regarding the entity which is publicly available, including annual financial reports and third-party audits, and which is sought in the written request.

4 On the written request of the other party, a Party shall promptly provide the following information concerning assistance received by any of its state-owned enterprises:

a any financing or re-financing that the Party, or another of the Party's state-owned enterprises or state enterprises, has provided to the state-owned enterprise, including the amount of such financing and the terms on which it was provided;

b any loan guarantee that the Party, or another of the Party's state-owned enterprises or state enterprises, has provided to the state-owned enterprise, including fees associated with the guarantee and any other conditions associated with the guarantee;

c any forgiveness of debt or other financial liability that the Party, or another of the Party's state-owned enterprises or state enterprises, has provided to the state-owned enterprise;

d any goods or services that the Party, or another one of the Party's state-owned enterprises or state enterprises, has provided to the state-owned enterprise, and the conditions associated with such provision; and

e any export credit that the Party, or one of the Party's state-owned enterprises, has provided in support of the export of a good or service from one of the Party's state-owned enterprises, including the amount of such export credits, and the terms and conditions on which it was provided.

5 Both parties shall include in any written request under Article x.15 an explanation of how the activities of the state-owned enterprise may be affecting trade or investment between the Parties.

Article x.16: Anti-Competitive Market Distortions

1 The Parties agree that they will not, through laws, regulations, administrative practices or other Covered Actions, distort their markets in trade-restrictive or anti-competitive ways ("Anti-Competitive Market Distortions" or "ACMDs"), unless there is a clearly expressed regulatory goal which has been published in advance consistent with Chapter 14 of this Agreement (Regulatory Coherence).

2 The Parties agree that they may provide supports to regionally impoverished areas[10] in their territories, and that prior to providing these supports the Parties should consult with each other through the Competition Policy Sub-Committee.

3 The Parties agree that they will develop mechanisms to deal with ACMDs of the other Party, and that these measures may include imposing a duty that is correlated with the scale of the impact of the ACMD on competition

in the market, and that the imposition of such a duty, provided that it is consistent with the factors set out below it, shall not be deemed to be a violation of this agreement or of the rules of the World Trade Organization:

- a the complaining party must prove that there is an ACMD[11];
- b the complaining party must prove that there is an adverse effect, or damage to their interests;
- c the complaining party must adduce evidence of the scale of the adverse effect; and
- d the complaining party must produce evidence of damage, and evidence that the ACMD has caused the damage.

4 The Parties agree that they will use these ACMD mechanisms with respect to ACMDs in other jurisdictions, and will mutually defend any claims brought that such mechanisms violate WTO rules.

Article x.17

The corporate governance framework of each Party shall include provisions aiming at protecting and facilitating the effective exercise of shareholders' rights in publicly listed companies, ensuring timely and accurate disclosure on all material matters, including the financial situation, performance, ownership and governance of those companies.

Article x.18

The Parties will ensure that they maintain corporate governance rules which require all companies to disclose government supports, privileges or other benefits as part of any applicable securities filings.

Article x.19

1 The Parties shall adopt or maintain corporate governance mechanisms which ensure accountability of the management and board towards the shareholders, responsible, objective and independent board decision-making, and equal treatment of shareholders of the same class.

2 The Parties may provide that some corporate governance principles, but not those set out in x.17, may not be applied to companies outside regulated markets or early phase development of the company.

Article x.20: Sub-Committee on State-Owned Enterprises and Designated Monopolies

1 The Parties hereby establish a Sub-Committee on State-Owned Enterprises and Designated Monopolies, State Aids and ACMDs ("SOE Committee"), which comprised officials from both parties.

2 The Sub-Committee meet within one year of the date of entry into force of the Agreement, and at least annually thereafter, unless the Parties decide otherwise.
3 The Sub-Committee shall:
   a review and consider the operation and implementation of this chapter;
   b discuss, at a Party's request, the activities of any state-owned enterprise or designated monopoly of a Party specified in the request with a view to identifying any distortion of trade or investment between the Parties that may result from those activities;
   c provide a framework for consultations under this chapter;
   d develop cooperative efforts, as appropriate, to promote the principles underlying the obligations contained in this chapter and to contribute to the development of similar obligations in regional and multilateral institutions in which the Parties participate; and
   e undertake such other activities as the Sub-Committee may decide.
4 Prior to each Sub-Committee meeting, both parties shall invite, as appropriate, input from the public on matters related to state-owned enterprises or designated monopolies that may affect developing its meeting agenda.

Article x.21: Exceptions

1 Nothing in Article x.11 (Courts and Administrative Bodies), Article x.12 (Adverse Effects), Article x.13 (Injury) or Article x.16 (state aids and ACMDs) shall be construed to:
   a prevent the adoption or enforcement by any Party of measures to respond temporarily to a national or global economic emergency; or
   b apply to a state-owned enterprise for which a Party has taken measures on a temporary basis in response to a national or global economic emergency.
2 Article x.11 (Courts and Administrative Bodies), Article x.12 (Adverse Effects), Article x.13 (Injury), Article x.7 (Requirements for Transparency & Corporate Governance), Article x.20 (Committee on State-Owned Enterprises and Designated Monopolies) and Article x.22 (Dispute Settlement) shall not apply where the state-owned enterprise is:
   a established or maintained by a Party solely to provide essential services to the general public in its territory; or
   b subject to government mandates defining its public service function, such as universal service obligations, or requirements to provide services at below market rates or on a cost recovery basis which are not imposed on similarly situated private companies, except where that public services function is being fulfilled in a manner that unnecessarily damages competition or restricts trade.

3 Articles x.11 (Courts and Administrative Bodies), Article x.12 (Adverse Effects) and Article x.13 (Injury) shall not apply to a state-owned enterprise or designated monopoly that provides healthcare services or finances housing, including insurance or guarantees of residential loans or mortgage securities, except where such a state-owned enterprise or designated monopoly shall accord treatment to covered investments no less favourable than the treatment it accords to like enterprises which are investments of the Party's investors, and provided that these activities do not unnecessarily damage competition or restrict trade.

4 With respect to a state-owned enterprise of a Party that provides export credits, Article x.11 (Courts and Administrative Bodies), Article x.12 (Adverse Effects) and Article x.13 (Injury) shall not apply to:

   a the provision of export credits that fall within the scope of the Arrangement and are offered on terms consistent with the Arrangement, regardless of whether the Party is a Participant to the Arrangement; and

   b the provision of short-term insurance, guarantee or other financing with a repayment term of less than two years, provided that the state-owned enterprise charges premium rates or interest rates that are adequate to cover the long-term operating costs and losses of the program, determined on a net present value basis, under which the insurance, guarantee or other financing is provided.

Article x.22: Dispute Settlement

Any recourse to dispute settlement pursuant to Chapter 19 (Dispute Settlement) for any matter arising under this chapter shall be subject to Annex 15.1 of this chapter.

Annex x: Process for Developing Information Concerning State-Owned Enterprises and Designated Monopolies

1 Where a panel has been established pursuant to Chapter 19 (Dispute Settlement) to examine a matter arising under this chapter, the panel shall administer the process set out in paragraphs 2–4 aimed at developing information relevant to the claim, including data regarding the volume and value of relevant purchases or sales by the state-owned enterprise or designated monopoly in question, and information about that entity's relevant purchasing, sales and contracting procedures.[12] The process shall include procedures aimed at protecting information that is by nature confidential or which a disputing Party provides on a confidential basis.

2 The complaining Party may present written questions to the other Party within 60 days of the date on which the panel is established. The responding Party shall provide its responses to the questions to the complaining Party and the panel within 60 days from the date it receives the questions.

3 The complaining Party shall have 60 days from the date it receives the responses to its questions to review them and provide any additional questions related to the responses to the responding Party. The responding Party shall have 45 days from the date it receives the additional questions to provide its responses to the additional questions to the complaining Party and the panel.
4 If the complaining Party considers that the responding Party has failed to cooperate in the process, the complaining Party shall inform the panel and the responding Party in writing no later than 30 days from the date responses to the complaining Party are due and provide the basis for this view. The panel shall afford the responding Party an opportunity to reply to this view in writing.
5 The panel may seek additional information from a disputing Party that was not provided to the panel through the information development process carried out under this Annex, where the panel considers the information necessary to resolve the dispute. However, the panel shall not request additional information to complete the record where the information would support a Party's position and the absence of that information in the record is the result of that Party's non-cooperation in the information gathering process.

Comments

1 This chapter does a lot of heavy lifting in the areas of SOEs, state aids and government distortions. This is not only important for both parties but it also aligns both parties around the developing global consensus in the OECD and other venues to deal with the problem of market distortions. A high-level agreement on these points should be possible between the US and the UK and could be a template for dealing with these problems in China and other highly distorted markets.
2 These provisions are based on existing US-X agreements but we have drawn in language on state-owned enterprises from other FTAs, as well as competition language in the OECD Regulatory Toolkit and Competition Assessment.

The Competition Provisions also discuss market distortions which have been raised by the EU, the US and Japan in the WTO Declaration in Buenos Aires, December 2017. Here, the trilateral group is seeking to lower market distortions in third countries. A US-UK FTA could build on and improve on what has been agreed.

Notes

1 For greater certainty, this excludes activities undertaken by an enterprise which operates on a:
- ·not-for-profit basis; or
- ·cost recovery basis.

2 For greater certainty, non-commercial assistance does not include intra-group transactions within a corporate group including state-owned enterprises, e.g. between the parent and subsidiaries of the group, or among the group's subsidiaries, when normal accounting standards or business practices would require that the corporate entity prepares consolidated net financial statements of these intra-group transactions.
3 For greater certainty, nothing in Article x.2.2 shall be construed to preclude a Party from applying its competition laws to commercial activities outside its borders that have anti-competitive effects within its jurisdiction.
4 For the purposes of this Article, enforcement proceedings mean judicial or administrative proceedings following an investigation into alleged violation of the competition laws.
5 Nothing in this paragraph shall prevent a Party from requiring that a person against whom such an allegation is made be responsible for establishing certain elements in defence of the allegation.
6 For greater certainty, the laws or regulations a Party adopts or maintains to proscribe these activities can be civil or criminal in nature.
7 Examples of regulatory, administrative or other governmental authority include the power to expropriate, grant licenses, approve commercial transactions or impose quotas, fees or other charges.
8 Such as a Public Service Obligation. The Public Service Obligation shall be constructed in such a way as to be the most pro-competitive and least trade-restrictive consistent with regulatory goals. Violation of the principals shall be grounds for violation of this agreement.
9 For greater certainty, for the purpose of this chapter, the term "product" does not include financial instruments, including money.
10 Definition of regionally impoverished area.
11 Any measure can give rise to an ACMD, including laws, regulations, government actions or inactions, statements by regulators, made publicly and privately.
12 The presentation of written questions and responses pursuant to paragraphs 2 and 3 may commence prior to the date a panel is composed. Upon its composition, the complaining Party shall provide any questions it presented to the responding Party, and the responding Party shall provide any responses it provided to the complaining Party, to the panel.

INDEX

Note: **Bold** page numbers refer to tables; *italic* page numbers refer to figures and page numbers followed by "n" denote endnotes.